THE EMC
Write-In
READER

Reading Strategies and Test Practice

WILLOW LEVEL

EMCParadigm Publishing Company

Staff Credits

Editorial

Laurie Skiba
Managing Editor

Brenda Owens
Editor

Becky Palmer
Reading Specialist

Nichola Torbett
Associate Editor

Jennifer Joline Anderson
Associate Editor

Diana Moen
Associate Editor

Mary Curfman
Editorial Consultant

Paul Spencer
Art and Photo Researcher

Design and Production

Shelley Clubb
Production Manager

Matthias Frasch
*Cover Designer and
Production Specialist*

Jennifer Wreisner
Text Designer

Erica Tava
Production Specialist

Lisa Beller
Production Specialist

Sharon O'Donnell
Proofreader

ISBN 0-8219-2916-X
© 2004 EMC Corporation

Published by EMC/Paradigm Publishing
875 Montreal Way
St. Paul, Minnesota 55102
www.emcp.com
E-mail: educate@emcp.com

Printed in the United States of America
10 9 8 7 6 5 4 3 2   XXX 10 09 08 07 06 05

Consultants and Contributors

Maria Callis
Reading Specialist/Department Chair
Trafalgar Middle School
Cape Coral, Florida

Shari Carlson
English/Reading Instructor
Fridley Middle School
Fridley, Minnesota

T. Carolyn Coleman
Language Arts/Reading Instructor
Gwinnett County Schools
Lawrenceville, Georgia

Dr. Edmund J. Farrell
Emeritus Professor of English Education
University of Texas at Austin
Austin, Texas

Sharon Kremer
Language Arts Instructor
Denton High School
Denton, Texas

Lisa Larnerd
English Department Chairperson
Basic High School
Henderson, Nevada

Beth Lee
Language Arts Instructor
Heritage Middle School
Longmont, Colorado

Cecilia Lewis
Language Arts Instructor
Mariner High School
Cape Coral, Florida

John Oricchio
Educational Consultant
Port Washington, New York

John Owens
Literacy Specialist
Heritage Middle School
Longmont, Colorado

Mary Spychalla
English/Reading Instructor
Valley Middle School
Apple Valley, Minnesota

Contents

UNIT 8   READING INFORMATIONAL AND VISUAL MEDIA

UNIT 9   DEVELOPING VOCABULARY SKILLS

UNIT 10   TEST-TAKING STRATEGIES

APPENDICES

Overview of Skills

LITERARY TOOLS

INFORMATIONAL AND VISUAL MEDIA TOOLS

Overview of Features

The EMC Write-In Reader helps you to interact with reading selections as never before! This portable anthology guides you in using reading strategies—reading tools that help you get more meaning from what you read. Questions and tips in the margins prompt you to record your thoughts and notes as you read. Using selections from the *Literature and the Language Arts* textbook, *The EMC Write-In Reader* gives you an opportunity to complete rich reading tasks, expand your reading skills, and increase your test-taking abilities.

The EMC Write-In Reader shows you how to use reading strategies before, during, and after reading and includes activities that develop your comprehension, fluency, and vocabulary skills.

The EMC Write-In Reader helps you learn how reading strategies work, how to combine them, and how to apply them to any reading task. These eight active reading strategies help you interact with a text to create meaning.

1. Read with a Purpose
2. Connect to Prior Knowledge
3. Write Things Down
4. Make Predictions
5. Visualize
6. Use Text Organization
7. Tackle Difficult Vocabulary
8. Monitor Your Reading Progress

Detailed instruction on one reading strategy is carried through the before, during, and after stages of the reading process for each selection.

The EMC Write-In Reader offers a unique text organization, including

- an **introduction to reading** unit that defines and explains the reading process, the eight reading strategies, and fix-up strategies to use when you have trouble
- a unit focusing on **essential reading skills** and tasks evaluated on standardized tests
- a unit for each **genre,** or kind of text, with an introduction on how to apply reading strategies to that genre
- a unit on **vocabulary development** to help you unlock word meaning
- a unit on **standardized test practice** to help you prepare for state and national tests
- an appendix of **fluency activities** to build word recognition skills, silent reading fluency, and oral reading fluency
- an appendix containing a multitude of **reading strategy graphic organizers**

Become a successful, active reader with *The EMC Write-In Reader!*

BEFORE READING

1 Reader's Resource provides background information to help you **set a purpose** for reading.

2 The **Active Reading Strategy** gives you step-by-step instruction on how to use the reading strategy **before reading**.

3 A **Graphic Organizer** for each selection helps you to **visualize** and **understand text organization** as you read.

CONNECT

Reader's resource

1

"Rules of the Game" appears in Amy Tan's award-winning first novel *The Joy Luck Club*, published in 1989. The novel weaves together the stories of four mothers born and raised in China and their four American-born daughters, exploring the conflicts between these two generations. The setting for the story is San Francisco's Chinatown, where the immigrant women form the Joy Luck Club and begin meeting to play the Chinese game *mah jong*, to invest in stocks, and to tell their stories.

Word watch **4**

PREVIEW VOCABULARY

adversary	impart
ally	intricate
ancestral	malodorous
benevolently	prodigy
caption	pungent
concession	relent
deftly	replica
diminishing	retort
elaborate	solemnity
etiquette	successive
flourish	tout
fragrant	triumphant
graciously	vanity
humility	

Reader's journal **5**

What kinds of conflicts do you have with your parents? How do you resolve them?

_____

_____

"Rules of the Game"
by Amy Tan

2

Active READING STRATEGY

MAKE PREDICTIONS

Before Reading ▶ **MAKE FIRST PREDICTIONS**

❑ Read the Reader's Resource.
❑ Answer the Reader's Journal questions.
❑ In a small group, use these clues to make one or two preliminary predictions about what will happen in this story. Record your predictions in the graphic organizer below.

Graphic Organizer 3

Clues	Predictions	What Really Happens

4 WordWatch gives you the opportunity to **preview** the vocabulary Words for Everyday Use for the selection.

5 Reader's Journal helps you to **connect** with what you know and to your own life.

DURING READING

Rules of the Game
Amy Tan

I was six when my mother taught me the art of invisible strength. It was a strategy for winning arguments, respect from others, and eventually, though neither of us knew it at the time, chess games.

"Bite back your tongue," scolded my mother when I cried loudly, yanking her hand toward the store that sold bags of salted plums. At home, she said, "Wise guy, he not go against wind. In Chinese we say, Come from South, blow with wind—poom!—North will follow. Strongest wind

10   cannot be seen."

The next week I bit back my tongue as we entered the store with the forbidden candies. When my mother finished her shopping, she quietly plucked a small bag of plums from the rack and put it on the counter with the rest of the items.

My mother <u>imparted</u> her daily truths so she could help my older brothers and me rise above our circumstances. We lived in San Francisco's Chinatown. Like most of the other Chinese children who played in the back alleys of

> **words for everyday use**
>
> **im • part** (im part′) *vt.*, give or communicate the knowledge of. *The teacher imparted his lessons to the class.*

During Reading ▶ **6**

MAKE PREDICTIONS

❑ Follow along as your teacher reads aloud the first two sections of the text. Then review the predictions you made and record what has really happened. Make one or two new predictions.

❑ Continue reading on your own. Stop every time you come to a section break to review your predictions and record new ones in your graphic organizer.

7

NOTE THE FACTS ✐

What lesson does the narrator learn about wanting something?

She learned to keep

quiet about what she

wants.

NOTE THE FACTS ✐

Why does the narrator's mother give her children advice?

to help them better

themselves

---

6 During Reading instruction in the margin tells you how to apply the reading strategy as you read.

7 Note the Facts questions give you the space to **make notes** about factual information as you read (see example).

DURING READING

8 **Read Aloud** activities in the margins help you to **build fluency** by giving you the chance to speak and listen to ideas you are trying to understand.

9 **Fix-Up Ideas** help you get back on track if you encounter problems or lose focus.

10 **Mark the Text** activities ask you to **underline or highlight** information in the text to help you read actively and organize your thoughts (see example).

reading the foreign English symbols, seeming to search deliberately for nothing in particular.

210   "This American rules," she concluded at last. "Every time people come out from foreign country, must know rules. You not know, judge say, Too bad, go back. They not telling you why so you can use their way go forward. They say, Don't know why, you find out yourself. But they knowing all the time. Better you take it, find out why yourself." She tossed her head back with a satisfied smile.

I found out about all the whys later. I read the rules and looked up all the big words in a dictionary. I borrowed books from the Chinatown library. I studied each chess piece, trying to absorb the power each contained.

220   I learned about opening moves and why it's important to control the center early on; the shortest distance between two points is straight down the middle. I learned about the middle game and why tactics between two adversaries are like clashing ideas; the one who plays better has the clearest plans for both attacking and getting out of traps. I learned why it is essential in the endgame to have foresight, a mathematical understanding of all the possible moves, and patience; all weaknesses and advantages become evident to a strong <u>adversary</u> and are obscured to a tiring opponent. I

230   discovered that for the whole game one must gather invisible strengths and see the endgame before the game begins.

I also found out why I should never reveal "why" to others. A little knowledge withheld is a great advantage one should store for future use. That is the power of chess. It is a game of secrets in which one must show and never tell.

I loved the secrets I found within the sixty-four black and white squares. I carefully drew a handmade chessboard and pinned it to the wall next to my bed, where at night I would stare for hours at imaginary battles. Soon I no longer lost my games or Life Savers, but I lost my adversaries. Winston and

240   Vincent decided they were more interested in roaming the streets after school in their Hopalong Cassidy[5] cowboy hats.

---

11 5. **Hopalong Cassidy.** Fictional cowboy hero popularized by movies and television shows in the 1950s

> **words for everyday use**
>
> **ad • ver • sar • y** (ad′ ve(r) ser ē) *n.*, one that contends with or opposes. *His enemy was a worthy <u>adversary</u>.*

12

8

READ ALOUD

Read lines 208–214 aloud. How does Waverly's mother feel about American rules?

_____

_____

_____

_____

9

FIX-UP IDEA

Ask a Question
If you have difficulty understanding the story, try asking a question that expresses what you don't understand. Then reread the section to answer your question. If you still can't find an answer, ask a classmate or your teacher. Consider how the answer to your question might help you make a prediction or how it affects the predictions you have already made.

10

MARK THE TEXT

Underline or highlight what Waverly says is the power of chess.

11 **Footnotes** explain references, unusual usage, and uncommon terms or words.

12 **Words for Everyday Use** includes the definition and pronunciation for new vocabulary. A sample sentence demonstrates the use of the word in context.

A small weekend crowd of Chinese people and tourists would gather as I played and defeated my opponents one by one. My mother would join the crowds during these outdoor exhibition games. She sat proudly on the bench, telling my admirers with proper Chinese <u>humility</u>, "Is luck."

A man who watched me play in the park suggested that my mother allow me to play in local chess tournaments. My mother smiled <u>graciously</u>, an answer that meant nothing. I desperately wanted to go, but I bit back my tongue. I knew she would not let me play among strangers. So as we walked home I said in a small voice that I didn't want to play in the local tournament. They would have American rules. If I lost, I would bring shame on my family.

"Is shame you fall down nobody push you," said my mother.

During my first tournament, my mother sat with me in the front row as I waited for my turn. I frequently bounced my legs to unstick them from the cold metal seat of the folding chair. When my name was called, I leapt up. My mother unwrapped something in her lap. It was her chang, a small tablet of red jade which held the sun's fire. "Is luck," she whispered, and tucked it into my dress pocket. I turned to my opponent, a fifteen-year-old boy from Oakland. He looked at me, wrinkling his nose.

As I began to play, the boy disappeared, the color ran out of the room, and I saw only my white pieces and his black ones waiting on the other side. A light wind began blowing past my ears. It whispered secrets only I could hear.

"Blow from the South," it murmured. "The wind leaves no trail." I saw a clear path, the traps to avoid. The crowd rustled. "Shhh! Shhh!" said the corners of the room. The wind blew stronger. "Throw sand from the East to distract him." The knight came forward ready for the sacrifice. The wind hissed, louder and louder. "Blow, blow, blow. He cannot see. He is blind now. Make him lean away from the wind so he is easier to knock down."

290

300

310

320

---

words for everyday use

hu • mil • i • ty (hu mi′ le tē) *n.*, state of being humble, not possessing pride. *With <u>humility</u> she gave credit to her teacher.*

gra • cious • ly (grā′ shes lē) *adv.*, with kindness and courtesy. *The gentleman <u>graciously</u> offered his seat to the elderly woman.*

UNIT 3 / READING FICTION   **91**

NOTE THE FACTS

How does Waverly get her mother to let her play in tournaments?

_____

_____

_____

13

THINK AND REFLECT

How does this tactic relate to Mrs. Jong's advice at the beginning of the story? **(Synthesize)**

_____

_____

_____

Literary TOOLS   **14**

SYMBOL. A **symbol** is a thing that stands for or represents both itself and something else. In lines 317–324, how does the wind affect Waverly's game? As you read the rest of the story, notice when the wind is mentioned. How might the wind be a symbol?

_____

_____

_____

13 **Think and Reflect** questions deepen your understanding of what you are reading.

14 **Literary Tools** explain **literary techniques and concepts** and help you recognize these elements as you read.

AFTER READING

15 **After Reading** activities follow up on the reading strategy and help you to summarize, synthesize, and reflect on the material you have read.

16 **Reading Skills and Test Practice** develops essential reading skills assessed on standardized tests.

Reflect ON YOUR READING

15

After Reading ▸ ANALYZE YOUR PREDICTIONS

When you finish reading the story, review the predictions you made. If you haven't already done so, record what really happened. Think about how this strategy affected your reading experience. Did you find yourself reading more actively in order to find out if your predictions were correct? Did you focus more on the story's main events and ideas? Write a paragraph or two answering these questions and describing how the reading strategy changed how you read. When you finish, share your essay with a partner and discuss how making predictions affected your understanding and enjoyment of the selection.

Reading Skills and Test Practice **16**

IDENTIFY SYMBOLISM

Discuss with a partner how to best answer the following questions about symbolism in "The Rules of the Game."

1. Throughout the story, the wind symbolizes Waverly's
   a. unseen fear of losing.
   b. unacknowledged love for her brother.
   c. invisible strength.
   d. hidden dislike of her mother.

What is the correct answer to the question above? How were you able to eliminate other answers?

_____

_____

_____

2. The title of the story, "Rules of the Game," has a double meaning. In addition to the rules of chess, the title may refer to the rules of
   a. the Chinese calendar.
   b. life.
   c. etiquette.
   d. the neighborhood school.

What is the correct answer to the question above? How were you able to eliminate other answers?

_____

_____

_____

THINK-ALOUD
NOTES

_____

_____

_____

_____

_____

_____

_____

_____

_____

_____

_____

Investigate, Inquire, and Imagine

RECALL: GATHER FACTS
1a. How does Mrs. Jong react in public to the Christmas gift of a used chess game? What is her real opinion, which she expresses when the family gets home?

INTERPRET: FIND MEANING
1b. Why does Mrs. Jong act as she does in public when that is not the way she really feels?

ANALYZE: TAKE THINGS APART
2a. Make a list of references in the story to rules and games.

SYNTHESIZE: BRING THINGS TOGETHER
2b. Is there more than one game being played in this story? Explain. What is the broader meaning of the title?

EVALUATE: MAKE JUDGMENTS
3a. How good a communicator do you think Mrs. Jong is? What accounts for the communication problems between Waverly and her mother?

EXTEND: CONNECT IDEAS
3b. In what ways is the parent-child relationship complicated when the parent comes from a different culture?

Literary Tools

SYMBOL. A **symbol** is a thing that stands for or represents both itself and something else. The wind serves as an important symbol in this story. Waverly's mother says that a wise person does not go against the wind and that the "strongest wind cannot be seen." What does this mean?

_____

_____

How does Mrs. Jong's advice about the wind help Waverly win her first chess tournament?

_____

_____

How is the wind used as a symbol when Waverly accuses her mother of showing off?

_____

_____

What does Waverly's mother say right before the imaginary chess game at the end of the story? Who or what is the strongest wind at this point?

_____

_____

17 Investigate, Inquire, and Imagine questions further your understanding of the reading, from basic recall and interpret questions to those that ask you to analyze, synthesize, evaluate, and extend your ideas. Some questions also ask you to look at a specific point of view or a different perspective.

18 Literary Tools follows up on the literary techniques and concepts introduced during reading and asks you to apply your understanding.

AFTER READING

19 WordWorkshop activities apply vocabulary development concepts to the words from the selection.

WordWorkshop

WORDS WITH MULTIPLE MEANINGS. Many words have more than one meaning. Multiple meanings can develop in several ways. A word might gain a wider or narrower meaning over time. For example, the word *mail* once meant "payment or rent" but now is most often used to refer to anything sent by post. It also has a lesser-known meaning that refers to medieval armor made of metal links or plates. Words can also be used as new parts of speech. For example, *mail* as it is used above is a noun, but the word can also be used as a verb meaning "to send by post."

Each of the following words has multiple meanings. Look up each word in the dictionary. Notice that words used as more than one part of speech have separate boldfaced entries. Multiple meanings of a word that are all the same part of speech are listed in a single boldfaced entry. Choose two meanings for each word and write them on your own paper. Then write an original sentence that reflects each meaning.

1. ally
2. concession
3. elaborate
4. retort
5. vanity

20 Read-Write Connection gives you the opportunity to write about your responses to the selection.

Read-Write Connection

Was Waverly's anger at the end of the story justified? Why, or why not? What do you think her "next move" will be?

_____

_____

_____

_____

_____

_____

_____

21 Beyond the Reading activities extend the ideas, topics, and themes from the selection.

Beyond the Reading 21

TEACH A GAME. Research the rules of chess, *mah jong,* or some other game that you would like to learn. Use the Internet, books, and other publications to gather information. Then prepare a presentation in which you teach the class to play the game you have chosen.

GO ONLINE. Visit the EMC Internet Resource Center at **emcp.com** to find links and additional activities for this selection.

Unit ONE

Introduction to READING

PURPOSES OF READING

As a reader, you read for different purposes. You might **read for experience**—for insights into ideas, other people, and the world around you. You can also **read to learn**. This is the kind of reading done most often in school. When you read to learn, you may read textbooks, newspapers and newsmagazines, and visual "texts" such as art and photographs. The purpose of this type of reading is to gain knowledge. Third, you can **read for information**. When you read in this way, you are looking for specific data in sources such as reference materials, tables, databases, and diagrams.

Reading for Experience
READING LITERATURE

The most important reason to read literature is to educate your imagination. Reading literary works, which include fiction, nonfiction, poetry, and drama, will train you to think and feel in new ways. In the process of reading literary works and thinking about your own and others' responses to them, you will exercise your imagination as you encounter characters and situations that you would otherwise never know.

Reading to Learn
READING TEXTBOOKS AND NONFICTION

When you are reading to learn, you have two main goals: to expand your knowledge on a particular topic and to remember the information later. When you read to learn, you will often work with textbooks; reference books; periodicals such as newspapers, journals, and newsmagazines; and related art and photographs.

Textbooks provide a broad overview of a course of study in an objective, factual way. Other types of nonfiction works provide

NOTE THE FACTS

What are three purposes for reading?

_____

_____

_____

information about people, places, things, events, and ideas. Types of nonfiction include histories, biographies, autobiographies, and memoirs. Periodicals such as newspapers, journals, and newsmagazines contain an enormous amount of information about current events around the world. While few people have time to read everything that appears in news periodicals, it is important to stay aware of what is going on in the world around you.

Reading for Information

READING INTERNET, REFERENCE, AND VISUAL MATERIALS

When you are reading for information, you are looking for information that answers a specific, immediate question; that helps you learn how to do something; or that helps you make a decision or draw a conclusion about something. One of the most important things for you to learn in school is how to find, process, and think about the vast amount of information available to you in online and printed reference works, graphic aids, and other visual materials.

THE READING PROCESS

The reading process begins before you actually start to read. Before reading, you begin to develop your own purpose and expectations for what you are about to read. These are related to what you already know and what you have experienced. During reading, you use your natural habits and responses to help you understand what you are reading, perhaps by adjusting your initial purpose and expectations. After reading, you think and reflect on what you have read. All readers use a reading process, even if they don't think about it. By becoming aware of this process, you can become a more effective reader. The reading process can be broken down into three stages: before reading, during reading, and after reading.

Before Reading

Have a plan for reading actively. Before you begin to read, establish a plan for reading actively by setting a purpose, previewing the material, and connecting with what you already know.

- ❑ **Set a purpose** for reading. Know why you are reading and what information you seek. Are you reading for experience or enjoyment, reading to learn, or reading for specific information?
- ❑ **Preview** the organization of the material. Glance at any visuals and think about how they add to the meaning of the text. Skim headings and introductory paragraphs.
- ❑ **Connect** with what you know. Think about how what you are reading connects to your own life and to your prior experience.

Before Reading ➤

ASK YOURSELF

- ■ What's my purpose for reading this?
- ■ What is this going to be about?
- ■ How is this information organized?
- ■ What do I already know about the topic?
- ■ How can I apply this information to my life?

During Reading

Use reading strategies to read actively. Reading strategies are actions you can take on paper, in your head, or aloud that help you understand what you are reading. During reading, you will use reading strategies to read actively. Keep in mind that you will often use a combination of these strategies to read a single text.

❑ **Read aloud** to build reading fluency and give oral emphasis to ideas you are trying to understand. Hearing words aloud may help you untangle difficult ideas. Listen to your teacher read passages aloud, or read aloud by yourself or with a partner.

❑ **Write things down** to note your responses to what you are reading. Methods such as highlighting and marking a text, taking or making notes, and creating graphic organizers help you read actively and organize your thoughts. Underline or copy to your notebook the main points. Note unusual or interesting ideas or things you don't understand. Jot down words you need to define. Write your reactions to what you read.

❑ **Think and reflect** by asking questions to further your understanding of what you are reading. Asking questions helps you to pinpoint parts of the text that are confusing. You can ask questions in your head, or you may write them down.

Check your reading and use fix-up ideas. Monitor your reading comprehension by paying attention to how well you understand what you are reading. If you find yourself reading the words but not actually understanding what you are reading, get back on track by using a **fix-up idea** such as rereading, reading in shorter chunks, changing your reading rate, or trying a new reading strategy. A fix-up idea will be presented with each reading strategy accompanying the selections in this text. (For more information on fix-up ideas, see pages 14–15.)

After Reading

Reflect on your reading. After you finish reading, summarize, synthesize, and reflect on the material you have read.

■ **Summarize** what you have read to help identify, understand, and remember the main and supporting ideas in the text.

■ **Synthesize** different ideas in the material by pulling the ideas together and drawing conclusions about them. Reread any sections you don't remember clearly. Answer any questions you had.

■ **Extend** your reading by examining how your knowledge has grown and identifying questions you still have about the material.

During Reading

ASK YOURSELF

■ What is the best way to accomplish my purpose for reading?
■ What do I want or need to find out while I'm reading?
■ What is the essential information presented here?
■ What is the importance of what I am reading?

CHECK YOUR READING

■ Do I understand what I just read? Can I summarize it?
■ What can I do to make the meaning more clear?

After Reading

ASK YOURSELF

■ What did I learn from what I have read?
■ What is still confusing?
■ What do I need to remember from my reading?
■ What effect did this text have on my thinking?
■ What else do I want to know about this topic?

USING ACTIVE READING STRATEGIES

Reading actively means thinking about what you are reading as you read. A reading strategy, or plan, helps you read actively and search for meaning in what you are reading. As a reader, you are in charge of unlocking the meaning of each text you read. This book will introduce you to eight excellent strategies that develop active reading. The following strategies can be applied at each stage of the reading process: before, during, and after reading.

Active Reading Strategies

1. Read with a Purpose
2. Connect to Prior Knowledge
3. Write Things Down
4. Make Predictions
5. Visualize
6. Use Text Organization
7. Tackle Difficult Vocabulary
8. Monitor Your Reading Progress

As you become experienced with each of the reading strategies, you will be able to use two or three strategies at a time, instead of just one. By using multiple strategies, you will become a thoughtful, active, and successful reader—not only in your English language arts classes but also in other content areas, during testing situations, and beyond the classroom. You will learn which strategies work best for you and use these strategies in every reading task you encounter.

❶ Read with a Purpose

Before you begin reading, think about your reason for reading the material. You might be reading from a textbook to complete a homework assignment, skimming a magazine for information about one of your hobbies, or reading a novel for your own personal enjoyment. Know why you are reading and what information you seek. Decide on your purpose for reading as clearly as you can. Be aware that your purpose may change as you read.

Read with a Purpose

Before Reading	Establish a purpose for reading
During Reading	Read with this purpose in mind
After Reading	Reflect on how the purpose affected the reading experience

THE READING PROCESS

BEFORE READING
Have a plan for reading
- ❏ Set a purpose
- ❏ Preview
- ❏ Connect

DURING READING
Use reading strategies
- ❏ Read aloud
- ❏ Write things down
- ❏ Think and reflect
- ❏ Check your reading and use fix-up ideas

AFTER READING
Reflect on your reading
- ❏ Summarize
- ❏ Synthesize
- ❏ Extend

After you determine your purpose for reading, you can choose a method of reading that fits that purpose. Scanning, skimming, and close reading are three different ways of reading.

SCANNING. When you **scan,** you look through written material quickly to locate particular information. Scanning is useful when, for example, you want to find an entry in an index or a definition in a textbook chapter. To scan, simply run your eye down the page, looking for a key word or words. When you find the key words, slow down and read carefully.

SKIMMING. When you **skim,** you glance through material quickly to get a general idea of what it is about. Skimming is an excellent way to get a quick overview of material. It is useful for previewing a chapter in a textbook, for surveying material to see if it contains information that will be useful to you, and for reviewing material for a test or essay. When skimming, look at titles, headings, and words that appear in boldface or colored type. Also read topic sentences of paragraphs, first and last paragraphs of sections, and any summaries or conclusions. In addition, glance at illustrations, photographs, charts, maps, or other graphics.

READING CLOSELY. When you **read closely**, you read slowly and carefully, looking at each sentence and taking the time to absorb its meaning before going on. Close reading is appropriate, for example, when you are reading some poems for pleasure or studying a textbook chapter for the first time. If you encounter words that you do not understand, try to figure them out from context or look them up in a dictionary. You may want to record such words in a word study notebook. The act of writing a word will help you to remember it later. When reading for school, take notes using a rough outline form or other note-taking format. Outlining the material will help you to learn it.

Setting a purpose gives you something to focus on as you read. For example, you might read the user's manual for your new phone to find out how to program speed-dial numbers. Or, you might read a mystery novel to find out which character committed the crime.

A few of the purposes you might have for reading "Something Could Happen to You" by Esmeralda Santiago, Unit 7, page 378, might be to learn something about the author's life, to learn about challenges immigrants face in a new country, or to learn how different groups perceive race and ethnicity. You may also read to identify certain elements, such as dialogue between the characters that reveals ideas about cultural identity. From the following background information provided in the Reader's Resource for this selection, decide on a purpose for reading "Something Could Happen to You."

NOTE THE FACTS

What is the difference between scanning and skimming?

_____

_____

_____

_____

MARK THE TEXT

Go back over the pages in this unit and highlight or underline a colored head. Then underline the boldface headings beneath the colored heading. Marking the text in this way helps you keep track of key ideas.

THINK AND REFLECT

On the lines below, write a purpose you could have for reading "Something Could Happen To You." **(Connect)**

_____

_____

_____

"Something Could Happen to You" is a warning that young Esmeralda Santiago frequently hears from her mother when she moves to Brooklyn, a borough of New York City, from Puerto Rico. In this selection, taken from Santiago's memoir _Almost a Woman_ (1998), the author describes her initial reactions to her new city, neighborhood, extended family, and school.

❷ Connect to Prior Knowledge

Prior knowledge is what you already know or have already experienced before reading something. Before and during reading, think about what you already know about the topic or subject matter. By connecting to your prior knowledge, you can increase your interest in and understanding of what you read. The Reader's Journal activities that come before each selection in this book provide an opportunity to connect to experiences in your own life. Information in the Reader's Resource expands your knowledge of what you are about to read.

Connect to Prior Knowledge	
Before Reading	Think about what you already know about the topic
During Reading	Use what you already know about the topic to make inferences and predictions
After Reading	Describe how the reading experience expanded your knowledge of the topic

Read the Reader's Resource for the biographical article "Montgomery Boycott," Unit 7, page 318. Think about what you already know about the Civil Rights movement as you read background information about the boycott.

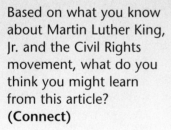

THINK AND REFLECT

Based on what you know about Martin Luther King, Jr. and the Civil Rights movement, what do you think you might learn from this article? **(Connect)**

_____

_____

_____

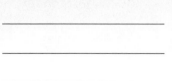

"Montgomery Boycott" is a nonfiction narrative by Coretta Scott King, the wife of Martin Luther King, Jr., that describes the refusal of African Americans in Montgomery, Alabama, to use the segregated city bus system. The Montgomery Boycott was an early action in the Civil Rights movement, in which African Americans demonstrated to use the same public facilities as whites, facilities such as lunch counters, bathrooms, and buses. Martin Luther King, Jr., who stressed nonviolent protest, became the leader in the fight for civil rights.

3 Write Things Down

Writing things down helps you pay attention to the words on a page. It is an excellent way to remember important ideas. Methods such as highlighting and marking or coding a text, taking or making notes, and creating graphic organizers help you read actively and organize your thoughts.

Write Things Down	
Before Reading	Have a plan for writing things down: sticky notes, handwritten notes, highlighters, or charts to fill in
During Reading	Use a method for writing things down; ask questions; respond
After Reading	Summarize things written down

Highlighting and marking a text helps you locate key ideas. Mark important ideas, things you would like to come back to, things that are confusing, things you like or dislike, and things with which you agree or disagree. In this Write-In Reader or a book you own, you may highlight the text itself. With other books you may need to use sticky notes and bookmarks to keep track of your thoughts.

As you read, find a way to connect to what you are reading by **coding** your reactions. Use the following system to keep track of your reactions in the margins or on sticky notes. Create additional notations for reactions you have that are not listed.

YES	I agree with this
NO	I disagree with this
?	I do not understand this
W	I wonder . . .
+	I like this part
–	I do not like this part
!	This is like something else I know
√	This seems important
∞	I need to come back and look at this
_____	_____

If you do not have sticky notes, keep track of your reactions in a chart like the one on the next page.

NOTE THE FACTS

What are some methods of writing things down?

_____

_____

_____

_____

MARK THE TEXT

Circle the things you can mark or highlight as you read.

Reading TIP

Additional ways to take notes:

■ outline
■ make lists
■ create a chart or diagram
■ write down main ideas and your responses
■ use a tape recorder

Reactions Chart

Page, Column, or Line Number:	Short Note about My Reactions
Ex: p. 6, col. 1	The boy in this story reminds me of a time when I visited a friend's house.

After reading, summarize your reactions and compare them to those of your classmates.

> Here is a summary of my reactions: I liked the story because it was funny, and because it showed the comfortable relationship between the two boys.
>
> Here is how my reactions were the same as those of my classmates: Most of my classmates thought the story was funny.
>
> Here is how my reactions were different from those of my classmates: I thought Boyd didn't recognize the prejudice the mother exhibited, but many of my classmates thought he did understand her behavior and was just being polite.

Taking or making notes helps you select ideas you consider important. *Paraphrase*, or write in your own words, what you have read and put it into notes you can read later. Taking or making notes is also a quick way for you to retell what you have just read. Since you cannot write in, mark up, or highlight information in a textbook or library book, make a response bookmark like the one on the next page and use it to record your thoughts and reactions. As you read, ask yourself questions, make predictions, react to ideas, identify key points, and/or write down unfamiliar words.

Response Bookmark

Page #	Questions, Predictions, Reactions, Key Points, and Unfamiliar Words
102	Yuck! Stewed tomatoes are awful.
	I bet Boyd will start making things up.
	New words for me: <u>kindling</u> and <u>foxhole</u>

Graphic organizers help you organize ideas as you read. For instance, if you are reading an essay that compares two authors, you might use a Venn diagram or a cluster chart to collect information about each author. If you are reading about an author's life, you may construct a time line. As you read a selection, create your own method for gathering and organizing information. You might use your own version of a common graphic organizer or invent a new way to show what the selection describes. Signal words in the text can help you construct an organizer. (See Appendix B at the back of this Write-In Reader for examples of these and other graphic organizers.)

NOTE THE FACTS

How can using a graphic organizer help you as you read?

_____

_____

_____

Signal Words	Common Graphic Organizer
descriptive words: *also, for instance, for example, in the beginning, in addition, the main reason, one point*	Character Chart, page B-8 Sensory Details Chart, page B-9 Summary Chart, page B-12
sequence words: *after, as before, next, now, on, first, second, finally*	Time Line, page B-10 Story Strip, page B-10 Plot Diagram, page B-11
comparison-and-contrast words: *as well as, but, either/or, likewise, on the other hand, similarly, not only/but*	Pro and Con Chart, page B-6 Cluster Chart, page B-7 Venn Diagram, page B-7
cause-and-effect words: *as a result, because, if/then, since, therefore, this led to*	Note-Taking Chart, page B-6 Cause-and-Effect Chart, page B-12 Drawing Conclusions Log, page B-13

After reading the following excerpt from the Central American myth the *Popol Vuh*, Unit 5, page 203, write down the answer to the question in the margin. Highlight or underline signal words that direct you to the answer.

Reading TIP

By learning to make predictions while you read, you become more engaged in what you're reading and you remember more information.

But they could not make them speak like men; they only hissed and screamed and cackled; they were unable to make words, and each screamed in a different way.

When the Creator and the Maker saw that it was impossible for them to talk to each other, they said: "It is impossible for them to say our names, the names of us, their Creators and Makers. This is not well," said the Forefathers to each other.

Then they said to them: "Because it has not been possible for you to talk, you shall be changed. We have changed our minds: Your food, your pasture, your homes, and your nests you shall have; they shall be the ravines and the woods, because it has not been possible for you to adore us or invoke us. There shall be those who adore us, we shall make other [beings] who shall be obedient. Accept your destiny: your flesh shall be torn to pieces. So shall it be. This shall be your lot." So they said, when they made known their will to the large and small animals which are on the face of the earth.

4 Make Predictions

When you **make predictions** during reading, you are making guesses about what the reading is going to be about or what might happen next. Before reading, make predictions based on clues from the page and from what you already know about the topic. Continue making predictions as you read. Remember, your predictions do not have to be correct. Pause during reading to gather information that helps you make more predictions and check predictions you have already made.

Make Predictions	
Before Reading	Gather information and make preliminary predictions
During Reading	Continue making predictions
After Reading	Analyze and verify predictions

Read the first two paragraphs from the short story "Rules of the Game" by Amy Tan, Unit 3, page 83. Look for clues that give you an idea about what will happen in this story.

I was six when my mother taught me the art of invisible strength. It was a strategy for winning arguments, respect from others, and eventually, though neither of us knew it at the time, chess games.

"Bite back your tongue," scolded my mother when I cried loudly, yanking her hand toward the store that sold bags of salted plums. At home, she said, "Wise guy, he not go against wind. In Chinese we say, Come from South, blow with wind—poom!— North will follow. Strongest wind cannot be seen."

Prediction Chart

Predictions	Clues	What Really Happens
The narrator will use "the art of invisible strength" to win at chess.	It was a strategy for winning arguments . . . and eventually . . . chess games	

5 Visualize

Reading is more than simply sounding out words. It is an active process that requires you to use your imagination. When you **visualize,** you form a picture or an image in your mind of what the text describes. Each reader's images will be different based on his or her prior knowledge and experience. Keep in mind that there are no "right" or "wrong" visualizations.

Visualize

Before Reading	Begin to picture what may happen
During Reading	Create mind pictures as you read
After Reading	Draw or summarize what you saw in your mind pictures

THINK AND REFLECT

Based on the clues in the excerpt, make a **prediction** about what might happen later in the story. Record your prediction in the first column of the chart. In the second column, tell what clues led you to make this prediction. After you read the rest of the story, you would be able to record what really happened in the story and to compare that to your original predictions. **(Predict)**

Read the following excerpt from Guy de Maupassant's "The Necklace," Unit 3, page 73. Pay attention to how Maupassant describes a woman's reaction to a diamond necklace in "a black satin box." As you read, think about what makes the woman behave in such an immoderate, or excessive, way.

THINK AND REFLECT

Make notes or draw pictures to convey the images you pictured in your mind while reading this passage. (Visualize)

> Suddenly she discovered in a black satin box a superb necklace of diamonds, and her heart beat fast with an immoderate desire. Her hands trembled as she took them up. She placed them about her throat, against her dress, and remained in ecstasy before them. Then she asked in a hesitating voice full of anxiety:
> "Could you lend me this? Only this?"
> "Why, yes, certainly."
> She fell upon the neck of her friend, embraced her with passion, then went away with her treasure.

6 Use Text Organization

Text organization refers to the different ways a text may be presented or organized. If you are aware of the ways different texts are organized, you will find it easier to understand what you read. For example, familiarity with typical plot elements—the exposition, rising action, climax, falling action, and resolution—is important for understanding the events in a short story or novel. Focusing on signal words and text patterns is important for understanding nonfiction and informational text. For instance, transition words, such as *first*, *second*, *next*, *then*, and *finally*, might indicate that an essay is written in chronological, or time, order.

Use Text Organization	
Before Reading	Preview organizational features (look over headings, pictures, format)
During Reading	Be aware of organizational features as you read
After Reading	Discuss how the text organization affected your reading experience

In this excerpt from "The Five Ages of Man," Unit 5, page 195, look for signal words that identify three of the five ages of man. Underline each age and circle what happened to each.

Next came a silver race, eaters of bread, likewise divinely created. The men were utterly subject to their mothers and dared not disobey them, although they might live to be a hundred years old. They were quarrelsome and ignorant, and never sacrificed to the gods but, at least, did not make war on one another. Zeus destroyed them all.

Next came a brazen race, who fell like fruits from the ash-trees, and were armed with brazen weapons. They ate flesh as well as bread, and delighted in war, being insolent and pitiless men. Black Death has seized them all.

The fourth race of man was brazen too, but nobler and more generous, being begotten by the gods on mortal mothers. They fought gloriously in the siege of Thebes, the expedition of the Argonauts, and the Trojan War. These became heroes, and dwell in the Elysian Fields.

THINK AND REFLECT

What signal words help you keep track of the ages of man? How does the organization of each paragraph help you keep track of what happened to each age?

_____

_____

_____

_____

7 Tackle Difficult Vocabulary

How do you deal with new or unfamiliar words as you read? Learning how to tackle difficult vocabulary on your own leads to improved reading comprehension. In some cases, you may want to identify and define new vocabulary before reading. Use context clues to guess meanings, find definitions in the dictionary, and decode words by recognizing common word parts.

Tackle Difficult Vocabulary

Before Reading	Have a plan for tackling difficult words
During Reading	Use context, word structure, footnotes, or a dictionary; ask for help
After Reading	Describe how vocabulary affected your reading experience

Read the following excerpt from "The Man Who Mistook His Wife for a Hat" by Oliver Sacks, Unit 7, page 333. Note any unfamiliar vocabulary you encounter. Record the word or words in your notebook. Then, go back to the word in the text and use both context clues (words nearby that provide hints about the meaning) and word parts to unlock the meaning. If necessary, consult a dictionary.

Reading TIP

If you take the time to learn new words, you increase your ability to understand what you read in class and on standardized tests. One of the best ways to learn new words is to **associate an image** with the meaning of a new word. For instance, you might associate the word _neurological_ with an image of a person's brain. What image might you associate with the word _ophthalmoscope_ if you know that _ophthalmo_ is a Greek root meaning "eye" and _scope_ is a Greek root meaning "an instrument for viewing and observing"?

> What a lovely man, I thought to myself. How can there be anything seriously the matter? Would he permit me to examine him?
>
> "Yes, of course, Dr. Sacks."
>
> I stilled my disquiet, his perhaps too, in the soothing routine of a neurological exam—muscle strength, co-ordination, reflexes, tone… It was while examining his reflexes—a trifle abnormal on the left side—that the first bizarre experience occurred. I had taken off his left shoe and scratched the sole of his foot with a key—a frivolous-seeming but essential test of a reflex—and then, excusing myself to screw my ophthalmoscope together, left him to put on the shoe himself. To my surprise, a minute later, he had not done this.

THINK AND REFLECT

Based on the context clues, what might the definition of *frivolous* be? (Apply)

_____

_____

READ ALOUD

Reading fluency is your ability to read something quickly and easily. Increase your reading fluency by rereading a 100–150-word passage aloud several times. Reread the passage until you are able to read through it in less than a minute without making any mistakes. Read the passage to a partner and have your partner track your errors, or read the passage into a tape recorder, play back your recording, and keep track of your own errors. For additional fluency practice, see Appendix A.

⑧ Monitor Your Reading Progress

All readers occasionally have difficulty as they read. The key to reading success is being aware of these difficulties. As you read, **monitor**, or pay attention to, your progress, stopping frequently to check how well you are understanding what you are reading. If you encounter problems or lose focus, use a **fix-up idea** to regain understanding. Readers who know how to apply fix-up ideas are well on the way to reading independence. They know when they are having a problem and are able to adjust and get back on track.

USING FIX-UP IDEAS

The following **fix-up ideas** can help you "fix up" any confusion or lack of attention you experience as you read. You probably use many of these already.

- **Reread.** If you don't understand a sentence, paragraph, or section the first time through, go back and reread it. Each time you reread a text, you understand and remember more.

- **Read in shorter chunks.** Break a long text into shorter chunks. Read through each "chunk." Then go back and make sure you understand that section before moving on.

- **Read aloud.** If you are having trouble keeping your focus, try reading aloud to yourself. Go somewhere private and read aloud, putting emphasis and expression in your voice. Reading aloud may help you to untangle difficult text by talking your way through it.

- **Ask questions.** As you read, stop and ask yourself questions about the text. These questions help you pinpoint things that are confusing or things you want to come back to later. You can ask questions in your head, or jot them down in the margins or on a piece of paper.

- **Change your reading rate.** Your reading rate is how fast or slow you read. Good readers adjust their rate to fit the situation. Read quickly, when you just need an overview, or if the reading task is easy. Slow down and read carefully when a text is difficult or contains a lot of description.

- **Create a mnemonic device.** A mnemonic (ni mä′ nik) device is a memory trick that helps you memorize specific information in a text. One memory trick is to make up an acronym, or abbreviation, to help you remember items in a list. For example, the acronym *HOMES* can help you remember the names of the five great lakes, Huron, Ontario, Michigan, Erie, and Superior. Another memory trick is to create a short sentence or rhyme. For instance, if you need to remember that in the eardrum, the anvil comes before the stirrup, remember "the letter *a* comes before the letter *s*."

Monitor Your Reading Progress

Before Reading	Be aware of fix-up ideas that ease reading problems
During Reading	Use fix-up ideas
After Reading	Evaluate the fix-up ideas used

As you read, use your classmates as resources to help you uncover the meaning in a selection. Working with a partner or a small group can increase your understanding of what you read.

THINK ALOUD. When you **think aloud**, you communicate your thoughts aloud to your classmates about what you are reading. Thinking aloud helps you share ideas about the text and ways in which to read it.

SHARE FIX-UP IDEAS. When you **share gix-up ideas**, you and your classmates can figure out ways to deal with difficult sections of a text.

Unit 1 READING Review

Choose and Use Reading Strategies

Before reading the excerpt below, review with a partner how to use each of these reading strategies (see pages 4–15).

1. Read with a Purpose
2. Connect to Prior Knowledge
3. Write Things Down
4. Make Predictions
5. Visualize
6. Use Text Organization
7. Tackle Difficult Vocabulary
8. Monitor Your Reading Progress

Now apply at least two of these reading strategies as you read "Ice and Light" from *Arctic Dreams* by Barry Lopez. Use the margins and mark up the text to show you are using the reading strategies to read actively.

> At first it seems that, except for a brief few weeks in autumn, the Arctic is without color. Its land colors are the colors of deserts, the ochers and siennas of stratified soils, the gray-greens of sparse plant life on bare soil. On closer inspection, however, the monotonic rock of the polar desert is seen to harbor the myriad greens, reds, yellows, and oranges of lichens. The whites of tundra swans and of sunlit ice in black water are pure and elegant. Occasionally, there is brilliant coloring—as with wildflowers in the summer, or a hillside of willow and bearberry in the fall; or a slick of vegetable oils shining with the iridescent colors of petroleum on a tundra puddle; or the bright face of a king eider. But the bright colors are more often only points in a season, not brushstrokes; and they are absorbed in the paler casts of the landscape.

On Your Own

Apply the reading strategies you have learned in this unit to your own reading. Select a passage from your favorite book, magazine, or newspaper, and try one of the following activities.

FLUENTLY SPEAKING. Reread a 100–150-word passage aloud several times. Reread the passage until you are able to read through it in less than a minute without making any mistakes. Read the passage to a partner and have your partner track your errors, or read the passage into a tape recorder, play back your recording, and keep track of your own errors.

PICTURE THIS. As you read, create a drawing, painting, sculpture, or other visual representation of the images that come into your mind.

PUT IT IN WRITING. Write an informal essay about the reading passage you have selected. Explain why you like to read this type of material. Discuss what you like about it and why you find it interesting. How does this passage relate to your own life?

Unit TWO

ESSENTIAL READING SKILLS

READING SKILLS

Each of the reading strategies we've discussed in Unit 1 helps you learn to think, question, and respond while you read. By using the eight active reading strategies, you will be able to demonstrate your mastery of the following reading skills:

- Identify the Author's Purpose
- Find the Main Idea
- Make Inferences
- Use Context Clues
- Analyze Text Organization
- Identify Sequence of Events
- Compare and Contrast
- Evaluate Cause and Effect
- Classify and Reorganize Information
- Distinguish Fact from Opinion
- Interpret Visual Aids
- Understand Literary Elements
- Draw Conclusions

Using these skills as you read helps you to become an independent, thoughtful, and active reader who can accomplish tasks evaluated on tests, particularly standardized tests. Standardized test practice connected to these skills follows each selection in this book.

Reading TIP

For more practice on test-taking skills, see Unit 10, Test-Taking Strategies, pages 469–482.

To **identify the author's purpose**, ask yourself

- Why did the author create this piece of writing?
- Is the author simply sharing information or trying to convince me of something?
- Is he or she writing to entertain or trying to make a point?

Identify the Author's Purpose

A writer's **purpose** is his or her aim or goal. Being able to figure out an author's purpose, or purposes, is an important reading skill. An author may write with one or more of the purposes listed in the following chart. A writer's purpose corresponds to a specific mode, or type, of writing. A writer can choose from a variety of forms while working within a mode.

Purposes of Writing

Purpose	Mode	Writing Forms
to reflect	personal/ expressive writing	diary entry, personal letter, autobiography, personal essay
to entertain, to describe, to enrich, and to enlighten	imaginative/ descriptive writing	poem, character sketch, play
to tell a story, to narrate a series of events	narrative writing	short story, biography, legend, myth, history
to inform, to explain	informative/ expository writing	news article, research report, expository essay, book review
to persuade	persuasive/ argumentative writing	editorial, petition, political speech, persuasive essay

Once you identify what the author is trying to do, you can evaluate, or judge, how well the author achieved that purpose. For example, you may judge that the author of a persuasive essay made a good and convincing argument. Or, you may decide that the novel you are reading has a boring plot. In other words, the author has done a bad job of entertaining you!

Read the following paragraph from David Quammen's essay "The Last Bison," Unit 7, page 351, and try to determine what the essay is about. Is the author trying to entertain, persuade, inform, or reflect? What information leads you to this answer?

It happened quickly. First there were 60 million, roaming the prairies and plains, blanketing whole valleys almost shoulder to shoulder for miles, the greatest abundance of any species of large mammal that modern humankind ever had the privilege to behold. And then, in 1889, there were (by one informed estimate) just 541 bison surviving throughout all the United States.

Find the Main Idea

The **main idea** is a brief statement of what you think the author wants you to know, think, or feel after reading the text. In some cases, the main idea will actually be stated. Check the first and last paragraphs for a sentence that sums up the entire passage. Usually, the author will not tell you what the main idea is, and you will have to infer it.

In general, nonfiction texts have main ideas; literary texts (poems, short stories, novels, plays, and personal essays) have themes. Sometimes, however, the term *main idea* is used to refer to the theme of a literary work, especially an essay or poem. Both deal with the central idea in a written work.

A good way to find the main or overall idea of a whole selection (or part of a selection) is to gather important details into a Main Idea Map like the one below. Use the details to determine the main or overall thought or message. This will help you to draw conclusions about the main idea when you finish reading.

Main Idea Map

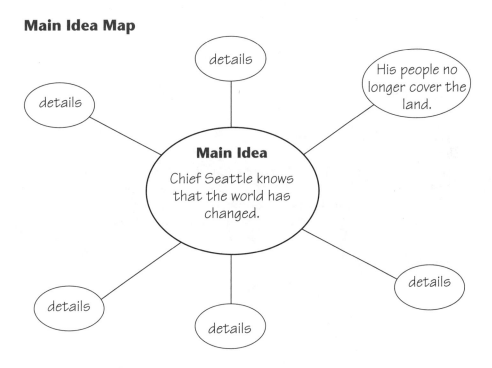

Reading TIP

To **infer the main idea**, ask yourself

- Who or what is this passage about?
- What does the author want me to know, think, feel, or do about this "who" or "what"?
- If I had to tell someone in one sentence what this passage is about, what would I say?

Make Inferences

By paying close attention to what you read, you will be able to make inferences about what the writer is trying to communicate. **Making an inference** means putting together the clues given in the text with your own prior knowledge.

Reading TIP

As you make inferences, remember that each inference needs to fit with all of the clues in the text and with your prior knowledge.

Inference Chart

Text	What I Infer
"and what people wanted to happen could happen—all you had to do was say it."	Words had strange consequences. They could make anything happen.

Use Context Clues

You can often figure out the meaning of an unfamiliar word by using context clues. **Context clues** are words and phrases near a difficult word that provide hints about its meaning. The context in which a word is used may help you guess what it means without having to look it up in the dictionary.

The following table explains different kinds of context clues and includes words that signal each type of clue. Look for these words in the sentences around an unfamiliar word to see if they signal a context clue.

Reading TIP

Sometimes you can determine the meaning of a word by using the context as a clue. For example, the word choice or mood of a passage in general may help you determine the meaning of a particular word.

Context Clues

comparison clue	shows a comparison, or how the unfamiliar word is like something that might be familiar to you
signal words	*and, like, as, just as, as if, as though*

EXAMPLE

"[T]he mountain bison were more hardy. . . . They would face into a driving blizzard in open country and stand their ground—waiting, enduring, indomitable. They were the living exempla of the word *stalwart*"—from "The Last Bison" by David Quammen. (The word *stalwart* is compared to the characteristics of a mountain bison; thus, the word must mean "something strong and enduring.")

contrast clue	shows that something contrasts, or differs in meaning, from something else
signal words	*but, nevertheless, on the other hand, however, although, though, in spite of*

"Melanocytes, the body's pigment cells . . . cluster together to form moles. Most are *innocuous*. But in some people, ultraviolet radiation [from the sun] appears to help trigger melanocytes to multiply and turn cancerous"—from "Beware the Unruly Sun" by Claudia Kalb. (If radiation causes some melanocytes to turn cancerous or become harmful, *innocuous* must describe ones that are not cancerous and "not harmful," that is, ones that are "harmless.")

restatement clue	uses different words to express the same idea
signal words	*that is, in other words, or namely*

EXAMPLE

"Between the acting of a dreadful thing / And the first motion, all the interim is / Like a *phantasma* or a hideous dream"—from *Julius Cæsar* by William Shakespeare. (The context directly restates that a *phantasma* is a "hideous dream.")

examples clue	gives examples of other items to illustrate the meaning of something
signal words	*including, such as, for example, for instance, especially, particularly*

EXAMPLE

"It reflected not only the needs of his *vocation*—he taught nineteenth- and twentieth-century literature—but a book lover's sensibility as well."—from "Into the Electronic Millennium" by Sven Birkerts. (The interspersed sentence provides a definition of *vocation* by giving an example that shows that it means "a person's occupation.")

cause-and-effect clue	tells you that something happened as a result of something else
signal words	*if/then, when/then, thus, therefore, because, so, as a result of, consequently, since*

EXAMPLE

"Daily newspapers, with their long columns of print, struggle against declining sales. Fewer and fewer people under the age of fifty read them. . . . But if the printed sheet is heading for *obsolescence*, people are tuning in to the signals. The screen is where the information and entertainment wars will be fought"—from "Into the Electronic Millenium" by Sven Birkerts. (If daily newspapers, or printed sheets, are suffering declining sales and fewer and fewer people are reading them, the word *obsolescence* must describe something that is "no longer used.")

NOTE THE FACTS

What does a restatement clue do? Write an example of a restatement clue.

_____

_____

_____

_____

Analyze Text Organization

Writing can be organized in different ways. To be an effective reader you need to know how to analyze how the text is organized. When you analyze something, you break it down into parts and then think about how the parts are related to each other and to the whole.

Reading TIP

Transition words connect ideas. They indicate how a text is organized. Look for words that
- describe main points (descriptive words)
- show sequence (sequence words)
- show comparison and contrast (comparison-and-contrast words)
- show cause and effect (cause-and-effect words)

Chronological or Time Order

Events are given in the order in which they happen or should be done. Events are connected by transition words such as *first, second, next, then, furthermore,* and *finally.* Chronological order is often used to relate a narrative, as in a short story; to write a how-to article on a topic like building a bird feeder; or to describe a process, such as what happens when a volcano erupts.

Spatial or Location Order

Parts are described in order of their location in space, for example, from back to front, left to right, or top to bottom. Descriptions are connected by transition words or phrases such as *next to, beside, above, below, beyond,* and *around.* Spatial order could be used for an article that discusses a project's physical aspects, such as describing the remodeling of a kitchen, or for a descriptive passage in literature, as in establishing the setting of a science fiction story set in a space station.

Order of Importance

Details are listed from least important to most important or from most important to least important; transition phrases are used such as *more important, less important, most important,* and *least important.* For example, a speech telling voters why they should elect you class president could build from the least important reason to the most important reason.

Comparison-and-Contrast Order

Details of two subjects are presented in one of two ways. In the first method, the characteristics of one subject are presented, followed by the characteristics of the second subject. This method could be used to organize an essay that compares and contrasts two fast-food chains, and to tell why one is superior to the other.

In the second method, both subjects are compared and contrasted with regard to one quality, then with regard to a second quality, and so on. An essay organized according to this method could compare the platforms of two political parties issue by issue: the environment, the economy, and so forth. Ideas are connected by transition words and phrases that indicate similarities or differences, such as *likewise, similarly, in contrast, a different kind, on the other hand,* and *another difference.*

Cause-and-Effect Order

One or more causes are followed by one or more effects, or one or more effects are followed by one or more causes. Transition words and phrases that indicate cause and effect include *one cause, another effect, as a result, consequently,* and *therefore.* Cause-and-effect organization might be used for a public health announcement warning about the dangers of playing with fire or an essay discussing the outbreak of World War I and the events that led up to it.

Classification or Sorting Order

Items are classified, or grouped, in categories to show how one group is similar to or different from another. Items in the same category should share one or more characteristics. For example, Edgar Allan Poe, Agatha Christie, and Stephen King can be classified together as mystery writers. Transition words that indicate classification order are the same words that indicate comparison-and-contrast order, words such as *likewise, similarly, in contrast, a different kind,* and *another difference.*

Identify Sequence of Events

Sequence refers to the order in which things happen. When you read certain types of writing, such as a short story, a novel, a biography of a person's life, or a history book, keep track of the sequence of events. You might do this by making a time line or a sequence map.

Time Line

To make a time line, draw a line and divide it into equal parts like the one on the next page. Label each part with a date or a time. Then add key events at the right places along the time line.

METHODS OF TEXT ORGANIZATION
- Chronological order
- Spatial order
- Order of importance
- Comparison-and-contrast order
- Cause-and-effect order
- Classification order

NOTE THE FACTS

How can you keep track of the sequence of events?

_____

_____

_____

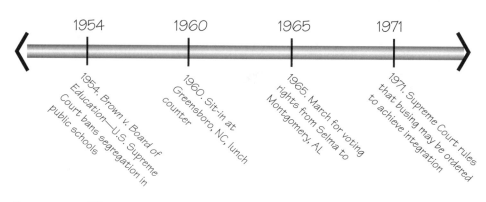

1954   1960   1965   1971

1954: Brown v. Board of Education—U.S. Supreme Court bans segregation in public schools

1960: Sit-in at Greensboro, NC, lunch counter

1965: March for voting rights from Selma to Montgomery, AL

1971: Supreme Court rules that busing may be ordered to achieve integration

Sequence Map

In each box, draw pictures that represent key events in a selection. Then write a caption under each box that explains each event. Draw the events in the order in which they occur.

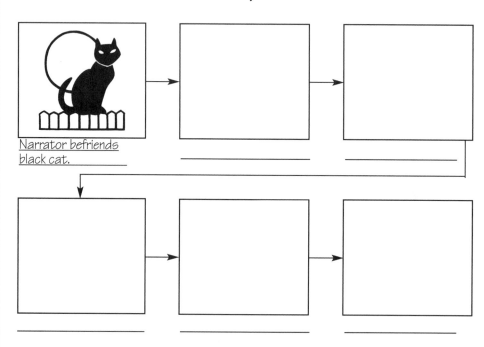

Narrator befriends black cat.

NOTE THE FACTS

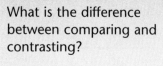

What is the difference between comparing and contrasting?

_____

_____

_____

_____

Compare and Contrast

Comparing and contrasting are closely related processes. When you **compare** one thing to another, you describe similarities between the two things; when you **contrast** two things, you describe their differences. To compare and contrast, begin by listing the features of each subject. Then go down both lists and check whether each feature is shared or not. You can also show similarities and differences in a Venn diagram. A Venn diagram uses two slightly overlapping circles. The outer part of each circle shows what aspects of two things are different from each other. The inner, or shared, part of each circle shows what aspects the two things share.

Venn Diagram

Write down ideas about Topic 1 in the first circle and ideas about Topic 2 in the second circle. The area in which the circles overlap should contain ideas common to both topics.

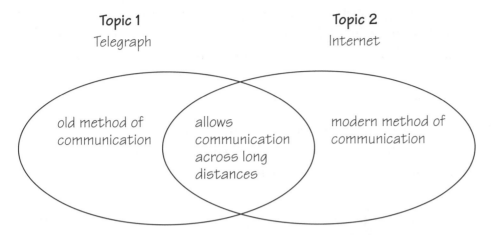

Topic 1
Telegraph

Topic 2
Internet

old method of communication

allows communication across long distances

modern method of communication

Evaluate Cause and Effect

When you evaluate **cause and effect**, you are looking for a logical relationship between a cause or causes and one or more effects. A writer may present one or more causes followed by one or more effects, or one or more effects followed by one or more causes. Transitional, or signal, words and phrases that indicate cause and effect include *one cause, another effect, as a result, because, since, consequently,* and *therefore.* As a reader, you determine whether the causes and effects in a text are reasonable. A graphic organizer like the one below will help you to recognize relationships between causes and effects.

MARK THE TEXT

Highlight or underline what you do when you evaluate cause and effect.

Cause-and-Effect Chart

Keep track of what happens in a story and why in a chart like the one below. Use cause-and-effect signal words to help you identify causes and their effects.

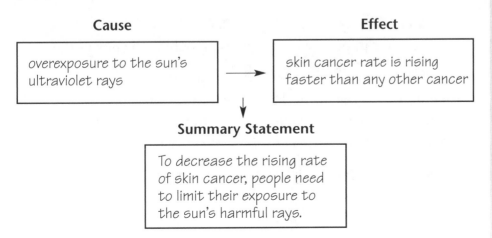

Cause

overexposure to the sun's ultraviolet rays

Effect

skin cancer rate is rising faster than any other cancer

Summary Statement

To decrease the rising rate of skin cancer, people need to limit their exposure to the sun's harmful rays.

Classify and Reorganize Information

To **classify** is to put into classes or categories. Items in the same category should share one or more characteristics. A writer may group, or categorize, things to show similarities and name the categories to clarify how one group is similar or different from another. For example, whales can be classified by their method of eating as *baleen* or *toothed*, or by their types such as *orca* or *blue*. Classifying or reorganizing the information into categories as you read increases your understanding.

The key step in classifying is choosing categories that fit your purpose. Take classification notes in a chart like the one below to help you organize separate types or groups and sort their characteristics.

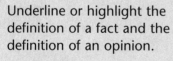

NOTE THE FACTS

What is the key step in classifying?

_____

_____

_____

Classification Chart

Category 1 Electronic Media	Category 2 Multimedia	Category 3 Technical Writing
Items in Category webzines; e-books; computer news services; web-based newspapers	**Items in Category** games; learning software; presentation software; reference materials; web pages	**Items in Category** instruction manuals; how-to instructional guides; procedural memos
Details and Characteristics distribute news online	**Details and Characteristics** uses combination of text, sound, pictures, animation, and video	**Details and Characteristics** scientific or process-oriented writing

Distinguish Fact from Opinion

A **fact** is a statement that could be proven by direct observation or a reliable reference guide. Every statement of fact is either true or false. The following statement is an example of fact:

> Edgar Allan Poe wrote "The Black Cat." (This statement is a fact that can be proven by getting a published copy of the story to see who the author is.)

An **opinion** is a statement that expresses an attitude or desire, not a fact about the world. One common type of opinion statement is a *value statement*. A value statement expresses an attitude toward something.

> Poe's story "The Black Cat" is ghastly and shocking. (The adjectives used to describe Poe's story express a personal attitude or opinion that cannot be proven.)

MARK THE TEXT

Underline or highlight the definition of a fact and the definition of an opinion.

Value statements often include judgment words such as the following:

attractive	honest	ugly
awesome	junk	unattractive
beautiful	kind	valuable
cheap	mean	wonderful
dishonest	nice	worthless
excellent	petty	
good	treasure	

NOTE THE FACTS

What are value statements? What are three words you could add to the chart at left?

_____

_____

_____

_____

A **policy statement** is an opinion that tells not what is but what someone believes should be. Such statements usually include words like *should, should not, ought, ought not, must,* or *must not.*

> You **should** use sunscreen to prevent melanoma.
> You **must not** ignore the signs of skin cancer.

A **prediction** makes a statement about the future. Because the future is unpredictable, most predictions can be considered opinions.

> New research will find a cure for melanoma.
> Computers may soon be able to diagnose skin cancer.

When evaluating a fact, ask yourself whether it can be proven through direct observation or by checking a reliable source such as a reference book or an unbiased expert. An opinion is only as good as the facts that support it. When reading or listening, be critical about the statements that you encounter. It may be helpful to make a chart like the one below to help distinguish fact from opinion as you read.

Reading **TIP**

To **distinguish fact from opinion**, ask yourself: Is this a fact, or is this an opinion? If it is a statement of fact, can it be proven or does it seem likely? If it is an opinion, can it be supported by facts?

Fact or Opinion Chart

Fact: Dr. Thomas Harvey, a pathologist in Wichita, Kansas, stored pieces of Einstein's brain in two glass jars.	**Opinion:** Albert Einstein was the smartest person who ever lived.
Proof: People can verify that Dr. Harvey, a Princeton pathologist, received pieces of Einstein's brain after Einstein's death in 1955.	**Support:** Einstein was smart, but it is impossible to prove that he was the smartest who ever lived.
Fact:	**Opinion:**
Proof:	**Support:**

Interpret Visual Aids

Visual aids are charts, graphs, pictures, illustrations, photos, maps, diagrams, spreadsheets, and other materials that present information. Many writers use visual aids to present data in understandable ways. Information visually presented in tables, charts, and graphs can help you find information, see trends, discover facts, and uncover patterns.

Reading Graphics	
Before Reading	■ Determine the subject of the graphic by reading the title, headings, and other textual clues.
	■ Determine how the data are organized, classified, or divided by reading the labels along rows or columns.
During Reading	■ Survey the data and look for trends by comparing columns and rows, noting changes among information fields, looking for patterns, or studying map sections.
	■ Use legends, keys, and other helpful sections in the graphic.
After Reading	■ Check footnotes or references for additional information about the data and their sources.
	■ List conclusions or summarize the data.

Pie Chart

A **pie chart** is a circle that stands for a whole group or set. The circle is divided into parts to show the divisions of the whole. When you look at a pie chart, you can see the relationships of the parts to one another and to the whole.

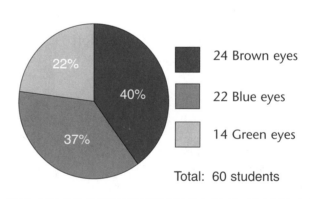

22%

40%

37%

24 Brown eyes

22 Blue eyes

14 Green eyes

Total: 60 students

EYE COLOR DISTRIBUTION IN ONE CLASSROOM

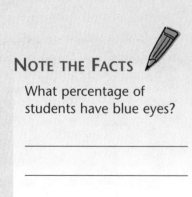

NOTE THE FACTS

What are two things you can do with graphics at the during-reading stage?

_____

_____

_____

_____

NOTE THE FACTS

What percentage of students have blue eyes?

_____

_____

Bar Graph

A **bar graph** compares amounts of something by representing the amounts as bars of different lengths. In the bar graph below, each bar represents the number of coats collected by several schools for a coat donation. To read the graph, simply imagine a line drawn from the edge of the bar to the bottom of the graph. Then read the number. For example, the bar graph below shows that Woodland collected 600 coats for the coat donation program.

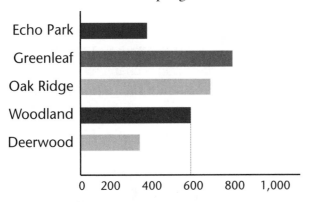

NUMBER OF COATS COLLECTED FOR COAT DONATION

NOTE THE FACTS

Which school collected the most coats for the coat donation? How many coats did they collect?

_____

_____

Map

A **map** is a representation, usually on a surface such as paper or a sheet of plastic, of a geographic area showing various significant features of that area.

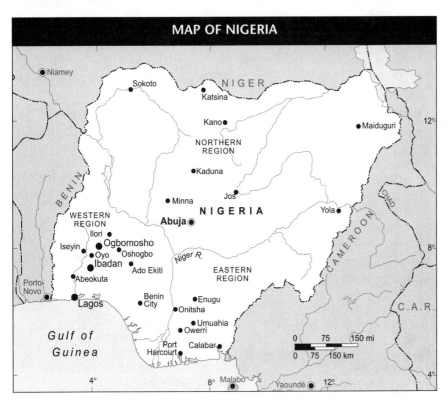

NOTE THE FACTS

What city lies closest to the mouth of the Niger River on the Gulf of Guinea?

_____

_____

Understand Literary Elements

Literary elements are the terms and techniques that are used in literature. When you read literature, you need to be familiar with the literary terms and reading skills listed below. These literary elements are explained in more detail in Unit 3, Reading Fiction, pages 36–38. Other literary elements are described in Units 4–7. Here are descriptions of the reading skills needed for some of the most common literary elements.

Reading TIP

An author's **writing style** can affect tone and mood. For example, sentence length, sentence variety, vocabulary difficulty (the number of mono-, bi-, and polysyllabic words), and the connotation (the association a word has in addition to its literal meaning) of words help determine the tone and mood.

- **RECOGNIZE MOOD AND TONE. Mood** is the atmosphere or emotion conveyed by a literary work. A writer creates mood by using concrete details to describe the setting, characters, or events. The writer can evoke in the reader an emotional response—such as fear, discomfort, longing, or anticipation—by working carefully with descriptive language and sensory details. The mood of a work might be dark, mysterious, gloomy, cheerful, inspiring, or peaceful. **Tone** is the writer's attitude toward the subject or toward the reader of a work. Examples of different tones that a work may have include familiar, ironic, playful, sarcastic, serious, and sincere.

- **UNDERSTAND POINT OF VIEW. Point of view** is the vantage point, or perspective, from which a story or narrative is told. Stories are typically written from the following points of view:

first-person point of view	narrator uses words such as *I* and *we*
second-person point of view	narrator uses *you*
third-person point of view	narrator uses words such as *he, she, it,* and *they*

- **ANALYZE CHARACTER AND CHARACTERIZATION. A character** is a person (or sometimes an animal) who takes part in the action of a story. **Characterization** is the literary techniques writers use to create characters and make them come alive. Writers use the following techniques to create characters:

Reading TIP

A **character chart** can be used as a graphic organizer to keep track of character development as you read. See the example in Appendix B, page B-8.

direct description	describing the physical features, dress, and personality of the character
behavior	showing what characters say, do, or think
interaction with others	showing what other characters say or think about them
internal state	revealing the character's private thoughts and emotions

- **EXAMINE PLOT DEVELOPMENT.** The plot is basically what happens in a story. A **plot** is a series of events related to a *central conflict*, or struggle. A typical plot involves the introduction of a conflict, its development, and its eventual resolution. The elements of plot include the following:

exposition	sets the tone or mood, introduces the characters and setting, and provides necessary background information
inciting incident	introduces a central conflict with or within one or more characters
rising action	develops a central conflict with or within one or more characters and develops toward a high point of intensity
climax	marks the highest point of interest or suspense in the plot at which something decisive happens
falling action	details the events that follow the climax
resolution	marks the point at which the central conflict is ended or resolved
dénouement	includes any material that follows the resolution and that ties up loose ends

Reading TIP

A graphic organizer called a **plot diagram** can be used to chart the plot of a literature selection. Refer to the example in Appendix B, page B-11.

Draw Conclusions

When you **draw conclusions,** you are gathering pieces of information and then deciding what that information means.

This passage from a *Newsweek* magazine article, "Beware the Unruly Sun," Unit 8, page 401, describes the rise of skin cancer in America.

> In the United States, the incidence of melanoma is rising faster than almost any other cancer, striking Americans at twice the rate today as it did two decades ago. This year alone more than 44,000 people are expected to be diagnosed, and 7,300 could die. "The increase is absolutely astounding," says Dr. Martin Weinstock, chair of the American Cancer Society's (ACS) skin-cancer advisory group. "This is a major public-health problem."

The key idea in this passage is that the number of deaths from skin cancer is rising very rapidly. Several supporting points,—"twice the rate" of twenty years ago, "the increase is astounding," and "a major public-health problem"— lead to the overall conclusion that something is causing the death rates to increase rapidly.

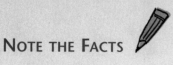
What kind of graphic organizer can help you draw conclusions? What can it help you track?

_____

_____

_____

Drawing conclusions is an essential part of reading. As you read, it may be helpful to use a graphic organizer such as a chart or log to keep track of the information you find and the conclusions you draw.

Drawing Conclusions Log

Key Idea	Key Idea	Key Idea
Cancer death rates are high		
Supporting Points	**Supporting Points**	**Supporting Points**
"twice the rate" of twenty years ago		
"the increase is astounding"		
"a major public-health problem"		
Overall Conclusion	**Overall Conclusion**	**Overall Conclusion**
Something is causing a huge increase in cancer death rates.		

Unit 2 **READING** Review

Choose and Use Reading Skills

Before reading the excerpt below, review with a partner how to use each of these essential reading skills.

- Identify the Author's Purpose
- Find the Main Idea
- Make Inferences
- Use Context Clues
- Analyze Text Organization
- Identify Sequence of Events
- Compare and Contrast

- Evaluate Cause and Effect
- Classify and Reorganize Information
- Distinguish Fact from Opinion
- Interpret Visual Aids
- Understand Literary Elements
- Draw Conclusions

After a stroke left him almost totally paralyzed, writer Jean-Dominique Bauby was forced to live in a diving bell, a diving apparatus consisting of a container open only at the bottom and supplied with compressed air by a hose. Read this excerpt from his book *The Diving Bell and the Butterfly* and note how you can use some of the reading skills discussed in this unit. After you finish reading the excerpt, answer the questions that follow.

I am fading away. Slowly but surely. Like the sailor who watches the home shore gradually disappear, I watch my past recede. My old life still burns within me, but more and more of it is reduced to the ashes of memory.

Yet since taking up residence in my diving bell, I have made two brief trips to the world of Paris medicine to hear the verdict pronounced on me from the diagnostic heights. On the first occasion, my emotions got the better of me when my ambulance happened to pass the ultra modern high-rise where I once followed the reprehensible calling of editor in chief of a famous women's magazine. First I recognized the building next door—a sixties antiquity, now scheduled to be demolished, according to the billboard out front. Then I saw our own glass façade, airily reflecting clouds and airplanes. On the sidewalk were a few of those familiar-looking faces that one passes every day for ten years without ever being able to put a name to them. When I thought I glimpsed someone I actually knew, walking behind a woman with her hair in a bun and a burly man in work clothes, I nearly unscrewed my head to see. Perhaps someone had caught sight of my ambulance from our sixth floor offices. I shed a few tears as we passed the corner café where I used to drop in for a bite. I can weep quite discreetly. People think my eye is watering.

1. What do you think is the author's purpose? What type of writing does he use? What ideas does the author want to communicate?

_____

_____

_____

2. Why does Bauby cry during his first trip back to Paris? What does this reveal about him?

_____

_____

3. How can you guess the meaning of the word *facade* by using context clues?

_____

_____

4. Make a prediction about what might happen to the narrator on his second trip back to Paris. What might he experience? Why do you think so?

_____

_____

On Your Own

FLUENTLY SPEAKING. Select a 100–150-word passage from a book, magazine, or newspaper that you are currently reading. Working with a partner, take turns reading the passage aloud several times. Break it down into shorter sections and alternate reading paragraphs or sentences. Use the Oral Reading Skills: Repeated Reading Record in Appendix A, page A-12, to chart your progress.

PICTURE THIS. Find an article that contains data of some sort. Think about how this data can be presented using a visual aid, such as a table, chart, or graph. Do you notice any trends or patterns in the information? Draw a visual aid, such as a pie chart or bar graph, to present the information in a more understandable way.

PUT IT IN WRITING. Read a short article from a magazine or newspaper. Now go back and reread the first and last paragraphs. Write a summary of the main idea. What is it that the author wants you to know, think, feel, or do after reading this text? Is the main idea stated, or did you have to infer it?

Unit THREE

REReading
Fiction

FICTION

Fiction is prose writing that tells an invented or imaginary story. *Prose* is writing that uses straightforward language and differs from poetry in that it doesn't have a rhythmic pattern. Some fiction, such as the historical novel, is based on fact, while other forms, such as the fantasy tale, are highly unrealistic. Fictional works may vary in structure and length.

Forms of Fiction

The oldest form of fiction is the stories told in the oral, or folk, tradition, which include myths, legends, and fables. The most common types of fiction are short stories, novels, and novellas.

THE SHORT STORY. A **short story** is a brief work of fiction that tells a story. It usually focuses on a single episode or scene and involves a limited number of characters. Although a short story contains all the main elements of fiction—character, setting, plot, and theme—it may not fully develop each element. Sometimes writers of the short story may focus on creating mood rather than telling a story. The selections in this unit are examples of short stories.

THE NOVEL. A **novel** is a long work of fiction that usually has more complex elements than a short story. Its longer format allows the elements of fiction to be more fully developed. The modern novel deals with the reality of human experience, often in an imaginative or romantic way. A **novella** is a work of fiction that is longer than a typical short story but shorter than a typical novel.

Types of fiction include **romances,** tales that feature the adventures of such legendary figures as Alexander the Great and King Arthur; **historical fiction,** which is partly based on actual historical events and is partly invented; and **science fiction,** imaginative literature based on scientific principles, discoveries, or laws that often deals with the future, the distant past, or worlds other than our own.

Reading TIP

The term fiction comes from the Latin *fictio,* meaning something invented.

NOTE THE FACTS

List the three most common types of fiction.

_____

_____

_____

Elements of Fiction

CHARACTER. A **character** is a person (or sometimes an animal) who takes part in the action of a story. The following are some useful terms for describing characters.

protagonist (main character)	central figure in a story
antagonist	character who struggles against the protagonist
major character	character with a significant role in the action of the story
minor character	character who plays a lesser role
one-dimentional character (flat character)	character who exhibits a single dominant quality (character trait)
three dimensional character (full or rounded character)	character who exhibits the complexity of traits of a human being
static character	character who does not change during the course of the story
dynamic character	character who does change during the course of the story
stock character	character found again and again in different literary works

CHARACTERIZATION. **Characterization** is the literary techniques writers use to create characters and make them come alive. Three major techniques are used to create characters:

direct description	describing the physical features, dress, and personality of the character
behavior	showing what the character says or does
interaction with others	showing what other characters say or think about the character
internal state	revealing the character's private thoughts and emotions

SETTING. The **setting** of a work of fiction is the time and place in which the events take place. In fiction, setting is most often revealed by description of landscape, scenery, buildings, weather, and season. Setting reveals important information about the time period, geographical location, cultural environment, and physical conditions in which the characters live.

NOTE THE FACTS

What is a character who exhibits a single dominant quality called?

_____

_____

_____

Reading TIP

A writer may use an *internal monologue* to reveal a character's private thoughts and emotions, and to shed light on a character's motives. **Motivation** is the force that moves a character to think, feel, or behave in a certain way. For example, a character may be motivated by greed, love, or friendship.

MOOD AND TONE. Mood is the atmosphere or emotion created by a literary work. A writer creates mood by using concrete details to describe the setting, characters, or events. The mood of a work might be dark, mysterious, gloomy, cheerful, inspiring, or peaceful.

Tone is the writer's attitude toward the subject or toward the reader of a work. The tone of a work might be familiar, ironic, playful, sarcastic, serious, or sincere.

POINT OF VIEW. Point of view is the vantage point from which a story or narrative is told. You need to consider point of view to understand the perspective from which the events in the story are being told. Stories are typically written from the following points of view:

first-person point of view	narrator uses words such as *I* and *we*
second-person point of view	narrator uses *you*
third-person point of view	narrator uses words such as *he, she, it*, and *they*

Most of the literature you read will be told from either the first-person or third-person point of view. In stories written from a first-person point of view, the narrator may be a participant or a witness of the action. In stories told from a third-person point of view, the narrator generally stands outside the action. In some stories, the narrator's point of view is *limited*. In such stories the narrator can reveal only his or her private, internal thoughts or those of a single character. In other stories, the narrator's point of view is *omniscient*. In such stories the narrator can reveal the private, internal thoughts of any character.

CONFLICT. A conflict is a struggle between two forces in a literary work. A plot involves the introduction, development, and eventual resolution of a conflict. A struggle that takes place between a character and some outside force is called an *external conflict*. A struggle that takes place within a character is called an *internal conflict*.

PLOT. When you read short stories or novels, it helps to know the parts of a plot. The plot is basically what happens in a story. A **plot** is a series of events related to a central conflict, or struggle. A typical plot involves the introduction of a conflict, its development, and its eventual resolution. The elements of plot include the following:

Reading TIP

The writer can create mood, or cause in the reader an emotional response—such as fear, discomfort, or longing—by working carefully with descriptive language and sensory details.

Reading TIP

One side of the central conflict in a work of fiction is usually taken by the main character. That character may struggle against another character, against the forces of nature, against society or social norms, against fate, or against some elements within himself or herself.

exposition	sets the tone or mood, introduces the characters and setting, and provides necessary background information
inciting incident	event that introduces a central conflict
rising action	develops a central conflict and rises toward a high point of intensity
climax	the high point of interest or suspense in the plot where something decisive happens
falling action	the events that follow the climax
resolution	the point at which the central conflict is ended or resolved
dénouement	any material that follows the resolution and that ties up loose ends

Use a **plot diagram** like the one below to chart the plot of a literature selection.

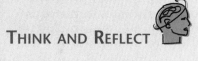

THINK AND REFLECT

In which part of the plot would you expect some kind of turning point to occur? **(Apply)**

_____

_____

_____

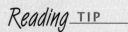

Reading **TIP**

Plots rarely contain all the elements in precisely this order. Elements of exposition may be introduced at any time in a work. Plots can exhibit many possible variations. If you understand the purpose of each element, you will be able to identify them whenever they appear.

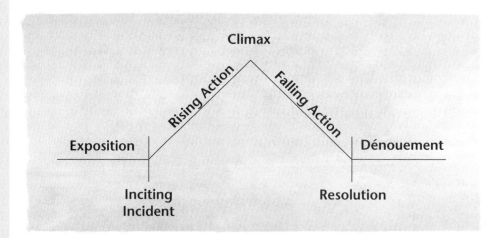

Become an Active Reader

The instruction in this unit gives you an in-depth look at how to use one active reading strategy for each story. Questions and tips in the margins keep your attention focused on reading actively. White space in the margins allows you to add your own comments and strategy ideas. Brief margin notes guide your use of additional strategies. Learning how to use several strategies in combination will ensure your understanding of what you are reading. When you have difficulty, use fix-up ideas to correct the problem. For further information about the active reading strategies, see Unit 1, pages 4–15.

Active Reading Strategy Checklists

When reading fiction, you need to be aware of the plot (or what happens), the characters, and the setting. The following checklists offer things to consider as you read fiction.

1 **READ WITH A PURPOSE.** Before reading about imagined events and characters, give yourself a purpose, or something to look for, as you read. Say to yourself

- ❑ I want to look for . . .
- ❑ I need to learn what happens to . . .
- ❑ I want to experience what it is like in . . .
- ❑ I want to understand . . .

2 **CONNECT TO PRIOR KNOWLEDGE.** Being aware of what you already know and thinking about it as you read can help you keep track of what's happening and will increase your knowledge. As you read, say to yourself

- ❑ I already know this about the story . . .
- ❑ This part of the story reminds me of . . .
- ❑ I think this part of the story is like . . .
- ❑ My experience tells me that . . .
- ❑ I like this description because . . .

3 **WRITE THINGS DOWN.** As you read short stories or novels, writing things down is very important. Possible ways to write things down include

- ❑ Underline characters' names.
- ❑ Write messages on sticky notes.
- ❑ Highlight the setting.
- ❑ Create a graphic organizer to keep track of plot elements.
- ❑ Use a code in the margin that shows how you respond to the characters, setting, or events. For instance, you can mark a description you like with a "+."

4 **MAKE PREDICTIONS.** Because fiction includes information about characters, settings, and events, make predictions about these story elements. Your predictions will help you think about what lies ahead. Make predictions like the following:

- ❑ I predict that this character will . . .
- ❑ The setting of this story makes me think that . . .
- ❑ I bet there will be a conflict between . . .
- ❑ This event in the story makes me guess that . . .

Reading **TIP**

Sometimes a purpose will be a directive from a teacher: "Look for foreshadowing." Other times you can set your own purpose by previewing the title, the opening paragraphs, and the instructional information for the story.

Reading **TIP**

Instead of writing down a short response, use a symbol or a short word to indicate your response. Use codes like the ones listed below.

+	I like this.
–	I don't like this.
√	This is important.
Yes	I agree with this.
No	I disagree with this.
?	I don't understand this.
!	This is like something I know.
↩	I need to come back to this later.

5 VISUALIZE. Visualizing, or allowing the words on the page to create images in your mind, is one of the most important things to do while reading fiction. Become part of the action. "See" what the author describes. Make statements like

❑ I imagine the setting to look like . . .
❑ This description of the main character makes me . . .
❑ I picture that this is what happens in this section . . .
❑ I envision myself in the action by . . .

6 USE TEXT ORGANIZATION. Fiction writing has a plot that you can follow. Use the plot, or the series of events, to keep track of what is happening. Say to yourself

❑ The exposition, or introduction, tells me . . .
❑ The central conflict centers on . . .
❑ The climax, or high point of interest, occurs when . . .
❑ The resolution, or the outcome, of this story lets me know . . .
❑ Signal words like *first*, *then*, and *finally* explain . . .

7 TACKLE DIFFICULT VOCABULARY. Difficult words in a story can get in the way of your ability to follow the events in a work of fiction. Use aids that a text provides, consult a dictionary, or ask someone about words you do not understand. When you come across a word you do not know, say to yourself

❑ The context tells me that this word means . . .
❑ A dictionary definition provided in the story shows that the word means . . .
❑ My work with the word before class helps me know that the word means . . .
❑ A classmate said that the word means . . .
❑ I can skip knowing the exact meaning of this word because . . .

8 MONITOR YOUR READING PROGRESS. All readers encounter difficulty when they read, especially if the reading material is not self-selected. When you have to read something, note problems you are having and fix them. The key to reading success is knowing when you are having difficulty. To fix problems, say to yourself

❑ Because I do not understand this part, I will . . .
❑ Because I am having trouble staying interested in the story, I will . . .
❑ Because the words are too hard, I will . . .
❑ Because the story is very long, I will . . .
❑ Because I cannot remember what I have just read, I will . . .

Fix-Up Ideas

- Reread
- Ask a question
- Read in shorter chunks
- Read aloud
- Retell
- Work with a partner
- Unlock difficult words
- Vary your reading rate
- Choose a new reading strategy
- Create a mnemonic device

How to Use Reading Strategies with Fiction

Use the following excerpts to discover how you might use reading strategies as you read fiction.

Excerpt 1. Note how a reader uses active reading strategies while reading this excerpt from "Rules of the Game" by Amy Tan.

WRITE THINGS DOWN

I will underline references to the wind as I read.

MAKE PREDICTIONS

Because the narrator talks about "chess games," I think that "Rules of the Game" will be about playing chess.

I was six when my mother taught me the art of invisible strength. It was a strategy for winning arguments, respect from others, and eventually, though neither of us knew it at the time, chess games.

"Bite back your tongue," scolded my mother when I cried loudly, yanking her hand toward the store that sold bags of salted plums. At home, she said, "Wise guy, he not go against wind. In Chinese we say, Come from South, blow with wind—poom!—North will follow. Strongest wind cannot be seen."

The next week I bit back my tongue as we entered the store with the forbidden candies. When my mother finished her shopping, she quietly plucked a small bag of plums from the rack and put it on the counter with the rest of the items.

MONITOR YOUR READING PROGRESS

I don't understand the mother's Chinese saying. I'll mark it and try to figure it out later.

CONNECT TO PRIOR KNOWLEDGE

The narrator wants to eat a bag of "salted plums." This doesn't sound very good to me.

Excerpt 2. Note how a reader uses active reading strategies while reading this excerpt from "The Black Cat" by Edgar Allan Poe.

READ WITH A PURPOSE

Poe writes horror stories. I want to discover if a black cat does something horrifying.

VISUALIZE

I envision a large mean black cat with thick fur standing on end.

I married early, and was happy to find in my wife a disposition not <u>uncongenial</u> with my own. Observing my partiality for domestic pets, she lost no opportunity of procuring those of the most agreeable kind. We had birds, goldfish, a fine dog, rabbits, a small monkey, and a *cat*.

This <u>latter</u> was a remarkably large and beautiful animal, entirely black, and sagacious to an astonishing degree. In speaking of his intelligence, my wife, who at heart was not a little tinctured[7] with superstition, made frequent <u>allusion</u> to the ancient popular notion, which regarded all black cats as witches in disguise. Not that she was ever *serious* upon this point—and I mention the matter at all for no better reason than that it happens, just now, to be remembered.

USE TEXT ORGANIZATION

Because the title of the story is "The Black Cat," the fact that the narrator's wife had a cat may be an important event.

TACKLE DIFFICULT VOCABULARY

Rereading after I study the footnotes and the definitions at the bottom of the page will help me understand the passage.

Reader's resource

First published in 1843, **"The Black Cat"** is considered one of Poe's greatest horror tales. In this story the narrator, whose sanity is in question, is haunted by a black cat. "The Black Cat" can be read in one of two ways—as a tale about supernatural events told by a sane narrator, or as a tale in which an insane narrator relates his hallucinations.

Word watch

PREVIEW VOCABULARY

allusion	incumbent
anomalous	inscrutability
apparition	intemperate
atrocity	jeopardize
aversion	latter
bravado	lime
cherish	odious
conflagration	perverseness
conjointly	premises
consign	procure
constitute	remorse
debauch	render
deliberate	repose
docility	reverberation
equivocal	solicit
expedient	succinctly
expound	succumb
goaded	uncongenial
imperceptible	ungovernable
inclination	

Reader's journal

Recall the scariest horror story you've read or the scariest horror film you've seen. What aspects of the story or film did you find most frightening? Why?

"The Black Cat"

by Edgar Allan Poe

Active READING STRATEGY

TACKLE DIFFICULT VOCABULARY

Before Reading PREVIEW AND LEARN SELECTION VOCABULARY

❏ Work with a partner to preview the selection. Read the Reader's Resource.
❏ Preview WordWatch and write down the Words for Everyday Use and the footnoted terms that appear on the selection pages.
❏ Study the vocabulary words and footnoted terms. Begin by pronouncing each word out loud, using a dictionary to help you with unfamiliar footnoted terms, if necessary.
❏ Then, choose ten words that you are unfamiliar with and write out their definitions in your notebook, using the format in the graphic organizer below. Organize this word study neatly in your notebook so that you can easily refer to the words while you read.

Graphic Organizer

Word: _____

Pronunciation: _____

Origins: _____

_____

Definition: _____

Sentence: _____

_____

Drawing:

The Black Cat

Edgar Allan Poe

For the most wild yet most homely[1] narrative which I am about to pen, I neither expect nor <u>solicit</u> belief. Mad indeed would I be to expect it, in a case where my very senses reject their own evidence. Yet, mad am I not—and very surely do I not dream. But tomorrow I die, and today I would unburden my soul. My immediate purpose is to place before the world, plainly, <u>succinctly</u>, and without comment, a series of mere household events. In their consequences, these events have terrified—have tortured—have destroyed me. Yet I will not attempt to <u>expound</u> them. To me, they have presented little but horror—to many they will seem less terrible than *baroques.*[2] Hereafter, perhaps, some intellect may be found which will reduce my phantasm[3] to the commonplace—some intellect more calm, more logical, and far less excitable than my own, which will perceive, in the circumstances I detail with awe, nothing more than an ordinary succession of very natural causes and effects.

10

---

1. **homely.** Simple, plain
2. **baroques.** Grotesque or whimsical designs, in the style of the Baroque period (*circa* 1600–1750)
3. **phantasm.** Specter or ghost

words for everyday use

so • lic • it (sə lis´it) *vt.,* ask earnestly or pleadingly. *I wish to <u>solicit</u> your advice about an important matter.*

suc • cinct • ly (suk siŋkt´lē) *adv.,* in a concise manner. *After <u>succinctly</u> explaining the procedure, the physician asked if anyone had any questions.*

ex • pound (eks pound´) *vt.,* explain in detail point by point. *The audience wilted from boredom as the speaker continued to <u>expound</u> the details of his scientific theory.*

During Reading

HANDLE DIFFICULT VOCABULARY WHILE YOU READ

- ❑ Begin reading the selection independently. Use the footnotes and vocabulary definitions or refer to your word study notebook if you forget the meaning of any difficult words.
- ❑ Jot down any new vocabulary words that keep you from understanding the story.
- ❑ Before moving on, use context clues, a dictionary, or another method to unlock the meaning of these difficult words.
- ❑ Continue using the strategy as you read, pausing as necessary to unlock the meaning of difficult words.

READ ALOUD

Read the first paragraph aloud. Pause and try to paraphrase each sentence in your own words to help set the stage for the tale the narrator is about to tell.

Literary TOOLS

FLASHBACK. A **flashback** is a section of a literary work that presents an event or series of events that occurred earlier than the current time in the work. As you read, note how Poe uses flashbacks in "The Black Cat."

What makes the speaker "the jest of his companions"? How is the speaker indulged by his parents? How does he spend most of his time?

_____

_____

_____

_____

Use THE STRATEGY

TACKLE DIFFICULT VOCABULARY. Remember to record in your word study notebook any unfamiliar words you encounter. You can work with these words later in order to become more familiar with them and to expand your personal vocabulary.

From my infancy I was noted for the docility and humanity of my disposition. My tenderness of heart was even so conspicuous as to make me the jest of my companions. I was especially fond of animals, and was indulged by my parents with a great variety of pets. With these I spent most of my time, and never was so happy as when feeding and caressing them. This peculiarity of character grew with my growth, and, in my manhood, I derived from it one of my principal sources of pleasure. To those who have cherished an affection for a faithful and sagacious[4] dog, I need hardly be at the trouble of explaining the nature or the intensity of the gratification thus derivable.[5] There is something in the unselfish and self-sacrificing love of a brute, which goes directly to the heart of him who has had frequent occasion to test the paltry friendship and gossamer fidelity[6] of mere *Man*.

I married early, and was happy to find in my wife a disposition not uncongenial with my own. Observing my partiality for domestic pets, she lost no opportunity of procuring those of the most agreeable kind. We had birds, goldfish, a fine dog, rabbits, a small monkey, and a *cat*.

This latter was a remarkably large and beautiful animal, entirely black, and sagacious to an astonishing degree. In speaking of his intelligence, my wife, who at heart was not a little tinctured[7] with superstition, made frequent allusion to the ancient popular notion, which regarded all black cats as witches in disguise. Not that she was ever *serious* upon this point—and I mention the matter at all for no better reason than that it happens, just now, to be remembered.

---

4. **sagacious.** Wise
5. **derivable.** Received
6. **paltry . . . fidelity.** *Paltry*—almost worthless; *gossamer fidelity*—light, flimsy loyalty
7. **tinctured.** Stained

words for everyday use

do • cil • i • ty (dō sil´ə tē) *n.*, state of being easily managed. *Maria picked the smallest puppy from the litter because of his docility and sweet face.*

cher • ish (cher´ish) *vt.*, hold dear. *They cherish their quiet evenings spent sitting on the front porch.*

un • con • ge • ni • al (un kən jēn´yəl) *adj.*, incompatible. *Tomatoes and potatoes are uncongenial companion plants in the garden.*

lat • ter (lat´ər) *adj.*, last mentioned. *Of all their children, Mary, Joseph, and Jasmine, the latter looks most like her mother.*

al • lu • sion (ə lü´ zhən) *n.*, indirect reference. *The poet frequently made allusion to youth, a topic with which he was obsessed.*

Pluto[8]—this was the cat's name—was my favorite pet and playmate. I alone fed him, and he attended me wherever I went about the house. It was even with difficulty that I could prevent him from following me through the streets.

50

Our friendship lasted, in this manner, for several years, during which my general temperament and character—through the instrumentality of the Fiend Intemperance[9]—had (I blush to confess it) experienced a radical alteration for the worse. I grew, day by day, more moody, more irritable, more regardless of the feelings of others. I suffered[10] myself to use <u>intemperate</u> language to my wife. At length, I even offered her personal violence. My pets, of course, were made to feel the change in my disposition. I not only neglected, but ill-used them. For Pluto, however,

60

I still retained sufficient regard to restrain me from maltreating him, as I made no scruple of maltreating the rabbits, the monkey, or even the dog, when, by accident, or through affection, they came in my way. But my disease grew upon me—for what disease is like Alcohol!—and at length even Pluto, who was now becoming old, and consequently somewhat peevish[11]—even Pluto began to experience the effects of my ill temper.

One night, returning home, much intoxicated, from one

70

of my haunts about town, I fancied that the cat avoided my presence. I seized him; when, in his fright at my violence, he inflicted a slight wound upon my hand with his teeth. The fury of a demon instantly possessed me.[12] I knew myself no longer. My original soul seemed, at once, to take its flight from my body; and a more than fiendish malevolence, gin-nurtured,[13] thrilled every fiber of my frame. I took from my waistcoat-pocket a penknife, opened it, grasped the poor beast by the throat, and deliberately cut one of its eyes from

---

8. **Pluto.** The cat was named for the Greek god of the underworld, whom the Romans called Pluto.
9. **Fiend Intemperance.** Substance abuse, particularly of alcohol
10. **suffered.** Allowed
11. **peevish.** Cranky; bad-tempered
12. **possessed me.** Held me
13. **gin-nurtured.** Caused by drinking gin, a hard liquor

words for everyday use

in • tem • per • ate (in tem′pər it) *adj.*, lacking restraint. *Because of her <u>intemperate</u> spending practices, Allison decided against opening another charge account.*

MARK THE TEXT

Highlight or underline the sentence that tells which pet is the speaker's favorite.

NOTE THE FACTS

What happens to the speaker's temperament? Why? How does this affect the pets?

_____

_____

_____

_____

NOTE THE FACTS

How does the speaker feel the next day about having hurt the cat?

_____

_____

_____

_____

FIX-UP IDEA

Reread
If dealing with difficult vocabulary affects your comprehension of the selection, try rereading sections of the text when you feel lost. Continue to pause when you encounter difficult words, and work to uncover their meanings. Once you feel comfortable with the words in a section, reread that section, going as far back in the story as necessary.

80 the socket! I blush, I burn, I shudder, while I pen the damnable <u>atrocity</u>.

When reason returned with the morning—when I had slept off the fumes of the night's <u>debauch</u>—I experienced a sentiment half of horror, half of remorse, for the crime of which I had been guilty; but it was, at best, a feeble and <u>equivocal</u> feeling, and the soul remained untouched. I again plunged into excess, and soon drowned in wine all memory of the deed.

In the meantime the cat slowly recovered. The socket of the lost eye presented, it is true, a frightful appearance, but 90 he no longer appeared to suffer any pain. He went about the house as usual, but, as might be expected, fled in extreme terror at my approach. I had so much of my old heart left, as to be at first grieved by this evident dislike on the part of a creature which had once so loved me. But this feeling soon gave place to irritation. And then came, as if to my final and irrevocable overthrow,[14] the spirit of <u>PERVERSENESS</u>. Of this spirit philosophy takes no account. Yet I am not more sure that my soul lives, than I am that perverseness is one of the primitive impulses of the human 100 heart—one of the indivisible primary faculties, or sentiments, which give direction to the character of Man. Who has not, a hundred times, found himself committing a vile or a stupid action, for no other reason than because he knows he should *not?* Have we not a perpetual <u>inclination</u>, in the teeth of our best judgment, to violate that which is *Law,* merely because we understand it to be such? This spirit of perverseness, I say, came to my final overthrow. It was this unfathomable[15] longing of the soul *to vex itself*—to offer violence to its own nature—to do wrong for the

---

14. **irrevocable overthrow.** Unavoidable downfall
15. **unfathomable.** Not thoroughly understood

words for everyday use

a • troc • i • ty (ə träs´ə tē) *n.,* cruel or evil act. *The prisoner of war remembered the <u>atrocity</u> committed against him for the rest of his life.*

de • bauch (dē bôch´) *n.,* extreme indulgence of one's appetites. *After eating an entire gallon of chocolate almond fudge ice cream, the twins paid for their <u>debauch</u> with severe stomach aches.*

e • quiv • o • cal (ē kwiv´ə kəl) *adj.,* uncertain; undecided. *Because of my experiences with both his fury and his kindness, I maintained an <u>equivocal</u> opinion.*

per • verse • ness (pər vurs´nəs) *n.,* deviation from what is considered right or good. *Children who commit acts of <u>perverseness</u> often become seriously troubled adults.*

in • cli • na • tion (in´ klə nā´ shən) *n.,* tendency. *On such a dreary morning, her <u>inclination</u> to stay in bed was understandable.*

110   wrong's sake only—that urged me to continue and finally to consummate[16] the injury I had inflicted upon the unoffending brute. One morning, in cold blood, I slipped a noose about its neck and hung it to the limb of a tree;—hung it with the tears streaming from my eyes, and with the bitterest remorse at my heart;—hung it *because* I knew that it had loved me, and *because* I felt it had given me no reason of offense;—hung it *because* I knew that in so doing I was committing a sin—a deadly sin that would so <u>jeopardize</u> my immortal soul as to place it—if such a thing were possible—

120   even beyond the reach of the infinite mercy of the Most Merciful and Most Terrible God.

    On the night of the day on which this most cruel deed was done, I was aroused from sleep by the cry of fire. The curtains of my bed were in flames. The whole house was blazing. It was with great difficulty that my wife, a servant, and myself, made our escape from the <u>conflagration</u>. The destruction was complete. My entire worldly wealth was swallowed up, and I resigned myself thenceforward[17] to despair.

130   I am above the weakness of seeking to establish a sequence of cause and effect, between the disaster and the atrocity. But I am detailing a chain of facts—and wish not to leave even a possible link imperfect. On the day succeeding the fire, I visited the ruins. The walls, with one exception, had fallen in. This exception was found in a compartment wall, not very thick, which stood about the middle of the house, and against which had rested the head of my bed. The plastering had here, in great measure, resisted the action of the fire—a fact which I attributed to its having been

140   recently spread. About this wall a dense crowd were collected, and many persons seemed to be examining a particular portion of it with very minute and eager attention. The words "strange!" "singular!" and other similar expressions, excited my curiosity. I approached and

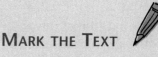

MARK THE TEXT

Mark the text that tells why the speaker hangs the cat.

NOTE THE FACTS

What happens to the speaker the night after the death of the cat? What is the speaker's mindset after this event?

_____

_____

_____

_____

---

16. **consummate.** Bring to completion
17. **thenceforward.** From then on

words for everyday use	**jeop • ard • ize** (jep´ər dīz´) *vt.,* risk; endanger. *The thunder and darkening sky could* <u>jeopardize</u> *our plans for an outdoor picnic.* **con • fla • gra • tion** (kän´ flə grā´ shən) *n.,* large, destructive fire. *To the horror of the villagers, the* <u>conflagration</u> *jumped the water barriers and burned a destructive path toward the village.*

saw, as if graven in *bas-relief* [18] upon the white surface, the figure of a gigantic *cat*. The impression was given with an accuracy truly marvellous. There was a rope about the animal's neck.

150 When I first beheld this <u>apparition</u>—for I could scarcely regard it as less—my wonder and my terror were extreme. But at length reflection came to my aid. The cat, I remembered, had been hung in a garden adjacent to the house. Upon the alarm of fire, this garden had been immediately filled by the crowd—by some one of whom the animal must have been cut from the tree and thrown, through an open window, into my chamber.[19] This had probably been done with the view of arousing me from sleep. The falling of other walls had compressed the victim of my cruelty into the substance of the freshly-spread plaster; the

160 <u>lime</u> of which, with the flames, and the *ammonia* from the carcass,[20] had then accomplished the portraiture as I saw it.

Although I thus readily accounted to my reason,[21] if not altogether to my conscience, for the startling fact just detailed, it did not the less fail to make a deep impression upon my fancy.[22] For months I could not rid myself of the phantasm of the cat; and, during this period, there came back into my spirit a half-sentiment that seemed, but was not, <u>remorse</u>. I went so far as to regret the loss of the animal, and to look about me, among the vile haunts which

170 I now habitually frequented, for another pet of the same species, and of somewhat similar appearance, with which to supply its place.

One night as I sat, half stupefied, in a den of more than infamy,[23] my attention was suddenly drawn to some black

---

18. **graven in *bas-relief*.** Carved so that it stands out against a wall or flat surface
19. **chamber.** Room
20. ***ammonia* from the carcass.** Colorless, strong-smelling gas made of nitrogen and hydrogen; it is a compound produced by a decaying human or animal body.
21. **accounted to my reason.** Explained to myself
22. **fancy.** Imagination
23. **den of more than infamy.** Tavern with a particularly bad reputation

words for everyday use

ap • pa • ri • tion (ap´ə rish´ən) *n.*, anything that appears suddenly, or in an extraordinary way. *She blinked her eyes, but she couldn't shake from view the <u>apparition</u> of the young, smiling woman.*

lime (līm) *n.*, calcium oxide, a white substance used in making mortar and cement. *Some soils naturally contain a high percentage of <u>lime</u>.*

re • morse (ri môrs´) *n.*, deep sense of guilt. *The convict showed no apparent <u>remorse</u> for her crime.*

object, <u>reposing</u> upon the head of one of the immense hogsheads[24] of gin, or of rum, which <u>constituted</u> the chief furniture of the apartment. I had been looking steadily at the top of this hogshead for some minutes, and what now caused me surprise was the fact that I had not sooner
180 perceived the object thereupon. I approached it, and touched it with my hand. It was a black cat—a very large one—fully as large as Pluto, and closely resembling him in every respect but one. Pluto had not a white hair upon any portion of his body; but this cat had a large, although indefinite splotch of white, covering nearly the whole region of the breast.

Upon my touching him, he immediately arose, purred loudly, rubbed against my hand, and appeared delighted with my notice. This, then, was the very creature of which I was in
190 search. I at once offered to purchase it of the landlord; but this person made no claim to it—knew nothing of it—had never seen it before.

I continued my caresses, and when I prepared to go home, the animal evinced a disposition[25] to accompany me. I permitted it to do so; occasionally stooping and patting it as I proceeded. When it reached the house it domesticated itself at once, and became immediately a great favorite with my wife.

For my own part, I soon found a dislike to it arising
200 within me. This was just the reverse of what I had anticipated; but—I know not how or why it was—its evident fondness for myself rather disgusted and annoyed me. By slow degrees these feelings of disgust and annoyance rose into the bitterness of hatred. I avoided the creature; a certain sense of shame, and the remembrance of my former deed of cruelty, preventing me from physically abusing it. I did not, for some weeks, strike, or otherwise violently ill use it; but gradually—very gradually—I came to look upon it with unutterable

---

24. **hogsheads.** Large barrels holding from sixty-three to one hundred and forty gallons
25. **evinced a disposition.** Appeared to want

words for everyday use

re • pose (ri pōz´) *vt.*, lie, rest, or be supported on. *While <u>reposing</u> in her hammock, the ever-hopeful gardener dreamed of giant tomatoes and succulent sweet corn.*

con • sti • tute (kän´ stə to͞ot´) *vt.*, form the components or elements of. *Wheat flour, bananas, and oatmeal <u>constituted</u> the primary ingredients of the banana bread.*

NOTE THE FACTS

What does the speaker do with the cat that he sees?

_____

_____

WHAT DO YOU WONDER?

_____

_____

_____

_____

210   loathing, and to flee silently from its <u>odious</u> presence, as from the breath of a pestilence.[26]

What added, no doubt, to my hatred of the beast, was the discovery, on the morning after I brought it home, that, like Pluto, it also had been deprived of one of its eyes. This circumstance, however, only endeared it to my wife, who, as I have already said, possessed, in a high degree, that humanity of feeling which had once been my distinguishing trait,[27] and the source of many of my simplest and purest pleasures.

220   With my <u>aversion</u> to this cat, however, its partiality for myself seemed to increase. It followed my footsteps with a pertinacity[28] which it would be difficult to make the reader comprehend. Whenever I sat, it would crouch beneath my chair, or spring upon my knees, covering me with its loathsome caresses. If I arose to walk it would get between my feet and thus nearly throw me down, or, fastening its long and sharp claws in my dress, clamber, in this manner, to my breast. At such times, although I longed to destroy it with a blow, I was yet withheld from so doing, partly by a

230   memory of my former crime, but chiefly—let me confess it at once—by absolute *dread* of the beast.

This dread was not exactly a dread of physical evil—and yet I should be at a loss how otherwise to define it. I am almost ashamed to own—yes, even in this felon's cell, I am almost ashamed to own—that the terror and horror with which the animal inspired me, had been heightened by one of the merest chimeras[29] it would be possible to conceive. My wife had called my attention, more than once, to the character of the mark of white hair, of which I have spoken,

240   and which constituted the sole visible difference between the strange beast and the one I had destroyed. The reader will remember that this mark, although large, had been originally very indefinite; but, by slow degrees—degrees nearly

---

26. **pestilence.** Communicable disease
27. **distinguishing trait.** Identifying characteristic
28. **pertinacity.** Persistence
29. **chimeras.** Illusions or fabrications of the mind

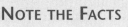

words for everyday use

o • di • ous (ō′ dē əs) *adj.*, disgusting; offensive. *Opinion polls indicated that the public believed the candidate was an <u>odious</u> man.*

a • ver • sion (ə vʉr′zhən) *n.*, loathing or revulsion. *Heidi's <u>aversion</u> toward television was not shared by many of her friends.*

imperceptible, and which for a long time my reason struggled to reject as fanciful—it had, at length, assumed a rigorous distinctness of outline. It was now the representation of an object that I shudder to name—and for this, above all, I loathed, and dreaded, and would have rid myself of the monster *had I dared*—it was now, I say, the image

250 of a hideous—of a ghastly thing—of the GALLOWS![30]—oh, mournful and terrible engine of Horror and of Crime—of Agony and of Death!

And now was I indeed wretched beyond the wretchedness of mere Humanity. And *a brute beast*—whose fellow I had contemptuously destroyed—*a brute beast* to work out for *me*—for me, a man fashioned in the image of the High God—so much of insufferable woe! Alas! neither by day nor by night knew I the blessing of rest any more! During the former the creature left me no moment alone, and in the

260 latter I started hourly from dreams of unutterable fear to find the hot breath of *the thing* upon my face, and its vast weight—an incarnate nightmare that I had no power to shake off—incumbent eternally upon my *heart!*

Beneath the pressure of torments such as these the feeble remnant of the good within me succumbed. Evil thoughts became my sole intimates[31]—the darkest and most evil of thoughts. The moodiness of my usual temper increased to hatred of all things and of all mankind; while from the sudden, frequent, and ungovernable outbursts of a fury to

270 which I now blindly abandoned myself, my uncomplaining wife, alas, was the most usual and the most patient of sufferers.

One day she accompanied me, upon some household errand, into the cellar of the old building which our poverty

---

30. **GALLOWS.** Upright frames used for hanging people
31. **intimates.** Close friends

MAKE PREDICTIONS. What later event might be foreshadowed by the black cat's white mark?

_____

_____

_____

_____

THINK AND REFLECT

Why does the speaker develop a hatred for all living things? **(Interpret)**

_____

_____

_____

words for everyday use

im • per • cep • ti • ble (im´pər sep´tə bəl) *adj.*, subtle; so as not to be easily perceived. *A slight breeze brought some relief, although it was nearly imperceptible to the laborers working in the sun.*

in • cum • bent (in kum´ bənt) *n.*, lying or pressing with its weight on something else. *Incumbent on the young boy's heart was the death of his beloved dog.*

suc • cumb (sə kum´) *vi.*, give way to; yield. *Several of the hikers succumbed to the heat.*

un • gov • ern • a • ble (un guv´ ərn ə bəl) *adj.*, unable to be controlled. *The child's ungovernable behavior distressed his parents greatly.*

NOTE THE FACTS

What happens when the speaker tries to hit the cat with an ax?

_____

_____

_____

_____

compelled us to inhabit. The cat followed me down the steep stairs, and, nearly throwing me headlong, exasperated me to madness. Uplifting an axe, and forgetting in my wrath the childish dread which had hitherto stayed my hand, I aimed a blow at the animal, which, of course, would have

280 proved instantly fatal had it descended as I wished. But this blow was arrested by the hand of my wife. <u>Goaded</u> by the interference into a rage more than demoniacal, I withdrew my arm from her grasp and buried the axe in her brain. She fell dead upon the spot without a groan.

This hideous murder accomplished, I set myself forthwith, and with entire deliberation, to the task of concealing the body. I knew that I could not remove it from the house, either by day or by night, without the risk of being observed by the neighbors. Many projects entered my mind. At one

290 period I thought of cutting the corpse into minute fragments, and destroying them by fire. At another, I resolved to dig a grave for it in the floor of the cellar. Again, I <u>deliberated</u> about casting it in the well in the yard—about packing it in a box, as if merchandise, with the usual arrangements, and so getting a porter to take it from the house. Finally I hit upon what I considered a far better <u>expedient</u> than either of these. I determined to wall it up in the cellar, as the monks of the Middle Ages are recorded to have walled up their victims.

300 For a purpose such as this the cellar was well adapted. Its walls were loosely constructed, and had lately been plastered throughout with a rough plaster, which the dampness of the atmosphere had prevented from hardening. Moreover, in one of the walls was a projection, caused by a false chimney, or fireplace, that had been filled up and made to resemble the rest of the cellar. I made no doubt that I could readily displace the bricks at this point, insert the corpse, and wall the whole up as before, so that no eye could detect any thing suspicious.

MARK THE TEXT

Highlight or underline where the speaker decides to hide the body.

words for everyday use

goad • ed (gōd´əd) *part.,* prodded into action. *Threats from the Department of Health <u>goaded</u> the negligent landlord into making improvements.*

de • lib • er • ate (di lib´ər āt´) *vt.,* think about or consider carefully. *With only thirty seconds left in the final quarter, the coach <u>deliberated</u> about the team's last play.*

ex • pe • di • ent (ek spē´ dē ənt) *n.,* resource suited to the occasion. *The young designer's idea proved to be a more efficient <u>expedient</u> than the previous solution.*

310   And in this calculation I was not deceived. By means of a crowbar I easily dislodged the bricks, and, having carefully deposited the body against the inner wall, I propped it in that position, while with little trouble I relaid the whole structure as it originally stood. Having <u>procured</u> mortar, sand, and hair, with every possible precaution, I prepared a plaster which could not be distinguished from the old, and with this I very carefully went over the new brick-work. When I had finished, I felt satisfied that all was right. The wall did not present the slightest appearance of having been

320 disturbed. The rubbish on the floor was picked up with the minutest care. I looked around triumphantly, and said to myself: "Here at least, then, my labor has not been in vain."

     My next step was to look for the beast which had been the cause of so much wretchedness; for I had, at length, firmly resolved to put it to death. Had I been able to meet with it at the moment, there could have been no doubt of its fate; but it appeared that the crafty animal had been alarmed at the violence of my previous anger, and forbore[32] to present itself in my present mood. It is impossible to describe or to

330 imagine the deep, the blissful sense of relief which the absence of the detested creature occasioned[33] in my bosom. It did not make its appearance during the night; and thus for one night, at least, since its introduction into the house, I soundly and tranquilly slept; aye, *slept* even with the burden of murder upon my soul.

     The second and the third day passed, and still my tormentor came not. Once again I breathed as a freeman. The monster, in terror, had fled the <u>premises</u> for ever! I

340 should behold it no more! My happiness was supreme! The guilt of my dark deed disturbed me but little. Some few inquiries had been made, but these had been readily answered. Even a search had been instituted—but of course nothing was to be discovered. I looked upon my future felicity[34] as secured.

---

32. **forbore.** Decided not
33. **occasioned.** Caused
34. **felicity.** Happiness

words for everyday use	**pro • cure** (prō kyo͞or´) *vt.*, get or obtain. *After he <u>procured</u> his meager rations of bacon, beans, and tinned milk, the elderly pensioner walked home.* **prem • is • es** (prem´ is əs) *n.*, house and its land. *The realtor couldn't recall how long the <u>premises</u> had been vacated.*

DRAW A PICTURE

THINK AND REFLECT

What false securities allow the narrator to remain calm after the murder? (Interpret)

_____

_____

_____

_____

NOTE THE FACTS

Who comes to the speaker's house? What do they do? What is the speaker's reaction?

_____

_____

_____

_____

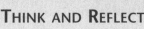

THINK AND REFLECT

What makes the speaker do what he does when the visitors are about to leave?

_____

_____

_____

_____

Upon the fourth day of the assassination, a party of the police came, very unexpectedly, into the house, and proceeded again to make rigorous investigation of the premises. Secure, however, in the inscrutability of my place

350 of concealment, I felt no embarrassment whatever. The officers bade[35] me accompany them in their search. They left no nook or corner unexplored. At length, for the third or fourth time, they descended into the cellar. I quivered not in a muscle. My heart beat calmly as that of one who slumbers in innocence. I walked the cellar from end to end. I folded my arms upon my bosom, and roamed easily to and fro. The police were thoroughly satisfied and prepared to depart. The glee at my heart was too strong to be restrained. I burned to say if but one word, by way of

360 triumph, and to render doubly sure their assurance of my guiltlessness.

"Gentlemen," I said at last, as the party ascended the steps, "I delight to have allayed your suspicions. I wish you all health and a little more courtesy. By the bye, gentlemen, this—this is a very well-constructed house," (in the rabid desire to say something easily, I scarcely knew what I uttered at all),—"I may say an *excellently* well-constructed house. These walls—are you going, gentlemen?—these walls are solidly put together";
and here, through the mere frenzy of bravado, I rapped heavily

370 with a cane which I held in my hand, upon that very portion of the brickwork behind which stood the corpse of the wife of my bosom.

But may God shield and deliver me from the fangs of the Arch-Fiend! No sooner had the reverberation of my blows sunk into silence, than I was answered by a voice from within the tomb!—by a cry, at first muffled and broken, like the

---

35. **bade.** Asked

words for everyday use

in • scru • ta • bil • i • ty (in skrōōt´ə bil´ə tē) *n.*, complete obscurity. *The famous actor's inscrutability was achieved with the aid of a masterful disguise.*

ren • der (ren´ dər) *vt.*, cause to be or become. *To render the squawking parrot silent, she threw a pillowcase over its cage.*

bra • va • do (brə vä´ dō) *n.*, false courage. *In a show of bravado, the circus clown stood tall and puffed out his chest.*

re • ver • ber • a • tion (ri vʉr´ bər ā´ shən) *n.*, echoed sound. *The reverberation from the bass guitar could be felt throughout the amphitheater.*

sobbing of a child, and then quickly swelling into one long, loud, and continuous scream, utterly <u>anomalous</u> and inhuman—a howl—a wailing shriek, half of horror and half of triumph, such as might have arisen only out of hell, <u>conjointly</u> from the throats of the damned in their agony and of the demons that exult in the damnation.

380

Of my own thoughts it is folly to speak. Swooning, I staggered to the opposite wall. For one instant the party on the stairs remained motionless, through extremity of terror and awe. In the next a dozen stout arms were toiling at the wall. It fell bodily. The corpse, already greatly decayed and clotted with gore, stood erect before the eyes of the spectators. Upon its head, with red extended mouth and solitary eye of fire, sat the hideous beast whose craft had seduced me into murder, and whose informing voice had <u>consigned</u> me to the hangman. I had walled the monster up within the tomb. ■

390

NOTE THE FACTS

Where had the cat been?

_____

_____

_____

_____

words for everyday use

a • nom • a • lous (ə näm´ə ləs) *adj.*, inconsistent or contradicting. *The appearance of the entire family, seated together at the kitchen table for breakfast, was an* <u>anomalous</u> *sight.*

con • joint • ly (kən joint´ lē) *adv.*, in a united or combined manner. *The baritone and tenor sections* <u>conjointly</u> *sang the final verses of the song.*

con • sign (kən sīn´) *vt.*, hand over or deliver. *After she had* <u>consigned</u> *the telegram to its recipient, the messenger rode away on her bicycle.*

Reflect ON YOUR READING

➤ ADD NEW WORDS TO YOUR PERSONAL VOCABULARY

When you finish reading, get together with your partner again to discuss the challenging words you encountered. Compare the additional vocabulary words each of you wrote down while reading, and discuss how the words affected your understanding and enjoyment of the selection. Then, choose twenty-five words from your list and create an original sentence for each word. By using these words to express your own thoughts, you will make them a part of your personal vocabulary, meaning that you will be able to remember them and use them in the future.

Reading Skills and Test Practice

USE CONTEXT CLUES

Discuss with a partner how to answer the following questions about words in context.

1. Read this sentence from the selection:

   No sooner had the reverberation of my blows sunk into silence, than I was answered by a voice from within the tomb!

   What does *reverberation* mean?
   a. sharp pain
   b. echoed sound
   c. excessive force
   d. aftershock

What is the correct answer to the question above? How were you able to eliminate the other answers? How did your application of the reading strategy help you answer the question?

_____

_____

_____

_____

2. Read this passage from the selection:

   On the night of the day on which this most cruel deed was done, I was aroused from sleep by the cry of fire. The curtains of my bed were in flames. The whole house was blazing. It was with great difficulty that my wife, a servant, and myself, made our escape from the conflagration.

What does *conflagration* mean?
a. large estate
b. frightening situation
c. destructive fire
d. area of confinement

What is the correct answer to the question above? How were you able to eliminate the other answers? How did your application of the reading strategy help you answer the question?

_____

_____

_____

_____

Investigate, Inquire, and Imagine

RECALL: GATHER FACTS
1a. What is the narrator's "immediate purpose" in writing his "most wild yet most homely narrative"?

INTERPRET: FIND MEANING
1b. What is the probable reason that the narrator would be "mad" to expect readers to believe his tale?

ANALYZE: TAKE THINGS APART
2a. Identify specific details that are particularly effective in creating an atmosphere of horror in the story.

SYNTHESIZE: BRING THINGS TOGETHER
2b. What is the narrator's definition of *perverseness*? What acts of perversity does the narrator commit? In what way is the telling of the story an act of perversity on the part of the narrator?

EVALUATE: MAKE JUDGMENTS
3a. In your opinion, is the narrator reliable? Why, or why not?

EXTEND: CONNECT IDEAS
3b. Do you think Poe wrote this story simply to engage readers by appealing to their fascination for the morbid? Or do you think Poe had a deeper message? If so, what might this message be?

Literary Tools

FLASHBACK. A **flashback** is a section of a literary work that presents an event or series of events that occurred earlier than the current time in the work. With what final event does the story open? Where is the narrator as he "pens" his tale?

_____

_____

_____

WordWorkshop

USING VOCABULARY TO WRITE A STORY. Using your own paper, write a short story using as many of the vocabulary words from the selection as you can (refer to the list in WordWatch on page 42). Each time you use a vocabulary word, underline it. You may change the form of the word as needed—for example, *allusions* instead of *allusion* or *docile* instead of *docility*. When you are finished, meet with a classmate and exchange stories. Check to make sure each word is used properly in your classmate's story. For an extra challenge, try writing your story using the vocabulary words in the order they appear in the WordWatch list.

> **EXAMPLE**
> She kept making allusions to her favorite songs, but the most <u>anomalous</u> thing about her was her claim that she had seen an <u>apparition</u> of such <u>atrocity</u> that even she had needed to turn away. This was an unusual occurrence for someone who harbored few <u>aversions</u> . . .

Read-Write Connection

What aspect of this story did you find most horrifying? Why?

_____

_____

_____

_____

_____

_____

_____

_____

_____

_____

Beyond the Reading

VIRTUAL TOUR. To learn more about Poe's life and writing career, take a virtual tour of the **Edgar Allan Poe Museum** online. Use your search engine to search for "Edgar Allan Poe Museum" or go to **www.poemuseum.org**. Read one or more of Poe's other short stories found on the site under "Selected Works," and compare and contrast the plot, characters, or themes to "The Black Cat."

GO ONLINE. Visit the EMC Internet Resource Center at **emcp.com** to find links and additional activities for this selection.

"The Open Window"

by Saki

Active READING STRATEGY

MAKE PREDICTIONS

Before Reading ➤ MAKE PRELIMINARY PREDICTIONS

- ❑ Read the Reader's Resource and the Reader's Journal sections on this page.
- ❑ Preview the Prediction Chart below before you begin reading.
- ❑ As you read, you will keep a detailed written record of your predictions in your chart. By keeping track of this process, you will be able to evaluate the effect that making predictions has on your reading experience.

Graphic Organizer

My Predictions	Reasons	Evidence	What Really Happened

CONNECT

Reader's resource

In "The Open Window," a young woman tries to enliven a formal meeting by telling a made-up story and watching the effect it has on her guest. Hector Hugh Munro (1870–1916), who took the pseudonym Saki from a character in Edward Fitzgerald's translation of the *Rubáiyát of Omar Khayyám*, is mostly known for his witty short stories, of which this selection is an example.

Word watch

PREVIEW VOCABULARY

convey	ghastly
delusion	imminent
duly	migrate
engulf	self-possessed
falteringly	

Reader's journal

Think about a social situation in which you were expected to behave in a certain way. Did you behave in the manner expected of you? Why, or why not?

_____

_____

_____

REVISE PREDICTIONS AND MAKE NEW PREDICTIONS

❏ Begin reading the selection independently. Look for details that might confirm or refute your preliminary predictions. Also, as new information is revealed in the text, jot down a few new predictions about future story events.

❏ When you come across information in the text that confirms a prediction, write down those details from the text next to your prediction and note that it proved true.

❏ When you find that a prediction you made was wrong, use the story details to revise your prediction or to make a new one. Again, write down those story details in your chart.

NOTE THE FACTS

What are Framton Nuttel's feelings on formal social situations?

_____

_____

_____

_____

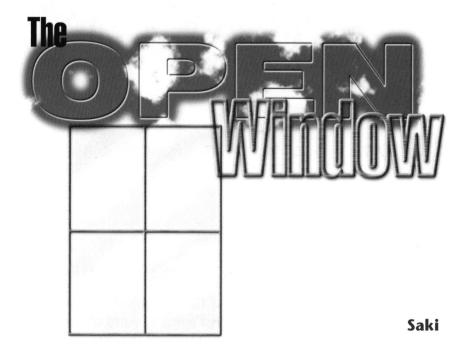

The OPEN Window

Saki

"My aunt will be down presently,[1] Mr. Nuttel," said a very <u>self-possessed</u> young lady of fifteen; "in the meantime you must try and put up with me."

Framton Nuttel endeavored[2] to say the correct something which should <u>duly</u> flatter the niece of the moment without unduly discounting[3] the aunt that was to come. Privately he doubted more than ever whether these formal visits on a succession of total strangers would do much towards helping the nerve cure which he was supposed to be undergoing.

10   "I know how it will be," his sister had said when he was preparing to <u>migrate</u> to this rural retreat; "you will bury yourself down there and not speak to a living soul, and your nerves will be worse than ever from moping. I shall just give you letters of introduction to all the people I know there. Some of them, as far as I can remember, were quite nice."

---

1. **presently**. Soon; in a little while
2. **endeavored**. Tried; attempted
3. **unduly discounting**. Improperly disregarding

words for everyday use

self- • pos • sessed (self´ pə zesd´) adj., confident, composed. A <u>self-possessed</u> speaker in any situation, she was undaunted by the hecklers in the audience.

du • ly (dōō´ lē) adv., as required, sufficiently. The bold applicant asked the company president if she was <u>duly</u> impressed with his qualifications.

mi • grate (mī´grāt´) vi., move from one place to another. In early winter, flocks of birds <u>migrate</u> south to warmer climates.

Framton wondered whether Mrs. Sappleton, the lady to whom he was presenting one of the letters of introduction, came into the nice division.

"Do you know many of the people round here?" asked the niece when she judged that they had had sufficient silent communion.[4]

"Hardly a soul," said Framton. "My sister was staying here, at the rectory,[5] you know, some four years ago, and she gave me letters of introduction to some of the people here."

He made the last statement in a tone of distinct regret.

"Then you know practically nothing about my aunt?" pursued the self-possessed young lady.

"Only her name and address," admitted the caller. He was wondering whether Mrs. Sappleton was in the married or widowed state. An undefinable something about the room seemed to suggest masculine habitation.

"Her great tragedy happened just three years ago," said the child; "that would be since your sister's time."

"Her tragedy?" asked Framton; somehow in this restful country spot tragedies seemed out of place.

"You may wonder why we keep that window wide open on an October afternoon," said the niece, indicating a large French window that opened on to a lawn.

"It is quite warm for the time of the year," said Framton; "but has that window got anything to do with the tragedy?"

"Out through that window, three years ago to a day, her husband and her two young brothers went off for their day's shooting. They never came back. In crossing the moor to their favorite snipe-shooting[6] ground they were all three <u>engulfed</u> in a treacherous piece of bog.[7] It had been that dreadful wet summer, you know, and places that were safe in other years gave way suddenly without warning. Their bodies were never recovered. That was the dreadful part of it." Here the child's voice lost its self-possessed note and became <u>falteringly</u> human.

20

30

40

---

4. **communion.** Sharing of thoughts
5. **rectory.** A residence of a parish priest
6. **snipe-shooting.** Bird-hunting
7. **bog.** Wet, spongy ground

words for everyday use	**en • gulf** (en gulf´) *vt.*, swallow up. *The foamy waves <u>engulfed</u> the children's sand castle.* **fal • ter • ing • ly** (fôl´ tər iŋ lē) *adv.*, uncertainly, unsteadily. *Not expecting a gesture of kindness, he <u>falteringly</u> took her hand.*

Literary TOOLS

IRONY. Irony is a difference between appearance and reality. As you read, look for examples of irony in "The Open Window."

THINK AND REFLECT

Why do you think Vera asks Framton about the "people round here"? about her aunt? **(Interpret)**

_____

_____

Reading TIP

In "The Open Window" the character of Framton Nuttel is created through *direct description* and *portrayal of behavior*, two techniques of characterization. Placed opposite the ineffective and earnest character of Nuttel is Vera. Note Vera's rather unconventional approach to formal visits and polite conversation with strangers.

READ ALOUD

Read aloud lines 41–60. What explanation does the girl give for the open window?

_____

_____

MAKE PREDICTIONS. When you find information in the text that confirms a prediction, write down those details next to your prediction in your Prediction Chart, and note that it proved true. When you find that a prediction you made was wrong, use the story details to revise your prediction or to make a new one. Again, write down those story details in your chart.

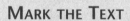

MARK THE TEXT

Underline or highlight what Framton thinks is a good topic of conversation.

50 "Poor aunt always thinks that they will come back some day, they and the little brown spaniel that was lost with them, and walk in at that window just as they used to do. That is why the window is kept open every evening till it is quite dusk. Poor dear aunt, she has often told me how they went out, her husband with his white waterproof coat over his arm, and Ronnie, her youngest brother, singing, 'Bertie, why do you bound?'[8] as he always did to tease her, because she said it got on her nerves. Do you know, sometimes on still, quiet evenings like this, I almost get a creepy feeling that they will 60 all walk in through that window—"

She broke off with a little shudder. It was a relief to Framton when the aunt bustled into the room with a whirl of apologies for being late in making her appearance.

"I hope Vera has been amusing you?" she said.

"She has been very interesting," said Framton.

"I hope you don't mind the open window," said Mrs. Sappleton briskly; "my husband and brothers will be home directly from shooting, and they always come in this way. They've been out for snipe in the marshes today, so they'll 70 make a fine mess over my poor carpets. So like you men-folk, isn't it?"

She rattled on cheerfully about the shooting and the scarcity of birds, and the prospects for duck in the winter. To Framton, it was all purely horrible. He made a desperate but only partially successful effort to turn the talk on to a less <u>ghastly</u> topic; he was conscious that his hostess was giving him only a fragment of her attention, and her eyes were constantly straying past him to the open window and the lawn beyond. It was certainly an unfortunate coincidence that he should have 80 paid his visit on this tragic anniversary.

"The doctors agree in ordering me complete rest, an absence of mental excitement, and avoidance of anything in the nature of violent physical exercise," announced Framton, who labored under the tolerably widespread <u>delusion</u> that total strangers and chance acquaintances are

---

8. **'Bertie . . . bound?'** Line from a popular song

> **words for everyday use**
>
> ghast • ly (gast´ lē) *adj.*, horrible; frightful. *The <u>ghastly</u> wound on his leg required over fifty stitches.*
>
> de • lu • sion (di lōō´ zhən) *n.*, false belief or opinion. *Suffering from paranoia, the patient lived with the <u>delusion</u> that others wished him harm.*

hungry for the least detail of one's ailments and infirmities,[9] their cause and cure. "On the matter of diet they are not so much in agreement," he continued.

"No?" said Mrs. Sappleton, in a voice which only replaced a yawn at the last moment. Then she suddenly brightened into alert attention—but not to what Framton was saying.

"Here they are at last!" she cried. "Just in time for tea, and don't they look as if they were muddy up to the eyes!"

Framton shivered slightly and turned towards the niece with a look intended to <u>convey</u> sympathetic comprehension. The child was staring out through the open window with dazed horror in her eyes. In a chill shock of nameless fear Framton swung around in his seat and looked in the same direction.

In the deepening twilight three figures were walking across the lawn towards the window; they all carried guns under their arms, and one of them was additionally burdened with a white coat hung over his shoulders. A tired brown spaniel kept close at their heels. Noiselessly they neared the house, and then a hoarse young voice chanted out of the dusk: "I said, Bertie, why do you bound?"

Framton grabbed wildly at his stick and hat; the hall-door, the gravel-drive, and the front gate were dimly noted stages in his headlong retreat. A cyclist coming along the road had to run into the hedge to avoid <u>imminent</u> collision.

"Here we are, my dear," said the bearer of the white mackintosh,[10] coming in through the window; "fairly muddy, but most of it's dry. Who was that who bolted out as we came up?"

"A most extraordinary man, a Mr. Nuttel," said Mrs. Sappleton; "could only talk about his illnesses, and dashed off without a word of good-bye or apology when you arrived. One would think he had seen a ghost."

FIX-UP IDEA

Read Aloud
If you are having trouble making predictions, try hearing the selection read aloud and working with others to make predictions. You might work in a small group or with your entire class to read the selection aloud, making and revising predictions as you read.

Reading STRATEGY
REVIEW

TACKLE DIFFICULT VOCABULARY. Record in your word study notebook any unfamiliar words you encounter. You can work with these words later in order to gain more familiarity with them and to expand your personal vocabulary.

---

9. **infirmities.** Physical weaknesses or defects
10. **mackintosh.** Waterproof outer coat

words for everyday use

con • vey (kən vā´) vt., make known. *To <u>convey</u> her disbelief at the jury's decision, the defense attorney shook her head and arched her eyebrows.*

im • mi • nent (im´ ə nənt) adj., impending; threatening. *The dark clouds and high humidity suggested an <u>imminent</u> thunderstorm.*

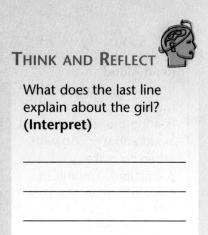

THINK AND REFLECT

What does the last line explain about the girl? (Interpret)

_____

_____

_____

120 "I expect it was the spaniel," said the niece calmly; "he told me he had a horror of dogs. He was once hunted into a cemetery somewhere on the banks of the Ganges by a pack of pariah dogs,[11] and had to spend the night in a newly dug grave with the creatures snarling and grinning and foaming just above him. Enough to make any one lose their nerve."

Romance at short notice was her speciality. ■

---

11. **Ganges . . . dogs.** *Ganges*—river in India; *pariah dogs*—outcast dogs, rejected by others

Reflect ON YOUR READING

After Reading ➤ ## ANALYZE YOUR PREDICTIONS

When you finish reading, review the predictions you made as you read the selection. Think about the information that led you to make your predictions and the details that confirmed or refuted them. Analyze the process by answering the following questions:

Were the incorrect predictions misguided, or did the story have a twist or surprise?

_____

_____

Did your predictions become more "on-target" as more story details were revealed? In other words, did you have to revise fewer predictions toward the end of the story than you did in the beginning?

_____

_____

Work with a partner to discuss your prediction-making experience. Compare your record of predictions with your partner's record, and discuss how the prediction-making process affected your reading experience.

Reading Skills and Test Practice

COMPARE AND CONTRAST CHARACTERS
READ, THINK, AND EXPLAIN. Discuss with a partner how to compare and contrast characters.

1. How are Vera and Mr. Nuttel alike? Use details from the text to support your ideas.

_____

_____

2. How are Vera and Mr. Nuttel different? Use details from the text to support your ideas.

_____

_____

REFLECT ON YOUR RESPONSE. Compare your response to that of your partner. How were you able to compare and contrast characters?

**THINK-ALOUD
NOTES**

_____

_____

_____

_____

_____

_____

_____

_____

_____

_____

_____

Investigate, Inquire, and Imagine

RECALL: GATHER FACTS
1a. Why does Framton make "formal visits on a succession of total strangers"? Why does his sister give him letters of introduction to people she knows?

→ INTERPRET: FIND MEANING
1b. What might this suggest about the character of Framton?

ANALYZE: TAKE THINGS APART
2a. Review the story and note the various tactics Vera employs to create "romance at short notice."

→ SYNTHESIZE: BRING THINGS TOGETHER
2b. What is the purpose of Vera's story about Framton Nuttel's "horror of dogs"?

PERSPECTIVE: LOOK AT OTHER VIEWS →
3a. What is Saki saying about the social conventions of the time period?

EMPATHY: SEE FROM INSIDE
3b. Imagine yourself in Framton's place—new to an unfamiliar community with a doctor's orders to avoid mental excitement and physical exertion. You discover Vera's lie. Do you confront her? If so, what will you say? Will you continue to try meeting other members of the community using letters of introduction? Why, or why not?

Literary Tools

IRONY. **Irony** is a difference between appearance and reality. Types of irony include the following:

dramatic irony	something is known by the reader or audience but is unknown to the characters
verbal irony	a statement is made that implies its opposite
irony of situation	an event occurs that violates the expectations of the characters, the reader, or the audience

Which forms of irony occur in "The Open Window"? Explain your answer. Cite specific examples of irony that occur in the story. How important to the success of this story is the author's use of irony? Explain your answer. Use your own paper as needed.

_____

_____

_____

WordWorkshop

Word Map. Make a Word Map for each of the following Words for Everyday Use from "The Open Window." Refer to the Word Map graphic organizer in Appendix B on page B-15 and review the definitions found at the bottom of the pages of the story. Write the vocabulary word in the first box. Beneath the word or phrase include its definition, word parts you recognize, and several synonyms. Use a dictionary if needed. In the two boxes at the bottom, write a sentence that uses the word or phrase and create a drawing that helps you remember it.

1. falteringly
2. ghastly
3. delusion
4. convey
5. imminent

Read-Write Connection

Why do you think Vera does what she does?

_____

_____

_____

_____

_____

_____

_____

_____

Beyond the Reading

Research Moors. The word *moor* is a clue to the setting of the story, which may take place in rural Scotland or another part of Great Britain. Locate photographs of moors in travel books about Great Britain and gather information about the animals and plants that live in this environment. How does the setting add to the story "The Open Window"?

Go Online. Visit the EMC Internet Resource Center at **emcp.com** to find links and additional activities for this selection.

Reader's resource

French writer Guy de Maupassant, 1850–1893, is famous for his short stories about the lives of ordinary French people. Many of his stories contain **irony**—situations in which appearances, or what *seems* to be true, are actually very different from reality. In **"The Necklace,"** Madame Loisel learns a serious lesson about appearances when she borrows a beautiful necklace to wear to a fancy ball.

Word watch

PREVIEW VOCABULARY

chagrin	inestimable
elated	nocturnal
finesse	odious
homage	stupefied
immoderate	suppleness
incessantly	usurer

Reader's journal

Have you ever envied the apparent wealth or material possessions of someone else? Would having those things make your life better? Why, or why not?

_____

_____

_____

"The Necklace"

by Guy de Maupassant

Active READING STRATEGY

WRITE THINGS DOWN

Before Reading → **DEVISE A PLAN FOR RECORDING INFORMATION**

❑ Read the Reader's Resource. Work with a partner to discuss the material presented.

❑ A **character** is a person who figures in the action of the work. A *protagonist,* or *main character,* is the central literary figure in a literary work. **Motivation** is the force that moves a character to think, feel, or behave in a certain way.

❑ Review the graphic organizer below. As you read, keep track in your graphic organizer of the forces that motivate the protagonist, Madame Loisel, to behave as she does.

Graphic Organizer

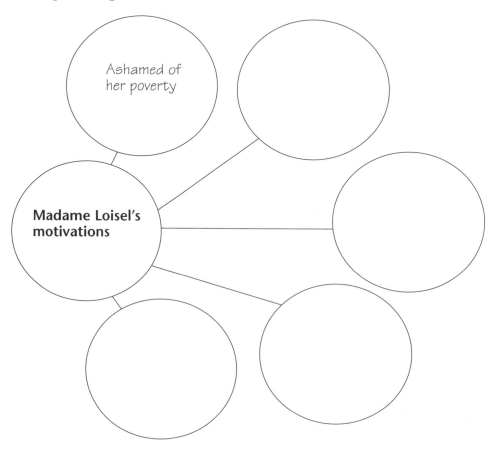

Ashamed of her poverty

Madame Loisel's motivations

The Necklace

Guy de Maupassant

She was one of those pretty, charming young ladies; born, as if through an error of destiny, into a family of clerks. She had no dowry,[1] no hopes, no means of becoming known, appreciated, loved, and married by a man either rich or distinguished; and she allowed herself to marry a petty clerk in the office of the Board of Education.

She was simple, not being able to adorn herself, but she was unhappy, as one out of her class; for women belong to no caste, no race, their grace, their beauty and their charm serving them in the place of birth and family. Their inborn <u>finesse</u>, their instinctive elegance, their <u>suppleness</u> of wit, are their only aristocracy, making some daughters of the people the equal of great ladies.

She suffered <u>incessantly</u>, feeling herself born for all delicacies and luxuries. She suffered from the poverty of her apartment, the shabby walls, the worn chairs and the faded stuffs. All these things, which another woman of her station would not have noticed, tortured and angered her. The sight of the little Breton,[2] who made this humble home, awoke in her sad regrets and desperate dreams. She thought of quiet antechambers with their oriental hangings lighted by high bronze torches and of the two great footmen in short trousers

10

20

---

1. **dowry.** Wealth to be given by a bride to her husband when she marries
2. **Breton** (brē´ tən). Someone from Brittany, a rural province of France

words for everyday use

fi • nesse (fə nes´) *n.*, ability to handle difficult situations diplomatically. *When nations are in conflict, they do better to rely on the <u>finesse</u> of diplomats and negotiators than on violence and threats to settle their differences.*

sup • ple • ness (sup´əl nes) *n.*, flexibility. *I considered myself very flexible, but the <u>suppleness</u> of my new yoga instructor was far greater than mine.*

in • ces • sant • ly (in ses´ ənt lē) *adv.*, constantly, endlessly. *City dwellers who vacation in the country sometimes find they miss the traffic that roars <u>incessantly</u>, night and day, along the city streets.*

During Reading

RECORD STORY DETAILS

❑ Follow along in your text as your teacher reads aloud the first section of "The Necklace." Record all details that you think are important. Before moving on, jot down your opinions of, or reactions to, Madame Loisel.

❑ Read the remainder of the selection independently. Continue to look for important details, including details about the characters.

❑ Write down these details, along with your reactions to the characters and the events taking place in the story.

NOTE THE FACTS

Into what kind of family is Madame Loisel born?

_____

_____

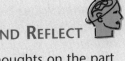

THINK AND REFLECT

What thoughts on the part of Madame Loisel show that she feels she should have been born to an aristocratic life? **(Interpret)**

_____

_____

_____

_____

MARK THE TEXT

Underline or highlight the ways in which the husband differs from his wife.

THINK AND REFLECT

In what way would you characterize the desires of the young woman? (Synthesize)

_____

_____

Literary TOOLS

FORESHADOWING.
Foreshadowing is the act of presenting materials that hint at events to occur later in the story. As you read, pay close attention to clues that foreshadow events to come, and based on those clues, anticipate how the story will end.

who sleep in the large armchairs, made sleepy by the heavy air from the heating apparatus. She thought of large drawing rooms hung in old silks, of graceful pieces of furniture carrying bric-a-brac[3] of <u>inestimable</u> value and of the little perfumed coquettish apartments made for five o'clock chats with most intimate friends, men known and sought after, whose attention all women envied and desired.

30   When she seated herself for dinner before the round table, where the tablecloth had been used three days, opposite her husband who uncovered the tureen with a delighted air, saying: "Oh! the good potpie! I know nothing better than that," she would think of the elegant dinners, of the shining silver, of the tapestries[4] peopling the walls with ancient personages and rare birds in the midst of fairy forests; she thought of the exquisite food served on marvelous dishes, of the whispered gallantries, listened to with the smile of the Sphinx[5] while eating the rose-colored flesh of the trout or a chicken's wing.

40   She had neither frocks nor jewels, nothing. And she loved only those things. She felt that she was made for them. She had such a desire to please, to be sought after, to be clever and courted.

She had a rich friend, a schoolmate at the convent,[6] whom she did not like to visit. She suffered so much when she returned. And she wept for whole days from <u>chagrin</u>, from regret, from despair and disappointment.

◆   ◆   ◆

50   One evening her husband returned, <u>elated</u>, bearing in his hand a large envelope.

"Here, he said, "here is something for you."

---

3. **bric-a-brac.** Decorations
4. **tapestries.** Woven wall hangings
5. **Sphinx.** In Greek myth, a creature with the body of a lion and the head of a woman that demanded that passersby in Thebes answer its riddles
6. **convent.** Residence for Catholic nuns; sometimes also a school for girls

words for everyday use

in • es • ti • ma • ble (in es´ tə mə bəl) *adj.,* too valuable to be measured; invaluable. *The value of a gift can be estimated in dollars and cents, but the value of the generosity behind the gift is <u>inestimable</u>.*

cha • grin (shə grin´) *n.,* feeling of severe embarrassment and annoyance. *The artist felt <u>chagrin</u> when her painting was described in the local papers as "second-rate."*

e • lat • ed (ē lāt´ed) *part.,* filled with joy. *Suzie's parents were <u>elated</u> when she decided to finish school rather than drop out.*

She quickly tore open the wrapper and drew out a printed card on which were inscribed these words:

The Minister of Public Instruction and Madame George Ramponneau ask the honor of M. and Mme.[7] Loisel's company Monday evening, January 18, at the Minister's residence.

60 Instead of being delighted, as her husband had hoped, she threw the invitation spitefully upon the table, murmuring:

"What do you suppose I want with that?"

"But, my dearie, I thought it would make you happy. You never go out, and this is an occasion, and a fine one! I had a great deal of trouble to get it. Everybody wishes one, and it is very select; not many are given to employees. You will see the whole official world there."

She looked at him with an irritated eye and declared impatiently: "What do you suppose I have to wear to such a thing as that?"

70 He had not thought of that; he stammered:

"Why, the dress you wear when we go to the theater. It seems very pretty to me."

He was silent, <u>stupefied</u>, in dismay, at the sight of his wife weeping. Two great tears fell slowly from the corners of her eyes toward the corners of her mouth; he stammered:

"What is the matter? What is the matter?"

By a violent effort she had controlled her vexation and responded in a calm voice, wiping her moist cheeks:

"Nothing. Only I have no dress and consequently I cannot
80 go to this affair. Give your card to some colleague whose wife is better filled out than I."

He was grieved but answered:

"Let us see, Matilda. How much would a suitable costume cost, something that would serve for other occasions, something very simple?"

She reflected for some seconds, making estimates and thinking of a sum that she could ask for without bringing with it an immediate refusal and a frightened exclamation from the economical clerk.

---

7. **M. and Mme.** Abbreviations for "Monsieur" and "Madame," French for Mr. and Mrs.

words for everyday use

stu • pe • fied (stoo´ pə fīd) *adj.,* stunned; bewildered. *He stood <u>stupefied</u> with horror as all his hard-earned cash blew away in the wind.*

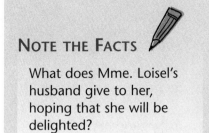

NOTE THE FACTS

What does Mme. Loisel's husband give to her, hoping that she will be delighted?

_____

_____

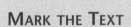
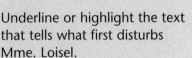

MARK THE TEXT

Underline or highlight the text that tells what first disturbs Mme. Loisel.

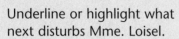

THINK AND REFLECT

What actions on the part of the husband show that he places his wife's happiness above his own? (Interpret)

_____

_____

_____

_____

MARK THE TEXT

Underline or highlight what next disturbs Mme. Loisel.

NOTE THE FACTS

What does Mme. Loisel resolve to do?

_____

_____

_____

90 Finally she said in a hesitating voice: "I cannot tell exactly, but it seems to me that four hundred francs[8] ought to cover it."

He turned a little pale, for he had saved just this sum to buy a gun that he might be able to join some hunting parties the next summer, on the plains at Nanterre,[9] with some friends who went to shoot larks up there on Sunday. Nevertheless, he answered:

"Very well. I will give you four hundred francs. But try to have a pretty dress."

100

◆   ◆   ◆

The day of the ball approached, and Mme. Loisel seemed sad, disturbed, anxious. Nevertheless, her dress was nearly ready. Her husband said to her one evening: "What is the matter with you? You have acted strangely for two or three days."

And she responded: "I am vexed not to have a jewel, not one stone, nothing to adorn myself with. I shall have such a 110 poverty-laden look. I would prefer not to go to this party."

He replied: "You can wear some natural flowers. At this season they look very chic. For ten francs you can have two or three magnificent roses."

She was not convinced. "No," she replied, "there is nothing more humiliating than to have a shabby air in the midst of rich women."

Then her husband cried out: "How stupid we are! Go and find your friend Madame Forestier and ask her to lend you her jewels. You are well enough acquainted with her to do this."

120 She uttered a cry of joy. "It is true!" she said. "I had not thought of that."

The next day she took herself to her friend's house and related her story of distress. Mme. Forestier went to her closet with the glass doors, took out a large jewel case, brought it, opened it and said: "Choose, my dear."

She saw at first some bracelets, then a collar of pearls, then a Venetian cross of gold and jewels and of admirable workmanship. She tried the jewels before the glass,

8. **francs.** French currency
9. **Nanterre** (nän • ter´). Suburb of Paris, France

hesitated, but could neither decide to take them nor leave
130   them. Then she asked:
       "Have you nothing more?"
       "Why, yes. Look for yourself. I do not know what will
       please you."
       Suddenly she discovered in a black satin box a superb
       necklace of diamonds, and her heart beat fast with an
       <u>immoderate</u> desire. Her hands trembled as she took them
       up. She placed them about her throat, against her dress, and
       remained in ectasy before them. Then she asked in a
       hesitating voice full of anxiety:
140   "Could you lend me this? Only this?"
       "Why, yes, certainly."
       She fell upon the neck of her friend, embraced her with
       passion, then went away with her treasure.

                        ◆   ◆   ◆

       The day of the ball arrived. Mme. Loisel was a great
       success. She was the prettiest of all, elegant, gracious,
       smiling and full of joy. All the men noticed her, asked her
150   name and wanted to be presented. All the members of the
       Cabinet wished to waltz with her. The minister of education
       paid her some attention.
       She danced with enthusiasm, with passion, intoxicated with
       pleasure, thinking of nothing, in the triumph of her beauty,
       in the glory of her success, in a kind of cloud of happiness
       that came of all this <u>homage</u> and all this admiration, of all
       these awakened desires and this victory so complete and
       sweet to the heart of woman.
       She went home toward four o'clock in the morning. Her
160   husband had been half asleep in one of the little salons[10]
       since midnight, with three other gentlemen whose wives
       were enjoying themselves very much.
       He threw around her shoulders the wraps they had carried
       for the coming home, modest garments of everyday wear,

---

10. **little salons.** Little rooms or booths alongside a ballroom floor

words for everyday use	**im • mod • er • ate** (im mäd´ ər it) *adj., excessive, unrestrained. Immoderate praise can be embarrassing.* **hom • age** (häm´ ij) *n., action to show honor or respect. The film industry paid homage to the aging actor by giving him a special award in recognition of his many excellent film roles.*

THINK AND REFLECT

What does Mme. Loisel borrow? How does she feel about this object? **(Interpret)**

_____

_____

_____

_____

NOTE THE FACTS

Was Mme. Loisel's night a success? Why was it so enjoyable?

_____

_____

_____

_____

Use THE STRATEGY

WRITE THINGS DOWN. As you read, keep track in your graphic organizer of the forces that motivate the protagonist, Mme. Loisel, to behave as she does.

MAKE PREDICTIONS. As you read, look for details that might foreshadow events to occur later in the story. Based on those clues, write down your predictions about what you think will happen. Also, as new information is revealed in the text, jot down a few new predictions about future story events. When you come across information in the text that confirms a prediction, write down those details from the text next to your prediction and note that it proved true.

WHAT DO YOU WONDER?

_____

_____

_____

_____

whose poverty clashed with the elegance of the ball costume. She felt this and wished to hurry away in order not to be noticed by the other women who were wrapping themselves in rich furs.

170   Loisel detained her. "Wait," said he. "You will catch cold out there. I am going to call a cab."

But she would not listen and descended the steps rapidly. When they were in the street they found no carriage, and they began to seek for one, hailing the coachmen whom they saw at a distance.

They walked along toward the Seine,[11] hopeless and shivering. Finally they found on the dock one of those old <u>nocturnal</u> coupés[12] that one sees in Paris after nightfall, as if they were ashamed of their misery by day.

It took them as far as their door in Martyr Street,[13] and

180 they went wearily up to their apartment. It was all over for her. And on his part he remembered that he would have to be at the office by ten o'clock.

She removed the wraps from her shoulders before the glass for a final view of herself in her glory. Suddenly she uttered a cry. Her necklace was not around her neck.

Her husband, already half undressed, asked: "What is the matter?"

She turned toward him excitedly:

"I have—I have—I no longer have Madame Forestier's

190 necklace."

He arose in dismay: "What! How is that? It is not possible."

And they looked in the folds of the dress, in the folds of the mantle, in the pockets, everywhere. They could not find it.

He asked: "You are sure you still had it when we left the house?"

"Yes, I felt it in the vestibule as we came out."

---

11. **Seine** (sān). River that runs through Paris
12. **coupés** (kü pās´). Carriages
13. **Martyr Street.** A martyr is someone who dies for a good cause

words for everyday use

noc • tur • nal (näk tʉr´ nəl) *adj.*, active at night. *The exterminator told Ellen that the noise she heard in her walls at night must be a mouse and not a squirrel, because mice are <u>nocturnal</u> but squirrels are active only during the day.*

"But if you had lost it in the street we should have heard it
200 fall. It must be in the cab."

"Yes. It is probable. Did you take the number?"

"No. And you, did you notice what it was?"

"No."

They looked at each other, utterly cast down. Finally Loisel
dressed himself again.

"I am going," said he, "over the track where we went on
foot, to see if I can find it."

And he went. She remained in her evening gown, not
having the force to go to bed, stretched upon a chair,
210 without ambition or thoughts.

Toward seven o'clock her husband returned. He had
found nothing.

He went to the police and to the cab offices and put an
advertisement in the newspapers, offering a reward; he did
everything that afforded them a suspicion of hope.

She waited all day in a state of bewilderment before this
frightful disaster. Loisel returned at evening, with his face
harrowed[14] and pale, and had discovered nothing.

"It will be necessary," said he, "to write to your friend that
220 you have broken the clasp of the necklace and that you will
have it repaired. That will give us time to turn around."

She wrote as he dictated.

◆　　◆　　◆

At the end of a week they had lost all hope. And Loisel,
older by five years, declared:

"We must take measures to replace this jewel."

The next day they took the box which had inclosed it to
230 the jeweler whose name was on the inside. He consulted his
books.

"It is not I, madame," said he, "who sold this necklace; I
only furnished the casket."[15]

Then they went from jeweler to jeweler, seeking a necklace
like the other one, consulting their memories, and ill, both of
them, with chagrin and anxiety.

In a shop of the Palais-Royal they found a chaplet of
diamonds which seemed to them exactly like the one they

---

14. **harrowed.** Lined
15. **casket.** Case

NOTE THE FACTS

What emotions does
Mme. Loisel feel about the
lost necklace? What does
the couple decide to do
about it?

_____

_____

_____

_____

ASK A QUESTION

_____

_____

_____

_____

FIX-UP IDEA

Read in Chunks
If you have difficulty identifying and recording story details, try reading the selection in shorter sections. Read one paragraph at a time, pausing after each to review it and to look for important details that describe characters and/or plot events. Once you record those details, you can move on to the next paragraph.

240 had lost. It was valued at forty thousand francs. They could get it for thirty-six thousand.

They begged the jeweler not to sell it for three days. And they made an arrangement by which they might return it for thirty-four thousand francs if they found the other one before the end of February.

Loisel possessed eighteen thousand francs which his father had left him. He borrowed the rest.

He borrowed it, asking for a thousand francs of one, five hundred of another, five louis of this one and three louis of 250 that one. He gave notes, made ruinous promises, took money of <u>usurers</u> and the whole race of lenders. He compromised his whole existence, in fact, risked his signature without even knowing whether he could make it good or not, and, harassed by anxiety for the future, by the black misery which surrounded him and by the prospect of all physical privations and moral torture, he went to get the new necklace, depositing on the merchant's counter thirty-six thousand francs.

When Mme. Loisel took back the jewels to Mme. Forestier the latter said to her in a frigid tone:

260 "You should have returned them to me sooner, for I might have needed them."

She did open the jewel box as her friend feared she would. If she should perceive the substitution what would she think? What should she say? Would she take her for a robber?

◆   ◆   ◆

Mme. Loisel now knew the horrible life of necessity. She did her part, however, completely, heroically. It was 270 necessary to pay this frightful debt. She would pay it. They sent away the maid; they changed their lodgings; they rented some rooms under a mansard roof.[16]

---

16. **mansard roof.** Roof with two slopes on each of the four sides, named for French architect François Mansard (1598–1666)

words for everyday use

u • sur • er (yōō′ zhər ər) *n.*, person who lends at an extremely high interest rate. *The Italian poet Dante, like most medieval Christians, considered lending money at interest immoral and believed the <u>usurers</u> who did this would suffer torment in hell after death.*

She learned the heavy cares of a household, the <u>odious</u> work of a kitchen. She washed the dishes, using her rosy nails upon the greasy pots and the bottoms of the stewpans. She washed the soiled linen, the chemises and dishcloths, which she hung on the line to dry; she took down the refuse to the street each morning and brought up the water, stopping at each landing to breathe. And, clothed like a woman of the people, she went to the grocer's, the butcher's and the fruiterer's with her basket on her arm, shopping, haggling to the last sou her miserable money.

Every month it was necessary to renew some notes, thus obtaining time, and to pay others.

The husband worked evenings, putting the books of some merchants in order, and nights he often did copying at five sous a page.

And this life lasted for ten years.

At the end of ten years they had restored all, all, with interest of the usurer, and accumulated interest, besides.

Mme. Loisel seemed old now. She had become a strong, hard woman, the crude woman of the poor household. Her hair badly dressed, her skirts awry, her hands red, she spoke in a loud tone and washed the floors in large pails of water. But sometimes, when her husband was at the office, she would seat herself before the window and think of that evening party of former times, of that ball where she was so beautiful and so flattered.

How would it have been if she had not lost that necklace? Who knows? Who knows? How singular is life and how full of changes! How small a thing will ruin or save one!

◆   ◆   ◆

One Sunday, as she was taking a walk in the Champs Elysées to rid herself of the cares of the week, she suddenly perceived a woman walking with a child. It was Mme. Forestier, still young, still pretty, still attractive. Mme.

280

290

300

MARK THE TEXT

Underline or highlight the text that tells how losing the necklace has changed Mme. Loisel's life.

READ ALOUD

Read aloud the highlighted text. In what ways has Mme. Loisel remained the same? What knowledge has she gained?

_____

_____

_____

_____

words for everyday use

o • di • ous (ō′ dē əs) adj., hateful and offensive. *When he was young, he did not mind heavy tasks like carrying water or digging holes, but he thought raking leaves was <u>odious</u> and unbearable.*

THINK AND REFLECT

Whom does Mme. Loisel blame for her misery? Is her blame well placed? (**Evaluate**)

_____

_____

_____

_____

Loisel was affected. Should she speak to her? Yes, certainly.
310 And now that she had paid, she would tell her all. Why not?

She approached her. "Good morning, Jeanne."

Her friend did not recognise her and was astonished to be so familiarly addressed by this common personage. She stammered:

"But, madame—I do not know—You must be mistaken."

"No, I am Matilda Loisel."

Her friend uttered a cry of astonishment: "Oh! my poor Matilda! How you have changed."

"Yes, I have had some hard days since I saw you, and some
320 miserable ones—and all because of you."

"Because of me? How is that?"

"You recall the diamond necklace that you loaned me to wear to the minister's ball?"

"Yes, very well."

"Well, I lost it."

"How is that, since you returned it to me?"

"I returned another to you exactly like it. And it has taken us ten years to pay for it. You can understand that it was not easy for us who have nothing. But it is finished, and I am
330 decently content."

Mme. Forestier stopped short. She said:

"You say that you bought a diamond necklace to replace mine?"

"Yes. You did not perceive it then? They were just alike."

And she smiled with a proud and simple joy. Mme. Forestier was touched and took both her hands as she replied:

"Oh, my poor Matilda! Mine were false. They were not
340 worth over five hundred francs!" ■

Reflect ON YOUR READING

After Reading ➤ EVALUATE CHARACTER MOTIVATION

When you finish reading the selection, review the notes you took while reading. Look closely at the details you recorded about Mme. Loisel, and compare those character details to the events of the story's plot. Then consider these questions: What aspects of Mme. Loisel's character, or personality, motivate her to do the things she does in this story? How is Mme. Loisel different from M. Loisel and Mme. Forestier? Do you think Mme. Loisel would be content if she were as financially comfortable as Mme. Forestier? Why, or why not? How do you think Mme. Loisel will react to Mme. Forestier's revelation at the end of the story? Answer these questions in a brief essay. Be sure to include details from the selection to support your ideas. When you have finished writing, share your essay with a partner and discuss any differences in opinions.

Reading Skills and Test Practice

IDENTIFY IRONY
Discuss with a partner how to best answer the following questions about irony.

1. Mme. Loisel has always dreamed of attending grand social functions. What is ironic about her refusal to attend one?
   a. Mme. Loisel believes that she is too poor.
   b. Mme. Loisel realizes that she does not know how to dance.
   c. Mme. Loisel dislikes the woman who sent the invitation.
   d. Mme. Loisel's husband cannot attend.

What is the correct answer to the question above? How were you able to eliminate the other answers?

_____

2. Read these final lines from the story.
   "Oh, my poor Matilda! Mine were false. They were not worth over five hundred francs!"

   These lines are ironic because Matilda

   a. wants to keep the necklace.
   b. wore the necklace only once.
   c. needlessly toiled to replace the necklace.
   d. left her husband over the necklace.

What is the correct answer to the question above? How were you able to eliminate the other answers?

_____

_____

_____

_____

_____

_____

_____

_____

_____

_____

_____

_____

Investigate, Inquire, and Imagine

RECALL: GATHER FACTS
1a. What does Mme. Loisel feel she must have in order to make her ball ensemble complete?

INTERPRET: FIND MEANING
1b. What actions on the part of Mme. Loisel emphasize her feeling of triumph at the dance?

ANALYZE: TAKE THINGS APART
2a. *Irony of situation* exists in a literary work when an event occurs that violates the expectations of the characters, the reader, or the audience. Identify the irony of situation in "The Necklace."

SYNTHESIZE: BRING THINGS TOGETHER
2b. How is Mme. Loisel's life symbolized by the necklace?

EVALUATE: MAKE JUDGMENTS
3a. Why do you think that Mme. Loisel chose to tell Mme. Forestier the truth when she saw her walking? Do you think Mme. Loisel was justified in blaming Mme. Forestier for the hardships she had suffered? Why, or why not?

EXTEND: CONNECT IDEAS
3b. What sort of relationship between human beings and their social environment is described in this story?

WordWorkshop

WORD WEB. Create a word web in which you list words that could describe Mme. Loisel at different stages in the story.

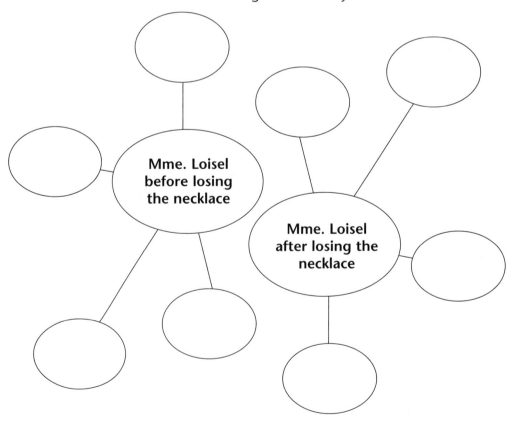

Literary Tools

FORESHADOWING. **Foreshadowing** is the act of presenting materials that hint at events to occur later in the story. Is the ending of the story a complete surprise, or is the diamond necklace's falseness partly foreshadowed? What clues does the author provide to foreshadow it?

_____

_____

_____

_____

_____

Read-Write Connection

Imagine that you are Mme. Loisel. What would you have done when you found out you had lost the borrowed necklace? How would you feel after finding out the original diamond necklace was false?

_____

_____

_____

_____

_____

_____

_____

_____

Beyond the Reading

NINETEENTH-CENTURY STYLE. Research the clothing and hairstyles worn by women and men of the middle and upper classes in the late nineteenth century, in both Europe and the United States. Then create a poster, full-size cutout, or drawings to present your findings, and label or discuss specific details shown on your visuals.

GO ONLINE. Visit the EMC Internet Resource Center at **emcp.com** to find links and additional activities for this selection.

Reader's resource

"**Rules of the Game**" appears in Amy Tan's award-winning first novel *The Joy Luck Club,* published in 1989. The novel weaves together the stories of four mothers born and raised in China and their four American-born daughters, exploring the conflicts between these two generations. The setting for the story is San Francisco's Chinatown, where the immigrant women form the Joy Luck Club and begin meeting to play the Chinese game *mah jong,* to invest in stocks, and to tell their stories.

Word watch

PREVIEW VOCABULARY

adversary	impart
ally	intricate
ancestral	malodorous
benevolently	prodigy
caption	pungent
concession	relent
deftly	replica
diminishing	retort
elaborate	solemnity
etiquette	successive
flourish	tout
fragrant	triumphant
graciously	vanity
humility	

Reader's journal

What kinds of conflicts do you have with your parents? How do you resolve them?

_____

_____

"Rules of the Game"

by Amy Tan

Active READING STRATEGY

MAKE PREDICTIONS

Before Reading ➤ **MAKE FIRST PREDICTIONS**

❏ Read the Reader's Resource.
❏ Answer the Reader's Journal questions.
❏ In a small group, use these clues to make one or two preliminary predictions about what will happen in this story. Record your predictions in the graphic organizer below.

Graphic Organizer

Clues	Predictions	What Really Happens

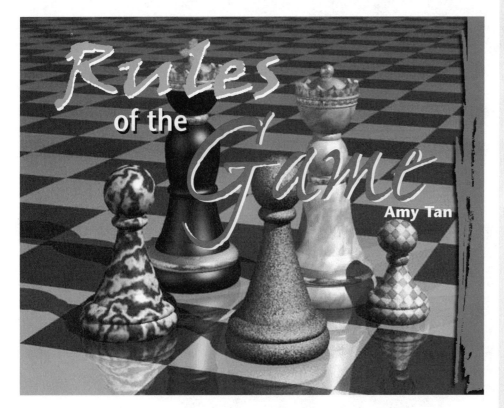

Rules of the Game

Amy Tan

MAKE PREDICTIONS

❑ Follow along as your teacher reads aloud the first two sections of the text. Then review the predictions you made and record what has really happened. Make one or two new predictions.

❑ Continue reading on your own. Stop every time you come to a section break to review your predictions and record new ones in your graphic organizer.

I was six when my mother taught me the art of invisible strength. It was a strategy for winning arguments, respect from others, and eventually, though neither of us knew it at the time, chess games.

"Bite back your tongue," scolded my mother when I cried loudly, yanking her hand toward the store that sold bags of salted plums. At home, she said, "Wise guy, he not go against wind. In Chinese we say, Come from South, blow with wind—poom!—North will follow. Strongest wind cannot be seen."

10   The next week I bit back my tongue as we entered the store with the forbidden candies. When my mother finished her shopping, she quietly plucked a small bag of plums from the rack and put it on the counter with the rest of the items.

My mother <u>imparted</u> her daily truths so she could help my older brothers and me rise above our circumstances. We lived in San Francisco's Chinatown. Like most of the other Chinese children who played in the back alleys of

NOTE THE FACTS

What lesson does the narrator learn about wanting something?

_____

_____

_____

NOTE THE FACTS

Why does the narrator's mother give her children advice?

_____

_____

_____

words for everyday use

im • part (im part′) vt., give or communicate the knowledge of. *The teacher imparted his lessons to the class.*

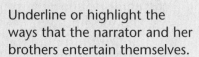

Underline or highlight the ways that the narrator and her brothers entertain themselves.

20 restaurants and curio[1] shops, I didn't think we were poor. My bowl was always full, three five-course meals every day, beginning with a soup full of mysterious things I didn't want to know the names of.

We lived on Waverly Place, in a warm, clean, two-bedroom flat that sat above a small Chinese bakery specializing in steamed pastries and dim sum.[2] In the early morning, when the alley was still quiet, I could smell <u>fragrant</u> red beans as they were cooked down to a pastry sweetness. By daybreak, our flat was heavy with the odor of fried sesame balls and sweet curried chicken crescents. From

30 my bed, I would listen as my father got ready for work, then locked the door behind him, one-two-three clicks.

At the end of our two-block alley was a small sandlot playground with swings and slides well-shined down the middle with use. The play area was bordered by wood-slat benches where old-country people sat crackling roasted watermelon seeds with their golden teeth and scattering the husks to an impatient gathering of gurgling pigeons. The best playground, however, was the dark alley itself. It was crammed with daily mysteries and adventures. My brothers

40 and I would peer into the medicinal herb shop, watching old Li dole out onto a stiff sheet of white paper the right amount of insect shells, saffron-colored seeds, and <u>pungent</u> leaves for his ailing customers. It was said that he once cured a woman dying of an <u>ancestral</u> curse that had eluded the best of American doctors. Next to the pharmacy was a printer who specialized in gold-embossed wedding invitations and festive red banners.

Farther down the street was Ping Yuen Fish Market. The front window displayed a tank crowded with doomed

50 fish and turtles struggling to gain footing on the slimy

---

1. **curio.** Something considered rare or unusual
2. **dim sum.** Traditional Chinese food consisting of a variety of items such as fried dumplings, chicken, or rice balls

words for everyday use

fra • grant (fra′ grent) *adj.*, marked by fragrance or pleasant odor. *The room was filled with the sweet smell of the <u>fragrant</u> flowers.*

pun • gent (pun′ jent) *adj.*, sharp or pointed. *The aged cheese had a <u>pungent</u> odor.*

an • ces • tral (an ses′ trel) *adj.*, relating to or inherited from an ancestor or family member. *She lived in her family's <u>ancestral</u> home.*

green-tiled sides. A hand-written sign informed tourists, "Within this store, is all for food, not for pet." Inside, the butchers with their bloodstained white smocks <u>deftly</u> gutted the fish while customers cried out their orders and shouted, "Give me your freshest," to which the butchers always protested, "All are freshest." On less crowded market days, we would inspect the crates of live frogs and crabs which we were warned not to poke, boxes of dried cuttlefish, and row upon row of iced prawns,[3] squid, and slippery fish. The

60   sanddabs made me shiver each time; their eyes lay on one flattened side and reminded me of my mother's story of a careless girl who ran into a crowded street and was crushed by a cab. "Was smash flat," reported my mother.

At the corner of the alley was Hong Sing's, a four-table café with a recessed stairwell in front that led to a door marked "Tradesmen." My brothers and I believed the bad people emerged from this door at night. Tourists never went to Hong Sing's, since the menu was printed only in Chinese. A Caucasian man with a big camera once posed me and my

70   playmates in front of the restaurant. He had us move to the side of the picture window so the photo would capture the roasted duck with its head dangling from a juice-covered rope. After he took the picture, I told him he should go into Hong Sing's and eat dinner. When he smiled and asked me what they served, I shouted, "Guts and duck's feet and octopus gizzards!" Then I ran off with my friends, shrieking with laughter as we scampered across the alley and hid in the entryway grotto[4] of the China Gem Company, my heart pounding with hope that he would chase us.

80   My mother named me after the street that we lived on: Waverly Place Jong, my official name for important American documents. But my family called me Meimei, "Little Sister." I was the youngest, the only daughter. Each morning before school, my mother would twist and yank on my thick black hair until she had formed two tightly wound

---

3. **prawns.** Edible crustaceans resembling shrimp
4. **grotto.** Cave or artificial recess or structure built to resemble a cave

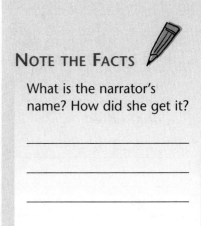

NOTE THE FACTS

What is the narrator's name? How did she get it?

_____
_____
_____

pigtails. One day, as she struggled to weave a hard-toothed comb through my disobedient hair, I had a sly thought.

I asked her, "Ma, what is Chinese torture?" My mother shook her head. A bobby pin was wedged between her lips. She wetted her palms and smoothed the hair above my ear, then pushed the pin in so that it nicked sharply against my scalp.

"Who say this word?" she asked without a trace of knowing how wicked I was being. I shrugged my shoulders and said, "Some boy in my class said Chinese people do Chinese torture."

"Chinese people do many things," she said simply. "Chinese do business, do medicine, do painting. Not lazy like American people. We do torture. Best torture."

My older brother Vincent was the one who actually got the chess set. We had gone to the annual Christmas party held at the First Chinese Baptist Church at the end of the alley. The missionary ladies had put together a Santa bag of gifts donated by members of another church. None of the gifts had names on them. There were separate sacks for boys and girls of different ages.

One of the Chinese parishioners had donned a Santa Claus costume and a stiff paper beard with cotton balls glued to it. I think the only children who thought he was the real thing were too young to know that Santa Claus was not Chinese. When my turn came up, the Santa man asked me how old I was. I thought it was a trick question; I was seven according to the American formula and eight by the Chinese calendar. I said I was born on March 17, 1951. That seemed to satisfy him. He then solemnly asked if I had been a very, very good girl this year and did I believe in Jesus Christ and obey my parents. I knew the only answer to that. I nodded back with equal <u>solemnity</u>.

Having watched the other children opening their gifts, I already knew that the big gifts were not necessarily the nicest ones. One girl my age got a large coloring book of

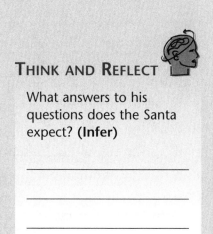

THINK AND REFLECT

How does Mrs. Jong turn Waverly's insult around? **(Infer)**

_____

_____

_____

THINK AND REFLECT

What answers to his questions does the Santa expect? **(Infer)**

_____

_____

_____

words for everyday use

so • lem • ni • ty (sə lem′ ne tē) *n.*, deep seriousness; formal or solemn observance. *The mourners were filled with <u>solemnity</u> at the funeral.*

biblical characters, while a less greedy girl who selected a smaller box received a glass vial of lavender toilet water.

130   The sounds of the box were also important. A ten-year-old boy had chosen a box that jangled when he shook it. It was a tin globe of the world with a slit for inserting money. He must have thought it was full of dimes and nickels, because when he saw that it had just ten pennies, his face fell with such undisguised disappointment that his mother slapped the side of his head and led him out of the church hall, apologizing to the crowd for her son who had such bad manners he couldn't appreciate such a fine gift.

       As I peered into the sack, I quickly fingered the remaining
140   presents, testing their weight, imagining what they contained. I chose a heavy, compact one that was wrapped in shiny silver foil and a red satin ribbon. It was a twelve-pack of Life Savers and I spent the rest of the party arranging and rearranging the candy tubes in the order of my favorites. My brother Winston chose wisely as well. His present turned out to be a box of <u>intricate</u> plastic parts; the instructions on the box proclaimed that when they were properly assembled he would have an authentic miniature <u>replica</u> of a World War II submarine.

150   Vincent got the chess set, which would have been a very decent present to get at a church Christmas party, except it was obviously used and, as we discovered later, it was missing a black pawn and a white knight. My mother graciously thanked the unknown benefactor, saying, "Too good. Cost too much." At which point, an old lady with fine white, wispy hair nodded toward our family and said with a whistling whisper, "Merry, merry Christmas."

       When we got home, my mother told Vincent to throw the chess set away. "She not want it. We not want it," she said,
160   tossing her head stiffly to the side with a tight, proud smile. My brothers had deaf ears. They were already lining up the chess pieces and reading from the dog-eared instruction book.

---

words for everyday use

in • tri • cate (in' tri ket) *adj.*, complicated, having many complex parts. *It was an <u>intricate</u> puzzle with over one thousand tiny pieces.*

rep • li • ca (re' pli kə) *n.*, exact copy or reproduction. *The painting was a <u>replica</u> of the original.*

_____

_____

_____

MARK THE TEXT

Underline or highlight Mrs. Jong's reaction to the chess set.

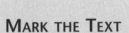

THINK AND REFLECT

Why does the white-haired woman whisper a special "Merry Christmas" to the Jongs? **(Interpret)**

_____

_____

_____

I watched Vincent and Winston play during Christmas week. The chessboard seemed to hold <u>elaborate</u> secrets waiting to be untangled. The chessmen were more powerful than old Li's magic herbs that cured ancestral curses. And my brothers wore such serious faces that I was sure something was at stake that was greater than avoiding the

170 tradesman's door to Hong Sing's.

"Let me! Let me!" I begged between games when one brother or the other would sit back with a deep sigh of relief and victory, the other annoyed, unable to let go of the outcome. Vincent at first refused to let me play, but when I offered my Life Savers as replacements for the buttons that filled in for the missing pieces, he <u>relented</u>. He chose the flavors: wild cherry for the black pawn and peppermint for the white knight. Winner could eat both.

As our mother sprinkled flour and rolled out small doughy

180 circles for the steamed dumplings that would be our dinner that night, Vincent explained the rules, pointing to each piece. "You have sixteen pieces and so do I. One king and queen, two bishops, two knights, two castles, and eight pawns. The pawns can only move forward one step, except on the first move. Then they can move two. But they can only take men by moving crossways like this, except in the beginning, when you can move ahead and take another pawn."

"Why?" I asked as I moved my pawn. "Why can't they

190 move more steps?"

"Because they're pawns," he said.

"But why do they go crossways to take other men? Why aren't there any women and children?"

"Why is the sky blue? Why must you always ask stupid questions?" asked Vincent. "This is a game. These are the rules. I didn't make them up. See. Here. In the book." He jabbed a page with a pawn in his hand. "Pawn. P-A-W-N. Pawn. Read it yourself."

My mother patted the flour off her hands. "Let me see

200 book," she said quietly. She scanned the pages quickly, not

NOTE THE FACTS

What does Waverly do to get her brothers to let her play chess?

_____

_____

_____

WHAT DO YOU WONDER?

_____

_____

_____

_____

words for everyday use

e • la • bor • ate (i la' be ret) *adj.*, marked by complexity, fullness of detail. *The man went to <u>elaborate</u> measures to plan every detail of his trip.*

re • lent (ri lent') *vi.*, give in or slacken. *Tired of Greg's pleading, Lora <u>relented</u> and told him the secret.*

reading the foreign English symbols, seeming to search deliberately for nothing in particular.

"This American rules," she concluded at last. "Every time people come out from foreign country, must know rules. You not know, judge say, Too bad, go back. They not telling you why so you can use their way go forward. They say, Don't know why, you find out yourself. But they knowing all the time. Better you take it, find out why yourself." She tossed her head back with a satisfied smile.

I found out about all the whys later. I read the rules and looked up all the big words in a dictionary. I borrowed books from the Chinatown library. I studied each chess piece, trying to absorb the power each contained.

I learned about opening moves and why it's important to control the center early on; the shortest distance between two points is straight down the middle. I learned about the middle game and why tactics between two adversaries are like clashing ideas; the one who plays better has the clearest plans for both attacking and getting out of traps. I learned why it is essential in the endgame to have foresight, a mathematical understanding of all the possible moves, and patience; all weaknesses and advantages become evident to a strong <u>adversary</u> and are obscured to a tiring opponent. I discovered that for the whole game one must gather invisible strengths and see the endgame before the game begins.

I also found out why I should never reveal "why" to others. A little knowledge withheld is a great advantage one should store for future use. That is the power of chess. It is a game of secrets in which one must show and never tell.

I loved the secrets I found within the sixty-four black and white squares. I carefully drew a handmade chessboard and pinned it to the wall next to my bed, where at night I would stare for hours at imaginary battles. Soon I no longer lost my games or Life Savers, but I lost my adversaries. Winston and Vincent decided they were more interested in roaming the streets after school in their Hopalong Cassidy[5] cowboy hats.

---

5. **Hopalong Cassidy.** Fictional cowboy hero popularized by movies and television shows in the 1950s

words for everyday use

ad • ver • sar • y (ad′ ve(r) ser ē) *n.*, one that contends with or opposes. *His enemy was a worthy <u>adversary</u>.*

READ ALOUD

Read lines 208–214 aloud. How does Waverly's mother feel about American rules?

_____

_____

_____

_____

FIX-UP IDEA

Ask a Question
If you have difficulty understanding the story, try asking a question that expresses what you don't understand. Then reread the section to answer your question. If you still can't find an answer, ask a classmate or your teacher. Consider how the answer to your question might help you make a prediction or how it affects the predictions you have already made.

MARK THE TEXT

Underline or highlight what Waverly says is the power of chess.

On a cold spring afternoon, while walking home from school, I detoured through the playground at the end of our alley. I saw a group of old men, two seated across a folding table playing a game of chess, others smoking pipes, eating peanuts, and watching. I ran home and grabbed Vincent's chess set, which was bound in a cardboard box with rubber bands. I also carefully selected two prized rolls of Life Savers. I came back to the park and approached a man who was observing the game.

"Want to play?" I asked him. His face widened with surprise and he grinned as he looked at the box under my arm.

"Little sister, been a long time since I play with dolls," he said, smiling <u>benevolently</u>. I quickly put the box down next to him on the bench and displayed my <u>retort</u>.

Lau Po, as he allowed me to call him, turned out to be a much better player than my brothers. I lost many games and many Life Savers. But over the weeks, with each <u>diminishing</u> roll of candies, I added new secrets. Lau Po gave me the names. The Double Attack from the East and West Shores. Throwing Stones on the Drowning Man. The Sudden Meeting of the Clan. The Surprise from the Sleeping Guard. The Humble Servant Who Kills the King. Sand in the Eyes of Advancing Forces. A Double Killing Without Blood.

There were also the fine points of chess <u>etiquette</u>. Keep captured men in neat rows, as well-tended prisoners. Never announce "Check" with <u>vanity</u>, lest someone with an unseen sword slit your throat. Never hurl pieces into the sandbox after you have lost a game, because then you must find them again, by yourself, after apologizing to all around you. By the end of the summer, Lau Po had taught me all he knew, and I had become a better chess player.

250

260

270

THINK AND REFLECT

What do the names in the paragraph at right refer to? **(Infer)**

_____

_____

_____

words for everyday use

be • nev • o • lent • ly (be nev′ lent lē) *adv.*, with kindness or goodwill. *She benevolently gave donations to the poor.*

re • tort (ri tort′) *n.*, quick, witty, or cunning reply. *He gave a quick retort to the insult.*

di • min • ish • ing (de mi′ nish ing) *adj.*, becoming smaller or less. *The poor investment gave diminishing returns.*

et • i • quette (e′ ti ket) *n.*, proper social conduct or procedure. *She displayed good etiquette at the tea party.*

van • i • ty (va′ ne tē) *n.*, inflated pride in oneself; conceit. *The boy accepted his trophy with a show of vanity.*

A small weekend crowd of Chinese people and tourists would gather as I played and defeated my opponents one by one. My mother would join the crowds during these outdoor exhibition games. She sat proudly on the bench, telling my admirers with proper Chinese <u>humility</u>, "Is luck."

A man who watched me play in the park suggested that my mother allow me to play in local chess tournaments. My mother smiled <u>graciously</u>, an answer that meant nothing. I desperately wanted to go, but I bit back my tongue. I knew she would not let me play among strangers. So as we walked home I said in a small voice that I didn't want to play in the local tournament. They would have American rules. If I lost, I would bring shame on my family.

"Is shame you fall down nobody push you," said my mother.

During my first tournament, my mother sat with me in the front row as I waited for my turn. I frequently bounced my legs to unstick them from the cold metal seat of the folding chair. When my name was called, I leapt up. My mother unwrapped something in her lap. It was her chang, a small tablet of red jade which held the sun's fire. "Is luck," she whispered, and tucked it into my dress pocket. I turned to my opponent, a fifteen-year-old boy from Oakland. He looked at me, wrinkling his nose.

As I began to play, the boy disappeared, the color ran out of the room, and I saw only my white pieces and his black ones waiting on the other side. A light wind began blowing past my ears. It whispered secrets only I could hear.

"Blow from the South," it murmured. "The wind leaves no trail." I saw a clear path, the traps to avoid. The crowd rustled. "Shhh! Shhh!" said the corners of the room. The wind blew stronger. "Throw sand from the East to distract him." The knight came forward ready for the sacrifice. The wind hissed, louder and louder. "Blow, blow, blow. He cannot see. He is blind now. Make him lean away from the wind so he is easier to knock down."

290

300

310

320

NOTE THE FACTS

How does Waverly get her mother to let her play in tournaments?

_____

_____

_____

THINK AND REFLECT

How does this tactic relate to Mrs. Jong's advice at the beginning of the story? (**Synthesize**)

_____

_____

_____

Literary TOOLS

SYMBOL. A **symbol** is a thing that stands for or represents both itself and something else. In lines 317–324, how does the wind affect Waverly's game? As you read the rest of the story, notice when the wind is mentioned. How might the wind be a symbol?

_____

_____

_____

<table>
<tr><td rowspan="3">words for everyday use</td><td>hu • mil • i • ty (hu mi' le tē) n., state of being humble, not possessing pride. With <u>humility</u> she gave credit to her teacher.</td></tr>
<tr><td>gra • cious • ly (grā' shes lē) adv., with kindness and courtesy. The gentleman <u>graciously</u> offered his seat to the elderly woman.</td></tr>
</table>

NOTE THE FACTS

How does Waverly's mother show that she values Waverly's chess skill?

_____

_____

_____

"Check," I said, as the wind roared with laughter. The wind died down to little puffs, my own breath.

330 My mother placed my first trophy next to a new plastic chess set that the neighborhood Tao[6] society had given to me. As she wiped each piece with a soft cloth, she said, "Next time win more, lose less."

"Ma, it's not how many pieces you lose," I said. "Sometimes you need to lose pieces to get ahead."

"Better to lose less, see if you really need."

At the next tournament, I won again, but it was my mother who wore the <u>triumphant</u> grin.

"Lost eight piece this time. Last time was eleven. What I tell you? Better off lose less!" I was annoyed, but I couldn't

340 say anything.

I attended more tournaments, each one further away from home. I won all games, in all divisions. The Chinese bakery downstairs from our flat displayed my growing collection of trophies in its window, amidst the dust-covered cakes that were never picked up. The day after I won an important regional tournament, the window encased a fresh sheet cake with whipped-cream frosting and red script saying, "Congratulations, Waverly Jong, Chinatown Chess Champion." Soon after that, a flower shop, headstone

350 engraver, and funeral parlor offered to sponsor me in national tournaments. That's when my mother decided that I no longer had to do the dishes. Winston and Vincent had to do my chores.

"Why does she get to play and we do all the work," complained Vincent.

"Is new American rules," said my mother. "Meimei play, squeeze all her brains out for win chess. You play, worth squeeze towel."

By my ninth birthday, I was a national chess champion. I

360 was still some 429 points away from grand master status, but I was <u>touted</u> as the Great American Hope, a child <u>prodigy</u>

---

6. **Tao.** Chinese mystical philosophy founded in the 6th century BC

words for everyday use	**tri • um • phant** (trī em(p)′ fent) *adj.*, victorious, or relating to triumph. *The school held a celebration for the <u>triumphant</u> football team.* **tout** (taut′) *vi.*, praise or publicize loudly. *Jill was <u>touted</u> for her scholastic abilities.* **prod • i • gy** (prä′ de jē) *n.*, highly talented child or youth. *His exceptional acting ability made him a child <u>prodigy</u>.*

and a girl to boot. They ran a photo of me in *Life* magazine next to a quote in which Bobby Fisher said, "There will never be a woman grand master." "Your move, Bobby," said the <u>caption</u>.

The day they took the magazine picture I wore neatly plaited[7] braids clipped with plastic barrettes trimmed with rhinestones. I was playing in a large high school auditorium that echoed with phlegmy coughs and the squeaky wooden floors. Seated across from me was an American man, about the same age as Lau Po, maybe fifty. I remember that his sweaty brow seemed to weep at my every move. He wore a dark, <u>malodorous</u> suit. One of his pockets was stuffed with a great white kerchief on which he wiped his palm before sweeping his hand over the chosen chess piece with great <u>flourish</u>.

In my crisp pink-and-white dress with scratchy lace at the neck, one of two my mother had sewn for these special occasions, I would clasp my hands under my chin, the delicate points of my elbows poised lightly on the table in the manner my mother had shown me for posing for the press. I would swing my patent leather shoes back and forth like an impatient child riding on a school bus. Then I would pause, suck in my lips, twirl my chosen piece in midair as if undecided, and then firmly plant it in its new threatening place, with a triumphant smile thrown back at my opponent for good measure.

I no longer played in the alley of Waverly Place. I never visited the playground where the pigeons and old men gathered. I went to school, then directly home to learn new chess secrets, cleverly concealed advantages, more escape routes.

But I found it difficult to concentrate at home. My mother had a habit of standing over me while I plotted out my games. I think she thought of herself as my protective <u>ally</u>.

370

380

390

7. **plaited.** Woven or braided

words for everyday use

cap • tion (kap′ shen) *n.*, heading or comment accompanying a photograph. *The <u>caption</u> below the photograph explained what was happening.*

mal • o • dor • ous (mal ō′ der es) *adj.*, having a bad odor. *The rotten fish made the room smell <u>malodorous</u>.*

flour • ish (fler′ ish) *n.*, bold sweeping gesture. *The traffic guard waved his arms with a <u>flourish</u>.*

al • ly (a′ lī) *n.*, one that is associated with another as a helper. *The doctor had become Ty's <u>ally</u> in his battle against cancer.*

Reading STRATEGY REVIEW

VISUALIZE. As you read lines 366–386, create a picture in your mind of the game between Waverly and the American man.

MARK THE TEXT

Underline the words that tell you what Waverly gives up to play chess.

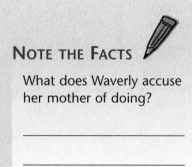
Use THE STRATEGY

MAKE PREDICTIONS. Write down a prediction about why Mrs. Jong wants Waverly to come with her. Revisit your prediction after you reach the next Note the Facts question.

_____

_____

_____

_____

Her lips would be sealed tight, and after each move I made, a soft "Hmmmmph" would escape from her nose.

"Ma, I can't practice when you stand there like that," I said one day. She retreated to the kitchen and made loud 400 noises with the pots and pans. When the crashing stopped, I could see out of the corner of my eye that she was standing in the doorway. "Hmmmph!" Only this one came out of her tight throat.

My parents made many <u>concessions</u> to allow me to practice. One time I complained that the bedroom I shared was so noisy that I couldn't think. Thereafter, my brothers slept in a bed in the living room facing the street. I said I couldn't finish my rice; my head didn't work right when my stomach was too full. I left the table with half-finished bowls 410 and nobody complained. But there was one duty I couldn't avoid. I had to accompany my mother on Saturday market days when I had no tournament to play. My mother would proudly walk with me, visiting many shops, buying very little. "This my daughter Wave-ly Jong," she said to whoever looked her way.

One day after we left a shop I said under my breath, "I wish you wouldn't do that, telling everybody I'm your daughter." My mother stopped walking. Crowds of people with heavy bags pushed past us on the sidewalk, bumping 420 into first one shoulder, then another.

"Aiii-ya. So shame be with mother?" She grasped my hand even tighter as she glared at me.

I looked down. "It's not that, it's just so obvious. It's just so embarrassing."

"Embarrass you be my daughter?" Her voice was cracking with anger.

"That's not what I meant. That's not what I said."

"What you say?"

I knew it was a mistake to say anything more, but I heard 430 my voice speaking, "Why do you have to use me to show off? If you want to show off, then why don't you learn to play chess?"

words for everyday use

con • ces • sion (ken se′ shen) *n.*, something granted as a right or privilege. *Many <u>concessions</u> were made by both sides in order to reach an agreement.*

My mother's eyes turned into dangerous black slits. She had no words for me, just sharp silence.

I felt the wind rushing around my hot ears. I jerked my hand out of my mother's tight grasp and spun around, knocking into an old woman. Her bag of groceries spilled to the ground.

"Aii-ya! Stupid girl!" my mother and the woman cried. Oranges and tin cans careened down the sidewalk. As my 440 mother stooped to help the old woman pick up the escaping food, I took off.

I raced down the street, dashing between people, not looking back as my mother screamed shrilly, "Meimei! Meimei!" I fled down an alley, past dark, curtained shops and merchants washing the grime off their windows. I sped into the sunlight, into a large street crowded with tourists examining trinkets and souvenirs. I ducked into another dark alley, down another street, up another alley. I ran until it hurt and I realized I had nowhere to go, that I was not 450 running from anything. The alleys contained no escape routes.

My breath came out like angry smoke. It was cold. I sat down on an upturned plastic pail next to a stack of empty boxes, cupping my chin with my hands, thinking hard. I imagined my mother, first walking briskly down one street or another looking for me, then giving up and returning home to await my arrival. After two hours, I stood up on creaking legs and slowly walked home.

The alley was quiet and I could see the yellow lights 460 shining from our flat like two tiger's eyes in the night. I climbed the sixteen steps to the door, advancing quietly up each so as not to make any warning sounds. I turned the knob; the door was locked. I heard a chair moving, quick steps, the locks turning—click! click! click!—and then the door opened.

"About time you got home," said Vincent. "Boy, are you in trouble."

He slid back to the dinner table. On a platter were the remains of a large fish, its fleshy head still connected to 470 bones swimming upstream in vain escape. Standing there waiting for my punishment, I heard my mother speak in a dry voice.

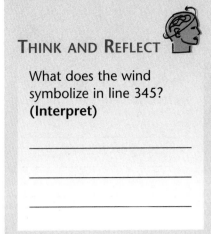

THINK AND REFLECT

What does the wind symbolize in line 345? (Interpret)

_____

_____

_____

NOTE THE FACTS

Why does Waverly decide to go home?

_____

_____

_____

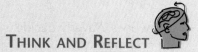
THINK AND REFLECT

Who is Waverly's opponent in this game? **(Infer)**
What does the game symbolize about Waverly's relationship to this opponent? **(Interpret)**

_____

_____

_____

_____

"We're not concerning this girl. This girl not have concerning for us."

Nobody looked at me. Bone chopsticks clinked against the insides of bowls being emptied into hungry mouths.

I walked into my room, closed the door, and lay down on my bed. The room was dark, the ceiling filled with shadows
480 from the dinnertime lights of neighboring flats.

In my head, I saw a chessboard with sixty-four black and white squares. Opposite me was my opponent, two angry black slits. She wore a triumphant smile. "Strongest wind cannot be seen," she said.

Her black men advanced across the plane, slowly marching to each <u>successive</u> level as a single unit. My white pieces screamed as they scurried and fell off the board one by one. As her men drew closer to my edge, I felt myself growing light. I rose up into the air and flew out the
490 window. Higher and higher, above the alley, over the tops of tiled roofs, where I was gathered up by the wind and pushed up toward the night sky until everything below me disappeared and I was alone.

I closed my eyes and pondered my next move. ■

words for everyday use	suc • ces • sive (sək se′ siv) *adj.*, following in order. *He took the required classes in* <u>successive</u> *order.*

Reflect ON YOUR READING

After Reading ➤ ANALYZE YOUR PREDICTIONS

When you finish reading the story, review the predictions you made. If you haven't already done so, record what really happened. Think about how this strategy affected your reading experience. Did you find yourself reading more actively in order to find out if your predictions were correct? Did you focus more on the story's main events and ideas? Write a paragraph or two answering these questions and describing how the reading strategy changed how you read. When you finish, share your essay with a partner and discuss how making predictions affected your understanding and enjoyment of the selection.

Reading Skills and Test Practice

IDENTIFY SYMBOLISM
Discuss with a partner how to best answer the following questions about symbolism in "The Rules of the Game."

1. Throughout the story, the wind symbolizes Waverly's
   a. unseen fear of losing.
   b. unacknowledged love for her brother.
   c. invisible strength.
   d. hidden dislike of her mother.

What is the correct answer to the question above? How were you able to eliminate the other answers?

_____

_____

_____

2. The title of the story, "Rules of the Game," has a double meaning. In addition to the rules of chess, the title may refer to the rules of
   a. the Chinese calendar.
   b. life.
   c. etiquette.
   d. the neighborhood school.

What is the correct answer to the question above? How were you able to eliminate the other answers?

_____

_____

_____

THINK-ALOUD NOTES

_____

_____

_____

_____

_____

_____

_____

_____

_____

_____

_____

Investigate, Inquire, and Imagine

RECALL: GATHER FACTS ➔
1a. How does Mrs. Jong react in public to the Christmas gift of a used chess game? What is her real opinion, which she expresses when the family gets home?

INTERPRET: FIND MEANING
1b. Why does Mrs. Jong act as she does in public when that is not the way she really feels?

ANALYZE: TAKE THINGS APART ➔
2a. Make a list of references in the story to rules and games.

SYNTHESIZE: BRING THINGS TOGETHER
2b. Is there more than one game being played in this story? Explain. What is the broader meaning of the title?

EVALUATE: MAKE JUDGMENTS ➔
3a. How good a communicator do you think Mrs. Jong is? What accounts for the communication problems between Waverly and her mother?

EXTEND: CONNECT IDEAS
3b. In what ways is the parent-child relationship complicated when the parent comes from a different culture?

Literary Tools

SYMBOL. A **symbol** is a thing that stands for or represents both itself and something else. The wind serves as an important symbol in this story. Waverly's mother says that a wise person does not go against the wind and that the "strongest wind cannot be seen." What does this mean?

_____

_____

How does Mrs. Jong's advice about the wind help Waverly win her first chess tournament?

_____

_____

How is the wind used as a symbol when Waverly accuses her mother of showing off?

_____

_____

What does Waverly's mother say right before the imaginary chess game at the end of the story? Who or what is the strongest wind at this point?

_____

_____

WordWorkshop

WORDS WITH MULTIPLE MEANINGS. Many words have more than one meaning. Multiple meanings can develop in several ways. A word might gain a wider or narrower meaning over time. For example, the word *mail* once meant "payment or rent" but now is most often used to refer to anything sent by post. It also has a lesser-known meaning that refers to medieval armor made of metal links or plates. Words can also be used as new parts of speech. For example, *mail* as it is used above is a noun, but the word can also be used as a verb meaning "to send by post."

Each of the following words has multiple meanings. Look up each word in the dictionary. Notice that words used as more than one part of speech have separate boldfaced entries. Multiple meanings of a word that are all the same part of speech are listed in a single boldfaced entry. Choose two meanings for each word and write them on your own paper. Then write an original sentence that reflects each meaning.

1. ally
2. concession
3. elaborate
4. retort
5. vanity

Read-Write Connection

Was Waverly's anger at the end of the story justified? Why, or why not? What do you think her "next move" will be?

_____

_____

_____

_____

_____

_____

_____

Beyond the Reading

TEACH A GAME. Research the rules of chess, *mah jong,* or some other game that you would like to learn. Use the Internet, books, and other publications to gather information. Then prepare a presentation in which you teach the class to play the game you have chosen.

GO ONLINE. Visit the EMC Internet Resource Center at **emcp.com** to find links and additional activities for this selection.

"After You, My Dear Alphonse"
by Shirley Jackson

Reader's resource

In **"After You, My Dear Alphonse"** Shirley Jackson shows that assuming things about another person can be a subtle, yet powerful form of prejudice. The saying "After you, my dear Alphonse" originated with a comic strip that first appeared in 1905. The expression is generally used humorously in a situation where two people go back and forth, suggesting the other go first, as a way of being polite. "After You, My Dear Alphonse" was published in Jackson's short story collection *The Lottery* in 1949.

Word watch

PREVIEW VOCABULARY

foreman	kindling
foxhole	stewed
impulse	

Reader's journal

When have you made an assumption about another person, only to discover later that you were wrong?

_____

_____

_____

Active READING STRATEGY

WRITE THINGS DOWN

Before Reading ➤ **FIND A METHOD FOR RECORDING INFORMATION**

❏ Read the Reader's Resource, and study the definition of *stereotype* in Literary Tools on page 101.
❏ Preview the graphic organizer below and prepare to record the assumptions Mrs. Wilson makes about Boyd based on her stereotypes of African Americans.

Graphic Organizer

Assumptions	Stereotypes
Johnny made Boyd carry the wood	Whites order African Americans around

After You, My Dear Alphonse

Shirley Jackson

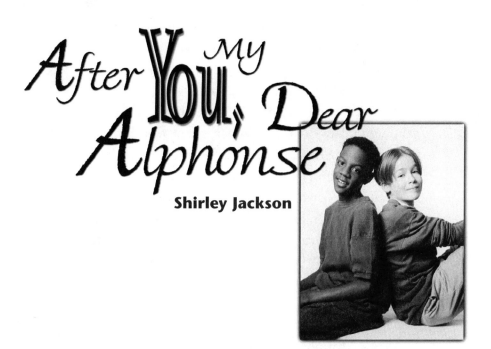

During Reading

RECORD AND ORGANIZE INFORMATION

❑ Read the selection independently.
❑ Use the selection's margin questions to help you identify the assumptions made by Mrs. Wilson.
❑ Record appropriate details in your Assumptions and Stereotypes Chart. Remember that you can find Mrs. Wilson's assumptions in the text, but you will most likely have to make inferences, putting the clues from the text with your own prior knowledge, in order to fill in the Stereotypes column of your chart.

Literary TOOLS

STEREOTYPE. A **stereotype** is an idea that many people have about a thing or a group that may often be untrue or only partly true. As you read, think about the stereotypes Mrs. Wilson has about African Americans.

Mrs. Wilson was just taking the gingerbread out of the oven when she heard Johnny outside talking to someone.

"Johnny," she called, "you're late. Come in and get your lunch."

"Just a minute, Mother," Johnny said. "After you, my dear Alphonse."

"After *you*, my dear Alphonse," another voice said.

"No, after *you*, my dear Alphonse," Johnny said.

Mrs. Wilson opened the door. "Johnny," she said. "You come in this minute and get your lunch. You can play after you've eaten."

Johnny came in after her, slowly. "Mother," he said, "I brought Boyd home for lunch with me."

"Boyd?" Mrs. Wilson thought for a moment. "I don't believe I've met Boyd. Bring him in, dear, since you've invited him. Lunch is ready."

"Boyd!" Johnny yelled. "Hey, Boyd, come on in!"

"I'm coming. Just got to unload this stuff."

"Well, hurry, or my mother'll be sore."[1]

"Johnny, that's not very polite to either your friend or your mother," Mrs. Wilson said. "Come sit down, Boyd."

10

20

NOTE THE FACTS

Who is Johnny's friend?

_____

_____

---

1. **sore.** Angry

As she turned to show Boyd where to sit, she saw he was a Negro boy, smaller than Johnny but about the same age. His arms were loaded with split <u>kindling</u> wood. "Where'll I put this stuff, Johnny?" he asked.

Mrs. Wilson turned to Johnny. "Johnny," she said, "what did you make Boyd do? What is that wood?"

30

"Dead Japanese," Johnny said mildly. "We stand them in the ground and run over them with tanks."

"How do you do, Mrs. Wilson?" Boyd said.

"How do you do, Boyd? You shouldn't let Johnny make you carry all that wood. Sit down now and eat lunch, both of you."

"Why shouldn't he carry the wood, Mother? It's his wood. We got it at his place."

"Johnny," Mrs. Wilson said, "go on and eat your lunch."

40

"Sure," Johnny said. He held out the dish of scrambled eggs to Boyd. "After you, my dear Alphonse."

"After *you*, my dear Alphonse," Boyd said.

"After *you*, my dear Alphonse," Johnny said. They began to giggle.

"Are you hungry, Boyd?" Mrs. Wilson asked.

"Yes, Mrs. Wilson."

"Well, don't you let Johnny stop you. He always fusses about eating, so you just see that you get a good lunch. There's plenty of food here for you to have all you want."

50

"Thank you, Mrs. Wilson."

"Come on, Alphonse," Johnny said. He pushed half the scrambled eggs onto Boyd's plate. Boyd watched while Mrs. Wilson put a dish of <u>stewed</u> tomatoes beside his plate.

"Boyd don't eat tomatoes, do you, Boyd?" Johnny said.

"*Doesn't* eat tomatoes, Johnny. And just because you don't like them, don't say that about Boyd. Boyd will eat *anything*."

"Bet he won't," Johnny said, attacking his scrambled eggs.

"Boyd wants to grow up and be a big, strong man so he can work hard," Mrs. Wilson said. "I'll bet Boyd's father

60

eats stewed tomatoes."

THINK AND REFLECT

Why does Mrs. Wilson think Boyd is carrying the wood? **(Infer)**

_____

_____

_____

MARK THE TEXT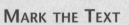

Underline or highlight what Mrs. Wilson assumes about Boyd's eating habits.

words for everyday use	kin • dling (kind′ liŋ) *adj.*, small pieces of wood or paper used to start a fire. *Janet used <u>kindling</u> sticks placed beneath the large logs to get the fire going.*
	stewed (stüd) *adj.*, cooked with simmering heat. *Bill's uncle ate <u>stewed</u> prunes for breakfast that he simmered the night before.*

"My father eats anything he wants to," Boyd said.

"So does mine," Johnny said. "Sometimes he doesn't eat hardly anything. He's a little guy, though. Wouldn't hurt a flea."

"Mine's a little guy, too," Boyd said.

"I'll bet he's strong, though," Mrs. Wilson said. She hesitated. "Does he . . . work?"

"Sure," Johnny said. "Boyd's father works in a factory."

70 "There, you see?" Mrs. Wilson said. "And he certainly has to be strong to do that—all that lifting and carrying at a factory."

"Boyd's father doesn't have to," Johnny said. "He's a foreman."

Mrs. Wilson felt defeated. "What does your mother do, Boyd?"

"My mother?" Boyd was surprised. "She takes care of us kids."

"Oh. She doesn't work, then?"

80 "Why should she?" Johnny said through a mouthful of eggs. "You don't work."

"You really don't want any stewed tomatoes, Boyd?"

"No, thank you, Mrs. Wilson," Boyd said.

"No, thank you, Mrs. Wilson, no, thank you, Mrs. Wilson, no, thank you, Mrs. Wilson," Johnny said. "Boyd's sister's going to work, though. She's going to be a teacher."

"That's a very fine attitude for her to have, Boyd." Mrs. Wilson restrained an impulse to pat Boyd on the head. "I imagine you're all very proud of her?"

90 "I guess so," Boyd said.

"What about all your other brothers and sisters? I guess all of you want to make just as much of yourselves as you can."

"There's only me and Jean," Boyd said. "I don't know yet what I want to be when I grow up."

"We're going to be tank drivers, Boyd and me," Johnny said. "Zoom." Mrs. Wilson caught Boyd's glass of milk as

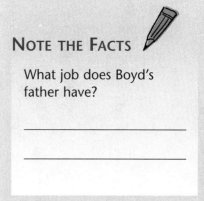

words for everyday use	**fore • man** (fôr′ mən) *n.,* person in charge of other workers or a section of a plant. *The foreman informed his workers of the production quota for the shift.*
	im • pulse (im′ pəls) *n.,* sudden spontaneous inclination to an unpremeditated action. *Jan's impulse was to throw a glass of water in her date's face after his rude remark.*

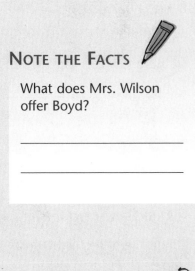

NOTE THE FACTS

What does Mrs. Wilson offer Boyd?

_____

_____

THINK AND REFLECT

What attitude underlies Mrs. Wilson's seemingly generous gestures? **(Infer)**

_____

_____

_____

_____

Johnny's napkin ring, suddenly transformed into a tank, plowed heavily across the table.

100 "Look, Johnny," Boyd said. "Here's a <u>foxhole</u>. I'm shooting at you."

Mrs. Wilson, with the speed born of long experience, took the gingerbread off the shelf and placed it carefully between the tank and the foxhole.

"Now eat as much as you want to, Boyd," she said. "I want to see you get filled up."

"Boyd eats a lot, but not as much as I do," Johnny said. "I'm bigger than he is."

"You're not much bigger," Boyd said. "I can beat you
110 running."

Mrs. Wilson took a deep breath. "Boyd," she said. Both boys turned to her. "Boyd, Johnny has some suits that are a little too small for him, and a winter coat. It's not new, of course, but there's lots of wear in it still. And I have a few dresses that your mother or sister could probably use. Your mother can make them over into lots of things for all of you, and I'd be very happy to give them to you. Suppose before you leave I make up a big bundle and then you and Johnny can take it over to your mother right away . . ." Her
120 voice trailed off as she saw Boyd's puzzled expression.

"But I have plenty of clothes, thank you," he said. "And I don't think my mother knows how to sew very well, and anyway I guess we buy about everything we need. Thank you very much, though."

"We don't have time to carry that old stuff around, Mother," Johnny said. "We got to play tanks with the kids today."

Mrs. Wilson lifted the plate of gingerbread off the table as Boyd was about to take another piece. "There are many
130 little boys like you, Boyd, who would be very grateful for the clothes someone was kind enough to give them."

"Boyd will take them if you want him to, Mother," Johnny said.

"I didn't mean to make you mad, Mrs. Wilson," Boyd said.

"Don't think I'm angry, Boyd. I'm just disappointed in you, that's all. Now let's not say anything more about it."

She began clearing the plates off the table, and Johnny took Boyd's hand and pulled him to the door. "Bye, Mother," Johnny said. Boyd stood for a minute, staring at Mrs. Wilson's back.

"After you, my dear Alphonse," Johnny said, holding the door open.

"Is your mother still mad?" Mrs. Wilson heard Boyd ask in a low voice.

"I don't know," Johnny said. "She's screwy sometimes."

"So's mine," Boyd said. He hesitated. "After *you*, my dear Alphonse." ■

THINK AND REFLECT

How does Mrs. Wilson feel when Boyd rejects the clothes? How can you tell? **(Interpret)**

_____

_____

_____

_____

Reflect ON YOUR READING

When you finish reading the selection, review your Assumptions and Stereotypes Chart. Then, write a one-page summary of the selection. In your summary, identify the assumptions revealed by Mrs. Wilson's remarks and reactions to Boyd and explain what stereotypes these assumptions reflect. When you're finished, share your summary with a partner, and discuss your impressions of "After You, My Dear Alphonse."

Reading Skills and Test Practice

IDENTIFY THE MAIN IDEA

READ, THINK, AND EXPLAIN. Discuss with a partner how to identify the main idea.

1. In this selection, Mrs. Wilson makes many untrue assumptions about Boyd. Identify one of these assumptions and explain why the assumption is false based on what you know about Boyd. Use details from the text to support your ideas.

   _____

   _____

   _____

   _____

2. Write a one-sentence summary of your interpretation of the message the author wants the reader to take away from this selection. Use text details to explain how you uncovered this message.

   _____

   _____

   _____

   _____

REFLECT ON YOUR RESPONSE. Compare your response to that of your partner. How were you able to identify the main idea?

   _____

   _____

THINK-ALOUD NOTES

_____

_____

_____

_____

_____

_____

_____

_____

_____

_____

_____

Investigate, Inquire, and Imagine

RECALL: GATHER FACTS
1a. Whom does Johnny invite home for lunch?

INTERPRET: FIND MEANING
1b. How does Mrs. Wilson's behavior change once she sees Boyd is African American?

ANALYZE: TAKE THINGS APART
2a. Identify proof that Johnny and Boyd are not aware of Mrs. Wilson's racist attitudes.

SYNTHESIZE: BRING THINGS TOGETHER
2b. Why doesn't Boyd get angry with Mrs. Wilson?

EVALUATE: MAKE JUDGMENTS
3a. Mrs. Wilson tells Boyd, "I'm just disappointed in you." Evaluate the cause of Mrs. Wilson's disappointment.

EXTEND: CONNECT IDEAS
3b. What role did Mrs. Wilson want Boyd to play? Have you ever played a role to meet someone else's expectations? Explain.

Literary Tools

STEREOTYPE. A **stereotype** is an idea that many people have about a thing or a group that may often be untrue or only partly true. Review the Assumptions and Stereotypes Chart you completed as you read. How does Boyd defy the stereotypes presented in the story? What is his experience with stereotypes?

_____

_____

_____

_____

_____

_____

_____

_____

_____

_____

_____

_____

_____

WordWorkshop

CONTRACTIONS. **Contractions** combine two words by shortening and joining them with an apostrophe.

EXAMPLES   isn't, aren't, don't, can't

In the following sentences from the story, underline each contraction and rewrite it as the two words from which it is derived. If a contraction is used incorrectly, write the contraction that should be used and the two words from which it is derived.

1. "Bring him in dear, since you've invited him."

_____

2. "Well, hurry, or my mother'll be sore."

_____

3. "Where'll I put this stuff, Johnny?" he asked.

_____

4. "Boyd don't eat tomatoes, do you, Boyd?" Johnny said.

_____

5. "I'll bet Boyd's father eats stewed tomatoes."

_____

Read-Write Connection

If you were Johnny, what would you say to your mother about what happened at lunch? Would you be angry or happy with how she treated Boyd?

_____

_____

_____

Beyond the Reading

"THE LOTTERY." Learn more about Shirley Jackson by reading another of her stories. One story you might consider reading is her most famous and controversial story, "The Lottery." Write a brief essay that summarizes the story that you chose to read and identifies its main themes. Close the essay with your personal reaction to the story.

GO ONLINE. Visit the EMC Internet Resource Center at **emcp.com** to find links and additional activities for this selection.

"Dead Men's Path"

by Chinua Achebe

Active READING STRATEGY

USE TEXT ORGANIZATION

Before Reading ▶ **PREVIEW THE SELECTION**

❑ Read the Reader's Resource and skim the Words for Everyday Use and footnotes at the bottom of the selection pages.

❑ Work with a partner to preview the margin questions for the selection. Discuss the information you've previewed, what the title of the selection might mean, and what you think the story will be about.

❑ Preview the Main Idea Map below. After you have considered and discussed this prereading information, make one or two predictions about what the main idea, or theme, of this story might be.

Graphic Organizer

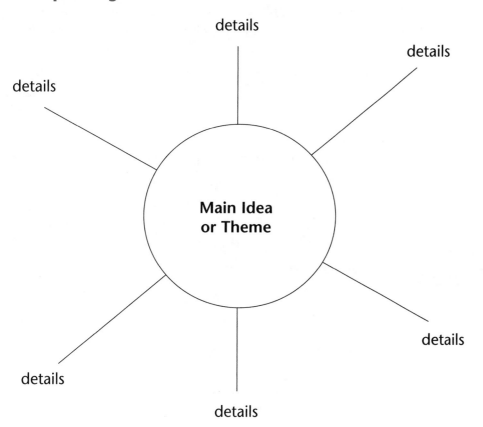

CONNECT

Reader's resource

"Dead Men's Path" is the story of a "progressive" African headmaster (principal) who takes on a new job in a village where the people are superstitious and cling to traditional tribal ways. The story addresses the cultural conflicts between "new" British ideas and "old" African customs. "Dead Men's Path" was published in Chinua Achebe's short story collection *Girls at War* (1972).

Word watch

PREVIEW VOCABULARY

denigration
eradicate
pivotal
propitiate
superannuated

Reader's journal

What customs are important in your culture? How far would you go to preserve them?

_____

_____

_____

_____

FIND THE MAIN IDEA

❑ Follow along in your text as your teacher reads the first part of the selection aloud.

❑ Write down what you believe to be the main idea, or theme, in the center circle of your Main Idea Map.

❑ As you read, record any details that support the main idea in the graphic organizer.

READ ALOUD

Read aloud the highlighted first paragraph. What is Obi's opinion of the other headmasters in the mission field?

_____

_____

_____

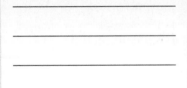

Literary TOOLS

NARRATOR. A **narrator** is one who tells a story. Something to consider is the reliability of the narrator. As you read, determine whether or not the narrator of "Dead Men's Path" is reliable. In other words, can you trust everything that he says?

Dead Men's Path

Chinua Achebe

Michael Obi's hopes were fulfilled much earlier than he had expected. He was appointed headmaster of Ndume Central School in January 1949. It had always been an unprogressive school, so the Mission authorities decided to send a young and energetic man to run it. Obi accepted this responsibility with enthusiasm. He had many wonderful ideas and this was an opportunity to put them into practice. He had had sound secondary school education which designated him a "<u>pivotal</u> teacher" in the official records 10 and set him apart from the other headmasters in the mission field. He was outspoken in his condemnation of the narrow views of these older and often less-educated ones.

"We shall make a good job of it, shan't we?" he asked his young wife when they first heard the joyful news of his promotion.

"We shall do our best," she replied. "We shall have such beautiful gardens and everything will be just *modern* and delightful . . ." In their two years of married life she had become completely infected by his passion for "modern 20 methods" and his <u>denigration</u> of "these old and <u>superannuated</u> people in the teaching field who would be

words for everyday use	**piv • o • tal** (pi′ və təl) *adj.*, on which something depends. *The <u>pivotal</u> new evidence helped to solve the crime.* **den • i • gra • tion** (de ni grā′ shən) *n.*, belittling. *Christa's <u>denigration</u> of Mary's Christmas tradition of making original homemade cards hurt Mary's feelings.* **su • per • an • nu • at • ed** (sü pər an′ yə wāt əd) *adj.*, old-fashioned; outdated. *Typewriters are considered <u>superannuated</u> since the invention of the personal computer.*

better employed as traders in the Onitsha[1] market." She began to see herself already as the admired wife of the young headmaster, the queen of the school.

The wives of the other teachers would envy her position. She would set the fashion in everything . . . Then, suddenly, it occurred to her that there might not be other wives. Wavering between hope and fear, she asked her husband, looking anxiously at him.

30 "All our colleagues are young and unmarried," he said with enthusiasm which for once she did not share. "Which is a good thing," he continued.

"Why?"

"Why? They will give all their time and energy to the school."

Nancy was downcast. For a few minutes she became skeptical about the new school; but was only for a few minutes. Her little personal misfortune could not blind her to her husband's happy prospects. She looked at him as he
40 sat folded up in a chair. He was stoop-shouldered and looked frail. But he sometimes surprised people with sudden bursts of physical energy. In his present posture, however, all his bodily strength seemed to have retired behind his deep-set eyes, giving them an extraordinary power of penetration. He was twenty-six, but looked thirty or more. On the whole, he was not unhandsome.

"A penny for your thoughts, Mike," said Nancy after a while, imitating the woman's magazine she read.

"I was thinking what a grand opportunity we've got at last
50 to show these people how a school should be run."

Ndume School was backward in every sense of the word. Mr. Obi put his whole life into the work, and his wife hers too. He had two aims. A high standard of teaching was insisted upon, and the school compound[2] was to be turned into a place of beauty. Nancy's dream-gardens came to life with the coming of the rains, and blossomed. Beautiful hibiscus and allamanda hedges in brilliant red and yellow marked out the carefully tended school compound
60 from the rank neighborhood bushes.

---

1. **Onitsha.** Commercial center in Nigeria
2. **compound.** Enclosed space within a building or group of buildings

THINK AND REFLECT

Is Nancy more influenced by modern Western culture or by traditional African culture? Explain. (Interpret)

_____

_____

_____

FIX-UP IDEA

Use Margin Questions
If you are having difficulty applying the reading strategy, use the questions in the margins to help you identify the main ideas in the selection. Read the first question on a page; then begin reading the text to find the answer. Jot down the answer, and consider whether that detail connects to the theme.

MARK THE TEXT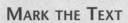

Underline or highlight Obi's two foremost goals.

NOTE THE FACTS

What does Obi see one night as he is admiring his work?

_____

_____

Reading STRATEGY REVIEW

MAKE PREDICTIONS.
Foreshadowing is the act of presenting materials that hint at events to occur later in a story. As you read lines 71–79, think about what the teacher's statements might foreshadow. Make a prediction about what you think will happen in the story. Look for information that will confirm or refute your prediction. Keep a written record of your ideas.

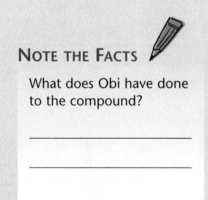

NOTE THE FACTS

What does Obi have done to the compound?

_____

_____

One evening as Obi was admiring his work he was scandalized to see an old woman from the village hobble right across the compound, through a marigold flower bed and the hedges. On going up there he found faint signs of an almost disused path from the village across the school compound to the bush on the other side.

"It amazes me," said Obi to one of his teachers who had been three years in the school, "that you people allowed the villagers to make use of this footpath. It is simply
70 incredible." He shook his head.

"The path," said the teacher apologetically, "appears to be very important to them. Although it is hardly used, it connects the village shrine with their place of burial."

"And what has that got to do with the school?" asked the headmaster.

"Well, I don't know," replied the other with a shrug of the shoulders. "But I remember there was a big row some time ago when we attempted to close it."

"That was some time ago. But it will not be used now,"
80 said Obi as he walked away. "What will the Government Education Officer think of this when he comes to inspect the school next week? The villagers might, for all I know, decide to use the schoolroom for a pagan ritual during the inspection."

Heavy sticks were planted closely across the path at the two places where it entered and left the school premises. These were further strengthened with barbed wire.

Three days later the village priest of *Ani* called on the
90 headmaster. He was an old man and walked with a slight stoop. He carried a stout walking stick which he usually tapped on the floor, by way of emphasis, each time he made a new point in his argument.

"I have heard," he said after the usual exchange of cordialities, "that our ancestral footpath has recently been closed . . ."

"Yes," replied Mr. Obi. "We cannot allow people to make a highway of our school compound."

"Look, here, my son," said the priest bringing down his
100 walking stick, "this path was here before you were born and before your father was born. The whole life of this village depends on it. Our dead relatives depart by it and our

ancestors visit us by it. But most important, it is the path of children coming in to be born . . ."

Mr. Obi listened with a satisfied smile on his face.

"The whole purpose of our school," he said finally, "is to <u>eradicate</u> just such beliefs as that. Dead men do not require footpaths. The whole idea is just fantastic. Our duty is to teach your children to laugh at such ideas."

110 "What you say may be true," replied the priest, "but we follow the practices of our fathers. If you reopen the path we shall have nothing to quarrel about. What I always say is: let the hawk perch and let the eagle perch." He rose to go.

"I am sorry," said the young headmaster. "But the school compound cannot be a thoroughfare. It is against our regulations. I would suggest your constructing another path, skirting our premises. We can even get our boys to help in building it. I don't suppose the ancestors will find the little detour too burdensome."

120 "I have no more words to say," said the old priest, already outside.

Two days later a young woman in the village died in childbed. A diviner[3] was immediately consulted and he prescribed heavy sacrifices to <u>propitiate</u> ancestors insulted by the fence.

Obi woke up the next morning among the ruins of his work. The beautiful hedges were torn up not just near the path but right round the school, the flowers trampled to death and one of the school buildings pulled down . . . That

130 day, the white Supervisor came to inspect the school and wrote a nasty report on the state of the premises but more seriously about the "tribal-war situation developing between the school and the village, arising in part from the misguided zeal of the new headmaster." ■

---

3. **diviner.** Religious person to whom prophetic powers are attributed

---

| words for everyday use | **e • rad • i • cate** (i raʹ də kāt) vt., do away with. *Because she wants to <u>eradicate</u> illiteracy, Mrs. Koslowski volunteers to tutor adults who want to learn to read.*
pro • pi • ti • ate (prō piʹ shē āt) vt., win or regain the good will of. *After disobeying an order, the soldier <u>propitiated</u> her captain by giving him tickets to a concert.* |

NOTE THE FACTS

What does the priest say is the most important purpose of the path for the villagers?

_____

_____

_____

NOTE THE FACTS

What happens two days after the priest's visit? How do the villagers respond?

_____

_____

_____

_____

THINK AND REFLECT

How is the Supervisor's report ironic? (**Analyze**)

_____

_____

_____

Reflect ON YOUR READING

When you have finished reading, review your Main Idea Map. Then, write a brief essay in which you identify the theme of this story and support it with details found in the text. Include in your essay an example of a prediction that you were able to confirm based on story details or any that you had to revise as new information was revealed. When you complete your essay, share it with a partner. Discuss any similarities or differences the two of you experienced in your applications of reading strategies.

THINK-ALOUD NOTES

Reading Skills and Test Practice

COMPARE AND CONTRAST IDEAS AND RECOGNIZE CAUSE AND EFFECT

READ, THINK, AND EXPLAIN. Discuss with a partner how to compare and contrast and how to recognize cause and effect.

1. How are Michael Obi's beliefs different from those of the village elders? Use details from the text to explain your answer.

_____

_____

_____

_____

2. What is the effect of the clashing of beliefs between Michael Obi and the village elders? Use details from the text to explain your answer.

_____

_____

_____

_____

REFLECT ON YOUR RESPONSE. Compare your response to that of your partner. How were you able to compare and contrast ideas and recognize cause and effect?

_____

_____

_____

_____

Investigate, Inquire, and Imagine

RECALL: GATHER FACTS
1a. How does the priest explain the importance of the path to the village?

INTERPRET: FIND MEANING
1b. Is Obi or the priest more tolerant of the other's beliefs? Explain.

ANALYZE: TAKE THINGS APART
2a. Analyze Obi's motivations in valuing the flowerbeds and hedges more than the villagers' beliefs.

SYNTHESIZE: BRING THINGS TOGETHER
2b. What does the path symbolize to the villagers?

EVALUATE: MAKE JUDGMENTS
3a. Evaluate whether the Ani community was justified in destroying the flowerbeds, hedges, and school building.

EXTEND: CONNECT IDEAS
3b. The destruction of the school property might have been avoided if the priest and Obi could have reached a compromise. Describe a conflict in your personal life, in government, in fiction, or in the movies. Tell what each side wanted and explain how the conflict was resolved.

WordWorkshop

WORD ROOTS. A **word root** is a word part that cannot stand alone as a complete word. Still, word roots, many of which descend from Greek and Latin words, carry and contribute meaning to complete words. Refer to the list of common word roots found in Unit 9 on pages 454–456. Using the following words from the selection, complete the chart below for each word, providing the word root, definition, and other examples. You may use a dictionary to identify words and to confirm that your examples use the word root as its meaning is listed in the chart. One example has been done for you.

Word	Root	Meaning of Root	Word Definition	Examples
superannuated opportunity prospect incredible promotion physical	ann	year	outdated	annual, anniversary

Keep a running list by noting other words that you come across that contain common word roots. Knowing the meanings of these key words can help you decipher meaning in unfamiliar words.

Literary Tools

Narrator. A **narrator** is one who tells a story. Whose opinion is presented in the sentence "Ndume School was backward in every sense of the word"? How reliable is the narrator of "Dead Men's Path"? With whom do the narrator's sympathies lie?

_____

_____

_____

_____

_____

_____

Read-Write Connection

If you were Michael Obi, how might you have avoided the destruction of school property?

_____

_____

_____

_____

_____

_____

_____

_____

Beyond the Reading

Missionaries. Investigate the part that missionaries have played in the history of Africa. What positive and negative effects have they had on the welfare of native Africans? In discussing these effects, cite specific individuals, countries, and impacts. Present the results of your research in a written essay, a pro and con chart, or a short debate.

Go Online. Visit the EMC Internet Resource Center at **emcp.com** to find links and additional activities for this selection.

"The Pedestrian"

by Ray Bradbury

Active READING STRATEGY

CONNECT TO PRIOR KNOWLEDGE

Before Reading ➤ **ACTIVATE PRIOR KNOWLEDGE**

❑ Read the Reader's Resource and skim the other selection pages, including the questions in the margins.

❑ Then, write a brief description of our world as we know it. Think about the activities and habits of people during the day and how those activities and habits are different at night.

❑ Preview the Venn Diagram below. Be prepared to fill in the graphic organizer as you read.

Graphic Organizer

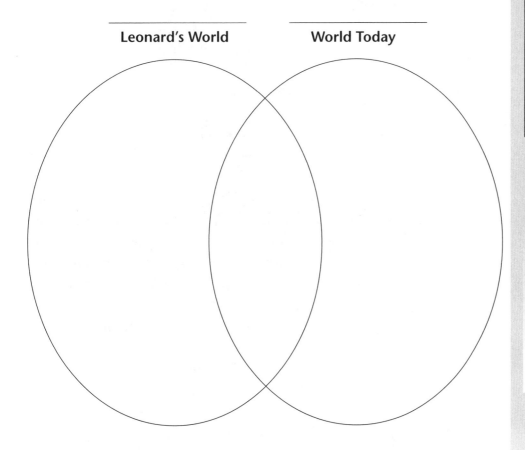

Leonard's World   World Today

CONNECT

Reader's resource

Science fiction is highly imaginative fiction containing fantastic elements based upon scientific principles, discoveries, or laws. Often, science fiction deals with the future, the distant past, or with worlds other than our own. The genre allows writers to suspend or alter certain elements of reality in order to create fascinating and sometimes instructive alternatives. **"The Pedestrian"** is set in the year AD 2053. As you read the selection, consider the ways in which the world Bradbury created is similar to the world you know.

Word watch

PREVIEW VOCABULARY

alibi   revue
illumination   riveted
jockey

Reader's journal

What do you think an automated world might be like?

_____

_____

_____

During Reading

Make Connections while Reading

❑ Begin reading the selection independently. Look for details about the world of AD 2053, and think about how that world compares with the world you live in today.

❑ As you read, write down details about Leonard's world in the left-hand circle of the Venn Diagram, and details about the world today in the right-hand circle. If there are any similarities, write those in the middle where the circles intersect. Jot down your ideas and explain any connections you can make.

Read Aloud

Read aloud the first highlighted paragraph. Who else is in Leonard's world? What might the phrase "as good as alone" indicate?

_____

_____

_____

Mark the Text

Underline or highlight to what Leonard compares walking through the dark city.

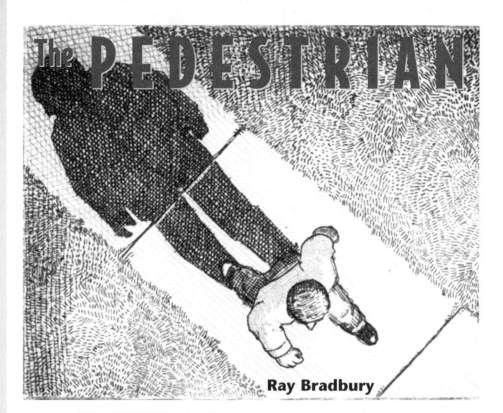

The PEDESTRIAN

Ray Bradbury

To enter out into that silence that was the city at eight o'clock of a misty evening in November, to put your feet upon that buckling concrete walk, to step over grassy seams and make your way, hands in pockets, through the silences, that was what Mr. Leonard Mead most dearly loved to do. He would stand upon the corner of an intersection and peer down long moonlit avenues of sidewalk in four directions, deciding which way to go, but it really made no difference; he was alone in this world of AD 2053, or as good as alone, and with a final decision made, a path selected, he would stride off, sending patterns of frosty air before him like the smoke of a cigar.

Sometimes he would walk for hours and miles and return only at midnight to his house. And on his way he would see the cottages and homes with their dark windows, and it was not unequal to walking through a graveyard where only the faintest glimmers of firefly light appeared in flickers behind the windows. Sudden gray phantoms seemed to manifest upon inner room walls where a curtain was still undrawn against the night, or there were whisperings and murmurs where a window in a tomb-like building was still open.

Mr. Leonard Mead would pause, cock his head, listen, look, and march on, his feet making no noise on the lumpy walk. For long ago he had wisely changed to sneakers when

10

20

strolling at night, because the dogs in intermittent squads would parallel his journey with barkings if he wore hard heels, and lights might click on and faces appear and an entire street be startled by the passing of a lone figure, himself, in the early November evening.

30   On this particular evening he began his journey in a westerly direction, toward the hidden sea. There was a good crystal frost in the air; it cut the nose and made the lungs blaze like a Christmas tree inside; you could feel the cold light going on and off, all the branches filled with invisible snow. He listened to the faint push of his soft shoes through autumn leaves with satisfaction, and whistled a cold quiet whistle between his teeth, occasionally picking up a leaf as he passed, examining its skeletal pattern in the infrequent lamplights as he went on, smelling its rusty smell.

40   "Hello, in there," he whispered to every house on every side as he moved. "What's up tonight on Channel 4, Channel 7, Channel 9? Where are the cowboys rushing, and do I see the United States Cavalry over the next hill to the rescue?"

The street was silent and long and empty, with only his shadow moving like the shadow of a hawk in midcountry. If he closed his eyes and stood very still, frozen, he could imagine himself upon the center of a plain, a wintry, windless American desert with no house in a thousand miles, and only dry river beds, the streets, for company.

50   "What is it now?" he asked the houses, noticing his wrist watch. "Eight-thirty P.M.? Time for a dozen assorted murders? A quiz? A <u>revue</u>? A comedian falling off the stage?"

Was that a murmur of laughter from within a moonwhite house? He hesitated, but went on when nothing more happened. He stumbled over a particularly uneven section of sidewalk. The cement was vanishing under flowers and grass. In ten years of walking by night or day, for thousands of miles, he had never met another person walking, not once in all that time.

60   He came to a cloverleaf intersection which stood silent where two main highways crossed the town. During the day

words for everyday use

re • vue (ri vyü´) n., musical show parodying topical matters. *In the highly amusing political <u>revue</u> now playing at an off-Broadway theater, the politicians look like wolves who prey on sheeplike voters.*

Literary TOOLS

MOOD. Mood, or *atmosphere,* is the emotion expressed in a literary work. Think about what emotions you feel as you read this story. Pay attention to the sensory details the author uses to create this mood.

NOTE THE FACTS

Where does Leonard imagine himself to be?

_____

_____

_____

MARK THE TEXT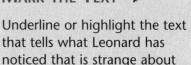

Underline or highlight the text that tells what Leonard has noticed that is strange about his walks.

it was a thunderous surge of cars, the gas stations open, a great insect rustling and a ceaseless <u>jockeying</u> for position as the scarab-beetles,[1] a faint incense puttering from their exhausts, skimmed homeward to the far directions. But now these highways, too, were like streams in a dry season, all stone and bed and moon radiance.

He turned back on a side street, circling around toward his home. He was within a block of his destination when the lone car turned a corner quite suddenly and flashed a fierce white cone of light upon him. He stood entranced, not unlike a night moth, stunned by the <u>illumination</u>, and then drawn toward it.

A metallic voice called to him:

"Stand still. Stay where you are! Don't move!"

He halted.

"Put up your hands!"

"But—" he said.

"Your hands up! Or we'll shoot!"

The police, of course, but what a rare, incredible thing; in a city of three million, there was only *one* police car left, wasn't that correct? Ever since a year ago, 2052, the election year, the force had been cut down from three cars to one. Crime was ebbing; there was no need now for the police, save for this one lone car wandering and wandering the empty streets.

"Your name?" said the police car in a metallic whisper. He couldn't see the men in it for the bright light in his eyes.

"Leonard Mead," he said.

"Speak up!"

"Leonard Mead!"

"Business or profession?"

"I guess you'd call me a writer."

"No profession," said the police car, as if talking to itself. The light held him fixed, like a museum specimen, needle thrust through chest.

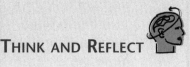

THINK AND REFLECT

Why does the police car say he has no profession? (Interpret)

_____

_____

_____

---

1. **scarab-beetles.** Any of a family of large, brightly colored beetles

"You might say that," said Mr. Mead. He hadn't written in years. Magazines and books didn't sell any more. Everything went on in the tomblike houses at night now, he thought, continuing his fancy. The tombs, ill-lit by television light, where the people sat like the dead, the gray or multicolored lights touching their faces, but never really touching *them*.

"No profession," said the phonograph voice, hissing. "What are you doing out?"

"Walking," said Leonard Mead.

"Walking!"

"Just walking," he said simply, but his face felt cold.

"Walking, just walking, walking?"

"Yes sir."

"Walking where? For what?"

"Walking for air. Walking to see."

"Your address!"

"Eleven South Saint James Street."

"And there is air *in* your house, you have an *air conditioner*, Mr. Mead?"

"Yes."

"And you have a viewing screen in your house to see with?"

"No."

"No?" There was a crackling quiet that in itself was an accusation.

"Are you married, Mr. Mead?"

"No."

"Not married," said the police voice behind the fiery beam. The moon was high and clear among the stars and the houses were gray and silent.

"Nobody wanted me," said Leonard Mead with a smile.

"Don't speak unless you're spoken to!"

Leonard Mead waited in the cold night.

"Just *walking*, Mr. Mead?"

"Yes."

"But you haven't explained for what purpose."

"I explained; for air, and to see, and just to walk."

"Have you done this often?"

"Every night for years."

The police car sat in the center of the street with its radio throat faintly humming.

"Well, Mr. Mead," it said.

"Is that all?" he asked politely.

USE THE STRATEGY

CONNECT TO PRIOR KNOWLEDGE. As you read, compare the actions of Leonard Mead with those of the other people in his world. How is Leonard different?

_____

_____

_____

_____

FIX-UP IDEA

Ask Questions
If you have difficulty applying the reading strategy, ask yourself questions about what you have read to help focus on the selection's main ideas. Then go back and reread until you find the answers. Asking questions will help you identify the elements of Leonard Mead's world. From these details, you can work to understand how that world is different from our present world.

NOTE THE FACTS

Why does Leonard walk?

_____

_____

_____

THINK AND REFLECT

Where does the police car take Leonard? Why is he seen as possessing "regressive tendencies"? (Interpret)

_____

_____

_____

MARK THE TEXT

Underline or highlight the text that tells what is different about Leonard's house.

"Yes," said the voice. "Here." There was a sigh, a pop.

140 The back door of the police car sprang wide. "Get in."

"Wait a minute, I haven't done anything!"

"Get in."

"I protest!"

"Mr. Mead."

He walked like a man suddenly drunk. As he passed the front window of the car he looked in. As he had expected there was no one in the front seat, no one in the car at all.

"Get in."

He put his hand to the door and peered into the back seat,

150 which was a little cell, a little black jail with bars. It smelled of <u>riveted</u> steel. It smelled of harsh antiseptic; it smelled too clean and hard and metallic. There was nothing soft there.

"Now if you had a wife to give you an <u>alibi</u>," said the iron voice. "But—"

"Where are you taking me?"

The car hesitated, or rather gave a faint whirring click, as if information, somewhere, was dropping card by punch-slotted card[2] under electric eyes. "To the Psychiatric Center for Research on Regressive Tendencies."[3]

160 He got in. The door shut with a soft thud. The police car rolled through the night avenues, flashing its dim lights ahead.

They passed one house on one street a moment later, one house in an entire city of houses that were dark, but this one particular house had all of its electric lights brightly lit, every window a loud yellow illumination, square and warm in the cool darkness.

"That's *my* house," said Leonard Mead.

No one answered him.

170 The car moved down the empty river-bed streets and off away, leaving the empty streets with empty sidewalks, and no sound and no motion all the rest of the chill November night. ■

---

2. **punch-slotted card.** Cards with tiny perforations were used for entering data in early computers.
3. **Regressive Tendencies.** Moving back to earlier behavior patterns or habits

words for everyday use

riv • et • ed (riv´it əd) adj., fastened with metal pins called rivets. Bridges are commonly made of <u>riveted</u> steel beams.

al • i • bi (al´ə bī´) n., excuse; proof of activities. When I accused Dwight of robbing the candy machine, he offered as his <u>alibi</u> the evidence that he had been on vacation with his family at the time of the crime.

Reflect ON YOUR READING

When you finish reading, review your notes and finalize your ideas about how Bradbury's world of 2053 differs from our world today. Where would Leonard be more comfortable—in that world or in our present world? Compare and contrast these two worlds in a brief essay, using details from the selection to support your ideas. When you have finished writing, share your essay with a partner, and discuss any differences in your comparisons.

Reading Skills and Test Practice

IDENTIFY SETTING AND MOOD

Discuss with a partner how to answer the following questions about setting and mood.

1. Which of the following words would *not* be used to describe the setting of "The Pedestrian"?
   a. void of activity
   b. quiet
   c. ruined
   d. eerie

What is the correct answer to the question above? How were you able to eliminate the other answers? How did your application of the reading strategy help you answer the question?

_____

_____

_____

2. Which word best describes the mood of "The Pedestrian"?
   a. somber
   b. heartbreaking
   c. peaceful
   d. lighthearted

What is the correct answer to the question above? How were you able to eliminate the other answers? How did your application of the reading strategy help you answer the question?

_____

_____

_____

THINK-ALOUD NOTES

_____

_____

_____

_____

_____

_____

_____

_____

_____

_____

_____

Investigate, Inquire, and Imagine

RECALL: GATHER FACTS
1a. What does Leonard Mead like to do at night? What does he learn to do to be less noticeable?

INTERPRET: FIND MEANING
1b. Why does Leonard want to avoid drawing attention to himself? Why are the streets deserted?

ANALYZE: TAKE THINGS APART
2a. Why is crime ebbing in this large city?

SYNTHESIZE: BRING THINGS TOGETHER
2b. What are the people in this city lacking? What does Leonard have that they do not?

EVALUATE: MAKE JUDGMENTS
3a. What comment might Bradbury be making about society? How valid is this comment? Explain.

EXTEND: CONNECT IDEAS
3b. Now that we have entered the twenty-first century, how accurate is Bradbury with some of his predictions and warnings? In what ways are his predictions true? In what ways have his predictions not yet come to pass?

Literary Tools

MOOD. **Mood,** or *atmosphere,* is the emotion expressed in a literary work. The writer can bring about in the reader an emotional response—such as fear, discomfort, longing, or anticipation—by working carefully with descriptive language and sensory details. Fill in the Sensory Details Chart below with the sensory details the author uses to create the mood in this story. What kind of mood does this descriptive language create? What emotions did you feel as you read this story?

Sight	Sound	Touch/Feeling	Taste	Smell

WordWorkshop

HOMOGRAPHS. **Homographs** are words that are spelled the same, but have different meanings and often, different pronunciations. *Homograph* literally means "written the same." It comes from the Greek roots *homo*, meaning "same," and *graph*, meaning "to write."

EXAMPLES   *lock* (of hair) and *lock* (as on a door)

bass (the fish) and *bass* (having a low pitch)

In this selection, the Word for Everyday Use *jockey* is an example of a homograph. *Jockey* can mean "to maneuver for position" as in the story, or it can mean "one who rides a horse in a race." Try to think of five more examples of homographs and write the words and their different meanings in the chart below.

Word	Meaning #1	Meaning #2
1.		
2.		
3.		
4.		
5.		

Read-Write Connection

What do you find most disturbing about the world in which Mr. Mead lives? Explain your answer using your own paper.

Beyond the Reading

PREDICT THE FUTURE. Bradbury envisions a world in which no one reads and writers are out of work. Do some research on "e-books," or electronic books, and then write an opinion essay predicting the future of books, reading, writing, or libraries in American society. In the future do you think people will read less? Will books as we know them disappear? If so, what will take their place? Will people still go to libraries and bookstores for reading material?

GO ONLINE. Visit the EMC Internet Resource Center at **emcp.com** to find links and additional activities for this selection.

Unit 3 READING Review

Choose and Use Reading Strategies

Before reading the excerpt below, review with a partner how to use each of these reading strategies with fiction.

1. Read with a Purpose
2. Connect to Prior Knowledge
3. Write Things Down
4. Make Predictions
5. Visualize
6. Use Text Organization
7. Tackle Difficult Vocabulary
8. Monitor Your Reading Progress

Now apply at least two of these reading strategies as you read this excerpt from the opening paragraph of the story "A Very Old Man with Enormous Wings" by Gabriel García Márquez. Use the margins and mark up the text to show how you are using the reading strategies to read actively.

On the third day of rain they had killed so many crabs inside the house that Pelayo had to cross his drenched courtyard and throw them into the sea, because the newborn child had a temperature all night and they thought it was due to the stench. The world had been sad since Tuesday. Sea and sky were a single ash-gray thing and the sands of the beach, which on March nights glimmered like powdered light, had become a stew of mud and rotten shellfish. The light was so weak at noon that when Pelayo was coming back to the house after throwing away the crabs, it was hard for him to see what it was that was moving and groaning in the rear of the courtyard. He had to go very close to see that it was an old man, a very old man, lying face down in the mud, who, in spite of his tremendous efforts, couldn't get up, impeded by his enormous wings.

Literary Tools

Select the best literary element on the right to complete each sentence on the left. Write the correct letter in the blank.

_____1. The wind serves as an important ____ in the story "Rules of the Game."

_____2. In "The Open Window," the fact that Nuttel expects to calm himself through social interaction but ends up highly agitated is an example of ____.

_____3. Mrs. Wilson appears to believe several ____ about African Americans in "After You, My Dear Alphonse."

_____4. In "The Black Cat," the narrator uses ____ to relate the story of the black cat.

_____5. Mme. Forestier's lack of concern over loaning a diamond necklace to Mme. Loisel in "The Necklace," is ____ for what happens at the end of the story.

_____6. Bradbury uses descriptive language and sensory details to create a suspenseful ____ in "The Pedestrian."

_____7. In the story "Dead Men's Path," the ____ could be considered unreliable because the story is presented from Obi's point of view.

a. flashback, 43

b. foreshadowing, 70

c. irony, 61

d. mood, 119

e. narrator, 110

f. stereotype, 101

g. symbol, 91

WordWorkshop

UNIT 3 WORDS FOR EVERYDAY USE

adversary, 89
alibi, 122
allusion, 44
ally, 93
ancestral, 84
anomalous, 55
apparition, 48
atrocity, 46
aversion, 50
benevolently, 90
bravado, 54
caption, 93
chagrin, 70
cherish, 44
concession, 94
conflagration, 47
conjointly, 55
consign, 55
constitute, 49
convey, 63
debauch, 46
deftly, 85
deliberate, 52
delusion, 62
denigration, 110
diminishing, 90

docility, 44
duly, 60
elaborate, 88
elated, 70
engulf, 61
equivocal, 46
eradicate, 113
etiquette, 90
expedient, 52
expound, 43
falteringly, 61
finesse, 69
flourish, 93
foreman, 103
foxhole, 104
fragrant, 84
ghastly, 62
goaded, 52
graciously, 91
homage, 73
humility, 91
illumination, 120
imminent, 63
immoderate, 73
impart, 83

imperceptible, 51
impulse, 103
incessantly, 69
inclination, 46
incumbent, 51
inestimable, 70
inscrutability, 54
intemperate, 45
intricate, 87
jeopardize, 47
jockey, 120
kindling, 102
latter, 44
lime, 48
malodorous, 93
migrate, 60
nocturnal, 74
odious, 50, 77
perverseness, 46
pivotal, 110
premises, 53
procure, 53
prodigy, 92
propitiate, 113
pungent, 84

relent, 88
remorse, 48
render, 54
replica, 87
repose, 49
retort, 90
reverberation, 54
revue, 119
riveted, 122
self-possessed, 60
solemnity, 86
solicit, 43
stewed, 102
stupefied, 71
successive, 96
succinctly, 43
succumb, 51
superannuated, 110
suppleness, 69
tout, 92
triumphant, 92
uncongenial, 44
ungovernable, 51
usurer, 76
vanity, 90

WORD FIND. From the definitions given below, identify these ten words from the list of Unit 3 Words for Everyday Use. Then find these words in the following Word Find Puzzle. The words may be found by reading forward, backward, diagonally, or vertically. If you need to look up a definition, refer to the page number following each word.

_____ 1. inflated pride in oneself; conceit
_____ 2. praise or publicize loudly
_____ 3. swallow up
_____ 4. deep sense of guilt
_____ 5. sharp or pointed
_____ 6. active at night
_____ 7. risk; endanger
_____ 8. a sudden spontaneous action
_____ 9. proper social conduct or procedure
_____ 10. victorious

P	E	A	M	S	H	I	D	W	O	E	C	E	I	N
B	C	E	N	O	F	J	R	F	I	Y	O	T	S	I
F	O	O	R	L	M	E	I	L	T	A	I	I	T	H
S	M	E	U	X	U	O	R	I	A	O	L	Q	H	E
G	M	G	B	Y	I	P	N	O	K	N	E	U	T	W
Z	N	U	S	T	Y	A	R	T	O	P	J	E	B	T
E	O	V	E	X	V	R	L	L	E	N	C	T	R	N
N	C	V	N	I	C	D	U	H	I	D	R	T	N	E
O	T	N	C	E	R	I	M	P	U	L	S	E	C	G
K	O	G	E	Z	W	Z	O	E	T	T	S	E	H	N
U	U	I	S	E	P	E	S	R	O	M	E	R	V	U
L	R	E	L	A	R	A	P	X	U	F	R	I	M	P
T	N	A	H	P	M	U	I	R	T	N	D	R	Q	E
W	A	O	F	Z	F	E	U	G	Z	B	R	A	A	D
Q	L	F	M	O	F	S	N	E	I	C	E	T	H	H

On Your Own

FLUENTLY SPEAKING. Perform a choral reading with a small group. Find a part of one of the stories in this unit that would be fun for a group to read. Practice the piece aloud. Everyone in the group should use the same phrasing and speed. Have group members add notes to the text that help them pronounce the words and pause at appropriate times.

PUT IT IN WRITING. Several of the stories in this unit contain elements of irony, a difference between appearance and reality. Write your own short story that uses some form of irony. Review the different types of irony in Literary Tools on page 66.

Unit FOUR

READING Poetry

Defining the word *poetry* is difficult because poems take so many different forms. They do not have to be written down; some are chanted or sung. Some poems rhyme and have a consistent rhythm, but others do not.

Poetry differs from prose in that it packs more meaning into fewer words and often uses meter, rhyme, and rhythm more obviously. One thing that all poems have in common is that they use imaginative language carefully chosen and arranged to communicate experiences, thoughts, or emotions.

There are many different kinds of poetry. Some common kinds are listed below. The most common techniques of poetry involve imagery, shape, rhythm, sound, and meaning. Each of these techniques is also discussed below.

Forms of Poetry

NARRATIVE POETRY. A **narrative poem** is a poem that tells a story. "The Legend" in this unit is an example of a narrative poem.

DRAMATIC POETRY. A **dramatic poem** is a poem that relies heavily on dramatic elements such as monologue (speech by a single character) or dialogue (conversation involving two or more characters). Often dramatic poems tell stories as narrative poems do.

LYRIC POETRY. A **lyric poem** is a highly musical verse that expresses the emotions of a speaker. Many of the poems in this unit are lyric poems, including Marge Piercy's "Simple Song" and Mark Doty's "New Dog." **Sonnets, odes, free verse, elegies, haiku,** and **imagist poems** are all forms of lyric poetry.

NOTE THE FACTS

What is unique about the way words are used in poetry?

_____

_____

_____

NOTE THE FACTS

What are the three main forms of poetry introduced in this book?

_____

_____

_____

If a poem contains figurative
language, you might have to
read it several times to
understand its meaning.
Don't be discouraged if you
don't get it the first time
through.

Techniques of Poetry: Imagery

An **image** is language that creates a concrete representation of an object or experience. An image is also the vivid mental picture created in the reader's mind by that language. For example, in Rainer Maria Rilke's poem "The Gazelle," he describes the gazelle as "tensed, as if each leg were a gun / loaded with leaps, but not fired while your neck / holds your head still, listening. . . ." The pictures created in your mind of the tense animal are images. When considered in a group, images are called **imagery.** Poets use colorful, vivid language and figures of speech to create imagery. A **figure of speech** is language meant to be understood imaginatively instead of literally. The following are common figures of speech:

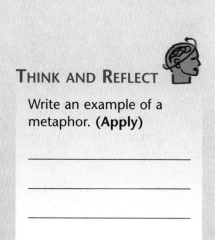

THINK AND REFLECT

Write an example of a metaphor. **(Apply)**

_____

_____

_____

Figures of Speech	Definitions	Examples
metaphor	figure of speech in which one thing is written about as if it were another	"the fishermen consciously become silhouettes in the postcard sunset"
simile	comparison using *like* or *as*	"as if each leg were a loaded gun"
personification	figure of speech in which an idea, animal, or thing is described as if it were a person	a tree that can move and speak

Techniques of Poetry: Shape

The shape of a poem is how it looks on the page. Poems are often divided into stanzas, or groups of lines. The following are some common types of stanzas:

Stanza Name	Number of Lines
couplet	two
triplet or tercet	three
quatrain	four
quintain	five
sestet	six
heptastich	seven
octave	eight

A **concrete poem**, or **shape poem**, is one with a shape that suggests its subject.

Techniques of Poetry: Rhythm

The **rhythm** is the pattern of beats or stresses in a line. A regular rhythmic pattern is called a **meter**. Units of rhythm are called **feet**. A **foot** consists of some combination of weakly stressed (˘) and strongly stressed (/) syllables, as follows:

Type of Foot	Pattern	Example
iamb, or **iambic foot**	˘ /	˘ / afraid
trochee, or **trochaic foot**	/ ˘	/ ˘ freedom
anapest, or **anapestic foot**	˘ ˘ /	˘ ˘ / in a flash
dactyl, or **dactylic foot**	/ ˘ ˘	/ ˘ ˘ feverish
spondee, or **spondaic foot**	/ /	/ / baseball

The following terms are used to describe the number of feet in a line of poetry.

Term	# of Feet	Example
monometer	one foot	˘ / Today ˘ / We play
dimeter	two feet	/ ˘ / ˘ Following | closely
trimeter	three feet	˘ / ˘ / ˘ / God shed | His light | on thee
tetrameter	four feet	/ ˘ / ˘ / ˘ / ˘ In the | greenest | of our | valleys
pentameter	five feet	˘ / ˘ / ˘ / A vast | re pub | lic famed| ˘ / ˘ / through ev | ry clime
hexameter or Alexandrine	six feet	˘ / ˘ / ˘ / In o | ther's eyes | we see | ˘ / ˘ / ˘ / ourselves | the truth | to tell

Reading STRATEGY
REVIEW

VISUALIZE. Draw a picture of what a shape poem about a tree might look like.

Reading TIP

Look for examples of poetry in your daily life. For example, song lyrics are a form of poetry in which rhythm is very important.

THINK AND REFLECT

List two additional words that would be an example of sight rhyme. (Apply)

_____

_____

_____

Techniques of Poetry: Sound

RHYME. **Rhyme** is the repetition of sounds at the ends of words. **End rhyme** is rhyme that occurs at the ends of lines. **Internal rhyme** occurs within lines. **Sight rhyme** occurs when two words are spelled similarly but pronounced differently, like _put_ and _rut_. **Rhyme scheme** is a pattern of end rhymes.

ALLITERATION. **Alliteration** is the repetition of initial consonant sounds. The following lines from Langston Hughes's "Dream Variations" contains three example of alliteration: "To whirl and to dance / Till the white day is done."

ASSONANCE. **Assonance** is the repetition of vowel sounds in stressed syllables that end with different consonant sounds as in "a girl _hears leaves_ rustle" in "The Gazelle."

CONSONANCE. **Consonance** is a kind of slant rhyme in which the ending consonant sounds match, but the preceding vowel sound does not, as in _wind_ and _sound_.

ONOMATOPOEIA. **Onomatopoeia** is the use of words or phrases that sound like the things to which they refer, like _caw_, _clink_, and _murmur_.

USING READING STRATEGIES WITH POETRY

Active Reading Strategy Checklists

The following checklists offer strategies for reading poetry.

1 READ WITH A PURPOSE. Before reading a poem, give yourself a purpose, or something to look for, as you read. Sometimes a purpose will be a directive from a teacher: "Pay attention to repeated words and phrases." Other times you can set your own purpose by previewing the title, the opening lines, and other information that are presented with the poem. Say to yourself
   ❑ I want to look for . . .
   ❑ I want to experience . . .
   ❑ I want to enjoy . . .
   ❑ I wonder . . .
   ❑ I want to see if . . .

2 CONNECT TO PRIOR KNOWLEDGE. Being aware of what you already know and thinking about it as you read can help you keep track of what's happening and will increase your knowledge. As you read, say to yourself

❑ I already know this about the poem's subject matter . . .
❑ This part of the poem reminds me of . . .
❑ I think this part of the poem is like . . .
❑ My experience tells me that . . .
❑ If I were the speaker, I would feel . . .
❑ I associate this image with . . .

3 WRITE THINGS DOWN. As you read poetry, write down how the poem helps you "see" what is described. Possible ways to write things down include:

❑ Underline words and phrases that appeal to your five senses.
❑ Write down your questions and comments.
❑ Highlight figures of speech and phrases you enjoy.
❑ Create a graphic organizer to keep track of your responses.
❑ Use a code in the margin that shows how you respond to the poem.

4 MAKE PREDICTIONS. Before you read a poem, use information about the author, the subject matter, and the title to make a guess about what a poem may describe. As you read, confirm or deny your predictions, and make new ones based on how the poem develops. Make predictions like the following:

❑ The title tells me that . . .
❑ I predict that this poem will be about . . .
❑ This poet usually writes about . . .
❑ I think the poet will repeat . . .
❑ These lines in the poem make me guess that . . .

5 VISUALIZE. Visualizing, or allowing the words on the page to create images in your mind, is extremely important while reading poetry. In order to visualize the words, change your reading pace and savor the words. Allow the words to affect all of your senses. Make statements such as

❑ The words help me see . . .
❑ The words help me hear . . .
❑ The words help me feel . . .
❑ The words help me taste . . .
❑ The words help me smell . . .

6 USE TEXT ORGANIZATION. When you read a poem, pay attention to punctuation and line breaks. Learn to chunk the lines in a poem so they make sense. Try reading all the way to the end of the sentence rather than stopping at each line break. Punctuation, rhythm, repetition, and line length offer clues that help you vary your reading rate and word emphasis. Say to yourself

Reading TIP

A simple code can help you remember your reactions to a poem. You can use
!   for "This is like something I have experienced"
?   for "I don't understand this"
✓   for "This seems important"

Reading TIP

Increase your enjoyment of poetry by reading it aloud.

❑ The punctuation in these lines helps me . . .
❑ The writer started a new stanza here because . . .
❑ The writer repeats this line because . . .
❑ The rhythm of this poem makes me think of . . .
❑ These short lines affect my reading speed by . . .

7 **TACKLE DIFFICULT VOCABULARY.** Difficult words in a poem can get in the way of your ability to respond to the poet's words and ideas. Use context clues that the lines provide, consult a dictionary, or ask someone about words you do not understand. When you come across a difficult word in a poem, say to yourself

❑ The lines near this word tell me that this word means . . .
❑ A definition provided with the poem shows that the word means . . .
❑ My work with the word before reading helps me know that the word means . . .
❑ A classmate said that the word means . . .

8 **MONITOR YOUR READING PROGRESS.** All readers encounter difficulty when they read, especially if the reading material is not self-selected. When you have to read something, take note of problems you are having and fix them. The key to reading success is knowing when you are having difficulty. To fix problems, say to yourself

❑ Because I don't understand this part, I will . . .
❑ Because I'm having trouble staying connected to the ideas in the poem, I will . . .
❑ Because the words in the poem are hard, I will . . .
❑ Because the poem is long, I will . . .
❑ Because I can't retell what the poem was about, I will . . .

Become an Active Reader

The instruction with the poems in this unit gives you an in-depth look at how to use one strategy with each poem. Brief margin notes guide your use of additional strategies. Using one active reading strategy will greatly increase your reading success and enjoyment. Use the space in the margins to add your own comments and strategy ideas. Learn how to use several strategies in combination to ensure your complete understanding of what you are reading. When you have difficulty, use a fix-up idea to solve your problem. For further information about the active reading strategies, see Unit 1, pages 4–15.

Reading **TIP**

If a poem has difficult vocabulary, read the poem, tackle the vocabulary you don't understand, and reread the poem.

FIX-UP IDEAS

■ Reread
■ Read in shorter chunks
■ Read aloud
■ Ask questions
■ Change your reading rate
■ Try a different reading strategy

How to Use Reading Strategies with Poetry

Use the following excerpts to discover how you might use reading strategies as you read poetry.

Excerpt 1. Notice how a reader uses active reading strategies while reading an excerpt from "Freeway 280" by Lorna Dee Cervantes.

VISUALIZE

I picture houses that look very small among flowers that have grown out of control.

CONNECT TO PRIOR KNOWLEDGE

"Man-high geraniums!" The little houses must have been abandoned or not well cared for.

Las casitas[1] near the gray cannery,
nestled amid wild abrazos[2] of climbing roses
and man-high red geraniums
are gone now. The freeway conceals it
all beneath a raised scar.

1. **Las casitas.** Little Houses (spanish)
2. **abrazos.** Embraces

MAKE PREDICTIONS

The writer calls the freeway a "raised scar," so I think "Freeway 280" will describe an ugly freeway.

READ WITH A PURPOSE

I want to discover how the writer describes a freeway.

Excerpt 2. Notice how a reader uses active reading strategies while reading this excerpt from "A Tree Telling of Orpheus" by Denise Levertov.

USE TEXT ORGANIZATION

By reading all the way to the period at the end of the sentence, I understand that the "all-night rain of music" is so quiet that it can barely be heard.

MONITOR YOUR READING PROGRESS

As I read, I say the words in my head the way the speaker might say them. I vary my speed and tone of voice.

The singer
    laughed till he wept to see us, he was so glad.
               At sunset
we came to this place I stand in, this knoll
with its ancient grove that was bare grass then.
    In the last light of that day his song became
farewell.
    He stilled our longing.
    He sang our sun-dried roots back into earth,
watered them: all-night rain of music so quiet
             we could almost
    not hear it in the
        moonless dark.
By dawn he was gone.

knoll (nōl) *n.*, mound; small hill. *I stopped to sit on the knoll in the woods and eat my sandwich.*

TACKLE DIFFICULT VOCABULARY

The definition of *knoll* at the bottom of the page helps me picture where the speaker is standing.

WRITE THINGS DOWN

The speaker compares the sound of the singing to a gentle rain. I can keep track of sensory details like this in a sensory detail chart.

Reader's resource

Langston Hughes's poetry and fiction is concerned with the lives of African Americans. Hughes (1902–1967) was a leading figure of the Harlem Renaissance. Roughly between 1920 and 1936, art, literature, and music by African-American artists flourished in Harlem, an area of New York City. Hughes's poetry reflects the natural, musical qualities of Harlem jazz from that time. **"Dream Variations"** deals with a common theme in Hughes's writing—African-American pride.

Reader's journal

When and where have you felt like celebrating life?

_____

_____

_____

_____

_____

_____

_____

"Dream Variations"

by Langston Hughes

Active READING STRATEGY

READ WITH A PURPOSE

Before Reading ➤ FIND A PURPOSE

❏ Read the Reader's Journal.
❏ Preview the definition of *mood* on page 170. Discuss the definition with a small group. What are some words that could be used to describe the mood of a poem or story?
❏ Preview the Emotionally Charged Words Chart below. You will use this chart to record words that have a strong emotional impact. One example has been done for you. Your purpose for reading will be to collect these words and use them to determine the mood of the poem.

Graphic Organizer

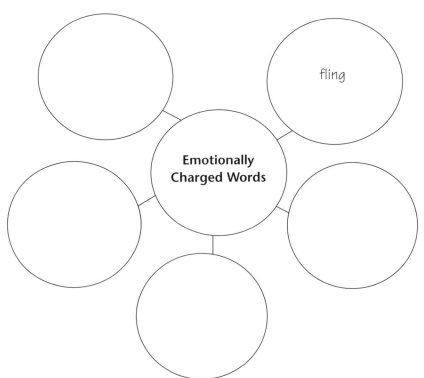

fling

Emotionally Charged Words

Dream VARIATIONS

Langston Hughes

READ WITH A PURPOSE

❑ Follow along as your teacher reads "Dream Variations" aloud. Notice how the poem makes you feel. Listen for powerful words and phrases.

❑ Now read the poem on your own. In your cluster chart, write down the words and phrases that make you feel something. These notes will help you uncover the mood of the poem.

MARK THE TEXT

Underline or highlight what the speaker wants to do during the day and in the evening.

To fling my arms wide
In some place of the sun,
To whirl and to dance
Till the white day is done.
5   Then rest at cool evening
Beneath a tall tree
While night comes on gently,
        Dark like me—
That is my dream!

10   To fling my arms wide
In the face of the sun,
Dance! Whirl! Whirl!
Till the quick day is done.
Rest at pale evening . . .
A tall, slim tree . . .
Night coming tenderly
        Black like me. ∎

FIX-UP IDEA

Connect to Prior Knowledge
If you are having trouble identifying emotionally charged words, try putting yourself in the speaker's place. Read each line. Then pause to imagine what it would feel like to be the speaker. Finally, identify the words in that line that helped you get the feeling, and write them in your chart.

Reflect ON YOUR READING

After Reading ▶ **DESCRIBE YOUR READING EXPERIENCE**

When you finish reading, work with a small group to review the words and phrases you wrote in your chart. Decide on the overall mood of the poem. Then write a brief essay explaining your interpretation of the mood. Be sure to explain not only how "Dream Variations" makes you feel but also which words and phrases created the strongest emotional reactions in you. Compare your essay to those of your group members. Discuss similarities and differences in your interpretation of the mood of the poem. Finally, discuss how finding a purpose for reading affected your reading experience.

Reading Skills and Test Practice

IDENTIFY MOOD AND TONE

1. Which of the following best describes the mood of "Dream Variations"?
   a. jubilant yet peaceful
   b. tense and apprehensive
   c. sad and lonely
   d. serious and somber

What is the correct answer to the question above? How were you able to eliminate the other answers? How did your use of the reading strategy help you answer the question?

_____

_____

_____

2. What is the speaker's tone in "Dream Variations"?
   a. angry
   b. ironic
   c. dejected
   d. hopeful

What is the correct answer to the question above? How were you able to eliminate the other answers? How did your use of the reading strategy help you answer the question?

_____

_____

_____

THINK-ALOUD NOTES

_____

_____

_____

_____

_____

_____

_____

_____

_____

_____

Investigate, Inquire, and Imagine

RECALL: GATHER FACTS
1a. What adjectives does the speaker use to describe day in lines 4 and 13? What adjectives does he use to describe evening in lines 5 and 14? What adverbs are used to describe the approach of night in lines 7 and 16?

→ INTERPRET: FIND MEANING
1b. What attitude does the speaker have toward daily life? How does the speaker feel about night? What emotions does the speaker associate with night and with being African American?

ANALYZE: TAKE THINGS APART
2a. Identify words and phrases in the poem that suggest the speaker might feel uncomfortable or out of place in his life as it is now.

→ SYNTHESIZE: BRING THINGS TOGETHER
2b. If dancing is a metaphor for something else, what is the speaker's real dream?

EVALUATE: MAKE JUDGMENTS
3a. Do you think the speaker's dream is realistic? Why, or why not?

→ EXTEND: CONNECT IDEAS
3b. What could the speaker do right now to bring his dream to life?

WordWorkshop

DENOTATION AND CONNOTATION. Words have both denotations and connotations. A **denotation** is the basic meaning of a word. A **connotation** is an emotional association attached to a word or expression. Think about how you feel about day and about night. In the graphic organizer below, make a list of words that express your feelings about each. Choose your words carefully. Then compare your words with those your classmates chose.

Words Describing Night	Words Describing Day

Literary Tools

REPETITION. **Repetition** is a writer's conscious reuse of a sound, word, phrase, sentence, or other element. What is repeated in this poem?

_____

_____

How is the reader affected by this repetition?

_____

_____

Read-Write Connection

How do you feel about the speaker's dream? Do you want the same thing, or do you have some other dream? If so, what would it be?

_____

_____

_____

_____

_____

_____

_____

_____

_____

_____

_____

Beyond the Reading

READ MORE DREAM POEMS. Langston Hughes has written several other poems on dreams, including "Dreams," "A Dream Deferred," and "The Dream Keeper." Find an anthology of Langston Hughes's poetry and read these three poems. Then read at least two other poems by Hughes. Think about why Hughes might have written so much about dreams and what his dreams might have been. Using details from the poems you have read, write an essay that answers these questions.

GO ONLINE. Visit the EMC Internet Resource Center at **emcp.com** to find links and additional activities for this selection.

"The Gazelle"

by Rainer Maria Rilke

Active READING STRATEGY

VISUALIZE

Before Reading ➤ **PREVIEW THE SELECTION**

❑ Read the Reader's Resource.
❑ Preview the Words for Everyday Use and the footnotes.
❑ Look at the picture of the gazelles on the next page. With a partner, brainstorm some words to describe the animals in the picture. Think of at least two comparisons you could make between the animals and other things that are familiar to you.
❑ Look over the Visualization Chart below. As you read, you will use this chart to sketch striking images from the poem.

Graphic Organizer

Lines

___4___

Lines

_____

Lines

_____

Lines

_____

Lines

_____

Lines

_____

CONNECT

Reader's resource

Rainer Maria Rilke (1875–1926) was a German poet considered to be one of the most important of the twentieth century. In his lyric poems, Rilke tries to express emotions and reactions that are almost impossible to put into words. In "**The Gazelle**," he attempts to capture the feeling he gets looking at these sensitive deer-like animals. One way that he tries to express this experience is by making creative comparisons.

Word watch

PREVIEW VOCABULARY

enchanted
feature
isolated

Reader's journal

Select an animal that you find beautiful or intriguing. What qualities and traits do you associate with the animal?

_____
_____
_____
_____
_____

VISUALIZE THE TEXT

❑ As your teacher reads the poem aloud, look at the photograph of the gazelles or close your eyes and allow the images to take shape in your mind. Jot down notes about what you saw.

❑ Take turns with a partner to reread each stanza of the poem. After each stanza, sketch the images in your graphic organizer. Then discuss them with your partner.

MARK THE TEXT

Underline or highlight the "enchanted thing" described in line 1.

NOTE THE FACTS

What causes the girl to turn and look in lines 13 and 14?

_____

_____

FIX-UP IDEA

Read Short Sections
This poem is made up of four short visual "scenes." If you are having trouble, read one scene at a time. Then stop to sketch that scene before moving on. When you finish the poem, you will identify what each scene has to do with a gazelle.

The Gazelle[1]

Gazella Dorcas[2]   **Rainer Maria Rilke**

Enchanted thing: how can two chosen words
ever attain the harmony of pure rhyme
that pulses through you as your body stirs?
Out of your forehead branch and lyre climb,

5   and all your features pass in simile,[3] through
the songs of love whose words, as light as rose-
petals, rest on the face of someone who
has put his book away and shut his eyes:

to see you: tensed, as if each leg were a gun
10   loaded with leaps, but not fired while your neck
holds your head still, listening: as when,

while swimming in some isolated place,
a girl hears leaves rustle, and turns to look:
the forest pool reflected in her face. ∎

---

1. **Gazelle.** Swift, timid, deer-like animal native to Africa
2. *Gazella Dorcas.* Scientific name of small, northern African gazelle with horns shaped like a lyre (a type of harp)
3. **all . . . simile.** All your features can be compared to other things

words for everyday use	**en • chant • ed** (en chant' əd) *adj.,* having magical powers. *The trees danced in the enchanted forest.*
	fea • ture (fē' chər) *n.,* distinct part or quality. *One feature that Carol liked about her house was the gabled roof.*
	i • so • lat • ed (ī' sə lāt' əd) *adj.,* separate; remote. *I love to picnic in isolated places that are far away from the city.*

Reflect ON YOUR READING

SYNTHESIZE IMAGES AND IDEAS

When you finish reading, review your sketches. Were you able to identify at least four images or "scenes" from the poem? Think about how each of these four images relates to the image of a gazelle. Below, write down a few notes for each image. Then discuss your ideas with a partner. Finally, discuss how visualizing helped you understand this difficult poem.

_____

_____

_____

_____

_____

Reading Skills and Test Practice

COMPARE AND CONTRAST IDEAS

1. In "The Gazelle," the gazelle is compared to all of the following except
   a. a loaded gun.
   b. a girl swimming in the forest.
   c. songs of love.
   d. a well-read book.

What is the correct answer to the question above? How were you able to eliminate the other answers? How did your use of the reading strategy help you to answer the question?

_____

_____

2. Which of the following qualities make the gazelle like a loaded gun?
   a. speed
   b. tension
   c. beauty
   d. color

What is the correct answer to the question above? How were you able to eliminate the other answers? How did your use of the reading strategy help you to answer the question?

_____

_____

THINK-ALOUD
NOTES

_____

_____

_____

_____

_____

_____

_____

_____

_____

_____

_____

Investigate, Inquire, and Imagine

RECALL: GATHER FACTS
1a. What pulses through the body of the gazelle in stanza 1?

→ INTERPRET: FIND MEANING
1b. How does the pulse in stanza 1 prepare the reader for the comparison in stanza 2?

ANALYZE: TAKE THINGS APART
2a. Compare and contrast the gazelle and the girl in stanza 4.

→ SYNTHESIZE: BRING THINGS TOGETHER
2b. Why does Rilke compare a girl "swimming in some isolated place" to a gazelle? What aspect of the gazelle is he trying to convey with this image?

EVALUATE: MAKE JUDGMENTS
3a. Which comparison in this poem do you find most effective? Why?

→ EXTEND: CONNECT IDEAS
3b. How does this poem relate to Rilke's goal of expressing feelings that are almost impossible to convey?

Literary Tools

INVERSION. An **inversion** is a poetic technique in which the normal order of words in a phrase is reversed or changed. Inversions can help you see the world in fresh and interesting ways. Consider the last line of the poem, "the forest pool reflected in her face." What would the line say if you switched the words *the forest pool* and *her face?*

_____

Which is the more common phrase?

_____

Why do you think the poet chose to invert these words?

_____

_____

Write two inversions of your own.

_____

_____

_____

_____

WordWorkshop

Synonyms and Antonyms. Synonym or antonym questions give you a word and ask you to select the word that has the same meaning (for a **synonym**) or the opposite meaning (for an **antonym**). You must select the best answer even if none is exactly correct. For this type of question, you should consider all the choices to see which is best. Read the following underlined words from the poem. From the choices listed after each one, circle the one most similar to the meaning of the underlined word as it is used in the poem.

1. <u>enchanted</u>: perfect, magical, quiet, beautiful
2. <u>attain</u>: take, complain, get, achieve
3. <u>pulses</u>: flows, beats, goes, runs
4. <u>feature</u>: thing, type, characteristic, distance
5. <u>isolated</u>: alone, far, together, equal

Read-Write Connection

Have you ever experienced something so beautiful that it was almost impossible to describe to someone? Choose such an experience and try to put it into words.

_____

_____

_____

_____

_____

_____

_____

_____

Beyond the Reading

Illustrate Animal Poems. Find at least five additional poems that have to do with animals. Read the poems. Then find or create an illustration for each. Your illustration should be not just a picture of the animal, but a picture that conveys the qualities of that animal that are reflected in the poem. Compile your poems and illustrations into a booklet to share with the class.

Go Online. Visit the EMC Internet Resource Center at **emcp.com** to find links and additional activities for this selection.

Reader's resource

Most of Emily Dickinson's work focuses on one aspect of life or human nature, such as love, death, or spirituality. Dickinson (1830–1886) is known for having lived a very private, secluded life in which she maintained contact only with her close friends and family. Because of the quiet life Dickinson led, people are often amazed at the power and diversity of her poetry. Only a few of Dickinson's poems were published in her lifetime, but her work has since been translated into other languages and read by millions of people around the world. **"Success is counted sweetest . . ."** presents Dickinson's view of the true nature of success, a view which people can really appreciate.

Reader's journal

When have you experienced success? How have you felt when you have wanted to succeed but have not?

_____

_____

_____

_____

_____

_____

_____

_____

"Success is counted sweetest . . ."
by Emily Dickinson

Active READING STRATEGY

WRITE THINGS DOWN

Before Reading ▶ PREVIEW THE POEM

❏ Read the Reader's Resource and respond to the Reader's Journal questions.
❏ Preview the footnotes.
❏ Preview the poem. Notice that this poem is made up of three sentences. Pay attention to where each sentence begins and ends. In the Main Ideas Chart below, you will write down the main idea of each sentence.

Graphic Organizer

Main Ideas
Sentence 1
Sentence 2
Sentence 3

Emily Dickinson

During Reading

WRITE DOWN MAIN IDEAS

❑ Follow along as your teacher reads the poem aloud. Underline or highlight words and phrases that seem especially important.

❑ Work with two other students to reread the poem one sentence at a time. After each sentence, pause to write down, on your own, what you think the main point of that sentence is. Use your own words.

Success is counted sweetest
By those who ne'er succeed.
To comprehend a nectar[1]
Requires sorest need.

5   Not one of all the purple Host
Who took the Flag today[2]
Can tell the definition
So clear of Victory

As he defeated—dying—
10   On whose forbidden ear
The distant strains of triumph
Burst agonized and clear! ■

MARK THE TEXT

Underline the person who can provide the clearest definition of victory.

FIX-UP IDEA

Tackle Difficult Vocabulary
If Dickinson's language gives you trouble, read the whole sentence once. Then find definitions for the words or phrases you don't know. Finally, reread the sentence, substituting the definitions for the difficult words or phrases.

---

1. **nectar.** Sweet liquid; here the speaker means "reward."
2. **purple Host / Who took the Flag today.** The speaker means "honored soldiers who won the battle."

Reflect ON YOUR READING

Compare the main ideas you identified with those your group members wrote down. Then, on your own paper, use your notes to write a group summary of the poem. You might rewrite the poem in your own words or write a paragraph in which you explain the poem's theme. Finally, discuss how your use of the reading strategy affected your reading experience.

Reading Skills and Test Practice

IDENTIFY THE THEME

Discuss with a partner how to answer the following questions about theme.

1. Which statement best describes the theme of "Success is counted sweetest . . ."?
   a. Only those who constantly fail can truly appreciate the value of succeeding.
   b. Those who are used to succeeding are likely to handle failure poorly.
   c. Success in war can never be measured because both sides suffer the loss of lives.
   d. It is unkind to celebrate success while those who have failed are present.

What is the correct answer to the question above? How were you able to eliminate the other answers? How did your application of the reading strategy help you answer the question?

_____

_____

2. What example does the poet use to illustrate her theme?
   a. soldiers waving a flag in victory after a difficult battle
   b. an athlete overcoming many obstacles to achieve success
   c. a defeated and dying soldier who hears the victors celebrating
   d. a hero who takes success for granted because he has never failed

What is the correct answer to the question above? How were you able to eliminate the other answers? How did your application of the reading strategy help you answer the question?

_____

_____

THINK-ALOUD NOTES

_____

_____

_____

_____

_____

_____

_____

_____

_____

_____

_____

Investigate, Inquire, and Imagine

RECALL: GATHER FACTS
1a. On whose ear are the sounds of triumph particularly painful and clear?

INTERPRET: FIND MEANING
1b. Why might the sounds of victory be clearer to certain people?

ANALYZE: TAKE THINGS APART
2a. How do the concepts of distance and need apply to the idea of success in this poem?

SYNTHESIZE: BRING THINGS TOGETHER
2b. How does the speaker feel about those who always win, those who never win, and their different ideas of victory?

PERSPECTIVE: LOOK AT OTHER VIEWS
3a. Much of Emily Dickinson's poetry is personal and subjective. Given what you know about her life, why do you think she was drawn to the subject of success?

EMPATHY: SEE FROM INSIDE
3b. If you were Emily Dickinson, what successes would you identify from your life?

Literary Tools

METER. The **meter** of a poem is its rhythmical pattern. Review the information about meter in the introduction to this unit. This poem is written primarily in *iambs*, which consist of an unstressed syllable followed by a stressed syllable, as in the words *afraid* and *release*. However, Dickinson varies the meter in this poem. Reread the poem, and mark the stress pattern. For example, the first line would look like this:

⌣ / ⌣ / ⌣ / ⌣
Success is counted sweetest

Where in the poem does the meter vary?

_____

_____

What word is emphasized because of this change? Why do you think Dickinson chose to emphasize this word?

_____

_____

WordWorkshop

ETYMOLOGIES. An **etymology** is the history of a word. In a dictionary entry, the etymology can be found in brackets, typically right after the part of speech. Use a dictionary to look up the etymologies of *triumph* and *victory*. Write the Latin word from which each English word comes, and then write the meaning of the Latin word.

1. triumph: _____

2. victory: _____

Now brainstorm a list of English words related to *victory* and *triumph*.

_____

_____

_____

_____

Read-Write Connection

Do you agree with the speaker of this poem about who appreciates success the most? Personally, do you appreciate success more when you have succeeded or when you have failed? Explain.

_____

_____

_____

_____

_____

_____

Beyond the Reading

EXPLORE IDEAS OF SUCCESS. Read another book, article, or poem on the topic of success. You might explore business books, biographies, or interviews with successful people who interest you. Then write an essay in which you explain the ideas of success expressed in the text you have read.

GO ONLINE. Visit the EMC Internet Resource Center at **emcp.com** to find links and additional activities for this selection.

"the waking"

by Theodore Roethke

Reader's resource

Theodore Roethke (1908–1963) wrote lyric poetry that expressed his deep respect for nature and the world in which he lived. **"The Waking"** is one of his most well-known poems. It comments on the speaker's process of learning as he or she goes through life. It also brings into question the idea of opposites such as waking and sleeping. Can one exist without the other?

Active READING STRATEGY

CONNECT TO PRIOR KNOWLEDGE

Before Reading ➤ **ACTIVATE PRIOR KNOWLEDGE**

❑ Respond to the Reader's Journal questions. Consider not only how you learn facts, details, and processes but also how you learn general lessons about life.

❑ Think about how pairs of opposites work. For example, we think of *asleep* and *awake* as opposites, but how do you know what *awake* means without thinking "not asleep"? With these ideas in mind, preview the definition of *paradox* in Literary Tools on page 154. Examples of paradox include: "We were rich and poor at the same time" and "Only those who have failed truly understand success." With your class, think of some other examples of paradox.

❑ Preview the graphic organizer below. As you read, you will use this chart to keep track of paradoxes in the poem and to explain what makes them paradoxical. One example has been done for you.

Reader's journal

How do you learn best, from example or from your own experience? Describe something you have "known" by feeling it rather than by thinking about it logically.

_____

_____

_____

_____

_____

_____

_____

Graphic Organizer

Paradoxical Statements	Explanations
I wake to sleep	A person wakes in order to be active, not in order to go back to sleep.

MAKE CONNECTIONS

❑ Follow along as your teacher reads the poem aloud. When your teacher finishes, jot down any connections you made between the poem and your own ideas.

❑ Reread the poem with a partner. Pause after each sentence to discuss what it might mean. Remember that many interpretations are possible. Notice the pairs of opposites mentioned by the speaker, and record in your chart any paradoxes you find.

FIX-UP IDEA

Ask a Question

Don't give up if you have trouble understanding this poem. Few people can say they fully understand it because it is written as a kind of riddle. Try making up a question about what you don't understand. Discuss the question with your partner. If you can't answer the question together, save it for the class discussion.

NOTE THE FACTS

How does the speaker learn?

_____

_____

the WAKING

Theodore Roethke

I wake to sleep, and take my waking slow.
I feel my fate in what I cannot fear.
I learn by going where I have to go.

We think by feeling. What is there to know?
5   I hear my being dance from ear to ear.
I wake to sleep, and take my waking slow.

Of those so close beside me, which are you?
God bless the Ground! I shall walk softly there,
And learn by going where I have to go.

10 Light takes the Tree; but who can tell us how?
The lowly worm climbs up a winding stair;
I wake to sleep, and take my waking slow.

Great Nature has another thing to do
To you and me; so take the lively air,
15 And, lovely, learn by going where to go.

This shaking keeps me steady. I should know.
What falls away is always. And is near.
I wake to sleep, and take my waking slow.
I learn by going where I have to go.   ■

Reflect ON YOUR READING

Take a moment to summarize in writing what you understand about this poem and how it relates to your prior knowledge and experiences. Discuss your summary with your partner. Then join another pair of students, and share your summaries with them. Together, see how much knowledge you can build. Also ask this group any questions you wrote about things you don't understand in the poem. Bring up any unanswered questions in a whole-class discussion of the poem.

_____

_____

_____

_____

Reading Skills and Test Practice

MAKE INFERENCES

Discuss with a partner how to answer the following questions that require you to make inferences.

1. The speaker of this poem prefers to learn by
   a. studying a textbook.
   b. listening to a lecture.
   c. observing nature.
   d. experiencing a variety of things.

What is the correct answer to the question above? How were you able to eliminate the other answers? How did your application of the reading strategy help you answer the question?

_____

_____

2. The speaker *most likely* views life as
   a. a wonderful, mysterious opportunity.
   b. a difficult and painful journey.
   c. a worthless experience determined by fate.
   d. a thrilling and dangerous ride.

What is the correct answer to the question above? How were you able to eliminate the other answers? How did your application of the reading strategy help you answer the question?

_____

_____

THINK-ALOUD
NOTES

_____

_____

_____

_____

_____

_____

_____

_____

_____

_____

Investigate, Inquire, and Imagine

RECALL: GATHER FACTS
1a. How does the speaker wake? What does Great Nature have, and to whom will this thing relate?

→ INTERPRET: FIND MEANING
1b. Most people wake and sleep every day. What "once in a lifetime" pair of opposites are hinted at by the ideas of waking and sleeping? What is the "thing" that Great Nature has in store?

ANALYZE: TAKE THINGS APART
2a. Identify details in the poem that show that the speaker loves life.

→ SYNTHESIZE: BRING THINGS TOGETHER
2b. What might it mean to "take the lively air," as the speaker recommends in line 14?

PERSPECTIVE: LOOK AT OTHER VIEWS →
3a. What does it mean to "think by feeling"? How is this related to the speaker's way of learning?

EMPATHY: SEE FROM INSIDE
3b. If you were the speaker, how would you explain your philosophy of life?

Literary Tools

PARADOX. A **paradox** is a seemingly contradictory statement, idea, or event. Often, paradoxes reveal a deeper truth. Review the graphic organizer you completed during reading. What do the speaker's paradoxes add to the meaning of this poem?

_____

_____

_____

_____

What deeper truths do they hint at?

_____

_____

_____

_____

WordWorkshop

SOUND AND SPELLING PATTERNS. Form a small group to do this activity. For each of the following words from "The Waking," brainstorm a list of at least ten words that rhyme. Try to think of words that have the same spelling pattern as the word given and also words that have a different spelling pattern. See how many different spelling patterns you can find for each rhyming word group.

EXAMPLE   **know**: go, doe, slow, crow, bow, beau, Thoreau, oh, though, Bordeaux

wake	sleep	ear	fate

Read-Write Connection

What would it mean for you to "take the lively air"? Describe things you might do if you were going to take Roethke's advice.

_____

_____

_____

_____

_____

Beyond the Reading

READ ABOUT SOMEONE "AWAKE." Find and read a book about someone who is living life fully. You can choose a fiction or a nonfiction selection. When you have finished the book, write an essay explaining how this character is "taking the lively air," as Roethke might put it.

GO ONLINE. Visit the EMC Internet Resource Center at **emcp.com** to find links and additional activities for this selection.

Reader's resource

"Simple Song," like most of Marge Piercy's poetry, is a free verse poem, meaning that it does not follow regular rhyme, meter, or stanza divisions. Piercy (1936–) explains that poetry is a part of her everyday life: "I make up poems for our cats. . . . I say poems to the peas and the day lilies. I make up poems for houses on the street in Cambridgeport." *Circles on the Water*, the collection in which "Simple Song" appears, reflects "little grace notes of thanksgiving and praise and cursing during the day." It is a collection of love poems, feminist poems, poems about animals and vegetables, and poems about living on Cape Cod.

Reader's journal

How do you respond to someone who seems similar to you? to someone who is different from you?

_____

_____

_____

_____

_____

_____

_____

_____

"Simple Song"

by Marge Piercy

Active READING STRATEGY

USE TEXT ORGANIZATION

Before Reading ▶ **PREVIEW THE SELECTION**

❏ Read the Reader's Resource.
❏ Look over the poem on page 157. How are the lines broken up? How many sentences make up this poem? Why do you think the poet decided to break up the lines this way?
❏ Preview the Main Ideas Chart below. You will use this graphic organizer to record the main idea of each stanza.

Graphic Organizer

Main Ideas
Stanza 1
Stanza 2
Stanza 3

Simple Song

Marge Piercy

During Reading ➤

USE TEXT ORGANIZATION

❑ As your teacher reads the poem aloud, try to identify how the main idea of stanza 1 is different from the main idea of stanza 2.

❑ When your teacher finishes reading aloud, study the poem on your own and record the main idea of each stanza in your graphic organizer.

NOTE THE FACTS

What do we say when we are moving toward someone (lines 1–5)? when we are leaving someone (lines 6–10)?

_____

_____

_____

When we are going toward someone we say
You are just like me
your thoughts are my brothers
word matches word
5   how easy to be together.

When we are leaving someone we say:
how strange you are
we cannot communicate
we can never agree
10 how hard, hard and weary to be together.

We are not different nor alike
But each strange in his leather body
sealed in skin and reaching out clumsy hands
and loving is an act
15 that cannot outlive
the open hand
the open eye
the door in the chest standing open. ■

FIX-UP IDEA

Visualize
If you have trouble with stanza 3, try visualizing the images in each line. Then consider what idea the images suggest. Write this idea in your Main Idea Chart for stanza 3.

Reflect ON YOUR READING

After Reading ➤ ANALYZE THE POEM'S STRUCTURE

How would you answer the question "What is this poem about?" Discuss your answer with a small group. Then, on your own paper, write a paragraph that answers the following questions about the poem's structure. How does the structure of the poem enhance its main ideas? How would the poem be different if it were just one long stanza? When you have finished writing, share your paragraph with your group.

**THINK-ALOUD
NOTES**

_____

_____

_____

_____

_____

_____

_____

_____

_____

_____

Reading Skills and Test Practice

COMPARE AND CONTRAST MAIN IDEAS
Discuss with a partner how to answer the following questions about comparing and contrasting main ideas.

1. What two ideas are contrasted in stanzas 1 and 2 of "Simple Song"?
   a. speaking to someone and touching someone
   b. loving someone and disliking someone
   c. believing someone is the same and believing someone is different
   d. being alone and being surrounded by people

What is the correct answer to the question above? How were you able to eliminate the other answers? How did your application of the reading strategy help you answer the question?

_____

_____

2. What is the main idea of the final stanza in the poem?
   a. People are too different to be able to stay together for long.
   b. People need to remain open to differences in order to have lasting love.
   c. People are too concerned with themselves to be able to truly give to others.
   d. When people are alone, they wish they had someone; when they are with someone, they wish they were alone.

What is the correct answer to the question above? How were you able to eliminate the other answers? How did your application of the reading strategy help you answer the question?

_____

_____

Investigate, Inquire, and Imagine

RECALL: GATHER FACTS
1a. In stanza 3, what word does the speaker use to describe each of us? What image does the speaker paint of a person?

→ **INTERPRET: FIND MEANING**
1b. What do this word and this image suggest about people's ability to relate to one another?

ANALYZE: TAKE THINGS APART
2a. What changes take place from stanza 1 to stanza 2? What phase of a relationship does each represent? What does the speaker mean when he or she says, in stanza 3, "We are not different nor alike"? What does the speaker say we are instead?

→ **SYNTHESIZE: BRING THINGS TOGETHER**
2b. What is the speaker saying about what brings people together and what pushes them apart? How does stanza 3 serve as a response to stanzas 1 and 2?

EVALUATE: MAKE JUDGMENTS
3a. Do you agree with the speaker that "loving is an act / that cannot outlive / the open hand / the open eye / the door in the chest standing open"? Do you agree that people are neither different nor alike? Explain your reasons for agreeing or disagreeing.

→ **EXTEND: CONNECT IDEAS**
3b. What could you conclude about the speaker's experience with love based on lines 14–18? What advice is the speaker giving about relationships?

Literary Tools

SPEAKER AND FIRST-PERSON POINT OF VIEW. The **speaker** is the character who speaks in, or narrates, a poem. The speaker and the writer of a poem are not necessarily the same person. **Point of view** is the vantage point from which a literary work is told. When a poem is written from the *first-person point of view,* the speaker uses words such as *I* and *we.* In poems from a *third-person point of view,* the speaker uses words such as *he, she, it,* and *they.* To whom is the speaker in "Simple Song" referring when he or she uses the word *we?*

_____

How might the poem be different if the speaker had used *I* instead of *we?*

_____

How might it be different if the poet had written in the third-person point of view*?*

_____

WordWorkshop

USING CONTEXT CLUES TO ANSWER SENTENCE COMPLETION QUESTIONS. When you approach sentence completion questions, look for context clues to help you answer the questions. Review the chart of context clues on pages 20–21. As you answer the questions below, look for signal words to help you.

1. While some people find differences frightening, I am _____ them.
   a. intrigued by
   b. protected from
   c. knowledgeable about
   d. intimidated by

2. Alicia is _____ by Jerome, as if he were an electrical current running through her.
   a. depressed
   b. infuriated
   c. energized
   d. amused

3. Images such as open hands, open doors, and open eyes are all ways of expressing _____ .
   a. frustration with other ways of thinking
   b. anger at people who are different
   c. willingness to entertain other views
   d. fascination with differences

Read-Write Connection

Do you have friends with whom it is "easy to be together"? What makes them so easy to get along with? Do you have any friends who are very different from you? How do you get along with them?

_____

_____

Beyond the Reading

READ ABOUT DIVERSITY. Read a book about a person whose background is different from yours. You could read a biography, an autobiography, a memoir, or a novel, in which the featured person is from a different racial or ethnic background, a different socioeconomic class, or a different country. Write an essay in which you discuss aspects of the person's life that are difficult for you to understand and aspects that seem similar to your own life.

GO ONLINE. Visit the EMC Internet Resource Center at **emcp.com** to find links and additional activities for this selection.

"New Dog"

by Mark Doty

Active READING STRATEGY

VISUALIZE

Before Reading ➤ **PREVIEW THE SELECTION**

❑ Read the Reader's Resource and respond to the Reader's Journal questions.

❑ Look at the photograph on the next page. This dog is a cocker spaniel, a breed of dog mentioned in the poem.

❑ Preview the graphic organizer below. You will use this Visualization Chart to sketch images from the poem. Notice that you will be asked to write down the line numbers below each sketch.

Graphic Organizer

Lines _____	Lines _____	Lines _____
Lines _____	Lines _____	Lines _____

CONNECT

Reader's resource

"New Dog" was published in 1995 in Mark Doty's collection of poems *Atlantis*. It tells about his friend Wally's dying wish for a new dog. In this poem, Doty (1953–) focuses closely on each moment. "Before Wally's diagnosis," says Doty, "lots of my work had been about memory and trying to gain some perspective on the past. Suddenly that was much less important and I felt pushed to pay attention to now, what I could celebrate or discern in the now."

Word watch

PREVIEW VOCABULARY

concatenation
tentative

Reader's journal

What assumptions do you have about dying people? How do you imagine they feel? What do you think they care about?

_____

_____

_____

VISUALIZE

- ❑ Read the poem independently. Go slowly, and give yourself time to imagine the people and dogs as you meet them. Imagine the scene the speaker describes. Also imagine the speaker and how he looks and feels as he watches this scene.
- ❑ Reread the poem, this time pausing to sketch the most striking images in your Visualization Chart.

New Dog

Mark Doty

NOTE THE FACTS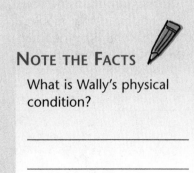

What is Wally's physical condition?

_____

_____

Jimi and Tony
can't keep Dino,
their cocker spaniel;
Tony's too sick,
the daily walks
more pressure
than pleasure,
one more obligation
that can't be met.

10   And though we already
have a dog, Wally
wants to adopt,
wants something small
and golden to sleep
next to him and
lick his face.
He's paralyzed now
from the waist down,

whatever's ruining him
20   moving upward, and

we don't know
how much longer
he'll be able to pet
a dog. How many men
want another attachment,
just as they're
leaving the world?

Wally sits up nights
and says, *I'd like*
30 *some lizards, a talking bird,*
some fish. A little rat.

So after I drive
to Jimi and Tony's
in the Village and they
meet me at the door and say,
We can't go through with it,
we can't give up our dog,
I drive to the shelter
—just to look—and there
40 is Beau: bounding and
practically boundless,
one brass <u>concatenation</u>
of tongue and tail,
unmediated energy,
too big, wild,

perfect. He not only
licks Wally's face
but bathes every
irreplaceable inch
50 of his head, and though
Wally can no longer
feed himself he can lift
his hand, and bring it
to rest on the rough gilt

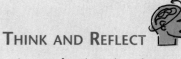

THINK AND REFLECT

A **paradox** is a situation or statement that seems to be contradictory. What paradox is expressed in lines 24–27? **(Interpret)**

_____

_____

MARK THE TEXT

Underline the words the speaker uses to describe Beau.

NOTE THE FACTS

How is Wally able to interact with the dog?

_____

_____

words for everyday use

con • cat • e • na • tion (kän ka tə nā' shən) *n.*, state of being linked together in a series or chain. *The <u>concatenation</u> of clues led the inspector to the murderer.*

flanks when they are,
for a moment, still.
I have never seen a touch
so deliberate.
It isn't about grasping;
60   the hand itself seems
almost blurred now,
softened, though
<u>tentative</u> only

because so much will
must be summoned,
such attention brought
to the work—which is all
he is now, this gesture
toward the restless splendor,
70   the unruly, the golden,
the animal, the new. ■

words for everyday use

ten • ta • tive (ten′ tə tiv) *adj.,* not fully worked out or developed. *Clarissa had <u>tentative</u> plans to play tennis in the afternoon.*

Reflect ON YOUR READING

After Reading ▶ SHARE YOUR VISUALIZATIONS

When you finish reading the poem, look over your sketches. Decide which image from the poem is your favorite. If you like, create a more detailed sketch of that image. When you are satisfied with your sketch, share it with a partner. Discuss why you like this image. Also talk about how your use of visualization affected your understanding of the poem.

Reading Skills and Test Practice

IDENTIFY THEME AND PARADOX

READ, THINK, AND EXPLAIN. Discuss with a partner how to identify theme and paradox.

1. A **theme** is a central idea in a literary work. Explain your interpretation of the theme of "New Dog." Use details from the poem to support your ideas.

_____

_____

_____

_____

_____

2. Identify the paradox in "New Dog." Cite the lines in the poem that present the paradox, and explain why the idea seems contradictory.

_____

_____

_____

_____

REFLECT ON YOUR RESPONSES. Compare your responses to those of your partner. How were you able to identify theme and paradox?

_____

_____

THINK-ALOUD NOTES

_____

_____

_____

_____

_____

_____

_____

_____

_____

_____

Investigate, Inquire, and Imagine

RECALL: GATHER FACTS
1a. What does Wally want, and why?

→ INTERPRET: FIND MEANING
1b. Why can the speaker say that Beau is "perfect" for the dying Wally?

ANALYZE: TAKE THINGS APART
2a. About his poetic inspiration, Mark Doty says, "I wait to be haunted, as it were, by an image. What happens is something I see registers on a deeper level than most experience does. A seal in the harbor, or the wreck of a fishing boat. I'll feel this tug in my memory. Then I'll begin describing it to try to capture it. In the process of describing it I begin to understand what it is about the image that's compelling. It's not enough to describe it; the image is a vehicle for something I'm trying to understand." Identify the compelling image of Wally that informs this poem.

→ SYNTHESIZE: BRING THINGS TOGETHER
2b. What is Mark Doty trying to understand by writing this poem?

EVALUATE: MAKE JUDGMENTS
3a. Evaluate the role the speaker plays in Wally's life.

→ EXTEND: CONNECT IDEAS
3b. Compare and contrast the attitude toward death in Mark Doty's "New Dog" and Garrett Hongo's "The Legend" (pages 169–170).

Literary Tools

LYRIC POEM. A **lyric poem** is a highly musical verse that expresses the emotions of a speaker. What emotions of the speaker are implied in this lyric poem?

_____

List at least four phrases that hint at the emotions of the speaker.

_____

_____

_____

_____

WordWorkshop

PREFIXES, SUFFIXES, AND WORD ROOTS. Understanding the meanings of common prefixes, suffixes, and word roots can help you unlock the meaning of unfamiliar words. A **prefix** is a letter or group of letters added to the beginning of a word to change its meaning. A **suffix** is a letter or group of letters added to the end of a word to change its meaning. A **word root** is a main word part that does not have a meaning in English unless a suffix or prefix is added to it. Skim the prefix, suffix, and word root charts on pages 452–456. Then, on your own paper, explain how a prefix, suffix, or word root helps you understand the meaning of the following words from "New Dog."

EXAMPLE attachment The suffix *–ment*, which can mean product or thing, tells me that an attachment is a product or thing to which someone is attached.

1. boundless
2. concatenation
3. unmediated
4. irreplaceable
5. unruly

Read-Write Connection

What process has the speaker been witnessing?

_____

_____

_____

_____

Beyond the Reading

EXPLORING THE CONNECTION WITH ANIMALS. Find and read an article or book about the relationship between a person or a group of people and one or more animals. For example, you might research how pets are being used as therapy in nursing homes, or you might read a memoir such as *Pack of Two* by Caroline Knapp about the relationship between a woman and her dog. Novels such as *Where the Red Fern Grows* or *Sounder* would also be good choices. Prepare an oral report for your class explaining the nature of the human-animal relationship in the text you have chosen.

GO ONLINE. Visit the EMC Internet Resource Center at **emcp.com** to find links and additional activities for this selection.

"The Legend"
by Garrett Hongo

Reader's resource

Garrett Hongo (1951–   ), a Japanese-American poet, was inspired to write **"The Legend"** after seeing a TV news story about an Asian man killed in an act of street violence. Hongo says the poem is about "my own needs for mercy, for a fulfillment to a broad, urban, and contemporary story that baffled me." The "weaver girl" at the end of the poem refers to an Asian myth in which she is the creator of the stars.

Word watch

PREVIEW VOCABULARY

array
mackinaw

Reader's journal

How do you react when you hear about violent acts in the news?

_____

_____

_____

_____

_____

Active READING STRATEGY

VISUALIZE

Before Reading ➤ PREVIEW THE SELECTION

❑ Read the Reader's Resource. Discuss why Garrett Hongo wrote this poem.

❑ Look over the Sensory Details Chart below. As you read, you will use this chart to record images from the poem that appeal to your senses of sight, sound, touch, taste, and smell.

Graphic Organizer

Sight	Sound	Touch	Taste	Smell
snowing softly				

The Legend

Garrett Hongo

In Chicago, it is snowing softly
and a man has just done his wash for the week.
He steps into the twilight of early evening,
carrying a wrinkled shopping bag
full of neatly folded clothes,
and, for a moment, enjoys
the feel of warm laundry and crinkled paper,
flannellike against his gloveless hands.
There's a Rembrandt[1] glow on his face,
10   a triangle of orange in the hollow of his cheek,
as a last flash of sunset
blazes the storefronts and lit windows of the street.

He is Asian, Thai or Vietnamese,
and very skinny, dressed as one of the poor
in rumpled suit pants and a plaid <u>mackinaw</u>,
dingy and too large.
He negotiates the slick of ice
on the sidewalk by his car,
opens the Fairlane's back door,
20   leans to place the laundry in,
and turns, for an instant,
toward the flurry of footsteps
and cries of pedestrians
as a boy—that's all he was—
backs from the corner package store

---

1. **Rembrandt.** (1606–1669) Dutch painter famous for his dramatic use
of color and of light and shadow

**words
for
everyday
use**   mack • i • naw (ma′ kə nô) *n.,* short coat made of heavy fabric. *The heavy fabric
of his* <u>mackinaw</u> *protected the man from the penetrating wind.*

VISUALIZE FROM TEXT DESCRIPTIONS

☐ As your teacher reads the poem aloud, close your eyes and imagine the scene described by the speaker. Think about how you would feel if you witnessed this scene. Note the weather, the time of day, and details about the man being described.

☐ In the graphic organizer, fill in the sensory details you remember. Then reread the poem on your own, filling in additional details.

NOTE THE FACTS

What has the man just finished?

_____

_____

MARK THE TEXT

Underline or highlight the details that tell you what the man looks like.

FIX-UP IDEA

Read Short Sections
Try reading the poem one stanza at a time. At the end of each stanza, pause to visualize what is happening. Then record sensory details in your chart. Reread the poem as many times as necessary to capture all of the sensory details.

shooting a pistol, firing it,
once, at the dumbfounded man
who falls forward,
grabbing at his chest.

30   A few sounds escape from his mouth,
a babbling no one understands
as people surround him
bewildered at his speech.
The noises he makes are nothing to them.
The boy has gone, lost
in the light <u>array</u> of foot traffic
dappling the snow with fresh prints.
Tonight, I read about Descartes'[2]
grand courage to doubt everything
40   except his own miraculous existence
and I feel so distinct
from the wounded man lying on the concrete
I am ashamed.

Let the night sky cover him as he dies.
Let the weaver girl cross the bridge of heaven
and take up his cold hands. ■

In Memory of Jay Kashiwamura.

---

2. **Descartes.** René Descartes (1596–1650), French philosopher who
said, "I think, therefore I am"

What can you tell about
the speaker from the fact
that he is reading
Descartes? **(Infer)**

_____

_____

NOTE THE FACTS

What happens to the
man?

_____

_____

Literary TOOLS

MOOD AND TONE. Mood is the
emotion created in the reader
by a literary work. Notice how
Hongo uses sensory details to
create the mood of this
poem. **Tone** is a writer's or
speaker's attitude toward the
subject or reader. Examples of
words that describe different
tones are *lighthearted, serious,
proud,* and *emphatic.* Notice
how the tone of this poem
changes from stanza 1 to
stanza 4.

Reflect ON YOUR READING

Review the details you recorded in the Sensory Details Chart. Then write a letter to a friend or family member describing what happened to the man on that Chicago street that evening. Use your own words, and include as many sensory details as you can in order to bring the scene to life in your reader's mind. When you finish writing, form a small group and take turns reading your letters aloud.

Reading Skills and Test Practice

IDENTIFY TONE

READ, THINK, AND EXPLAIN. Discuss with a partner how to identify tone. Then write essays answering the following questions. Use your own paper as needed.

1. Describe the tone that the poet takes toward his subject in the first few stanzas of "The Legend." Use details from the poem to support your ideas.

_____

_____

_____

_____

_____

2. How does the tone change near the end of the poem? Use details from the poem to support your ideas.

_____

_____

_____

_____

REFLECT ON YOUR RESPONSES. Compare your responses to those of your partner. How were you able to identify the tone?

_____

_____

THINK-ALOUD
NOTES

_____

_____

_____

_____

_____

_____

_____

_____

_____

_____

Investigate, Inquire, and Imagine

RECALL: GATHER FACTS
1a. What do the suffering man's noises mean to the bystanders? How does the speaker feel about the man?

INTERPRET: FIND MEANING
1b. What does the reaction of the bystanders reveal about them? Why does the speaker feel this way?

ANALYZE: TAKE THINGS APART
2a. Identify the associations you have with the title of this poem.

SYNTHESIZE: BRING THINGS TOGETHER
2b. Why do you think the poem is titled "The Legend"?

EVALUATE: MAKE JUDGMENTS
3a. Evaluate the speaker's attitude toward violence in modern society.

EXTEND: CONNECT IDEAS
3b. Robert Frost liked to distinguish between grievances (complaints) and griefs (sorrows). He even suggested that grievances, which are a form of propaganda, should be expressed only in prose, "leaving poetry to go its way in tears." In what ways does "The Legend" go its way in tears?

Literary Tools

MOOD. **Mood,** or *atmosphere*, is the emotion created in the reader by part or all of a literary work. The writer can evoke in the reader an emotional response such as fear, discomfort, longing, or anticipation. The writer creates the mood by working carefully with sensory details and descriptive language. What is the mood of stanza 1?

_____

_____

What phrases and words create this mood?

_____

_____

_____

_____

WordWorkshop

SENSORY ASSOCIATIONS WITH WORDS. Poetry has been defined as "imaginative language carefully chosen." One reason why the words in poems are so carefully chosen is that words have powerful **sensory associations**. For example, consider the difference between the word *dappled* and the word *spotted*. Which appeals to you more, and why? For each of the words below, identify at least two synonyms, or words that mean nearly the same thing. Then explain which word appeals to you the most, and why.

1. crinkled

_____

2. blaze

_____

3. skinny

_____

4. mackinaw

_____

5. dumbfounded

_____

Read-Write Connection

What emotion does the speaker probably feel when he imagines the victim in the hands of the weaver girl after his death? Explain.

_____

_____

_____

Beyond the Reading

READ ABOUT THE ASIAN-AMERICAN EXPERIENCE. Find and read another poem, story, novel, or memoir about one or more Asian Americans. Then create a project that demonstrates an important idea from the text you read. For example, you might compile a "soundtrack" that includes songs related to the text or plan a website that explores various aspects of the text.

GO ONLINE. Visit the EMC Internet Resource Center at **emcp.com** to find links and additional activities for this selection.

In 1973, Bernice Johnson Reagon (1942–) founded Sweet Honey in the Rock, a Grammy Award-winning African-American female singing group. With deep roots in spirituals, hymns, gospel, jazz, and blues, Sweet Honey in the Rock performs a cappella, or without accompaniment other than percussion instruments. Five African-American women join their powerful voices with handheld drums and rattles to sing about social justice, activism, love, and the history of African Americans and women. **"I Remember; I Believe"** is one of their songs.

Reader's journal

In what way are memories important?

_____

_____

_____

_____

_____

_____

_____

_____

"I REMEMBER; I BELIEVE"

by Bernice Johnson Reagon

Active READING STRATEGY

USE TEXT ORGANIZATION

Before Reading ➤ **PREVIEW THE SELECTION**

❏ With a partner, read the Reader's Resource. Notice that this selection is actually a song.

❏ "I Remember; I Believe" uses repetition to organize ideas. Preview the poem. What words do the first three lines of stanzas 1, 2, and 3 have in common? What word does the last line of each stanza have in common?

❏ Preview the cluster chart below. As you read, you will use the chart to record the things the speaker does not know. Add more circles as needed.

Graphic Organizer

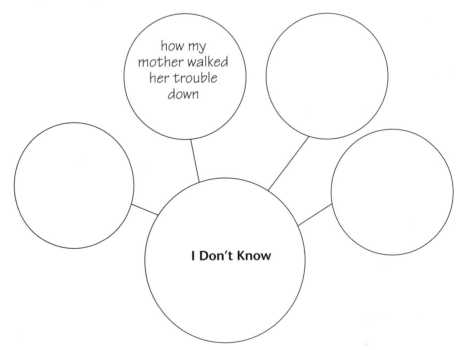

how my mother walked her trouble down

I Don't Know

I REMEMBER, I BELIEVE

Bernice Johnson Reagon

I don't know how my mother walked her trouble down
I don't know how my father stood his ground
I don't know how my people survived slavery
I do remember, that's why I believe

5   I don't know why the rivers overflow their banks
I don't know why the snow falls and covers the ground
I don't know why the hurricane sweeps thru the land
    every now and then
Standing in a rainstorm, I believe

I don't know why the angels woke me up this morning
    soon
10   I don't know why the blood still runs through my veins
I don't know how I rate to run another day
I am here still running, I believe

My God calls to me in the morning dew
The power of the universe knows my name
Gave me a song to sing and sent me on my way
15   I raise my voice for justice, I believe ■

During Reading

USE ORGANIZATIONAL FEATURES

- ❑ Listen as your teacher reads stanza 1 aloud. Then discuss what the speaker does not know. What do all of these things have in common?
- ❑ Read the rest of the song with your partner. Record what the speaker does not know, and discuss what the things in each stanza have to do with each other.

NOTE THE FACTS

Why does the speaker believe (line 4)?

_____

_____

READ ALOUD

Read the last stanza aloud. Use your voice to express the tone, or attitude, of the speaker.

FIX-UP IDEA

Connect to Prior Knowledge
If you have trouble, try putting yourself in the speaker's position. When you are standing in a rainstorm, does it matter whether you understand what causes weather? What does it mean to you to be "still running"? For what do you "raise your voice"?

Reflect ON YOUR READING

After Reading ➤ ANALYZE ORGANIZATIONAL FEATURES

Review the structure of "I Remember; I Believe." Then write a brief essay explaining how the parts fit together. In your essay, discuss how using the text's organizational features has affected your interpretation of the poem's theme or message. When you have finished writing, share your essay with your partner and compare your understandings of "I Remember; I Believe."

Reading Skills and Test Practice

IDENTIFY TONE AND THEME

Discuss with a partner how to answer the following questions about tone and theme.

1. Which word best describes the tone of "I Remember; I Believe"?
   a. confused
   b. angry
   c. determined
   d. playful

What is the correct answer to the question above? How were you able to eliminate the other answers? How did your application of the reading strategy help you answer the question?

_____

_____

2. Which of the following statements would *not* be considered a theme of "I Remember; I Believe"?
   a. Faith, or belief, triumphs over despair.
   b. Remembering injustice in the past brings hope for justice in the future.
   c. Even though you might not be able to understand how people survive tragedy, you can still believe in the value of surviving.
   d. This life offers so many hardships that you can't help losing your faith in the future.

What is the correct answer to the question above? How were you able to eliminate the other answers? How did your application of the reading strategy help you answer the question?

_____

_____

Investigate, Inquire, and Imagine

RECALL: GATHER FACTS
1a. What does the speaker not know about herself in stanza 3? What does she say she is going to do in stanza 4?

INTERPRET: FIND MEANING
1b. What do you think this speaker's attitude is toward life? How can you tell?

ANALYZE: TAKE THINGS APART
2a. What kinds of things does the speaker not know? Into what categories do these things fall?

SYNTHESIZE: BRING THINGS TOGETHER
2b. How is the speaker able to "believe" when she does not know why or how things are the way they are?

EVALUATE: MAKE JUDGMENTS
3a. Do you think the title is appropriate for this song? Why, or why not?

EXTEND: CONNECT IDEAS
3b. For decades after the Holocaust, many Holocaust survivors kept silent for various reasons—some say they wanted to forget; others wanted to hide their shame. Today, there is a whole genre of Holocaust literature that tells what happened during that time. Why do you think oppressed people want to remember their past? Why do you think they fight against silence?

Literary Tools

THEME. A **theme** is a central idea in a literary work. Themes commonly address universal topics that people around the world share—things like love, death, family, and friendship. What possible themes from this song can you name?

_____

_____

What is the speaker saying about memory and remembering the past?

_____

How does the repetition emphasize the themes in the song?

_____

_____

WordWorkshop

FIGURATIVE LANGUAGE. **Figurative language** is writing or speech meant to be understood imaginatively rather than literally. Many writers, especially poets, use figurative language to help readers see things in new ways. If you see a familiar word used in a way that does not make sense literally, the word might be used figuratively. To determine the figurative meaning of a word or phrase, use context clues. (Review "Using Context Clues" on pages 20–21 of this book.) Also think about the associations you have with the word's literal meaning. Answer the following questions on your own paper.

1. What does the speaker probably mean when she says her mother "walked her troubles down"?
2. When the speaker says her father "stood his ground," does she really mean he was standing up? If not, what does she mean?
3. What does the word *run* mean in lines 11 and 12?
4. If the speaker of this poem is Bernice Johnson Reagon, how does she literally "raise her voice for justice"? How could this phrase be interpreted figuratively?
5. Express one theme of this poem using figurative language.

Read-Write Connection

What, if anything, do you believe you are called to do? Do you believe you are put on this earth for a specific reason? If so, what is that reason? If not, why not?

_____

_____

_____

_____

Beyond the Reading

CREATE AN ANTHOLOGY OF HOPE. Use books of poetry and Internet sites such as the one sponsored by the Academy of American Poets to find at least ten poems that deal with social justice and reasons for hope. Group these poems in some way. You might categorize them by author, by theme, by topic, or by type of poetry. Collect the poems into a book. Write an introduction explaining why you chose these poems and why you grouped them the way you did. Keep one copy of the book. Find a place to leave a second copy where it is likely to be found by someone in need of hope.

GO ONLINE. Visit the EMC Internet Resource Center at **emcp.com** to find links and additional activities for this selection.

Unit 4 READING Review

Choose and Use Reading Strategies

Before reading the poem below, review with a partner how to use each of these reading strategies.

1. Read with a Purpose
2. Connect to Prior Knowledge
3. Write Things Down
4. Make Predictions
5. Visualize
6. Use Text Organization
7. Tackle Difficult Vocabulary
8. Monitor Your Reading Progress

Now apply at least two of these reading strategies as you read "Neutral Tones" by Thomas Hardy. Use the margins and mark up the text to show how you are using the reading strategies to read actively.

We stood by a pond that winter day,
And the sun was white, as though chidden[1] of God,
And a few leaves lay on the starving sod;
—They had fallen from an ash and were gray.

Your eyes on me were as eyes that rove
Over tedious riddles of years ago;
And some words played between us to and fro
On which lost the more by our love.

The smile on your mouth was the deadest thing
Alive enough to have strength to die;
And a grin of bitterness swept thereby
Like an ominous bird a-wing. . . .

Since then, keen lessons that love deceives,
And wrings with wrong, have shaped to me
Your face, and the God-curst sun, and a tree,
And a pond edged with grayish leaves.

---

1. **chidden.** Scolded mildly

WordWorkshop

array, 170
concatenation, 163
enchanted, 142
feature, 142
isolated, 142
mackinaw, 169
tentative, 164

1. List two prefixes found in the words above and identify the meaning of each.

   _____

2. List three suffixes found in the words above, and identify how they affect the meaning of the words in which they appear.

   _____

   _____

3. What word part does *tentative* share with *tender* and *tension?* Is this word part a prefix, a suffix, a base word, or a word root? Based on the meanings of the words, what do you think the word part means?

   _____

   _____

4. Use a dictionary to look up the etymology, or word history, of *isolated*. Based on this etymology, how is *isolated* related to *insulated*? How are they still related in meaning?

   _____

   _____

   _____

5. Name two words with the same prefix as *concatenation*. What does this prefix mean?

   _____

Literary Tools

Select the literary element from the column on the right that best completes each sentence on the left. Write the correct letter in the blank.

_____1. "He wore a head under his hat" is an example of _____.

_____2. The rhythmical pattern of a poem is called its _____.

_____3. In "New Dog," Wally's friend who takes care of him is the _____ of the poem.

_____4. A(n) _____ of the poem "Simple Song" is that relationships require openness.

_____5. To say that you are both hungry and overly full is to use a(n) _____.

_____6. Words and images help to create the _____, or atmosphere, of a poem.

_____7. The _____ of a literary work determines whether the narrator uses *I* or a third-person pronoun like *he, she*, or *they*.

_____8. A highly musical verse that expresses the emotions of a speaker is called a(n) _____.

a. theme, 177

b. meter, 149

c. mood, 172

d. speaker, 159

e. inversion, 144

f. point of view, 159

g. lyric poem, 166

h. paradox, 154

On Your Own

Look through poetry collections and search the Internet until you find a poem that you like. Then complete one of the following activities using the poem you have found.

FLUENTLY SPEAKING. Form a small group with others who like the poem you have selected. Prepare a choral reading of the poem. In a choral reading, several people read a text aloud together, using vocal effects to communicate the meaning of the poem. For example, you might divide the group into people with high voices and people with low voices. Each of the two groups would be responsible for reading certain lines of the poem. You could also alternate slow and fast lines or stanzas; alternate loud and soft lines; emphasize key words and phrases by reading them all together or in a louder or softer voice; pause for a certain number of silent beats before continuing; clap, snap your fingers, or make some other noise at the ends of certain lines or stanzas; or even read the poem in a round with overlapping voices. Rehearse the choral reading until the whole group is ready to perform it smoothly for the class.

PICTURE THIS. Imagine that the speaker of the poem you have chosen is taking an art class. The speaker's teacher has asked the speaker to create a drawing, painting, sculpture, or other visual representation of the feelings and ideas in the poem. Create the project the speaker would make. Be prepared to explain how the project is related to the poem.

PUT IT IN WRITING. Write an informal essay to persuade a friend to read the poem you have selected. Discuss any lines, images, or figures of speech that you especially like. Tell what you think the poem means, and why. When you turn in your essay, include a copy of the poem with it.

Unit FIVE

READING Folk Literature

FOLK LITERATURE

Human beings are storytelling creatures. Long before people invented writing, they were telling stories about the lives of their gods and heroes. The best of their stories were passed by word of mouth from generation to generation, from folk to folk. These early stories were told in the form of poems, songs, and what we would now call prose tales.

Stories, poems, and songs passed by word of mouth from person to person are important elements of a group's culture. Eventually, many of these stories, poems, and songs that had been told out loud were written down. **Folk literature** is the written versions of these stories, poems, and songs. Folk literature is full of literary devices that helped storytellers remember the stories. These devices include the use of repetition, common phrases such as "once upon a time" and "they lived happily ever after," and familiar characters and events. Some common types of folk literature are defined below.

Types of Folk Literature

MYTHS. **Myths** are stories that explain objects or events in the natural world as resulting from the action of some supernatural force or entity, most often a god. Every early culture around the globe has produced myths. This unit includes two Greek myths, "The Five Ages of Man" and "Orpheus," told by Robert Graves, and a selection from the *Popol Vuh*, a sacred epic of Quiché Mayan mythology.

FOLK TALES. **Folk tales** are brief stories passed by word of mouth from generation to generation in a particular culture. "Popocatépetl and Ixtacihuatl," found in this unit, is an Aztec folk tale. **Fairy tales** are folk tales that contain supernatural beings, such as fairies, dragons, ogres, and animals with human qualities. **Tall tales** are colorful

MARK THE TEXT

Highlight or underline eight types of folk literature. Start here and continue on the next page.

THINK AND REFLECT

Cinderella, Puss in Boots, and Snow White are well-known fairy tale characters. What others can you think of?

_____

_____

_____

stories that depict the exaggerated wild adventures of North American folk heroes. Many of these heroes and stories revolve around the American frontier and the Wild West.

PARABLES. **Parables** are very brief stories told to teach a moral lesson. Some of the most famous parables are those told by Jesus in the Bible.

FABLES. **Fables** are brief stories, often with animal characters, told to express a moral. Famous fables include those of Æsop and Jean de La Fontaine.

FOLK SONGS. **Folk songs** are traditional or composed songs typically made up of stanzas, a refrain, and a simple melody. They express commonly shared ideas or feelings and may be narrative (tell a story) or lyrical (express an emotion). Traditional folk songs are anonymous songs that have been transmitted orally.

LEGENDS. **Legends** are stories that have been passed down through time. These stories are popularly thought of as historical but without evidence that the events occurred. Examples in this unit are "Sundiata Keita, the Legend and the King" and an excerpt from *King Arthur and His Knights of the Round Table*.

USING READING STRATEGIES WITH FOLK LITERATURE

Active Reading Strategy Checklists

In the stories, poems, and songs that are a part of folk literature, storytellers want to entertain their audience and to pass along cultural ideas and beliefs. The following checklists offer strategies for reading folk literature.

1 READ WITH A PURPOSE. Give yourself a purpose, or something to look for, as you read. Often, you can set a purpose for reading by previewing the title, the opening lines, and instructional information. Other times, a teacher may set your purpose: "Write down tricks that one character plays on another." To read with a purpose, say to yourself

❏ I want to look for . . .
❏ I want to find out what happens to . . .
❏ I want to understand how . . .
❏ The message of this selection is . . .

2 **CONNECT TO PRIOR KNOWLEDGE.** Connect to what you already know about a particular culture and its storytelling traditions. To connect to prior knowledge, say to yourself

- ❏ I know that this type of folk literature has . . .
- ❏ The events in this selection remind me of . . .
- ❏ Something similar I've read is . . .
- ❏ I can connect to this part of the selection because . . .

3 **WRITE THINGS DOWN.** Create a written record of the cultural ideas and beliefs that a storyteller passes along. To keep a written record

- ❏ Underline characters' names.
- ❏ Write down your thoughts about the story.
- ❏ Highlight what the characters do and think.
- ❏ Create a graphic organizer to keep track of events.
- ❏ Use a code to respond to what happens.

4 **MAKE PREDICTIONS.** Use information about the title and subject matter to guess what a folk literature selection will be about. As you read, confirm or deny your predictions, and make new ones based on what you learn. To make predictions, say to yourself

- ❏ The title tells me that the selection will be about . . .
- ❏ I predict that this character will . . .
- ❏ Tales from this cultural tradition usually . . .
- ❏ The conflict between the characters will be resolved by . . .
- ❏ I think the selection will end with . . .

5 **VISUALIZE.** Visualizing, or allowing the words on the page to create images in your mind, helps you understand a storyteller's account. In order to visualize what happens in a folk literature selection, imagine that you are the storyteller. Read the words in your head with the type of expression and feeling that the storyteller might use with an audience. Make statements such as

- ❏ I imagine the characters sound like . . .
- ❏ My sketch of what happens includes . . .
- ❏ I picture this sequence of events . . .
- ❏ I envision the characters as . . .

Reading TIP

Instead of writing down a short response, use a symbol or a short word to indicate your response. Use codes like the ones listed below.

+	I like this.
–	I don't like this.
√	This is important.
Yes	I agree with this.
No	I disagree with this.
?	I don't understand this.
!	This is like something I know.
ᎧᏗ	I need to come back to this later.

Reading TIP

Sketching story events helps you remember and understand them.

6 USE TEXT ORGANIZATION. When you read folk literature, pay attention to transition or signal words such as *first, if/then,* and *on the other hand.* These words identify important ideas and text patterns. Stop occasionally to retell what you have read. Say to yourself

- ❑ What happens first is . . .
- ❑ There is a conflict between . . .
- ❑ The high point of interest is . . .
- ❑ I can summarize this section by . . .
- ❑ The message of this selection is that . . .

7 TACKLE DIFFICULT VOCABULARY. Difficult words can hinder your ability to understand folk literature. Use context, consult a dictionary, or ask someone about words you do not understand. When you come across a difficult word, say to yourself

- ❑ The words around the difficult word tell me it must mean . . .
- ❑ A dictionary definition shows that the word in this context means . . .
- ❑ My work with the word before reading helps me know that the word means . . .
- ❑ A classmate said that the word means . . .

8 MONITOR YOUR READING PROGRESS. Almost all readers encounter some difficulty when they read, especially if they are reading assigned material and not something they have chosen on their own. When you are assigned to read folk literature, note the problems you are having and fix them. The key to reading success is knowing when you are having difficulty. To fix problems, say to yourself

- ❑ Because I don't understand this part, I will . . .
- ❑ Because I'm having trouble staying connected, I will . . .
- ❑ Because the words are hard, I will . . .
- ❑ Because this selection is long, I will . . .
- ❑ Because I can't retell what this section was about, I will . . .

Become an Active Reader

The instruction with the folk literature in this unit gives you an in-depth look at how to use one major strategy with each folk literature selection. Learn how to combine several strategies to ensure your complete understanding of what you are reading. When you have difficulty, use fix-up ideas to fix a problem. For further information about the active reading strategies, including the fix-up ideas, see Unit 1, pages 4–15.

Reading TIP

If the words in a selection are difficult to pronounce, practice saying them aloud before you read.

FIX-UP IDEAS

Whenever you feel your attention is failing, or if you do not understand what you are reading, use a fix-up idea.

- ■ Reread
- ■ Ask a question
- ■ Read in shorter chunks
- ■ Read aloud
- ■ Retell
- ■ Work with a partner
- ■ Unlock difficult words
- ■ Vary your reading rate
- ■ Choose a new reading strategy
- ■ Create a mnemonic device

How to Use Reading Strategies with Folk Literature

Use the following excerpts to discover how you might use reading strategies as you read folk literature.

Excerpt 1. Note how a reader uses active reading strategies while reading this excerpt from "Popocatépetl and Ixtachihuatl" retold by Julie Piggott.

USE TEXT ORGANIZATION

This part sets up a conflict between the characters.

VISUALIZE

The story takes place in ancient Mexico, so I picture Ixta and Popo with dark hair and long gowns.

The man with whom Ixta was in love was also in love with her. Had they been allowed to marry, their state could have been doubly joyous. His name was Popocatépetl, and Ixta and his friends all called him Popo. He was a warrior in the service of the emperor, tall and strong, with a capacity for gentleness, and very brave. He and Ixta loved each other very much, and while they were content and even happy when they were together, true joy was not theirs because the Emperor continued to insist that Ixta should not be married when the time came for her to take on her father's responsibilities.

MAKE A PREDICTION

Something bad may happen to Ixta because her father won't allow her to marry.

CONNECT TO PRIOR KNOWLEDGE

Popo and Ixta remind me of Romeo and Juliet.

Excerpt 2. Note how a reader uses active reading strategies while reading this excerpt from "Sundiata Keita, the Legend and the King" by Patricia and Fredrick McKissack.

MONITOR YOUR READING PROGRESS

Rereading the opening lines helps me understand them.

TACKLE DIFFICULT VOCABULARY

I can use the definition and the footnotes to follow what's happening.

At a time when the Mande[1] people needed a leader one came, and his name was Sogolon-Djata, a member of the Keita clan, who had ruled in Mali for three centuries. Maghan Kon Fatta, the king, was his father, and his mother was Sogolon Kedjou, a hunchback. In the rapidly spoken language of the Mandinka,[2] his name Sogolon-Djata, became Sundiata, "The Hungering Lion."

Sundiata Keita is the King Arthur and George Washington of Mali.[3] He was a warrior-king who united a weak and scattered people, and, under his benevolent leadership, ushered in a glorious period of peace and prosperity.

WRITE THINGS DOWN

I'm going to underline words that show why Sundiata is an important king.

READ WITH A PURPOSE

I want to find out why Sundiata is "the King Arthur and George Washington of Mali."

---

1. **Mande.** Any member of a group of people native to western Africa
2. **Mandinka.** Subgroup of the Mande
3. **Mali.** Inland nation in western Africa

Reader's resource

The Netsilik Inuit, who call themselves the "people of the seal," live in a remote area of Canada above the Arctic Circle, in one of the bleakest regions of the world. Winters there last ten months, the temperature drops to 50 degrees Fahrenheit below zero, and the ocean freezes solid.

Like other Inuit peoples living in the Arctic and subarctic areas of Canada, Greenland, Alaska, and Siberia, the Netsilik are well adapted to this harsh environment and live in close harmony with nature.

As is true of many peoples around the globe, the Inuit have felt modern civilization encroaching on their traditional way of life. The poem **"Magic Words"** expresses the belief of Nalungiaq, a Netsilik priest or shaman, that at one time words had magical powers that they no longer have today.

Reader's journal

How is magic similar to the imagination?

_____

_____

_____

_____

_____

"MAGIC WORDS"

by Nalungiaq, translated by Edward Field

Active READING STRATEGY

VISUALIZE

Before Reading ▶ **PREVIEW THE SELECTION**

❏ Read the Reader's Resource.
❏ Create in your mind a visual image of the Netsilik Inuit world. Describe your visual image to a partner, beginning with the words "I see."
❏ Imagine what elements of the Inuit world might be considered magical, for example, the fog or the sounds of wild animals.
❏ Respond to Inuit ideas in the margins. Add ideas about the Inuit world to the Venn Diagram below.

Graphic Organizer

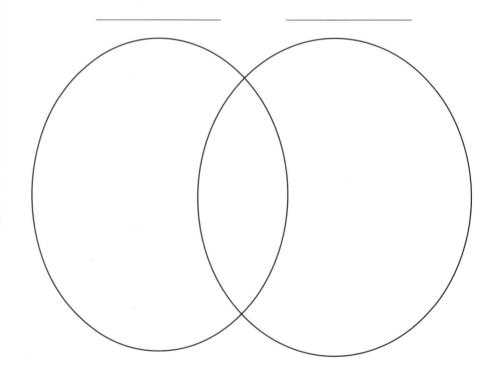

The World in Earliest Times   The World Today

MAGIC WORDS

Nalungiaq

During Reading ➤

CREATE VISUALIZATIONS FROM TEXT

❑ Create visual images of the Inuit world as your teacher reads the poem aloud. Close your eyes as you listen, allowing the details of the poem to enter your images. Imagine that you are making a movie in your mind and that your teacher's voice is describing the action.

❑ Read the poem again. Make your mind pictures more vivid and complete as you read on your own.

Literary TOOLS

FOLK TRADITION. A work from the **folk tradition** is a story that is passed by word of mouth from generation to generation. In traditional cultures around the globe, ideas, values, beliefs, customs, news, and histories are transmitted orally. Often, the works in the folk tradition contain miraculous or magical elements. Highlight or underline magical elements as you read.

WHAT DO YOU WONDER?

_____

_____

_____

_____

In the very earliest times,
when both people and animals lived on earth,
a person could become an animal if he wanted to
and an animal could become a human being.
5   Sometimes we were people
and sometimes animals
and there was no difference.
All spoke the same, the universal tongue.
That was a time when words were like magic.
10   The mind had mysterious powers,
and a word uttered by chance
might have consequences.
It would suddenly come alive
and what people wanted to happen could happen—
15   all you had to do was say it.
Nobody could explain this.
That's just the way it was. ■

Reflect ON YOUR READING

When you finish reading the poem, replay some of the images you created in your mind. Choose your favorite scene, and sketch it on your own paper. Do not worry about your drawing ability. Label objects in your sketch if you think they will be unclear. At the top or bottom, write down the words from the poem that your picture illustrates. Share your sketch with a partner, and discuss similarities or differences in your visualizations.

Reading Skills and Test Practice

IDENTIFY THE AUTHOR'S PURPOSE AND TONE
Discuss with your group how best to answer the following cause-and-effect questions.

1. What might the author's main purpose have been for sharing "Magic Words"?
   a. to preserve aspects of her culture's beliefs and history
   b. to convince readers that the Inuit people are magical
   c. to remind people that animals and humans once lived harmoniously
   d. to entertain readers with an anecdote about magic

What is the correct answer to the question above? How were you able to eliminate the other answers? How did your application of the reading strategy help you?

_____

_____

2. Which of the following best describes the tone of "Magic Words"?
   a. sarcastic
   b. playful
   c. melancholy
   d. matter of fact

What is the correct answer to the question above? How were you able to eliminate the other answers? How did your application of the reading strategy help you?

_____

_____

Investigate, Inquire, and Imagine

RECALL: GATHER FACTS
1a. According to the speaker, what strange consequences used to result from a word "uttered by chance"?

→ INTERPRET: FIND MEANING
1b. What was magical about words in the earlier time?

ANALYZE: TAKE THINGS APART
2a. What evidence does the speaker offer that people in earlier times lived in close harmony with nature and had powers they do not have today?

→ SYNTHESIZE: BRING THINGS TOGETHER
2b. Does the speaker believe that life is harder or easier for people today? Explain.

EVALUATE: MAKE JUDGMENTS
3a. Do you believe that people today view themselves as deeply connected to animals and the natural world? What aspects of modern life make such connections less direct than they once were?

→ EXTEND: CONNECT IDEAS
3b. In what sense do words still perform magically every time a person reads a poem, story, or play?

Literary Tools

FOLK TRADITION. A work from the **folk tradition** is a story that is passed by word of mouth from generation to generation. How, according to the shaman, did the old world differ from the world today? Use your Venn Diagram from page 188 to write a brief paragraph that compares the past to the present.

_____

_____

_____

_____

_____

_____

_____

_____

_____

_____

WordWorkshop

TRANSCRIPTION AND TRANSLATION. Nalungiaq, an Inuit (Eskimo) woman, reported that she learned the song "Magic Words" from an elderly uncle named Unaraluk. Unaraluk was a shaman, a kind of sorcerer or priest. Danish explorer Knud Rasmussen first wrote down the song. Rasmussen, who was part Inuit and spoke the Inuit language, lived for some time with the Netsilik people during his expedition across arctic America, known as the Fifth Thule Expedition (1921–1924). He collected many Netsilik legends and tales in the desire to learn about the unique view such an isolated people had developed of their world and the universe. American poet Edward Field translated many of Rasmussen's stories.

People who **transcribe** text, like Rasmussen, try to write down word for word everything that is said, without leaving anything out or rewording it. **Translators**, like Field, try to preserve the original meaning of the text while using different words to express ideas.

How might "Magic Words" have been affected by having been retold so many times, then transcribed and translated into an entirely different language?

_____

_____

Why is it important to avoid rewording or changing the original meaning of the text?

_____

_____

Read-Write Connection

In what ways do words have power?

_____

_____

_____

_____

Beyond the Reading

THE INUIT CULTURE. Research the culture of the Inuit. Choose one aspect of daily life or history that particularly interests you. Inuit topics you might research include their language, hunting and fishing techniques, their population and location, or their beliefs and traditions. Write a brief report of your findings.

GO ONLINE. Visit the EMC Internet Resource Center at **emcp.com** to find links and additional activities for this selection.

from *The Greek Myths*

"The Five Ages of Man" and "Orpheus"

by Robert Graves

Active READING STRATEGY

WRITE THINGS DOWN

Before Reading ➡ DEVISE A PLAN FOR ORGANIZING INFORMATION

❑ Review the titles of these excerpts from *The Greek Myths*. Consider what information might be presented in each.

❑ With a partner, discuss methods you might use to record important details in each excerpt. For example, the title "The Five Ages of Man" suggests that five items will be discussed and explained. You might use a graphic organizer that identifies the five ages and provides space to record details about each. For "Orpheus," you might create a cluster chart that lists the name "Orpheus" in the center and details about Orpheus in the outer circles.

❑ Create a graphic organizer for each excerpt that fits the details you gather. You may use the suggestions above, use ideas you and your partner produce, or look in Appendix B for other possible charts and graphs you might use.

Graphic Organizer

"The Five Ages of Man"	"Orpheus"

CONNECT

Reader's resource

"The Five Ages of Man" and **"Orpheus"** appear in Robert Graves's book *The Greek Myths*, a dictionary-style work that contains retellings of many classic Greek myths. These myths probably grew out of Greece's early feudal culture of the Mycenaean Age (1580–1100 BC). "The Five Ages of Man" traces the history of humankind. "Orpheus" describes events in the life of the mythical poet and musician Orpheus.

READ ALOUD

PRONUNCIATION KEY
Orpheus (ōr′ fē əs)
Dionysus (dī′ ō nī səs)
Maenads (mē′ nadz)
Mycenaean (mī sēn′ ē an)

Word watch

PREVIEW VOCABULARY
degenerate   reverently
insolent   spontaneously
plaintive

Reader's journal

On your own paper, list places where you have seen the influence of Greek mythology. These might be pictures used in advertisements, names of sports teams, or even descriptions of characters in a book, movie, or television show.

ORGANIZE INFORMATION AS YOU READ

❑ Follow along in your text as your teacher reads the first two paragraphs of the first excerpt, "The Five Ages of Man," aloud. Discuss which details are the most important and why. Record these details in your graphic organizer.

❑ Read the rest of the excerpts from *The Greek Myths* on your own. Look for important details as you read. Record these details in your organizers, or highlight key ideas and add them to your graphic organizers later.

READ ALOUD

PRONOUNCIATION KEY

Zeus (züs). King of all the gods

Hera (hārə). Zeus's wife

Athene (ə the′ nə). Goddess of wisdom

Hades (hā′ dēz). The god of the underworld

Helius (hē′ lē əs), or Apollo. The sun god

Prometheus (prō mē′ thē əs). Punished by Zeus for giving fire to humans

Cronus (crō nəs). Zeus's father

MARK THE TEXT

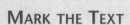

Underline or highlight details that describe each of the five ages of man. Circle what happened to each age. Begin on this page and continue on the next page.

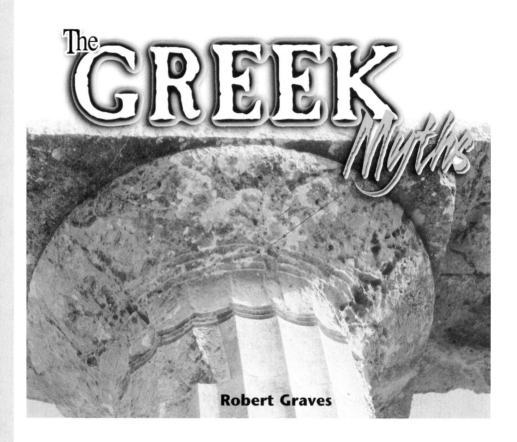

The GREEK Myths

Robert Graves

THE FIVE AGES OF MAN

Some deny that Prometheus created men, or that any man sprang from a serpent's teeth.[1] They say that Earth bore them <u>spontaneously</u>, as the best of her fruits, especially in the soil of Attica, and that Alalcomeneus was the first man to appear, by Lake Copais in Boeotia,[2] before even the Moon was created. He acted as Zeus's counsellor on the occasion of his quarrel with Hera, and as tutor to Athene while she was still a girl.

These men were the so-called golden race, subjects of
10 Cronus, who lived without cares or labour, eating only acorns, wild fruit, and honey that dripped from the trees,

---

THE FIVE AGES OF MAN
1. **Prometheus . . . serpent's teeth.** Reference to other Greek creation myths
2. **Boeotia.** (Vo ē′ shə). District in east-central Greece

words for everyday use	**spon • ta • ne • ous • ly** (spän tā′ nē əs lē) *adv.,* in a natural way, without outside influence. *Jacob's love for painting developed <u>spontaneously</u>; his parents did not push him to develop his artistic talents.*

drinking the milk of sheep and goats, never growing old, dancing, and laughing much; death, to them, was no more terrible than sleep. They are all gone now, but their spirits survive as genii[3] of happy music retreats, givers of good fortune, and upholders of justice.

20   Next came a silver race, eaters of bread, likewise divinely created. The men were utterly subject to their mothers and dared not disobey them, although they might live to be a hundred years old. They were quarrelsome and ignorant, and never sacrificed to the gods but, at least, did not make war on one another. Zeus destroyed them all.

    Next came a brazen[4] race, who fell like fruits from the ash-trees, and were armed with brazen weapons. They ate flesh as well as bread, and delighted in war, being <u>insolent</u> and pitiless men. Black Death has seized them all.

30   The fourth race of man was brazen too, but nobler and more generous, being begotten by the gods on mortal mothers. They fought gloriously in the siege of Thebes, the expedition of the Argonauts, and the Trojan War. These became heroes, and dwell in the Elysian Fields.[5]

    The fifth race is the present race of iron, unworthy descendants of the fourth. They are <u>degenerate</u>, cruel, unjust, malicious, libidinous, unfilial,[6] treacherous.

ORPHEUS

Orpheus, son of the Thracian King Oeagrus and the Muse Calliope,[1] was the most famous poet and musician who ever lived. Apollo presented him with a lyre, and the Muses taught him its use, so that he not only enchanted wild beasts, but made the trees and rocks move from their places to follow the sound of his music. At Zone

---

THE FIVE AGES OF MAN
  3. **genii.** Guardian spirits
  4. **brazen.** Brass
  5. **Elysian Fields.** Paradise for virtuous people after death
  6. **unfilial.** Unlike a loving, respectful son or daughter

ORPHEUS
  1. **Calliope** (kə lī′ ə pē′). Muse of eloquence and epic poetry

words for everyday use

in • so • lent (in′ sə lənt) *adj.*, boldly disrespectful. *The <u>insolent</u> student talked back to his teacher.*

de • gen • er • ate (dē jen′ ər it) *adj.*, having sunk below a former condition. *He had sunk to such <u>degenerate</u> lows that he would steal from his own mother.*

FIX-UP IDEA

Read Short Sections at a Time
If you have difficulty figuring out which details are important, read the excerpt one paragraph at a time. Pause after each paragraph to identify important details. Write the details down before you move on to the next paragraph. Use this strategy throughout the selection. Use this method with the next selection, "Orpheus," as well.

Literary TOOLS

MYTH. A **myth** is a story that explains objects or events in the natural world. The objects or events are the result of actions by some supernatural force or entity, most often a god. Myths are found in every early culture. As you read this Greek myth, note Orpheus's special skills and the effect his skill has on things in the natural world. What is his special skill? What effect does it have? Record these details in your "Orpheus" graphic organizer.

TACKLE DIFFICULT VOCABULARY.
Work with a partner to tackle
unfamiliar words and phrases.
Use context clues to see that
difficult phrases such as
"settled among the savage
Cicones of Thrase" and "the
passage which opens at
Aornum in Thesprotis" are
merely naming people and
places in Greece. You do not
need to know all of the details
about these people and
places. Get a general idea of
what the words are referring
to, and then continue reading.
Once you have unlocked the
meaning, reread paragraphs
that contain difficult words
and phrases.

Use THE STRATEGY

WRITE THINGS DOWN. Continue
to record important details
about Orpheus in your
graphic organizer.

in Thrace[2] a number of ancient mountain oaks are still
standing in the pattern of one of his dances, just as he left
them.

10   After a visit to Egypt, Orpheus joined the Argonauts,[3]
with whom he sailed to Colchis, his music helping them to
overcome many difficulties—and, on his return, married
Eurydice, whom some called Agriope, and settled among
the savage Cicones of Thrace.

    One day, near Tempe, in the valley of the river Peneius,
Eurydice met Aristaeus, who tried to force her. She trod on
a serpent as she fled, and died of its bite; but Orpheus
boldly descended into Tartarus,[4] hoping to fetch her back.
He used the passage which opens at Aornum in Thesprotis
20   and, on his arrival, not only charmed the ferryman Charon,
the Dog Cerberus,[5] and the three Judges of the Dead with
his <u>plaintive</u> music, but temporarily suspended the tortures
of the damned; and so far soothed the savage heart of Hades
that he won leave to restore Eurydice to the upper world.
Hades made a single condition: that Orpheus might not
look behind him until she was safely back under the light of
the sun. Eurydice followed Orpheus up through the dark
passage, guided by the sounds of his lyre, and it was only
when he reached the sunlight again that he turned to see
30   whether she were still behind him, and so lost her forever.

    When Dionysus invaded Thrace, Orpheus neglected to
honour him, but taught other sacred mysteries and
preached the evil of sacrificial murder to the men of Thrace,
who listened <u>reverently</u>. Every morning he would rise to
greet the dawn on the summit of Mount Pangaeum,
preaching that Helius, whom he named Apollo, was the

---

  2. **Thrace.** Ancient region in the Balkan Peninsula of Greece, north of
the Aegean Sea
  3. **Argonauts.** Men who sail with the hero Jason to search for the
Golden Fleece in Greek myth
  4. **Tartarus.** Infernal abyss below Hades, which is the home of the dead,
and ruled by Hades, the god of the underworld
  5. **Charon, the Dog Cerberus (sar´ bar as).** Charon was the boatman who led the
dead across the river Styx into Hades; Cerberus was a three-headed dog who
guarded the gate of Hades.

**words
for
everyday
use**
plain • tive (plān´ tiv) *adj.*, mournful; sad. *At the funeral, the pastor read the eulogy
in a <u>plaintive</u> voice.*
rev • er • ent • ly (rev´ ər ənt lē) *adv.*, in a manner suggesting deep respect, love,
or awe. *At the church service, the altar boy lit the candles <u>reverently</u>.*

greatest of all gods. In vexation, Dionysus set the Maenads[6] upon him at Deium in Macedonia. First waiting until their husbands had entered Apollo's temple, where Orpheus served as priest, they seized the weapons stacked outside, burst in, murdered their husbands, and tore Orpheus limb from limb. His head they threw into the river Hebrus, but it floated, still singing, down to the sea, and was carried to the island of Lesbos.

80

Tearfully, the Muses collected his limbs and buried them at Leibethra, at the foot of Mount Olympus,[7] where the nightingales now sing sweeter than anywhere else in the world. The Maenads had attempted to cleanse themselves of Orpheus's blood in the river Helicorn; but the River-god dived under the ground and disappeared for the space of nearly four miles, emerging with a different name, the Baphyra. Thus he avoided becoming an accessory to the murder. ■

90

THINK AND REFLECT

Why do the "nightingales now sing sweeter"? **(Interpret)**

_____

_____

_____

---

6. **Maenads** (mē′ nadz). Wild group of women who worshipped Dionysus, the god of revelry
7. **Mount Olympus.** Mountain where the gods live

Reflect ON YOUR READING

Share your graphic organizer with a partner. Compare the methods of organization, as well as the details each of you recorded. Discuss the benefits and drawbacks of the methods of organization you and your partner chose, and add to your notes any information you may have missed.

Reading Skills and Test Practice

COMPARE AND CONTRAST

READ, THINK, AND EXPLAIN. Discuss with your partner how to compare and contrast ideas in the excerpts from *The Greek Myths*. Use your own paper as needed.

1. Compare the two brazen races discussed in "The Five Ages of Man," and explain how they are similar to and different from each other.

   _____

   _____

   _____

   _____

2. Compare details in "The Five Ages of Man" and "Orpheus." Based on the information presented in each, Orpheus was most likely a member of what race? Explain your reasoning.

   _____

   _____

   _____

   _____

REFLECT ON YOUR RESPONSE. Compare your response to that of your partner. How did you compare and contrast ideas?

   _____

   _____

   _____

   _____

THINK-ALOUD
NOTES

_____

_____

_____

_____

_____

_____

_____

_____

_____

_____

_____

Investigate, Inquire, and Imagine

RECALL: GATHER FACTS
1a. Who is Orpheus? For what is he best known? What happens to Orpheus at the hands of Dionysus?

INTERPRET: FIND MEANING
1b. How do Orpheus's talents help him during his life? Why is Dionysus angry with Orpheus?

ANALYZE: TAKE THINGS APART
2a. Analyze how the materials and qualities associated with each successive race in "The Five Ages of Man" evolve, or change.

SYNTHESIZE: BRING THINGS TOGETHER
2b. Based on your analysis, what can you infer about classical Greek attitudes toward the state of human nature in their own time? What did they probably think had happened to human nature over time?

EVALUATE: MAKE JUDGMENTS
3a. Based on the different stories about Orpheus, what is your opinion of Orpheus's character? What is your opinion of Zeus? of Dionysus?

EXTEND: CONNECT IDEAS
3b. Based on these selections from *The Greek Myths,* what can you conclude about the Greeks' view of their gods? about the world in general?

Literary Tools

MYTH. A **myth** is a story that explains objects or events in the natural world. The objects or events are the result of actions by some supernatural force or entity, most often a god. Record the names and actions of the gods in both myths in a cluster chart like the one below.

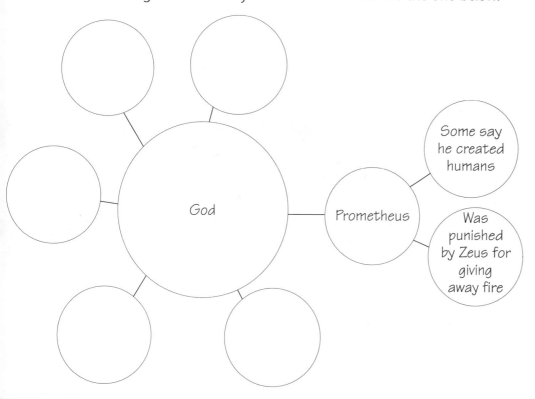

WordWorkshop

PREFIXES AND SUFFIXES. Use a dictionary and your knowledge of the vocabulary words to fill in the blanks in the two charts below.

Prefix	Meaning of Prefix	Sample Word	Meaning of Sample Word
		degenerate	
		unfilial	
pre–			
anti–			
hetero–			

Suffix	Meaning of Suffix	Sample Word	Meaning of Sample Word
		reverently	
		spontaneously	
–ish			
–ment			
–ful			
–less			

Read-Write Connection

Which excerpt did you find more interesting, "The Five Ages of Man" or "Orpheus"? Why?

_____

_____

_____

_____

_____

Beyond the Reading

MYTHOLOGICAL ART. Mythological stories and characters have inspired artists throughout the centuries. With a partner, conduct research on artwork inspired by a figure from Greek mythology. Photocopy or create an illustration of the artwork. Read more about the character or myth the artwork depicts. Share your research with the class.

GO ONLINE. Visit the EMC Internet Resource Center at **emcp.com** to find links and additional activities for this selection.

from the POPOL VUH

Anonymous, English version by Delia Goetz and Sylvanus G. Morley, from the Spanish translation by Adrián Recinos

Active READING STRATEGY

TACKLE DIFFICULT VOCABULARY

Before Reading ➤ **PREVIEW DIFFICULT WORDS**

❑ Work with a partner to preview the words in WordWatch. Add each word, its phonetic spelling, and its definition to the graphic organizer below.

❑ Have your partner use the phonetic spellings to the check your pronunciation.

❑ Read each word and its definition one more time before you begin reading.

❑ As you read, add other words that you do not know to the chart. Use another sheet of paper if you run out of room below.

Graphic Organizer

Word or Phrase	Phonetic Spelling	Definition
Example: condemn	[kən dem']	denounce; convict

CONNECT

Reader's resource

The *Popol Vuh* or "The Book of the Community" is a sacred epic of the Quiché Maya, a people who inhabited present-day Guatemala at the beginning of the eleventh century. The original *Popol Vuh*, written between 1554 and 1558, was destroyed by Spanish conquerors who believed that such native texts were pagan and evil. A translation survived. This excerpt from the translation recounts why humans and other creatures were created.

Word watch

PREVIEW VOCABULARY

condemn	ravine
diviner	soothsayer
invoke	venerate

Reader's journal

Throughout history, people have tried to explain the creation of the world. How do you believe the world was created?

_____

_____

_____

TACKLE DIFFICULT WORDS WHILE READING

❑ Begin reading the selection silently. Use your graphic organizer as needed.

❑ If a difficult word is not in your graphic organizer or in the footnotes, add it to your graphic organizer. Try to determine its meaning from the context or look it up in a dictionary. Once you understand the word, resume reading.

Reading STRATEGY
REVIEW

USE TEXT ORGANIZATION.
Look for words like *then*, *promptly*, *thus*, and *so it was* to keep track of the sequence of events. What two kinds of small animals are the first to be created?

_____

_____

Use THE STRATEGY

TACKLE DIFFICULT VOCABULARY. Remember to add words you do not know to your graphic organizer.

from the

POPOL VUH

Anonymous

Then they made the small wild animals, the guardians of the woods, the spirits of the mountains,[1] the deer, the birds, pumas, jaguars, serpents, snakes, vipers, guardians of the thickets.

And the Forefathers asked: "Shall there be only silence and calm under the trees, under the vines? It is well that hereafter there be someone to guard them."

So they said when they meditated and talked. Promptly the deer and the birds were created. Immediately they gave homes to the deer and the birds. "You, deer, shall sleep in the fields by the river bank and in the <u>ravines</u>. Here you shall be amongst the thicket, amongst the pasture; in the woods you shall multiply, you shall walk on four feet and they will support you. Thus be it done!" So it was they spoke.

Then they also assigned homes to the birds big and small. "You shall live in the trees and in the vines. There you shall make your nests; there you shall multiply; there you shall

10

---

1. **spirits of the mountains.** In ancient times the Maya believed that forests were filled with spirits that acted as guardians.

words for everyday use   ra • vine (rə vēn') *n.*, long, deep hollow in the earth's surface. *Loliwag River dried up after the Conifer Dam was built, but a deep <u>ravine</u> marks where the water used to flow.*

increase in the branches of the trees and in the vines." Thus
the deer and the birds were told; they did their duty at once,
and all sought their homes and their nests.

And the creation of all the four-footed animals and the
birds being finished, they were told by the Creator and the
Maker[2] and the Forefathers: "Speak, cry, warble, call, speak
each one according to your variety, each, according to your
kind." So was it said to the deer, the birds, pumas, jaguars,
and serpents.

"Speak, then, our names, praise us, your mother, your
father. <u>Invoke</u> then, Huracán, Chipi-Caculhá,
Raxa-Caculhá,[3] the Heart of Heaven, the Heart of Earth,
the Creator, the Maker, the Forefathers; speak, invoke us,
adore us," they were told.

But they could not make them speak like men; they only
hissed and screamed and cackled; they were unable to make
words, and each screamed in a different way.

When the Creator and the Maker saw that it was
impossible for them to talk to each other, they said: "It is
impossible for them to say our names, the names of us, their
Creators and Makers. This is not well," said the Forefathers
to each other.

Then they said to them: "Because it has not been possible
for you to talk, you shall be changed. We have changed our
minds: Your food, your pasture, your homes, and your nests
you shall have; they shall be the ravines and the woods,
because it has not been possible for you to adore us or
invoke us. There shall be those who adore us, we shall make
other [beings] who shall be obedient. Accept your destiny:
your flesh shall be torn to pieces. So shall it be. This shall
be your lot." So they said, when they made known their will
to the large and small animals which are on the face of the
earth.

20

30

40

50

---

2. **Creator and the Maker.** Mother and father gods, also known as
Tzacol and Bitol and many other names
3. **Huracán, Chipi-Caculhá, Raxa-Caculhá** (hü rä kän';
chē pē kä kül hä'; rä shä kä kül hä'). Thunder and lightning gods who
together make up the Heart of Heaven

words for everyday use

in • voke (in vōk') vt., call on for blessing, help, inspiration, or support. *"Help me,
Master of Sums,"* <u>invoked</u> Dudley as he picked up his algebra test.

FIX-UP IDEA

Reread
If difficult vocabulary
makes the *Popol Vuh* hard
to understand, pause to
review the meanings of
difficult words in one
section. Once you feel that
you understand the
meanings of the words in
that section, reread the
section. Then go on to
another section of the
text. Repeat this process
as needed.

NOTE THE FACTS

What caused the Creators
to change their creation?

_____

_____

_____

CONNECT TO PRIOR KNOWLEDGE. How are the Creators and Makers in this story similar to creators in other stories you have heard or read?

_____

_____

_____

Literary TOOLS

CHRONOLOGICAL ORDER. **Chronological order** is the arrangement of details in the order of their occurrence. Review what the gods have created so far by going back and circling their creations.

They wished to give them another trial; they wished to make another attempt; they wished to make [all living things] adore them.

But they could not understand each other's speech; they could succeed in nothing, and could do nothing. For this reason they were sacrificed, and the animals which were on earth were <u>condemned</u> to be killed and eaten.

60 For this reason another attempt had to be made to create and make men by the Creator, the Maker, and the Forefathers.

"Let us try again! Already dawn draws near: Let us make him who shall nourish and sustain us! What shall we do to be invoked, in order to be remembered on earth? We have already tried with our first creations, our first creatures; but we could not make them praise and <u>venerate</u> us. So, then, let us try to make obedient, respectful beings who will nourish and sustain us." Thus they spoke.

Then was the creation and the formation. Of earth, of mud, they made [man's] flesh. But they saw that it was not 70 good. It melted away, it was soft, did not move, had no strength, it fell down, it was limp, it could not move its head, its face fell to one side, its sight was blurred, it could not look behind. At first it spoke, but had no mind. Quickly it soaked in the water and could not stand.

And the Creator and the Maker said: "Let us try again because our creatures will not be able to walk nor multiply. Let us consider this," they said.

Then they broke up and destroyed their work and their creation. And they said: "What shall we do to perfect it, in 80 order that our worshipers, our invokers, will be successful?"

Thus they spoke when they conferred again: "Let us say again to Xpiyacoc, Xmucané,[4] Hunahpú-Vuch, Hunahpú-Utiú:[5] 'Cast your lot again. Try to create again.'"

---

4. **Xpiyacoc, Xmucané** (shēp yä kōk´; shmü kä nä´). Old man and woman, Grandfather and Grandmother; a Creator-couple responsible for making the material things of the world

5. **Hunahpú-Vuch, Hunahpú-Utiú** (hü nä pü´ üch; hü nä pü´ ü tyü´). Other names for the Grandfather and Grandmother. Hunahpú-Vuch was goddess of the dawn; Hunahpú-Utiú was god of the night.

words for everyday use	
	con • demn (kən dem´) *vt.*, pronounce judgment against; sentence. *The armed robber was <u>condemned</u> to twenty years in prison.*
	ven • er • ate (ven´ ər āt) *vt.*, worship. *Chloe <u>venerated</u> Gordie until she found out what a scoundrel he was.*

In this manner the Creator and the Maker spoke to Xpiyacoc and Xmucané.

Then they spoke to those <u>soothsayers</u>, the Grandmother of the Day, the Grandmother of the Dawn, as they were called by the Creator and the Maker, and whose names were Xpiyacoc and Xmucané.

90 And said Huracán, Tepeu, and Gucumatz[6] when they spoke to the soothsayer, to the Maker, who are the <u>diviners</u>: "You must work together and find the means so that man, whom we shall make, man, whom we are going to make, will nourish and sustain us, invoke and remember us."

"Enter, then, into council, grandmother, grandfather, our grandmother, our grandfather, Xpiyacoc, Xmucané, make light, make dawn, have us invoked, have us adored, have us remembered by created man, by made man, by mortal man. Thus be it done.

100 "Let your nature be known, Hunahpú-Vuch, Hunahpú-Utiú, twice mother, twice father, Nim-Ac, Nima-Tziís,[7] the master of emeralds, the worker in jewels, the sculptor, the carver, the maker of beautiful plates, the maker of green gourds, the master of resin, the master Toltecat,[8] grandmother of the sun, grandmother of dawn, as you will be called by our works and our creatures.

"Cast the lot with your grains of corn and the *tzité*.[9] Do it thus, and we shall know if we are to make, or carve his mouth and eyes out of wood." Thus the diviners were told.

110 They went down at once to make their divination, and cast their lots with the corn and the *tzité*. "Fate! Creature!" said an old woman and an old man. And this old man was the one who cast the lots with *tzité*, the one called Xpiyacoc.

---

6. **Tepeu, and Gucumatz** (tā pā ü′; gü kü mätz′). Other names for the Creator and the Maker. Tepeu meant king; Gucumatz was a serpent covered with green feathers, the equivalent of the Mexican Kukulcán and the Aztec Quetzalcoatl.
7. **Nim-Ac, Nima-Tziís** (nēm äk′; nē mä′ tzē ēs′). Other names for the Creator and the Maker. Nim-Ac was the Father and Nima-Tziís was the Mother.
8. **Toltecat** (tôl′ te kät). Silversmith, worker of silver—a valued occupation
9. *tzité* (tzē tā′). Tree whose wood is used for making fences. The red grains of its fruit are used for fortunetelling, along with the grains of corn.

| words for everyday use | sooth • say • er (sōōth′ sā ər) n., person who professes to foretell the future. *Marcel asked the <u>soothsayer</u> what the future held for him.* |
| | di • vin • er (də vīn′ ər) n., one who tries to foretell the future. *Unhappy with the soothsayer's prediction, he tried another <u>diviner</u> whose answer pleased him.* |

Use **THE STRATEGY**

TACKLE DIFFICULT VOCABULARY. Who are the diviners? What do they do?

_____

_____

_____

Use **THE STRATEGY**

TACKLE DIFFICULT VOCABULARY. Write down a synonym for *tzité*.

_____

_____

_____

Use THE STRATEGY

TACKLE DIFFICULT VOCABULARY. Continue to add words you do not know to your graphic organizer.

READ ALOUD

Read lines 129–147 aloud with a partner. Practice reading lines in a way that shows how the creator gods felt about their creation.

THINK AND REFLECT

Do the first humans satisfy the Creators? Why, or why not? **(Evaluate)**

_____

_____

_____

And the old woman was the diviner, the maker, called Chiracán Xmucané.

Beginning the divination, they said: "Get together, grasp each other! Speak, that we may hear." They said, "Say if it is well that the wood be got together and that it be carved by the Creator and the Maker, and if this [man of wood] is he
120 who must nourish and sustain us when there is light when it is day!

"Thou, corn; thou, *tzité*; thou, fate; thou, creature; get together, take each other," they said to the corn, to the *tzité*, to fate, to the creature. "Come to sacrifice here, Heart of Heaven; do not punish Tepeu and Gucumatz!"[10]

Then they talked and spoke the truth: "Your figures of wood shall come out well; they shall speak and talk on earth."

"So may it be," they answered when they spoke.

And instantly the figures were made of wood. They
130 looked like men, talked like men, and populated the surface of the earth.

They existed and multiplied; they had daughters, they had sons, these wooden figures; but they did not have souls, nor minds, they did not remember their Creator, their Maker; they walked on all fours, aimlessly.

They no longer remembered the Heart of Heaven and therefore they fell out of favor. It was merely a trial, an attempt at man. At first they spoke, but their face was without expression; their feet and hands had no strength;
140 they had no blood, nor substance, nor moisture, nor flesh; their cheeks were dry, their feet and hands were dry, and their flesh was yellow.

Therefore, they no longer thought of their Creator nor their Maker, nor of those who made them and cared for them.

These were the first men who existed in great numbers on the face of the earth. ■

---

10. **"Come . . . Gucumatz!"** The speakers are inviting the Heart of Heaven to join in the casting of lots and ensure the success of the diviners.

Reflect ON YOUR READING

When you finish reading, rejoin your partner to discuss the vocabulary in the selection from the *Popol Vuh*. With your partner, write a new story that uses all of the words in your graphic organizer.

Reading Skills and Test Practice

RECOGNIZE CAUSE AND EFFECT

Discuss with your partner how to answer the following questions about cause and effect.

1. What caused the Creators to be displeased with their first creation, the animals?
   a. The animals ate things they were not supposed to eat.
   b. The animals could not produce offspring.
   c. The animals were unable to speak in praise of their Makers.
   d. The animals were made out of wood and had no substance.

What is the correct answer to the question above? How were you able to eliminate the other answers? How did your application of the reading strategy help you?

_____

_____

_____

_____

2. Because the Creators were displeased with them, the animals were
   a. wiped off the face of the Earth.
   b. condemned to be killed and eaten.
   c. changed into a new race of men.
   d. displaced from their homes and forced to wander the Earth aimlessly.

What is the correct answer to the question above? How were you able to eliminate the other answers? How did your application of the reading strategy help you?

_____

_____

_____

_____

THINK-ALOUD NOTES

_____

_____

_____

_____

_____

_____

_____

_____

_____

_____

_____

Investigate, Inquire, and Imagine

RECALL: GATHER FACTS
1a. From what material do the Creators attempt to make the first humans? What qualities are lacking in the second group of humans?

INTERPRET: FIND MEANING
1b. Why is the creation of the first humans considered a failure?

ANALYZE: TAKE THINGS APART
2a. Compare the second group of humans to the Creators' previous creations. What suggests that the Creators think the second group of humans is at least a partial success?

SYNTHESIZE: BRING THINGS TOGETHER
2b. What suggests that humans were created to be a higher order of beings than the other creatures?

EVALUATE: MAKE JUDGMENTS
3a. In this creation story, what kind of relationship is established between the earthly and spiritual worlds? What is your opinion of the Creators? Explain.

EXTEND: CONNECT IDEAS
3b. Design a third group of humans that would satisfy the desires of the Creators. What abilities and attributes would this third group possess? Of what materials would you make these new humans?

Literary Tools

CHRONOLOGICAL ORDER. **Chronological order** is the arrangement of details in the order of their occurrence. Recall that writers, or storytellers, may use signal words such as *then, next,* and *before* to guide readers through the sequence of events. Why would chronological order be an appropriate organization for a creation story? What signal words can you identify in the selection from the *Popol Vuh?* Use signal words to retell the story of creation told in the *Popol Vuh.* Use your own paper as needed.

_____

_____

_____

_____

Read-Write Connection

What ideas or beliefs expressed in this myth seemed strange or unfamiliar to you? Which of your beliefs might seem strange to a person from the ancient Mayan culture? Use your own paper as needed.

WordWorkshop

USING CONTEXT CLUES. **Context clues,** or words surrounding a new word, can often help you estimate the meaning of unfamiliar words as you read. One type of context clue is restatement, when the author reveals the meaning of a word by using different words to express the same idea.

Imagine that you are the Creator or the Maker referred to in the *Popol Vuh*. Determine the effectiveness of your "creation" by examining it within the context of its surroundings. Now, instead of trying to create human beings from doubtful materials, you will create sentences that show the meaning of words used in the myth. Rewrite each sentence from the *Popol Vuh* below, using restatement to define the underlined word.

EXAMPLE
Sentence from the Myth: So they said when they meditated and talked.
Restatement: So they said when they meditated and talked, for they needed to ponder and discuss the matter thoughtfully.

1. "You, deer, shall sleep in the fields by the river bank and in the <u>ravines</u>."

   _____

2. So was it said to the deer, the birds, <u>pumas</u> . . .

   _____

3. "<u>Invoke</u>, then, Huracán, Chipi-Caculhá, Raxa-Caculha, the Heart of Heaven . . ."

   _____

4. This shall be your <u>lot</u>.

   _____

5. For this reason they were sacrificed, and the animals that were on earth were <u>condemned</u> to be killed or eaten.

   _____

Beyond the Reading

MYTHS. Cultures from around the world have created their own unique myths, and many focus on the creation of animals and humans. Find a myth from another culture that explains how humans and animals were created. Retell this myth by creating a story strip or sequence of events chart that lists events in the myth in the order in which they occur.

GO ONLINE. Visit the EMC Internet Resource Center at **emcp.com** to find links and additional activities for this selection.

"Popocatépetl and Ixtacihuatl"

Retold by Julie Piggott

Reader's resource

"Popocatépetl and Ixtacihuatl" is an Aztec tale that explains the origin of a snow-capped volcano called Popocatépetl, or "smoking mountain," and its twin peak, Ixtacihuatl, or "white woman." "Popocatépetl and Ixtacihuatl" takes place in Tenochtitlan, a city built in approximately 1325, roughly on the site where Mexico City now stands.

Word watch

PREVIEW VOCABULARY

adamant	edifice
apprehensive	emit
behest	refute
besiege	resinous
brandish	trebly
brine	unanimous
decree	vanquish

READ ALOUD

PRONUNCIATION KEY
Popocatépetl (pō′ pō ka tā′ pet′ l)
Ixtacihuatl (ēs′ tä sē′ wä təl)
Tenochtitlan (tā nōch′ tēt län′)

Reader's journal

Discuss stories you know that deal with young lovers who meet with difficulty or opposition.

_____

_____

Active READING STRATEGY

MAKE PREDICTIONS

Before Reading → **MAKE PRELIMINARY PREDICTIONS**

❑ Read the Reader's Resource.
❑ Discuss the title, the information in the Reader's Resource, and your answer to the Reader's Journal topic.
❑ With a partner, brainstorm predictions about what may happen in the myth. Record two or three predictions in the graphic organizer below.

Graphic Organizer

Clues	Predictions	Adjustments/ Confirmations of My Predictions

Popocatépetl and Ixtacihuatl

Retold by Julie Piggott

During Reading

REVISE PREDICTIONS AND MAKE NEW PREDICTIONS

❑ Follow along in the text as your teacher reads the first page of "Popocatépetl and Ixtacihuatl" aloud. When your teacher finishes reading, review the predictions you made. Were any of your predictions confirmed? Do any predictions need to be revised, based on new information you learned?

❑ Write one or two new predictions about Ixta or the Emperor.

❑ Continue reading the selection independently. Keep your predictions in mind as you read, and look for information in the text that confirms or refutes your predictions. Record details that confirm or refute your predictions, and look for details that can help you make new predictions.

There was once an Aztec emperor in Tenochtitlan. He was very powerful. Some thought he was wise as well, while others doubted his wisdom. He was born a ruler and a warrior; and he kept at bay those tribes living in and beyond the mountains surrounding the Valley of Mexico, with its huge lake called Texcoco in which Tenochtitlan was built. His power was absolute, and the splendor in which he lived was very great.

It is not known for how many years the Emperor ruled Tenochtitlan, but it is known that he lived to a great age. However, it was not until he was in his middle years that his wife gave him an heir, a girl. The Emperor and Empress loved the princess very much, and she was their only child. She was a dutiful daughter and learned all she could from her father about the art of ruling, for she knew that when he died, she would reign in his stead in Tenochtitlan.

Her name was Ixtacihuatl. Her parents and her friends called her Ixta. She had a pleasant disposition and, as a result, she had many friends. The great palace where she lived with the Emperor and Empress rang with their laughter when they came to the parties her parents gave for

10

20

NOTE THE FACTS

Why does the princess learn all she can from her father?

_____

_____

_____

_____

Use THE STRATEGY

MAKE PREDICTIONS. The Emperor forbids Ixta to marry her lover. Add a prediction to your chart about what might happen to Ixta and her lover.

Literary TOOLS

FORESHADOWING.
Foreshadowing is the act of presenting materials that hint at events that may occur later in the story. Foreshadowing may take the form of plot elements, such as something a character says or does, or it may be embodied in the mood the writer creates. How do the lines 42–52 foreshadow what might happen?

_____

_____

_____

her. As well as being a delightful companion, Ixta was also very pretty, even beautiful.

Her childhood was happy, and she was content enough when she became a young woman. But by then she was fully aware of the great responsibilities which would be hers when her father died, and she became serious and studious and did not enjoy parties as much as she had done when 30 younger.

Another reason for her being so serious was that she was in love. This in itself was a joyous thing, but the Emperor forbade her to marry. He wanted her to reign and rule alone when he died, for he trusted no one, not even his wife, to rule as he did except his much loved only child, Ixta. This was why there were some who doubted the wisdom of the Emperor; for, by not allowing his heiress to marry, he showed a selfishness and shortsightedness toward his daughter and his empire which many considered was not 40 truly wise. An emperor, they felt, who was not truly wise could not also be truly great or even truly powerful.

The man with whom Ixta was in love was also in love with her. Had they been allowed to marry, their state could have been doubly joyous. His name was Popocatépetl, and Ixta and his friends all called him Popo. He was a warrior in the service of the Emperor, tall and strong, with a capacity for gentleness, and very brave. He and Ixta loved each other very much, and while they were content and even happy when they were together, true joy was not theirs because the 50 Emperor continued to insist that Ixta should not be married when the time came for her to take on her father's responsibilities.

This unfortunate but moderately happy relationship between Ixta and Popo continued for several years, the couple pleading with the Emperor at regular intervals and the Emperor remaining constantly <u>adamant</u>. Popo loved Ixta no less for her father's stubbornness; and she loved him no less while she studied, as her father demanded she should do, the art of ruling in preparation for her reign.

words for everyday use

ad • a • mant (ad′ ə mənt) *adj.,* unshakeable; not giving in. *Luan begged me to reconsider, but I remained <u>adamant</u> in my decision.*

60   When the Emperor became very old, he also became ill. In his feebleness, he channeled all his failing energies toward instructing Ixta in statecraft,[1] for he was no longer able to exercise that craft himself. So it was that his enemies, the tribes who lived in the mountains and beyond, realized that the great Emperor in Tenochtitlan was great no longer, for he was only teaching his daughter to rule and not ruling himself.

The tribesmen came nearer and nearer to Tenochtitlan until the city was <u>besieged</u>. At last the Emperor realized himself that he was great no longer, that his power was

70   nearly gone, and that his domain was in dire peril.[2]

Warrior though he long had been, he was now too old and too ill to lead his fighting men into battle. At last he understood that, unless his enemies were frustrated in their efforts to enter and lay waste to Tenochtitlan, not only would he no longer be Emperor but his daughter would never be Empress.

Instead of appointing one of his warriors to lead the rest into battle on his behalf, he offered a bribe to all of them. Perhaps it was that his wisdom, if wisdom he had, had

80   forsaken him; or perhaps he acted from fear. Or perhaps he simply changed his mind. But the bribe he offered to whichever warrior succeeded in lifting the siege of Tenochtitlan and defeating the enemies in and around the Valley of Mexico was both the hand of his daughter and the equal right to reign and rule, with her, in Tenochtitlan. Furthermore, he decreed that directly he learned that his enemies had been defeated, he would instantly cease to be Emperor himself. Ixta would not have to wait until her father died to become Empress; and, if her father should die

90   of his illness or old age before his enemies were <u>vanquished</u>, he further <u>decreed</u> that he who overcame the surrounding

1. **statecraft.** Ability, wisdom, and methods of someone who manages public affairs
2. **dire peril.** Great danger

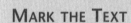

Use THE STRATEGY

MAKE PREDICTIONS. Reread lines 67–70. Add a prediction to your chart about what will happen if the Emperor loses his power.

MARK THE TEXT

Underline or highlight words or phrases that describe the Emperor's bribe.

words for everyday use	be • siege (bē sēj´) vt., close in on and attack. *As the defendant left the courtroom he was <u>besieged</u> with angry shouts from the crowd and questions from reporters.*
	van • quish (van´ kwish) vt., conquer. *After their enemies were <u>vanquished</u>, the warriors celebrated with a joyous banquet.*
	de • cree (dē krē´) vt., order officially. *Ms. Kwillian <u>decreed</u> that anyone talking during the test would fail.*

enemies should marry the princess whether he, the Emperor, lived or not.

Ixta was fearful when she heard of her father's bribe to his warriors, for the only one whom she had any wish to marry was Popo; and she wanted to marry him, and only him, very much indeed.

Use **THE STRATEGY**

MAKE PREDICTIONS. Reread lines 98–101. Add a prediction to your chart on what the warriors will do.

The warriors, however, were glad when they heard of the 100 decree. There was not one of them who would not have been glad to have the princess as his wife, and they all relished the chance of becoming Emperor.

And so the warriors went to war at their ruler's <u>behest</u>, and each fought <u>trebly</u> hard; for each was fighting not only for the safety of Tenochtitlan and the surrounding valley, but for the delightful bride and for the right to be the Emperor himself.

Even though the warriors fought with great skill, and even though each one exhibited a courage he did not know he possessed, the war was a long one. The Emperor's enemies were firmly entrenched around Lake Texcoco and 110 Tenochtitlan by the time the warriors were sent to war; and as battle followed battle, the final outcome was uncertain.

Reading **STRATEGY**
REVIEW

VISUALIZE. Use the footnotes to visualize the warriors' weapons. Sketch three of their weapons.

The warriors took a variety of weapons with them; wooden clubs edged with sharp blades of obsidian,[3] obsidian machetes,[4] javelins[5] which they hurled at their enemies from troughed throwing boards,[6] bows and arrows, slings and spears set with obsidian fragments, and lances, too. Many of them carried shields woven from wicker and covered in tough hide and most wore armor made of thick 120 quilted cotton soaked in <u>brine</u>.

The war was long and fierce. Most of the warriors fought together and in unison, but some fought alone. As time went on, natural leaders emerged and, of these, undoubtedly Popo

---

3. **obsidian.** Hard, black volcanic rock
4. **machetes.** Heavy-bladed knives
5. **javelins.** Throwing spears
6. **throwing boards.** Hollowed, narrow wooden paddle with which to throw

words for everyday use

be • hest (bē hest') *n.*, command. *Sarah took out the garbage at her father's <u>behest</u>.*

tre • bly (treb' lē) *adv.*, extremely; three times as. *After hearing of Amy's accomplishments on the flute, piano, and guitar, I was <u>trebly</u> impressed.*

brine (brīn) *n.*, salt water. *After swimming in the ocean, Loren washed the <u>brine</u> from her clothes.*

was the best. Finally, it was he, <u>brandishing</u> his club and shield, who led the great charge of running warriors across the valley, with their enemies fleeing before them to the safety of the coastal plains and jungles beyond the mountains.

130   The warriors acclaimed Popo as the man most responsible for the victory; and, weary though they all were, they set off for Tenochtitlan to report to the Emperor and for Popo to claim Ixta as his wife at last.

    But a few of those warriors were jealous of Popo. Since they knew none of them could rightly claim the victory for himself (the decision among the Emperor's fighting men that Popo was responsible for the victory had been <u>unanimous</u>), they wanted to spoil for him and for Ixta the delights which the Emperor had promised.

140   These few men slipped away from the rest at night and made their way to Tenochtitlan ahead of all the others. They reached the capital two days later, having traveled without sleep all the way, and quickly let it be known that, although the Emperor's warriors had been successful against his enemies, the warrior Popo had been killed in battle.

    It was a foolish and cruel lie which those warriors told their Emperor, and they told it for no reason other than that they were jealous of Popo.

    When the Emperor heard this, he demanded that Popo's
150 body be brought to him so that he might arrange a fitting burial. He knew the man his daughter had loved would have died courageously. The jealous warriors looked at one another and said nothing. Then one of them told the Emperor that Popo had been killed on the edge of Lake Texcoco and that his body had fallen into the water and no man had been able to retrieve it. The Emperor was saddened to hear this.

    After a little while, he demanded to be told which of his warriors had been responsible for the victory; but none of
160 the fighting men before him dared claim the successful

words for everyday use

bran • dish (bran′ dish) *vt.,* wave; exhibit. *Minerva proudly <u>brandished</u> the first copy of the newspaper with her picture on the front page.*

u • nan • i • mous (yōō nan′ ə məs) *adj.,* in complete agreement. *I expected Lionel to oppose the proposition, but the decision was <u>unanimous</u>.*

TACKLE DIFFICULT VOCABULARY.
Write synonyms for difficult
words in the margins. Writing
a synonym in the text helps
you keep on reading.

FIX-UP IDEA

Ask a Question
If you have difficulty
making predictions about
what will happen,
underline key details and
events in the selection. Ask
how the key details or
events you underline
might influence future
events. In line 183,
"Princess Ixtacihuatl did
not wish to live if
Popocatépetl was dead,
and so she died herself" is
an important event you
should underline. What
might happen now that
Princess Ixta is dead?
Think of an answer to your
question, and then read to
see if your guess is right.

MARK THE TEXT
Underline or highlight what
Popo does when he learns
about Ixta.

outcome of the war for himself, for each knew the others
would <u>refute</u> him. So they were silent. This puzzled the
Emperor, and he decided to wait for the main body of his
warriors to return and not to press the few who had brought
the news of the victory and of Popo's death.

Then the Emperor sent for his wife and his daughter and
told them their enemies had been overcome. The Empress
was thoroughly excited and relieved at the news. Ixta was
only <u>apprehensive</u>. The Emperor, seeing her anxious face,
170   told her quickly that Popo was dead. He went on to say that
the warrior's body had been lost in the waters of Lake
Texcoco; and again it was as though his wisdom had left
him, for he spoke at some length of his not yet being able to
tell Ixta who her husband would be and who would become
Emperor when the main body of warriors returned to
Tenochtitlan.

But Ixta heard nothing of what he told her, only that her
beloved Popo was dead. She went to her room and lay
down. Her mother followed her and saw at once she was
180   very ill. Witch doctors were sent for, but they could not
help the princess, and neither could her parents. Her illness
had no name, unless it was the illness of a broken heart.
Princess Ixtacihuatl did not wish to live if Popocatépetl was
dead, and so she died herself.

The day after her death, Popo returned to Tenochtitlan
with all the other surviving warriors. They went straight to
the palace and, with much cheering, told the Emperor that
his enemies had been routed and that Popo was the
undoubted victor of the conflict.

190   The Emperor praised his warriors and pronounced Popo
to be the new Emperor in his place. When the young man
asked first to see Ixta, begging that they should be married
at once before being jointly proclaimed Emperor and
Empress, the Emperor had to tell Popo of Ixta's death and
how it had happened.

Popo spoke not a word.

**words
for
everyday
use**   re • fute (ri fyo͞ot') *vt.,* prove to be wrong. *Angela <u>refuted</u> Tony's accusation that she
was lazy by showing him the work she had done on their project while he was
sleeping.*
ap • pre • hen • sive (ap' rē hen' siv) *adj.,* fearful; nervous. *Despite hours spent
studying, Paul was <u>apprehensive</u> that he might not pass the test.*

He gestured the assembled warriors to follow him, and together they sought out the few jealous men who had given the false news of his death to the Emperor. With the army

200 of warriors watching, Popo killed each one of them in single combat with his obsidian studded club. No one tried to stop him.

That task accomplished, Popo returned to the palace and, still without speaking and still wearing his stiff cotton armor, went to Ixta's room. He gently lifted her body and carried it out of the palace and out of the city, and no one tried to stop him doing that either. All the warriors followed him in silence.

When he had walked some miles, he gestured to them

210 again, and they built a huge pile of stones in the shape of a pyramid. They all worked together and they worked fast, while Popo stood and watched, holding the body of the princess in his arms. By sunset the mighty <u>edifice</u> was finished. Popo climbed it alone, carrying Ixta's corpse with him. There, at the very top, under the heap of stones, he buried the young woman he had loved so well and for so long and who had died for the love of him.

That night Popo slept alone at the top of the pyramid by Ixta's grave. In the morning he came down and spoke for

220 the first time since the Emperor had told him the princess was dead. He told the warriors to build another pyramid, a little to the southeast of the one which held Ixta's body, and to build it higher than the other.

He told them, too, to tell the Emperor on his behalf that he, Popocatépetl, would never reign and rule in Tenochtitlan. He would keep watch over the grave of the Princess Ixtacihuatl for the rest of his life.

The messages to the Emperor were the last words Popo ever spoke. Well before the evening, the second mighty pile

230 of stones was built. Popo climbed it and stood at the top, taking a torch of <u>resinous</u> pine wood with him.

And when he reached the top, he lit the torch, and the warriors below saw the white smoke rise against the blue

USE THE STRATEGY

MAKE PREDICTIONS. Reread lines 209–217. Predict what Popo will do next.

THINK AND REFLECT

Who is responsible for what happened to Ixta and Popo? **(Evaluate)**

_____

_____

_____

words for everyday use

ed • i • fice (ed′ i fis) n., structure. *The old abandoned building was torn down to make room for a new edifice.*

res • in • ous (rez′ ən əs) adj., having resin—a clear, yellowish-brown substance that comes from trees or plants. *Joan built a fire using resinous wood and it smoked quite a bit.*

sky; and they watched as the sun began to set, and the smoke turned pink and then a deep red, the color of blood.

So Popocatépetl stood there, holding the torch of memory of Ixtacihuatl, for the rest of his days.

240 The snows came, and, as the years went by, the pyramids of stone became high, white-capped mountains. Even now the one called Popocatépetl <u>emits</u> smoke in memory of the princess whose body lies in the mountain which bears her name. ∎

Reflect ON YOUR READING

ANALYZE PREDICTIONS

When you finish reading, review the predictions you made as you read the selection. Think about the information that led you to make your predictions and the details that confirmed or refuted them. Did your predictions become more "on target" as more story details were revealed? Compare your predictions with your partner's, and discuss how the process of making predictions added to your reading experience.

Reading Skills and Test Practice

IDENTIFY CONFLICT AND RESOLUTION

Discuss with your partner how to answer the following questions about conflict and resolution.

1. Which statement best describes the central conflict between the Emperor and Ixta?
   a. The Emperor did not feel Ixta was fit to rule the kingdom after his death.
   b. Ixta wanted to rule the kingdom immediately; she did not want to wait until the Emperor's death.
   c. The Emperor forbade Ixta to marry anyone, for he wanted her to rule alone.
   d. The Emperor forbade Ixta to marry Popo, but she was allowed to marry another warrior.

What is the correct answer to the question above? How were you able to eliminate the other answers? How did your application of the reading strategy help you?

_____

_____

2. Which statement best describes the resolution of the main conflict in "Popocatépetl and Ixtacihuatl"?
   a. After many hardships, Popo and Ixta marry and rule Tenochtitlan together.
   b. Popo is killed in battle, and Ixta dies from grief.
   c. Popo is successful in defeating the Emperor's enemies, winning Ixta's hand in marriage and the right to rule Tenochtitlan with her.
   d. Popo buries Ixta in a huge pyramid, and he himself dies atop a twin pyramid.

What is the correct answer to the question above? How were you able to eliminate the other answers? How did your application of the reading strategy help you?

_____

_____

THINK-ALOUD NOTES

_____

_____

_____

_____

_____

_____

_____

_____

_____

_____

_____

Investigate, Inquire, and Imagine

RECALL: GATHER FACTS
1a. After Popo's victory, how do some of his fellow warriors behave? How does Ixta respond to the news about Popo's performance in battle? What does she do? Why?

INTERPRET: FIND MEANING
1b. What emotion drives some of the warriors to betray Popo? Why does Popo refuse to rule Tenochtitlan? What does he do instead?

ANALYZE: TAKE THINGS APART
2a. How are the reactions of Popo and Ixta to their separation similar? How are their reactions different?

SYNTHESIZE: BRING THINGS TOGETHER
2b. What do the two pyramids become? Why do you think the people of Tenochtitlan developed this story?

EVALUATE: MAKE JUDGMENTS
3a. Which people are to blame for the tragic end of the two lovers? Who is most at fault? Why? What could have been done to prevent the tragedy?

EXTEND: CONNECT IDEAS
3b. What morals, or messages, can be taken from this story? What does the story tell you about the values of the Aztec people?

Literary Tools

FORESHADOWING. **Foreshadowing** is the act of presenting materials that hint at events to occur later in the story. Find three examples of foreshadowing in "Popocatépetl and Ixtacihuatl." What is foreshadowed?

Example of Foreshadowing	Prediction
Some doubt the Emperor's wisdom.	The Emperor may do something foolish.

Read-Write Connection

How do you feel when you have played by the rules, only to lose to someone who cheats or plays unfairly? Use your own paper to answer this question.

WordWorkshop

<small>USING CONTEXT CLUES.</small> The following words are found in "Popocatépetl and Ixtacihuatl." Write down how each word is used in the story. Use the page number listed to locate each word. Use clues in the text to define each in your own words. Then note the dictionary definition. Use the example as a guide.

<small>EXAMPLE</small>
adamant, page 212
Sentence: This unfortunate but moderately happy relationship between Ixta and Popo continued for several years, the couple pleading with the Emperor at regular intervals and the Emperor remaining constantly _adamant_.
Sentence Clues/Definition from Context: "Remains" and "constantly" hint that the Emperor has an iron will and is unwilling to change. Therefore, _adamant_ must mean something like "resistant to changing one's mind or opinion."
Dictionary Definition: unshakeable; not giving in

1. splendor, page 211

   Sentence:_____

   Sentence Clues: _____

   Dictionary Definition: _____

2. disposition, page 211

   Sentence:_____

   Sentence Clues: _____

   Dictionary Definition: _____

3. forsaken, page 213

   Sentence:_____

   Sentence Clues: _____

   Dictionary Definition: _____

4. acclaimed, page 215

   Sentence:_____

   Sentence Clues: _____

   Dictionary Definition: _____

Beyond the Reading

<small>UNEARTHING INFORMATION.</small> Read more about topics related to "Popocatépetl and Ixtacihuatl." Among the topics to consider are volcanoes, star-crossed lovers, myths that explain natural elements, the Aztec culture, or Aztec myths. Share your information in a written, oral, or illustrated presentation.

<small>GO ONLINE.</small> Visit the EMC Internet Resource Center at **emcp.com** to find links and additional activities for this selection.

Reader's resource

King Arthur and His Knights of the Round Table, like other Arthurian legends, is set in England in approximately the fifth or sixth century AD. This excerpt, from Roger Lancelyn Green's first of four volumes about King Arthur, retells the story of Arthur's birth and rise to leadership. Like many other chronicles of King Arthur, Green's story is based primarily on Thomas Malory's *Le Morte d'Arthur.* However, Green adds material from several other texts—British, French, and even Latin poetry, prose, and analysis—to present a complete picture of the Arthur story. Notice that Green uses British spellings such as *centre* for *center* and *armour* for *armor.*

Word watch

PREVIEW VOCABULARY

churl	ravage
homage	vengeance

Reader's journal

In your opinion, what qualities are important for leadership?

_____

_____

_____

from King Arthur and His Knights of the Round Table

Retold by Roger Lancelyn Green

Active READING STRATEGY

CONNECT TO PRIOR KNOWLEDGE

Before Reading ➤ ACTIVATE PRIOR KNOWLEDGE

❑ Read the Reader's Resource. Discuss what you know about King Arthur.
❑ Use a K-W-L Chart to organize what you know, what you want to know, and what you learned.
❑ Fill in the first two columns before you begin reading.

Graphic Organizer

What I *Know* about King Arthur	What I *Want* to Know about King Arthur	What I Have *Learned* about King Arthur

Retold by Roger Lancelyn Green

CHAPTER I

THE TWO SWORDS

After wicked King Vortigern had first invited the Saxons
to settle in Britain and help him to fight the Picts and
Scots, the land was never long at peace. Although so much
of it was covered with thick forests, much also was beautiful
open country, with little villages and towns, country houses
and cottages, as the Romans had left it not many years
before. Having once seen it, the Saxons could never again
be contented with their savage, unfruitful homes in
Germany and Denmark; and year by year more and more of
10   them came stealing across the North Sea in their long ships,
to kill or drive out the Britons and settle in their homes.

Vortigern was dead, and Aurelius Ambrosius, last of the
Romans, was dead too, when Uther Pendragon, whom
some call the brother of Ambrosius, led the Britons. He
defeated the Saxons in many battles, and brought peace to
the southern lands where he was king—to London, and to
Winchester, which was then called Camelot, and to
Cornwall where Gorlois his loyal follower was duke. But
Uther fell in love with Gorlois's wife, the lovely Igrayne,
20   and there was battle between them, until Gorlois fell, and
Uther married his widow.

He visited her first in the haunted castle of Tintagel, the
dark castle by the Cornish sea, and Merlin the enchanter
watched over their love. One child was born to Uther and
Igrayne—but what became of that baby boy only the wise

CONNECT TO PRIOR
KNOWLEDGE

❑ Follow along in the text
as your teacher reads
aloud the first three
paragraphs of the excerpt
from *King Arthur and His
Knights of the Round Table*
(through line 28 on page
224).

❑ Discuss the information
presented in this section.
Add what you learn to
your K-W-L Chart before
you continue reading.

❑ Read the rest of the
selection on your own.
Try to connect the new
information presented in
the legend with what you
already know about
Arthurian stories.
Continue recording
information in your K-W-L
Chart as you read.

Reading STRATEGY
REVIEW

USE TEXT ORGANIZATION.
Keep track of the plot by
listing important things
that happen. What
important things have
happened so far?

_____

_____

_____

_____

_____

MARK THE TEXT

Underline or highlight what happens to the son of Uther and Igrayne.

DRAW A PICTURE

Create a family tree that shows what happened to the children of Igrayne and Gorlois.

Literary TOOLS

LEGEND. A **legend** is a story coming down from the past, often based on real events or characters from older times. Unlike myths, legends are popularly regarded as historical; however, they may contain elements that are fantastic or unverifiable. What elements of a legend do you note so far?

_____

_____

_____

Merlin could have told, for he carried it away by a secret path down the cliff side in the dead of night, and no word was spoken of its fate.

30   Uther had no other children, though Igrayne and Gorlois had three daughters; two of these were grown-up when Igrayne became queen, and were married—Morgawse to Lot, King of Orkney,[1] and Elaine to Nantres, King of Garlot: they had sons who in after days were among the bravest Knights of the Round Table. But the third daughter, Morgana le Fay, was still only a child, and she was sent to school in a nunnery; yet, by some means, she learnt much magic, which she used wickedly.

King Uther Pendragon had only a little while of happiness with the fair Igrayne, for soon the Saxons made war against

40   him once more, and sent a traitor to serve him, who poisoned the King and many of his followers.

Then the land fell upon days more evil and wretched than any which had gone before. King Uther's knights fought amongst themselves, quarrelling as to who should rule; and the Saxons, seeing that there was no strong man to lead the Britons against them, conquered more and more of Britain.

Years of strife and misery went by, until the appointed time was at hand. Then Merlin, the good enchanter, came out from the deep, mysterious valleys of North Wales,

50   which in those days was called Gwynedd, through Powys or South Wales, and passed on his way to London. And so great was his fame that neither Saxon nor Briton dared molest him.

Merlin came to London and spoke with the Archbishop; and a great gathering of knights was called for Christmas Day—so great that all of them could not find a place in the abbey church, so that some were forced to gather in the churchyard.

In the middle of the service, there arose suddenly a

60   murmur of wonder outside the abbey: for there was seen, though no man saw it come, a great square slab of marble-stone in the churchyard, and on the stone an anvil[2] of iron, and set point downwards a great, shining sword of steel thrust deeply into the anvil.

_____

1. **Orkney.** Region of Scotland
2. **anvil.** Heavy iron block on which metal is hammered into shape

"Stir not till the service be done," commanded the Archbishop when this marvel was made known to him. "But pray the more unto God that we may find a remedy for the sore wounds of our land."

When the service was ended the Archbishop and the lords and knights who had been within the abbey came out to see the wonder of the sword. Round about the anvil they found letters of gold set in the great stone, and the letters read thus:

WHOSO PULLETH OUT THIS SWORD FROM THIS STONE AND ANVIL IS THE TRUE-BORN KING OF ALL BRITAIN.

When they saw this, many and many a man tried to pull out the sword—but not one of them could stir it a hair's breadth.

"He is not here," said the Archbishop. "But doubt not that God will send us our King. Let messengers be sent through all the land to tell what is written on the stone: and upon New Year's Day we will hold a great tournament, and see whether our King is amongst those who come to joust. Until then, I counsel that we appoint ten knights to guard the stone, and set a rich pavilion over it."

All this was done, and upon New Year's Day a great host of knights met together. But none as yet could draw forth the sword out of the stone. Then they went all a little way off, and pitched tents, and held a tournament or sham fight, trying their strength and skill at jousting with long lances of wood, or fighting with broad-swords.

It happened that among those who came was the good knight Sir Ector, and his son Kay, who had been made a knight not many months before; and with them came Arthur, Sir Kay's young brother, a youth of scarcely sixteen years of age.

Riding to the jousts, Sir Kay found suddenly that he had left his sword in his lodgings, and he asked Arthur to ride back and fetch it for him.

"Certainly I will," said Arthur, who was always ready to do anything for other people, and back he rode to the town. But Sir Kay's mother had locked the door, and gone out to see the tournament, so that Arthur could not get into the lodgings at all.

This troubled Arthur very much. "My brother Kay must have a sword," he thought, as he rode slowly back. "It will

CONNECT TO PRIOR KNOWLEDGE. Have you heard of the sword-in-the-stone story before? What do you think happens to the sword?

_____

_____

_____

Reading STRATEGY REVIEW

TACKLE DIFFICULT VOCABULARY. Use the context to determine the meaning of the words *joust* (lines 83 and 90) and *sham* (line 89).

Take a Break
If you have difficulty understanding the events, take a break to organize your thoughts and make new connections. Review your K-W-L Chart, and read the details you have collected. Reread sections if the details are unclear to you. When you feel confident about your knowledge of the selection thus far, resume your reading.
    Take a break to review your notes whenever you become confused or cannot remember what you have read. Reread lines 111–118. Add to your chart what Arthur does.

NOTE THE FACTS

What does Kay know about the sword that Arthur does not know? What does Kay try to claim?

_____

_____

_____

DRAW A PICTURE

Sketch what you think the sword and the anvil look like.

be a shame and a matter for unkind jests if so young a knight comes to the jousts without a sword. But where can I find him one? . . . I know! I saw one sticking in an anvil in the churchyard, I'll fetch that: it's doing no good there!"

110

So Arthur set spurs to his horse and came to the churchyard. Tying his horse to the stile, he ran to the tent which had been set over the stone—and found that all ten of the guardian knights had also gone to the tournament. Without stopping to read what was written on the stone, Arthur pulled out the sword at a touch, ran back to his horse, and in a few minutes had caught up with Sir Kay and handed it over to him.

Arthur knew nothing of what sword it was, but Kay had

120

already tried to pull it from the anvil, and saw at a glance that it was the same one. Instantly he rode to his father Sir Ector, and said:

"Sir! Look, here is the sword out of the stone! So you see I must be the true-born King of all Britain!"

But Sir Ector knew better than to believe Sir Kay too readily. Instead, he rode back with him to the church, and there made him swear a solemn oath with his hands on the Bible to say truly how he came by the sword.

"My brother Arthur brought it to me," said Kay, with a

130

sigh.

"And how did *you* get the sword?" asked Sir Ector.

"Sir, I will tell you," said Arthur, fearing that he had done wrong. "Kay sent me to fetch his sword, but I could not come to it. Then I remembered having seen this sword sticking uselessly into an anvil in the churchyard. I thought it could be put to a better use in my brother's hand—so I fetched it."

"Did you find no knights guarding the sword?" asked Sir Ector.

140

"Never a one," said Arthur.

"Well, put the sword back into the anvil, and let us see you draw it out," commanded Sir Ector.

"That's easily done," said Arthur, puzzled by all this trouble over a sword, and he set it back easily into the anvil.

Then Sir Kay seized it by the hilt and pulled his hardest: but struggle and strain as he might, he could not move it by a hair's breadth. Sir Ector tried also, but with no better success.

150   "Pull it out," he said to Arthur.

And Arthur, more and more bewildered, put his hand to the hilt and drew forth the sword as if out of a well-greased scabbard.[3]

"Now," said Sir Ector, kneeling before Arthur and bowing his head in reverence, "I understand that you and none other are the true-born King of this land."

"Why? Oh, why is it I? Why do you kneel to me, my father?" cried Arthur.

"It is God's will that whoso might draw forth the sword
160 out of the stone and out of the anvil is the true-born King of Britain," said Sir Ector. "Moreover, though I love you well, you are no son of mine. For Merlin brought you to me when you were a small child, and bade me bring you up as my own son!"

"Then if I am indeed King," said Arthur, bowing his head over the cross-hilt of the sword, "I hereby pledge myself to the service of God and of my people, to the righting of wrongs, to the driving-out of evil, to the bringing of peace and plenty to my land . . . Good sir, you have been as a
170 father to me since ever I can remember, be still near me with a father's love and a father's counsel and advice . . . Kay, my foster-brother, be you seneschal[4] over all my lands and a true knight of my court."

After this they went to the Archbishop and told him all. But the knights and barons were filled with rage and jealousy, and refused to believe that Arthur was the true-born King. So the choice was put off until Easter; and at Easter once more until Whitsun, or Pentecost[5] as it then was called: but still, though many kings and knights
180 came to try their strength, Arthur alone could pull out the sword.

Then all the people cried: "Arthur! We will have Arthur! By God's will he is our King! God save King Arthur!" And they knelt down before him, the noble and the humble together, the rich and the poor, and cried him mercy for delaying him so long. And Arthur forgave them readily, and

---

3. **scabbard.** Case or sheath for a sword
4. **seneschal.** Person in charge of lands or resources
5. **Whitsun, or Pentecost.** Christian festival seven Sundays after Easter

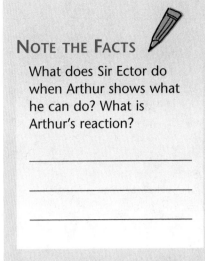

NOTE THE FACTS

What does Sir Ector do when Arthur shows what he can do? What is Arthur's reaction?

_____

_____

_____

MARK THE TEXT

Underline or highlight the pledge that Arthur makes.

TACKLE DIFFICULT VOCABULARY.
Use the Words for Everyday
Use to determine the meaning
of the words *homage* (line
190) and *ravaged* (line 197).

NOTE THE FACTS

What does Merlin do to
protect Arthur?

_____

_____

_____

kneeling down himself he gave the wondrous sword to the
Archbishop and received of him the high and holy order of
Knighthood. And then came all the earls and barons, the

190 knights and squires, and did <u>homage</u> to Arthur, swearing to
serve and obey him as was their duty.

King Arthur now gathered together all the hosts of
Britain, and with the pick of the older knights who had
served his father and the younger knights whose chief desire
was to show their courage and loyalty, he set out to do battle
with the Saxons and to punish all those thieves and robbers
who had <u>ravaged</u> the land for many years, doing cruel and
shameful deeds.

Before long he had brought peace and safety to the

200 southern parts of Britain, making his capital at Camelot. But
the other kings who ruled then in and about Britain—the
Kings of Orkney and Lothian, of Gwynedd and Powys, of
Gorre and Garlot—grew jealous of this unknown boy who
was calling himself King of all Britain, and sent word that
they were coming to visit him with gifts—but that their gifts
would be given with sharp swords between the head and
shoulders.

Then Merlin came suddenly to Arthur and led him to the
city of Caerleon in South Wales, into a strong tower well

210 provisioned for a siege. The hostile kings came also to
Caerleon and surrounded the tower: but they could not
break in, to kill Arthur and his faithful followers.

Merlin came out of the tower after fifteen days, stood
upon the steps in the gateway and asked all the angry kings
and knights why they came in arms against King Arthur.

"Why have you made that boy, that Arthur, our King?"
they shouted.

"Be silent and listen, all of you!" commanded Merlin, and
a great quiet fell upon all who were gathered together, an

220 awe and a wonder as the good enchanter spoke to them.

"I will tell you of wondrous things," he said. "Arthur is
indeed your King, the rightful King of all this land—yes,

words for everyday use	**hom • age** (häm′ ij) *n.*, acts done to show honor and respect. *Jergen knelt in* <u>*homage*</u> *before the king.*
	rav • age (rav′ ij) *vt.*, destroy; ruin. *The storm* <u>*ravaged*</u> *the towns up and down the shore, leaving behind a wake of destruction and despair.*

and of Wales too, of Ireland and Scotland and Orkney also, and of Armorica[6] beyond the sea; and he shall rule other lands also. He is the true and only son of the good King Uther Pendragon! Of his birth and of the things which should befall when he was King, I knew by my holy arts. Uther came to Tintagel in the form of Gorlois three hours after Gorlois was dead: then and thus he comforted the

230 Lady Igrayne and won her to be his wife. But, so my knowledge told me, their son, this Arthur, was born to great and wondrous things. A little while after his birth at dark Tintagel, Uther, who hearkened to my words, gave the child into my care, and I bore him to Avalon, the Land of Mystery. And the Dwellers in Avalon—you know them not, but you would call them Fairies and Elves—cast a pure and great enchantment upon the child, a magic most strong. Three gifts they gave to Arthur: that he should be the best of all knights; that he should be the greatest king this land

240 shall ever know; and that he should live long—longer than any man shall ever know. These, the virtues of a good and generous prince, the Dwellers in Avalon gave to Arthur. And in Avalon the elves are forging Excalibur to be the sword of his right—the clean flashing blade that shall be raised only in the cause of right, shining on the earth until the time comes when they shall call it back again. . . . Arthur is your King! Year by year as he reigns, his kingdom shall grow—not Britain, nor the islands of the seas, no, nor Armorica and Gaul[7]—but Logres,[8] the land of blessing,

250 God's Kingdom upon earth, which Arthur shall show you for a little space before the darkness falls again."

There was silence for a while when Merlin had finished speaking, for all those who heard him felt that they were at the beginning of a time of wonders, and that Arthur was more than just a King who ruled because his father had been King, or because he was the strongest man amongst them.

Suddenly they all knelt before him where he stood above Merlin on the steps of the tower, and with one voice

260 promised to be his true and faithful subjects all the days of their lives.

---

6. **Armorica.** Brittany, in France
7. **Gaul.** France
8. **Logres.** Kingdom of Britain ruled by Arthur

This section of the text is very long, without any paragraph breaks. Learn to read (silently in your head) as though you are one of the characters. In this section, read as though you are Merlin telling other kings and knights about Arthur. Underline important things you, as Merlin, say about Arthur.

NOTE THE FACTS

How do the people feel about Arthur after Merlin's speech?

_____

_____

_____

MARK THE TEXT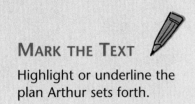

Highlight or underline the
plan Arthur sets forth.

WHAT DO YOU
WONDER?

_____

_____

_____

Then the Archbishop set the crown upon Arthur's head,
and the people cheered him once more: and this was the
real beginning of his reign.

"Tomorrow we will begin to collect our forces," said King
Arthur. "And when all are gathered together, we march to the
north and to the east to do battle with the Saxons and drive
them out of Britain. Then we will build castles and set guards
along the coast so that never again may they invade us: we will
270 rebuild the churches which they have destroyed, and build
new ones to the glory of God; and our knights shall ride about
the country punishing all those who break the peace and do ill
to any. And if any man or woman, be he or she the greatest or
the least of my subjects, be in any trouble, or have complaint
against any man, let them come to me, and never shall their
sorrow go uncomforted and their wrong unrighted."

King Arthur feasted that day in the great castle of
Caerleon: but before ever the feast was ended there befell
the first of the marvelous adventures that were to happen in
280 the wonderland of Logres during his reign.

Suddenly into the courtyard there rode a young squire,
leading another horse, across the saddle of which lay the
body of a knight but newly slain.

"Vengeance, lord King!" cried the squire, when Arthur
came from the hall to learn what this might mean. "Give me
vengeance! Here lies Sir Miles, dead upon his steed, as
goodly a knight and as brave as any in the land. In the forest
not many leagues[9] from here King Pellinore has set up his
pavilion beside the high road, by a well of fresh water, and
290 he goes about to slay all knights that pass this way. Where-
fore I pray you that my master be honourably buried, and
that some knight ride out to avenge his death."

There was a certain squire in Arthur's court, whose name
was Gryflet, no older than Arthur himself, and now he fell
on his knees before the King and begged him for all his
service to make him a knight so that he might go out and
fight with Pellinore.

---

9. **leagues.** Units of measurement equal to about three miles

**words
for
everyday
use**   **ven • geance** (ven' jəns) *n.*, return of an injury for an injury; revenge. *I tried to*
make Arden forgive and forget, but she was out for <u>vengeance</u>.

"You are not old enough yet for such a battle," said King Arthur, "nor have you grown great enough in strength."

300   "Yet, make me a knight!" begged Gryflet.

"My lord," said Merlin quietly to Arthur, "it were a great pity to lose Gryflet, for he would be a passing good man when he comes of age, and would be your faithful knight all his life . . . Pellinore is the strongest man in the world now bearing arms, and surely Gryflet will be slain if they come to sword strokes."

King Arthur nodded, and turned again to his young squire: "Gryflet," he said, "kneel, and I will make you a knight according to your wish." And when this was done, he

310   went on: "And now, Sir Gryflet, since I have made you knight, surely you owe me a gift."

"My lord, whatever you shall ask is yours," said Gryflet.

"Promise me then," commanded Arthur, "by your honour as a knight, that when you come upon King Pellinore by the well in the forest, you joust but with your spears and, on horseback or on foot, fight with him in no other wise."[10]

"That will I promise you," said Gryflet; and then he took his horse in great haste, snatched up his spear, slung his

320   shield on his left arm, and went off in a cloud of dust until he came to the well-side in the forest. And there he saw a rich pavilion, and before it a horse ready saddled and bridled, and at the side a tree on which hung a shield painted in bright colours, and by it a great spear.

Sir Gryflet hit the shield with the butt of his own spear so hard that it came clattering to the ground, and King Pellinore came out of the pavilion—a tall, strong man as fierce as a lion.

"Sir knight!" he cried, "why smote you down my shield?"

330   "Sir, for that I would joust with you!" answered Gryflet.

"It were better that you did not," said King Pellinore. "You are but a new, young knight, and not so strong as I!"

"In spite of that, I will joust with you," repeated Gryflet.

"Well, this is by no desire of mine," said King Pellinore as he buckled on his armour, "but let things fall as they must. Whose knight are you?"

Reading STRATEGY REVIEW

MAKE PREDICTIONS. From what you know about heroic tales, what do you think will happen to Pellinore?

_____

_____

_____

MARK THE TEXT

Highlight or underline what Arthur has Gryflet promise.

_____

10. **in no other wise.** In no other way

"Sir, I am one of King Arthur's court!" cried Gryflet. And with that they rode away in either direction along the road, then turned their horses, set their spears in rest, and

340 galloped at one another as hard as they could. Sir Gryflet's spear struck the shield of King Pellinore and broke all to pieces: but King Pellinore's spear went straight through Gryflet's shield, deep into his side, and there broke off short. And Sir Gryflet and his horse fell upon the ground.

King Pellinore came and bent over Sir Gryflet, who lay still where he had fallen, and unloosed his helmet. "Well, this was a brave youth," said Pellinore, "and if he lives, will be a mighty knight." Then he placed Gryflet across the saddle, and the horse galloped back to Caerleon with none

350 to guide it.

Arthur was very wroth when he saw how badly hurt was Sir Gryflet, and at once he put on his own armour, closed the vizor of his helmet so that no one could see his face, and with spear in hand rode hard into the forest to be revenged upon King Pellinore.

But on his way he found three robbers attacking Merlin, and they seemed like to beat him to death with great clubs.

"Fly, <u>churls</u>!" cried Arthur, riding at them furiously, and the three cowards turned and fled when they saw the knight

360 charging at them.

"Ah, Merlin," said Arthur, "for all your wisdom and your magic, you would have been murdered in a few minutes if I had not come to your rescue!"

"Not so," answered Merlin, smiling his mysterious smile. "Easily could I have saved myself, had I willed it. It is you who draw near to your death—for you go towards it in your pride, if God does not aid you."

But Arthur would not take heed of Merlin's wisdom, and rode fiercely on until he came to the rich pavilion by the

370 well. And there sat King Pellinore upon his great war-horse, waiting for him.

"Sir knight!" cried Arthur, "why stand you here, fighting and striking down all the knights who ride this way?"

words for everyday use

churl (churl) *n.*, surly, mean person. *"What a <u>churl</u>!" Helen sputtered after the cashier slammed down her change with a <u>surly</u> glare.*

"It is my custom to do so," answered Pellinore sternly. "And if any man would make me change my custom, let him try at his peril!"

"I will make you change it!" cried Arthur.

"And I will defend my custom," replied Pellinore quietly.

Then they drew apart, and came riding together at full
380 tilt, so hard that both spears shivered into little pieces as each hit the centre of the other's shield. Arthur would have drawn his sword then, but Pellinore said:

"Not so, let us run together with spears yet again."

"So I would," said Arthur, "if I had another spear!"

"I have plenty," answered Pellinore, and he shouted to his squire to bring two out of the pavilion.

Once more the two kings jousted together; and once more their spears broke into fragments without either of them being struck from his horse. A third time they jousted, and
390 Arthur's spear broke, but King Pellinore's struck him so hard in the middle of the shield that horse and man fell to the earth.

But Arthur sprang to his feet in a great fury, drawing his sword and shouting defiance at Pellinore, who thereupon came down from his horse and drew his own sword. Then began a fierce battle, with many great strokes; they hacked and hewed at one another, cutting pieces off their shields and armour, and suffering each of them so many wounds that the trampled grass in front of the pavilion was stained
400 with red. They rested once, and then charged each other again: but their swords met together with so mighty a crash that Arthur's broke in two, leaving him with the useless hilt in his hand.

"Ah-ha!" cried King Pellinore. "Now you are in my power, to slay or spare as I will! And I will kill you forthwith, unless you kneel and yield to me, confessing yourself to be a knight of little worth."

"There are two ways with that," cried Arthur, mad with shame and fury. "Death is welcome when it comes; but to
410 yield—never!" And with that he leapt in under Pellinore's sword, seized him round the waist and hurled him to the ground. They struggled there for a while, but Pellinore was still the strongest, and presently he tore off Arthur's helmet and took up his sword to cut his head off also.

Reading STRATEGY REVIEW

MAKE PREDICTIONS. What will happen when Arthur and Pellinore fight?

_____

_____

_____

THINK AND REFLECT

What does Arthur think of surrender? What does that tell you about his values? (Analyze)

_____

_____

_____

MARK THE TEXT

Underline or highlight words or phrases that show how Pellinore's anger is stopped.

But Merlin came suddenly and laid his hand on Pellinore's shoulder: "Knight," he said, "hold your hand and do not strike this stroke. For if you do the hope of Logres dies, and you put this land of Britain into the greatest ruin and desolation that ever a country suffered."

420   "Who is it?" asked Pellinore.

"This is King Arthur!" said Merlin.

For a moment Pellinore was tempted to strike the blow: for he feared that if Arthur lived, he would never forgive him for what he had done. But Merlin smiled quietly, and placed his hand on Pellinore's head. And at once all the anger and fear went from his mind, and he sank back quietly against the tree beside the well of clear water, and passed into a deep sleep.

Merlin helped King Arthur, who was sorely wounded, to
430   mount his horse, and led him away into the forest.

"Alas, Merlin, what have you done?" asked Arthur; for now he had put from him all the pride and wilfulness which had so nearly caused his death. "You have killed this good knight by your magic—and I would rather have lost my kingdom than that one so brave and mighty should die thus."

"Cease to trouble," said Merlin. "For all things work by the will of God and to the glory of Logres. He is more like to live than you are, for you are sorely wounded, and he
440   does but sleep . . . I told you how mighty a fighter he was. This is King Pellinore who in time to come shall do you good service. And his sons, Sir Tor and Sir Lamorak, shall be among the bravest of your knights."

Then Merlin brought Arthur to a hermitage where lived a good old man who was a clever leech, or healer of wounds. And in three days he was nearly cured, and could ride once more and fight as strongly as ever.

"Alas," said Arthur as they rode through the forest. "Now I have no sword."

450   "Let not that trouble you," said Merlin. "There was no virtue in the sword which is lost: it has served its purpose. But near here your own sword awaits you: it was made in Avalon by fairy craft, made for you alone until you must return it ere you journey to Avalon yourself. It is called Excalibur, and none may stand against its stroke: and with it you shall bring freedom and peace to Logres. This is the

Use THE STRATEGY

CONNECT TO PRIOR KNOWLEDGE. What is the meaning of a leech today? What does *leech* mean in this story?

_____

_____

_____

hour appointed when Excalibur shall be placed in your hand—for now you will grasp its hilt in all humility, and draw it only to defend the right."

460   Deeper and deeper into the forest they went, and before long the hills rose on either side until they were riding through a narrow valley that wound through dark mountains. And at last they came to a narrow pass in the rocks, and beyond it, in a cup of the mountains, Arthur saw a strange lake. All around it the hills rose darkly and desolately, but the lake water was of the clearest, sunniest blue, and the shore was covered thickly in fresh green grass and flowers. Over the brow of a little rise beyond the lake, the mountains opened out into a great plain, and beyond it

470 was water, half hidden in mist, and broken with many islands.

    "This is the Lake of the Fairy Palace," said Merlin, "and beyond the lake, over the brow of the hill yonder, lies the plain of Camlann where the last battle shall be fought, and you shall fall beneath the stroke of the Evil Knight. And beyond the plain lies Avalon, hidden in the mist and the mysterious waters . . . Go down now and speak with the Lady of the Lake, while I wait for you here."

    Leaving his horse with Merlin, Arthur went down the

480 steep path to the side of the magic lake. Standing on the shore, he looked out across the quiet blue water—and there in the very centre of the Lake he saw an arm clothed in white samite[11] with a hand holding above the surface a wondrous sword with a golden hilt set with jewels, and a jewelled scabbard and belt.

    And then Arthur saw a beautiful damsel dressed in pale blue silk with a golden girdle, who walked across the water until she stood before him on the shore.

    "I am the Lady of the Lake," she said, "and I am come to

490 tell you that your sword Excalibur awaits you yonder. Do you wish to take the sword and wear it at your side?"

    "Damsel," said Arthur, "that is indeed my wish."

    "For long I have guarded the sword," said the Lady of the Lake. "Give me but a gift when I shall come to ask you for one, and the sword shall be yours."

---

11. **samite.** Heavy silk cloth, often interwoven with gold or silver, commonly worn in the Middle Ages

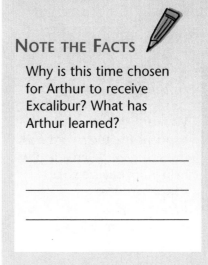

NOTE THE FACTS

Why is this time chosen for Arthur to receive Excalibur? What has Arthur learned?

_____

_____

_____

MARK THE TEXT

Underline or highlight what is going to happen to Arthur.

Reading STRATEGY
            REVIEW

VISUALIZE. Picture what Arthur saw in the "very centre of the Lake." Continue your visualization by picturing what the "beautiful damsel" does.

NOTE THE FACTS

Name some elements of fantasy that have appeared in the story so far.

_____

_____

_____

THINK AND REFLECT

What advice does Merlin give Arthur? Does Arthur heed the advice? What change in Arthur does his reaction to Merlin's advice demonstrate? **(Evaluate)**

_____

_____

_____

"By my faith," answered Arthur, "I swear to give you whatsoever gift you shall ask for."

"Enter into this boat, then," said the Lady of the Lake.
500 And Arthur saw a barge floating on the water before him, into which he stepped. The Lady of the Lake stood on the shore behind him, but the barge moved across the water as if unseen hands drew it by the keel, until Arthur came beside the arm clothed in white samite. Leaning out, he took the sword and the scabbard: and at once the arm and the hand which had held it sank quietly out of sight beneath the blue waters.

Then the barge brought Arthur to the shore where the Lady of the Lake had stood: but now she was gone also. He
510 tied the barge to a tree-root which curved over the water-side, and strode joyfully up the steep path to the pass, buckling the sword Excalibur to his side as he went.

Merlin awaited him with the horses, and together they rode away into the forest, and back by many winding paths until they drew near the river which lay between them and Caerleon, and came to the straight, paved road leading to the city.

"In a little while," said Merlin, "King Pellinore will come riding towards us. For he has ceased to do battle with all
520 who pass through the forest, having seen a Questing Beast which he must follow now for many years."

"Then I will fight with him once more," cried Arthur. "Now that I have so good a sword as Excalibur maybe I shall overcome and slay him!"

Merlin shook his head: "Let him pass," he said, "for so I counsel you. He is a brave knight and a mighty, and in days to come he will do you good service, and he and his sons shall be among the bravest in your court."

"I will do as you advise me," said Arthur. But he looked
530 upon the sword Excalibur, and sighed.

"Which like you better, the sword or the scabbard?" asked Merlin.

"I like the sword!" cried Arthur.

"Then are you the more unwise," said Merlin gravely. "The scabbard is worth ten such swords: for while you wear that magic scabbard you shall lose but little blood, however sorely you are wounded. Keep well that scabbard, and have good care of it after I am gone from you, for a certain

wicked lady who is nearly related to you shall seek to steal
540   both sword and scabbard."

They rode on, and in a little while met King Pellinore—
who rode past as if he had not seen them.

"I marvel," said Arthur, "that he did not even speak to us!"

"He saw you not," answered Merlin, "for my magic was
upon him. But had you striven to stay him in your pride,
then he would have seen you well enough."

Before long they came to Caerleon, and his knights
welcomed Arthur joyfully. And when they heard of his
adventures, they were surprised that he should thus have
550   gone into danger alone. But all the bravest and noblest of
them rejoiced exceedingly that they had such a king, one
who would risk his life in an adventure as other ordinary
knights did. ■

Use THE STRATEGY

CONNECT TO PRIOR
KNOWLEDGE. What warning
does Merlin give Arthur?
What do you think might
happen based on what
you know about King
Arthur?

_____

_____

_____

Reflect ON YOUR READING

When you finish reading, examine the notes you made as you read. Review your K-W-L Chart, filling in the chart with information you gathered as you read. Then, write a brief essay summarizing the most important parts of your K-W-L Chart. In your essay, explain what you knew before you began reading, what you learned as you read, and what more you would like to learn about King Arthur, Merlin, and the knights. When you finish writing, share your essay with a partner, and discuss how you gathered information for the K-W-L Chart.

Reading Skills and Test Practice

ANALYZE CHARACTER DEVELOPMENT

READ, THINK, AND EXPLAIN. Discuss with a partner how to analyze character development in the following passage. Then, use your own paper as needed to answer the questions.

> "Then if I am indeed King," said Arthur, bowing his head over the cross-hilt of the sword, "I hereby pledge myself to the service of God and of my people, to the rightings of wrongs, to the driving-out of evil, to the bringing of peace and plenty to my land. . . ."

1. What does this passage suggest about Arthur's character? Use details from the passage to support your analysis.

_____

_____

_____

2. Does Arthur honor his vow at all times? Or does he make decisions that betray this pledge? Go back to the story and find details that support your ideas.

_____

_____

_____

REFLECT ON YOUR RESPONSE. Compare your response to that of your partner. What helped you analyze Arthur's character development?

_____

_____

THINK-ALOUD NOTES

_____

_____

_____

_____

_____

_____

_____

_____

_____

_____

_____

_____

_____

Investigate, Inquire, and Imagine

RECALL: GATHER FACTS
1a. When and where were the terms set out to select Britain's new king? What were those terms? How were they met and by whom?

→ INTERPRET: FIND MEANING
1b. How does Arthur envision his new role? How does he hope to change Britain's situation? What promises does he make to the people?

ANALYZE: TAKE THINGS APART
2a. Analyze the role Merlin plays in Arthur's early years and his transformation to king. What special gifts does Arthur have because of Merlin's guidance? What signs of magic are there in Merlin's interaction with Arthur?

→ SYNTHESIZE: BRING THINGS TOGETHER
2b. How does Arthur's relationship with Merlin change by the end of the selection?

EVALUATE: MAKE JUDGMENTS
3a. Why do you think the people of Britain believe Arthur's claim to the throne? Why is his leadership so attractive?

→ EXTEND: CONNECT IDEAS
3b. What can you infer from this story about the rest of Arthur's life and reign as king?

Literary Tools

LEGEND. A **legend** is a story coming down from the past, often based on real events or characters from older times. Unlike myths, legends are popularly regarded as historical; however, they may contain elements that are fantastic or unverifiable. Use the cluster chart below to list elements in the King Arthur story that make it a legend.

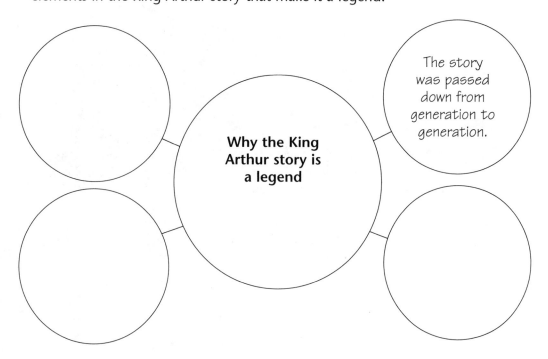

The story was passed down from generation to generation.

Why the King Arthur story is a legend

WordWorkshop

Synonyms. The word **synonym** is from the Greek for "same + name." Synonyms are words or expressions from the same language that have the same or nearly the same meaning in some or all senses.

Match each of the following words from *King Arthur and His Knights of the Round Table* with the word that has the most similar meaning. Use the context in the story or a dictionary to figure out the meaning of words you do not know. The number behind each word indicates on which page the word appears in the story.

_____1. churl, 232   a. destroy
_____2. homage, 228   b. a nasty person
_____3. ravage, 228   c. knightly combat
_____4. vengeance, 230   d. a horse's headgear
_____5. joust, 231   e. great anger
_____6. sham, 225   f. a knight's assistant
_____7. hilt, 235   g. revenge
_____8. squire, 230   h. imitation
_____9. bridle, 231   i. a sword's handle
_____10.wroth, 232   j. honor

Read-Write Connection

If you had lived in King Arthur's time, would you have supported him as a king? Would you have wanted to serve in his court? Why, or why not?

_____

_____

_____

_____

_____

Beyond the Reading

Further Tales of the Round Table. With a small group of your classmates, read additional excerpts from *King Arthur and His Knights of the Round Table*. Hold a class storytelling festival. Have groups of students share different stories about King Arthur's adventures.

Go Online. Visit the EMC Internet Resource Center at **emcp.com** to find links and additional activities for this selection.

"Sundiata Keita, the Legend and the King"
from The Royal Kingdoms of Ghana, Mali, and Songhay: Life In Medieval Africa
by Patricia and Fredrick McKissack

Active READING STRATEGY

READ WITH A PURPOSE

Before Reading ➤ **ESTABLISH A PURPOSE FOR READING**

❑ Read the Reader's Resource.
❑ Consider this question with a partner: "What do I want to learn from reading this selection?" Use *who, what, where, when, why,* and *how* questions to create a purpose for reading. For example, you might ask: who is Sundiata, what kind of king was he, where did he live, when did he reign, or how did he overcome his disability. Create a chart like the one below in your notebook. Write a purpose for reading "Sundiata Keita, the Legend and the King" on the first line of the chart you create.
❑ As you read, gather important details in the story. Revise or change your purpose if important details do not match your purpose.

Graphic Organizer

My purpose for reading "Sundiata Keita, the Legend and the King":
Important details in "Sundiata Keita, the Legend and the King": ▶ ▶ ▶ ▶ ▶
Revisions or changes to my purpose:
What I learned from reading "Sundiata Keita, the Legend and the King":

READ WITH A PURPOSE IN MIND

❑ Follow along in the text as your teacher reads the first five paragraphs of the selection aloud, through line 41. After the oral reading, discuss with the class some of the important ideas presented thus far.

❑ Make a list of details you consider important so far, and add them to your chart.

❑ Read the rest of the selection silently. Keep in mind why you are reading, and identify and record important details that help you achieve your purpose. You may revise your purpose for reading if additional information changes your outlook.

Reading STRATEGY
REVIEW

TACKLE DIFFICULT VOCABULARY. If you are uncertain what the word *hunchback* means, consult a dictionary or ask a classmate.

Sundiata Keita
the Legend and the King

Patricia and Fredrick McKissack

At a time when the Mande[1] people needed a leader one came, and his name was Sogolon-Djata, a member of the Keita clan, who had ruled in Mali for three centuries. Maghan Kon Fatta, the king, was his father, and his mother was Sogolon Kedjou, a hunchback. In the rapidly spoken language of the Mandinka,[2] his name, Sogolon-Djata, became Sundiata, "The Hungering Lion."

Sundiata Keita is the King Arthur and George Washington of Mali.[3] He was a warrior-king who united a

10 weak and scattered people, and, under his benevolent leadership, ushered in a glorious period of peace and prosperity. However, Arthur is a mythical king; there is no evidence that he ever lived. There are many legends about Washington, but he was definitely a real person. Sundiata's story is full of legend, but he, too, really lived. Like Washington, he is honored as a great man, the founder of his nation. As we learn more about him, we will be able to see him as a person with good and bad sides. Sundiata should be seen as a three-dimensional man of his time and

20 not just a mythic figure.

---

1. **Mande.** Any member of a group of people native to western Africa
2. **Mandinka.** Subgroup of the Mande
3. **Mali.** Inland nation in western Africa

words for everyday use

be • nev′ • o • lent (bə nev′ ə lənt) *adj.*, kindly or charitable. *The benevolent queen allowed her subjects to pay her in taxes only what they could afford, and her kindness was rewarded with loyal support.*

The Keita griots[4] of Mali, who preserved the history and wisdom of their great kings, have told the story of Sundiata for centuries. Mamadou Kouyate, from the village of Djeliba Koro, begins the tale:

Listen then, sons of Mali, children of the black people, listen to my word, for I am going to tell you of Sundiata, the father of the Bright Country, of the savanna[5] land, the ancestor of those who draw the bow, the master of a hundred <u>vanquished</u> kings.

30   Two hunters told Maghan Kon Fatta that if he married Sogolon, their son would be a leader without equal, and so the king did. The day Sundiata was born a storm foretold of his greatness. "The lion child, the buffalo child is born," said the midwife.[6] "The Almighty has made the thunder peal, the white sky has lit up and the earth has trembled."

    Maghan Kon Fatta favored Sundiata and his mother, which angered his first wife, Sassouma Berete. Sassouma's jealousy of Sogolon was matched only by her hatred of Sundiata. She plotted to destroy them both to make sure

40 her son, Prince Dankaran Touman, would become king after King Fatta died.

    As Sundiata grew, the situation took an odd twist. Sundiata was seven years old, yet he couldn't walk! People were shocked and surprised to see a boy his age crawling around like a baby. Sassouma used every opportunity to embarrass Sogolon and hurl insults at her son. She pushed her beautiful child up front during all ceremonies, so he could be seen and adored.

    As long as the king lived, Sundiata was protected and

50 Sassouma's scheming was kept in check, but Maghan Kon Fatta died when Sundiata was very young. Against Fatta's wishes, the royal council was <u>coerced</u> into making Touman

Use THE STRATEGY

READ WITH A PURPOSE. Highlight or underline details that help you meet your purpose. Many details about Sundiata are revealed in the opening paragraphs.

NOTE THE FACTS

How did Sassouma Berete feel about Sundiata and his mother? What did she plan to do?

_____

_____

_____

---

4. **griots.** Storytellers, bards from West Africa
5. **savanna.** Flat grassland
6. **midwife.** Person who assists women in childbirth

words for everyday use

van • quished (vaŋ′ kwishd) *adj.*, beaten or conquered in battle. *The <u>vanquished</u> ruler was sent by his conquerer to live in another kingdom.*

co • erce (kō ʉrs′) *vt.*, force by intimidation to do something. *The police detective was able to <u>coerce</u> a confession out of the suspect by threatening to arrest her family.*

FIX-UP IDEA

Read Aloud

If you are having difficulty reading with a purpose, read the story aloud with a small group of students. Have your group decide on a purpose for reading, and assign group members to read different sections of the text aloud. For example, one student might read the narrative, another might read the indented sections of text, and two students might read the dialogue between Sumanguru and Sundiata. While one group member reads the story aloud, the other group members should record important ideas and events that help the group achieve its purpose for reading.

MARK THE TEXT

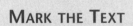

Underline or highlight how Sundiata learned to walk.

the mansa,[7] and Sassouma became the power behind the throne.

Free to carry out her threats, she did her best to humiliate Sogolon and her children. Sogolon was forced to live in a storage hut out behind the palace and Sassouma encouraged children to tease and poke fun at them. In spite of her efforts, Sundiata made two friends, Manding Bory, his half-brother, and Balla Fasseke, his teacher.

Just at this time, Sumanguru's army captured Mali. He spared the lives of Touman, who could be controlled through his mother, and Sundiata, who seemed harmless. Before leaving the city Sumanguru mocked the Mandinka, saying they were a weak and spineless people, like their king's son.

Balla Fasseke was sent as an <u>envoy</u> to Sumanguru, but after hearing Balla Fasseke speak, the king decided to keep him there to be his personal griot. After that Sundiata was determined to overcome his physical handicap.

With the help of a blacksmith—remember the power of the blacksmiths—who made braces for his legs, and the loving support of his family, Sundiata learned to walk upright. On that day his mother sang:

Oh, day, what a beautiful day,
Oh, day, day of joy;
Allah Almighty, you never created a finer day.
So my son is going to walk!

Through <u>rigorous</u> exercise and hard work the young prince grew tall and strong and became a very good archer. A prince needed to be fit, but Sogolon taught her son that a good ruler also needed to be wise. She taught Sundiata to respect Mandinka customs and traditions, their history and law.

When Sassouma heard that Sundiata could walk, she went to the Nine Witches of Mali and asked them to kill him.

60

70

80

---

7. **mansa.** Heir to the throne

words for everyday use

en • voy (än′ voi) *n.*, agent who transacts diplomatic business. *The president sent a diplomatic <u>envoy</u> on a mission to England in order to complete the business transaction.*

rig • or • ous (rig′ ər əs) *adj.*, extremely harsh or severe. *Her <u>rigorous</u> training schedule called for waking up at five o'clock in the morning and running six miles before breakfast.*

They tried, but Sundiata's kind heart weakened the witches' powers. Knowing that Sassouma would not stop until she had killed Sundiata, Sogolon fled with her children. Sundiata hated to leave his friends, but he had to go.

90

No one would take them in, because they were afraid of Sassouma's revenge. At last they found refuge with the distant king of Mema. Mema was probably what was left of the old kingdom of Ghana.[8] There Sundiata lived in exile, where he distinguished himself as a warrior-hunter.

Over the years, Sumanguru's taxes increased so much that Mali couldn't pay them. Sumanguru's army advanced against the Mandinka people at Kangaba. Touman and Sassouma fled, but loyal subjects sent a message to Sundiata, asking him to come home. The Mandinka warriors weren't afraid to fight, but they needed a general.

100

The king of Mema loved Sundiata as a son, so he raised an army with troops and cavalry to help fight the wicked ruler. Even the king's sons joined Sundiata. With Sogolon's blessings, the young prince of Mali was at last ready to fulfill his destiny.

All along the way, the Mandinka army scored victory after victory against Sumanguru's forces. As the people were freed, they joined Sundiata in his march against the oppressive Susu[9] regime.

110

After five years, the two armies met in the plain of Kirina (Krina).[10] Sundiata pitched his camp at Dayala in the valley of the Niger.[11] Sumanguru's army stood at Kirina. The night before the battle, Sumanguru visited Sundiata in the form of an owl, a bird of ill omen among the Mande.

SUMANGURU: I am the king of Mali by force of arms. My rights have been established by conquest.

SUNDIATA: Then I will take Mali from you by force of arms and chase you from my kingdom.

SUMANGURU: Know that I am the wild yam of the rocks; nothing will make me leave Mali.

Use THE STRATEGY

READ WITH A PURPOSE. Learn more about Sundiata and what he does to make Mali great.

Literary TOOLS

DIALOGUE. Dialogue is conversation involving two or more people or characters. Note in the dialogue how Sundiata and Sumanguru try to outdo each other.

---

8. **Ghana.** Nation in Africa
9. **Susu.** Agricultural people living mainly in the African nations of Guinea and Sierra Leone
10. **plain of Kirina (Krina).** Wide, open flatlands in Mali
11. **Niger.** River that flows from the northeast border of Guinea through Mali, Niger, and Nigeria, where it empties into the Atlantic Ocean

NOTE THE FACTS

Who wins the argument between Sundiata and Sumanguru? What does he say?

_____

_____

_____

MARK THE TEXT

Underline or highlight what happens to Sumanguru.

120   SUNDIATA: Know that I have in my camp seven master smiths who will shatter the rocks. Then, yam, I will eat you.

SUMANGURU: I am the poisonous mushroom that made the fearless vomit.

SUNDIATA: As for me I am the ravenous cock, the poison does not matter to me.

SUMANGURU: Behave yourself, little boy, or you will burn your foot, for I am the red-hot cinder.

SUNDIATA: But me, I am the rain that extinguishes the cinder; I am the <u>boisterous</u> torrent that will carry you off.

130   SUMANGURU: I am the mighty silk-cotton tree that looks from on high on the tops of other trees.

SUNDIATA: And I, I am the creeper that climbs to the top of the forest giant.

SUMANGURU: Enough of this argument. You shall not have Mali.

SUNDIATA: Know that there is not room for two kings on the same skin, Sumanguru; you will let me have your place.

Sumanguru was shaken by Sundiata's self-confidence, although he was sure his magic would protect him. But
140   Sundiata's blacksmith was also a well-known wizard. He made a poison from the blood of a white rooster stolen from Sumanguru's camp. Then he dipped the rooster's nail into the blood and fastened it to an arrow.

In the story the griots tell, the battle at Kirina is a classic tale of good versus evil. The Mandinka warriors fought nobly. When the battle looked like it was going against the Susu, Sumanguru hid behind his men. At just the right moment, Sundiata shot the arrow. It barely grazed Sumanguru's shoulder, but it was enough. Seeing the
150   rooster nail caused him to tremble and scream. Then, turning his horse toward the mountains, he fled. Sundiata followed, but Sumanguru was never heard from again. Some say he was swallowed by the mountains. Without their leader the Susu army was defeated and <u>dispersed</u>.

| words for everyday use | bois • ter • ous (bois′ tər əs) *adj.*, stormy or turbulent. *The <u>boisterous</u> baseball fans became even rowdier after their team won the World Series.* |
| | dis • perse (dis pʉrs′) *vi.*, break up and scatter about. *The crowd <u>dispersed</u> peacefully after the fireworks display, going their separate ways with little trouble.* |

Sundiata was reunited with Balla Fasseke, who became his griot, and his good friend and half-brother, Manding Bory. The griot hailed him, saying, "Sundiata, Maghan Sundiata, hail, king of Mali, in the name of the twelve kings of the Bright Country, I salute you as Mansa." To celebrate their
160 liberation, Balla Fasseke wrote a song that griots still sing:

> *Niama,[12] Niama, Niama,*
> *You, you serve as a shelter for all,*
> *All come to seek <u>refuge</u> under you.*
> *And as for you, Niama,*
> *Nothing serves you for shelter,*
> *God alone protects you.*

Sundiata crushed the Susu's stronghold, forever destroying the Susu and their dynasty.

Because of his courage and leadership, Sundiata was
170 chosen to be mansa of Mali, which he ruled from 1230 to 1255. Mali means "the hippopotamus," which is often used in association with Sundiata, as are the lion, the symbol of the Keita clan, and the buffalo of his mother's clan.

According to the griots' story, Sundiata began his rule by first moving his seat of government from Kangaba to Niani, the place of his birth. Then he established a solid hold over the gold and salt trade that had been the source of Ghana's wealth. ∎

----

12. *Niama.* Mande word that could mean "leader"

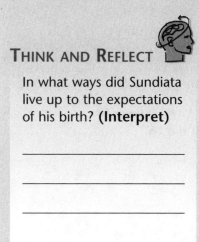

THINK AND REFLECT

In what ways did Sundiata live up to the expectations of his birth? **(Interpret)**

_____

_____

_____

words for everyday use

ref • uge (ref' yo͞oj) n., place of shelter and safety. *The store's awning was our <u>refuge</u> from the sudden downpour.*

Reflect ON YOUR READING

➤ **EVALUATE THE READING STRATEGY**

When you have finished reading, discuss the ideas you recorded, and explain how the ideas helped you accomplish your reading goal. Then, use your own paper to write a brief essay summarizing your experience of reading with a purpose.

Reading Skills and Test Practice

IDENTIFY THE AUTHORS' PURPOSE

With a partner, discuss how to answer the following questions about the authors' purpose. Read the following passage from the story to answer both questions. Circle the letter of the correct answer for each.

THINK-ALOUD NOTES

> Sundiata Keita is the King Arthur and George Washington of Mali. . . . However, Arthur is a mythical king; there is no evidence that he ever lived. There are many legends about Washington, but he was definitely a real person. Sundiata's story is full of legend, but he, too, really lived. Like Washington, he is honored as a great man, the founder of his nation. As we learn more about him, we will be able to see him as a person with good and bad sides. Sundiata should be seen as a three-dimensional man of his time and not just a mythic figure.

1. Why do Patricia and Fredrick McKissack compare Sundiata to King Arthur and George Washington?
   a. to illustrate that heroes all over the world are the same
   b. to convince readers that Sundiata is better than other heroes
   c. to help readers understand Sundiata's status in Africa by providing familiar comparisons
   d. to entertain readers with stories they already enjoy

2. Why do the McKissacks address the reader directly at the end of the passage?
   a. to persuade readers to believe only the facts about Sundiata and to disregard any legends
   b. to explain that they will present an objective view of Sundiata and that readers should remain objective while reading
   c. to persuade readers that Sundiata was better than King Arthur and George Washington because Sundiata was both real and legendary
   d. to challenge readers by distracting them from the main narrative of the story

Investigate, Inquire, and Imagine

RECALL: GATHER FACTS
1a. What surprised people about the seven-year-old Sundiata? Who helped him overcome this problem? Where did Sundiata go when he was forced to leave? Why did he come back?

INTERPRET: FIND MEANING
1b. How did Sundiata's problem affect the way other people viewed him? Why did Sundiata leave his friends and his home? What was the battle like between the Mandinka and Sumanguru and his army?

ANALYZE: TAKE THINGS APART
2a. Compare Sundiata to Sumanguru. What does each king's actions and behavior tell you about each of them?

SYNTHESIZE: BRING THINGS TOGETHER
2b. What qualities made Sundiata a good leader? What accomplishments in his early life are especially admirable?

EVALUATE: MAKE JUDGMENTS
3a. Do you think that the authors are successful in portraying Sundiata as a "man of his time" or do they only show him as a "mythic figure"? Explain.

EXTEND: CONNECT IDEAS
3b. How was Sundiata's future greatness predicted from the time of his birth? How did God's will fit into his destiny? In what ways did Sundiata represent the transformation from humble being to one of exceptional status?

Literary Tools

DIALOGUE. **Dialogue** is conversation involving two or more people or characters. Answer the following questions about the dialogue in "Sundiata Keita, the Legend and the King."

1. How does the dialogue between Sundiata and Sumanguru affect the story? What kinds of images are included in the dialogue?

   _____

   _____

3. Who emerges as the winner of the argument? What does the argument foreshadow or predict?

   _____

   _____

5. Griots, or storytellers, often acted out the stories they told. How could this dialogue be acted out to make it entertaining?

   _____

   _____

WordWorkshop

USE CONTEXT CLUES. Fill in each blank with the most appropriate word from the words listed below. You may not use every word, and you may have to change the tense of a word.

benevolent   boisterous   coerce   disperse   envoy   refuge   rigorous

1. The hunted quail took _____ in the underbrush.
2. _____ from all the Latin American countries met in Quito, Ecuador, for a diplomatic meeting.
3. Although hockey practice was _____, Ryan looked forward to the workout each day during the season.
4. On the last day of school, the class was so _____ that they were practically bouncing off the walls.
5. The chickens that had gathered around me as I fed them _____ in alarm when I accidentally dropped the bucket.

Read-Write Connection

Do you think Sundiata would be a good leader? Why, or why not? Would you want Sundiata to be your ruler? Use your own paper as needed.

_____

_____

_____

_____

_____

_____

_____

_____

Beyond the Reading

MEETING CHALLENGES. Read more about a person who overcame a physical challenge. Create a time line or story strip that describes how the person met the challenge.

GO ONLINE. Visit the EMC Internet Resource Center at **emcp.com** to find links and additional activities for this selection.

Unit 5 **READING** Review

Choose and Use Reading Strategies

Before reading a passage from *Le Morte d'Arthur* by Sir Thomas Malory, review and discuss with a partner how to use reading strategies with folk literature.

1. Read with a Purpose
2. Connect to Prior Knowledge
3. Write Things Down
4. Make Predictions
5. Visualize
6. Use Text Organization
7. Tackle Difficult Vocabulary
8. Monitor Your Reading Progress

Next, apply at least two of these reading strategies as you read the passage below. Use the margins and mark up the text to show how you are using the reading strategies to read actively. Pay particular attention to the strange phrasing in the first line. How can you figure out what it means?

And when Sir Mordred heard Sir Arthur, he ran until him with his sword drawn in his hand. And there King Arthur smote Sir Mordred under the shield, with a foin of his spear, throughout the body, more than a fathom. And when Sir Mordred felt that he had his death's wound he thrust himself with the might that he had up to the bur of King Arthur's spear. And right so he smote his father Arthur, with his sword holden in both his hands, on the side of the head, that the sword pierced the helmet and the brain pan, and therewithal Sir Mordred fell stark dead to the earth; and the noble Arthur fell in a swoon to the earth and there he swooned ofttimes.

And Sir Lucan the Butler and Sir Bedevere ofttimes heave him up. And so weakly they led him betwixt them both, to a little chapel not far from the seaside. And when the king was there he thought him well eased. Then heard they people cry in the field.

"Now go thou, Sir Lucan," said the king, "and do me to wit what betokens that noise in the field."

WordWorkshop

Unit 5 Words for Everyday Use

ANALOGIES. Standardized tests may evaluate your word knowledge by using **analogy questions**. Analogy questions are word problems that ask you to identify the relationships between given pairs of words. Here is an example of an analogy question.

ROBIN : BIRD :: FROG : REPTILE

In an analogy question, a single colon (:) means "is to" or "is related to," and a double colon (::) means "as" or "in the same way that." ROBIN : BIRD :: FROG : REPTILE would be read:

"A robin is to a bird as a frog is to a reptile."

Here are some common relationships used in analogy questions.

Relationship	Example
Synonyms	FRAUDULENT : DECEITFUL
Antonyms	POOR : AFFLUENT
Part and whole	CHAPTER : BOOK
Cause and effect	FALL : INJURY
Description	LEMON : SOUR
Thing and category	ROBIN : BIRD
Thing and what it's used for	MEDICINE : ILLNESS
Thing or person and what it lacks	COWARD : VALOR
Thing or person and where it can be found	COOK : KITCHEN
Degrees of the same thing	AMUSING : HILARIOUS

With a partner, choose five vocabulary words and create an analogy question for each. For each question, identify the relationship between the words. Use at least three different relationships.

Adamant : Uncertain :: Strong : Weak   (Antonyms)

1. _____ : _____ :: _____ : _____ (_____)

2. _____ : _____ :: _____ : _____ (_____)

3. _____ : _____ :: _____ : _____ (_____)

4. _____ : _____ :: _____ : _____ (_____)

5. _____ : _____ :: _____ : _____ (_____)

Literary Tools

Select a literary element from the column on the right that best completes each sentence on the left. Write the correct letter in the blank.

_____1. Visualizing who is speaking helps readers follow a(n) _____ between two characters in a story or play.

_____2. A time line for "The Five Ages of Man" would show how to list the ages in _____.

_____3. *King Arthur and His Knights of the Round Table* is defined as a(n) _____ because it contains elements of history and fantasy.

_____4. "But a few of those warriors were jealous of Popo" is an example of _____ because readers fear that the warriors will do something bad to Popo later in the story.

_____5. Legends, myths, and fairy tales, stories that have been passed down from generation to generation, are part of a culture's _____.

_____6. Orpheus's death explains why "nightingales now sing sweeter than anywhere else in the world" and illustrates why "Orpheus" is defined as a(n) _____.

a. folk tradition, 191

b. myth, 199

c. chronological order, 208

d. foreshadowing, 220

e. legend, 239

f. dialogue, 249

On Your Own

FLUENTLY SPEAKING. Find a children's picture book that retells a song or story from the folk tradition. Make an audio recording of the book for younger children to hear. Record the story and listen to your reading. Note corrections you would like to make to your reading, and rerecord the story. Do this rereading and rerecording two or three times. When you record your final reading, make sure that you use lots of expression in your voice to help younger readers understand what happens.

PICTURE THIS. Make quick sketches of the main characters in each of the selections in this unit. Use descriptions in the selections to make your sketches. Choose three or four of your sketches and include them in a picture that tells a new story.

PUT IT IN WRITING. With one or two classmates, choose one of the selections in this unit and rewrite it as a short drama. You may add scenes to your drama that show what might have happened after the selection you read ended. Act out your drama for the class.

Unit SIX

READING Drama

DRAMA

A **drama**, or *play*, is a story told through characters played by actors. Early groups of people around the world enacted ritual scenes related to hunting, warfare, or religion. From these, drama arose. Western drama as we know it began in ancient Greece.

Types of Drama

Most dramas can be classified as either comedies or tragedies. A **comedy** originally was any work with a happy ending. The term is widely used today to refer to any humorous work, especially one prepared for the stage or screen. A **tragedy** initially was a drama that told the story of the fall of a person of high status. Scenes from *The Tragedy of Julius Cæsar* by William Shakespeare appear in this unit. In recent years, the word *tragedy* has been used to describe any play about the downfall of a central character, or *protagonist*, who wins the audience's sympathies.

Elements of Drama

THE PLAYWRIGHT AND THE SCRIPT. The author of a play is the **playwright.** A playwright has limited control in deciding how his or her work is presented. Producers, directors, set designers, and actors all interpret a playwright's work and present their interpretations to the audience.

SCRIPT. A **script** is the written text from which a drama is produced. It contains dialogue and stage directions and may be divided into acts and scenes. Scripts for teleplays (television dramas), screenplays (film dramas), and radio plays, such as Lucille Fletcher's *The Hitchhiker* in this unit, include detailed instruction for how the play should be broadcast or filmed. Because *The Hitchhiker* is a radio play, you will find detailed sound effects.

NOTE THE FACTS

What is a tragedy?

_____

_____

_____

When might a playwright
want a character to speak
in a soliloquy?

_____

_____

_____

_____

Reading STRATEGY
REVIEW

VISUALIZE. Using the Parts of a
Stage diagram, mark where
actors would go if stage
directions told them to *enter
right*.

DIALOGUE. The speech of the actors in a play is called **dialogue.** In a play, dialogue appears after the names of characters. A speech given by one character is called a **monologue.** A speech given by a character alone on stage is called a **soliloquy.** A statement intended to be heard by the audience but not by other characters on the stage is called an **aside.**

ACTS AND SCENES. An **act** is a major part of a play. One-act, three-act, and five-act plays are all common. The plays of ancient Rome and of Elizabethan England, including Shakespeare's *The Tragedy of Julius Cæsar* in this unit, were typically divided into five **acts.** *The Hitchhiker* by Lucille Fletcher is a play with just one act. A **scene** is a short section of a drama, and typically begins with the entrance of one or more characters. The number of scenes in each act may vary.

STAGE DIRECTIONS. Stage directions are notes included in a script to describe how the playwright wants something to be presented or performed onstage. Stage directions can describe lighting, costumes, music, sound effects, or other elements of a play. They can also describe entrances and exits, gestures, tone of voice, or other elements related to the acting of a play. Stage directions sometimes provide background information. In stage directions, the parts of the stage are described from the actor's point of view, as shown in the diagram below. Paying attention to the stage directions can help you understand the action in a play even when you cannot see it performed.

THE PARTS OF A STAGE

Up Right	Up Center	Up Left
Right Center	Center	Left Center
Down Right	Down Center	Down Left

SPECTACLE. The **spectacle** includes all the elements of the drama that are presented to the audience's senses. The set, props, special effects, lighting, and costumes are all part of the spectacle.

Active Reading Strategy Checklists

When reading drama, be aware of the plot (what happens), the setting, the characters, the dialogue (what the characters say), and the stage directions (how the characters say their lines and the actions they take onstage). The following checklists offer things to consider as you read drama.

1 READ WITH A PURPOSE. Before reading drama, give yourself a purpose, or something to look for, as you read. Sometimes a purpose will be a directive from a teacher: "Chart the way Mark Antony changes the mood of the crowd." Other times you can set your own purpose by previewing the opening lines and instructional information. Say to yourself

- ❏ I want to look for . . .
- ❏ I need to learn what happens to . . .
- ❏ I want to experience how . . .
- ❏ I want to understand why . . .
- ❏ I want to figure out what causes . . .

2 CONNECT TO PRIOR KNOWLEDGE. Being aware of what you already know and thinking about it as you read can help you understand the characters and events. As you read, say to yourself

- ❏ The setting is a lot like . . .
- ❏ What happens here is similar to what happens in . . .
- ❏ This character is like . . .
- ❏ The ending reminds me of . . .
- ❏ I like this description because . . .

3 WRITE THINGS DOWN. As you read drama, write down important ideas that the author is sharing with readers. Possible ways to write things down include

- ❏ Underline important information in the stage directions.
- ❏ Write down your ideas about how the characters might say their lines.
- ❏ Highlight lines you want to read aloud.
- ❏ Create a graphic organizer to keep track of people and events.
- ❏ Use a code in the margin that shows how you respond to the action.

Reading **TIP**

Become an actor! Practice reading parts of the play aloud using a voice that expresses what the characters feel.

USE A CODE

Here's a way to code the text.
- **+** I like this
- **–** I don't like this
- **√** This is important
- **Yes** I agree with this
- **No** I disagree with this
- **?** I don't understand this
- **W** I wonder . . .
- **!** This is like something I know
- **↝** I need to come back to this later

Create additional code marks to note other reactions you have.

4 MAKE PREDICTIONS. As you read drama, use information in the stage directions and the dialogue to make guesses about what will happen next. Make predictions like the following:

- ❏ The title makes me predict that . . .
- ❏ The stage directions make me think that . . .
- ❏ I think the selection will end with . . .
- ❏ I think there will be a conflict between . . .
- ❏ The dialogue makes me guess that . . .

5 VISUALIZE. Visualizing, or allowing the words on the page to create images in your mind, helps you understand the action and how the characters may say their lines. In order to visualize the setting, the characters, and the action, make statements such as

- ❏ The setting and props . . .
- ❏ This character speaks . . .
- ❏ This character's movements are . . .
- ❏ This character wears . . .
- ❏ Over the course of the play, this character's behavior . . .
- ❏ The words help me see, hear, feel, smell, taste . . .

Reading TIP

Sketch what the setting and the characters look like. The sketch will help you envision the action.

6 USE TEXT ORGANIZATION. When you read drama, pay attention to the dialogue, the characters, and the action. Learn to stop occasionally and retell what you have read. Say to yourself

- ❏ The stage directions help me pay attention to . . .
- ❏ The exposition, or introduction, is about . . .
- ❏ The central conflict centers on . . .
- ❏ The climax, or high point of interest, occurs when . . .
- ❏ The resolution, or the outcome, of the play is that . . .
- ❏ My summary of this scene is . . .

Reading TIP

Insert synonyms for difficult words into the dialogue as you read. If you are unsure about a synonym that will work, ask a classmate about the synonym he or she would use.

7 TACKLE DIFFICULT VOCABULARY. Difficult words in drama can get in the way of your ability to understand the characters and events. Use context, consult a dictionary, or ask someone about words you do not understand. When you come across a difficult word in a drama, say to yourself

- ❏ The lines near this word tell me that this word means . . .
- ❏ A dictionary definition shows that the word means . . .
- ❏ My work with the word before reading helps me know that the word means . . .
- ❏ A classmate said that the word means . . .
- ❏ This word is pronounced . . .

8 MONITOR YOUR READING PROGRESS. All readers encounter difficulty when they read, especially if the reading material is not self-selected. When you have to read something, note problems you are having and fix them. The key to reading success is knowing when you are having difficulty. To fix problems, say to yourself

- ❏ Because I don't understand this part, I will . . .
- ❏ Because I'm having trouble staying connected to what I'm reading, I will . . .
- ❏ Because the words in the play are too hard, I will . . .
- ❏ Because the play is long, I will . . .
- ❏ Because I can't retell what happened here, I will . . .

Become an Active Reader

The instruction with the drama selections in this unit gives you an in-depth look at how to use one strategy with each selection. Brief margin notes guide your use of additional strategies. Using one active reading strategy will greatly increase your reading success and enjoyment. Use the white space in the margins to add your own comments and strategy ideas. Learn how to use several strategies in combination to ensure your complete understanding of what you are reading. When you have difficulty, try a fix-up idea. For further information about the active reading strategies, see Unit 1, pages 4–15.

FIX-UP IDEAS

- ■ Reread
- ■ Ask a question
- ■ Read in shorter chunks
- ■ Read aloud
- ■ Retell
- ■ Work with a partner
- ■ Unlock difficult words
- ■ Vary your reading rate
- ■ Choose a new reading strategy
- ■ Create a mnemonic device

How to Use Reading Strategies with Drama

Use the following excerpts to discover how you might use reading strategies as you read drama.

Excerpt 1. Note how a reader uses active reading strategies while reading this excerpt from *The Tragedy of Julius Cæsar* by William Shakespeare.

CONNECT TO PRIOR KNOWLEDGE

I've heard the opening lines of this speech before.

MONITOR YOUR READING PROGRESS

Reading Antony's speech aloud helps me start to understand his feelings about Cæsar.

ANTONY. Friends, Romans, countrymen, lend me your ears!
I come to bury Cæsar, not to praise him.
The evil that men do lives after them,
The good is oft <u>interred</u> with their bones;
So let it be with Cæsar. The noble Brutus
Hath told you Cæsar was ambitious;
If it were so, it was a <u>grievous</u> fault,
And grievously hath Cæsar answer'd it.
Here, under leave of Brutus and the rest
(For Brutus is an honorable man,
So are they all, all honorable men),
Come I to speak in Cæsar's funeral.

TACKLE DIFFICULT VOCABULARY

The definitions of *interred* and *grievous* at the bottom of the page help me understand this excerpt.

VISUALIZE

I imagine myself in Antony's place, giving a speech at the front of the Roman Forum.

Excerpt 2. Note how a reader uses active reading strategies while reading this excerpt from *The Hitchhiker* by Lucille Fletcher.

WRITE THINGS DOWN

I'm going to keep track of Adams's sightings of the hitchhiker by <u>underlining</u> each encounter.

MAKE PREDICTIONS

Adams has already seen the hitchhiker twice, so I think he'll pick up the hitchhiker.

SOUND. Auto hum.
MUSIC. In.
ADAMS. *(narrating)* I was in excellent spirits. The drive ahead of me, even the loneliness, seemed like a lark. But I reckoned without *him*.
MUSIC. Changes to something weird and empty.
ADAMS. *(narrating)* Crossing Brooklyn Bridge that morning in the rain, <u>I saw a man leaning against the cables</u>. He seemed to be waiting for a lift. There were spots of fresh rain on his shoulders. He was carrying a cheap overnight bag in one hand. He was thin, nondescript, with a cap pulled down over his eyes. He stepped off the walk right in front of me and, if I hadn't swerved hard, I'd have hit him.
SOUND. Terrific skidding.
MUSIC. In.
ADAMS. *(narrating)* I would have forgotten him completely, except that just an hour later, while crossing the Pulaski Skyway over the Jersey flats, <u>I saw him again</u> . . .

USE TEXT ORGANIZATION

The stage directions help me understand the action.

READ WITH A PURPOSE

The music lets me know that something spooky is going to happen. I want to find out what the spooky thing is going to be.

from The Tragedy of Julius Cæsar

by William Shakespeare

Active READING STRATEGY

WRITE THINGS DOWN

Before Reading ▶ **PREVIEW THE SELECTION**

❏ Read the Reader's Resource on page 262.
❏ Preview the cast of characters on page 262. Pay particular attention to which characters will conspire against Julius Cæsar.
❏ Note that the play is divided into five acts and multiple scenes, although the selection you will read includes only act 2, scenes 2 and 3, and act 3, scenes 1 and 2.
❏ As you read, you will be recording summaries of each scene. Work with the Summarize Sections Chart below.

Graphic Organizer

On your own paper, create a chart like the one below. Label each act and scene and summarize each section. You will need to summarize act 2, scenes 2 and 3, and act 3, scenes 1 and 2.

Summary of act 2, scene 2:
.
Summary of act 2, scene 3:
Summary of act 3, scene 1:
Summary of act 3, scene 2:

CONNECT

Word watch

PREVIEW VOCABULARY

amiss	imminent
bequeath	inter
commonwealth	lament
cur	malice
decree	portent
discourse	puissant
entrails	reverence
expound	utterance
grievous	valiant
horrid	valor

Reader's journal

What makes a person honorable?

_____

_____

_____

_____

Note: Characters who will appear in the scenes you will read are marked in **bold** type.

Julius Cæsar

TRIUMVIRS (RULING THREE-PERSON LEADERSHIP) AFTER THE DEATH OF CÆSAR
Octavius Cæsar
Mark Antony
M. Aemilius Lepidus

SENATORS
Cicero
Publius
Popilius Lena

CONSPIRATORS AGAINST CÆSAR
Marcus Brutus
Cassius
Casca
Trebonius
Caius Ligarius
Decius Brutus
Metellus Cimber
Cinna

Flavius and Murellus, tribunes
Artemidorus of Cnidos, a teacher of rhetoric
Soothsayer
Cinna, a poet
Another Poet

FRIENDS TO BRUTUS AND CASSIUS
Lucilius, Titinius, Messala, Young Cato, Volumnius, Flavius

SERVANTS TO BRUTUS
Varrus, Clitus, Claudio, Strato, Lucius, Dardanius

Pindarus, servant to Cassius
Calphurnia, wife to Cæsar
Portia, wife to Brutus
Senators, Citizens, Guards, Attendants, etc.

Setting: 44 BC at Rome; near Sardis; near Philippi

Reader's resource

THE TRAGEDY OF JULIUS CÆSAR. A **tragedy** traditionally tells of the fall of a noble character or characters. The selection you are about to read chronicles the fall of Julius Cæsar, a popular Roman leader born around 100 BC. Although the common people, or plebeians, loved Cæsar, members of the nobility began to fear him. Determined not to let Cæsar make himself king and overthrow the republic, a group of conspirators assassinated Cæsar in the year 44 BC.

In Shakespeare's play, Julius Cæsar isn't the only tragic character. The play also tells of the fall of Marcus Brutus, a man who believed he was doing the right thing by killing Cæsar, preventing him from becoming a dictator and so preserving the Roman republic.

As you read the selection from the play, look for the way fortunes change for Cæsar, Brutus, and Brutus's rival, Mark Antony.

WILLIAM SHAKESPEARE AND HIS WORLD. William Shakespeare (1564–1616) is often called the greatest playwright who ever lived. Even now, nearly 400 years after his death, his plays are still popular. In Shakespeare's time, people from all levels of society attended the theater. Shakespeare wrote his plays to provide something for everyone: lyrical poetry, philosophical ideas, physical comedy, and swashbuckling sword fights.

William Shakespeare was born to Mary Arden and John Shakespeare in Stratford-upon-Avon, a small English village on the banks of the river Avon. In 1582, at the age of 18, Shakespeare married the 28-year-old Anne Hathaway, who was also from the same town. The couple had three children.

By 1592, Shakespeare was living in London, England's largest city, and working in the theater. Shakespeare's theater company, the Lord Chamberlain's Men, became the most popular acting troupe in London. They performed at the Globe Theater and in a small indoor theater called Blackfriars, and put on regular performances at the court of Queen Elizabeth I. After Elizabeth's death in 1603, the troupe changed their name to the King's Men in honor of their new patron and ruler, King James I.

Dividing his time between Stratford-upon-Avon and London, Shakespeare managed to write at least 36 plays and some of the finest poetry in the English language. His plays include comedies such as *The Taming of the Shrew* and *Much Ado About Nothing;* histories such as *Richard the Third* and *Henry the Fifth;* tragedies such as *Hamlet, Othello, King Lear,* and *Macbeth;* and romances such as *The Winter's Tale* and *The Tempest. The Tragedy of Julius Cæsar,* which is both a history and a tragedy, was first performed on September 21, 1599, at the Globe Theater.

Shakespeare retired in or around 1611 and returned to Stratford-upon-Avon, a wealthy and successful man. He died at age 52, but his plays have lived on to delight audiences through the ages and around the world.

from *The*

Tragedy of Julius Cæsar

William Shakespeare

ACT 2

SCENE 2: THE HOME OF JULIUS CÆSAR

Thunder and lightning. Enter JULIUS CÆSAR *in his nightgown.*

CÆSAR. Nor[1] heaven nor earth have been at peace tonight.
Thrice hath Calphurnia in her sleep cried out,
"Help, ho! they murther[2] Cæsar!" Who's within?

Enter a SERVANT.

SERVANT. My lord?
5 **CÆSAR.** Go bid the priests do present sacrifice,[3]
And bring me their opinions of success.[4]
SERVANT. I will, my lord. *Exit.*

Enter CALPHURNIA.

CALPHURNIA. What mean you, Cæsar? Think you to walk
forth?
You shall not stir out of your house today.
10 **CÆSAR.** Cæsar shall forth; the things that threaten'd me

---

1. **Nor.** Neither
2. **murther.** Murder
3. **do present sacrifice.** Immediately perform a sacrifice (and read the omens)
4. **opinions of success.** Predictions about whether I shall be successful

WRITE THINGS DOWN

As you read the selection, you will identify and record details that help you track characters' actions in several key scenes of the play. To help yourself understand the play,

❑ Assign characters and read your parts aloud. You can change characters at the change of scenes.
❑ When you are not reading out loud, follow along in the text.
❑ As you read, record summaries of each scene in the Summarize Sections Chart on page 261. At the end of each page and scene, write a summary of what has happened so far. Record important information about the setting and the characters.

NOTE THE FACTS

What has Calphurnia, Cæsar's wife, cried out in her sleep?

_____

_____

_____

Read aloud Calphurnia's dialogue in the highlighted text, lines 13–26. Then read Cæsar's dialogue in the next highlighted box, lines 32–37. What omens does Calphurnia report? What is Cæsar's response?

_____

_____

_____

FIX-UP IDEA

Ask a Question
Before reading a page, review the questions in the margins, like the one above. Then, as the play is read aloud, jot down your answers to the questions. Use these answers to help you fill in your Summarize Sections chart.

THINK AND REFLECT

What does Cæsar mean in line 33 when he says that "[t]he valiant never taste of death but once"? Do you agree with him? What does Cæsar's attitude reveal about his character? **(Infer and Extend)**

_____

_____

_____

Ne'er look'd but on my back; when they shall see
The face of Cæsar, they are vanished.

CALPHURNIA.   Cæsar, I never stood on ceremonies,[5]
Yet now they fright[6] me. There is one within,
15   Besides the things that we have heard and seen,
Recounts most <u>horrid</u> sights seen by the watch.[7]
A lioness hath whelped[8] in the streets,
And graves have yawn'd and yielded up their dead;
Fierce fiery warriors fight upon the clouds
20   In ranks and squadrons and right form[9] of war,
Which drizzled blood upon the Capitol;
The noise of battle hurtled in the air;
Horses did neigh, and dying men did groan,
And ghosts did shriek and squeal about the streets.
25   O Cæsar, these things are beyond all use,[10]
And I do fear them.

CÆSAR.   What can be avoided
Whose end is purpos'd by the mighty gods?
Yet Cæsar shall go forth; for these predictions
Are to the world in general as to Cæsar.[11]
30   **CALPHURNIA.**   When beggars die there are no comets seen;
The heavens themselves blaze forth the death of princes.

CÆSAR.   Cowards die many times before their deaths,
The valiant never taste of death but once.
Of all the wonders that I yet have heard,
35   It seems to me most strange that men should fear,
Seeing that death, a necessary end,
Will come when it will come.

Enter a SERVANT.

What say the augurers?[12]

---

5. **stood on ceremonies.** Believed in omens
6. **fright.** Frighten
7. **watch.** Watchman
8. **whelped.** Given birth
9. **right form.** Proper formations
10. **beyond all use.** Outside of all normal experience
11. **Are to . . . Cæsar.** Apply as much to the rest of the world as they do to me
12. **augurers.** Religious officials of ancient Rome who foretold the future
by reading signs and omens

words for everyday use   hor • rid (hōr´ id) *adj.,* terrible; horrible. *The smell of the garbage after two days in the sun was absolutely* <u>horrid</u>.

SERVANT. They would not have you to stir forth today.
Plucking the <u>entrails</u> of an offering forth,
40 They could not find a heart within the beast.
  CÆSAR. The gods do this in shame of cowardice;
Cæsar should be a beast without a heart
If he should stay at home today for fear.
No, Cæsar shall not; Danger knows full well
45 That Cæsar is more dangerous than he.
We are two lions litter'd[13] in one day,
And I the elder and more terrible;
And Cæsar shall go forth.
  CALPHURNIA.   Alas, my lord,
Your wisdom is consum'd in confidence.
50 Do not go forth today; call it my fear
That keeps you in the house, and not your own.
We'll send Mark Antony to the Senate house
And he shall say you are not well today.
Let me, upon my knee, prevail in this.
55 **CÆSAR.** Mark Antony shall say I am not well,
And for thy humor[14] I will stay at home.

Enter DECIUS.

Here's Decius Brutus; he shall tell them so.
  DECIUS. Cæsar, all hail! Good morrow, worthy Cæsar,
I come to fetch you to the Senate house.
60 **CÆSAR.** And you are come in very happy time
To bear my greeting to the senators,
And tell them that I will not come today.
Cannot, is false; and that I dare not, falser:
I will not come today. Tell them so, Decius.
  CALPHURNIA. Say he is sick.
65 **CÆSAR.**   Shall Cæsar send a lie?
Have I in conquest stretch'd mine arm so far,
To be afeard to tell greybeards the truth?
Decius, go tell them Cæsar will not come.

---

13. **litter'd.** Born
14. **for thy humor.** At your insistence, to please you

> **words for everyday use**
>
> **en • trails** (en´ trālz) *n. pl.,* inner organs, viscera. *The movie was so frightening Eric could feel it in his <u>entrails</u>; he felt so nauseous that he could not watch it anymore.*

Reading **STRATEGY**
                REVIEW

READ WITH A PURPOSE. As you read the play, set your own purpose for reading, one that keeps you interested. What do you want to find out? What do you want to understand?

_____

_____

_____

_____

_____

NOTE THE FACTS

What does Calphurnia beg of Cæsar? What does Cæsar agree to do?

_____

_____

_____

Reading **TIP**

Note that there are two characters named Brutus in this play. Decius Brutus, who appears here, is a minor character. He is usually called Decius. The major character of Marcus Brutus is most often referred to as Brutus.

NOTE THE FACTS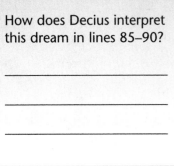

What has Calphurnia dreamed? What will Cæsar do because of this?

_____

_____

_____

 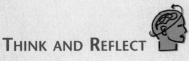
THINK AND REFLECT

What motives might Decius have in interpreting the dream this way? **(Infer)**

_____

_____

_____

DECIUS. Most mighty Cæsar, let me know some cause,

70 Lest I be laugh'd at when I tell them so.

CÆSAR. The cause is in my will, I will not come:

That is enough to satisfy the Senate.

But for your private satisfaction,

Because I love you, I will let you know.

75 Calphurnia here, my wife, stays[15] me at home:

She dreamt tonight she saw my statue,

Which, like a fountain with an hundred spouts,

Did run pure blood; and many lusty Romans

Came smiling and did bathe their hands in it.

80 And these does she apply for[16] warnings and <u>portents</u>

And evils <u>imminent</u>, and on her knee

Hath begg'd that I will stay at home today.

DECIUS. This dream is all <u>amiss</u> interpreted,

It was a vision fair and fortunate.

85 Your statue spouting blood in many pipes,

In which so many smiling Romans bath'd,

Signifies that from you great Rome shall suck

Reviving blood, and that great men shall press

For tinctures, stains, relics, and cognizance.[17]

90 This by Calphurnia's dream is signified.

CÆSAR. And this way have you well <u>expounded</u> it.

DECIUS. I have, when you have heard what I can say;

And know it now: the Senate have concluded

To give this day a crown to mighty Cæsar.

95 If you shall send them word you will not come,

Their minds may change. Besides, it were a mock

Apt to be render'd,[18] for someone to say

"Break up the Senate till another time,

When Cæsar's wife shall meet with[19] better dreams."

---

15. **stays.** Keeps
16. **apply for.** Explain as
17. **tinctures . . . cognizance.** Signs showing their allegiance to Cæsar
18. **mock . . . render'd.** Something likely to be said in mockery
19. **meet with.** Have

words for everyday use

por • tent (pôr´ tent´) *n.*, sign; omen. *We interpreted the thunder as a <u>portent</u> of doom.*

im • mi • nent (im´ ə nənt) *adj.*, about to occur. *When we heard the thunder, we knew that lightning was <u>imminent</u>.*

a • miss (ə mis´) *adv.*, wrongly; improperly. *When we smelled smoke after lightning struck the house, we knew that something was <u>amiss</u>.*

ex • pound (eks pound´) *vt.*, explain; give more information about. *We tried to <u>expound</u> the danger we were in to the fire department as clearly and quickly as possible.*

100 If Cæsar hide himself, shall they not whisper,
    "Lo Cæsar is afraid"?
    Pardon me, Cæsar, for my dear, dear love
    To your proceeding[20] bids me tell you this;
    And reason to my love is liable.[21]

105 **CÆSAR.**   How foolish do your fears seem now, Calphurnia!
    I am ashamed I did yield to them.
    Give me my robe, for I will go.

    Enter BRUTUS, LIGARIUS, METELLUS, CASCA, TREBONIUS,
       CINNA, *and* PUBLIUS.

    And look where Publius is come to fetch me.
    PUBLIUS.   Good morrow, Cæsar.
    CÆSAR.   Welcome, Publius.

110 What, Brutus, are you stirr'd so early too?
    Good morrow, Casca. Caius Ligarius,
    Cæsar was ne'er so much your enemy
    As that same ague[22] which hath made you lean.
    What is't a' clock?[23]
    BRUTUS.   Cæsar, 'tis strucken[24] eight.

115 **CÆSAR.**   I thank you for your pains and courtesy.

    Enter ANTONY.

    See, Antony, that revels long a-nights,
    Is notwithstanding up. Good morrow, Antony.
    ANTONY.   So to most noble Cæsar.
    CÆSAR.   Bid them prepare within;
    I am to blame to be thus waited for.

120 Now, Cinna; now, Metellus; what, Trebonius:
    I have an hour's talk in store for you;
    Remember that you call on me today;
    Be near me, that I may remember you.
    TREBONIUS.   Cæsar, I will; [*aside*] and so near will I be,

125 That your best friends shall wish I had been further.
    CÆSAR.   Good friends, go in, and taste some wine with me,
    And we, like friends, will straightway go together.

---

20. **proceeding.** Advancing, moving forward
21. **reason . . . liable.** My thinking is based upon my love for you
22. **ague.** Fever
23. **What is't a' clock.** What time is it?
24. **'tis strucken.** It has struck

NOTE THE FACTS

What does Cæsar ultimately decide to do?

_____

_____

_____

Literary TOOLS

FORESHADOWING.
Foreshadowing presents material that hints at events to come. What is foreshadowed by Calphurnia's dream?

_____

_____

_____

Reading TIP

The line numbering in this play may be confusing to you. Shakespeare's dialogue is written in a kind of unrhymed poetry called **blank verse,** in which each line has ten syllables (give or take a few). In many cases, lines are split between two or more characters. For example, Antony's words "So to most noble Cæsar" and Cæsar's words "Bid them prepare within" together make up line 118.

BRUTUS. [*Aside.*] That every like is not the same,[25]
O Cæsar,
130   The heart of Brutus earns[26] to think upon!

Exeunt.

SCENE 3: A STREET IN ROME NEAR THE CAPITOL

Enter ARTEMIDORUS *reading a paper.*

ARTEMIDORUS. "Cæsar, beware of Brutus; take heed of Cassius; come not near Casca; have an eye to Cinna; trust not Trebonius; mark well Metellus Cimber; Decius Brutus loves thee not; thou hast wrong'd Caius Ligarius. There is but one mind in all these men, and it is bent against Cæsar. If thou beest[1] not immortal, look about you; security gives way to conspiracy. The mighty gods defend thee!
                    Thy lover,[2]
                        Artemidorus."

Here will I stand till Cæsar pass along,
And as a suitor[3] will I give him this.
10   My heart laments that virtue cannot live
Out of the teeth of emulation.[4]
If thou read this, O Cæsar, thou mayest live;
If not, the Fates with traitors do contrive.

Exit.

ACT 2, SCENE 2
25. **every like . . . same.** Being like something is not being identical with it. Brutus is saying that some of those present resemble friends but are not true friends.
26. **earns.** Grieves

ACT 2, SCENE 3
1. **thou beest.** You are
2. **lover.** Friend
3. **as a suitor.** Like someone asking a favor
4. **Out of . . . emulation.** Outside the destructive reach (the bite) of rivalry

words for everyday use

la • ment (lə ment´) *vt.*, regret deeply; grieve. *The mourners* lamented *the passing of their beloved friend.*

Use THE STRATEGY

WRITE THINGS DOWN. Take time now to summarize the events of scene 2 in your Summarize Sections Chart.

READ ALOUD

Read aloud Artemidorus's warnings in the highlighted box in lines 1–7. Then highlight or underline the text that tells Cæsar what he should beware.

THINK AND REFLECT

What does Artemidorus mean when he says that his "heart laments that virtue cannot live / Out of the teeth of emulation" in lines 12–13? Give a modern-day example that illustrates his lament. **(Interpret)**

_____

_____

_____

_____

_____

ACT 3
SCENE 1: ROME; IN FRONT OF THE CAPITOL

Flourish. Enter CÆSAR, BRUTUS, CASSIUS, CASCA, DECIUS, METELLUS, TREBONIUS, CINNA, ANTONY, LEPIDUS, ARTEMIDORUS, PUBLIUS, POPILIUS, *and the* SOOTHSAYER.

CÆSAR. The ides of March[1] are come.

SOOTHSAYER. Ay, Cæsar, but not gone.

ARTEMIDORUS. Hail, Cæsar! Read this schedule.

5 **DECIUS.** Trebonius doth desire you to o'er-read
(At your best leisure) this his humble suit.

ARTEMIDORUS. O Cæsar, read mine first; for mine's a suit
That touches Cæsar nearer. Read it, great Cæsar.

CÆSAR. What touches us ourself shall be last serv'd.

ARTEMIDORUS. Delay not, Cæsar, read it instantly.

CÆSAR. What, is the fellow mad?

10 **PUBLIUS.**   Sirrah, give place.[2]

CASSIUS. What, urge you your petitions in the street?
Come to the Capitol.

CÆSAR enters the Capitol, the rest following.

POPILIUS. I wish your enterprise today may thrive.

CASSIUS. What enterprise, Popilius?

POPILIUS.   Fare you well.

Leaves him and joins CÆSAR.

15 **BRUTUS.** What said Popilius Lena?

CASSIUS. He wish'd today our enterprise might thrive.
I fear our purpose is discovered.

BRUTUS. Look how he makes to[3] Cæsar; mark him.

CASSIUS. Casca, be sudden, for we fear prevention.

20 Brutus, what shall be done? If this be known,
Cassius or Cæsar never shall turn back,
For I will slay myself.

BRUTUS.   Cassius, be constant;[4]
Popilius Lena speaks not of our purposes,
For look he smiles, and Cæsar doth not change.

ACT 3, SCENE 1
1. **ides of March.** Fifteenth of March
2. **Sirrah, give place.** Get out of the way (said to Artemidorus). *Sirrah* was a term used to address an inferior.
3. **makes to.** Heads toward
4. **constant.** Steady

THINK AND REFLECT

Why does Artemidorus want Cæsar to read his note first? What might have happened if Cæsar had followed Artemidorus's request? **(Infer)**

_____

_____

_____

NOTE THE FACTS

What worries those conspiring against Cæsar?

_____

_____

_____

READ ALOUD

Read aloud the highlighted text in lines 25–26. What does Trebonius do?

_____

_____

_____

NOTE THE FACTS

What does Cæsar warn Metellus Cimber not to do? What will Cæsar not tolerate?

_____

_____

_____

Literary TOOLS

MOTIVATION. A **motivation** is a force that moves a character to think, feel, or behave in a certain way. What motivates Cæsar to respond to Metellus Cimber as he does? What does he want others to know about him? What does this say about his character?

_____

_____

_____

25   **CASSIUS.**   Trebonius knows his time; for look you, Brutus,
He draws Mark Antony out of the way.

Exeunt ANTONY _and_ TREBONIUS.

DECIUS.   Where is Metellus Cimber? Let him go
And presently prefer[5] his suit to Cæsar.
BRUTUS.   He is address'd;[6] press near and second him.
30   **CINNA.**   Casca, you are the first that rears your hand.
CÆSAR.   Are we all ready? What is now amiss
That Cæsar and his Senate must redress?
METELLUS.   Most high, most mighty, and most <u>puissant</u> Cæsar,
Metellus Cimber throws before thy seat
An humble heart.   _Kneeling._
35   **CÆSAR.**   I must prevent thee, Cimber.
These couchings and these lowly courtesies[7]
Might fire the blood of ordinary men,
And turn preordinance and first decree[8]
Into the law of children.[9] Be not fond
40   To[10] think that Cæsar bears such rebel[11] blood
That will be thaw'd from the true quality
With that which melteth fools—I mean sweet words,
Low-crooked curtsies, and base spaniel fawning.
Thy brother by <u>decree</u> is banished;
45   If thou dost bend, and pray, and fawn for him,
I spurn[12] thee like a <u>cur</u> out of my way.
Know, Cæsar doth not wrong, nor without cause
Will he be satisfied.[13]
     METELLUS.   Is there no voice more worthy than my own,
50   To sound more sweetly in great Cæsar's ear

---

5. **presently prefer.** Immediately present
6. **address'd.** Ready
7. **courtesies.** Bows
8. **preordinance and first decree.** Earlier made laws
9. **the law of children.** Children's games to be changed at whim
10. **fond / To.** So absurd as to
11. **rebel.** Rebellious
12. **spurn.** Kick
13. **Will he be satisfied.** Moved to change his mind

For the repealing of my banish'd brother?
BRUTUS.   I kiss thy hand, but not in flattery, Cæsar;
Desiring thee that Publius Cimber may
Have an immediate freedom of repeal.[14]
CÆSAR.   What, Brutus?
55   **CASSIUS.**   Pardon, Cæsar! Cæsar, pardon!
As low as to thy foot doth Cassius fall,
To beg enfranchisement[15] for Publius Cimber.
CÆSAR.   I could be well mov'd, if I were as you;
If I could pray to move, prayers would move me;
60   But I am constant as the northern star,
Of whose true-fix'd and resting quality
There is no fellow[16] in the firmament.[17]
The skies are painted with unnumb'red sparks,
They are all fire, and every one doth shine;
65   But there's but one in all doth hold his place.
So in the world: 'tis furnish'd well with men,
And men are flesh and blood, and apprehensive;[18]
Yet in the number I do know but one
That unassailable holds on his rank,[19]
70   Unshak'd of motion; and that I am he,
Let me a little show it, even in this—
That I was constant Cimber should be banish'd
And constant do remain to keep him so.
CINNA.   O Cæsar—
CÆSAR.   Hence! Wilt thou lift up Olympus?[20]
DECIUS.   Great Cæsar—
75   **CÆSAR.**   Doth not Brutus bootless[21] kneel?
CASCA.   Speak hands for me!

They stab CÆSAR.

CÆSAR.   *Et tu,*[22] *Brute?*—Then fall Cæsar!

Dies.

CINNA.   Liberty! Freedom! Tyranny is dead!

---

14. **freedom of repeal.** Permission to be recalled from exile
15. **enfranchisement.** Here, Cassius means reinstatement as a full citizen
16. **fellow.** Equal
17. **firmament.** Sky
18. **apprehensive.** Capable of reason
19. **holds on his rank.** Holds his position
20. **Olympus.** In Greek myth, the mountain that is home to the gods
21. **bootless.** In vain
22. *Et tu.* Latin for *and you*

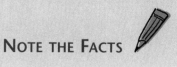

NOTE THE FACTS

What do Brutus and Cassius ask of Cæsar? How does Cæsar respond? To what does he compare himself?

_____

_____

_____

MARK THE TEXT

Underline Cæsar's last words and circle the name of the person to whom he directs them. Underline what Cinna and the other killer shout after Cæsar is dead.

Run hence, proclaim, cry it about the streets.

80 **CASSIUS.**   Some to the common pulpits,[23] and cry out,
"Liberty, freedom, and enfranchisement!"[24]

BRUTUS.   People and senators, be not affrighted;[25]
Fly not, stand still; ambition's debt is paid.

CASCA.   Go to the pulpit, Brutus.

DECIUS.   And Cassius too.

85 **BRUTUS.**   Where's Publius?

CINNA.   Here, quite confounded with[26] this mutiny.

METELLUS.   Stand fast together, lest some friend of Cæsar's
Should chance[27]—

BRUTUS.   Talk not of standing. Publius, good cheer,
90 There is no harm intended to your person,
Nor to no Roman else.[28] So tell them, Publius.

CASSIUS.   And leave us, Publius, lest that the people,
Rushing on us, should do your age some mischief.

BRUTUS.   Do so, and let no man abide[29] this deed,
95 But we the doers.

Exeunt all but the Conspirators.
Enter TREBONIUS.

CASSIUS.   Where is Antony?

TREBONIUS.   Fled to his house amaz'd.
Men, wives, and children stare, cry out, and run,
As[30] it were doomsday.

BRUTUS.   Fates, we will know your pleasures.
That we shall die, we know, 'tis but the time,
100 And drawing days out, that men stand upon.[31]

CASCA.   Why, he that cuts off twenty years of life
Cuts off so many[32] years of fearing death.

BRUTUS.   Grant that, and then is death a benefit;
So are we Cæsar's friends, that have abridg'd
105 His time of fearing death. Stoop, Romans, stoop,
And let us bathe our hands in Cæsar's blood

---

23. **pulpits.** Platforms for public speakers
24. **enfranchisement.** Full citizenship rights
25. **affrighted.** Frightened
26. **confounded with.** Overwhelmed by
27. **chance.** Happen
28. **no Roman else.** Any other Roman
29. **abide.** Suffer the consequences of
30. **As.** As if
31. **stand upon.** Worry about
32. **so many.** As many

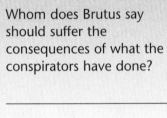

NOTE THE FACTS

Whom does Brutus say should suffer the consequences of what the conspirators have done?

_____

_____

_____

READ ALOUD

Read aloud the highlighted text in lines 103–110. What does Brutus suggest the conspirators do?

_____

_____

_____

Up to the elbows, and besmear our swords;
Then walk we forth, even to the marketplace,[33]
110 And waving our red weapons o'er our heads,
Let's all cry, "Peace, freedom, and liberty!"

CASSIUS.   Stoop then, and wash. How many ages hence
Shall this our lofty scene be acted over
In states unborn and accents[34] yet unknown!

BRUTUS.   How many times shall Cæsar bleed in sport,[35]
115 That now on Pompey's basis[36] lies along
No worthier than the dust!

CASSIUS.   So oft as that shall be,
So often shall the knot[37] of us be call'd
The men that gave their country liberty.

DECIUS.   What, shall we forth?

CASSIUS.   Ay, every man away.
120 Brutus shall lead, and we will grace his heels
With the most boldest and best hearts of Rome.

Enter a SERVANT.

BRUTUS.   Soft, who comes here? A friend of Antony's.

SERVANT.   Thus, Brutus, did my master bid me kneel;
Thus did Mark Antony bid me fall down;
125 And being prostrate, thus he bade me say:
Brutus is noble, wise, valiant, and honest;
Cæsar was mighty, bold, royal, and loving.
Say, I love Brutus, and I honor him;
Say, I fear'd Cæsar, honor'd him, and lov'd him.
130 If Brutus will vouchsafe that Antony
May safely come to him, and be resolv'd
How Cæsar hath deserv'd to lie in death,
Mark Antony shall not love Cæsar dead
So well as Brutus living; but will follow
135 The fortunes and affairs of noble Brutus

---

33. **marketplace.** The Forum
34. **accents.** Languages
35. **in sport.** In entertainments, such as plays
36. **Pompey's basis.** Pedestal of Pompey's statue
37. **knot.** Group

words for everyday use

val • iant (val′yənt) *adj.*, full of courage; brave. *The valiant knight fought off eight opponents after he had been wounded.*

NOTE THE FACTS

How does Cassius think Cæsar's killer's will be regarded in the future?

_____

_____

_____

NOTE THE FACTS

What does Antony want Brutus to do? What does he promise Brutus in return?

_____

_____

_____

Thorough the hazards of this untrod[38] state
With all true faith. So says my master Antony.

BRUTUS.   Thy master is a wise and valiant Roman,
I never thought him worse.

140 Tell him, so please him come unto this place,
He shall be satisfied; and, by my honor,
Depart untouch'd.

SERVANT.   I'll fetch him presently.[39]

Exit SERVANT.

BRUTUS.   I know that we shall have him well to friend.[40]

CASSIUS.   I wish we may; but yet have I a mind

145 That fears him much; and my misgiving still
Falls shrewdly to the purpose.[41]

Enter ANTONY.

BRUTUS.   But here comes Antony. Welcome, Mark Antony!

ANTONY.   O mighty Cæsar! dost thou lie so low?
Are all thy conquests, glories, triumphs,[42] spoils,

150 Shrunk to this little measure? Fare thee well!
I know not, gentlemen, what you intend,
Who else must be let blood,[43] who else is rank;[44]
If I myself, there is no hour so fit
As Cæsar's death's hour, nor no instrument

155 Of half that worth as those your swords, made rich
With the most noble blood of all this world.
I do beseech ye, if you bear me hard,[45]
Now, whilst your purpled hands do reek and smoke,[46]
Fulfill your pleasure. Live a thousand years,

160 I shall not find myself so apt to die;
No place will please me so, no mean[47] of death,
As here by Cæsar, and by you cut off,
The choice and master spirits of this age.

BRUTUS.   O Antony! beg not your death of us.

---

38. **untrod.** Not previously explored, new
39. **presently.** At once
40. **well to friend.** As a good friend
41. **misgiving . . . purpose.** Doubts usually prove to be well-founded.
42. **triumphs.** Processions
43. **let blood.** Bled, as was done in the past to cure disease
44. **rank.** Sick
45. **bear me hard.** Dislike me
46. **smoke.** Steam with warm blood
47. **mean.** Means

Reading STRATEGY
          REVIEW

USE TEXT ORGANIZATION.
Because much of the
dialogue in this play is
poetry, you should chunk
the lines so they make
sense. A sentence doesn't
always stop at the end of
a line. Instead, it ends only
when you see a period,
question mark, or
exclamation point. A
comma or semicolon
signals that you should
slow down in your
reading. Read aloud the
text in the highlighted
box on this page. How
does Antony react when
he sees Cæsar's body?
What does he beg the
conspirators to do if they
dislike him?

_____

_____

_____

_____

165 Though now we must appear bloody and cruel,
As by our hands and this our present act
You see we do, yet see you but our hands,
And this the bleeding business they have done.
Our hearts you see not, they are pitiful;[48]

170 And pity to the general wrong of Rome—
As fire drives out fire, so pity pity—
Hath done this deed on Cæsar.[49] For your part,
To you our swords have leaden points, Mark Antony;
Our arms in strength of <u>malice</u>, and our hearts

175 Of brothers' temper, do receive you in
With all kind love, good thoughts, and <u>reverence</u>.
CASSIUS.   Your voice shall be as strong as any man's
In the disposing of new dignities.[50]
BRUTUS.   Only be patient till we have appeas'd

180 The multitude, beside themselves with fear,
And then we will deliver[51] you the cause
Why I, that did love Cæsar when I strook him,
Have thus proceeded.

ANTONY.   I doubt not of your wisdom.
Let each man render me his bloody hand.

185 First, Marcus Brutus, will I shake with you;
Next, Caius Cassius, do I take your hand;
Now, Decius Brutus, yours; now yours, Metellus;
Yours, Cinna; and, my valiant Casca, yours;
Though last, not least in love, yours, good Trebonius.

190 Gentlemen all—alas, what shall I say?
My credit[52] now stands on such slippery ground
That one of two bad ways you must conceit[53] me,
Either a coward or a flatterer.
That I did love thee, Cæsar, O, 'tis true;

195 If then thy spirit look upon us now,
Shall it not grieve thee dearer than thy death,

---

48. **pitiful.** Full of pity
49. **pity to . . . Cæsar.** Our pity for Rome caused us to act as we have.
50. **dignities.** Titles, public offices
51. **deliver.** Explain to
52. **credit.** Reputation
53. **conceit.** Perceive

words for everyday use	**mal • ice** (mal´is) *n.*, desire to do harm. *The reporter told the politician privately that she had no feelings of <u>malice</u>, she was just doing her job.*
	rev • er • ence (rev´ər əns) *n.*, feelings of respect, care, or love. *The children looked at their grandmother with <u>reverence</u> and love.*

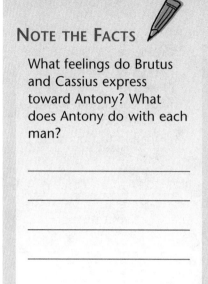

NOTE THE FACTS

What feelings do Brutus and Cassius express toward Antony? What does Antony do with each man?

_____

_____

_____

_____

MARK THE TEXT

Read lines 183–193 out loud. Underline the two "bad ways" Antony worries the conspirators will perceive him.

EXTENDED METAPHOR. An **extended metaphor** is a point-by-point presentation of one thing as though it were another. Circle the thing that Antony calls Cæsar in line 204. How does Shakespeare extend this metaphor? In other words, what else does he say happened to the object he compares to Cæsar?

_____

_____

_____

_____

NOTE THE FACTS

What loyalty does Antony pledge to the conspirators?

_____

_____

_____

To see thy Antony making his peace,
Shaking the bloody fingers of thy foes,
Most noble! in the presence of thy corse?[54]

200 Had I as many eyes as thou hast wounds,
Weeping as fast as they stream forth thy blood,
It would become me better than to close
In terms of friendship with thine enemies.
Pardon me, Julius! Here wast thou bay'd,[55] brave hart,[56]

205 Here didst thou fall, and here thy hunters stand,
Sign'd in thy spoil, and crimson'd in thy lethe.[57]
O world! thou wast the forest to this hart,
And this indeed, O world, the heart of thee.
How like a deer, strooken[58] by many princes,

210 Dost thou here lie!
CASSIUS.   Mark Antony—
ANTONY.   Pardon me, Caius Cassius!
The enemies of Cæsar shall say this:
Then, in a friend, it is cold modesty.
CASSIUS.   I blame you not for praising Cæsar so,

215 But what compact mean you to have with us?
Will you be prick'd in number[59] of our friends,
Or shall we on, and not depend on you?
ANTONY.   Therefore I took your hands, but was indeed
Sway'd from the point, by looking down on Cæsar.

220 Friends am I with you all, and love you all,
Upon this hope, that you shall give me reasons
Why, and wherein, Cæsar was dangerous.
BRUTUS.   Or else were this a savage spectacle.
Our reasons are so full of good regard

225 That were you, Antony, the son of Cæsar,
You should be satisfied.
ANTONY.   That's all I seek,
And am, moreover, suitor[60] that I may
Produce his body to the marketplace,
And in the pulpit, as becomes a friend,

---

54. **corse.** Body
55. **bay'd.** Chased down, brought to bay
56. **hart.** Deer, with a pun to *heart*
57. **lethe.** Blood. In Greek myth, Lethe was a river from which the dead in Hades drank, causing them to forget and to give up their former lives.
58. **strooken.** Struck
59. **prick'd in number.** Counted as one
60. **suitor.** Petitioner

230 Speak in the order of[61] his funeral.

BRUTUS.   You shall, Mark Antony.

CASSIUS.   Brutus, a word with you.

Aside to Brutus. You know not what you do. Do not consent

That Antony speak in his funeral.

Know you how much the people may be mov'd

By that which he will utter?

235 **BRUTUS.**   By your pardon—

I will myself into the pulpit first,

And show the reason of our Cæsar's death.

What Antony shall speak, I will protest

He speaks by leave and by permission;

240 And that we are contented Cæsar shall

Have all true rites and lawful ceremonies.

It shall advantage[62] more than do us wrong.

CASSIUS.   I know not what may fall,[63] I like it not.

BRUTUS.   Mark Antony, here take you Cæsar's body.

245 You shall not in your funeral speech blame us,

But speak all good you can devise of Cæsar,

And say you do't by our permission;

Else shall you not have any hand at all

About his funeral. And you shall speak

250 In the same pulpit whereto I am going,

After my speech is ended.

ANTONY.   Be it so;

I do desire no more.

BRUTUS.   Prepare the body then, and follow us.

Exeunt. Manet ANTONY.

ANTONY.   O, pardon me, thou bleeding piece of earth,[64]

255 That I am meek and gentle with these butchers!

Thou art the ruins of the noblest man

That ever lived in the tide of times.

Woe to the hand that shed this costly blood!

Over thy wounds now do I prophesy

260 (Which like dumb mouths do ope[65] their ruby lips

---

61. **in the order of.** In the ceremonies conducted for
62. **advantage.** Help, aid
63. **may fall.** May occur
64. **thou . . . earth.** Cæsar
65. **ope.** Open

NOTE THE FACTS

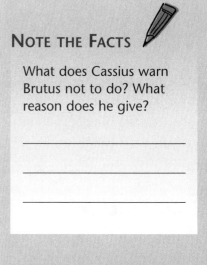

What does Cassius warn Brutus not to do? What reason does he give?

_____

_____

_____

MARK THE TEXT

Underline or highlight the terms Brutus outlines for Antony to abide by in his speech.

Reading **STRATEGY**
                  REVIEW

MAKE PREDICTIONS. Based on the emotions Antony expresses in lines 254–275, what do you predict Antony will do or say in his speech?

_____

_____

_____

_____

To beg the voice and <u>utterance</u> of my tongue)
A curse shall light upon the limbs of men;
Domestic fury and fierce civil strife
Shall cumber[66] all the parts of Italy;
265 Blood and destruction shall be so in use,
And dreadful objects so familiar,
That mothers shall but smile when they behold
Their infants quartered with the hands of war;
All pity chok'd with custom of[67] fell[68] deeds;
270 And Cæsar's spirit, ranging[69] for revenge,
With Ate[70] by his side come hot from hell,
Shall in these confines with a monarch's voice
Cry "Havoc!" and let slip[71] the dogs of war,
That this foul deed shall smell above the earth
275 With carrion men, groaning for burial.

Enter Octavio's[72] SERVANT.

You serve Octavius Cæsar, do you not?
SERVANT. I do, Mark Antony.
ANTONY. Cæsar did write for him to come to Rome.
SERVANT. He did receive his letters and is coming,
280 And bid me say to you by word of mouth—
O Cæsar!— [_Seeing the body._]
ANTONY. Thy heart is big; get thee apart and weep.
Passion, I see, is catching, for mine eyes,
Seeing those beads of sorrow stand in thine,
285 Began to water. Is thy master coming?
SERVANT. He lies tonight within seven leagues of Rome.
ANTONY. Post[73] back with speed, and tell him what hath chanc'd.[74]

READ ALOUD

With a partner, read aloud the highlighted text on this page. Who is coming to Rome? What message does Antony send this person?

_____

_____

_____

---

66. **cumber.** Help, aid
67. **with custom of.** By familiarity with
68. **fell.** Terrible; cruel
69. **ranging.** Roving
70. **Ate.** Greek goddess of conflict
71. **let slip.** Unhook from their leashes
72. _Octavio's._ Gaius Octavius, grand nephew and heir to Julius Cæsar; later Augustus Cæsar, the first of the Roman emperors
73. **Post.** Ride
74. **chanc'd.** Happened

ut • ter • ance (ut´ər əns) _n.,_ speech. _The <u>utterances</u> of the poet were so beautiful that all her listeners left feeling radiant._

Here is a mourning Rome, a dangerous Rome,
No Rome of safety for Octavius yet;
290   Hie hence,[75] and tell him so. Yet stay awhile,
Thou shalt not back till I have borne this corse
Into the marketplace. There shall I try,
In my oration, how the people take
The cruel issue[76] of these bloody men,
295   According to the which[77] thou shalt <u>discourse</u>
To young Octavius of the state of things.
Lend me your hand.   *Exeunt with* CÆSAR'S *body.*

SCENE 2: THE ROMAN FORUM

Enter BRUTUS *and* CASSIUS *with the* PLEBEIANS.[1]

PLEBEIANS.   We will be satisfied! Let us be satisfied!
BRUTUS.   Then follow me, and give me audience, friends.
Cassius, go you into the other street,
And part the numbers.[2]
5   Those that will hear me speak, let 'em stay here;
Those that will follow Cassius, go with him;
And public reasons shall be rendered
Of Cæsar's death.
1. PLEBEIAN.   I will hear Brutus speak.
2. PLEBEIAN.   I will hear Cassius, and compare their
reasons,
10   When severally[3] we hear them rendered.

Exit Cassius with some of the Plebeians.
Brutus goes into the pulpit.

3. PLEBEIAN.   The noble Brutus is[4] ascended; silence!

---

75. **Hie hence.** Hurry from here
76. **issue.** Consequences
77. **the which.** The outcome of which (Antony plans to use his speech as an
occasion to test the attitudes of the people about the killing of Cæsar)

ACT 3, SCENE 2
 1. **PLEBEIANS.** Common people
 2. **part the numbers.** Divide the crowd
 3. **severally.** Separately
 4. **is.** Has

words for everyday use

dis • course (dis´kôrs´) *vi.,* speak. *Listening to the professor <u>discourse</u> upon almost any topic was an illuminating experience.*

NOTE THE FACTS

What do the plebeians demand? How will Brutus and Cassius fulfill the demand?

_____

_____

_____

_____

Read aloud Brutus's speech in the highlighted box. What does Brutus say would have happened had Cæsar not been killed? What was Cæsar's crime?

_____

_____

_____

BRUTUS. Be patient till the last.⁵
Romans, countrymen, and lovers,⁶ hear me for my cause, and be silent, that you may hear. Believe me for mine honor,
15 and have respect to⁷ mine honor, that you may believe. Censure⁸ me in your wisdom, and awake your senses, that you may the better judge. If there be any in this assembly, any dear friend of Cæsar's, to him I say, that Brutus' love to Cæsar was no less than his. If then that friend demand why
20 Brutus rose against Cæsar, this is my answer: Not that I lov'd Cæsar less, but that I lov'd Rome more. Had you rather Cæsar were living, and die all slaves, than that Cæsar were dead, to live all freemen? As Cæsar lov'd me, I weep for him; as he was fortunate, I rejoice at it; as he was valiant,
25 I honor him; but, as he was ambitious, I slew him. There is tears for his love; joy for his fortune; honor for his <u>valor</u>; and death for his ambition. Who is here so base⁹ that would be a bondman?¹⁰ If any, speak, for him have I offended. Who is here so rude¹¹ that would not be a Roman? If any,
30 speak, for him have I offended. Who is here so vile that will not love his country? If any, speak, for him have I offended. I pause for a reply.

ALL. None, Brutus, none.

BRUTUS. Then none have I offended. I have done no
35 more to Cæsar than you shall do to Brutus. The question of his death is enroll'd¹² in the Capitol: his glory not extenuated,¹³ wherein he was worthy; nor his offences enforc'd,¹⁴ for which he suffer'd death.

Enter MARK ANTONY *and others with Cæsar's body.*

Here comes his body, mourn'd by Mark Antony, who,
40 though he had no hand in his death, shall receive the benefit

---

5. **last.** End
6. **lovers.** Friends
7. **to.** For
8. **Censure.** Judge
9. **base.** Low
10. **bondman.** Servant, slave
11. **so rude.** Barbarous

12. **question . . . is enroll'd.** Reasons for his death have been recorded
13. **extenuated.** Lessened
14. **enforc'd.** Forced, exaggerated

words for everyday use

val • or (val´ər) n., courage or bravery. *In some medieval works, women are portrayed as knights of great <u>valor</u>.*

of his dying, a place in the <u>commonwealth</u>, as which of you
shall not? With this I depart, that, as I slew my best lover[15]
for the good of Rome, I have the same dagger for myself,
when it shall please my country to need my death.

45   **ALL.**   Live, Brutus, live, live!

  1. PLEBEIAN.   Bring him with triumph home unto his
house.

  2. PLEBEIAN.   Give him a statue with his ancestors.

  3. PLEBEIAN.   Let him be Cæsar.

  4. PLEBEIAN.   Cæsar's better parts
Shall be crown'd in Brutus.

  1. PLEBEIAN.   We'll bring him to his house
With shouts and clamors.

50   **BRUTUS.**   My countrymen—

  2. PLEBEIAN.   Peace, silence! Brutus speaks.

  1. PLEBEIAN.   Peace ho!

  BRUTUS.   Good countrymen, let me depart alone,
And, for my sake, stay here with Antony.
Do grace to Cæsar's corpse, and grace his speech

55 Tending to Cæsar's glories, which Mark Antony
(By our permission) is allow'd to make.
I do entreat you, not a man depart,
Save I alone, till Antony have spoke.[16]   *Exit.*

  1. PLEBEIAN.   Stay ho, and let us hear Mark Antony.

60   **3. PLEBEIAN.**   Let him go up into the public chair,
We'll hear him. Noble Antony, go up.

  ANTONY.   For Brutus' sake, I am beholding to you.

                         Goes into the pulpit.

  4. PLEBEIAN.   What does he say of Brutus?

  3. PLEBEIAN.   He says, for Brutus' sake
He finds himself beholding to us all.

  4. PLEBEIAN.   'Twere best he speak no harm of Brutus
65   here!

  1. PLEBEIAN.   This Cæsar was a tyrant.

---

15. **lover.** Friend
16. **have spoke.** Has spoken

NOTE THE FACTS

What does Brutus offer to do? How do the people respond?

_____

_____

_____

MARK THE TEXT

Underline the opinion the crowd has of Cæsar after Brutus's speech.

Read aloud the highlighted text on this page. What does Antony say is the purpose of his speech? What does he say will live on after Cæsar dies, and what will be buried with Cæsar?

_____

_____

Literary TOOLS

BLANK VERSE AND IAMBIC PENTAMETER. Blank verse is unrhymed poetry written in iambic pentameter. An **iambic pentameter** line consists of five feet, each containing two syllables. The first syllable has a weak beat or stress and the second has a strong stress:

ˇ / ˇ / ˇ /
If it | were so, | it is |

ˇ / ˇ /
a grie | vous fault,

Compare the format of Antony's speech on this page with Brutus's speech on page 280. Which speech does Shakespeare write in prose? Which speech uses blank verse? Why do you think Shakespeare presents the words of these two men so differently?

MARK THE TEXT

Underline the three reasons Antony gives to show that Cæsar was not ambitious.

3. PLEBEIAN.   Nay, that's certain:
We are blest that Rome is rid of him.
2. PLEBEIAN.   Peace, let us hear what Antony can say.
ANTONY.   You gentle Romans—
ALL.   Peace ho, let us hear him.

70   **ANTONY.**   Friends, Romans, countrymen, lend me your ears!
I come to bury Cæsar, not to praise him.
The evil that men do lives after them,
The good is oft <u>interred</u> with their bones;
So let it be with Cæsar. The noble Brutus
75   Hath told you Cæsar was ambitious;
If it were so, it was a <u>grievous</u> fault,
And grievously hath Cæsar answer'd it.
Here, under leave of Brutus and the rest
(For Brutus is an honorable man,
80   So are they all, all honorable men),
Come I to speak in Cæsar's funeral.
He was my friend, faithful and just to me;
But Brutus says he was ambitious,
And Brutus is an honorable man.
85   He hath brought many captives home to Rome,
Whose ransoms did the general coffers[17] fill;
Did this in Cæsar seem ambitious?
When that the poor have cried, Cæsar hath wept;
Ambition should be made of sterner stuff:
90   Yet Brutus says he was ambitious,
And Brutus is an honorable man.
You all did see that on the Lupercal
I thrice presented him a kingly crown,
Which he did thrice refuse. Was this ambition?
95   Yet Brutus says he was ambitious,
And sure[18] he is an honorable man.
I speak not to disprove what Brutus spoke,
But here I am to speak what I do know.

_____

17. **general coffers.** The treasury of the republic
18. **sure.** Certainly

| words for everyday use | **in • ter** (in tər´) vt., bury. _Since the sailors were not able to <u>inter</u> their comrade's remains, they gave him an honorable burial at sea._ |
| | **griev • ous** (grēv´əs) adj., very serious; grave. _That is not just a slight mistake— that's a <u>grievous</u> error!_ |

You all did love him once, not without cause;

100 What cause withholds you then to mourn for him?
O judgment! thou art fled to brutish beasts,
And men have lost their reason. Bear with me,
My heart is in the coffin there with Cæsar,
And I must pause till it come back to me.

1. PLEBEIAN.   Methinks there is much reason in his
105   sayings.
2. PLEBEIAN.   If thou consider rightly of the matter,
Cæsar has had great wrong.
3. PLEBEIAN.   Has he, masters?
I fear there will a worse come in his place.
4. PLEBEIAN.   Mark'd ye his words? He would not take the
    crown,
110 Therefore 'tis certain he was not ambitious.
1. PLEBEIAN.   If it be found so, some will dear abide it.[19]
2. PLEBEIAN.   Poor soul, his eyes are red as fire with
    weeping.
3. PLEBEIAN.   There's not a nobler man in Rome than
    Antony.
4. PLEBEIAN.   Now mark him, he begins again to speak.
115 **ANTONY.**   But yesterday the word of Cæsar might
Have stood against the world; now lies he there,
And none so poor to[20] do him reverence.
O masters! if I were dispos'd to stir
Your hearts and minds to mutiny and rage,
120 I should do Brutus wrong, and Cassius wrong,
Who (you all know) are honorable men.
I will not do them wrong; I rather choose
To wrong the dead, to wrong myself and you,
Than I will wrong such honorable men.
125 But here's a parchment with the seal of Cæsar,
I found it in his closet, 'tis his will.
Let but the commons hear this testament—
Which, pardon me, I do not mean to read—
And they would go and kiss dead Cæsar's wounds,
130 And dip their napkins in his sacred blood;
Yea, beg a hair of him for memory,
And dying, mention it within their wills,

Reading STRATEGY
REVIEW

VISUALIZE. Illustrate the facial expressions of the plebeians, showing their emotions as they consider Antony's assessment of Cæsar.

Literary TOOLS

REPETITION AND IRONY. Repetition is the writer's conscious reuse of a sound, word, phrase, sentence, or other element. **Irony** is a difference between appearance and reality. What word does Antony repeat many times to describe the conspirators, especially Brutus? What does he really want the crowd to think? What makes Antony's description ironic?

_____

_____

_____

_____

Bequeathing it as a rich legacy
Unto their issue.²¹

135 **4. PLEBEIAN.** We'll hear the will. Read it, Mark Antony.

ALL. The will, the will! we will hear Cæsar's will.

ANTONY. Have patience, gentle friends, I must not read it.
It is not meet²² you know how Cæsar lov'd you:
You are not wood, you are not stones, but men;

140 And, being men, hearing the will of Cæsar,
It will inflame you, it will make you mad.
'Tis good you know not that you are his heirs,
For if you should, O, what would come of it?

4. PLEBEIAN. Read the will, we'll hear it, Antony.

145 You shall read us the will, Cæsar's will.

ANTONY. Will you be patient? Will you stay²³ awhile?
I have o'ershot myself²⁴ to tell you of it.
I fear I wrong the honorable men
Whose daggers have stabb'd Cæsar; I do fear it.

150 **4. PLEBEIAN.** They were traitors; honorable men!

ALL. The will! the testament!

2. PLEBEIAN. They were villains, murderers. The will,
read the will!

ANTONY. You will compel me then to read the will?
Then make a ring about the corpse of Cæsar,

155 And let me show you him that made the will.
Shall I descend? and will you give me leave?²⁵

ALL. Come down.

2. PLEBEIAN. Descend.

3. PLEBEIAN. You shall have leave.

ANTONY *comes down from the pulpit.*

160 **4. PLEBEIAN.** A ring, stand round.

1. PLEBEIAN. Stand from the hearse, stand from the body.

2. PLEBEIAN. Room for Antony, most noble Antony.

ANTONY. Nay, press not so upon me, stand far off.

---

21. **issue.** Descendants, heirs
22. **meet.** Proper, suitable
23. **stay.** Wait
24. **o'ershot myself.** Gone too far
25. **give me leave.** Allow me to

words for everyday use be • queath (bē kwēth´) vt., hand down; pass on. *My grandfather bequeathed his gold pocket watch to my father.*

NOTE THE FACTS
What does Antony say when the plebeians insist on hearing Cæsar's will?

THINK AND REFLECT
How does Antony build his case and turn the plebeians against the conspirators? (Synthesize)

ALL. Stand back; room, bear back!

165 ANTONY. If you have tears, prepare to shed them now.
You all do know this mantle. I remember
The first time ever Cæsar put it on;
'Twas on a summer's evening, in his tent,
That day he overcame the Nervii.

170 Look, in this place ran Cassius' dagger through;
See what a rent the envious Casca made;
Through this the well-beloved Brutus stabb'd,
And as he pluck'd his cursed steel away,
Mark how the blood of Cæsar followed it,

175 As rushing out of doors to be resolv'd
If Brutus so unkindly²⁶ knock'd or no;
For Brutus, as you know, was Cæsar's angel.
Judge, O you gods, how dearly Cæsar lov'd him!
This was the most unkindest cut of all;

180 For when the noble Cæsar saw him stab,
Ingratitude, more strong than traitors' arms,
Quite vanquish'd him. Then burst his mighty heart,
And in his mantle muffling up his face,
Even at the base of Pompey's statue

185 (Which all the while ran blood) great Cæsar fell.
O, what a fall was there, my countrymen!
Then I, and you, and all of us fell down,
Whilst bloody treason flourish'd over us.
O now you weep, and I perceive you feel

190 The dint²⁷ of pity. These are gracious drops.
Kind souls, what weep you when you but behold
Our Cæsar's vesture²⁸ wounded? Look you here,

Lifting CÆSAR'S *mantle.*

Here is himself, marr'd as you see with traitors.
1. PLEBEIAN. O piteous spectacle!

195 2. PLEBEIAN. O noble Cæsar!
3. PLEBEIAN. O woeful day!
4. PLEBEIAN. O traitors, villains!
1. PLEBEIAN. O most bloody sight!
2. PLEBEIAN. We will be reveng'd!

200 ALL. Revenge! About! Seek! Burn! Fire! Kill!

---

26. **unkindly.** Unnaturally
27. **dint.** Stroke
28. **vesture.** Clothing

NOTE THE FACTS

What does Antony show the crowd?

_____

_____

_____

READ ALOUD

Read aloud the highlighted text on this page. What does Antony say was the "most unkindest cut of all" for Cæsar? What does he say actually killed Cæsar?

_____

_____

_____

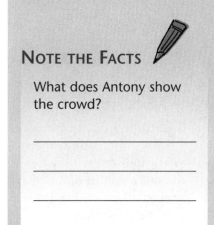

MARK THE TEXT

Circle the words that Antony now calls the conspirators.

NOTE THE FACTS

What does Antony say he did not mean to do? According to Antony, how does he differ from Brutus?

_____

_____

_____

_____

Literary TOOLS

IRONY. Irony is a difference between appearance and reality. How does Antony use irony to his advantage?

_____

_____

_____

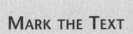

MARK THE TEXT

Underline or highlight what Cæsar has left to the people in his will.

Slay! Let not a traitor live!

ANTONY.   Stay, countrymen.

1. PLEBEIAN.   Peace there, hear the noble Antony.

2. PLEBEIAN.   We'll hear him, we'll follow him, we'll die with him.

205   **ANTONY.**   Good friends, sweet friends, let me not stir you up
To such a sudden flood of mutiny.
They that have done this deed are honorable.
What private griefs they have, alas, I know not,
That made them do it. They are wise and honorable,
210   And will no doubt with reasons answer you.
I come not, friends, to steal away your hearts.
I am no orator, as Brutus is;
But (as you know me all) a plain blunt man
That love[29] my friend, and that they know full well
215   That gave me public leave to speak of him.
For I have neither wit, nor words,[30] nor worth,
Action, nor utterance, nor the power of speech
To stir men's blood; I only speak right on.[31]
I tell you that which you yourselves do know,
220   Show you sweet Cæsar's wounds, poor, poor, dumb mouths,
And bid them speak for me. But were I Brutus,
And Brutus Antony, there were an Antony
Would ruffle up your spirits, and put a tongue
In every wound of Cæsar, that should move
225   The stones of Rome to rise and mutiny.

ALL.   We'll mutiny.

1. PLEBEIAN.   We'll burn the house of Brutus.

3. PLEBEIAN.   Away then, come, seek the conspirators.

ANTONY.   Yet hear me, countrymen, yet hear me speak.

ALL.   Peace ho, hear Antony, most noble Antony!

230   **ANTONY.**   Why, friends, you go to do you know not what.
Wherein hath Cæsar thus deserv'd your loves?
Alas you know not! I must tell you then:
You have forgot the will I told you of.

ALL.   Most true. The will! Let's stay and hear the will.

235   **ANTONY.**   Here is the will, and under Cæsar's seal:
To every Roman citizen he gives,
To every several man, seventy-five drachmas.

---

29. **That love.** Loved
30. **words.** Fluency; ease with words
31. **right on.** Directly, from the heart, not as a trained speaker

2. PLEBEIAN.   Most noble Cæsar! we'll revenge his death.

3. PLEBEIAN.   O royal Cæsar!

240   **ANTONY.**   Hear me with patience.

ALL.   Peace ho!

ANTONY.   Moreover, he hath left you all his walks,
His private arbors and new-planted orchards,
On this side Tiber;[32] he hath left them you,
245   And to your heirs for ever—common pleasures,[33]
To walk abroad and recreate[34] yourselves.
Here was a Cæsar! when comes such another?

1. PLEBEIAN.   Never, never! Come, away, away!
We'll burn his body in the holy place,
250   And with the brands fire the traitors' houses.
Take up the body.

2. PLEBEIAN.   Go fetch fire.

3. PLEBEIAN.   Pluck down benches.

4. PLEBEIAN.   Pluck down forms,[35] windows,[36] anything.

Exeunt PLEBEIANS *with the body.*

255   **ANTONY.**   Now let it work. Mischief, thou art afoot,
Take thou what course thou wilt!

Enter SERVANT.

How now, fellow?

SERVANT.   Sir, Octavius is[37] already come to Rome.

ANTONY.   Where is he?

SERVANT.   He and Lepidus are at Cæsar's house.

260   **ANTONY.**   And thither will I straight to visit him;
He comes upon a wish.[38] Fortune is merry,
And in this mood will give us any thing.

SERVANT.   I heard him say, Brutus and Cassius
Are rid[39] like madmen through the gates of Rome.

265   **ANTONY.**   Belike[40] they had some notice[41] of the people,
How I had mov'd them. Bring me to Octavius.

Exeunt.

---

32. **this side Tiber.** On this side of the Tiber river
33. **pleasures.** Public places of rest and relaxation
34. **recreate.** Enjoy
35. **forms.** Benches
36. **windows.** Shutters
37. **is.** Has
38. **upon a wish.** As I wished
39. **Are rid.** Have ridden
40. **Belike.** Most likely
41. **notice.** News

NOTE THE FACTS

What else does Antony say Cæsar has left the people?

_____

_____

_____

READ ALOUD

Read aloud the highlighted text on this page. What does the mob leave to do?

_____

_____

_____

THINK AND REFLECT

By the end of this scene, what has Antony accomplished? What does this reflect about Antony's character? **(Synthesize and Infer)**

_____

_____

_____

_____

_____

Reflect ON YOUR READING

After Reading **SUMMARIZE THE SELECTION**

After you finish reading, work with a small group to complete your Summarize Sections Chart for all scenes in the selection. How have fortunes changed for Cæsar, Brutus, and Antony? What character trait in each man has led to the outcome he experienced?

Reading Skills and Test Practice

COMPARE AND CONTRAST

READ, THINK, AND EXPLAIN. Compare and contrast the speeches of Brutus and Cæsar and the end results of each. Use evidence from the text to support your answer.

_____

_____

_____

_____

_____

_____

REFLECT ON YOUR RESPONSE. Compare your response with that of a partner. Talk about how the information you wrote down while reading helped you write your response.

_____

_____

_____

_____

_____

Investigate, Inquire, and Imagine

RECALL: GATHER FACTS
1a. As Brutus ends his speech, what does he tell the crowd about Antony? What does this reveal about how much Brutus trusts Antony?

→ INTERPRET: FIND MEANING
1b. Why do you think Brutus allows Antony to give a funeral speech for Cæsar, despite Cassius's warnings? What does this action reveal about Brutus? Is this action a mistake? Why, or why not?

ANALYZE: TAKE THINGS APART
2a. Compare the speeches delivered by Brutus and Mark Antony before the plebeians. Analyze the content and purpose of each speech as well as its tone and style. How are the speeches similar, and how are they different?

→ SYNTHESIZE: BRING THINGS TOGETHER
2b. What conclusions do you draw about the character of each man based on their speeches?

EVALUATE: MAKE JUDGMENTS
3a. Evaluate the impact of Mark Antony's speech on the crowd. What do you think he hoped to accomplish in his speech? Why? Using evidence from the text of the speech, explain whether or not he reached his goal.

→ EXTEND: CONNECT IDEAS
3b. When have you been part of a crowd that acted in ways each person would not have acted if alone? When is mob mentality dangerous? What examples of mob mentality can you recall from history or recent world and national events? Can mob influence ever be positive?

Literary Tools

MOTIVATION. A **motivation** is a force that moves a character to think, feel, or behave in a certain way. Review your completed Summarize Sections Chart. What motivates Cæsar, Brutus, and Antony to behave as they do? How is each man motivated to act? What is the end result of such motivations and actions?

_____

_____

_____

_____

_____

_____

WordWorkshop

WORD RACE. Working with two classmates, practice reading the twenty vocabulary words from the selection aloud. Have one person time how many seconds it takes you to read the entire list. Have another person keep track of the words you mispronounce. Compete with another team to see which team pronounces the same list of words the fastest with the fewest errors. Then read the word list again, seeing who can read the words the loudest, softest, and with the most emotion.

amiss	expound	portent
bequeath	grievous	puissant
commonwealth	horrid	reverence
cur	imminent	utterance
decree	inter	valiant
discourse	lament	valor
entrails	malice	

Read-Write Connection

What do you predict will happen next for Antony and Brutus? What would you advise each person to do?

_____

_____

_____

_____

_____

_____

_____

Beyond the Reading

READ MORE OF THE PLAY. Get a complete copy of *The Tragedy of Julius Cæsar* from your teacher or a library and finish reading it. Before you start, go back over the cast of characters at the beginning of act 1 and predict what will happen to each person. What will become of the conspirators? What will Antony do next? When you finish reading the play, go back and see if your predictions came true.

GO ONLINE. Visit the EMC Internet Resource Center at **emcp.com** to find links and additional activities for this selection.

THE HITCHHIKER

by Lucille Fletcher

Active READING STRATEGY

USE TEXT ORGANIZATION

Before Reading ➤ **PREVIEW THE SELECTION**

❏ Form a group of three or four. Then read the Reader's Resource and discuss how this play might be different than one meant to be performed on stage.

❏ Preview the selection. Look over the list of characters on page 292. Notice that segments of the play are divided by music and that sound effects are included in the text. Why is some of the text italicized?

❏ Preview the information in Literary Tools on page 294. Make sure everyone in your group understands the definitions of *foreshadowing* and *suspense*. Then examine the Suspenseful Events Chart below. As you read, you will label suspenseful events from the text on the appropriate spot on the road.

Graphic Organizer

CONNECT

Reader's resource

The Hitchhiker is about a cross-country drive that quickly turns eerie. It is one of several radio plays written by Lucille Fletcher (1912–). A radio play is meant to be heard and depends entirely on sound to convey what is happening. Notice how sound effects, music, and the characters' words carefully paint a picture of each scene so that the listener can visualize what is happening.

Word watch

PREVIEW VOCABULARY

nondescript
ominous
outset
phosphorescent

Reader's journal

Do you enjoy ghost stories and thrillers? Why do you think such stories are so popular?

_____

_____

_____

_____

_____

_____

USE TEXT ORGANIZATION

❑ Read the play aloud with your class. Assign parts using the list of characters below. Pay close attention to the descriptions of sound effects and music.

❑ Using cues such as music, sound effects, and dialogue, look for suspenseful moments in the text. Record suspenseful events in your graphic organizer.

CHARACTERS

Orson Welles, narrator
Ronald Adams
Mother
Voice
Mechanic
Henry
Woman
Girl
Gallup Operator
Long Distance Operator
Albuquerque Operator
New York Operator
Mrs. Whitney

NOTE THE FACTS

How will this ghost story be different from most?

_____

_____

_____

_____

THE HITCHHIKER

Lucille Fletcher

WELLES. (*narrating*)   Good evening, this is Orson Welles. . . .

MUSIC.   *In.*

WELLES.   Personally I've never met anybody who didn't like a good ghost story, but I know a lot of people who think there are a lot of people who don't like a good ghost story. For the benefit of these, at least, I go on record at the <u>outset</u> of this evening's entertainment with the sober assurance that, although blood may be curdled on the program, none will be
10   spilt. There's no shooting, knifing, throttling, axing, or poisoning here. No clanking chains, no cobwebs, no bony and/or hairy hands appearing from secret panels or, better yet, bedroom curtains. If it's any part of that dear old <u>phosphorescent</u> foolishness that people who don't like ghost stories don't like, then again, I promise you we haven't got it. What we do have is a thriller. If it's half as good as we think it is, you can call it a shocker, and we present it proudly and without apologies. After all, a story doesn't have to appeal to the heart—it can also appeal to the spine. Sometimes you

words for everyday use	
	out • set (outʹsetʹ) *n.*, beginning; start. *Though he tried his best, Randall knew from the <u>outset</u> that he would never persuade the queen of the prom to join his rock band.*
	phos • pho • res • cent (fäsʹfə reʹsənt) *adj.*, luminescent, giving off light. *Warm sea waters often glow at night when <u>phosphorescent</u> plankton are agitated.*

20 want your heart to be warmed—sometimes you want your spine to tingle. The tingling, it's to be hoped, will be quite audible as you listen tonight to *The Hitchhiker*—That's the name of our story, *The Hitchhiker*—

SOUND. *Automobile wheels humming over concrete road.*

MUSIC. *Something weird and shuddery.*

ADAMS. (*narrating*) I am in an auto camp[1] on Route Sixty-Six just west of Gallup, New Mexico. If I tell it, perhaps it will help me. It will keep me from going mad. But I must tell this quickly. I am not mad now. I feel perfectly
30 well, except that I am running a slight temperature. My name is Ronald Adams. I am thirty-six years of age, unmarried, tall, dark, with a black mustache. I drive a 1940 Ford V-8, license number 6V-7989. I was born in Brooklyn.[2] All this I know. I know that I am, at this moment, perfectly sane. That it is not I who has gone mad—but something else—something utterly beyond my control. But I must speak quickly . . . very quickly. At any moment the link with life may break. This may be the last thing I ever tell on earth . . . the last night I ever see the stars. . . .

40 **MUSIC.** *In.*

ADAMS. (*narrating*) Six days ago I left Brooklyn to drive to California. . . .

MOTHER. Goodbye, son. Good luck to you, my boy. . . .

ADAMS. Goodbye, mother. Here—give me a kiss, and then I'll go. . . .

MOTHER. I'll come out with you to the car.

ADAMS. No. It's raining. Stay here at the door. Hey—what is this? Tears? I thought you promised me you wouldn't cry.

MOTHER. I know dear. I'm sorry. But I—do hate to see
50 you go.

ADAMS. I'll be back. I'll only be on the coast three months.

MOTHER. Oh—it isn't that. It's just—the trip. Ronald—I really wish you weren't driving.

ADAMS. Oh—mother. There you go again. People do it every day.

MOTHER. I know. But you'll be careful, won't you. Promise me you'll be extra careful. Don't fall asleep—or drive fast—or pick up any strangers on the road. . . .

---

1. **auto camp.** Highway rest area
2. **Brooklyn.** One of the five boroughs of New York City; located south of the island of Manhattan

READ ALOUD

Read the highlighted passage aloud. Use your voice to capture Adams's mood. How can you tell something is wrong?

_____

_____

_____

NOTE THE FACTS

What does Adams's mother fear?

_____

_____

Use THE STRATEGY

USE TEXT ORGANIZATION. Notice how the music is used to set the mood of each section. What does the music in line 73 signal about what is about to happen?

_____

_____

_____

ADAMS. Lord, no. You'd think I was still seventeen to hear you talk—

MOTHER. And wire me as soon as you get to Hollywood, won't you, son?

ADAMS. Of course I will. Now don't you worry. There isn't anything going to happen. It's just eight days of perfectly simple driving on smooth, decent, civilized roads, with a hotdog or a hamburger stand every ten miles. . . . *(Fade)*

SOUND. *Auto hum.*

MUSIC. *In.*

ADAMS. *(narrating)* I was in excellent spirits. The drive ahead of me, even the loneliness, seemed like a lark. But I reckoned without *him.*

MUSIC. *Changes to something weird and empty.*

ADAMS. *(narrating)* Crossing Brooklyn Bridge that morning in the rain, I saw a man leaning against the cables. He seemed to be waiting for a lift. There were spots of fresh rain on his shoulders. He was carrying a cheap overnight bag in one hand. He was thin, <u>nondescript</u>, with a cap pulled down over his eyes. He stepped off the walk right in front of me and, if I hadn't swerved hard, I'd have hit him.

SOUND. *Terrific skidding.*

MUSIC. *In.*

ADAMS. *(narrating)* I would have forgotten him completely, except that just an hour later, while crossing the Pulaski Skyway over the Jersey flats,[3] I saw him again. At least, he looked like the same person. He was standing now, with one thumb pointing west. I couldn't figure out how he'd got there, but I thought probably one of those fast trucks had picked him up, beaten me to the Skyway, and let him off. I didn't stop for him. Then—late that night, I saw him again.

MUSIC. *Changing.*

ADAMS. *(narrating)* It was on the New Pennsylvania Turnpike between Harrisburg and Pittsburgh. It's two

---

3. **Pulaski Skyway . . . Jersey flats.** Name of an overpass that crosses a marshy area in northeastern New Jersey

words for everyday use

non • de • script (nän´di skript´) *adj.,* lacking in recognizable characteristics or qualities. *The house was so <u>nondescript</u> that I wasn't sure I would recognize it.*

hundred and sixty-five miles long, with a very high speed limit. I was just slowing down for one of the tunnels—when I saw him—standing under an arc light by the side of the road. I could see him quite distinctly. The bag, the cap, even the spots of fresh rain spattered over his shoulders. He hailed me this time. . . .

100   **VOICE.** (*very spooky and faint*)   Hall-ooo. . . . (*It echoes as though coming through the tunnel.*) Hall-ooo. . . !

ADAMS. (*narrating*)   I stepped on the gas like a shot. That's lonely country through the Alleghenies, and I had no intention of stopping. Besides, the coincidence, or whatever it was, gave me the willies. I stopped at the next gas station.

SOUND.   *Auto tires screeching to stop . . . horn honk.*

MECHANIC.   Yes, sir.

ADAMS.   Fill her up.

MECHANIC.   Certainly, sir. Check your oil, sir?

110   **ADAMS.**   No, thanks.

SOUND.   *Gas being put into car.*

MECHANIC.   Nice night, isn't it?

ADAMS.   Yes. It—hasn't been raining here recently, has it?

MECHANIC.   Not a drop of rain all week.

ADAMS.   I suppose that hasn't done your business any harm.

MECHANIC.   Oh—people drive through here all kinds of weather. Mostly business, you know. There aren't many pleasure cars out on the Turnpike this season of the year.

ADAMS.   I suppose not. (*casually*) What about hitchhikers?

120   **MECHANIC.** (*laughing*)   Hitchhikers here?

ADAMS.   What's the matter? Don't you ever see any?

MECHANIC.   Not much. If we did, it'd be a sight for sore eyes.

ADAMS.   Why?

MECHANIC.   A guy'd be a fool who started out to hitch rides on this road. Look at it. It's two hundred and sixty-five miles long, there's practically no speed limit, and it's a straightaway. Now what car is going to stop to pick up a guy under those conditions? Would you stop?

130   **ADAMS.**   No. (*He answers slowly, with puzzled emphasis.*) Then you've never seen anybody?

MECHANIC.   Nope. Mebbe they get the lift before the Turnpike starts—I mean, you know—just before the toll house—but then it'd be a mighty long ride. Most cars wouldn't want to pick up a guy for that long a ride. And you

THINK AND REFLECT

Why does Adams ask about the rain? (**Infer**)

_____

_____

_____

THINK AND REFLECT

How do the mechanic's answers make Adams feel? (**Interpret**)

_____

_____

_____

know—this is pretty lonesome country here—mountains, and woods. . . . You ain't seen anybody like that, have you?

ADAMS.   No. *(quickly)* Oh no, not at all. It was—just a—technical question.′

140   **MECHANIC.**   I see. Well—that'll be just a dollar forty-nine—with the tax.

. . . *(Fade)*

SOUND.   *Auto hum up.*

MUSIC.   *Changing.*

ADAMS. *(narrating)*   The thing gradually passed from my mind, as sheer coincidence. I had a good night's sleep in Pittsburgh. I did not think about the man all next day—until just outside of Zanesville, Ohio, I saw him again.

MUSIC.   *Dark,* <u>ominous</u> *note.*

150   **ADAMS.** *(narrating)*   It was a bright sun-shiny afternoon. The peaceful Ohio fields, brown with the autumn stubble, lay dreaming in the golden light. I was driving slowly, drinking it in, when the road suddenly ended in a detour. In front of the barrier, he was standing.

MUSIC.   *In.*

ADAMS. *(narrating)*   Let me explain about his appearance before I go on. I repeat. There was nothing sinister about him. He was as drab as a mud fence. Nor was his attitude menacing. He merely stood there, waiting, almost drooping

160   a little, the cheap overnight bag in his hand. He looked as though he had been waiting there for hours. Then he looked up. He hailed me. He started to walk forward.

VOICE. *(far off)* Hall-ooo . . . Hall-ooo. . . .

ADAMS. *(narrating)*   I had stopped the car, of course, for the detour. And for a few moments, I couldn't seem to find the new road. I knew he must be thinking that I had stopped for him.

VOICE. *(sounding closer now)*   Hall-ooo . . . Hallll . . . ooo. . . .

SOUND.   *Gears jamming . . . sound of motor turning over hard*

170   *. . . nervous accelerator.*

VOICE. *(closer)*   Hall . . . oooo. . . .

ADAMS. *(with panic in his voice)*   No. Not just now. Sorry. . . .

words for everyday use

om • i • nous (äm´ə nəs) *adj.,* threatening, sinister. *The captain of the field hockey team thought the buzzards circling overhead at the start of the game were* <u>ominous</u>.

VOICE. (*closer*)   Going to California?

SOUND.   *Starter starting . . . gears jamming.*

ADAMS. (*as though sweating blood*)   No. Not today. The other way. Going to New York. Sorry . . . sorry. . . .

SOUND.   *Car starts with squeal of wheels on dirt . . . into auto hum.*

MUSIC.   *In.*

180   **ADAMS.** (*narrating*)   After I got the car back onto the road again, I felt like a fool. Yet the thought of picking him up, of having him sit beside me was somehow unbearable. Yet, at the same time, I felt, more than ever, unspeakably alone.

SOUND.   *Auto hum up.*

ADAMS. (*narrating*)   Hour after hour went by. The fields, the towns ticked off, one by one. The lights changed. I knew now that I was going to see him again. And though I dreaded the sight, I caught myself searching the side of the road, waiting for him to appear.

190   **SOUND.**   *Auto hum up . . . car screeches to a halt . . . impatient honk two or three times . . . door being unbolted.*

SLEEPY MAN'S VOICE.   Yep? What is it? What do you want?

ADAMS. (*breathless*)   You sell sandwiches and pop here, don't you?

VOICE. (*cranky*)   Yep. We do. In the daytime. But we're closed up now for the night.

ADAMS.   I know. But—I was wondering if you could possibly let me have a cup of coffee—black coffee.

VOICE.   Not at this time of night, mister. My wife's the

200   cook and she's in bed. Mebbe further down the road—at the Honeysuckle Rest. . . .

SOUND.   *Door squeaking on hinges as though being closed.*

ADAMS.   No—no. Don't shut the door. (*shakily*) Listen—just a minute ago, there was a man standing here—right beside this stand—a suspicious looking man. . . .

WOMAN'S VOICE. (*from distance*)   Henry? Who is it, Henry?

HENRY.   It's nobuddy, mother. Just a feller thinks he wants a cup of coffee. Go back into bed.

ADAMS.   I don't mean to disturb you. But you see, I was

210   driving along—when I just happened to look—and there he was. . . .

HENRY.   What was he doing?

ADAMS.   Nothing. He ran off—when I stopped the car.

THINK AND REFLECT

Why does Henry react negatively to Adams? **(Infer)**

_____

_____

_____

MARK THE TEXT

Underline or highlight words that contribute to the mood of lines 227–237. How would you describe this mood? What does Adams plan to do?

_____

—

_____

_____

Reading STRATEGY
REVIEW

VISUALIZE. Picturing what is happening as you read will help you get more from your reading. Form mental images of what happens in lines 240–269.

HENRY. Then what of it? That's nothing to wake a man in the middle of his sleep about. (*sternly*) Young man, I've got a good mind to turn you over to the local sheriff.

ADAMS. But—I—

HENRY. You've been taking a nip,[4] that's what you've been doing. And you haven't got anything better to do than to

220 wake decent folk out of their hard-earned sleep. Get going. Go on.

ADAMS. But—he looked as though he were going to rob you.

HENRY. I ain't got nothin' in this stand to lose. Now—on your way before I call out Sheriff Oakes. (*Fade*)

SOUND. *Auto hum up.*

ADAMS. (*narrating*) I got into the car again, and drove on slowly. I was beginning to hate the car. If I could have found a place to stop . . . to rest a little. But I was in the Ozark

230 Mountains of Missouri now. The few resort places there were closed. Only an occasional log cabin, seemingly deserted, broke the monotony of the wild wooded landscape. I had seen him at that roadside stand; I knew I would see him again—perhaps at the next turn of the road. I knew that when I saw him next, I would run him down. . . .

SOUND. *Auto hum up.*

ADAMS. But I did not see him again until late next afternoon. . . .

SOUND. *Warning system at train crossing.*

240 **ADAMS.** (*narrating*) I had stopped the car at a sleepy little junction just across the border into Oklahoma—to let a train pass by—when he appeared, across the tracks, leaning against a telephone pole.

SOUND. *Distant sound of train chugging . . . bell ringing steadily.*

ADAMS. (*narrating, very tensely*) It was a perfectly airless, dry day. The red clay of Oklahoma was baking under the southwestern sun. Yet there were spots of fresh rain on his shoulders. I couldn't stand that. Without thinking, blindly, I

250 started the car across the tracks.

SOUND. *Train chugging closer.*

ADAMS. (*narrating*) He didn't even look up at me. He was staring at the ground. I stepped on the gas hard, veering the

---

4. **taking a nip.** Having a drink of something alcoholic

wheel sharply toward him. I could hear the train in the distance now, but I didn't care. Then something went wrong with the car. It stalled right on the tracks.

SOUND. *Train chugging closer. Above this, sound of car stalling.*

ADAMS. (*narrating*)   The train was coming closer. I could hear its bell ringing, and the cry of its whistle. Still he stood there. And now—I knew that he was beckoning—beckoning me to my death.

SOUND. *Train chugging close. Whistle blows wildly. Then train rushes up and by with pistons going.*

ADAMS. (*narrating*)   Well—I frustrated him that time. The starter had worked at last. I managed to back up. But when the train passed, he was gone. I was all alone in the hot dry afternoon.

SOUND. *Train retreating. Crickets begin to sing in background.*

MUSIC. *In.*

ADAMS. (*narrating*)   After that, I knew I had to do something. I didn't know who this man was or what he wanted of me. I only knew that from now on, I must not let myself be alone on the road for one single moment.

SOUND. *Auto hum up. Slow down. Stop. Door opening.*

ADAMS.   Hello, there. Like a ride?

GIRL.   Well, what do you think? How far you going?

ADAMS.   Amarillo . . . I'll take you all the way to Amarillo.

GIRL.   Amarillo, Texas?

ADAMS.   I'll drive you there.

GIRL.   Gee!

SOUND. *Door closes—car starts.*

MUSIC. *In.*

GIRL.   Mind if I take off my shoes? My dogs[5] are killing me.

ADAMS.   Go right ahead.

GIRL.   Gee, what a break this is. A swell car, a decent guy, and driving all the way to Amarillo. All I been getting so far is trucks.

ADAMS.   Hitchhike much?

GIRL.   Sure. Only it's tough sometimes, in these great open spaces, to get the breaks.

ADAMS.   I should think it would be. Though I'll bet if you get a good pick-up in a fast car, you can get to places faster than—say, another person, in another car?

260

270

280

290

---

5. **dogs.** Feet (slang)

WHAT DO YOU WONDER?

_____

_____

_____

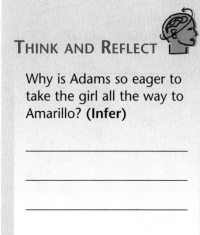

THINK AND REFLECT

Why is Adams so eager to take the girl all the way to Amarillo? **(Infer)**

_____

_____

_____

THINK AND REFLECT

Reread lines 295–300. Why is Adams asking the girl this question? (Infer)

_____

_____

_____

GIRL. I don't get you.

ADAMS. Well, take me, for instance. Suppose I'm driving across the country, say, at a nice steady clip of about forty-five miles an hour. Couldn't a girl like you, just standing beside the road, waiting for lifts, beat me to town after town—provided she got picked up every time in a car doing
300   from sixty-five to seventy miles an hour?

GIRL. I dunno. Maybe and maybe not. What difference does it make?

ADAMS. Oh—no difference. It's just a—crazy idea I had sitting here in the car.

GIRL. (*laughing*) Imagine spending your time in a swell car thinking of things like that!

ADAMS. What would you do instead?

GIRL. (*admiringly*) What would I do? If I was a good-looking fellow like yourself? Why—I'd just enjoy
310   myself—every minute of the time. I'd sit back, and relax, and if I saw a good-looking girl along the side of the road . . . (*sharply*) Hey! Look out!

ADAMS. (*breathlessly*) Did you see him too?

GIRL. See who?

ADAMS. That man. Standing beside the barbed wire fence.

GIRL. I didn't see—anybody. There wasn't nothing but a bunch of steers—and the barbed wire fence. What did you think you was doing? Trying to run into the barbed wire fence?

320   **ADAMS.** There was a man there, I tell you . . . a thin gray man, with an overnight bag in his hand. And I was trying to—run him down.

GIRL. Run him down? You mean—kill him?

ADAMS. He's a sort of—phantom. I'm trying to get rid of him—or else prove that he's real. But (*desperately*) you say you didn't see him back there? You're sure?

GIRL. (*queerly*) I didn't see a soul. And as far as that's concerned, mister . . .

ADAMS. Watch for him the next time, then. Keep
330   watching. Keep your eyes peeled on the road. He'll turn up again—maybe any minute now. (*excitedly*) There. Look there—

SOUND. *Auto sharply veering and skidding. Girl screams.*

SOUND. *Crash of car going into barbed wire fence. Frightened lowing of steer.*

NOTE THE FACTS

What did Adams do that scared the girl? Why did he do this?

_____

_____

_____

GIRL. How does this door work? I—I'm gettin' outta here.

ADAMS. Did you see him that time?

GIRL (*sharply*) No. I didn't see him that time. And personally, mister, I don't expect never to see him. All I want
340 to do is to go on living—and I don't see how I will very long driving with you—

ADAMS. I'm sorry. I—I don't know what came over me. (*frightened*) Please—don't go. . . .

GIRL. So if you'll excuse me, mister—

ADAMS. You can't go. Listen, how would you like to go to California? I'll drive you to California.

GIRL. Seeing pink elephants all the way? No thanks.

ADAMS. (*desperately*) I could get you a job there. You wouldn't have to be a waitress. I have friends there—my
350 name is Ronald Adams—You can check up.

SOUND. *Door opens.*

GIRL. Uhn-hunh. Thanks just the same.

ADAMS. Listen. Please. For just one minute. Maybe you think I am half cracked. But this man. You see, I've been seeing this man all the way across the country. He's been following me. And if you could only help me—stay with me—until I reach the coast—

GIRL. You know what I think you need, big boy? Not a girl friend. Just a good dose of sleep. . . . There, I got it now.
360 **SOUND.** *Door opens . . . slams.*

ADAMS. No. You can't go.

GIRL. (*screams*) Leave your hands offa me, do you hear! Leave your—

ADAMS. Come back here, please, come back.

SOUND. *Struggle . . . slap . . . footsteps running away on gravel . . . lowing of steer.*

ADAMS. (*narrating*) She ran from me, as though I were a monster. A few minutes later, I saw a passing truck pick her up. I knew then that I was utterly alone.
370 **SOUND.** *Lowing of steer up.*

ADAMS. (*narrating*) I was in the heart of the great Texas prairies. There wasn't a car on the road after the truck went by. I tried to figure out what to do, how to get hold of myself. If I could find a place to rest. Or even, if I could sleep right here in the car for a few hours, along the side of the road . . . I was getting my winter overcoat out of the back seat to use as a blanket, (Hall-ooo), when I saw him

FIX-UP IDEA

Connect to Prior Knowledge
If you have trouble understanding why the characters behave as they do, try putting yourself in their positions. What associations do you have with hitchhikers? How would you feel if you were Adams? if you were the girl?

THINK AND REFLECT

Why does the girl run away? **(Infer)**

_____

_____

coming toward me (Hall-ooo), emerging from the herd of moving steer . . .

380   **VOICE.**   Hall-ooo . . . Hall-oooo . . .

SOUND.   *Auto starting violently . . . up to steady hum.*

MUSIC.   *In.*

ADAMS. (*narrating*)   I didn't wait for him to come any closer. Perhaps I should have spoken to him then, fought it out then and there. For now he began to be everywhere. Whenever I stopped, even for a moment—for gas, for oil, for a drink of pop, a cup of coffee, a sandwich—he was there.

MUSIC.   *Faster.*

390   **ADAMS.** (*narrating*)   I saw him standing outside the auto camp in Amarillo that night, when I dared to slow down. He was sitting near the drinking fountain in a little camping spot just inside the border of New Mexico.

MUSIC.   *Faster.*

ADAMS. (*narrating*)   He was waiting for me outside the Navajo Reservation,[6] where I stopped to check my tires. I saw him in Albuquerque where I bought twelve gallons of gas . . . I was afraid now, afraid to stop. I began to drive faster and faster. I was in lunar landscape now—the great

400   arid mesa country of New Mexico. I drove through it with the indifference of a fly crawling over the face of the moon.

MUSIC.   *Faster.*

ADAMS. (*narrating*)   But now he didn't even wait for me to stop. Unless I drove at eighty-five miles an hour over those endless roads—he waited for me at every other mile. I would see his figure, shadowless, flitting before me, still in its same attitude, over the cold and lifeless ground, flitting over dried-up rivers, over broken stones cast up by old glacial upheavals, flitting in the pure and cloudless air. . . .

410   **MUSIC.**   *Strikes sinister note of finality.*

ADAMS. (*narrating*)   I was beside myself when I finally reached Gallup, New Mexico, this morning. There is an auto camp here—cold, almost deserted at this time of year. I went inside, and asked if there was a telephone. I had the feeling that if only I could speak to someone familiar, someone I loved, I could pull myself together.

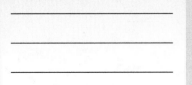

THINK AND REFLECT

Reread lines 403–409. What does this passage confirm or deny about Adams's previous theory that the hitchhiker was getting fast rides and so staying ahead of him?

_____

_____

_____

---

6. **Navajo Reservation.** Land reserved for the Navajo tribe by the United States government during the period of westward expansion, similar to other reservations for Native American tribes

SOUND.   *Nickel put in slot.*

OPERATOR.   Number, please?

ADAMS.   Long distance.

420   **SOUND.**   *Return of nickel: buzz.*

LONG DISTANCE.   This is long distance.

ADAMS.   I'd like to put in a call to my home in Brooklyn, New York. My name is Ronald Adams. The number there is Beechwood 2-0828.

LONG DISTANCE.   Thank you. What is your number?

ADAMS.   312.

ALBUQUERQUE OPR.   Albuquerque.

LONG DISTANCE.   New York for Gallup. (*Pause*)

NEW YORK OPR.   New York.

430   **LONG DISTANCE.**   Gallup, New Mexico, calling Beechwood 2-0828. (*Fade*)

ADAMS.   I had read somewhere that love could banish demons. It was the middle of the morning. I knew Mother would be home. I pictured her, tall, white-haired, in her crisp house dress, going about her tasks. It would be enough, I thought, merely to hear the even calmness of her voice. . . .

LONG DISTANCE.   Will you please deposit three dollars and eighty-five cents for the first three minutes? When you have deposited a dollar and a half, will you please wait until

440   I have collected the money?

SOUND.   *Clunk of six coins.*

LONG DISTANCE.   All right, deposit another dollar and a half.

SOUND.   *Clunk of six coins.*

LONG DISTANCE.   Will you please deposit the remaining twelve cents?

SOUND.   *Clunk of four coins.*

LONG DISTANCE.   Ready with Brooklyn—go ahead, please.

ADAMS.   Hello.

450   **MRS. WHITNEY.**   Mrs. Adams's residence.

ADAMS.   Hello. Hello—Mother?

MRS. WHITNEY. (*very flat and rather proper . . . dumb, too, in a flighty sort of way*) This is Mrs. Adams's residence. Who is it you wished to speak to, please?

ADAMS.   Why—who's this?

MRS. WHITNEY.   This is Mrs. Whitney.

ADAMS.   Whitney? I don't know any Mrs. Whitney. Is this Beechwood 2-0828?

NOTE THE FACTS

Why does Adams make the telephone call?

_____

_____

MAKE A NOTE

_____

_____

_____

_____

NOTE THE FACTS

Where is Adams's mother? Why?

_____

_____

READ ALOUD

With a partner, read the highlighted section aloud. What confusing information does Mrs. Whitney give Adams?

_____

_____

MRS. WHITNEY.   Yes.

460   ADAMS.   Where's my mother? Where's Mrs. Adams?

MRS. WHITNEY.   Mrs. Adams is not at home. She is still in the hospital.

ADAMS.   The hospital!

MRS. WHITNEY.   Yes. Who is this calling please? Is it a member of the family?

ADAMS.   What's she in the hospital for?

MRS. WHITNEY.   She's been prostrated[7] for five days. Nervous breakdown. But who is this calling?

ADAMS.   Nervous breakdown? But—my mother was never

470   nervous . . .

MRS. WHITNEY.   It's all taken place since the death of her oldest son, Ronald.

ADAMS.   The death of her oldest son, Ronald. . . ? Hey— what is this? What number is this?

MRS. WHITNEY.   This is Beechwood 2-0828. It's all been very sudden. He was killed just six days ago in an automobile accident on the Brooklyn Bridge.

OPERATOR. (breaking in)   Your three minutes are up, sir. (Silence)

480   OPERATOR.   Your three minutes are up, sir. (pause) Your three minutes are up, sir. (fade) Sir, your three minutes are up. Your three minutes are up, sir.

ADAMS. (narrating in a strange voice) And so, I am sitting here in this deserted auto camp in Gallup, New Mexico. I am trying to think. I am trying to get hold of myself. Otherwise, I shall go mad . . . Outside it is night—the vast, soulless night of New Mexico. A million stars are in the sky. Ahead of me stretch a thousand miles of empty mesa, mountains, prairies—desert. Somewhere among them, he is

490   waiting for me. Somewhere I shall know who he is, and who . . . I . . . am. . . .

MUSIC.   Up.   ■

---

7. **prostrated.** The character means *prostrate*, lying flat.

Reflect ON YOUR READING

ANALYZE TEXT ORGANIZATION

Meet again with your before-reading group. Compare your Suspenseful Events Charts and discuss the following questions:

- How was suspense built throughout this radio play?
- Which elements helped to signal a suspenseful event?
- Which event do you think was the **climax**, or the point of highest suspense?
- How did the use of the reading strategy help you answer these questions?

Reading Skills and Test Practice

IDENTIFY CONFLICT AND RESOLUTION

Discuss with a partner how to answer the following questions about conflict and resolution.

1. Which of the following statements describes the central conflict in *The Hitchhiker?*
   a. Adams's mother does not want him to drive to California but he does anyway.
   b. Adams refuses to let the female hitchhiker leave his car.
   c. Adams is haunted by the same hitchhiker over and over as he travels across the country.
   d. Adams is plagued by a variety of hitchhikers as he travels across the country.

What is the correct answer to the question above? How were you able to eliminate the other answers? How did your application of the reading strategy help you answer the question?

_____

2. Which of the following statements describes the resolution of the conflict in the play?
   a. Adams tries to hit the hitchhiker and scares the female hitchhiker he has with him.
   b. Adams learns that he himself was killed in an automobile accident on the Brooklyn Bridge.
   c. Adams learns that the hitchhiker is an old highway legend.
   d. Adams's fear of the hitchhiker overwhelms him so he returns home.

What is the correct answer to the question above? How were you able to eliminate the other answers? How did your application of the reading strategy help you answer the question?

_____

THINK-ALOUD NOTES

_____
_____
_____
_____
_____
_____
_____
_____
_____
_____

Investigate, Inquire, and Imagine

RECALL: GATHER FACTS
1a. What does Adams tell his mother just before he leaves Brooklyn? What does he see as he is crossing the Brooklyn Bridge in the rain? What does he do as a result?

INTERPRET: FIND MEANING
1b. What really happened to Adams on the Brooklyn Bridge? Were his mother's fears justified?

ANALYZE: TAKE THINGS APART
2a. What makes the figure beside the road so frightening?

SYNTHESIZE: BRING THINGS TOGETHER
2b. Given the way the play ends, who is the figure beside the road?

EVALUATE: MAKE JUDGMENTS
3a. Do you agree with the narrator that this is a spine-tingling tale? Why, or why not?

EXTEND: CONNECT IDEAS
3b. Compare this radio play to Edgar Allan Poe's story "The Black Cat" (Unit 3, page 43). In what way is Adams similar to the narrator in that story? What other stories have you read that have similar narrators or characters?

Literary Tools

FORESHADOWING AND SUSPENSE. **Foreshadowing** presents material that hints at events to come. **Suspense** is a feeling of expectation, anxiousness, or curiosity created by questions raised in the mind of the reader, viewer, or listener. A writer evokes these questions through emotion-producing concrete details. By raising questions, the writer keeps the audience engaged in the action, wondering how the questions will be answered. How does the conversation between Adams and his mother at the beginning of the play foreshadow later events?

_____

_____

What things about the hitchhiker raise questions in Adams's mind and the minds of listeners?

_____

_____

What two questions does Adams have at the end of the play? What do you think the answers to these questions might be?

_____

_____

WordWorkshop

USING NEW VOCABULARY. In order to make words your own, you need to use them in your speech and writing. On your own paper, write the first two paragraphs of a ghost story. Use at least five of the following words from *The Hitchhiker* in your paragraphs. Use a dictionary or context clues from the story to determine the meaning of words that are unfamiliar to you.

audible	nondescript	sinister
beckon	ominous	sober
curdle	outset	throttle
junction	phosphorescent	veer

Read-Write Connection

At what point did you begin to doubt what Adams was seeing? What clues told you something was strange about his story?

_____

_____

_____

_____

_____

_____

_____

_____

Beyond the Reading

EXPLORE RADIO PLAYS. Read one or more one-act plays from the many anthologies that are available. Then form a group and work together to adapt one of the one-act plays as a radio play. You will need to add music, sound effects, and possibly even some dialogue to make the play understandable without any visuals. Then assign parts and record the play for your class.

GO ONLINE. Visit the EMC Internet Resource Center at **emcp.com** to find links and additional activities for this selection.

Unit 6 READING Review

Choose and Use Reading Strategies

Before reading the drama passage below, review with a partner how to use each of these reading strategies.

❶ Read with a Purpose
❷ Connect to Prior Knowledge
❸ Write Things Down
❹ Make Predictions
❺ Visualize
❻ Use Text Organization
❼ Tackle Difficult Vocabulary
❽ Monitor Your Reading Progress

Now apply at least two of these reading strategies as you read the following excerpt from *The Tragedy of Julius Cæsar*, act 1, scene 2. Mark up the text to show how you are using reading strategies to read actively.

> **BRUTUS.** Another general shout!
> I do believe that these applauses are
> For some new honors that are heap'd on Cæsar.
>
> 135 **CASSIUS.** Why, man, he doth bestride the narrow world
> Like a Colossus,[43] and we petty men
> Walk under his huge legs, and peep about
> To find ourselves dishonorable graves.
> Men at some time are masters of their fates;
> 140 The fault, dear Brutus, is not in our stars,[44]
> But in ourselves, that we are <u>underlings</u>.
> Brutus and Cæsar: what should be in that "Cæsar"?
> Why should that name be sounded more than yours?
> Write them together, yours is as fair a name;
> 145 Sound them, it doth become[45] the mouth as well;
> Weigh them, it is as heavy; conjure[46] with 'em,
> "Brutus" will start a spirit[47] as soon as "Cæsar."
>
> ---
> 43. **Colossus.** Gigantic statue, like that of the Colossus of Rhodes, under whose legs ships sailed
> 44. **stars.** Reference to the belief that human destiny is governed by the stars
> 45. **become.** Suit
> 46. **conjure.** Do magic, call up spirits
> 47. **start a spirit.** Call up a ghost, inspire people

Literary Tools

Select the best literary element on the right to complete each sentence on the left. Write the correct letter in the blank.

1. When Antony talks about Brutus and the conspirators one way but expects his listeners to understand that he means the opposite, Antony is using _____.

2. A reader who is driven to keep reading by questions in his or her mind is experiencing ___.

3. Unrhymed iambic pentameter is called ___.

4. A comparison that is continued for several lines is called a(n) ___.

5. The fact that Adams's mother worries that something bad will happen to him on the road is ___ of his fatal accident.

6. A(n) ___, such as Cæsar's desire to be viewed as a strong leader, moves a character to think, feel, or behave in a certain way.

7. ___ results when the audience knows something a character doesn't know.

8. A line of poetry that has five feet, each of which contains one weak beat followed by one strong beat, is written in ___.

9. The fall of a noble character like Julius Cæsar would be depicted in a(n) ___, a type of play.

10. Antony's conscious reuse of the words *wrong* and *honorable* as he speaks about what Brutus and Cassius have done is an example of ___.

a. blank verse, 282

b. dramatic irony, 294

c. extended metaphor, 276

d. foreshadowing, 306

e. iambic pentameter, 282

f. irony, 283

g. motivation, 289

h. repetition, 283

i. suspense, 306

j. tragedy, 255

WordWorkshop

UNIT 6 WORDS FOR EVERYDAY USE

amiss, 266	grievous, 282	outset, 292
bequeath, 284	horrid, 264	phosphorescent, 292
commonwealth, 281	imminent, 266	portent, 266
cur, 270	inter, 282	puissant, 270
decree, 270	lament, 268	reverence, 275
discourse, 279	malice, 275	utterance, 278
entrails, 265	nondescript, 294	valiant, 273
expound, 266	ominous, 296	valor, 280

USING NEW VOCABULARY. On your own paper, answer each of the following questions with a paragraph. Paragraphs can be brief, but they should show that you understand the meaning of each italicized word. When you have finished, read your answers aloud to a partner, and then compare them to his or her answers.

1. Could a situation be both *ominous* and *nondescript?* both *horrid* and *nondescript?* If it could, give an example. If it couldn't, explain why.
2. Explain how a *decree* could be interpreted *amiss.* What kind of *discoursing* would likely result? Might it cause someone to *expound* on the decree? Why, or why not?
3. Identify something that might be a *portent* of *imminent* danger and explain its significance.
4. Describe a *puissant* person acting with *valor.* Might this action involve *malice?* Why, or why not?
5. Write a paragraph using the following words correctly: *cur, entrails, inter, utterance,* and *reverence.*

On Your Own

FLUENTLY SPEAKING. Find a scene from a play that you like by going to the library and looking through drama anthologies, screenplays, and scripts. Then work with a small group to do a dramatic reading of one scene. Introduce the scene with background information that will help your audience understand what the scene is about. Practice your lines until you and the other actors can present the play smoothly and with appropriate feeling.

PICTURE THIS. Draw a cartoon of one of the most memorable scenes from the selections you have read in this unit. Add cartoon bubbles that show the characters expressing thoughts that were not in the original selection.

PUT IT IN WRITING. Write a short story that modernizes one or more of the themes of *The Tragedy of Julius Cæsar,* such as ambition or betrayal. Base at least one character in your story on a character from Shakespeare's play.

Unit SEVEN

READING Nonfiction

NONFICTION

NONFICTION. **Nonfiction** is writing about real people, places, things, and events. It can also explore thoughts and ideas. Categories of nonfiction writing follow.

Forms of Nonfiction

ARTICLE. An **article** is a brief work of nonfiction on a specific topic. You can find articles in encyclopedias, newspapers, and magazines.

AUTOBIOGRAPHY. An **autobiography** is the story of a person's life told by that person. Consequently, autobiographies are told from the first-person point of view. "Something Could Happen to You" by Esmeralda Santiago is an example of an autobiography.

BIOGRAPHY. A **biography** is the story of a person's life told by another person. Although biographies are told from a third-person point of view, autobiographical excerpts such as **letters**, **diaries**, and **journals** may be included. "Montgomery Boycott" by Coretta Scott King is a biographical account of Martin Luther King, Jr.'s involvement in the Civil Rights movement.

DOCUMENTARY WRITING. **Documentary writing** is writing that records an event or subject in accurate detail. A profile of the Jazz Age or a report on human rights abuses in China would be examples of documentary writing.

ESSAY. An **essay**, originally meaning "a trial or attempt," is a short nonfiction work that explores a single subject and is typically a more lasting work than an article. Among the many types of essays are personal and expository essays. A **personal**, or **expressive, essay** deals with the life or interests of the writer. Personal essays are often, but not always, written in the first person. An **expository essay** features the developed ideas of the writer on a certain topic.

Reading TIP

You will often read nonfiction to learn or to read for information. The purpose of this type of reading is to gain knowledge.

NOTE THE FACTS

What are two types of essays?

_____

_____

_____

CONNECT TO PRIOR KNOWLEDGE. What types of histories have you read in social studies class?

_____

_____

_____

THINK AND REFLECT

Write another example of how-to writing. **(Apply)**

_____

_____

_____

Reading TIP

A nonfiction work can have more than one purpose. For example, in a memoir a writer could entertain with a story, then inform the reader about his or her reaction to a historical event. In a letter a writer could reflect on an anecdote, then persuade the reader to take action to help save the rainforest, for example.

HISTORY. A **history** is an account of past events. To write their histories, writers may use **speeches, sermons, contracts, deeds, constitutions, laws, political tracts**, and other types of public records. Coretta Scott King's "Montgomery Boycott" is an example of a history.

HOW-TO WRITING. **How-to writing** is writing that explains a procedure or strategy. A manual that explains how to operate a DVD player is an example of how-to writing.

MEMOIR. A **memoir** is a nonfiction narration that tells a story autobiographically or biographically. Memoirs are based on a person's experiences and reactions to events. "Something Could Happen to You" by Esmeralda Santiago is an example of a memoir.

SPEECH. A **speech** is a public address that was originally delivered orally. Chief Seattle's "Yonder sky that has wept tears of compassion . . ." is an example of a speech.

Purposes and Methods of Writing in Nonfiction

PURPOSE. A writer's **purpose**, or *aim*, is a writer's reason for writing. The following chart classifies modes, or categories, of prose writing by purpose.

Modes and Purposes of Writing

Mode	Purpose	Writing Forms
personal/ expressive writing	to reflect	diary entry, memoir, personal letter, autobiography, personal essay
imaginative/ descriptive writing	to entertain, to describe, to enrich, and to enlighten	poem, character sketch, play, short story
narrative writing	to tell a story, to narrate a series of events	short story, biography, legend, myth, history
informative/ expository writing	to inform, to explain	news article, research report, expository essay, book review
persuasive/ argumentative writing	to persuade	editorial, petition, political speech, persuasive essay

Types of Nonfiction Writing

In order to write effectively, a writer can choose to organize a piece of writing in different ways. The following chart describes types of writing that are commonly used in nonfiction, and tells how they are organized.

Type of Writing	Description
narration	Narrative writing tells a story or describes events. It may use chronological, or time, order.
dialogue	Dialogue reveals people's actual speech, which is set off with quotation marks.
description	Descriptive writing tells how things look, sound, smell, taste, or feel, often using spatial order.
exposition	Expository writing presents facts or opinions and is sometimes organized in one of these ways: ■ **Analysis** breaks something into its parts and shows how the parts are related. ■ **Classification** places subjects into categories according to what they have in common. ■ **Comparison-and-contrast order** presents similarities as it compares two things and differences as it contrasts them. ■ **How-to writing** presents the steps in a process or directions on how to do something.

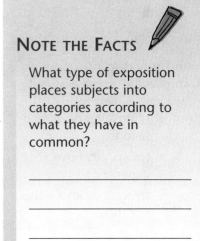

NOTE THE FACTS

What type of exposition places subjects into categories according to what they have in common?

_____

_____

_____

Active Reading Strategy Checklists

When reading nonfiction, it is important to know that the author is telling you about true events. The following checklists offer things to consider when reading nonfiction selections.

1 READ WITH A PURPOSE. Before reading nonfiction, give yourself a purpose, or something to look for, as you read. Sometimes a purpose will be a directive from a teacher: "Find out what the author experienced on her trip to Arkansas." Other times you can set your own purpose by previewing the title, the opening lines, and instructional information. Say to yourself

- ❏ This selection will be about . . .
- ❏ I will keep track of . . .
- ❏ The author wants readers to know . . .
- ❏ The author wrote this to . . .

2 CONNECT TO PRIOR KNOWLEDGE. Being aware of what you already know and calling it to mind as you read can help you understand a writer's views. As you read, say to yourself

- ❏ I already know this about the author's ideas . . .
- ❏ These things in the selection are similar to something I have experienced . . .
- ❏ Something similar I've read is . . .
- ❏ I agree with this because . . .

3 WRITE THINGS DOWN. As you read nonfiction, write down or mark important points that the author makes. Possible ways to keep a written record include

- ❏ Underline the author's key ideas.
- ❏ Write down your thoughts about the author's ideas.
- ❏ Highlight the author's main points and supporting details.
- ❏ Create a graphic organizer to keep track of ideas.
- ❏ Use a code to respond to the author's ideas.

Reading TIP

To connect to your prior knowledge, compare what you are reading to

- things you have read before
- things you have experienced
- things you know about the topic

Reading TIP

A simple code can help you remember your reactions to what you are reading. You can use

! for "This is like something I have experienced"

? for "I don't understand this"

✓ for "This seems important"

4 **MAKE PREDICTIONS.** Before you read a nonfiction selection, use information about the author, the subject matter, and the title to guess what the selection will be about. As you read, confirm or deny your predictions, and make new ones based on what you learn. Make predictions like the following:

❑ What will come next is . . .
❑ The author will support ideas by . . .
❑ I think the selection will end with . . .
❑ The title tells me that the selection will be about . . .

5 **VISUALIZE.** Visualizing, or allowing the words on the page to create images in your mind, helps you understand the author's message. In order to visualize what a selection is about, imagine that you are the narrator. Read the words in your head with the type of expression that the author means to put behind them. Make statements such as

❑ This parts helps me envision how . . .
❑ My sketch of this part would include . . .
❑ This part helps me see how . . .
❑ This part changes my views on . . .
❑ The author connects ideas by . . .

6 **USE TEXT ORGANIZATION.** When you read nonfiction, pay attention to the main idea and supporting details. Learn to stop occasionally and retell what you have read. Say to yourself

❑ The writer's main point is . . .
❑ The writer supports the main point by . . .
❑ In this section, the writer is saying that . . .
❑ I can summarize this section by . . .
❑ I can follow the events because . . .

7 **TACKLE DIFFICULT VOCABULARY.** Difficult words can hinder your ability to understand a writer's message. Use context, consult a dictionary, or ask someone about words you do not understand. When you come across a difficult word in nonfiction, say to yourself

❑ The lines near this word tell me that this word means . . .
❑ A dictionary definition shows that the word means . . .
❑ My work with the word before reading helps me know that the word means . . .
❑ A classmate said that the word means . . .

Reading TIP

Read nonfiction carefully the first time through. Take notes as you read. After you finish reading, reread your notes. Mark them up and make additions or corrections. Rereading your notes and clarifying them helps you remember what you've read.

Reading TIP

Skim a selection before you read it. Make a list of words that might slow you down, and write synonyms for each in the margins. As you read, use the synonyms in place of the words.

FIX-UP IDEAS

- Reread
- Ask a question
- Read in shorter chunks
- Read aloud
- Retell
- Work with a partner
- Unlock difficult words
- Vary your reading rate
- Choose a new reading strategy
- Create a mnemonic device

8 MONITOR YOUR READING PROGRESS. All readers encounter difficulty when they read, especially if the reading material is not self-selected. When you have to read something, take note of problems you are having and fix them. The key to reading success is knowing when you are having difficulty. To fix problems, say to yourself

- ❏ Because I don't understand this part, I will . . .
- ❏ Because I'm having trouble staying connected to the ideas in the selection, I will . . .
- ❏ Because the words in the selection are too hard, I will . . .
- ❏ Because the selection is long, I will . . .
- ❏ Because I can't retell what the selection was about, I will . . .

Become an Active Reader

The instruction with the nonfiction selections in this unit gives you an in-depth look at how to use one strategy. Brief margin notes guide your use of additional strategies. Using one active reading strategy at a time will greatly increase your reading success and enjoyment. Learn how to use several strategies in combination to ensure your complete understanding of what you are reading. When you have difficulty, use active reading solutions to fix a problem. For further information about the active reading strategies, see Unit 1, pages 4–15.

How to Use Reading Strategies with Nonfiction

Use the following excerpts to discover how you might use reading strategies as you read nonfiction.

Excerpt 1. Note how a reader uses active reading strategies while reading this excerpt from "Montgomery Boycott" by Coretta Scott King.

READ WITH A PURPOSE

I want to learn more about the Civil Rights movement.

VISUALIZE

I can see myself on one of these buses. I would not be happy to have to get off the bus and reboard in the rear.

CONNECT TO PRIOR KNOWLEDGE

I know that Martin Luther King, Jr. was a minister and a Civil Rights leader and that Coretta Scott King was his wife.

MAKE PREDICTIONS

I think the boycott will be successful. I think King will talk about Rosa Parks next.

Of all the facets of segregation in Montgomery,[1] the most degrading were the rules of the Mongomery City Bus Lines. This Northern-owned corporation outdid the South itself. Although seventy percent of its passengers were black, it treated them like cattle—worse than that, for nobody insults a cow. The first seats on all buses were reserved for whites. Even if they were unoccupied and the rear seats crowded, Negroes would have to stand at the back in case some white might get aboard; and if the front seats happened to be occupied and more white people boarded the bus, black people seated in the rear were forced to get up and give them their seats. Furthermore—and I don't think Northerners ever realized this—Negroes had to pay their fares at the front of the bus, get off, and walk to the rear door to board again. Sometimes the bus would drive off without them after they had paid their fare.

Excerpt 2. Note how a reader uses active reading strategies while reading this excerpt from "The Man Who Mistook His Wife for a Hat" by Oliver Sacks.

WRITE THINGS DOWN

I'm going to keep a list of odd things Dr. P. says and does.

TACKLE DIFFICULT VOCABULARY

The footnote helps me understand how Dr. P. reacts to a flower.

MONITOR YOUR READING PROGRESS

Rereading after I know the meaning of the footnoted and underlined words makes reading easier.

USE TEXT ORGANIZATION

Dr. P.'s dialogue explains the way he sees the flower.

I had stopped at a florist on my way to his [Dr. P.'s] apartment and bought myself an extravagant red rose for my buttonhole. Now I removed this and handed it to him. He took it like a botanist or morphologist[16] given a specimen, not like a person given a flower.

"About six inches in length," he commented. "A convoluted red form with a linear green attachment."

---

16. **botanist or morphologist.** Botanist (bä´ tə nist)—one who studies plants; morphologist (mȯr fä´ lə jist)—biologist who studies the form and structure of animals and plants

"Montgomery Boycott"
by Coretta Scott King

"**Montgomery Boycott**" is a nonfiction narrative by Coretta Scott King, the wife of Martin Luther King, Jr., that describes the refusal of African Americans in Montgomery, Alabama, to use the segregated city bus system. The Montgomery boycott was an early action in the Civil Rights movement, in which African Americans demonstrated to use the same public facilities as whites, facilities such as lunch counters, bathrooms, and buses. Martin Luther King, Jr., who stressed non-violent protest, became the leader in the fight for civil rights.

Active READING STRATEGY

CONNECT TO PRIOR KNOWLEDGE

Before Reading → **ACTIVATE PRIOR KNOWLEDGE**

❏ Read the Reader's Resource.
❏ Discuss with several classmates what you know about the Civil Rights movement and the social and economic conditions that led to it.
❏ Fill in the first two columns of the K-W-L Chart below.

Graphic Organizer

What I *Know*	What I *Want* to Learn	What I Have *Learned*

Word watch

PREVIEW VOCABULARY

aptly	exaltation
coercion	exposé
coherently	irate
comply	oppression
coordinate	serene
degrading	unethical
devoid	

Reader's journal

What injustices do you feel are worth protesting?

_____

_____

_____

Montgomery boycott

Coretta Scott King

O f all the facets of segregation in Montgomery,[1] the most <u>degrading</u> were the rules of the Montgomery City Bus Lines. This Northern-owned corporation outdid the South itself. Although seventy percent of its passengers were black, it treated them like cattle—worse than that, for nobody insults a cow. The first seats on all buses were reserved for whites. Even if they were unoccupied and the rear seats crowded, Negroes would have to stand at the back in case some whites might get aboard; and if the front seats happened to be occupied and more white people boarded the bus, black people seated in the rear were forced to get up and give them their seats. Furthermore—and I don't think Northerners ever realized this—Negroes had to pay their fares at the front of the bus, get off, and walk to the rear door to board again. Sometimes the bus would drive off without them after they had paid their fare. This would

10

---

1. **Montgomery.** Capital of Alabama, located on the Alabama River in the south central part of the state

words for everyday use

de • grad • ing (dē grād´iŋ) *adj.*, depriving of dignity. *The use of whites-only water fountains was another <u>degrading</u> aspect of segregation.*

During Reading

CONNECT TO PRIOR KNOWLEDGE

❑ Read the selection on your own, taking time to reflect on prior knowledge you have about the names, organizations, and events it describes.
❑ Write down additional things you know as you read about them in the "What I Know" column of the graphic organizer.
❑ As you learn something new that you deem important, write it in the "What I Have Learned" section of the graphic organizer.

NOTE THE FACTS

What did the bus segregation laws require?

_____

_____

Literary TOOLS

AIM. A writer's **aim** is his or her purpose, or goal. As you read, try to determine Mrs. King's aim in writing this selection.

NOTE THE FACTS

According to lines 30–45, what incident finally sparked a response?

_____

_____

_____

happen to elderly people or pregnant women, in bad weather or good, and was considered a great joke by the drivers. Frequently the white bus drivers abused their
20 passengers, called them niggers, black cows, or black apes. Imagine what it was like, for example, for a black man to get on a bus with his son and be subjected to such treatment.

There had been one incident in March 1955 when fifteen-year-old Claudette Colvin refused to give up her seat to a white passenger. The high school girl was handcuffed and carted off to the police station. At that time Martin[2] served on a committee to protest to the city and bus-company officials. The committee was received politely—and nothing was done.

30 The fuel that finally made that slow-burning fire blaze up was an almost routine incident. On December 1, 1955, Mrs. Rosa Parks, a forty-two-year-old seamstress whom my husband <u>aptly</u> described as "a charming person with a radiant personality," boarded a bus to go home after a long day working and shopping. The bus was crowded, and Mrs. Parks found a seat at the beginning of the Negro section. At the next stop more whites got on. The driver ordered Mrs. Parks to give her seat to a white man who boarded; this meant that she would have to stand all the way home. Rosa Parks was not
40 in a revolutionary frame of mind. She had not planned to do what she did. Her cup had run over. As she said later, "I was just plain tired, and my feet hurt." So she sat there, refusing to get up. The driver called a policeman, who arrested her and took her to the courthouse. From there Mrs. Parks called E. D. Nixon, who came down and signed a bail bond[3] for her.

Mr. Nixon was a fiery Alabamian. He was a Pullman porter[4] who had been active in A. Philip Randolph's Brotherhood of Sleeping Car Porters and in civil-rights activities. Suddenly he also had had enough; suddenly, it

---

2. **Martin.** Dr. Martin Luther King, Jr. (1929–1968), leader of the American Civil Rights movement who was assassinated in 1968
3. **bail bond.** Formal pledge to pay the full amount of bail assigned by the court if the prisoner being released does not appear in court as scheduled
4. **Pullman porter.** Attendant in a railroad car that has seats that can be converted to berths for sleeping

words for everyday use   apt • ly (apt´lē) adv., fittingly. *She was <u>aptly</u> described in the yearbook as charming, popular, and smart, adjectives that fit her perfectly.*

seemed, almost every Negro in Montgomery had had
enough. It was spontaneous combustion. Phones began
ringing all over the Negro section of the city. The Women's
Political Council suggested a one day boycott of the buses as
a protest. E. D. Nixon courageously agreed to organize it.

The first we knew about it was when Mr. Nixon called my
husband early in the morning of Friday, December 2. He
had already talked to Ralph Abernathy.[5] After describing the
incident, Mr. Nixon said, "We have taken this type of thing
too long. I feel the time has come to boycott the buses. It's
the only way to make the white folks see that we will not
take this sort of thing any longer."

Martin agreed with him and offered the Dexter Avenue
Church as a meeting place. After much telephoning, a
meeting of black ministers and civic leaders was arranged
for that evening. Martin said later that as he approached his
church Friday evening, he was nervously wondering how
many leaders would really turn up. To his delight, Martin
found over forty people, representing every segment of
Negro life, crowded into the large meeting room at Dexter.
There were doctors, lawyers, businessmen, federal-
government employees, union leaders, and a great many
ministers. The latter were particularly welcome, not only
because of their influence, but because it meant that they
were beginning to accept Martin's view that "Religion deals
with both heaven and earth. . . . Any religion that professes
to be concerned with the souls of men and is not concerned
with the slums that doom them, the economic conditions
that strangle them, and the social conditions that cripple
them, is a dry-as-dust religion." From that very first step,
the Christian ministry provided the leadership of our
struggle, as Christian ideals were its source.

The meeting opened with brief devotions.[6] Then, because
E. D. Nixon was away at work, the Reverend L. Roy
Bennett, president of the Interdenominational[7] Ministerial
Alliance, was made chairman. After describing what had
happened to Mrs. Parks, Reverend Bennett said, "Now is the
time to move. This is no time to talk; it is time to act."

---

5. **Ralph Abernathy.** A leader of the Civil Rights movement
6. **devotions.** Prayers
7. **Interdenominational.** Cooperative effort among leaders of different
religious groups

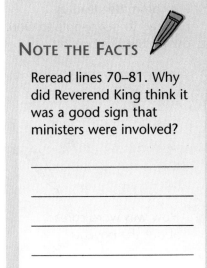

NOTE THE FACTS

What course of action was
suggested?

_____

_____

Reading TIP

Note in the highlighted
paragraph that the author
uses a chronological method
of organization.

NOTE THE FACTS

Reread lines 70–81. Why
did Reverend King think it
was a good sign that
ministers were involved?

_____

_____

_____

_____

Martin told me after he got home that the meeting was almost wrecked because questions or suggestions from the floor were cut off. However, after a stormy session, one thing was clear: however much they differed on details, everyone was unanimously for a boycott. It was set for Monday, December 5. Committees were organized; all the ministers present promised to urge their congregations to take part. Several thousand leaflets were printed on the church mimeograph machine[8] describing the reasons for the boycott and urging all Negroes not to ride buses "to work, to town, to school, or anyplace on Monday, December 5." Everyone was asked to come to a mass meeting at the Holt Street Baptist Church on Monday evening for further instructions. The Reverend A. W. Wilson had offered his church because it was larger than Dexter and more convenient, being in the center of the Negro district.

Saturday was a busy day for Martin and the other members of the committee. They hustled around town talking with other leaders, arranging with the Negro-owned taxi companies for special bulk fares and with the owners of private automobiles to get the people to and from work. I could do little to help because Yoki was only two weeks old, and my physician, Dr. W. D. Pettus, who was very careful, advised me to stay in for a month. However, I was kept busy answering the telephone, which rang continuously, and <u>coordinating</u> from that central point the many messages and arrangements.

Our greatest concern was how we were going to reach the fifty thousand black people of Montgomery, no matter how hard we worked. The white press, in an outraged <u>exposé</u>, spread the word for us in a way that would have been impossible with only our resources.

As it happened, a white woman found one of our leaflets, which her Negro maid had left in the kitchen. The <u>irate</u>

---

8. **mimeograph machine.** Early form of copy machine that used a roller with ink on it

MARK THE TEXT

Underline or highlight how the committee leaders planned to get people to work during the bus boycott.

NOTE THE FACTS

How was word spread about the boycott?

_____

_____

_____

woman immediately telephoned the newspapers to let the white community know what the blacks were up to. We laughed a lot about this, and Martin later said that we owed them a great debt.

On Sunday morning, from their pulpits, almost every Negro minister in town urged people to honor the boycott.

Martin came home late Sunday night and began to read the morning paper. The long articles about the proposed boycott accused the NAACP[9] of planting Mrs. Parks on the bus—she had been a volunteer secretary for the Mont-gomery chapter—and likened the boycott to the tactics of the White Citizens' Councils.[10] This upset Martin. That awesome conscience of his began to gnaw at him, and he wondered if he were doing the right thing. Alone in his study, he struggled with the question of whether the boycott method was basically unchristian. Certainly it could be used for <u>unethical</u> ends. But, as he said, "We are using it to give birth to freedom . . . and to urge men to <u>comply</u> with the law of the land. Our concern was not to put the bus company out of business, but to put justice in business." He recalled Thoreau's words, "We can no longer lend our cooperation to an evil system," and he thought, "He who accepts evil without protesting against it is really cooperating with it." Later Martin wrote, "From this moment on I conceived of our movement as an act of massive noncooperation. From then on I rarely used the word *boycott*."

<u>Serene</u> after his inner struggle, Martin joined me in our sitting room. We wanted to get to bed early, but Yoki began crying and the telephone kept ringing. Between interrup-tions we sat together talking about the prospects for the success of the protest. We were both filled with doubt. Attempted boycotts had failed in Montgomery and other

---

9. **NAACP.** National Association for the Advancement of Colored People
10. **White Citizens' Councils.** Groups started in Mississippi in 1954 that had the goal of defeating desegregation in the South

words for everyday use

un • eth • i • cal (un eth´i kəl) *adj.,* not conforming to moral standards. *Plagiarism, or using the words and ideas of others without their permission, is <u>unethical</u> and can result in students being expelled from school.*

com • ply (kəm plī´) *vi.,* act in accordance with rule, command, or request. *The judge gave him thirty days to <u>comply</u> with the bicycle helmet law and warned him he would have to pay a fine if he refused.*

se • rene (sə rēn´) *adj.,* calm, peaceful. *Nature preserves are often considered to be <u>serene</u> places, allowing for quiet reflection.*

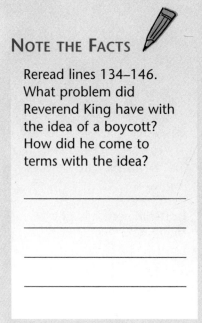

NOTE THE FACTS

Reread lines 134–146. What problem did Reverend King have with the idea of a boycott? How did he come to terms with the idea?

_____

_____

_____

_____

Use THE STRATEGY

CONNECT TO PRIOR KNOWLEDGE. Think about other types of "massive noncooperation" that have occurred in U.S. history. For example, you might have heard of some incidents that took place during the 1960s. Write these examples in the first column of the graphic organizer.

cities. Because of changing times and tempers, this one seemed to have a better chance, but it was still a slender hope. We finally decided that if the boycott was 60 percent effective we would be doing all right, and we would be satisfied to have made a good start.

A little after midnight we finally went to bed, but at five-thirty the next morning we were up and dressed again. 160 The first bus was due at 6 o'clock at the bus stop just outside our house. We had coffee and toast in the kitchen; then I went into the living room to watch. Right on time, the bus came, headlights blazing through the December darkness, all lit up inside. I shouted, "Martin! Martin, come quickly!" He ran in and stood beside me, his face lit with excitement. There was not one person on that usually crowded bus!

We stood together waiting for the next bus. It was empty too, and this was the most heavily traveled line in the whole 170 city. Bus after empty bus paused at the stop and moved on. We were so excited we could hardly speak <u>coherently</u>. Finally Martin said, "I'm going to take the car and see what's happening in other places in the city."

He picked up Ralph Abernathy, and they cruised together around the city. Martin told me about it when he got home. Everywhere it was the same. A few white people and maybe one or two blacks in otherwise empty buses. Martin and Ralph saw extraordinary sights—the sidewalks crowded with men and women trudging to work; the students of Alabama 180 State College walking or thumbing rides; taxi cabs with people clustered in them. Some of our people rode mules; others went in horse-drawn buggies. But most of them were walking, some making a round trip of as much as twelve miles. Martin later wrote, "As I watched them I knew that there is nothing more majestic than the determined courage of individuals willing to suffer and sacrifice for their freedom and dignity."

Martin rushed off again at nine o'clock that morning to attend the trial of Mrs. Parks. She was convicted of

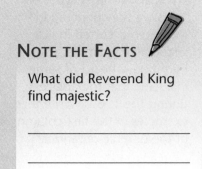

NOTE THE FACTS

What did Reverend King find majestic?

_____

_____

words for everyday use	**co • her • ent • ly** (kō hir´ənt lē) *adv.*, in a way capable of being understood. *The teacher tried to show his students how to write more <u>coherently</u> because their thoughts were always confused and disorganized when they put them down on paper.*

190   disobeying the city's segregation ordinance and fined ten dollars and costs. Her young attorney, Fred D. Gray, filed an appeal. It was one of the first clearcut cases of a Negro being convicted of disobeying the segregation laws—usually the charge was disorderly conduct or some such thing.

      The leaders of the movement called a meeting for three o'clock in the afternoon to organize the mass meeting to be held that night. Martin was a bit late, and as he entered the hall, people said to him, "Martin, we have elected you to be our president. Will you accept?"

200   It seemed that Rufus A. Lewis, a Montgomery business-man, had proposed Martin, and he had been unanimously elected. The people knew, and Martin knew, that the post was dangerous, for it meant being singled out to become the target of the white people's anger and vengeance. Martin said, "I don't mind. Somebody has to do it, and if you think I can, I will serve."

      Then other officers were elected. Rev. L. Roy Bennett became vice-president; Rev. E. N. French, corresponding secretary; Mrs. Erna A. Dungee, financial secretary; and E.

210 D. Nixon, treasurer. After that they discussed what to call the organization. Someone suggested the Negro Citizens' Committee. Martin did not approve, because that sounded like an organization of the same spirit as the White Citizens' Council. Finally, Ralph Abernathy proposed calling the organization the Montgomery Improvement Association, the MIA, and this name was unanimously approved.

      Fear was an invisible presence at the meeting, along with courage and hope. Proposals were voiced to make the MIA a sort of secret society, because if no names were mentioned it would be safer for the leaders. E. D. Nixon opposed that

220 idea. "We're acting like little boys," he said. "Somebody's name will be known, and if we're afraid, we might just as well fold up right now. The white folks are eventually going to find out anyway. We'd better decide now if we are going to be fearless men or scared little boys."

      That settled that question. It was also decided that the protest would continue until certain demands were met. Ralph Abernathy was made chairman of the committee to draw up the demands.

230   Martin came home at six o'clock. He said later that he was nervous about telling me he had accepted the presidency of

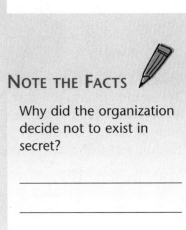

NOTE THE FACTS

What was new about Mrs. Parks's case?

_____

_____

_____

NOTE THE FACTS

What organization was formed?

_____

_____

NOTE THE FACTS

Why did the organization decide not to exist in secret?

_____

_____

THINK AND REFLECT

Reread lines 243–245. What guided Reverend King's life? How can you tell? (Infer)

_____

_____

_____

_____

NOTE THE FACTS

What did Reverend King hope his speech would do?

_____

_____

_____

READ ALOUD

Read aloud the portions of Reverend King's speech that are highlighted. Identify the most important words and phrases and emphasize them.

the protest movement, but he need not have worried, because I sincerely meant what I said when I told him that night, "You know that whatever you do, you have my backing."

Reassured, Martin went to his study. He was to make the main speech at the mass meeting that night. It was now six-thirty, and—this was the way it was usually to be—he had only twenty minutes to prepare what he thought might
240 be the most decisive speech of his life. He said afterward that thinking about the responsibility and the reporters and television cameras, he almost panicked. Five minutes wasted and only fifteen minutes left. At that moment he turned to prayer. He asked God "to restore my balance and be with me in a time when I need Your guidance more than ever."

How could he make his speech both militant enough to rouse people to action and yet <u>devoid</u> of hate and resentment? He was determined to do both.

Martin and Ralph went together to the meeting. When
250 they got within four blocks of the Holt Street Baptist Church, there was an enormous traffic jam. Five thousand people stood outside the church listening to loudspeakers and singing hymns. Inside it was so crowded, Martin told me, the people had to lift Ralph and him above the crowd and pass them from hand to hand over their heads to the platform. The crowd and the singing inspired Martin, and God answered his prayer. Later Martin said, "That night I understood what the older preachers meant when they said, 'Open your mouth and God will speak for you.'"
260 First the people sang "Onward, Christian Soldiers" in a tremendous wave of five thousand voices. This was followed by a prayer and a reading of the Scriptures. Martin was introduced. People applauded; television lights beat upon him. Without any notes at all he began to speak. Once again he told the story of Mrs. Parks, and rehearsed some of the wrongs black people were suffering. Then he said, "But there comes a time when people get tired. We are here this evening to say to those who have mistreated us so long that

words
for
everyday
use

de • void (di void´) adj., completely without. Her blind date was <u>devoid</u> of charm, wit, or sophistication, and his utter lack of appeal made her wish the evening had never happened.

270 we are tired, tired of being segregated and humiliated, tired of being kicked about by the brutal feet of <u>oppression</u>."

The audience cheered wildly, and Martin said, "We have no alternative but to protest. We have been amazingly patient . . . but we come here tonight to be saved from the patience that makes us patient with anything less than freedom and justice."

Taking up the challenging newspaper comparison with the White Citizens' Council and the Klan,[11] Martin said, "They are protesting for the perpetuation of injustice in the community; we're protesting for the birth of justice . . .
280 their methods lead to violence and lawlessness. But in our protest there will be no cross burnings; no white person will be taken from his home by a hooded Negro mob and brutally murdered . . . we will be guided by the highest principles of law and order."

Having roused the audience for militant action, Martin now set limits upon it. His study of nonviolence and his love of Christ informed his words. He said, "No one must be intimidated to keep them from riding the buses. Our method must be persuasion, not <u>coercion</u>. We will only say to the
290 people, 'Let your conscience be your guide.' . . . Our actions must be guided by the deepest principles of the Christian faith. . . . Once again we must hear the words of Jesus, 'Love your enemies. Bless them that curse you. Pray for them that despitefully use you.' If we fail to do this, our protest will end up as a meaningless drama on the stage of history, and its memory will be shrouded in the ugly garments of shame. . . . We must not become bitter and end up by hating our white brothers. As Booker T. Washington[12] said, 'Let no man pull you so low as to make you hate him.'" Finally,
300 Martin said, "If you will protest courageously, and yet with dignity and Christian love, future historians will say, 'There

---

11. **the Klan.** Group begun as the Ku Klux Klan in Tennessee in 1866 for the purpose of militantly defeating any efforts of nonwhites to attain equal rights with white Americans
12. **Booker T. Washington.** (1856–1915) Founder of the teacher's college for African Americans that later became Tuskegee Institute

| words for everyday use | **op • pres • sion** (ə presh´ən) *n.*, something that holds down by unjust power. *South Africa's policy of <u>oppression</u> against blacks was called apartheid.* |
| | **co • er • cion** (kō ʉr´shən) *n.*, act of force through threats or violence. *The officer was accused of <u>coercion</u> because he threatened a suspect and forced him to confess to committing a crime.* |

MAKE A NOTE

_____

_____

_____

_____

NOTE THE FACTS

What will guide the movement?

_____

_____

_____

NOTE THE FACTS

What did Reverend King wish to avoid? What did Booker T. Washington warn against?

_____

_____

_____

_____

THINK AND REFLECT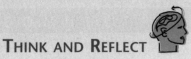

Reread lines 305–308.
How successful was
Reverend King's speech?
(Infer)

_____

_____

_____

lived a great people—a black people—who injected new meaning and dignity into the veins of civilization.' This is our challenge and our overwhelming responsibility."

As Martin finished speaking, the audience rose cheering in <u>exaltation</u>. And in that speech my husband set the keynote and the tempo of the movement he was to lead from

308 Montgomery onward. ■

words for everyday use	**ex • al • ta • tion** (eg´zôl tā´shən) _n._, feeling of great joy and pride. _The crowd roared in <u>exaltation</u> when the home team came from behind to win the game and cap its undefeated season._

Reflect ON YOUR READING

→ SYNTHESIZE YOUR CONNECTIONS

When you finish reading, review the notes in your graphic organizer. Take time to fill in the third column if you have not already done so. Compare your chart to the charts of students in your group. Discuss what you learned from the selection. Then write a paragraph about how you used your prior knowledge to help you read the selection.

_____

_____

_____

_____

_____

Reading Skills and Test Practice

IDENTIFY THE AUTHOR'S PURPOSE AND POINT OF VIEW
Discuss with a partner how to answer the following questions about the author's purpose and point of view.

1. Which of the following statements best describes the author's purpose for writing this selection?
   a. to entertain readers with memories from her past
   b. to persuade readers to join the Civil Rights movement
   c. to inform readers about an important event in American history
   d. to convince readers that her husband was a great man

Circle the correct answer to the question above. How were you able to eliminate the other answers? How did your application of the reading strategy help you answer the question?

_____

_____

2. From what point of view is "Montgomery Boycott" written?
   a. first person
   b. second person
   c. third-person limited
   d. third-person omniscient

Circle the correct answer to the question above. How were you able to eliminate the other answers? How did your application of the reading strategy help you answer the question?

_____

_____

THINK-ALOUD
NOTES

_____

_____

_____

_____

_____

_____

_____

_____

_____

_____

Investigate, Inquire, and Imagine

RECALL: GATHER FACTS
1a. What part of segregation did Coretta Scott King find the most degrading?

→ **INTERPRET: FIND MEANING**
1b. What laws allowed the mistreatment of African-American bus passengers? How did passengers react to such laws?

ANALYZE: TAKE THINGS APART
2a. Why was Reverend King insistent that the protests be nonviolent?

→ **SYNTHESIZE: BRING THINGS TOGETHER**
2b. Where did he get his ideas?

EVALUATE: MAKE JUDGMENTS
3a. In retrospect, was the Montgomery bus boycott a good decision for the organizers of the Civil Rights movement? Why, or why not?

→ **EXTEND: CONNECT IDEAS**
3b. In 1849, Henry David Thoreau wrote one of his most influential works, an essay entitled "Civil Disobedience." It grew out of a prison stay that resulted from his conscientious objection to paying a poll tax that supported the Mexican War, which Thoreau was against because he saw it as an effort to extend slavery. What do you think Martin Luther King, Jr. would have thought of Thoreau's behavior?

Literary Tools

AIM. A writer's **aim** is his or her purpose, or goal. Complete the chart below, listing facts that Mrs. King provides about her husband in the first column and her aim for its inclusion in the second column. What is Mrs. King's overall aim in writing about her husband?

Facts about Martin Luther King, Jr.	Aim
He offered the Dexter church as a early involvement meeting place.	To inform the reader of Martin's role in the boycott.

WordWorkshop

Prefixes, Suffixes, and Word Roots. Test your knowledge of commonly used prefixes, suffixes, and word roots. For each of the questions below, circle the letter of the meaning that accurately answers the question. You may want to refer to the lists of commonly used prefixes, word roots, and suffixes in Unit 9 on pages 452–456.

_____1. Which of the following prefixes means *before?*
   a. dis–   c. pre–
   b. re–   d. pro–
_____2. Which of the following suffixes means "capable of"?
   a. –ance   c. –ly
   b. –ible   d. –ous
_____3. Which of the following word roots means *draw* or *pull?*
   a. port   c. strict
   b. spect   d. tract
_____4. Which of the following word roots means *climb?*
   a. scend   c. vis
   b. dict   d. gress
_____5. Which of the following prefixes means "put into or onto" or "cause to be"?
   a. im–   c. mis–
   b. em–   d. de–

Read-Write Connection

Which people introduced in this selection do you admire? What about them do you find admirable?

_____

_____

_____

_____

Beyond the Reading

Researching Boycotts. Some people continue to boycott companies, sometimes because their products reflect substandard labor practices or cruelty to animals. Research a boycotting campaign, making sure to find answers to the following questions: When did the boycott occur? What were customers protesting? What was the stature of the company being boycotted? How long did the boycott last? What is the estimated loss of sales to the company? Were conditions improved after the boycott? Present your findings to the class.

Go Online. Visit the EMC Internet Resource Center at **emcp.com** to find links and additional activities for this selection.

Reader's resource

Oliver Sacks is a world-famous neurologist, a doctor who specializes in the study of the brain and nervous system. In **"The Man Who Mistook His Wife for a Hat,"** Dr. Sacks describes the puzzling case of a patient, whom he calls Dr. P., who suffers from visual agnosia—the inability to recognize familiar people and objects. Sacks describes his consultations with Dr. P. with sensitivity and humor.

Word watch

PREVIEW VOCABULARY

abstract	frivolous
acuity	genially
aghast	incisive
amiably	indomitable
apprehend	ingenious
celluloid	linear
cognition	omit
collusion	pathology
comply	peremptory
confabulate	placidly
construe	renounce
convoluted	schematic
deficit	stylized
degenerative	symmetry
diffidently	tenacity
elicit	torrid
farcical	trifle
forbear	verbatim

Reader's journal

What things do you find most amazing about the human brain?

"THE MAN WHO MISTOOK HIS WIFE FOR A HAT"

by Oliver Sacks

Active READING STRATEGY

TACKLE DIFFICULT VOCABULARY

Before Reading ➤ **PREVIEW AND LEARN SELECTION VOCABULARY**

❑ Read the Reader's Resource.
❑ With a partner, take turns pronouncing out loud the Words for Everyday Use and footnotes, as well as the definitions.
❑ Then create Word Maps like the one below on your own paper and fill them in with the Words for Everyday Use that you don't know.

Graphic Organizer

A Challenging Word or Phrase

Definition

Word Parts I Recognize	Synonyms

A Sentence That Contains the Word or Phrase

A Picture That Illustrates the Word or Phrase

THE MAN WHO MISTOOK HIS WIFE FOR A HAT

Oliver Sacks

Dr. P. was a musician of distinction, well-known for many years as a singer, and then, at the local School of Music, as a teacher. It was here, in relation to his students, that certain strange problems were first observed. Sometimes a student would present himself, and Dr. P. would not recognise him; or, specifically, would not recognise his face. The moment the student spoke, he would be recognised by his voice. Such incidents multiplied, causing embarrassment, perplexity, fear—and, sometimes, comedy. For not only did
10   Dr. P. increasingly fail to see faces, but he saw faces when there were no faces to see: <u>genially</u>, Magoo-like,[1] when in the street, he might pat the heads of water-hydrants and parking meters, taking these to be the heads of children; he would <u>amiably</u> address carved knobs on the furniture, and be astounded when they did not reply. At first these odd mistakes were laughed off as jokes, not least by Dr. P. himself. Had he not always had a quirky sense of humour, and been given to Zen-like paradoxes[2] and jests? His musical powers were as dazzling as ever; he did not feel ill—he had
20   never felt better; and the mistakes were so ludicrous—and so <u>ingenious</u>—that they could hardly be serious or betoken anything serious. The notion of there being "something the

---

1. **Magoo-like.** Mr. Magoo is a cartoon character often shown making silly mistakes because of his poor eyesight.
2. **given to Zen-like paradoxes.** Zen is a type of Buddhism native to Japan that emphasizes the use of intuition. Students of Zen learn to look at things from a different point of view. A paradox is something contradictory. Dr. P. tended to say and do things that were different or contrary to expectation.

words for everyday use	
	ge • nial • ly (jēn′yə lē) *adv.*, in a friendly way. *We had heard that Parisians were unfriendly, but the people we met in Paris behaved quite genially.*
	ami • a • bly (ām′yə blē) *adv.*, in a friendly way. *"Hello there, Mike!" Bill said amiably.*
	in • ge • nious (in jēn′yəs) *adj.*, original. *"What an ingenious idea!" I exclaimed to the inventor.*

During Reading

TACKLE DIFFICULT VOCABULARY WHILE YOU READ

❏ Read the selection independently, stopping to unlock the meaning of unfamiliar vocabulary words using context clues or your knowledge of word parts.

❏ If these strategies don't work, fill out a Word Map graphic organizer for each vocabulary word that you don't know. Then reread the paragraph in which the unfamiliar word appears.

NOTE THE FACTS

What did Dr. P. fail to see, or recognize? What did he sometimes mistakenly see?

_____

_____

_____

Reading TIP

Oliver Sacks is from England. Note that he uses the British spellings of words. For example, he uses *recognise* instead of the American *recognize; humour* instead of *humor; colour* instead of *color.*

matter" did not emerge until some three years later, when diabetes developed. Well aware that diabetes could affect his eyes, Dr. P. consulted an ophthalmologist, who took a careful history, and examined his eyes closely. "There's nothing the matter with your eyes," the doctor concluded. "But there is trouble with the visual parts of your brain. You don't need my help, you must see a neurologist." And so, as a result of this referral, Dr. P. came to me.

It was obvious within a few seconds of meeting him that there was no trace of dementia[3] in the ordinary sense. He was a man of great cultivation and charm, who talked well and fluently, with imagination and humour. I couldn't think why he had been referred to our clinic.

And yet there *was* something a bit odd. He faced me as he spoke, was oriented towards me, and yet there was something the matter—it was difficult to formulate. He faced me with his *ears,* I came to think, but not with his eyes. These, instead of looking, gazing, at me, "taking me in," in the normal way, made sudden strange fixations—on my nose, on my right ear, down to my chin, up to my right eye—as if noting (even studying) these individual features, but not seeing my whole face, its changing expressions, "me," as a whole. I am not sure that I fully realised this at the time—there was just a teasing strangeness, some failure in the normal interplay of gaze and expression. He saw me, he *scanned* me, and yet . . .

"What seems to be the matter?" I asked him at length.

"Nothing that I know of," he replied with a smile, "but people seem to think there's something wrong with my eyes."

"But *you* don't recognise any visual problems?"

"No, not directly, but I occasionally make mistakes."

I left the room briefly, to talk to his wife. When I came back Dr. P. was sitting placidly by the window, attentive, listening rather than looking out. "Traffic," he said, "street

---

3. **dementia** (di men[t]´ shə). Insanity

words for everyday use	**plac • id • ly** (pla´ səd lē) *adv.,* in a calm way. *Unlike most audiences, who erupted into cheers and wild applause, this audience sat* <u>placidly</u> *waiting for the band's first song.*

sounds, distant trains—they make a sort of symphony, do
they not? You know Honegger's *Pacific 234?*"[4]

60   What a lovely man, I thought to myself. How can there
be anything seriously the matter? Would he permit me to
examine him?

    "Yes, of course, Dr. Sacks."

    I stilled my disquiet, his perhaps too, in the soothing
routine of a neurological exam—muscle strength,
co-ordination, reflexes, tone . . . It was while examining his
reflexes—a <u>trifle</u> abnormal on the left side—that the first
bizarre experience occurred. I had taken off his left shoe
and scratched the sole of his foot with a key—a <u>frivolous</u>-
seeming but essential test of a reflex—and then, excusing
70   myself to screw my ophthalmoscope together, left him to
put on the shoe himself. To my surprise, a minute later, he
had not done this.

    "Can I help?" I asked.

    "Help what? Help whom?"

    "Help you put on your shoe."

    "Ach," he said, "I had forgotten the shoe," adding, *sotto
voce*,[5] "The shoe? The shoe?" He seemed baffled.

    "Your shoe," I repeated. "Perhaps you'd put it on."

    He continued to look downwards, though not at the shoe,
80   with an intense but misplaced concentration. Finally his
gaze settled on his foot: "That is my shoe, yes?"

    Did I mis-hear? Did he mis-see?

    "My eyes," he explained, and put a hand to his foot. "*This*
is my shoe, no?"

    "No, it is not. That is your foot. *There* is your shoe."

    "Ah! I thought that was my foot."

    Was he joking? Was he mad? Was he blind? If this was
one of his "strange mistakes," it was the strangest mistake I
had ever come across.

90   I helped him on with his shoe (his foot), to avoid further
complication. Dr. P. himself seemed untroubled, indifferent,

---

4. **Honegger's *Pacific 234*.** Symphony, or piece of music, written by
French composer Arthur Honegger (1892–1955)

5. ***sotto voce*** (sä´tō vō´ chə). Italian term meaning "under his breath; softly"

<table>
<tr><td>words
for
everyday
use</td><td>tri • fle (trī´fəl) n., to a small degree; slightly. I was a <u>trifle</u> annoyed when the pizza
arrived late, but I didn't complain.

friv • o • lous (fri´və ləs) adj., having little importance. Enough with the <u>frivolous</u>
details—let's get down to the important business of the day.</td></tr>
</table>

_____

_____

_____

_____

Use **THE STRATEGY**

**TACKLE DIFFICULT
VOCABULARY.** Remember to
use context clues to
unlock the meaning of
new words. Which word
in the sentence containing
frivolous is the word's
antonym?

_____

NOTE THE FACTS

What "strange mistake"
does Dr. P. make when
asked to put on his shoe?

_____

_____

_____

Reread lines 108–123. What does Dr. P. say he "sees" in the *National Geographic* picture? Does his description match the picture? What strange thing does he do next?

_____

_____

_____

_____

maybe amused. I resumed my examination. His visual <u>acuity</u> was good: he had no difficulty seeing a pin on the floor, though sometimes he missed it if it was placed to his left.

He saw all right, but what did he see? I opened out a copy of the *National Geographic Magazine*, and asked him to describe some pictures in it.

His responses here were very curious. His eyes would dart from one thing to another, picking up tiny features,
100 individual features, as they had done with my face. A striking brightness, a colour, a shape would arrest his attention and <u>elicit</u> comment—but in no case did he get the scene-as-a-whole. He failed to see the whole, seeing only details, which he spotted like blips on a radar screen. He never entered into relation with the picture as a whole— never faced, so to speak, *its* physiognomy.[6] He had no sense whatever of a landscape or scene.

I showed him the cover, an unbroken expanse of Sahara dunes.
110 "What do you see here?" I asked.

"I see a river," he said. "And a little guest-house with its terrace on the water. People are dining out on the terrace. I see coloured parasols here and there." He was looking, if it was "looking," right off the cover, into mid-air and <u>confabulating</u> non-existent features, as if the absence of features in the actual picture had driven him to imagine the river and the terrace and the coloured parasols.

I must have looked <u>aghast</u>, but he seemed to think he had done rather well. There was a hint of a smile on his face. He
120 also appeared to have decided that the examination was over, and started to look round for his hat. He reached out his hand, and took hold of his wife's head, tried to lift it off, to put it on. He had apparently mistaken his wife for a hat! His wife looked as if she was used to such things.

---

6. **physiognomy** (fĭ´zē ä[g]´ nə mē). Outward appearance; physical appearance

words for everyday use

a • cu • ity (a kyü´ə tē) *n.*, sharpness. *They called him "The Razor" because of his remarkable mental <u>acuity</u>.*

e • lic • it (ē li´sət) *vt.*, call forth or bring out. *The offensive statements <u>elicited</u> boos from the audience.*

con • fab • u • late (kən fa´byə lāt) *vt.*, fill in gaps in memory by fabricating, or inventing, information. *When asked what she had done last month, the little girl <u>confabulated</u> a circus on the moon.*

a • ghast (ə gast´) *adj.*, horrified; shocked. *Taro was <u>aghast</u> when he found that his friend had lied to him; he could not speak for a long time.*

I could make no sense of what had occurred, in terms of conventional neurology (or neuropsychology). In some ways he seemed perfectly preserved, and in others absolutely, incomprehensibly devastated. How could he, on the one hand, mistake his wife for a hat and, on the other, function, as apparently he still did, as a teacher at the Music School?

I had to think, to see him again—and to see him in his own familiar habitat, at home.

A few days later I called on Dr. P. and his wife at home, with the score of the *Dichterliebe* in my briefcase (I knew he liked Schumann),[7] and a variety of odd objects for the testing of perception. Mrs. P. showed me into a lofty apartment, which recalled fin-de-siècle Berlin.[8] A magnificent old Bösendorfer[9] stood in state in the centre of the room, and all round it were music-stands, instruments, scores . . . There were books, there were paintings, but the music was central. Dr. P. came in and, distracted, advanced with outstretched hand to the grandfather clock, but, hearing my voice, corrected himself, and shook hands with me. We exchanged greetings, and chatted a little of current concerts and performances. <u>Diffidently</u>, I asked him if he would sing.

"The *Dichterliebe!*" he exclaimed. "But I can no longer read music. You will play them, yes?"

I said I would try. On that wonderful old piano even my playing sounded right, and Dr. P. was an aged, but infinitely mellow Fischer-Dieskau,[10] combining a perfect ear and voice with the most <u>incisive</u> musical intelligence. It was clear that the Music School was not keeping him on out of charity.

Dr. P.'s temporal lobes were obviously intact: he had a wonderful musical cortex.[11] What, I wondered, was going

_____

_____

_____

_____

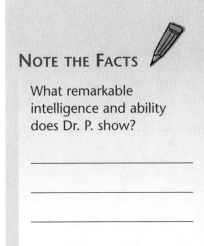

NOTE THE FACTS

What remarkable intelligence and ability does Dr. P. show?

_____

_____

_____

---

7. ***Dichterliebe . . . Schumann*** (shü´ män´). Symphony written by German composer Robert Schumann (1810–1856)

8. **fin-de-siècle** (fan de sē e´ kəl) **Berlin.** The décor of the apartment reminds him of Berlin, the capital of Germany, at the end of the nineteenth century.

9. **Bösendorfer.** Austrian-made grand piano

10. **Fischer-Dieskau** (fi´shər dēs´ kaù´). Dietrich Fischer-Dieskau (1925–), a famed German singer with a low, baritone voice

11. **temporal lobes . . . musical cortex.** The musical areas of Dr. P.'s brain were not damaged.

---

words for everyday use

dif • fi • dent • ly (di´fə dənt lē) *adv.,* in a hesitant, shy way. *"Maybe you'd like to go to the movies sometime or something?" Ramona asked <u>diffidently</u>.*

in • ci • sive (in sī´səv) *adj.,* sharp. *Bart's <u>incisive</u> criticism of my essay was maybe a little too cutting!*

NOTE THE FACTS

Reread lines 166–175.
How does Dr. P. respond
to abstract shapes and
schematic drawings?

_____

_____

_____

_____

MAKE A NOTE

_____

_____

_____

_____

on in his parietal and occipital lobes,[12] especially in those areas where visual processing occurred? I carry the Platonic solids[13] in my neurological kit, and decided to start with these.

160   "What is this?" I asked, drawing out the first one.

"A cube, of course."

"Now this?" I asked, brandishing another.

He asked if he might examine it, which he did swiftly and systematically: "A dodecahedron, of course. And don't bother with the others—I'll get the eikosihedron too."

<u>Abstract</u> shapes clearly presented no problems. What about faces? I took out a pack of cards. All of these he identified instantly, including the jacks, queens, kings, and the joker. But these, after all, are <u>stylized</u> designs, and it was

170 impossible to tell whether he saw faces or merely patterns. I decided I would show him a volume of cartoons which I had in my briefcase. Here, again, for the most part, he did well. Churchill's cigar, Schnozzle's nose: as soon as he had picked out a key feature he could identify the face. But cartoons, again, are formal and <u>schematic</u>. It remained to be seen how he would do with real faces, realistically represented.

    I turned on the television, keeping the sound off, and found an early Bette Davis film. A love scene was in progress. Dr. P. failed to identify the actress—but this could

180 have been because she had never entered his world. What was more striking was that he failed to identify the expressions on her face or her partner's, though in the course of a single <u>torrid</u> scene these passed from sultry yearning through passion, surprise, disgust and fury to a

---

12. **parietal and occipital lobes.** The parietal lobes, located in the central part of the brain, deal with bodily sensation; the occipital lobes, located in the back of the brain, contain the visual areas.
13. **Platonic solids.** Solid three-dimensional geometric shapes

words for everyday use

ab • stract (ab'strakt) *adj.*, having only a simple form and not representing a picture or narrative content. *Thuy did not like the <u>abstract</u> paintings, which just showed shapes and lines of color.*

styl • ized (stī'līzd) *adj.*, not realistic; conforming to a set pattern or design. *The company logo was a <u>stylized</u> sun: a yellow circle with six lines that represented rays.*

sche • mat • ic (ski ma' tik) *adj.*, following a set scheme or design. *The traveling speaker became bored quickly because her presentations were so <u>schematic</u>: the entire speech had to be said word-for-word.*

tor • rid (tôr'əd) *adj.*, hot; passionate. *Mom let me watch the R-rated movie but covered my eyes when the <u>torrid</u> love scenes came on.*

melting reconciliation. Dr. P. could make nothing of any of this. He was very unclear as to what was going on, or who was who or even what sex they were. His comments on the scene were positively Martian.

It was just possible that some of his difficulties were
190 associated with the unreality of a <u>celluloid</u>, Hollywood world; and it occurred to me that he might be more successful in identifying faces from his own life. On the walls of the apartment there were photographs of his family, his colleagues, his pupils, himself. I gathered a pile of these together and, with some misgivings, presented them to him. What had been funny, or <u>farcical</u>, in relation to the movie, was tragic in relation to real life. By and large, he recognised nobody: neither his family, nor his colleagues, nor his pupils, nor himself. He recognised a portrait of
200 Einstein, because he picked up the characteristic hair and moustache; and the same thing happened with one or two other people. "Ach, Paul!" he said, when shown a portrait of his brother. "That square jaw, those big teeth, I would know Paul anywhere!" But was it Paul he recognised, or one or two of his features, on the basis of which he could make a reasonable guess as to the subject's identity? In the absence of obvious "markers," he was utterly lost. But it was not merely the <u>cognition</u>, the *gnosis*,[14] at fault; there was something radically wrong with the whole way he
210 proceeded. For he approached these faces—even of those near and dear—as if they were abstract puzzles or tests. He did not relate to them, he did not behold. No face was familiar to him, seen as a "thou,"[15] being just identified as a set of features, an "it." Thus there was formal, but no trace of personal, gnosis. And with this went his indifference, or blindness, to expression. A face, to us, is a person looking out—we see, as it were, the person through his *persona*, his

---

14. *gnosis* (nōˊ səs). Greek term meaning "knowledge of truth"
15. "thou." "You"

THINK AND REFLECT

Reread lines 189–199. What do Dr. P.'s responses reveal about his ability to make sense of the visual world? **(Infer)**

_____

_____

_____

_____

FIX-UP IDEA

Write Things Down and Reread
If difficult medical terminology affects your comprehension of the selection, consider making a medical glossary. Write down the medical words you come across as you read the selection. Refer to the Words for Everyday Use and the footnotes, or look up the definitions in a dictionary if necessary. Then reread the passages that use these words.

face. But for Dr. P. there was no *persona* in this sense—no outward *persona*, and no person within.

220   I had stopped at a florist on my way to his apartment and bought myself an extravagant red rose for my buttonhole. Now I removed this and handed it to him. He took it like a botanist or morphologist[16] given a specimen, not like a person given a flower.

"About six inches in length," he commented. "A <u>convoluted</u> red form with a <u>linear</u> green attachment."

"Yes," I said encouragingly, "and what do you think it *is*, Dr. P. ?"

"Not easy to say." He seemed perplexed. "It lacks the
230   simple <u>symmetry</u> of the Platonic solids, although it may have a higher symmetry of its own . . . I think this could be an inflorescence or flower."

"Could be?" I queried.

"Could be," he confirmed.

"Smell it," I suggested, and he again looked somewhat puzzled, as if I had asked him to smell a higher symmetry. But he <u>complied</u> courteously, and took it to his nose. Now, suddenly, he came to life.

"Beautiful!" he exclaimed. "An early rose. What a heavenly
240   smell!" He started to hum "Die Rose, die Lillie . . ." Reality, it seemed, might be conveyed by smell, not by sight.

I tried one final test. It was still a cold day, in early spring, and I had thrown my coat and gloves on the sofa.

"What is this?" I asked, holding up a glove.

"May I examine it?" he asked, and, taking it from me, he proceeded to examine it as he had examined the geometrical shapes.

---

16. **botanist or morphologist.** Botanist (bä´ tə nist)—one who studies plants; morphologist (mȯr fä´ lə jist)—biologist who studies the form and structure of animals and plants

READ ALOUD

Read aloud the highlighted text on this page. What is comical about this scene?

_____

_____

_____

"A continuous surface," he announced at last, "infolded on itself. It appears to have"—he hesitated—"five outpouchings, if this is the word."

250

"Yes," I said cautiously. "You have given me a description. Now tell me what it is."

"A container of some sort?"

"Yes," I said, "and what would it contain?"

"It would contain its contents!" said Dr. P., with a laugh. "There are many possibilities. It could be a change-purse, for example, for coins of five sizes. It could . . ."

I interrupted the barmy[17] flow. "Does it not look familiar? Do you think it might contain, might fit, a part of

260

your body?"

No light of recognition dawned on his face.

No child would have the power to see and speak of "a continuous surface . . . infolded on itself," but any child, any infant, would immediately know a glove as a glove, see it as familiar, as going with a hand. Dr. P. didn't. He saw nothing as familiar. Visually, he was lost in a world of lifeless abstractions. Indeed he did not have a real visual world, as he did not have a real visual self. He could speak about things, but did not see them face-to-face. Hughlings Jackson,

270

discussing patients with aphasia and left-hemisphere lesions,[18] says they have lost "abstract" and "propositional" thought[19]—and compares them with dogs (or, rather, he compares dogs to patients with aphasia). Dr. P., on the other hand, functioned precisely as a machine functions. It wasn't merely that he displayed the same indifference to the visual word as a computer but—even more strikingly—he <u>construed</u> the world as a computer construes it, by means of key features and schematic relationships. The scheme might

---

17. **barmy.** Full of froth; lacking substance
18. **aphasia . . . lesions.** Aphasia (ə fā´zhə)—loss of ability to understand words and language; left-hemisphere lesions (lē´ zhənz)—lesions, or injuries, in the left side of the brain
19. **"abstract" and "propositional" thought.** These patients have lost the ability to think about ideas in the abstract or about things that might happen; they can only think about objects that are right in front of them or things that are happening right now. Like dogs, they live simply, and they live in the moment.

words for everyday use

con • strue (kən strü´) *vt.,* understand or explain the meaning of something using the circumstances or evidence. *Given the context clues in the sentence, which had to do with sea life, I was able to <u>construe</u> the meaning of the word* conch.

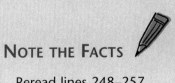

NOTE THE FACTS

Reread lines 248–257. How does Dr. P. describe the glove Dr. Sacks gives him? What does he think it is?

_____

_____

_____

WHAT DO YOU WONDER?

_____

_____

_____

_____

be identified—in an "identiti-kit" way—without the reality
280 being grasped at all.

The testing I had done so far told me nothing about Dr.
P.'s inner world. Was it possible that his visual memory and
imagination were still intact? I asked him to imagine
entering one of our local squares from the north side, to
walk through it, in imagination or in memory, and tell me
the buildings he might pass as he walked. He listed the
buildings on his right side, but none of those on his left. I
then asked him to imagine entering the square from the
south. Again he mentioned only those buildings that were
290 on the right side, although these were the very buildings he
had <u>omitted</u> before. Those he had "seen" internally before
were not mentioned now; presumably, they were no longer
"seen." It was evident that his difficulties with leftness, his
visual field <u>deficits</u>, were as much internal as external,
bisecting his visual memory and imagination.

What, at a higher level, of his internal visualisation?
Thinking of the almost hallucinatory intensity with which
Tolstoy visualises and animates his characters, I questioned
Dr. P. about *Anna Karenina*.[20] He could remember incidents
300 without difficulty, had an undiminished grasp of the plot,
completely omitted visual characteristics, visual narrative or
scenes. He remembered the words of the characters, but not
their faces; and though, when asked, he could quote, with
his remarkable and almost <u>verbatim</u> memory, the original
visual descriptions, these were, it became apparent, quite
empty for him, and lacked sensorial, imaginal, or emotional
reality. Thus there was an internal agnosia as well.

But this was only the case, it became clear, with certain sorts
of visualisation. The visualisation of faces and scenes, of visual
310 narrative and drama—this was profoundly impaired, almost
absent. But the visualisation of *schemata*[21] was preserved,

---

20. *Anna Karenina* (a´ nə kä re´ nə nä). Famous novel by Russian author Leo Tolstoy
21. *schemata* (skē mä´ tə). Schemes, set patterns

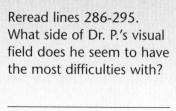

NOTE THE FACTS

Reread lines 286-295. What side of Dr. P.'s visual field does he seem to have the most difficulties with?

_____

_____

_____

MARK THE TEXT

Underline or highlight Dr. Sacks's additional diagnosis.

perhaps enhanced. Thus when I engaged him in a game of mental chess, he had no difficulty visualising the chessboard or the moves—indeed, no difficulty in beating me soundly.

Luria said of Zazetsky[22] that he had entirely lost his capacity to play games but that his "vivid imagination" was unimpaired. Zazetsky and Dr. P. lived in worlds which were mirror images of each other. But the saddest difference between them was that Zazetsky, as Luria said, "fought to regain his lost faculties with the <u>indomitable</u> <u>tenacity</u> of the damned," whereas Dr. P. was not fighting, did not know what was lost, did not indeed know that anything was lost. But who was more tragic, or who was more damned—the man who knew it, or the man who did not?

When the examination was over, Mrs. P. called us to the table, where there was coffee and a delicious spread of little cakes. Hungrily, hummingly, Dr. P. started on the cakes. Swiftly, fluently, unthinkingly, melodiously, he pulled the plates towards him, and took this and that, in a great gurgling stream, an edible song of food, until, suddenly, there came an interruption: a loud, <u>peremptory</u> rat-tat-tat at the door. Startled, taken aback, arrested, by the interruption, Dr. P. stopped eating, and sat frozen, motionless, at the table, with an indifferent, blind, bewilderment on his face. He saw, but no longer saw, the table; no longer perceived it as a table laden with cakes. His wife poured him some coffee: the smell titillated his nose, and brought him back to reality. The melody of eating resumed.

How does he do anything, I wondered to myself? What happens when he's dressing, goes to the lavatory, has a bath? I followed his wife into the kitchen and asked her how, for instance, he managed to dress himself. "It's just like the eating," she explained. "I put his usual clothes out, in all the usual places, and he dresses without difficulty,

---

22. **Luria . . . Zazetsky.** The author is quoting Alexander Romanovich Luria (1902–1977), a Russian neuropsychologist (psychologist who deals with neurology). Zazetsky was one of his patients.

words for everyday use

in • dom • i • ta • ble (in dä′mə tə bəl) *adj.*, not defeatable. *Superman is indomitable except if kryptonite is used against him.*

te • na • ci • ty (tə na′sə tē) *n.*, courage; quality of not giving up. *At first the principal said no, but after seeing the tenacity of the students, he agreed to change the policy.*

per • emp • to • ry (pə remp′tə rē) *adj.*, urgent; commanding. *The general barked a peremptory order for troops to move forward.*

NOTE THE FACTS

Reread lines 328–338. What happens to Dr. P.'s enjoyment of lunch when there is a knock at the door? What snaps him back to the act of eating?

_____

_____

_____

NOTE THE FACTS

Reread lines 356–362.
What does Dr. Sacks think
about Dr. P.'s final
paintings? What does he
think caused the change
in Dr. P.'s artistic style?

_____

_____

_____

THINK AND REFLECT

Reread lines 364–367.
Why do you think Dr. P.'s
wife disagrees with Dr.
Sacks so strongly? **(Infer)**

_____

_____

_____

_____

singing to himself. He does everything singing to himself.
But if he is interrupted and loses the thread, he comes to a
complete stop, doesn't know his clothes—or his own body.
He sings all the time—eating songs, dressing songs,
350 bathing songs, everything. He can't do anything unless he
makes it a song."

While we were talking my attention was caught by the
pictures on the walls.

"Yes," Mrs. P. said, "he was a gifted painter as well as a
singer. The School exhibited his pictures every year."

I strolled past them curiously—they were in chronological
order. All his earlier work was naturalistic and realistic, with
vivid mood and atmosphere, but finely detailed and concrete.
Then, years later, they became less vivid, less concrete, less
360 realistic and naturalistic; but far more abstract, even
geometrical and cubist.[23] Finally, in the last paintings, the
canvasses became nonsense, or nonsense to me—mere
chaotic lines and blotches of paint. I commented on this to
Mrs. P.

"Ach, you doctors, you're such philistines!"[24] she
exclaimed, "Can you not see *artistic development*—how he
<u>renounced</u> the realism of his earlier years, and advanced
into abstract, non-representational art?"

"No, that's not it," I said to myself (but <u>forbore</u> to say it to
370 poor Mrs. P.). He had indeed moved from realism to non-
representation to the abstract, but this was not the artist, but
the <u>pathology</u>, advancing—advancing towards a profound
visual agnosia, in which all powers of representation imagery,
all sense of the concrete, all sense of reality, were being
destroyed. This wall of paintings was a tragic pathological
exhibit, which belonged to neurology, not art.

---

23. **cubist.** In an abstract style, not meant to be realistic, such as some of
the works of Spanish artist Pablo Picasso (1881–1973)
24. **philistines** (fil´ ə stēnz). People who cannot understand artistic values;
ignorant people

words for everyday use

re • nounce (ri nouns´) *vt.*, give up or leave behind. *The vegetarian <u>renounced</u> eating meat.*

for • bear (fôr bar´) *v.*, hold back from, abstain. *We ask that you <u>forbear</u> going out with your friends until your grades improve.*

pa • tho • lo • gy (pa thä´ lə jē) *n.*, abnormality caused by disease. *Compulsive lying is sometimes caused by a <u>pathology</u>: hence the term "pathological liar."*

And yet, I wondered, was she not partly right? For there is often a struggle, and sometimes, even more interestingly, a <u>collusion</u> between the powers of pathology and creation. Perhaps, in his cubist period, there might have been both artistic and pathological development, colluding to engender an original form; for as he lost the concrete, so he might have gained in the abstract, developing a greater sensitivity to all the structural elements of line, boundary, contour—an almost Picasso-like power to see, and equally depict, those abstract organisations embedded in, and normally lost in, the concrete . . . Though in the final pictures, I feared, there was only chaos and agnosia.

We returned to the great music-room, with the Bösendorfer in the centre, and Dr. P. humming the last torte.

"Well, Dr. Sacks," he said to me. "You find me an interesting case, I perceive. Can you tell me what you find wrong, make recommendations?"

"I can't tell you what I find wrong," I replied, "but I'll say what I find right. You are a wonderful musician, and music is your life. What I would prescribe, in a case such as yours, is a life which consists entirely of music. Music has been the centre, now make it the whole, of your life."

This was four years ago—I never saw him again, but I often wondered how he <u>apprehended</u> the world, given his strange loss of image, visuality, and the perfect preservation of a great musicality. I think that music, for him, had taken the place of image. He had no body-image, he had body-music: this is why he could move and act as fluently as he did, but came to a total confused stop if the "inner music" stopped. And equally with the outside, the world . . .

In *The World as Representation and Will* Schopenhauer[25] speaks of music as "pure will." How fascinated he would have been by Dr. P., a man who had wholly lost the world as representation, but wholly preserved it as music or will.

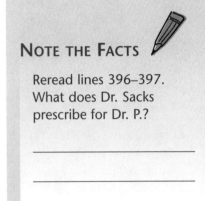

NOTE THE FACTS

Reread lines 396–397. What does Dr. Sacks prescribe for Dr. P.?

_____

_____

---

25. **Schopenhauer** (shō´ pən hau´ ər). Arthur Schopenhauer (1788–1860), German philosopher

words for everyday use

col • lu • sion (kə lü´ zhən) *n.*, secret cooperation; conspiracy. *I became nervous because my friends were whispering so much, but then I found the reason for their <u>collusion</u> was a surprise party for me!*

ap • pre • hend (a´ pri hend´) *v.*, grasp; understand. *Doug found it difficult to <u>apprehend</u> Carmen's point of view.*

And this, mercifully, held to the end—for despite the gradual advance of his disease (a massive tumour or <u>degenerative</u> process in the visual parts of his brain) Dr. P. lived and taught music to the last days of his life. ■

words for everyday use

de • gen • er • a • tive (di je' nə rə tiv) _adj._, something that degenerates, or destroys. _Alzheimer's is a <u>degenerative</u> disease that affects memory._

Reflect ON YOUR READING

After Reading ➤ **REVIEW DIFFICULT VOCABULARY**

When you finish reading, review the words you recorded in your Word Maps. Then, prepare a crossword puzzle using at least eight of these words (see the sample crossword puzzle in Appendix A, page A-2). Trade puzzles with a classmate, and try to complete his or her crossword puzzle. Ask your partner to correct the crossword puzzle you completed. Then write a paragraph evaluating how you tackled the difficult vocabulary in the selection.

Reading Skills and Test Practice

USE CONTEXT CLUES

Discuss with a partner how to answer the following questions about words in context.

1. Read the following passage from the selection:

   "Smell it," I suggested, and he again looked somewhat puzzled, as if I had asked him to smell a higher symmetry. But he complied courteously, and took it to his nose. Now, suddenly, he came to life.

   What does *complied* mean?
   a. interrupted
   b. refused
   c. understood
   d. obeyed

Circle the correct answer to the question above. How were you able to eliminate the other answers?

2. Read the following passage from the selection:

   I questioned Dr. P. about *Anna Karenina*. . . . He remembered the words of the characters, but not their faces; and though, when asked, he could quote, with his remarkable and almost verbatim memory, the original visual descriptions, these were, it became apparent, quite empty for him, and lacked sensorial, imaginal, or emotional reality.

   What does *verbatim* mean?
   a. faulty
   b. word for word
   c. automatic
   d. abstract

Circle the correct answer to the question above. How did your application of the reading strategy help you answer the question?

THINK-ALOUD
NOTES

_____

_____

_____

_____

_____

_____

_____

_____

_____

_____

Investigate, Inquire, and Imagine

RECALL: GATHER FACTS → INTERPRET: FIND MEANING
1a. Who is Dr. P.? What is wrong with him?

1b. Why can't Dr. P. accurately describe the landscape in the *National Geographic* photo? Why do you think Dr. P. invents details in the photo?

ANALYZE: TAKE THINGS APART → SYNTHESIZE: BRING THINGS TOGETHER
2a. Which tests are easy for Dr. P., and why? Which tests are difficult or impossible for him to perform, and why?

2b. How well will Dr. Sacks's prescription allow Dr. P. to function in the world?

EVALUATE: MAKE JUDGMENTS → EXTEND: CONNECT IDEAS
3a. How would you characterize Dr. Sacks's prescription for Dr. P.?

3b. What senses or areas of expertise would you rely on if you were diagnosed with visual agnosia? How would you want people to treat you if you had a disability? How do you think most people treat Dr. P.?

Literary Tools

NARRATIVE WRITING. **Narrative writing** is a type of nonfiction writing that often aims to make a point by sharing a story about an event or a series of events. Complete the chart below to list the occurrences in the case of Dr. P. and to tell what they reveal. One example has been done for you. What do these occurrences reveal in general about Dr. P.'s condition?

Occurrences in the Case of Dr. P.	What They Reveal
Dr. P. fails to recognize some of his students until they speak, and he sees faces where there are none.	Something might be wrong with Dr. P.'s vision.

WordWorkshop

SENTENCE COMPLETION. Complete each sentence with the Word for Everyday Use that makes the most sense in the sentence. You will need to change the part of speech of some words to make them fit the sentences. For a list of Words for Everyday Use, see WordWatch on page 332.

1. Court reporters record _____ the testimony and proceedings of court cases to provide an exact report.
2. The artist's style was marked by his use of startling color and perfect _____ of form.
3. Members of the community will have a greater sense of safety, once the police have _____ the person committing the burglaries.
4. The two dogs raced toward each other, circling and sniffing, their wagging tails signaling a(n) _____ meeting.
5. Mattie was known for her _____ comments, sometimes at the expense of other people's feelings.

Read-Write Connection

Do you think Dr. P. is aware of what he is missing? If you had visual agnosia, what would you miss seeing the most?

_____

_____

_____

_____

_____

Beyond the Reading

WRITING A CASE HISTORY. Read a review of and watch the based-on-fact 1990 movie *Awakenings*, starring Robin Williams and Robert De Niro. A case history is a record of the history, environment, and relevant details of a medical case. Write a case history of the character Leonard Lowe. What is his diagnosis? What are his symptoms? Which drug brings him back to life? How would you describe the changes in him? Include answers to these questions in your case history.

GO ONLINE. Visit the EMC Internet Resource Center at **emcp.com** to find links and additional activities for this selection.

Reader's resource

Bison, or American buffalo, once roamed in great herds over North America from the Appalachians to the Rockies. In 1850, there were still almost twenty million bison left roaming free. White Americans slaughtered the animals without concern in the late 1800s, almost wiping out the whole species. In **"The Last Bison,"** Quammen traces the history of the bison and the measures taken to save the species from extinction.

Word watch

PREVIEW VOCABULARY

abundance	flagrant
accession	hindsight
carnage	prodigious
defunct	stalwart
distinction	superfluous
enterprising	

Reader's journal

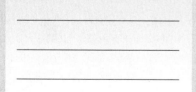

What impact do humans have on the natural environment?

_____

_____

_____

_____

"The Last Bison"

by David Quammen

Active READING STRATEGY

USE TEXT ORGANIZATION

Before Reading ➤ **PREVIEW THE SELECTION**

❏ Read the Reader's Resource.

❏ Join a class discussion about the various ways an essay can be organized. For example, one might organize ideas in chronological order, spatial order, order of importance, comparison-and-contrast order, cause-and-effect order, or part-by-part order. Review the methods of organization in Unit 2, pages 22–23. Work with the class to describe the main characteristics of these different methods of organization.

❏ As you read "The Last Bison," record the selection's main ideas in Main Idea Maps like the one below. Use a seperate Main Idea Map for each main idea. Try to identify the method Quammen uses to organize the essay.

Grapic Organizer

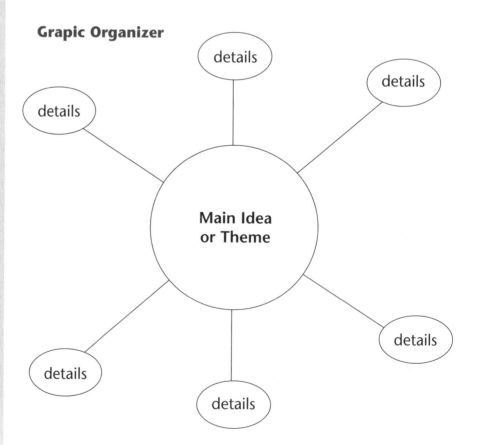

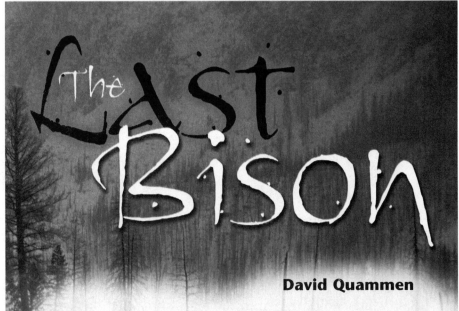

The Last Bison

David Quammen

I t happened quickly. First there were 60 million, roaming the prairies and plains, blanketing whole valleys almost shoulder to shoulder for miles, the greatest <u>abundance</u> of any species of large mammal that modern humankind ever had the privilege to behold. And then, in 1889, there were (by one informed estimate) just 541 bison surviving throughout all the United States.

The slaughter had been conducted with <u>prodigious</u> efficiency and prodigious waste. Sometimes the meat was
10 taken from a dead bison, sometimes only the hide, sometimes no more than the tongue, cut out and pickled in brine,[1] to be sent to New York in a barrel. Sometimes not even that: People shot them from train windows to relieve the boredom of crossing Nebraska by rail, and left them rotting untouched. In the 1870s, the wildest years of the <u>carnage</u>, certain booking agents for the railroads went so far as to advertise outings on that basis: "Ample time will be had for a grand BUFFALO HUNT. Buffaloes are so numerous along the road that they are shot from the cars

---

1. **brine.** Water saturated with salt

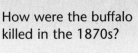

MARK THE TEXT

Underline or highlight what happened when the hunters went in search of buffalo in 1884.

NOTE THE FACTS

What interested "sport hunters"?

_____

_____

_____

20   nearly every day. On our last excursion our party killed twenty buffaloes in a hunt of six hours! Round trip tickets from Leavenworth,[2] only $10!" In Montana and the Dakotas, last refuge of the big herds, the trade in hides peaked around 1882 and then suddenly, two years later, the professional hunters were coming back from a frustrating season having seen no buffalo. None. They were gone or in hiding. Perhaps a final few desperate animals had retreated to high country, beyond the Absaroka Mountains, into Yellowstone Park.[3] At this point among the

30   thrill-seekers, the railroad excursionists, those idle souls back in Wichita and St. Louis and Philadelphia who collected trophies and fancied themselves "sport hunters," there was a measure of interest in that supposed <u>distinction</u> which would attach to the man who killed the last American bison.

But no one did. Miracle of our good fortune: No one did.

Why not? Partly because of natural human sloth:[4] As bison grew more rare, the stalking of one became a matter

40   of greater expense and inconvenience. Partly also because of collective good sense: Laws (belated and, at first, weak) were passed. And partly the last of the bison survived because they were not, for even an experienced and relentless hunter, so very easy to find. During that near brush with extinction at the end of the 1880s, when the species had fallen in this country to fewer than 600 individuals, and not many more in Canada, the high mountain meadows and steep woodlands of the Yellowstone plateau *did* shelter bison—probably more than 200 head, one-third of

50   the entire national remnant.

These Yellowstone animals were not newcomers, however, not fugitives lately arrived in flight from the massacre

---

2. **Leavenworth.** City in northeastern Kansas on the Missouri River
3. **Yellowstone Park.** National park of about 3,500 square miles located mainly in northwestern Wyoming
4. **sloth.** Laziness

words for everyday use

dis • tinc • tion (di stiŋk´shən) n., special recognition. *He earned the <u>distinction</u> of being the only man to win the marathon three years in a row and was recognized with a special award for his achievement.*

below. They were a distinct subspecies now known as mountain bison. They had been there all along.

And they were a little different, the mountain bison, a little more cagey than their lowland relatives, perhaps more than a little better adapted to avoid terminal confrontation with man. Fossil evidence shows that they were slightly larger, on average, than plains bison (which is to say, larger 60 than any animal on the continent), and yet from historical accounts we hear also that they were more agile and alert and wary. One observer in 1877 wrote: "These animals are by no means plentiful, and are moreover excessively shy, inhabiting the deepest, darkest defiles,[5] or the craggy, almost precipitous,[6] sides of mountains, inaccessible to any but the most practised mountaineers." Another writer, the park's superintendent in 1880, judged them "most keen of scent and difficult of approach of all mountain animals." The cloak of hair over their shoulders and hump was darker and finer 70 than on plains buffalo, the alignment of horns was minutely different and, most important, the mountain bison were more hardy.

They had the evolved capability[7] to endure those bitter and long winters in the high Yellowstone valleys—above 7,500 feet with deep snow and temperatures often below minus 25°—where a buffalo hunter, white or Indian, could too easily freeze to death in pursuit. They would face into a driving blizzard in open country and stand their ground—waiting, enduring, indomitable. They were living 80 exempla of the word _stalwart_. They would plow snow aside with the muzzles of their massive heads to reach edible grass underneath. They would use the Firehole River and other natural geo-thermal features of Yellowstone as high-ways and oases during the worst of the winter. And in sum-mer they climbed still higher, escaping the biting insects,

Use THE STRATEGY

USE TEXT ORGANIZATION. Remember to record the author's main ideas in your Main Idea Maps. Continue to look for clues that will reveal the essay's method of organization.

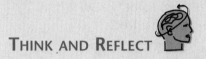

THINK AND REFLECT

What was the most important difference about the mountain buffalo? What effect could this have on the declining buffalo population? **(Interpret)**

_____

_____

_____

_____

---

5. **defiles.** Deep stone valleys between cliffs or rock outcroppings
6. **precipitous.** Almost vertical; steep or sheer
7. **evolved capability.** Practical ability developed over many generations
8. **sedges.** Grasslike plants with triangular leaves that grow in wet ground

words for everyday use

stal • wart (stôl´wərt) _adj.,_ strong; robust; unyielding. _Tonto was the trusted stalwart companion of the Lone Ranger._

THINK AND REFLECT

Why were the bison in Yellowstone so hard to hunt? (**Analyze**)

_____

_____

_____

NOTE THE FACTS

What did the government finally do? Why was this act almost too late?

_____

_____

_____

grazing the sedges[8] and grasses of subalpine meadows, venturing even onto the alpine tundra above timberline. Hannibal[9] would have worshipped these creatures.

But despite their reclusiveness, despite their agility and power, despite the legislation that in 1872 had made Yellowstone our first national park, the mountain bison were still poached for their heads and their hides. Snowshoes[10] and Sharps rifles made this possible, if not easy, and trophy heads were now bringing high enough prices to justify the ordeal. It was illegal but the law allowed only token penalties, and the park budget allowed only token enforcement. In 1894, after an especially <u>flagrant</u> poaching case was reported in the journal *Forest and Stream*, spawning further coverage in newspapers around the country and a tardy <u>accession</u> of public concern, Congress finally passed a law with penalties severe enough to protect the Yellowstone bison. Yet by then it was very nearly too late. Enforcement was still difficult in the Yellowstone backcountry, and by 1897 the entire park population had shrunk to less than twenty-five. These few animals were burdened with a double distinction. They were not only the last of the mountain bison. They were also the last wild bison, of any sort whatever, in all the United States.

Elsewhere the sole survivors were plains bison that had been preserved by <u>enterprising</u> ranchers for commercial stock-growing experiments. These private herds were dealt with like cattle: fed out on hay during hard weather, gathered periodically into corrals, the excess male calves castrated into steers. Saddled, some of them, for the amusement of their owners. Consigned to performing in rodeos. Cross-bred with domestic cattle. Doted on as

---

9. **Hannibal.** (*circa* 247–183 BC) North African general from the state of Carthage who crossed the Alps to invade Italy in 218 BC
10. **Snowshoes.** Flat, netted surfaces used for walking on snow

words for everyday use

fla • grant (flā´grənt) *adj.*, outrageous. *The referee called the basketball player for a <u>flagrant</u> foul after she wrapped her arms around an opposing player about to score.*
ac • ces • sion (ak sesh´ən) *n.*, outburst. *An unusual <u>accession</u> of public concern followed the report that the town's drinking water was unsafe; the general outburst led to an emergency meeting.*
en • ter • pris • ing (ent´ər prī´ziŋ) *adj.*, marked by an independent energetic spirit and by readiness to undertake an experiment. *He was considered an <u>enterprising</u> young businessman because he had ambitions of opening his own chain of restaurants.*

nostalgic curios. And routinely slaughtered for their meat. When the century turned, there were still many buffalo in the United States, and the number increasing, but the only wild and free-living holdouts[11] were those two dozen in Yellowstone.

And then in 1902, with well-meaning folk convinced that the little group was doomed, stock-ranching practices came also to Yellowstone. Congress put up $15,000, twenty-one plains bison were purchased from private herds in Texas and Montana, and an official "Buffalo Ranch" was established in the gorgeous Lamar Valley of the park's northeast corner. Hay was doled out, there were corrals and roundups, castrations and cullings.[12] It became—judged on its own terms—a successful operation. Many bison were raised at the Lamar Buffalo Ranch. Only <u>hindsight</u> could have shown us that it was an utterly <u>superfluous</u> enterprise.

Superfluous because, while this ranching proceeded in the Lamar, the two dozen wild bison went their own way, to the high woodlands and the tundra in summer, to the sheltered valleys and thermal areas in winter, and survived. Left alone, given nothing but peace, they saved themselves. Endured, as they always had done, and after two decades on the brink of extinction, began again to multiply naturally.

The Buffalo Ranch is long since <u>defunct</u>. Its buildings now house a thriving institute for the study of Yellowstone's ecosystem. And today in Yellowstone Park, along the Lamar and the Firehole, amid the bunchgrass and sage[13] of the Hayden Valley, across the Mirror Plateau above Specimen Ridge and at the headwaters of the Bechler River, there live about two thousand bison.

120

130

140

---

11. **holdouts.** Few remaining bison after the rest had been destroyed
12. **cullings.** Process of selecting, as for breeding
13. **bunchgrass and sage.** Tufts of grass and sagebrush, a composite plant with small flowers common in the dry, alkaline soil of western America

words for everyday use

hind • sight (hīnd´sīt´) n., ability to see, after an event, what should have been done. _"Hindsight is 20/20," his father told him after he failed the test and realized he should have studied harder for it._
su • per • flu • ous (sə pʉr´flōō əs) adj., unnecessary. _Nora thought she was a superfluous member of the committee, since she never had anything to contribute._
de • funct (dē fuŋkt´) adj., no longer existing. _Drive-in movie theaters are largely defunct; only a few still exist._

Reading STRATEGY REVIEW

UNLOCK DIFFICULT VOCABULARY. Remember to stop to unlock the meaning of unfamiliar vocabulary words using context clues or your knowledge of word parts. If these strategies don't work, fill out a Word Map graphic organizer, as you did for "The Man Who Mistook His Wife for a Hat" (see page 332) for each vocabulary word that you don't know. Then reread the passage in which the unfamiliar word appears.

MARK THE TEXT

Underline or highlight what happened to the survivors of the plains bison.

NOTE THE FACTS

Why was the Lamar Buffalo Ranch "superfluous"?

_____

_____

_____

_____

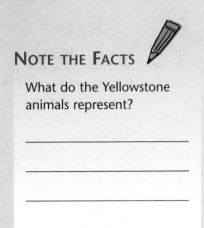
150   Despite some past interbreeding with—adulteration by[14]—the old Lamar herd of coddled flatland outsiders, the Yellowstone animals represent our best and only remnant of wild bison, mountain bison, America's most imposing and resolute and dignified beast. These creatures were made for greatness. They were made to scale the spine of a continent, on tiny hooves below huge shoulders, and stand facing the driven snow. They were made to last.   ■

---

14. **adulteration by.** Impurification by; weakening by

Reflect ON YOUR READING

After Reading ➤ ANALYZE THE SELECTION

When you have finished reading, join a small group to discuss your reading experience. Share your opinions on which method Quammen uses to organize this essay, and discuss the history of the bison that is presented in the selection. Then, work independently to write a critical review of this essay. In your review, discuss the content of the selection, as well as its method of organization. Remember to use the details from the text that you noted in your Main Idea Maps to support your opinions.

Reading Skills and Test Practice

IDENTIFY THE MAIN IDEA AND TONE

READ, THINK, AND EXPLAIN. Discuss with a partner how to identify the main idea and tone.

1. Summarize the main idea of "The Last Bison." Use details and specifics from the text to support your summary.

   _____

   _____

   _____

   _____

2. What is Quammen's tone in this essay? In other words, what emotional attitude toward the bison does the essay imply? Use details from the text to support your ideas.

   _____

   _____

   _____

   _____

REFLECT ON YOUR RESPONSE. Compare your response to that of your partner. How were you able to identify the main idea and tone?

   _____

   _____

   _____

   _____

THINK-ALOUD NOTES

_____

_____

_____

_____

_____

_____

_____

_____

_____

_____

Investigate, Inquire, and Imagine

RECALL: GATHER FACTS → INTERPRET: FIND MEANING
1a. What measures were taken to preserve the bison?

1b. Why didn't preservation measures work? What was responsible for saving the bison?

ANALYZE: TAKE THINGS APART → SYNTHESIZE: BRING THINGS TOGETHER
2a. How did humans upset the balance of nature? Why were their efforts to amend this disruption ineffective?

2b. How might the message of this essay be applied to current practices regarding the environment?

EVALUATE: MAKE JUDGMENTS → EXTEND: CONNECT IDEAS
3a. Evaluate whether Quammen remains impartial about the bison. What attitude does he take toward them?

3b. Do you favor hunters' rights or environmentalists' concerns? How might these two groups reach a compromise?

WordWorkshop

SENTENCE COMPLETION. Approaching a concept from different angles can help you understand it better. Rather than *answering* sentence completion questions, try approaching the questions from another angle—by creating a sentence completion vocabulary quiz for your classmates. Create 10 to 12 sentence completion questions that can be answered using the Words for Everyday Use from "The Last Bison." You may create questions that call for two Words for Everyday Use in one question. Make sure that you employ context clues such as:

- apposition: renaming something in different words
- restatement: expressing the same idea more than once using different language
- using language of comparison and contrast

Use the space below to make notes about your ideas for each of the Words for Everyday Use. Then write the quiz on your own paper.

_____

_____

_____

_____

_____

_____

Literary Tools

ESSAY. An **essay** is a brief work of prose nonfiction. A good essay develops a single idea, or *thesis*, and uses details to support it. Refer to your Main Idea Maps and review the details that Quammen uses as support. What is the main idea of this essay? How effectively does the author support this thesis? Explain your answer, using details from the text.

_____

_____

_____

_____

_____

_____

Read-Write Connection

Imagine what it would be like to be a Native American hunter who has come across bison carcasses left to rot in the plains. How would you respond?

_____

_____

_____

_____

_____

_____

_____

Beyond the Reading

HISTORY OF HUNTING. Research the history of hunting in the United States. How has hunting changed since the time of buffalo hunting? In what ways does hunting affect the environment? What animals are hunted most frequently? Why? Give a presentation on hunting and how it is regarded today as opposed to the time of the buffalo hunts.

GO ONLINE. Visit the EMC Internet Resource Center at **emcp.com** to find links and additional activities for this selection.

Reader's resource

Chief Seattle was chief of the Suquamish and Duwamish tribes in the northwestern United States during the nineteenth century. Soon after the organization of the Washington Territory in 1853, Governor Stevens spoke to Chief Seattle's people about a proposed treaty—one that would relocate the tribe to a reservation. **"Yonder sky that has wept tears of compassion . . ."** is Chief Seattle's response to the governor's speech. In this response, Chief Seattle reveals aspects of his people's cultural beliefs.

Word watch

PREVIEW VOCABULARY

disfigure	reproach
exempt	sequestered
molestation	stolidly
receding	verdant
remnant	

Reader's journal

Imagine that somebody wanted to take over your house or your town and make you move to another place. How would you respond?

_____

_____

_____

"YONDER SKY THAT HAS WEPT TEARS OF COMPASSION . . ."

by Chief Seattle

Active READING STRATEGY

WRITE THINGS DOWN

Before Reading ➤ ESTABLISH A PURPOSE FOR READING

❑ Read the Reader's Resource and hypothesize what Chief Seattle's purpose may have been in giving this speech.
❑ Fill in the Before Reading section of the Author's Purpose Chart below.
❑ Discuss with several classmates what you know about Native Americans—what their culture values, how they were treated historically, where they live today.

Graphic Organizer

Before Reading
Predict the author's purpose, the type of writing he or she uses, and the ideas he or she wants to communicate.

During Reading
Gather ideas that the author communicates to readers.

After Reading
Summarize the ideas the author communicates. Explain how these ideas help fulfill the author's purpose.

YONDER SKY
THAT HAS WEPT TEARS OF COMPASSION...

Chief Seattle

Yonder sky that has wept tears of compassion upon my people for centuries untold, and which to us appears changeless and eternal, may change. Today is fair. Tomorrow it may be overcast with clouds. My words are like the stars that never change. Whatever Seattle says the great chief at Washington[1] can rely upon with as much certainty as he can upon the return of the sun or the seasons. The white chief says that big chief at Washington sends us greetings of friendship and goodwill. This is kind

10 of him for we know he has little need of our friendship in return. His people are many. They are like the grass that covers vast prairies. My people are few. They resemble the scattering trees of a storm-swept plain. The great—and I presume—good white chief sends us word that he wishes to buy our lands but is willing to allow us enough to live comfortably. This indeed appears just, even generous, for the red man no longer has rights that he need respect, and the offer may be wise also, as we are no longer in need of an extensive country.

20 There was a time when our people covered the land as the waves of a wind-ruffled sea cover its shell-paved floor, but that time long since passed away with the greatness of tribes that are now but a mournful memory. I will not dwell on, nor mourn over, our untimely decay, nor <u>reproach</u> my

---

1. **great chief at Washington.** President of the United States

---

words for everyday use

re • proach (ri prōch´) vt., accuse, blame. *The minister <u>reproached</u> the boy for stealing from the collection plate.*

READ WITH A PURPOSE IN MIND

☐ Follow along in your text as your teacher reads aloud the first paragraph of the speech. As you listen, try to imagine the time and place in which the speech was given.

☐ Fill in the During Reading section of the Author's Purpose Chart, noting the main ideas that Chief Seattle expresses in the first paragraph.

☐ Read the remainder of the selection on your own, pausing periodically to fill in the graphic organizer.

NOTE THE FACTS

What does the white chief wish to do? How does Seattle feel about what the white chief wants?

_____

_____

_____

Reading TIP

A **transition** is a word, phrase, sentence, or paragraph used to connect ideas and to show relationships between them. Note the sentence transitions that Chief Seattle makes to connect one paragraph to the next. Think about how the last sentence in a paragraph relates to the first sentence in the next paragraph.

IMAGE AND IMAGERY. An **image** is language that creates a concrete representation of an object or an experience. The images in a literary work are referred to, collectively, as the work's **imagery**. As you read, look for examples of nature imagery in Chief Seattle's speech.

THINK AND REFLECT

Reread lines 35–38. What does Chief Seattle value over revenge? (Infer)

_____

_____

_____

NOTE THE FACTS

How does Seattle feel about God and His relationship to Seattle's people?

_____

_____

paleface brothers with hastening it as we too may have been somewhat to blame.

Youth is impulsive. When our young men grow angry at some real or imaginary wrong, and <u>disfigure</u> their faces with black paint, it denotes that their hearts are black, and that

30 they are often cruel and relentless, and our old men and old women are unable to restrain them. Thus it has ever been. Thus it was when the white man first began to push our forefathers westward. But let us hope that the hostilities between us may never return. We would have everything to lose and nothing to gain. Revenge by young men is considered gain, even at the cost of their own lives, but old men who stay at home in times of war, and mothers who have sons to lose, know better.

Our good father at Washington—for I presume he is now

40 our father as well as yours, since King George has moved his boundaries further north—our great and good father, I say, sends us word that if we do as he desires he will protect us. His brave warriors will be to us a bristling wall of strength, and his wonderful ships of war will fill our harbors so that our ancient enemies far to the northward—the Hydas and Tsimpsians—will cease to frighten our women, children, and old men. Then in reality will he be our father and we his children. But can that ever be? Your God is not our God! Your God loves your people and hates mine. He

50 folds his strong protecting arms lovingly about the pale face and leads him by the hand as a father leads his infant son— but He has forsaken His red children—if they really are His. Our God, the Great Spirit, seems also to have forsaken us. Your God makes your people wax strong every day. Soon they will fill all the land. Our people are ebbing away like a rapidly <u>receding</u> tide that will never return. The white man's God cannot love our people or He would protect them. They seem to be orphans who can look nowhere for help. How then can we be brothers? How can your God become

60 our God and renew our prosperity and awaken in us dreams of returning greatness? If we have a common heavenly

words for everyday use

dis • fig • ure (dis fig′yər) *vt.*, hurt the appearance of. *Her appearance became frightening after she decided to <u>disfigure</u> herself with fake scars and white makeup.*

re • ced • ing (ri sēd′iŋ) *adj.*, moving back. *His <u>receding</u> hairline made him look older than he was.*

father He must be partial—for He came to His paleface children. We never saw Him. He gave you laws but had no word for his red children whose teeming multitudes once filled this vast continent as stars fill the firmament.[2] No; we are two distinct races with separate origins and separate destinies. There is little in common between us.

To us the ashes of our ancestors are sacred and their resting place is hallowed ground.[3] You wander far from the graves of your ancestors and seemingly without regret. Your religion was written upon tables of stone by the iron finger of your God[4] so that you could not forget. The Red Man could never comprehend nor remember it. Our religion is the traditions of our ancestors—the dreams of our old men, given them in the solemn hours of night by the Great Spirit; and the visions of our sachems,[5] and is written in the hearts of our people.

Your dead cease to love you and the land of their nativity[6] as soon as they pass the portals of[7] the tomb and wander way beyond the stars. They are soon forgotten and never return. Our dead never forget the beautiful world that gave them being. They still love its <u>verdant</u> valleys, its murmuring rivers, its magnificent mountains, <u>sequestered</u> vales and verdant-lined lakes and bays, and ever yearn in tender, fond affection over the lonely hearted living, and often return from the Happy Hunting Ground[8] to visit, guide, console and comfort them.

Day and night cannot dwell together. The red man has ever fled the approach of the white man, as the morning mist flees before the morning sun.

However, your proposition seems fair and I think that my people will accept it and will retire to the reservation you

Use THE STRATEGY

READ WITH A PURPOSE.
To help you think of Chief Seattle's overall purpose, write down the purpose for each paragraph in his speech. Then think about what all the purposes have in common.

NOTE THE FACTS

How do Seattle's dead ancestors feel about the land? Why is the land important in Seattle's religion?

_____

_____

_____

MARK THE TEXT

Underline or highlight the term for Heaven in Chief Seattle's language.

---

2. **firmament.** Sky seen as an arch
3. **hallowed ground.** Sacred ground
4. **written . . . iron finger of your God.** Chief Seattle is referring to the stone tablets containing the Ten Commandments that, according to the Old Testament, were handed down from God to Moses.
5. **sachems.** Holy men
6. **nativity.** Birth
7. **portals of.** Opening to
8. **Happy Hunting Ground.** Heaven; place of afterlife

words for everyday use	
	ver • dant (vʉrd´ ʼnt) *adj.,* green; covered in vegetation. *When we saw the <u>verdant</u> hills of Vermont, we understood why it was called the Green Mountain State.*
	se • ques • tered (si kwes´tərd) *adj.,* secluded. *The <u>sequestered</u> valley was both beautiful and remote; its hidden lakes and secluded location made it a perfect spot for camping.*

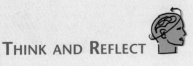

THINK AND REFLECT

Reread lines 93–95. What adjective characterizes the "words of nature"? (Infer)

_____

_____

THINK AND REFLECT

Reread line 111. How does Chief Seattle feel about the downfall of his people? (Infer)

_____

_____

NOTE THE FACTS

What demand does Seattle make?

_____

_____

offer them. Then we will dwell in peace, for the words of the great white chief seem to be the words of nature speaking to my people out of dense darkness.

It matters little where we pass the <u>remnant</u> of our days. They will not be many. The Indians' night promises to be dark. Not a single star of hope hovers above his horizon. Sad-voiced winds moan in the distance. Grim fate seems to

100 be on the red man's trail, and wherever he goes he will hear the approaching footsteps of his fell destroyer[9] and prepare <u>stolidly</u> to meet his doom, as does the wounded doe that hears the approaching footsteps of the hunter.

A few more moons. A few more winters—and not one of the descendants of the mighty hosts that once moved over this broad land or lived in happy homes, protected by the Great Spirit, will remain to mourn over the graves of a people—once more powerful and hopeful than yours. But why should I mourn at the untimely fate of my people?

110 Tribe follows tribe, and nation follows nation, like the waves of the sea. It is the order of nature, and regret is useless. Your time of decay may be distant, but it will surely come, for even the white man whose God walked and talked with him as friend with friend, cannot be <u>exempt</u> from the common destiny. We may be brothers after all. We will see.

We will ponder your proposition and when we decide we will let you know. But should we accept it, I here and now make this condition that we will not be denied the privilege without <u>molestation</u> of visiting at any time the tombs of our

120 ancestors, friends, and children. Every part of this soil is sacred in the estimation of my people. Every hillside, every valley, every plain and grove, has been hallowed by some sad or happy event in days long vanished. Even the rocks, which

---

9. **fell destroyer.** Cruel murderer

words for everyday use

rem • nant (rem´nənt) _n.,_ small remaining part. _The discount store sold me a carpet <u>remnant</u> at a reasonable price._

stol • id • ly (stäl´id lē) _adv.,_ in a way that shows little emotion or excitability. _He thought <u>stolidly</u> about the high school prom, and did not participate in excited conversations about it._

ex • empt (eg zempt´) _adj.,_ excused, released. _College students are usually <u>exempt</u> from paying back student loans until they complete their studies._

mo • les • ta • tion (mō´les tā´shən) _n.,_ interference with intent to trouble or harm. _Americans are guaranteed the right to have a free press without <u>molestation</u> from the government._

seem to be dumb and dead as they swelter in the sun along the silent shore, thrill with memories of stirring events connected with the lives of my people, and the very dust upon which you now stand responds more lovingly to their footsteps than to yours, because it is rich with the blood of our ancestors and our bare feet are conscious of the

130 sympathetic touch. Our departed braves, fond mothers, glad, happy-hearted maidens, and even our little children who lived here and rejoiced here for a brief season, will love these somber solitudes and at eventide[10] they greet shadowy returning spirits. And when the last red man shall have perished, and the memory of my tribe shall have become a myth among the white men, these shores will swarm with the invisible dead of my tribe, and when your children's children think themselves alone in the field, the store, the shop, upon the highway, or in the silence of the pathless

140 woods, they will not be alone. In all the earth there is no place dedicated to solitude. At night when the streets of your cities and villages are silent and you think them deserted, they will throng with the returning hosts that once filled them and still love this beautiful land. The white man will never be alone.

Let him be just and deal kindly with my people, for the dead are not powerless. Dead, did I say? There is no death, only a change of worlds. ■

---

10. **eventide.** Evening

FIX-UP IDEA

Read Aloud
If you have difficulty with the reading strategy, listen to the address being read aloud by a classmate or your teacher. As you listen, keep thinking about Chief Seattle's main purpose. As you continue to jot down notes about the speech's main ideas, also note your reactions to them.

READ ALOUD

Read aloud the highlighted text on this page. In what way will Seattle's people remain immortal?

_____

_____

_____

NOTE THE FACTS

In lines 147–148, how does Seattle say he views death?

_____

_____

Reflect ON YOUR READING

When you finish reading, complete the After Reading section of the graphic organizer. Then review your notes about the main ideas in the speech. Write a sentence about Chief Seattle's main purpose. Write a brief essay in which you expand on your opinion, giving examples from the speech. Finally, rejoin your group, taking turns to read your essays aloud and discuss your reading experience.

THINK-ALOUD NOTES

_____

_____

_____

_____

_____

_____

_____

_____

_____

_____

_____

Reading Skills and Test Practice

IDENTIFY CAUSE AND EFFECT

Discuss with a partner how to answer the following questions about cause and effect.

1. Read the following passage from the speech.

   There was a time when our people covered the land as waves of a wind-ruffled sea cover its shell-paved floor, but that time long since passed away with the greatness of tribes that are now but a mournful memory. I will not dwell on, nor mourn over, our untimely decay, nor reproach my paleface brothers with hastening it as we too may have been somewhat to blame.

   According to Chief Seattle, what is the cause of his people's "untimely decay"?

   a. the challenging climate of the land
   b. the coming of white men and, possibly, the actions of his own people
   c. the tendency of his people to dwell on memories
   d. the habit of his people to place blame on others for their problems

Circle the correct answer to the question above. How were you able to eliminate the other answers?

2. Read the following passage from the speech.

   Our good father at Washington—for I presume he is now our father as well as yours, since King George has moved his boundaries further north—our great and good father, I say, sends us word that if we do as he desires he will protect us.

   Which word or words in this passage suggest a cause-and-effect relationship?

   a. presume
   b. as well as
   c. since
   d. further

Circle the correct answer to the question above. How did your application of the reading strategy help you answer the question?

Investigate, Inquire, and Imagine

RECALL: GATHER FACTS →
1a. At the beginning of the speech, what is Chief Seattle referring to when he talks about the sky or weather changing? What things does he say are "changeless and eternal"?

INTERPRET: FIND MEANING
1b. What comparisons does Chief Seattle make in the first paragraph? Why does he make them?

ANALYZE: TAKE THINGS APART →
2a. As seen by Chief Seattle, compare and contrast his people's religion with that of the white people.

SYNTHESIZE: BRING THINGS TOGETHER
2b. How would you characterize Chief Seattle's remarks in the last paragraph? How do they summarize what he has been saying all along?

PERSPECTIVE: LOOK AT OTHER VIEWS →
3a. Compare and contrast the white people's relationship with nature to that of the Native Americans.

EMPATHY: SEE FROM INSIDE
3b. What does Chief Seattle reveal about himself in his speech?

Literary Tools

IMAGE AND IMAGERY. An **image** is language that creates a concrete representation of an object or an experience. The images in a literary work are referred to, collectively, as the work's **imagery**. Fill in the chart below to show natural images in the speech and whether they refer to earth, water, or sky. What does Chief Seattle's use of imagery reveal about him?

Image	Category
"Today is fair. Tomorrow it may be overcast with clouds."	Sky

WordWorkshop

ANTONYMS. Chief Seattle used many words with negative connotations when he described the decline of his people at the time the "paleface" nation was rapidly growing and becoming strong. Use a thesaurus to find an antonym (a word that has the *opposite* meaning) for each of Chief Seattle's words underlined in the sentences below. Then use each antonym in a sentence of your own.

> **EXAMPLE**
> ". . . I here and now make this condition that we will not be denied the privilege without <u>molestation</u> of visiting at any time the tombs of our ancestors, friends, and children."
>
> Antonym: *honor*
>
> Sentence: *The palefaces claim what they call the rightful honor to roam freely throughout this great land since it is they who will settle and tame the vast wilderness.*

1. "I will not dwell on, nor mourn over, our untimely decay, nor <u>reproach</u> my paleface brothers with hastening it as we too may have been somewhat to blame."
2. "When our young men grow angry at some real or imaginary wrong, and <u>disfigure</u> their faces with black paint, it denotes that their hearts are black, and that they are often cruel and relentless. . . ."
3. "Our people are ebbing away like a rapidly <u>receding</u> tide that will never return."
4. "It matters little where we pass the <u>remnant</u> of our days."
5. "Grim fate seems to be on the red man's trail, and wherever he goes he will hear the approaching footsteps of his fell destroyer and prepare <u>stolidly</u> to meet his doom, as does the wounded doe that hears the approaching footsteps of the hunter."

Read-Write Connection

To what idea in Chief Seattle's speech did you react the most strongly?

_____

_____

_____

Beyond the Reading

TYING ART TO LITERATURE. Read about Native American art and look for a Native American painting to illustrate this selection. Then write a paragraph explaining why the painting reflects the theme or content of the speech. Show the painting to a small group of your classmates and read your paragraph out loud.

GO ONLINE. Visit the EMC Internet Resource Center at **emcp.com** to find links and additional activities for this selection.

"shORt assignments"

by Anne Lamott

Active READING STRATEGY

CONNECT TO PRIOR KNOWLEDGE

Before Reading ▶ **ACTIVATE PRIOR KNOWLEDGE**

- ❏ Read the Reader's Resource.
- ❏ Take a moment to answer the Reader's Journal question by explaining your personal writing process. Reflect on a time when you were given a large writing project. What steps did you take to make it manageable?
- ❏ Preview the Reactions Chart below. As you read, use this chart to record your thoughts and reactions. Ask yourself questions, make predictions, react to ideas, identify key points, and/or write down unfamiliar words.

Graphic Organizer

Page #	Questions, Predictions, Reactions, Key Points, and Unfamiliar Words

CONNECT

Reader's resource

Anne Lamott's essay "**Short Assignments**" is taken from her book *Bird by Bird: Some Instructions on Writing and Life*. In *Bird by Bird*, Lamott wants to share "everything that has helped me along the way and what [writing] is like for me on a daily basis." If you follow her advice in the essay, you will have a strategy for how to attack a large writing assignment.

Word watch

PREVIEW VOCABULARY

arresting
leering

Reader's journal

What problems have you encountered when given a writing assignment?

_____

_____

_____

CONNECT WITH PRIOR KNOWLEDGE

❑ Read the essay on your own, stopping to record your reactions to Lamott's key points in the graphic organizer.

❑ Think about the problems you have with writing assignments. In the graphic organizer, write down these problems and any solutions Lamott offers to them.

❑ Note the things you have in common with Lamott's strategy, and things she mentions that you feel are worth trying.

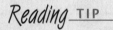

Reading TIP

Notice that Lamott's tone is sometimes humorous. Try to find other humorous passages in the essay and think about why she is using humor to talk about a serious topic.

SHORT assignments
from BIRD BY BIRD

Anne Lamott

The first useful concept is the idea of short assignments. Often when you sit down to write, what you have in mind is an autobiographical novel about your childhood, or a play about the immigrant experience, or a history of—oh, say—say women. But this is like trying to scale a glacier. It's hard to get your footing, and your fingertips get all red and frozen and torn up. Then your mental illnesses arrive at the desk like your sickest, most secretive relatives. And they pull up chairs in a semicircle around the computer, and they try

10 to be quiet but you know they are there with their weird coppery breath, <u>leering</u> at you behind your back.

What I do at this point, as the panic mounts and the jungle drums begin beating and I realize that the well has run dry and that my future is behind me and I'm going to have to get a job only I'm completely unemployable, is to stop. First I try to breathe, because I'm either sitting there panting like a lapdog or I'm unintentionally making slow asthmatic death rattles. So I just sit there for a minute, breathing slowly, quietly. I let my mind wander. After a

20 moment I may notice that I'm trying to decide whether or

words for everyday use	**leer • ing** (lēr' iŋ) *vi.*, casting a sidelong glance that is lascivious, knowing, or wanton. *Carol looked away from the stranger's <u>leering</u> expression. The stranger <u>leered</u> at Carol in a way that made her uncomfortable.*

not I am too old for orthodontia[1] and whether right now would be a good time to make a few calls, and then I start to think about learning to use makeup and how maybe I could find some boyfriend who is not a total and complete fixer-upper and then my life would be totally great and I'd be happy all the time, and then I think about all the people I should have called back before I sat down to work, and how I should probably at least check in with my agent and tell him this great idea I have and see if *he* thinks it's a good
30 idea, and see if *he* thinks I need orthodontia—if that is what he is actually thinking whenever we have lunch together. Then I think about someone I'm really annoyed with, or some financial problem that is driving me crazy, and decide that I must resolve this before I get down to today's work. So I become a dog with a chew toy, worrying it for a while, wrestling it to the ground, flinging it over my shoulder, chasing it, licking it, chewing it, flinging it back over my shoulder. I stop just short of actually barking. But all of this only takes somewhere between one and two minutes, so I
40 haven't actually wasted that much time. Still, it leaves me winded. I go back to trying to breathe, slowly and calmly, and I finally notice the one-inch picture frame that I put on my desk to remind me of short assignments.

It reminds me that all I have to do is to write down as much as I can see through a one-inch picture frame. This is all I have to bite off for the time being. All I am going to do right now, for example, is write that one paragraph that sets the story in my hometown, in the late fifties, when the trains were still running. I am going to paint a picture of it, in
50 words, on my word processor. Or all I am going to do is to describe the main character the very first time we meet her, when she first walks out the front door and onto the porch. I am not even going to describe the expression on her face when she first notices the blind dog sitting behind the wheel of her car—just what I can see through the one-inch picture frame, just one paragraph describing this woman, in the town where I grew up, the first time we encounter her.

E. L. Doctorow[2] once said that "writing a novel is like driving a car at night. You can see only as far as your

---

1. **orthodontia.** Branch of dentistry dealing with irregularities of the teeth and their correction (as by means of braces)
2. **E. L. Doctorow.** (1931–) American novelist

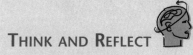

THINK AND REFLECT

Reread lines 19–38. Characterize the kind of thoughts that go through Lamott's mind. Why do these thoughts keep her from writing? **(Infer)**

_____

_____

_____

_____

NOTE THE FACTS

What helps Lamott to calm down enough to begin writing?

_____

_____

_____

READ ALOUD

Read aloud the highlighted text. How does E. L. Doctorow's quote offer good advice about writing and life?

_____

_____

_____

COLLOQUIALISM. A colloquialism is the use of informal language. Circle the colloquialism in line 73. Then look for examples of colloquialism as you read Lamott's essay.

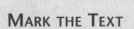

MARK THE TEXT

Underline or highlight the advice Lamott's father gives to his son.

FIX-UP IDEA

Use Margin Questions
If you have difficulty identifying Lamott's advice, use the questions in the margins to focus your attention on the essay's main points. First, read the question. Then, read until you locate the answer. Write down the answers in the margins.

60

headlights, but you can make the whole trip that way." You don't have to see where you're going, you don't have to see your destination or everything you will pass along the way. You just have to see two or three feet ahead of you. This is right up there with the best advice about writing, or life, I have ever heard.

So after I've completely exhausted myself thinking about the people I most resent in the world, and my more <u>arresting</u> financial problems, and, of course, the orthodontia, I remember to pick up the one-inch picture

70

frame and to figure out a one-inch piece of my story to tell, one small scene, one memory, one exchange. I also remember a story that I know I've told elsewhere but that over and over helps me to get a grip: thirty years ago my older brother, who was ten years old at the time, was trying to get a report on birds written that he'd had three months to write, which was due the next day. We were out at our family cabin in Bolinas, and he was at the kitchen table close to tears, surrounded by binder paper and pencils and unopened books on birds, immobilized by the hugeness of

80

the task ahead. Then my father sat down beside him, put his arm around my brother's shoulder, and said, "Bird by bird, buddy. Just take it bird by bird."

I tell this story again because it usually makes a dent in the tremendous sense of being overwhelmed that my students experience. Sometimes it actually gives them hope, and hope, as Chesterton[3] said, is the power of being cheerful in circumstances that we know to be desperate. Writing can be a pretty desperate endeavor, because it is about some of our deepest needs: our need to be visible, to

90

be heard, our need to make sense of our lives, to wake up and grow and belong. It is no wonder if we sometimes tend to take ourselves perhaps a bit too seriously. So here is another story I tell often.

---

3. **Chesterton.** G. K. Chesterton (1874–1936) was a British writer and critic.

words for everyday use

ar • rest • ing (ə rest′ iŋ) *adj.,* catching the attention; striking; impressive. *For officer Nelson, seeing the dog at the wheel of the Chevrolet was an <u>arresting</u> experience.*

In the Bill Murray[4] movie *Stripes*, in which he joins the army, there is a scene that takes place the first night of boot camp, where Murray's platoon is assembled in the barracks. They are supposed to be getting to know their sergeant, played by Warren Oates, and one another. So each man takes a few moments to say a few things about who he is and

100 where he is from. Finally it is the turn of this incredibly intense, angry guy named Francis. "My name is Francis," he says. "No one calls me Francis—anyone here calls me Francis and I'll kill them. And another thing. I don't like to be touched. Anyone here ever tries to touch me, I'll kill them," at which point Warren Oates jumps in and says, "Hey—lighten up, Francis."

This is not a bad line to have taped to the wall of your office.

Say to yourself in the kindest possible way, Look, honey,

110 all we're going to do for now is to write a description of the river at sunrise, or the young child swimming in the pool at the club, or the first time the man sees the woman he will marry. That is all we are going to do for now. We are just going to take this bird by bird. But we are going to finish this *one* short assignment. ■

---

4. **Bill Murray.** American film and television comedian

THINK AND REFLECT

Reread lines 101–106. What movie phrase helps keep Lamott and her students from taking themselves too seriously? What is she saying indirectly here? **(Infer)**

_____

_____

_____

_____

NOTE THE FACTS

What does Lamott suggest that readers should do with the movie phrase she quotes?

_____

_____

Reading STRATEGY
REVIEW

READ WITH A PURPOSE. Reading with a purpose in mind will make your reading of the selection more meaningful. Review the active reading strategy for "Yonder sky has wept tears of compassion . . ." on page 360. What do you think is Lamott's main purpose in writing this essay? What is your purpose in reading it?

_____

_____

Reflect ON YOUR READING

When you finish reading the essay, go back to your answer to the Reader's Journal question that you wrote before you began reading. Review your notes on Lamott's advice, and consider how you might apply that advice to help make your writing experiences go more smoothly. Then, write a "short assignment." Write about anything you want, but focus on viewing your subject through a "one-inch picture frame," as Lamott suggests. When you are done writing, share your short assignment with a small group and tell your classmates how you were able to apply the advice in the essay.

Reading Skills and Test Practice

IDENTIFY THE AUTHOR'S PURPOSE AND MAIN IDEA
Discuss with a partner how to answer the following questions about the author's purpose and main idea.

1. Which of the following best describes the author's purpose in writing this essay?
   a. to entertain readers with a humorous story of her own writing experience
   b. to persuade readers to be disciplined writers, always focused on their end goal
   c. to inform readers of the proper way to write
   d. to offer readers advice on how to approach writing with small goals in mind

Circle the correct answer to the question above. How were you able to eliminate the other answers? How did your application of the reading strategy help you answer the question?

_____

_____

2. Which statement best describes the main idea of this essay?
   a. Do not let a writing task overwhelm you; just take it step by step.
   b. When writing a short assignment, always try to focus on the bigger picture.
   c. When writing, try to remember the advice of successful writers.
   d. If you encounter writer's block, try meditating and thinking about your end goal.

Circle the correct answer to the question above. How were you able to eliminate the other answers? How did your application of the reading strategy help you answer the question?

_____

_____

THINK-ALOUD NOTES

_____

_____

_____

_____

_____

_____

_____

_____

_____

_____

Investigate, Inquire, and Imagine

RECALL: GATHER FACTS   →   INTERPRET: FIND MEANING

1a. What does Lamott say writers often have in mind when they first sit down to write?

1b. What does she mean when she compares one's first attempts at writing to "trying to scale a glacier"?

ANALYZE: TAKE THINGS APART   →   SYNTHESIZE: BRING THINGS TOGETHER

2a. Identify the potential obstacles writers face when starting a new writing project.

2b. What is the ultimate goal of Lamott's advice about "short assignments"? What does she want writers to be able to do?

EVALUATE: MAKE JUDGMENTS   →   EXTEND: CONNECT IDEAS

3a. Do you think Lamott's advice for writing is helpful? Why, or why not?

3b. How might Lamott's advice apply to other aspects of your own life? In what other circumstances might the "bird by bird" approach help you to reach your goals?

Literary Tools

COLLOQUIALISM. **Colloquialism** is the use of informal language. Complete the chart below with examples of colloquialisms from the selection and their equivalents in formal English. One example has been done for you. What tone does Lamott's use of colloquialisms create?

Colloquialisms	Formal English
Maybe I could find some boyfriend who is not a total and complete fixer-upper.	Maybe I could find some boyfriend who does not need much improvement.

WordWorkshop

Colloquialisms. Review the definition of *colloquialism* in Literary Tools on page 375. Rewrite the following sentences using more formal language in place of the colloquialisms.

1. My little brother has been screaming at the top of his lungs, and it is driving me nuts!

   _____

2. It really bugs Jean when her friends ask to use her plastic.

   _____

3. David is a couch potato who likes to chow down on pizza while watching TV.

   _____

4. Justin and Randy are going to kick back at the cabin this weekend and knock about the village.

   _____

5. Jan chickened out of the debate and caught a movie instead.

   _____

Read-Write Connection

What are some examples of short assignments Lamott would approve of if you were writing a short story?

_____

_____

_____

_____

Beyond the Reading

Using Creative Writing Tips. Lamott's advice on short assignments is applicable to nonfiction and fiction writing. Research other creative writing tips on the Internet. Then take one of the tips and use it as you write a short assignment for a short story, play, or screenplay.

Go Online. Visit the EMC Internet Resource Center at **emcp.com** to find links and additional activities for this selection.

"SOMETHING COULD HAPPEN TO YOU"
from *Almost a Woman*
by Esmeralda Santiago

Active READING STRATEGY

READ WITH A PURPOSE

Before Reading ▶ **SET A PURPOSE FOR READING**

- ❏ Form a small group with other classmates. Have one person read aloud the Reader's Resource.
- ❏ With your group, set a purpose for reading the selection.
- ❏ Fill in the before reading section of the Reader's Purpose Chart below.

Graphic Organizer

Before Reading
Set a purpose for reading. *(Example: I am going to find out what it was like for the author to move to New York.)*

During Reading
Take notes on what you learn. *(Example: Mami and Tata thought streets would be paved with gold.)*

After Reading
Reflect on your purpose and what you learned. *(Example: I want to see how hard it was for the author to move to a new country. I believe she and her family were very brave.)*

READ WITH A PURPOSE

- ❑ Follow along in the selection as your teacher reads aloud the beginning part.
- ❑ Read the remainder of the selection on your own.
- ❑ Keep your reading purpose in mind, and note relevant details in the during-reading section of the graphic organizer.

NOTE THE FACTS

Where did the author and her family come from?

_____

_____

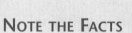 TOOLS

MEMOIR. A **memoir** is a nonfiction narration that tells a story. It can be autobiographical or biographical. As you read, pay attention to the formative experiences that Santiago recounts about her experiences as an immigrant.

"SOMETHING COULD HAPPEN TO YOU"

from *Almost a Woman*
Esmeralda Santiago

We came to Brooklyn in search of medical care for my youngest brother, Raymond, whose toes were nearly <u>severed</u> by a bicycle chain when he was four. In Puerto Rico, doctors wanted to amputate the often red and swollen foot, because it wouldn't heal. In New York, Mami hoped doctors could save it.

The day we arrived, a hot, humid afternoon had splintered into thunderstorms as the last rays of the sun dipped into the rest of the United States. I was thirteen and superstitious enough to
10 believe thunder and lightning held significance beyond the meteorological. I stored the sights and sounds of that dreary night into memory as if their meaning would someday be revealed in a flash of insight to forever transform my life. When the insight came, nothing changed, for it wasn't the weather in Brooklyn that was important, but the fact that I was there to notice it.

One hand tightly grasped by Mami, the other by six-year-old Edna, we squeezed and pushed our way through the crowd of travellers. Five-year-old Raymond clung to Mami's

words for everyday use

sev • er (se' vər) *vi.,* remove; cut. *Relations with her family were <u>severed</u> by Gong when she left China.*

20 other hand, his unbalanced <u>gait</u> drawing sympathetic smiles from people who moved aside to let us walk ahead of them.

At the end of the tunnel waited Tata, Mami's mother, in black lace and high heels, a pronged rhinestone pin on her left shoulder. When she hugged me, the pin pricked my cheek, pierced <u>subtle</u> flower-shaped indentations that I rubbed rhythmically as our taxi hurtled through drenched streets banked by high, angular buildings.

New York was darker than I expected, and, in spite of the cleansing rain, dirtier. Used to the sensual curves of rural
30 Puerto Rico, my eyes had to adjust to the regular, aggressive two-dimensionality of Brooklyn. Raindrops pounded the hard streets, captured the dim silver glow of street lamps, bounced against sidewalks in glistening sparks, then disappeared, like tiny <u>ephemeral</u> jewels, into the darkness. Mami and Tata teased that I was disillusioned because the streets were not paved with gold. But I had no such vision of New York. I was disappointed by the darkness, and fixed my hopes on the promise of light deep within the sparkling raindrops.

40 Two days later, I leaned against the wall of our apartment building on McKibbin Street wondering where New York ended and the rest of the world began. It was hard to tell. There was no horizon in Brooklyn. Everywhere I looked my eyes met a vertical maze of gray and brown straight-edged buildings with sharp corners and deep shadows. Every few blocks there was a cement playground surrounded by chain link fence. And in between, weedy lots mounded with garbage and rusting cars.

A girl came out of the building next door, a jump rope in
50 her hand. She appraised me shyly; I pretended to ignore her. She stepped on the rope, stretched the ends overhead as if to measure their length, then began to skip, slowly, grunting each time she came down on the sidewalk. Swish splat grunt swish, she turned her back to me, swish splat

THINK AND REFLECT

Reread lines 19–21. Why does Raymond walk with an "unbalanced gait"? **(Infer)**

_____

_____

_____

MARK THE TEXT

Underline or highlight the author's description of New York.

NOTE THE FACTS

What did the author see everywhere she looked in Brooklyn?

_____

_____

_____

words for everyday use	**gait** (gāt) *n.*, manner of walking or moving. *The tall man had a dignified <u>gait</u>.* **sub • tle** (sə' təl) *adj.*, difficult to perceive or understand. *The sound was so <u>subtle</u> that Julio couldn't be sure if his neighbors were home.* **ephem • er • al** (i fem' rəl) *adj.*, lasting briefly; temporary; fleeting. *The <u>ephemeral</u> beauty of the fireworks lasted for seconds only.*

Reading TIP

Ask a Spanish-speaking student to help you with the Spanish words in the selection, or make guesses based on the context of the passage containing the words.

READ ALOUD

Read aloud the highlighted text on this page. What does it reveal about Esmeralda's personality?

_____

_____

_____

THINK AND REFLECT

Reread lines 80–88. How does the author's mother caution her after learning she has gone outside to play? What kind of a parent is she? What is her attitude toward her new home? **(Infer)**

_____

_____

_____

_____

grunt swish, she faced me again and smiled. I smiled back and she hopped over.

"¿_Tú eres hispana?_" she asked, as she whirled the rope in lazy arcs.

"No, I'm Puerto Rican."

60 "Same thing. Puerto Rican, Hispanic. That's what we are here." She skipped a tight circle, stopped abruptly and shoved the rope in my direction. "Want a turn?"

"Sure." I hopped on one leg, then the other. "So, if you're Puerto Rican, they call you Hispanic?"

"Yeah. Anybody who speaks Spanish."

I jumped a circle, like she had done, but faster. "You mean, if you speak Spanish, you're Hispanic?"

"Well, yeah. No, I mean your parents have to be Puerto Rican or Cuban or something."

70 I whirled the rope to the right, then the left, like a boxer. "Okay, your parents are Cuban, let's say, and you're born here, but you don't speak Spanish. Are you Hispanic?"

She bit her lower lip. "I guess so," she finally said. "It has to do with being from a Spanish country. I mean, you or your parents, like, even if you don't speak Spanish, you're Hispanic, you know?" She looked at me uncertainly. I nodded and returned her rope.

But I didn't know. I'd always been Puerto Rican, and it hadn't occurred to me that in Brooklyn I'd be someone else.

80 Later, I asked. "Are we Hispanics, Mami?"

"Yes, because we speak Spanish."

"But a girl said you don't have to speak the language to be Hispanic."

She scrunched her eyes. "What girl? Where did you meet a girl?"

"Outside. She lives in the next building."

"Who said you could go out to the sidewalk? This isn't Puerto Rico. _Algo te puede suceder._"

"Something could happen to you" was a variety of dangers
90 outside the locked doors of our apartment. I could be mugged. I could be dragged into any of the dark, abandoned buildings on the way to or from school, and be raped and murdered. I could be accosted by gang members into whose turf I strayed. I could be seduced by men who preyed on unchaperoned girls too willing to talk to strangers. I listened to Mami's lecture with downcast eyes and the necessary,

respectful expression of humility. But inside, I quaked. Two days in New York, and I'd already become someone else. It wasn't hard to imagine that greater dangers lay ahead.

100   Our apartment on McKibbin Street was more substantial than any of our houses in Puerto Rico. Its marble staircase, plaster walls, and tiled floors were bound to the earth, unlike the wood and zinc rooms on stilts where I'd grown up. Chubby angels with bare buttocks danced around plaster wreaths on the ceiling. There was a bathtub in the kitchen with hot and cold running water, and a toilet inside a closet with a sink and a medicine chest.

    An alley between our bedroom window and the wall of the next building was so narrow that I stretched over to touch
110 the bricks and left my mark on the greasy soot that covered them. Above, a sliver of sky forced vague yellow light into the ground below, filled with empty detergent boxes, tattered clothes, unpaired shoes, bottles, broken glass.

    Mami had to go look for work, so Edna, Raymond, and I went downstairs to stay with Tata in her apartment. When we knocked on her door, she was just waking up. I sat at the small table near the cooking counter to read the newspapers that Don Julio, Tata's boyfriend, brought the night before. Edna and Raymond stood in the middle of the room and
120 stared at the small television on a low table. Tata switched it on, fiddled with the knobs and the antenna until the horizontal lines disappeared and black and white cartoon characters chased each other across a flat landscape. The kids sank to the floor cross-legged, their eyes on the screen. Against the wall, under the window, Tata's brother, Tío Chico, slept with his back to us. Every so often, a snore woke him, but he chewed his drool, mumbled, slept again.

    While Tata went to wash up in the hall bathroom, I tuned in to the television. A dot bounced over the words of a song
130 being performed by a train dancing along tracks, with dogs, cats, cows, and horses dangling from its windows and caboose. I was hypnotized by the dot skipping over words

---

Use THE STRATEGY

READ WITH A PURPOSE.
Make sure to stop at the end of each section to record notes on what you learn in the during-reading section of the graphic organizer. Also write down how the information in each section relates to your purpose for reading.

NOTE THE FACTS

Who is Tío Chico, and where does he sleep?

_____

_____

that looked nothing like they sounded. "Shilbee cominrun demuntin wenshecoms, toot-toot" sang the locomotive, and the ball dipped and rose over "She'll be coming 'round the mountain when she comes," with no toots. The animals, dressed in cowboy hats, overalls, and bandannas, waved pick axes and shovels in the air. The toot-toot was replaced by a bow-wow or a miaow-ow, or a moo-moo. It was joyous and

140 silly, and made Edna and Raymond laugh. But it was hard for me to enjoy it as I focused on the words whizzing by, on the dot jumping rhythmically from one syllable to the next, with barely enough time to connect the letters to the sounds, with the added distraction of an occasional neigh, bark, or the kids' giggles.

When Tata returned from the bathroom, she made coffee on the two-burner hot plate. Fragrant steam soon filled the small room, and, as she strained the grounds through a well-worn flannel filter, Tío Chico rose as if the aroma were an

150 alarm louder and more insistent than the singing animals on the television screen, the clanking of pots against the hot plate and counter, the screech of the chair legs as I positioned myself so that I could watch both Tata and the cartoons.

"Well, look who we have here," Tío Chico said as he stretched until his long, bony fingers scraped the ceiling. He wore the same clothes as the day before, a faded pair of dark pants and a short-sleeve undershirt, both wrinkled and giving off a <u>pungent</u> sweaty smell. He stepped over Edna

160 and Raymond, who barely moved to let him through. In two long-legged strides, he slipped out to the bathroom. As he shut the door, the walls closed in, as if his <u>lanky</u> body added dimension to the cramped room.

Tata hummed the cartoon music. Her big hands reached for a pan, poured milk, stirred briskly as it heated and frothed. I was <u>mesmerized</u> by her grace, by how she held her head, by the disheveled ash-color curls that framed her

<table>
<tr><td rowspan="3">words
for
everyday
use</td><td>pun • gent (pən' jənt) adj., causing a sharp sensation; prickly; acrid. Satya loved the fall's <u>pungent</u> smell of burning leaves.</td></tr>
<tr><td>lanky (lan' kē) adj., tall; spare; loose-jointed. The man was a surprisingly good dancer for being so <u>lanky</u>.</td></tr>
<tr><td>mes • mer • ize (mez' mə rīz) vt., hypnotize; fascinate. The children were <u>mesmerized</u> by the puppet show.</td></tr>
</table>

high cheekbones. She looked up with mischievous caramel eyes, and grinned without breaking her rhythm.

170   Tío Chico returned showered and shaved, wearing a clean shirt and pants as wrinkled as the ones he'd taken off. He dropped the dirty clothes in a corner near Tata's bed and made up his cot. Tata handed me a cup of sweetened *café con leche*, and, with a head gesture, indicated I should <u>vacate</u> the chair for Tío Chico.

    "No, no, that's okay," he said, "I'll sit here."

    He perched on the edge of the cot, elbows on knees, his fingers wrapped around the mug Tata gave him. Steam rose from inside his hands in a transparent spiral.

180   I couldn't speak English, so the school counselor put me in a class for students who'd scored low on intelligence tests, who had behavior problems, who were marking time until their sixteenth birthday when they could drop out. The teacher, a pretty black woman only a few years older than her students, pointed to a seat in the middle of the room. I didn't dare look anyone in the eyes. Grunts and mutters followed me, and, while I had no idea what they meant, they didn't sound friendly.

    The desk surface was elaborately carved. There were many
190 names, some followed by an apostrophe and a year. Several carefully rendered obscenities meant nothing to me, but I appreciated the workmanship of the shadowed letters, the <u>fastidious</u> edges around the *f* and *k*. I guessed a girl had written the cursive message whose *i*s were dotted with hearts and daisies. Below it, several lines of timid, chicken-scratch writing alternated with an aggressive line of block letters.

    I pressed my hands together under the desk to <u>subdue</u> their shaking, studied the straight lines and ragged curves chiseled into the desktop by those who sat there before me.
200 Eyes on the <u>marred</u> surface, I focused on the teacher's voice, on the unfamiliar waves of sound that crested over my head.

Reading STRATEGY REVIEW

USE TEXT ORGANIZATION.
Note that the selection is divided into five sections. What is the focus of each section?

_____
_____
_____
_____
_____

NOTE THE FACTS

What class was the author put in, and why?

_____
_____
_____
_____

---

words for everyday use

va • cate (vā′ cāt) *vt.*, deprive of an occupant; make free. *The electric guitarist set up his system once the drummer <u>vacated</u> the stage.*

fas • tid • i • ous (fa stiˊ dē əs) *adj.*, meticulous; showing attention to detail. *The <u>fastidious</u> sculptor makes busts so realistic that it looks as if real people are staring at you.*

sub • due (səb düˊ) *vt.*, bring under control; reduce the intensity or degree of. *The principal <u>subdued</u> the noisy class.*

marred (märd) *adj.*, damaged or defaced. *Painters were restoring the <u>marred</u> wall.*

THINK AND REFLECT

Reread lines 200–206. What reaction did the author have toward her teacher's words? What does this incident tell you about the kind of attention she was getting in school? **(Infer)**

_____

_____

_____

_____

NOTE THE FACTS

What song did the author learn by heart?

_____

_____

_____

_____

I wanted to float up and out of that classroom, away from the hostile air that filled every corner of it, every crevice. But the more I tried to disappear, the more present I felt, until, exhausted, I gave in, floated with the words, certain that if I didn't, I would drown in them.

On gym days, girls had to wear grass-green, cotton, short-sleeve, bloomer-leg, one-piece outfits that buttoned down the front to an elastic waistband covered with a sash too short to tie into anything but a bulky knot. Grass green didn't look good on anyone, least of all adolescent girls whose faces broke out in red pimples. The gym suit had elastic around the bottom to keep our panties from showing when we fell or sat. On those of us with skinny legs, the elastic wasn't snug enough, so the bloomers hung limply to our knees, where they flapped when we ran.

The uniform, being one piece, made it impossible to go to the bathroom in the three minutes between classes. Instead of wearing it all day, we could bring it to school and change before gym, but no one did, since boys periodically raided the locker room to see our underwear. Proper hygiene during "the curse" was impossible, as we needed at least three hands, so most girls brought notes from their mothers. The problem was that if you didn't wear the uniform on gym days, everyone knew you were menstruating.

One girl bought two gym suits, chopped off the bottom of one, seamed around the selvage, and wore the top part under her blouse so that no one could tell if she had her period or not. I asked Mami to do that for me, but she said we didn't have money to waste on such foolishness.

Friday mornings we had Assembly. The first thing we did was to press our right hands to our breasts and sing "The Star Spangled Banner." We were encouraged to sing as loud as we could, and within a couple of weeks, I learned the entire song by heart.

> Ojo sé. Can. Juice. ¿Y?
> Bye de don surly lie.
> Whassoprowow we hell
> Add debt why lie lass gleam in.
> Whosebrods tripe sand bye ¿Stars?

True de perro los ¡Ay!
Order am parts we wash,
Wha soga lang tree streem in.

I had no idea what the song said or meant, and no one bothered to teach me. It was one of the things I was supposed to know, and, like the daily recitation of "The Pledge of Allegiance," it had to be done with enthusiasm, or teachers gave out <u>demerits</u>. The pledge was printed in ornate letters on a poster under the flag in every classroom.

250 "The Star Spangled Banner," however, remained a mystery for years, its nonsense words the only song I could sing in English from beginning to end. ■

words for everyday use de • mer • it (di mer′ ət) *n.*, mark entailing a loss of privilege. *The teacher gave Assad a <u>demerit</u> for being late.*

Reflect ON YOUR READING

After Reading ▶ COMPARE READING AND WRITING PURPOSES

When you finish reading the selection, review the definition of *memoir* in Literary Tools on page 378, and write a statement as a group about Santiago's overall purpose for writing this selection. Then, write a brief essay in which you compare the author's writing purpose with your purpose for reading. When you have finished writing, share your essay with your group.

THINK-ALOUD NOTES

Reading Skills and Test Practice

USE CONTEXT CLUES

Discuss with a partner how to answer the following questions about words in context.

1. Read the following sentence from the selection.

   Raindrops pounded the hard streets, captured the dim silver glow of street lamps, bounced against sidewalks in glistening sparks, then disappeared, like tiny ephemeral jewels, into the darkness.

   What does *ephemeral* mean?
   a. rapid
   b. beautiful
   c. valuable
   d. temporary

Circle the correct answer to the question above. How were you able to eliminate the other answers? How did your application of the reading strategy help you answer the question?

2. Read the following sentences from the selection.

   I pressed my hands together under the desk to subdue their shaking, and studied the straight lines and ragged curves chiseled into the desktop by those who sat there before me. Eyes on the marred surface, I focused on the teacher's voice, on the unfamiliar waves of sound that crested over my head.

   What does *marred* mean?
   a. decorated
   b. distracted
   c. unfamiliar
   d. damaged

Circle the correct answer to the question above. How were you able to eliminate the other answers? How did your application of the reading strategy help you answer the question?

Investigate, Inquire, and Imagine

RECALL: GATHER FACTS →
1a. Why do the author and her family come to the United States?

INTERPRET: FIND MEANING
1b. What does the United States offer that Puerto Rico does not?

ANALYZE: TAKE THINGS APART →
2a. Analyze what the author learns about being Hispanic.

SYNTHESIZE: BRING THINGS TOGETHER
2b. Is the author proud of being Hispanic? Explain.

EVALUATE: MAKE JUDGMENTS →
3a. What are the author's greatest obstacles as a recent immigrant?

EXTEND: CONNECT IDEAS
3b. The Statue of Liberty, which many immigrants have passed on their way to the United States, has a poem by Emma Lazarus inscribed on its pedestal: "Give me your tired, your poor, / Your huddled masses yearning to breathe free, / The wretched refuse of your teeming shore. / Send these, the homeless, tempest-tost to me, / I lift my lamp beside the golden door!" Did the United States live up to its stated promise for Santiago?

Literary Tools

MEMOIR. A **memoir** is a nonfiction narration that tells a story. It can be autobiographical or biographical. Complete the cluster chart below to list the formative, or most important, experiences the author has shortly after coming to the United States. One example has been done for you. Is Santiago's memoir autobiographical or biographical?

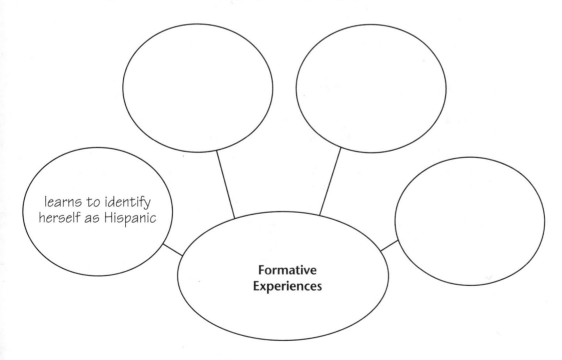

learns to identify herself as Hispanic

Formative Experiences

WordWorkshop

USING SUFFIXES. Complete each word in the left-hand column by adding one of the suffixes that follow. Then match the completed word with its definition in the right-hand column. Write the letter of the correct meaning next to the completed word.

–ed   –ate   –y   –al   –ent

1. lank_____   a. temporary

2. vac_____   b. tall

3. pung_____   c. fascinated

4. mesmeriz_____   d. make free

5. ephemer_____   e. acrid

Read-Write Connection

If you were the author, what would you find most upsetting about your first few months in Brooklyn?

_____

_____

_____

_____

_____

_____

_____

_____

Beyond the Reading

READING IMMIGRANT STORIES. Read an immigrant story about someone from a country other than Puerto Rico. Then compare and contrast this immigrant's experience with Santiago's. For what reason(s) did this person come to the United States? Did he or she have friends or family here? What was this person's initial reaction to the United States? How easily did he or she adjust to our culture? Did he or she have any problems with the language? These are some points to consider in yourcomparison-contrast essay.

GO ONLINE. Visit the EMC Internet Resource Center at **emcp.com** to find links and additional activities for this selection.

Unit 7 READING Review

Choose and Use Reading Strategies

Before reading the excerpt below, review with a partner how to use each of these reading strategies.

1. Read with a Purpose
2. Connect to Prior Knowledge
3. Write Things Down
4. Make Predictions
5. Visualize
6. Use Text Organization
7. Tackle Difficult Vocabulary
8. Monitor Your Reading Progress

Now apply at least two of these reading strategies as you read the excerpt from *How Reading Changed My Life* by Anna Quindlen. Use the margins and mark up the text to show how you are using the reading strategies to read actively.

> There is something in the American character that is even secretly hostile to the act of aimless reading, a certain hale and heartiness that is suspicious of reading as anything more than a tool for advancement. This is a country that likes confidence but despises hubris, that associates the "nose in the book" with the same sense of covert superiority that Ms. Winfrey's mother did. America is also a nation that prizes sociability and community, that accepts a kind of psychological domino effect: alone leads to loner, loner to loser. Any sort of turning away from human contact is suspect, especially one that interferes with the go-out-and-get-going ethos that seems to be at the heart of our national character. The image of American presidents that stick are those that portray them as men of action: Theodore Roosevelt on safari, John Kennedy throwing a football around with his brothers. There is only Lincoln as solace to the inveterate reader, a solitary figure sitting by the fire, saying, "My best friend is a person who will give me a book I have not read."

WordWorkshop

UNIT 7 WORDS FOR EVERYDAY USE

abstract, 338	defunct, 355	hindsight, 355	reproach, 361
abundance, 351	degenerative, 346	incisive, 337	schematic, 338
accession, 354	degrading, 319	indomitable, 343	sequestered, 363
acuity, 336	demerit, 385	ingenious, 333	serene, 323
aghast, 336	devoid, 326	irate, 322	sever, 378
amiably, 333	diffidently, 337	lanky, 382	stalward, 353
apprehend, 345	disfigure, 362	leering, 370	stolidly, 364
aptly, 320	distinction, 352	linear, 340	stylized, 338
arresting, 372	elicit, 336	marred, 383	subdue, 383
carnage, 351	enterprising, 354	mesmerize, 382	substantial, 381
celluloid, 339	ephemeral, 379	molestation, 364	subtle, 379
coercion, 327	exaltation, 328	omit, 342	superfluous, 355
cognition, 339	exempt, 364	oppression, 327	symmetry, 340
coherently, 324	exposé, 322	pathology, 344	tenacity, 343
collusion, 345	farcical, 339	peremptory, 343	torrid, 338
comply, 323, 340	fastidious, 383	placidly, 334	trifle, 335
confabulate, 336	flagrant, 354	prodigious, 351	unethical, 323
construe, 341	forbear, 344	pungent, 382	vacate, 383
convoluted, 340	frivolous, 335	receding, 362	verbatim, 342
coordinate, 322	gait, 379	remnant, 364	verdant, 363
deficit, 342	genially, 333	renounce, 344	

CONTEXT CLUES. Fill in the blank with the letter for the best word to complete the sentence.

_____ 1. It took three movers to put the_____ dresser in the moving van because it was so heavy.
  a. sequestered
  b. plummeting
  c. unwieldy

_____ 2. Mrs. Martinelli liked the_____ of her gated community where all the wealthy residents paid to have a security guard at the gate.
  a. exclusivity
  b. inclination
  c. coercion

_____ 3. For the_____ operation, Max wore a ski mask and black clothes so he wouldn't be detected.
  a. convoluted
  b. covert
  c. salvage

_____ 4. The party room was the_____ property of the townhome association and all the residents could sign up to use it.
  a. pungent
  b. degenerative
  c. communal

_____ 5. The stroke victim showed great_____ , not giving up until she could walk again.
     a. tenacity
     b. sustenance
     c. exaltation

_____ 6. Julie was_____ about eating only 800 calories a day and took her calorie counter with her everywhere.
     a. invincible
     b. obsessive
     c. subtle

_____ 7. Tim's piano teacher_____ him for not practicing, and the harsh words made him cry.
     a. supplanted
     b. construed
     c. reproached

_____ 8. Jess worked out at the gym only_____, so the girl at the desk didn't know her and always asked for her I.D.
     a. aptly
     b. sporadically
     c. stolidly

_____ 9. Kim slept soundly in the hotel room knowing her parents were in the_____ room.
     a. adjoining
     b. torrid
     c. destitute

_____10. Because of a bomb threat, all the students were told to_____ the school.
     a. sever
     b. assuage
     c. vacate

Literary Tools

Select the best literary element on the right to complete each sentence on the left. Write the correct letter in the blank.

_____ 1. If you tell your friends to "chow down" at your party, you are using a(n)_____.

_____ 2. When a writer's _____ is to persuade his readers, he might write an editorial.

_____ 3. In her _____, Katharine Hepburn talked about her acting career and the love of her life.

_____ 5. Oliver Sacks uses _____ to share the details of Dr. P.'s medical problem.

_____ 6. When Chief Seattle calls white people "grass that covers vast prairies," he is using _____.

_____ 6. A good _____ develops a single idea and uses details to support it.

a. memoir, 378

b. colloquialism, 372

c. narrative writing, 334

d. purpose or aim, 319

e. essay, 351

f. imagery, 362

On Your Own

FLUENTLY SPEAKING. Select an excerpt 15 to 20 lines long from one of the selections in this unit. Practice reading it aloud, having determined in advance the emotional impact you are striving for. On a piece of paper write down the emotions you want to elicit in your listener. Fold the paper. Then read your excerpt to a classmate. When you are done, ask him or her to write down the emotions that came to mind as you read. Compare the two papers to see if the information matches.

PICTURE THIS. Review the Words for Everyday Use from this unit listed in WordWorkshop on page 390. Choose a word and look up the definition on the page listed. Then, draw a sketch to help you remember this word. See page 462 in Unit 9 for an example.

PUT IT IN WRITING. Think about the stereotypes some Americans have about ethnic minorities. Choose one of the selections in this unit by a writer who represents an ethnic minority. Write a short essay in which you discuss how the selection dispels such stereotypes.

Unit EIGHT

READING
Informational
and Visual Media

INFORMATIONAL AND VISUAL MEDIA

Learning how to read online and print reference works, graphic aids, and other visuals will help you access, process, and think about the vast amount of information available to you.

Informational Media

Media are channels or systems of communication, information, or entertainment. *Mass media*, designed to reach the mass of the people, refers specifically to means of communication, such as newspapers, radio, or television. *Journalism* is the gathering, evaluating, and disseminating, through various media, of news and facts of current interest. Journalism has expanded from printed matter (newspapers and periodicals) to include radio, television, documentary films, the Internet, and computer news services.

Newspapers, issued on a daily or weekly basis, report the news, comment on the news, support various public policies, and furnish special information and advice to readers.

Periodicals, released at regular intervals, are publications that include journals, magazines, or newsletters. They feature material of special interest to particular audiences. "Beware the Unruly Sun" and "The Roots of Genius?" are examples in this unit of periodical articles.

Technical writing refers to scientific or process-oriented instructional writing that is of a technical or mechanical nature, such as **instruction manuals**, **how-to instructional guides**, and **procedural memos**. In this unit, "Into the Electronic Millennium" is a technical essay.

Reading TIP

The word *media* comes from a Latin word meaning "middle." The media are literally "in the middle." They pass information from their source to you. As you read texts from the media, consider whether they have altered or slanted the truth before passing information along to you.

Elements of Informational Media

NEWS ARTICLES. **News articles** are informational pieces of writing about a particular topic, issue, event, or series of events. They can be found in newspapers, periodicals, and on Internet sites such as news groups or information services.

EDITORIALS AND COMMENTARIES. An **editorial** is an article in a newspaper or periodical that gives the opinions of the editors or publishers. A **commentary** expresses the opinion of a participant or observer of a particular event.

ESSAYS. An **essay** is a brief work of nonfiction that need not be a complete treatment of a subject.

INTERVIEWS. An **interview** is a question and answer exchange between a reporter who wants information and the person who has that information.

REVIEWS. A **review**, or *critique*, is a critical evaluation of a work, such as a book, play, movie, musical performance, or recording.

Electronic Media

Electronic media includes online magazines and journals, known as **webzines** or **e-zines**, **computer news services**, and many **web-based newspapers** that are available on the **Internet**. In addition to handling web documents, the Internet also allows people to send e-mail, access archives of files, and participate in discussion groups.

Multimedia means presenting information using a combination of text, sound, pictures, animation, and video. Common multimedia computer applications include **games**, **learning software**, **presentation software**, **reference materials**, and **web pages**. Using multimedia can provide a varied and informative interactive experience.

Elements of Electronic Media

ELECTRONIC MAIL. **Electronic mail**, or **e-mail**, is used to send written messages between individuals or groups on the Internet. E-mail messages tend to be more informal and conversational in style than letters are.

WEB PAGES. A **web page** is an electronic "page" on the World Wide Web or Internet that may contain text, pictures, and sometimes animations related to a particular topic. A *website* is a collection of pages grouped together to organize the information offered by the person, company, or group that owns it.

Reading STRATEGY
REVIEW

CONNECT TO PRIOR KNOWLEDGE. What kinds of multimedia software have you used?

_____

_____

_____

NEWSGROUPS. Another use of e-mail is **listservs**, in which discussions on a particular subject are grouped together into **newsgroups** on a wide range of subjects. Messages to a newsgroup are accessible in the form of a list on a local news server that has a worldwide reach. Users can choose which messages they want to read and reply by posting messages to the newsgroup.

INFORMATION SERVICES. **Information services**, or *news services*, are providers of electronic news, information, and e-mail services.

BULLETIN BOARD SYSTEMS. A **bulletin board system**, or BBS, is an online service that allows users to post and read messages on a particular topic, converse in a *chat room*, play games with another person, and copy, or download, programs to their personal computers.

WEBZINES OR E-ZINES. **Webzines** or **e-zines** are periodicals that are available online. They may be available only online, or they may also be available in a printed magazine distributed by traditional methods.

ONLINE NEWSPAPERS. Many major newspapers are now available online. Past editions of the paper are usually accessible through an online archive.

Visual Media

Many books and news media rely on **visual arts**, such as **fine art**, **illustrations**, and **photographs**, to convey ideas. Critically viewing a painting or photograph can add meaning to your understanding of a text.

Elements of Visual Media

GRAPHIC AIDS. **Graphic aids** are visual materials with information such as **drawings**, **illustrations**, **diagrams**, **charts**, **graphs**, **maps**, and **spreadsheets**.

PHOTOGRAPHS. Photographs can accompany news stories or historical documents, serve as scientific evidence or works of art, and record everyday life. New photographic technology allows for digital formats to be stored on disk and downloaded to computers.

DIGITAL PHOTOGRAPHY. With **digital photography**, images are converted into a code of ones and zeroes that a computer can read. Digital photographs can be manipulated into new images.

PHOTOJOURNALISM. **Photojournalism** is documentary photography that tells a particular story in visual terms. Photojournalists, who usually work for newspapers and periodicals, cover cultural and news events in areas such as politics, war, business, sports, and the arts.

NOTE THE FACTS

What is the purpose of a newsgroup?

_____

_____

THINK AND REFLECT

Why might someone doubt the accuracy of a digital photograph? **(Infer)**

_____

_____

_____

VISUAL ARTS. The **visual arts** include painting, sculpture, drawing, printmaking, collage, photography, video, and computer-assisted art. With art, the artist tries to communicate with viewers, who may have different ideas about how to interpret the work. Learning about the location and time period of an artwork can contribute to a better understanding of it.

USING READING STRATEGIES WITH INFORMATIONAL AND VISUAL MEDIA

Active Reading Strategy Checklists

When reading informational and visual media, you will need to identify how the text is structured. Scan the material first. Headings, pictures, and directions will reveal what the selection wants to communicate. Use the following checklists when you read informational and visual media.

1 READ WITH A PURPOSE. Before reading informational and visual media, give yourself a purpose, or something to look for, as you read. Know why you are reading and what information you seek. Sometimes a purpose will be a directive from a teacher: "Keep track of risk factors that affect skin cancer." Other times you can set your own purpose by previewing the title, the opening and closing paragraphs, and instructional information. Say to yourself

❑ I need to look for . . .
❑ I must keep track of . . .
❑ I need to understand the writer's views on . . .
❑ It is essential that I figure out how . . .
❑ I want to learn what happened when . . .

2 CONNECT TO PRIOR KNOWLEDGE. Connect to information you already know about the writer's topic. As you read, build on what you know. Say to yourself

❑ I know this about the topic already . . .
❑ Other information I've read about this topic said . . .
❑ I've used similar visual aids by . . .
❑ I did something similar when . . .
❑ This information is like . . .

Reading TIP

Use titles, heads, charts, and pictures to preview the selection before you read it.

3 **WRITE THINGS DOWN.** As you read informational and visual media, write down or mark ideas that help you understand the writer's views. Possible ways to keep a written record include

❑ Underline information that answers a specific question.
❑ Write down steps in a process.
❑ Highlight conclusions the writer draws.
❑ Create a graphic organizer that shows how to do something.
❑ Use a code to respond to the writer's ideas.

4 **MAKE PREDICTIONS.** Before you read informational and visual media, use the title and subject matter to guess what the selection will be about. As you read, confirm or deny your predictions, and make new ones based on what you learn. Make predictions like the following:

❑ The title tells me that the selection will be about . . .
❑ Graphic aids show me that . . .
❑ I predict that the writer will want me to . . .
❑ This selection will help me . . .
❑ This writer will conclude by . . .

5 **VISUALIZE.** Visualizing, or allowing the words on the page to create images in your mind, helps you understand what informational and visual media is trying to communicate. In order to visualize what an informational and visual media selection is communicating, you need to picture the people, events, or procedure that a writer describes. Make statements such as

❑ I imagine these people will . . .
❑ A drawing of this part would include . . .
❑ I picture that this is happening in this section . . .
❑ I envision the situation as . . .

6 **USE TEXT ORGANIZATION.** When you read informational and visual media, pay attention to the text's structure. Learn to stop occasionally and retell what you have read. Say to yourself

❑ The title, headings, and pictures tell me this selection will be about . . .
❑ The writer's directions . . .
❑ There is a pattern to how the writer presents . . .
❑ The writer presents the information by . . .
❑ The writer includes helpful sections that . . .

Reading TIP

Instead of writing down a short response, use a symbol or a short word to indicate your response.
+   I like this
−   I don't like this
√   This is important
Yes I agree with this
No I disagree with this
?   I don't understand this
!   This is like something I know
☞   I need to come back to this later

Create your own code to note reactions you have.

Reading TIP

Drawing a diagram or creating a flow chart as you read can help you understand technical writing.

Reading TIP

Scan the first and last paragraphs, or any headings, pictures, and graphs, before you read. This will give you a quick picture of what the writer wants you to understand.

FIX-UP IDEAS

- Reread
- Ask a question
- Read in shorter chunks
- Retell
- Work with a partner
- Choose a new reading strategy
- Create a mnemonic device

7 TACKLE DIFFICULT VOCABULARY. Difficult words can hinder your ability to understand informational and visual media. Use context, consult a dictionary, or ask someone about words you do not understand. When you come across a difficult word in the selection, say to yourself

❏ The writer defines this word by . . .

❏ A dictionary definition shows that the word means . . .

❏ My work with the word before reading helps me know that the word means . . .

❏ A classmate said that the word means . . .

8 MONITOR YOUR READING PROGRESS. All readers encounter difficulty when they read, especially if they haven't chosen the reading material. When you have to read something, note problems you are having and fix them. The key to reading success is knowing when you are having difficulty. To fix problems, say to yourself

❏ Because I don't understand this part, I will . . .

❏ Because I'm having trouble staying connected to the ideas in the selection, I will . . .

❏ Because the words in the selection are too hard, I will . . .

❏ Because the selection is long, I will . . .

❏ Because I can't retell what the selection was about, I will . . .

Become an Active Reader

Active reading strategy instruction in this unit gives you an in-depth look at how to use one active reading strategy with each selection. Margin notes guide your use of this strategy and show you how to combine it with other strategies. Using just one reading strategy increases your chance of reading success. Learning how to use several strategies in combination increases your chance of success even more. Use the questions and tips in the margins to keep your attention focused on reading actively. Use the white space in the margins to jot down responses to what you are reading. For more information about the active reading strategies, see Unit 1, pages 1–15.

How to Use Reading Strategies with Informational and Visual Media

Read the following excerpts to discover ways to use reading strategies as you read informational and visual media.

Excerpt 1. Note how a reader uses active reading strategies while reading this excerpt from "Beware the Unruly Sun" by Claudia Kalb, page 401.

CONNECT TO PRIOR KNOWLEDGE

My grandfather had a cancerous spot removed from his face last year.

READ WITH A PURPOSE

I want to find out more about malignant melanoma.

VISUALIZE

I'm trying to imagine what the "funny-looking spot" looked like.

The summer sun. It warms the sand and the soul. But as Kathleen Black will remind you, those brilliant rays can also ravage the body. Just weeks before her 35th birthday last fall, Black was told that the funny-looking spot on her left shin—no bigger than a pencil eraser—was a deadly form of cancer called malignant melanoma. "Boy, those two words will echo in your brain," she says. "I saw my life flashing in front of me."

MAKE A PREDICTION

I predict that Kathleen Black will be okay, but the article will advise people to use sunscreen.

Excerpt 2. Note how a reader uses active reading strategies while reading this excerpt from "Into the Electronic Millennium" by Sven Birkerts, page 417.

MONITOR YOUR READING PROGRESS

Reading parts of the essay aloud helps me understand the complex sentence structures.

WRITE THINGS DOWN

As I read, I'm going to look for clues about how the author feels about electronic communication.

A change is upon us—nothing could be clearer.

The printed word is part of a <u>vestigial</u> order that we are moving away from—by choice and by societal compulsion. I'm not just talking about disaffected academics, either. This shift is happening throughout our culture, away from the patterns and habits of the printed page and toward a new world distinguished by its reliance on electronic communications.

This is not, of course, the first such shift in our long history. In Greece, in the time of Socrates, several centuries after Homer, the dominant oral culture was overtaken by the writing technology. And in Europe another epochal transition was effected in the late fifteenth century after Gutenberg invented movable type. In both cases the long-term societal effects were overwhelming, as they will be for us in the years to come.

---

ves tig i al (ve sti´ jē əl) *adj.*, showing a trace, mark, or visible sign left by something vanished or lost. *From the <u>vestigial</u> ruins, Daniel could imagine the temple as it looked in 45 BC.*

USE TEXT ORGANIZATION

The writer often places important ideas in the opening and closing sentences of each paragraph.

TACKLE DIFFICULT VOCABULARY

The definition of *vestigial* at the bottom of the page helps me understand this paragraph.

Reader's resource

Newsweek reporter Claudia Kalb warns about the medical risks of overexposure to the sun in the article **"Beware the Unruly Sun."** Kalb's informative article tells readers how to protect themselves from the sun, become familiar with types of skin cancer, and learn warning signs so that they can get help when needed.

Word watch

PREVIEW VOCABULARY

burrow	malignant
derive	pigment
detection	plummet
immune	precursor
innocuous	prognosis
lesion	ravage

Reader's journal

What are some precautions you take now to protect your future health?

_____

_____

_____

"Beware the Unruly Sun"

by Claudia Kalb

Active READING STRATEGY

READ WITH A PURPOSE

Before Reading ➤ DEVELOP A PURPOSE FOR READING

❏ Read the Reader's Resource.
❏ Discuss with a partner possible reasons for reading this article.
❏ Fill out the Before Reading section of the Reader's Purpose Chart.

Graphic Organizer

Before Reading
Set a purpose for reading. *(Example: I am going to learn how to avoid skin cancer.)*

During Reading
Take notes on what you learn. *(Example: funny looking spot—appearance of skin cancer)*

After Reading
Reflect on your purpose and what you learned. *(Example: I wanted to learn how to avoid skin cancer. From the notes that I took, I know to use sunscreen with SPF of 15 or higher.)*

BEWARE
the unruly Sun

Claudia Kalb

READ WITH A PURPOSE

❑ Read the article independently.
❑ Fill out the During Reading section of the graphic organizer with notes about the information in the article.

The summer sun. It warms the sand and the soul. But as Kathleen Black will remind you, those brilliant rays can also <u>ravage</u> the body. Just weeks before her 35th birthday last fall, Black was told that the funny-looking spot on her left shin—no bigger than a pencil eraser—was a deadly form of cancer called <u>malignant</u> melanoma. "Boy, those two words will echo in your brain," she says. "I saw my life flashing in front of me."

10   In the United States, the incidence of melanoma is rising faster than almost any other cancer, striking Americans at twice the rate today as it did two decades ago. This year alone more than 44,000 people are expected to be diagnosed, and 7,300 could die. "The increase is absolutely astounding," says Dr. Martin Weinstock, chair of the American Cancer Society's (ACS) skin-cancer advisory group. "This is a major public-health problem."

But there's good news, too. Melanoma offers its victims an unusual grace period: diagnosed early—before it's had time to <u>burrow</u> beneath the skin—it's almost totally curable.

20   New tools, including computer imaging are helping dermatologists[1] detect melanoma. And new treatments, such as therapeutic vaccines, are now being tested to fight

---

1. **dermatologists.** Doctors who specialize in skin

words for everyday use

rav • age (ra′ vij) *vt.,* destroy. *The fire <u>ravaged</u> the forest.*
ma • lig • nant (mə lig′ nənt) *adj.,* severe, rapidly growing, potentially deadly. *Because the tumor was <u>malignant</u>, she began treatment immediately.*
bur • row (bʉr′ ō) *vi.,* dig; tunnel; delve beneath. *The tiny animal <u>burrowed</u> under the hay.*

NOTE THE FACTS

What kind of cancer is rising faster than any other?

_____

_____

Reading TIP _____

An **acronym** is a word like ACS that is formed from the first letter of each successive word. You may want to make a list of the acronyms in the selection. Next to each acronym, note the word each letter stands for.

Use THE STRATEGY

READ WITH A PURPOSE. If new text information focuses your interest on another aspect of the article, revise your reading purpose and continue reading with the new purpose in mind.

NOTE THE FACTS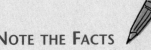

What are the risk factors for melanoma?

_____

_____

_____

NOTE THE FACTS

List the warning signs of malignant melanoma.

_____

_____

_____

against it. Most important, you can easily learn the warning signs—and possibly save your own life.

Melanocytes, the body's <u>pigment</u> cells, generally do good, not harm. They give our skin its natural color and, when struck by the sun, churn out additional pigment (or melanin) to darken and protect us. Melanocytes also cluster together to form moles. Most are <u>innocuous</u>. But in some
30   people, ultraviolet radiation[2] appears to help trigger melanocytes to multiply and turn cancerous, either in moles that already exist or in new skin <u>lesions</u>. More often than not, skin cancers turn out to be basal cell carcinoma or squamous cell carcinoma;[3] both are "nonmelanomas" and are usually not fatal. "It's the melanomas that kill," says Dr. John DiGiovanna, a dermatologist at Brown University School of Medicine. Accounting for just 4 percent of skin cancers, they cause six out of seven skin-cancer deaths.

Although no one is <u>immune</u> to melanoma, people with fair
40   skin and light eyes and hair are at greater risk. Other factors include having a large number of moles, a family history of melanoma and bad sunburns as a child—especially in the first 15 years of life. The best weapon against the disease is early <u>detection</u>. But don't rely on your GP:[4] most have minimal training in skin cancer. Use the ABCD test to check yourself regularly (the Skin Cancer Foundation has visuals at www.skincancer.org): Is the mole asymmetrical? Is its border uneven or ragged? Is there more than one color present? Is the diameter greater than 6 millimeters? Also look for
50   inflammation or bleeding. Check every inch of your body from your scalp down to the skin between your toes. Men are

2. **ultraviolet radiation.** Energy waves produced by the sun, extending from the violet, or short-wavelength, end of the visible light range to the X-ray region
3. **basal cell carcinoma and squamous cell carcinoma.** Types of skin cancer
4. **GP.** General Practitioner, or doctor

words for everyday use

pig • ment (pig′ mənt) *n.*, coloring matter in cells and tissue. *The <u>pigment</u> of the mole changed from tan to brown almost overnight.*

in • noc • u • ous (in nä′ kyə wəs) *adj.*, harmless. *It was a rude but <u>innocuous</u> comment.*

le • sion (lē′ zhən) *n.*, wound; flaw; abnormal change. *He noticed a red <u>lesion</u> on his arm and called the doctor.*

im • mune (i myün′) *adj.*, protected; resistant to a disease. *Few people are <u>immune</u> to the common cold.*

de • tec • tion (di tek′ shən) *n.*, discovery. *She visits the dentist regularly to ensure decay <u>detection</u>.*

Melanoma: Rising Rates

It's the least common of the three major skin cancers, but it accounts for the most deaths.

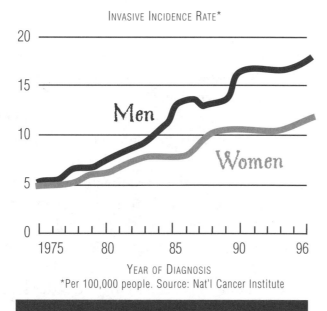

INVASIVE INCIDENCE RATE*

Men

Women

YEAR OF DIAGNOSIS
*Per 100,000 people. Source: Nat'l Cancer Institute

THINK AND REFLECT

Look at the graph. Are more men or more women developing melanoma? **(Interpret)**

_____

_____

more likely to develop melanoma on their trunks (probably because they go shirtless in the sun), women on their legs.

If you see anything suspicious, call your doctor. The American Academy of Dermatology (www.aad.org or 888-462-DERM) can help you find a skin specialist in your area; the ACS (www.cancer.org or 800-ACS-2345) offers information about what to expect during an exam. A key factor in prognosis is how deeply the melanoma has invaded the skin. At less than three quarters of a millimeter, your chances are better than 95 percent. Beyond four millimeters, the odds plummet to less than 50 percent. Says AAD president Dr. Darrell Rigel: "That little difference is a big difference in survival."

If you do have a mole biopsied,[5] request that it be read by a specialist called a dermatopathologist. "In less trained

60

---

5. **biopsied.** Examined body tissue, cells, and fluids

words for everyday use	prog • nos • is (präg nō′ səs) *n.*, act or art of foretelling the course of a disease. *The doctor's prognosis was hopeful.*
	plum • met (plə′ mət) *vi.*, fall or drop rapidly. *The value of the stock plummeted, and Mr. Robinson lost $10,000.*

Literary **TOOLS**

ARTICLE. An **article** is a brief work of nonfiction on a specific topic. As you read, pay attention to the main topics discussed in this article. Look for details supporting each main topic.

THINK AND REFLECT

Reread lines 60–62. How does the depth of the melanoma affect survival rates? What do these odds tell you about how to protect yourself? **(Infer)**

_____

_____

_____

_____

hands, there have been problems," says Rigel. Seek a second opinion if you have any concerns. Dorothy Shaffer, 42, was told in 1990 that the mole on her calf was "nothing to worry about." But the lab made a mistake. Now a disease that might have been licked is threatening her life. "If I see 45," she says, "I'll be lucky."

You may be able to help ward off melanoma. Start by using sunscreen with an SPF[6] of at least 15. Dr. Mark Pittelkow of the Mayo Clinic recommends newer products containing zinc and avobenzone. Pay special attention to the kids, too. Last week the ACS reported that 72 percent of 11- to 18-year-olds surveyed got sunburned last summer—a potential <u>precursor</u> to cancer. One third were wearing sunscreen at the time. The FDA[7] ruled last month that sunscreens can no longer be labeled "sunblocks" because they're incapable of absolute protection. Use them liberally (about a shot glass full) and repeatedly. Ditch products more than three years old. And try to avoid direct sun between 10 A.M. and 4 P.M.

The future of melanoma may be better for all of us soon. New digital imaging can take a magnified snapshot or Melanomagram, helping doctors see deeper into a lesion and track it over time. Computers may soon be able to "read" moles and help make diagnoses. A genetic test is on the horizon, too. Drugs <u>derived</u> from the body's own chemicals are now being used to boost the immune system to attack advanced melanoma, and therapeutic vaccines are being tested. "From 15 years ago until now, we've taken quantum leaps"[8] says DiGiovanna.

Health officials, who are launching skin cancer-awareness campaigns this summer, hope increased vigilance and new research will one day kill off melanoma for good. It all starts with people like Kathleen Black—her cancer turned out to be early stage. "I really feel like I've dodged a bullet," she says. Now it's your turn. ■

6. **SPF.** Sun Protection Factor
7. **FDA.** Food and Drug Administration
8. **quantum leaps.** Big steps; huge progress

words for everyday use

pre • cur • sor (pri kur' sər) *n.*, person or thing that comes before and indicates the approach of another. *The nausea was usually the <u>precursor</u> of a headache.*

de • rive (di rīv') *vi.*, take, receive, or make, especially from a specified source. *The expression is <u>derived</u> from Latin.*

Reflect ON YOUR READING

After Reading EVALUATE THE READING STRATEGY

When you finish reading, fill in the After Reading section of the graphic organizer. Compare your reading experience with your partner's. Discuss any remaining questions you have about the article and how it did or didn't satisfy your purpose. Finally, discuss how reading with a purpose affected how you read the article.

Reading Skills and Test Practice

INTERPRET GRAPHS

Discuss with a partner how to answer the following questions about interpreting the graph on page 403.

1. Which of the following statements is true based on the information in the graph?
   a. The graph illustrates the differences in the occurrence of two types of skin cancers.
   b. The graph shows how many people died from melanoma, not how many people were diagnosed with the disease.
   c. The graph shows how many people were diagnosed with melanoma, not how many people died from the disease.
   d. The graph illustrates the rising number of people diagnosed with skin cancer over a thirty-year period.

What is the correct answer to the question above? How were you able to eliminate the other answers? How did your application of the reading strategy help you answer the question?

____

____

2. Which of the following statements is true based on the information in the graph?
   a. Women's rates were leveling off in the late 1990s.
   b. Men's rates were dropping in the late 1990s.
   c. Both men's and women's rates began rising again in the late 1990s.
   d. Women's rates decreased sharply around 1987.

What is the correct answer to the question above? How were you able to eliminate the other answers? How did your application of the reading strategy help you answer the question?

____

____

THINK-ALOUD NOTES

Investigate, Inquire, and Imagine

RECALL: GATHER FACTS
1a. List the precautions that may protect you from melanoma.

INTERPRET: FIND MEANING
1b. How might you change your behavior based on these precautions?

ANALYZE: TAKE THINGS APART
2a. In the case of malignant melanoma, why are prevention and early detection crucial?

SYNTHESIZE: BRING THINGS TOGETHER
2b. What attitude does a person need to have in order to carry out the suggestions for prevention?

EVALUATE: MAKE JUDGMENTS
3a. Why is the sun the number one cause of melanoma?

EXTEND: CONNECT IDEAS
3b. What cultural values contribute to increasing cases of melanoma?

Literary Tools

ARTICLE. An **article** is a brief work of nonfiction on a specific topic. Fill in the graphic organizer below in order to organize some of the main points raised in the article.

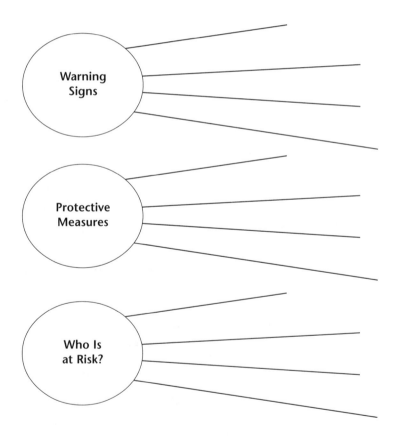

Why does the author begin and end with the story of Ms. Black?

_____

_____

WordWorkshop

WORD FAMILIES. A **word root** is a word part that cannot stand alone as a complete word. For each word root below, write a word from the selection that contains it.

1. *carcin/carcino:* tumor; cancer

_____

2. *melas:* black

_____

3. *derma:* skin

_____

4. *bio:* life

_____

5. *therapeuein:* to treat

_____

Read-Write Connection

How has reading this article influenced how you will spend a day in the sun?

_____

_____

_____

_____

Beyond the Reading

RESEARCHING SUN DEITIES. Many ancient peoples worshipped sun gods, recognizing the sun as a powerful life force. In Egypt, the sun god was called *Re* or *Ra*, and in India, *Surya*. Native American Indians performed a sun dance in honor of the sun. In ancient Rome, the sun god was *Apollo*, who drew his chariot across the sky. The Aztec religion called the sun gods *Huitzilopochtli* and *Tezcatlipoca* and built giant pyramids to honor them. Read more about one of these sun deities. Then create a project to show what you have learned. For example, you might interpret a poem, explain a work of art, or tell a story about one of these deities.

GO ONLINE. Visit the EMC Internet Resource Center at **emcp.com** to find links and additional activities for this selection.

Reader's resource

In **"How to Write a Letter,"** radio personality Garrison Keillor gives humorous tips on how to write an informal, personal letter. He also comments on why it is important to keep the art of letter writing alive for future generations. Garrison Keillor is the host of "A Prairie Home Companion," a weekly program that is broadcast on National Public Radio.

Word watch

PREVIEW VOCABULARY

anonymity   obligatory

Reader's journal

If you could write a personal letter to anyone right now, to whom would you send it? What would it say?

_____

_____

_____

_____

"How to Write a Letter"
by Garrison Keillor

Active READING STRATEGY

CONNECT TO PRIOR KNOWLEDGE

Before Reading ➤ ACTIVATE PRIOR KNOWLEDGE

❏ Read the Reader's Resource.
❏ Participate in a class discussion about letter writing. Share what you know about how to write a personal letter and the experiences you have had writing and receiving letters.
❏ Fill in the Before Reading section of the Connections Chart below.

Graphic Organizer

Before Reading
Read the selection title. Then skim the selection and answer the following questions.
1. What kind of selection is this (short story, essay, speech, etc.)?   _____
2. What do you think this selection will be about?   _____
3. List three facts or experiences related to the subject of this selection.   _____   _____

After Reading
Complete this section after reading the selection.
1. Did you guess correctly what the selection was about? Explain.   _____   _____
2. What did you learn from this selection that you did not know before reading it?   _____   _____

How to write a letter

Garrison Keillor

During Reading

CONNECT TO PRIOR KNOWLEDGE

❑ Follow along in the text as your teacher reads it aloud.

❑ As you listen, compare your ideas about letter writing with Keillor's. Use a code to mark thoughts and feelings with which you agree and disagree.

NOTE THE FACTS

How does Keillor describe himself?

_____

_____

Reading STRATEGY REVIEW

READ WITH A PURPOSE. Reading with a purpose will help you get more meaning from the selection. Review the Active Reading Strategy for "Beware the Unruly Sun" on page 400. Reread the current selection with a clear purpose in mind. What is your purpose for reading this selection?

_____

_____

We shy persons need to write a letter now and then, or else we'll dry up and blow away. It's true. And I speak as one who loves to reach for the phone, dial the number, and say, "Big Bopper here—what's shakin', babes?" The telephone is to shyness what Hawaii is to February, it's a way out of the woods, *and yet:* a letter is better.

Such a sweet gift—a piece of handmade writing in an envelope that is not a bill, sitting in our friend's path when she trudges home from a long day spent among wahoos and savages, a day our words will help repair. They don't need to be immortal, just sincere. She can read them twice and again tomorrow: *You're someone I care about, Corinne, and think of often and every time I do you make me smile.*

We need to write, otherwise nobody will know who we are. They will have only a vague impression of us as A Nice Person, because, frankly, we don't shine at conversation, we lack the confidence to thrust our faces forward and say, "Hi, I'm Heather Hooten: let me tell you about my week." Mostly we say "Uh-huh" and "Oh, really." People smile and look over our shoulder, looking for someone else to meet.

So a shy person sits down and writes a letter. To be known by another person—to meet and talk freely on the page—to be close despite distance. To escape from <u>anonymity</u> and be our own sweet selves and express the music of our souls.

words for everyday use

an • o • nym • i • ty (an' ə nim' ə tē) *n.*, quality or state of not being known. *Some writers use pen names to protect their <u>anonymity</u>.*

Reread lines 33–34. What is the first step in writing a letter? Why does guilt interfere with letter-writing? (Infer)

_____

_____

_____

Literary TOOLS

EXPOSITION. **Exposition** is a type of writing that presents facts or opinions in an organized manner. As you read, focus on the sequence of Keillor's advice for writing a letter.

Use THE STRATEGY

CONNECT TO PRIOR KNOWLEDGE. Think about a story you have read or seen on TV or at the movies in which a letter played an important role. What was the aim of the letter? Why were letters so important in that story? What does the story reveal about the role of written communication in our lives?

_____

_____

_____

_____

Same thing that moves a giant rock star to sing his heart out in front of 123,000 people moves us to take ballpoint in hand and write a few lines to our dear Aunt Eleanor. *We want to be known.* We want her to know that we have fallen in love, that we quit our job, that we're moving to New York, and we want to say a few things that might not get said in casual conversation: *Thank you for what you've meant to me, I am very happy right now.*

30

The first step in writing letters is to get over the guilt of *not* writing. You don't "owe" anybody a letter. Letters are a gift. The burning shame you feel when you see unanswered mail makes it harder to pick up a pen and makes for a cheerless letter when you finally do. *I feel bad about not writing, but I've been so busy,* etc. Skip this. Few letters are <u>obligatory</u>, and they are *Thanks for the wonderful gift and I am terribly sorry to hear about George's death* and *Yes, you're welcome to stay with us next month,* and not many more than that. Write those promptly if you want to keep your friends. Don't worry about the others, except love letters, of course. When your true love writes, *Dear Light of My Life, Joy of My Heart, O Lovely Pulsating Core of My Sensate[1] Life,* some response is called for.

40

Some of the best letters are tossed off in a burst of inspiration, so keep your writing stuff in one place where you can sit down for a few minutes and *(Dear Roy, I am in the middle of a book entitled* We Are Still Married *but thought I'd drop you a line. Hi to your sweetie, too)* dash off a note to a pal. Envelopes, stamps, address book, everything in a drawer so you can write fast when the pen is hot.

50

A blank white eight-by-eleven sheet can look as big as Montana if the pen's not so hot—try a smaller page and write boldly. Or use a note card with a piece of fine art on the front; if your letter ain't good, at least they get the Matisse.[2] Get a pen that makes a sensuous line, get a

---

1. *Sensate.* Appealing to the senses
2. *Matisse.* (1869–1954) Henri Matisse, French painter

words for everyday use

ob • lig • a • to • ry (əb lig′ ə tôr′ ē) *adj.,* required. *Military service is <u>obligatory</u> in some European countries.*

comfortable typewriter, a friendly word processor—
60 whichever feels easy to the hand.

Sit for a few minutes with the blank sheet in front of you,
and meditate on the person you will write to, let your
friend come to mind until you can almost see her or him in
the room with you. Remember the last time you saw each
other and how your friend looked and what you said and
what perhaps was unsaid between you, and when your
friend becomes real to you, start to write.

Write the salutation—*Dear You*—and take a deep breath
and plunge In. A simple declarative sentence[3] will do,
70 followed by another and another and another. Tell us what
you're doing and tell it like you were talking to us. Don't
think about grammar, don't think about lit'ry style; don't try
to write dramatically, just give us your news. Where did you
go, who did you see, what did they say, what do you think?

If you don't know where to begin, start with the present
moment: *I'm sitting at the kitchen table on a rainy Saturday
morning. Everyone is gone and the house is quiet.* Let your
simple description of the present moment lead to
something else, let the letter drift gently along.

80 The toughest letter to crank out is one that is meant to
impress, as we all know from writing job applications; if it's
hard work to slip off a letter to a friend, maybe you're
trying too hard to be terrific. A letter is only a report to
someone who already likes you for reasons other than your
brilliance. Take it easy.

Don't worry about form. It's not a term paper. When you
come to the end of one episode, just start a new paragraph.
You can go from a few lines about the sad state of pro
football to the fight with your mother to your fond
90 memories of Mexico to your cat's urinary-tract infection to
a few thoughts on personal indebtedness and on to the
kitchen sink and what's in it. The more you write, the
easier it gets, and when you have a True True Friend to
write to, a *compadre*,[4] a soul sibling, then it's like driving a
car down a country road, you just get behind the keyboard
and press on the gas.

---

3. **declarative sentence.** Sentence that makes a direct statement and
that is punctuated with a period
4. *compadre.* Spanish for close friend or pal

MARK THE TEXT

Underline or highlight the
questions Keillor thinks you
should answer in a letter.

THINK AND REFLECT

Reread lines 80–83. What
is the "toughest letter to
crank out"? If someone is
trying to impress a friend
in a letter, what does that
say about how the writer
feels about the friend?
(Infer)

_____

_____

_____

READ ALOUD

Read aloud the highlighted
text on this page. How
would you describe the
contents of this letter?

_____

_____

FIX-UP IDEA

Choose a New Strategy
If you have difficulty connecting to prior knowledge, choose another strategy such as writing down information, using the text's organization, or predicting what will come next.

NOTE THE FACTS

According to Keillor, what will your friend's grandkids feel when they read your letters in forty years?

_____

_____

Don't tear up the page and start over when you write a bad line—try to write your way out of it. Make mistakes and plunge on. Let the letter cook along and let yourself be bold. Outrage, confusion, love—whatever is in your mind, let it find a way to the page.

Writing is a means of discovery, always, and when you come to the end and write *Yours ever* or *Hugs and kisses*, you'll know something you didn't when you wrote *Dear Pal*.

Probably your friend will put your letter away and it'll be read again a few years from now—and it will improve with age. And forty years from now, your friend's grandkids will dig it out of the attic and read it, a sweet and precious relic *of the ancient eighties* that gives them a sudden clear glimpse of you and her and the world we old-timers knew. You will then have created an object of art. Your simple lines about where you went, who you saw, what they said, will speak to those children and they will feel in their hearts the humanity of our times.

You can't pick up a phone and call the future and tell them about our times. You have to pick up a piece of paper. ∎

Reflect ON YOUR READING

When you finish reading, fill in the After Reading section of the graphic organizer. Think about Keillor's advice for writing a personal letter. Then, on your own paper, write a letter to a friend or relative using Keillor's advice.

Reading Skills and Test Practice

IDENTIFY THE AUTHOR'S PURPOSE AND TONE

Discuss with a partner how to answer the following questions about the author's purpose and tone.

1. In your opinion, what is the author's main purpose in writing this essay?
   a. to persuade people to write more letters
   b. to inform people that letters are difficult to write
   c. to entertain readers with a fictional account of a letter-writing experience
   d. to inform people how to write a professional business letter

What is the correct answer to the question above? How were you able to eliminate the other answers? How did your application of the reading strategy help you answer the question?

_____

_____

2. Which of the following words best describes Keillor's tone in this essay?
   a. serious
   b. academic
   c. lighthearted
   d. respectful

What is the correct answer to the question above? How were you able to eliminate the other answers? How did your application of the reading strategy help you answer the question?

_____

_____

THINK-ALOUD NOTES

_____
_____
_____
_____
_____
_____
_____
_____
_____
_____
_____

Investigate, Inquire, and Imagine

RECALL: GATHER FACTS
1a. What type of person needs to write a letter? Why? What does such a person gain by writing a letter?

INTERPRET: FIND MEANING
1b. Keillor says, "The telephone is to shyness what Hawaii is to February . . . " How would you explain this comparison?

ANALYZE: TAKE THINGS APART
2a. What does Keillor mean by the "humanity of our times"?

SYNTHESIZE: BRING THINGS TOGETHER
2b. How would Keillor likely respond to seeing letters in the Library of Congress by great authors such as George Washington and Abigail Adams?

EVALUATE: MAKE JUDGMENTS
3a. Evaluate whether Keillor's view of work, described in paragraph 2, is realistic. What is his purpose in describing a workday in this manner?

EXTEND: CONNECT IDEAS
3b. According to British author E.M. Forster, "Letters have to pass two tests before they can be classed as good: they must express the personality both of the writer and of the recipient." Would Keillor agree or disagree with this statement? Why?

Literary Tools

EXPOSITION. **Exposition** is a type of writing that presents facts or opinions in an organized manner. Fill in the flow chart below with Keillor's tips for writing a personal letter. One example has been done for you.

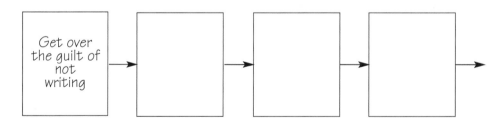

Does Keillor's essay express mainly facts or mainly opinions? Give one example of each.

_____

_____

_____

WordWorkshop

COLLOQUIALISMS. A **colloquialism** is an example of informal language. Keillor uses several colloquialisms in his essay. Rewrite each sentence below in more formal language.

1. Your friend's <u>grandkids</u> will dig your letter out of the attic and read it.

_____

2. Keep your writing <u>stuff</u> in one place.

_____

3. If your letter <u>ain't</u> good, at least they get the Matisse.

_____

4. Let the letter <u>cook along</u> and let yourself be bold.

_____

5. The toughest letter to <u>crank out</u> is one that is meant to impress.

_____

Read-Write Connection

Under what circumstances is e-mail an effective and appropriate substitute for a personal letter? Why would anyone write a personal letter in the age of e-mail?

_____

_____

_____

_____

_____

Beyond the Reading

EXPLORING *84 CHARING CROSS ROAD*. American writer Helene Hanff wrote letters to a bookseller in England. Read some of the letters in her book *84 Charing Cross Road* or watch the movie based on her book. Why did she write her letters? How would you characterize their contents? Did the letters change over time? What gift did she receive from writing her letters? Write a short composition addressing these questions.

GO ONLINE. Visit the EMC Internet Resource Center at **emcp.com** to find links and additional activities for this selection.

"Into the Electronic Millennium"

by Sven Birkerts

Active READING STRATEGY

TACKLE DIFFICULT VOCABULARY

Before Reading ➤ PREVIEW VOCABULARY

❑ Read the Reader's Resource.
❑ With a partner, take turns pronouncing each word in the Words for Everyday Use boxes on pages 418–425. Also read aloud the contextual sentences that use the new words.
❑ Read the definition for each footnote aloud.
❑ Preview the Word Concept Map below. You will use Word Concept Maps like this one to make associations with difficult words from this selection.

Graphic Organizer

Contextual sentence:

Likely contexts in which word might be used:

Synonyms:

Meaning:

Antonyms:

Word:

Examples:

Nonexamples:

Into the Electronic MILLENNIUM

Sven Birkerts

During Reading

TACKLE DIFFICULT
VOCABULARY

❑ Read the essay
independently.
❑ Use context clues and
your knowledge of word
parts to unlock the
meaning of difficult
words.
❑ Make a list of the words
from this selection that
you think you will have
difficulty remembering.

Some years ago, a friend and I comanaged a used and rare book shop in Ann Arbor, Michigan. We were often asked to appraise and purchase libraries—by retiring academics, widows, and disgruntled graduate students. One day we took a call from a professor of English at one of the community colleges outside Detroit.

When he answered the buzzer I did a double take—he looked to be only a year or two older than we were. "I'm selling everything," he said, leading the way through a large
10   apartment. As he opened the door of his study I felt a nudge from my partner. The room was wall-to-wall books and as neat as a chapel.

The professor had a remarkable collection. It reflected not only the needs of his vocation—he taught nineteenth- and twentieth-century literature—but a book lover's sensibility as well. The shelves were strictly arranged, and the books themselves were in superb condition. When he left the room we set to work inspecting, counting, and estimating. This is always a delicate procedure, for the buyer is at once
20   anxious to avoid insult to the seller and eager to get the goods for the best price. We adopted our usual strategy, working out a lower offer and a more generous fallback price. But there was no need to worry. The professor took our first offer without batting an eye.

As we boxed up the books, we chatted. My partner asked the man if he was moving. "No," he said, "but I am getting out." We both looked up. "Out of the teaching business, I mean. Out of books." He then said that he wanted to show

DRAW A PICTURE

NOTE THE FACTS

Why did the professor want
to sell his books?

_____

_____

us something. And indeed, as soon as the books were packed
30   and loaded, he led us back through the apartment and down
a set of stairs. When we reached the basement, he flicked on
the light. There, on a long table, displayed like an exhibit in
the Space Museum,[1] was a computer. I didn't know what
kind it was then, nor could I tell you now, fifteen years later.
But the professor was keen to explain and demonstrate.

While he and my partner hunched over the terminal, I
roamed to and fro, inspecting the shelves. It was purely a
reflex gesture, for they held nothing but thick binders
and paperbound manuals. "I'm changing my life," the ex-
40   professor was saying. "This is definitely where it's all going
to happen." He told us that he already had several good job
offers. And the books? I asked. Why was he selling them all?
He paused for a few beats. "The whole profession represents
a lot of pain to me," he said. "I don't want to see any of these
books again."

The scene has stuck with me. It is now a kind of marker in
my mental life. That afternoon I got my first serious <u>inkling</u>
that all was not well in the world of print and letters. All
sorts of <u>corroborations</u> followed. Our professor was by no
50   means an isolated case. Over a period of two years we met
with several others like him. New men and new women who
had glimpsed the future and had decided to get out while
the getting was good. The selling off of books was
sometimes done for financial reasons, but the need to burn
bridges was usually there as well. It was as if heading to the
future also required the destruction of tokens from the past.

A change is upon us—nothing could be clearer. The
printed word is part of a <u>vestigial</u> order that we are moving
away from—by choice and by societal compulsion. I'm not
60   just talking about disaffected academics, either. This shift is
happening throughout our culture, away from the patterns

---

1. **Space Museum.** The Smithsonian's National Air and Space Museum
in Washington, D.C.

words for everyday use

in • kling (iŋ′ kliŋ) *n.*, slight knowledge; vague notion. *Maria had an <u>inkling</u> that Justin would ask her to the dance.*

cor • rob • o • ra • tion (kə rä′ bə rä′ shən) *n.*, confirmation; something supported with evidence or authority. *The <u>corroboration</u> of the plaintiff's story by a key witness led to the conviction of the defendant.*

ves • tig • i • al (ve sti′ jē əl) *adj.*, showing a trace, mark, or visible sign left by something vanished or lost. *From the <u>vestigial</u> ruins Daniel could imagine the temple as it looked in 45 BC.*

READ ALOUD

Read aloud the highlighted text on this page. What future does the professor see?

_____

_____

THINK AND REFLECT

Reread lines 53–55. Other than for financial gain, why did the people Birkerts met want to sell their books? Why does he begin his essay with the anecdote of the English professor? **(Infer)**

_____

_____

_____

NOTE THE FACTS

What is changing in our culture (lines 60–63)?

_____

_____

_____

and habits of the printed page and toward a new world distinguished by its reliance on electronic communications.

This is not, of course, the first such shift in our long history. In Greece, in the time of Socrates, several centuries after Homer, the dominant oral culture was overtaken by the writing technology. And in Europe another epochal transition was effected in the late fifteenth century after Gutenberg invented movable type. In both cases the long-
70 term societal effects were overwhelming, as they will be for us in the years to come.

The evidence of the change is all around us, though possibly in the manner of the forest that we cannot see for the trees. The electronic media, while <u>conspicuous</u> in gadgetry, are very nearly invisible in their functioning. They have slipped deeply and irrevocably into our midst, creating sluices[2] and circulating through them. I'm not referring to any one product or function in isolation, such as television or fax machines or the networks that make them possible. I
80 mean the interdependent totality that has arisen from the <u>conjoining</u> of parts—the disk drives hooked to modems, transmissions linked to technologies of reception, recording, duplication, and storage. Numbers and codes and frequencies. Buttons and signals. And this is no longer "the future," except for the poor or the self-consciously atavistic[3]—it is now. Next to the new technologies, the scheme of things represented by print and the snail-paced linearity of the reading act looks <u>stodgy</u> and dull. Many educators say that our students are less and less able to read,
90 or analyze, or write with clarity and purpose. Who can blame the students? Everything they meet with in the world around them gives the signal: That was then, and electronic communications are now.

---

2. **sluices.** Channels to drain or carry off surplus water
3. **atavistic.** Showing a recurrence of or reversion to a past style, manner, outlook, or approach

Literary TOOLS

DICTION. Diction, when applied to writing, refers to word choice. Much of a writer's style is determined by his or her diction, the types of words that he or she chooses. As you read, try to categorize the type of words Birkerts chooses to use.

Use THE STRATEGY

TACKLE DIFFICULT VOCABULARY. Stop at the end of each page and reread the sentences in the text that contain new vocabulary. If you still don't understand a word or can't remember its meaning, add it to your list.

words for everyday use

con • spic • u • ous (kən spi′ kyü wəs) *adj.*, obvious to the eye or mind. *Jed's absence was <u>conspicuous</u> because it was his turn to give a speech.*
con • join • ing (kən join′ iŋ) *n.*, joining together separate entities for a common purpose. *Romeo and Juliet hoped that the <u>conjoining</u> of their two families would occur after their marriage.*
stodg • y (stä′ jē) *adj.*, moving in a slow plodding way. *The <u>stodgy</u> professor took his time in reaching the podium.*

Do I exaggerate? If all this is the case, why haven't we heard more about it? Why hasn't somebody stepped forward with a bow tie and a pointer stick to explain what is going on? Valid questions, but they also beg the question. They assume that we are all plugged into a total system—where else would that "somebody" appear if not on the
100   screen at the communal hearth?

Media theorist Mark Crispin Miller has given one explanation for our situation in his discussions of television in _Boxed In: The Culture of TV._ The medium, he proposes, has long since diffused itself throughout the entire system. Through sheer <u>omnipresence</u> it has vanquished the possibility of comparative perspectives. We cannot see the role that television (or, for our purposes, all electronic communications) has assumed in our lives because there is no independent ledge where we might secure our footing.
110   The medium has absorbed and <u>eradicated</u> the idea of a pretelevision past; in place of what used to be we get an ever-new and ever-renewable present. The only way we can hope to understand what is happening, or what has already happened, is by way of a severe and unnatural dissociation of sensibility.

To get a sense of the enormity of the change, you must force yourself to imagine—deeply and in nontelevisual terms—what the world was like a hundred, even fifty, years ago. If the feat is too difficult, spend some time with a novel
120   from the period. Read between the lines and reconstruct. Move through the sequence of a character's day and then <u>juxtapose</u> the images and sensations you find with those in the life of the average urban or suburban dweller today.

Inevitably, one of the first realizations is that a communications net, a soft and <u>pliable</u> mesh woven from invisible threads, has fallen over everything. The so-called natural world, the place we used to live, which served us so long as the yardstick for all measurements, can now only be perceived through a scrim.[4] Nature was then; this is now.

130 Trees and rocks have receded. And the great geographical Other, the faraway rest of the world, has been transformed by the pure possibility of access. The numbers of distance and time no longer mean what they used to. Every place, once unique, itself, is strangely shot through with radiations from every other place. "There" was then; "here" is now.

Think of it. Fifty to a hundred million people (maybe a conservative estimate) form their ideas about what is going on in America and in the world from the same basic package

140 of edited images—to the extent that the image itself has lost much of its once-fearsome power. Daily newspapers, with their long columns of print, struggle against declining sales. Fewer and fewer people under the age of fifty read them; computers will soon make packaged information a custom product. But if the printed sheet is heading for <u>obsolescence</u>, people are tuning in to the signals. The screen is where the information and entertainment wars will be fought. The communications <u>conglomerates</u> are waging bitter takeover battles in their zeal to establish global empires. As Jonathan

150 Crary has written in "The Eclipse of the Spectacle," "Telecommunications is the new arterial network <u>analogous</u> in part to what railroads were for capitalism in the nineteenth century. And it is this electronic substitute for geography that corporate and national entities are now carving up." Maybe one reason why the news of the change is not part of the common currency is that such news can only sensibly be communicated through the more analytic sequences of print.

---

4. **scrim.** Theater drop that appears opaque when a scene in front is lighted and transparent when a scene in back is lighted

words for everyday use	**ob • so • les • cence** (äb′ sə le′ sən(t)s) *n.*, process of becoming outdated or no longer in use. *The thesis of the book is that American companies plan on obsolescence so that consumers will have to replace products periodically.*
	con • glom • er • ate (kən gläm′ rət) *n.*, widely diversified corporation. *The conglomerate had software, toy, and music entertainment divisions.*
	a • nal • o • gous (ə na′ lə gəs) *adj.*, showing a likeness that permits one to draw a comparison. *A brain and a computer are analogous because both reason.*

Reading STRATEGY REVIEW

CONNECT TO PRIOR KNOWLEDGE. You already know some things about electronic media that will make reading the selection easier. Review the Active Reading Strategy for "How to Write a Letter" on page 408. Think about your personal experience with computers. Does the computer keep you from reading more print resources? Why, or why not?

_____

_____

_____

160   To underscore my point, I have been making it sound as if we were all abruptly walking out of one room and into another, leaving our books to the moths while we settle ourselves in front of our state-of-the-art terminals. The truth is that we are living through a period of overlap; one way of being is pushed athwart[5] another. Antonio Gramsci's often-cited sentence comes inevitably to mind: "The crisis consists precisely in the fact that the old is dying and the new cannot be born; in this interregnum,[6] a great variety of <u>morbid</u> symptoms appears." The old surely is dying, but I'm not so sure that the new is having any great difficulty being

170 born. As for the morbid symptoms, these we have in abundance. The overlap in communications modes, and the ways of living that they are associated with, invites comparison with the transitional epoch in ancient Greek society, certainly in terms of the relative degree of disturbance. Historian Eric Havelock designated that period as one of "proto-literacy," of which his fellow scholar Oswyn Murray has written:

   To him [Havelock] the basic shift from oral to literate culture was a slow process; for centuries, despite the

180 existence of writing, Greece remained essentially an oral culture. This culture was one which depended heavily on the encoding of information in poetic texts, to be learned by rote and to provide a cultural encyclopedia of conduct. It was not until the age of Plato[7] in the fourth century that the dominance of poetry in an oral culture was challenged in the final triumph of literacy.

   That challenge came in the form of philosophy, among other things, and poetry has never recovered its cultural primacy. What oral poetry was for the Greeks, printed books

190 in general are for us. But our historical moment, which we might call "proto-electronic," will not require a transition period of two centuries. The very essence of electronic

---

5. **athwart.** In opposition to
6. **interregnum.** Period of time between two reigns
7. **Plato.** Greek philosopher (*circa* 427–347 BC)

words for everyday use

mor • bid (môr' bəd) *adj.,* of, relating to, or characteristic of disease. *Because of her <u>morbid</u> condition, Mrs. Washburn sought a doctor's diagnosis.*

transmissions is to <u>surmount</u> impedances[8] and to hasten transitions. Fifty years, I'm sure, will suffice. As for what the conversion will bring—and *mean*—to us, we might glean a few clues by looking to some of the "morbid symptoms" of the change. But to understand what these <u>portend</u>, we need to remark a few of the more obvious ways in which our various technologies condition our senses and sensibilities.

200   I won't tire my reader with an extended rehash of the differences between the print orientation and that of electronic systems. Media theorists from Marshall McLuhan to Walter Ong to Neil Postman have discoursed upon these at length. What's more, they are reasonably common-sensical. I therefore will abbreviate.

The order of print is linear, and is bound to logic by the <u>imperatives</u> of syntax. Syntax is the substructure of <u>discourse</u>, a mapping of the ways that the mind makes sense through language. Print communication requires the active

210   engagement of the reader's attention, for reading is fundamentally an act of translation. Symbols are turned into their verbal referents and these are in turn interpreted. The print engagement is essentially private. While it does represent an act of communication, the contents pass from the privacy of the sender to the privacy of the receiver. Print also <u>posits</u> a time axis; the turning of pages, not to mention the vertical descent down the page, is a forward-moving succession, with earlier contents at every point serving as a ground for what follows. Moreover, the printed material is

220   static—it is the reader, not the book, that moves forward. The physical arrangements of print are in accord with our traditional sense of history. Materials are layered; they lend themselves to rereading—and to sustained attention. The

THINK AND REFLECT

Reread lines 194–197. What is Birkerts's attitude toward the change that took place in Greece and the changes that are occurring in our society today? How can you tell? (Infer)

_____

_____

_____

NOTE THE FACTS

How are we affected by the way information is presented (lines 209–242)?

_____

_____

_____

_____

_____

---

8. **impedances.** Hindrances; things that impede, or interfere with the progress of

words for everyday use

sur • mount (sər mount') *vt.*, overcome; prevail over. *Suzie was in such a good mood she felt she could <u>surmount</u> any obstacle that came her way.*

por • tend (pôr tend') *vt.*, give an omen or anticipatory sign of; indicate. *The black clouds <u>portend</u> a bad storm.*

im • per • a • tive (im per' ə tiv) *n.*, something that is obligatory. *The <u>imperatives</u> of the scientific approach were neglected in the study.*

dis • course (dis' kōrs) *n.*, verbal interchange of ideas; conversation. *Tim found the <u>discourse</u> of the guest speaker difficult to follow because he used a lot of compound-complex sentences and difficult vocabulary.*

pos • it (pä' zət) *vt.*, suggest; propose as an explanation. *Galileo <u>posited</u> the observation that bodies do not fall with velocities proportional to their weights.*

pace of reading is variable, with progress determined by the reader's focus and comprehension.

The electronic order is in most ways opposite. Information and contents do not simply move from one private space to another, but they travel along a network. Engagement is <u>intrinsically</u> public, taking place within a circuit of larger
230 connectedness. The vast resources of the network are always there, potential, even if they do not <u>impinge</u> on the immediate communication. Electronic communication can be passive, as with television watching, or interactive, as with computers. Contents, unless they are printed out (at which point they become part of the static order of print) are felt to be evanescent.[9] They can be changed or deleted with the stroke of a key. With visual media (television, projected graphs, highlighted "bullets") impression and image take precedence over logic and concept, and detail and linear
240 sequentiality are sacrificed. The pace is rapid, driven by jump-cut[10] <u>increments</u>, and the basic movement is laterally associative rather than vertically cumulative. The presentation structures the reception and, in time, the expectation about how information is organized.

Further, the visual and nonvisual technology in every way encourages in the user a heightened and ever-changing awareness of the present. It works against historical perception, which must depend on the inimical[11] notions of logic and sequential succession. If the print medium <u>exalts</u>
250 the word, fixing it into permanence, the electronic counterpart reduces it to a signal, a means to an end.

---

9. **evanescent.** Tending to vanish like vapor
10. **jump-cut.** Film term referring to the conclusion of a scene brought about by removing or accelerating the middle part
11. **inimical.** Hostile or unfriendly

words for everyday use

in • trin • si • cal • ly (in trin′ zi kə lē) *adv.*, in a manner showing the essential nature or constitution of a thing. *Intrinsically, a diamond is worth more if it is not flawed.*

im • pinge (im pinj′) *vi.*, have an effect. *The rain impinged on my decision to take a walk.*

in • cre • ment (in′ krə ment) *n.*, action or process of increasing in quantity or value. *Ted's wages increased in increments until he was finally making eight dollars an hour.*

ex • alt (ig zôlt′) *vt.*, elevate by praise or in estimation. *Joanna exalted her boyfriend and did not see him realistically.*

Transitions like the one from print to electronic media do not take place without rippling or, more likely, *reweaving* the entire social and cultural web. The tendencies outlined above are already at work. We don't need to look far to find their effects. We can begin with the newspaper headlines and the millennial lamentations[12] sounded in the op-ed[13] pages: that our educational systems are in decline; that our students are less and less able to read and comprehend their required texts, and that their aptitude scores have leveled off well below those of previous generations. Tag-line communication, called "bite-speak" by some, is destroying the last remnants of political discourse; spin doctors and media consultants are our new shamans.[14] As communications empires fight for control of all information outlets, including publishers, the latter have <u>succumbed</u> to the tyranny of the bottom line; they are less and less willing to publish work, however worthy, that will not make a tidy profit. And, on every front, funding for the arts is being cut while the arts themselves appear to be suffering a deep crisis of <u>relevance</u>. And so on.

Every one of these developments is, of course, over-determined, but there can be no doubt that they are connected, perhaps profoundly, to the transition that is underway. ■

260

270

---

12. **lamentations.** Acts or instances of expressing sorrow, mourning, or regret
13. **op-ed.** Page of special features usually opposite the editorial page of a newspaper
14. **shamans.** Priests who use magic for the purpose of curing the sick, divining the hidden, and controlling events

words for everyday use

suc • cumb (sə kum′) *vi.*, yield to superior strength or force or overpowering appeal or desire. *Rob <u>succumbed</u> to his desire for chocolate and ate a Hershey bar.*

rel • e • vance (re′ lə ven(t)s) *n.*, pertinence; relation to the matter at hand. *The geometry teacher was used to students questioning the <u>relevance</u> of geometry to their everyday lives.*

Reflect ON YOUR READING

After Reading ➤ OWN THE MEANINGS OF NEW WORDS

Form a group of three or four students. For each new word on your lists, fill out a Word Concept Map. Then work as a group to create a sentence completion test. Start by creating a contextual sentence for ten of the words. Then rewrite each sentence, replacing the vocabulary word with a blank. Provide four multiple-choice answers labeled *a, b, c,* and *d.* Trade tests with another group and work together to complete the new test.

Reading Skills and Test Practice

USE CONTEXT CLUES
Discuss with a partner how to answer the following questions about words in context.

1. Read the following sentence from the selection.

   The electronic media, while conspicuous in gadgetry, are very nearly invisible in their functioning.

   What does *conspicuous* mean?

   a. complicated
   b. visible
   c. unnatural
   d. complex

What is the correct answer to the question above? How were you able to eliminate the other answers? How did your application of the reading strategy help you answer the question?

_____

_____

2. Read the following sentence from the selection.

   Inevitably, one of the first realizations is that a communications net, a soft and pliable mesh woven from invisible threads, has fallen over everything.

   What does *pliable* mean?

   a. slow
   b. sturdy
   c. flexible
   d. delicate

What is the correct answer to the question above? How were you able to eliminate the other answers? How did your application of the reading strategy help you answer the question?

_____

_____

Investigate, Inquire, and Imagine

RECALL: GATHER FACTS
1a. Who was Gutenberg?

→ INTERPRET: FIND MEANING
1b. The selection you have just read is taken from a book called *The Gutenberg Elegies*. An elegy is a poem that expresses sorrow over a death. Why do you think Birkerts gave the book this title?

ANALYZE: TAKE THINGS APART
2a. Analyze Birkerts's prediction about how literacy will change.

→ SYNTHESIZE: BRING THINGS TOGETHER
2b. What is Birkerts's attitude about this change?

EVALUATE: MAKE JUDGMENTS
3a. Evaluate how realistically Birkerts portrays the electronic age in this essay.

→ EXTEND: CONNECT IDEAS
3b. Statistics from the book industry suggest that book buying is on the rise. What do you think would be Birkerts's reaction to this information?

Literary Tools

DICTION. **Diction,** when applied to writing, refers to word choice. Much of a writer's style is determined by his or her diction, the types of words that he or she chooses. Complete the cluster chart listing words that you think are characteristic of Birkerts's diction. One example has been done for you.

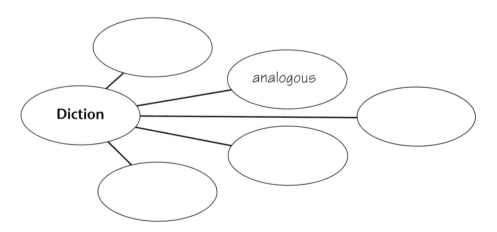

Looking at these words, what adjectives would you use to describe his diction in general?

_____

_____

WordWorkshop

PREFIXES AND SUFFIXES. For each of the following Words for Everyday Use, circle any prefix or suffix contained in the word. Give a brief definition of the prefix or suffix. With each prefix or suffix that you identify, create a new word and use it in a sentence. An example has been done for you.

> **EXAMPLE**   conglomerate
> prefix, if any, and its meaning: *con–; with; together*
> new word using prefix: *congregate*
> sentence: *The neighbors congregated at the local park on the day of the picnic.*
> suffix, if any, and its meaning: *–ate; one acted upon; function or rank*
> new word using suffix: *delegate*
> sentence: *She was chosen as a delegate at the convention.*

1. conspicuous

2. corroboration

3. discourse

4. eradicate

5. corroboration

Read-Write Connection

What do you think Birkerts would say about the immense expansion of Internet use that has occurred since this essay was published in 1994?

_____

_____

_____

_____

_____

_____

_____

Beyond the Reading

RESEARCHING MEDIA THEORY. Research a media theory by Marshall McLuhan, Walter Ong, or Neil Postman, whom Birkerts refers to in his essay. Then get together with other students in your class who researched the same theory. Think of an interesting way to introduce the theory to the rest of the class.

GO ONLINE. Visit the EMC Internet Resource Center at **emcp.com** to find links and additional activities for this selection.

from The Victorian Internet
by Tom Standage

Active READING STRATEGY

WRITE THINGS DOWN

Before Reading ➤ **DEVISE A PLAN FOR RECORDING INFORMATION**

❑ Read the Reader's Resource.
❑ Participate in a class discussion in which you share ways that you record information when reading—for example, taking notes, making an outline, marking key ideas, using sticky notes, or using graphic organizers.
❑ Take notes in the chart below as you read the selection.

Graphic Organizer

Section Heading or Page Number	Main Ideas and My Reactions
Summary of My Notes	

CONNECT

Reader's resource

In his book *The Victorian Internet* (1998), British journalist Tom Standage compares the nineteenth-century telegraph with the present-day Internet. By showing how closely they are related, he explains the significance of both. In this excerpt from the book, Standage points out commonalities of the two inventions and cautions against seeing new technology as a cure-all for society's ills.

Word watch

PREVIEW VOCABULARY

encrypt	obsolete
enmity	optimistic
explicitly	panacea
facilitate	protocol
generic	purport
gullibility	quintessentially
hype	skepticism
inaugurate	subsequently
laud	

Reader's journal

For what purposes do you use the Internet?

_____

_____

_____

NOTE THE FACTS

What is the technological foundation for the phone, fax, and Internet?

_____

_____

_____

Literary TOOLS

COMPARISON-CONTRAST. Comparison-contrast presents similarities as it compares two things and presents differences as it contrasts them. As you read, note the similarities between the telegraph and the Internet.

from The Victorian Internet

Tom Standage

Although it has now faded from view, the telegraph lives on within the communications technologies that have <u>subsequently</u> built up on its foundations: the telephone, the fax machine, and, more recently, the Internet. And, ironically, it is the Internet—despite being regarded as a <u>quintessentially</u> modern means of communication—that has the most in common with its telegraphic ancestor.

Like the telegraph network, the Internet allows people to communicate across great distances using interconnected networks. (Indeed, the <u>generic</u> term *internet* simply means a group of interconnected networks.) Common rules and <u>protocols</u> enable any sort of computer to exchange messages with any other—just as messages could easily be passed from one kind of telegraph apparatus (a Morse printer, say) to another (a pneumatic tube). The journey of an e-mail

10

words for everyday use

sub • se • quent • ly (sub' si kwent lē) *adv.*, following in order of time or place; succeeding. *The college <u>subsequently</u> put Josh on probation.*

quin • tes • sen • tial • ly (kwin' tə sen(t)' shəl ē) *adv.*, most purely. *Writer Jack Kerouac expressed the essence of the Beat Generation <u>quintessentially</u> in* On the Road.

ge • ner • ic (jə ner' ik) *adj.*, descriptive of all members of a group or category, not specific or individual, general. *She buys <u>generic</u> food brands because they are cheaper.*

pro • to • col (prō' tə kol) *n.*, established, precise, and correct procedures. *Lawyers must follow <u>protocol</u> to defend their clients.*

message, as it hops from mail server to mail server toward its destination, mirrors the passage of a telegram from one telegraph office to the next.

20   There are even echoes of the earliest, most primitive telegraphs—such as the optical system invented by Chappe[1]—in today's modems and network hardware. Every time two computers exchange an eight-digit binary number,[2] or byte, they are going through the same motions as an eight-panel shutter telegraph would have done two hundred years ago. Instead of using a codebook to relate each combination to a different word, today's computers use another agreed-upon protocol to transmit individual letters. This scheme, called ASCII (for American Standard Code for Information Interchange), says, for example, that a

30 capital "A" should be represented by the pattern 01000001; but in essence the principles are unchanged since the late eighteenth century. Similarly, Chappe's system had special codes to increase or reduce the rate of transmission, or to request that garbled information be sent again—all of which are features of modems today. The protocols used by modems are decided on by the ITU, the organization founded in 1865 to regulate international telegraphy. The initials now stand for International Telecommunication Union, rather than International Telegraph Union.

40   More striking still are the parallels between the social impact of the telegraph and that of the Internet. Public reaction to the new technologies was, in both cases, a confused mixture of <u>hype</u> and <u>skepticism</u>. Just as many Victorians[3] believed the telegraph would eliminate misunderstanding between nations and usher in a new era of world peace, an avalanche of media coverage has <u>lauded</u> the

---

1. **optical system invented by Chappe.** Claude Chappe (1763–1805) was a French inventor who, with his brother Ignace, made a visual signal line, a visual telegraph, between two points on the war front during the French revolution. The device had two arms that formed positions representing the alphabet.
2. **binary number.** Number that has two as its base
3. **Victorians.** People who lived during the period of Queen Victoria's reign in England (1837–1901)

| words for everyday use | **hype** (hīp) *n., slang,* promotion or attention from, for example, the media. *The <u>hype</u> about his first movie made him seem like a big star.*
 skep • ti • cism (skep′ tə si zəm) *n.,* attitude of doubt or suspended judgment. *Because of his <u>skepticism</u>, he didn't support the Internet until he had tried it himself.*
 laud (lôd) *vt.,* sing the praises of. *He was <u>lauded</u> for his performance in the play.* |

Reading TIP

Note that this selection focuses on the past in an effort to understand more clearly the present as well as the future direction of technological innovations.

Use THE STRATEGY

WRITE THINGS DOWN. Summarize the comparisons made in the first three paragraphs between the telegraph and the Internet.

_____

_____

_____

_____

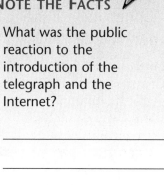

NOTE THE FACTS

What was the public reaction to the introduction of the telegraph and the Internet?

_____

_____

FIX-UP IDEA

Make Predictions
With a partner, make predictions about what other areas of comparison Standage is going to make between the telegraph and the Internet.

NOTE THE FACTS

What did Negroponte claim children will not know in the future?

_____

_____

NOTE THE FACTS

What kind of software is used today and what does it prevent?

_____

_____

_____

Internet as a powerful new medium that will transform and improve our lives.

Some of these claims sound oddly familiar. In his 1997
50 book _What Will Be: How the New World of Information Will Change Our Lives_, Michael Dertouzos of the Laboratory for Computer Science at the Massachusetts Institute of Technology wrote of the prospect of "computer-aided peace" made possible by digital networks like the Internet. "A common bond reached through electronic proximity may help stave off future flareups of ethnic hatred and national breakups," he suggested. In a conference speech in November 1997, Nicholas Negroponte, head of the MIT Media Laboratory, <u>explicitly</u> declared that the Internet
60 would break down national borders and lead to world peace. In the future, he claimed, children "are not going to know what nationalism is."

The similarities do not end there. Scam artists found crooked ways to make money by manipulating the transmission of stock prices and the results of horse races using the telegraph; their twentieth-century counterparts have used the Internet to set up fake "shop fronts" <u>purporting</u> to be legitimate providers of financial services, before disappearing with the money handed over by would-
70 be investors; hackers[4] have broken into improperly secured computers and made off with lists of credit card numbers.

People who were worried about inadequate security on the telegraph network, and now on the Internet, turned to the same solution: secret codes. Today software to compress files and <u>encrypt</u> messages before sending them across the Internet is as widely used as the commercial codes that flourished on the telegraph network. And just as the ITU placed restrictions on the use of telegraphic ciphers,[5] many governments today are trying to do the same with computer
80 cryptography, by imposing limits on the complexity of the encryption available to Internet users. (The ITU, it should

---

4. **hackers.** People who perform illegal activities and break-ins on computers
5. **ciphers.** Messages in code

words for everyday use

ex • plic • it • ly (ik spli′ sət lē) _adv._, clearly expressed, directly stated. _He <u>explicitly</u> stated there should be no photographs taken in the museum._

pur • port (pər pōrt′) _vt._, claim or imply something that might not be true. _The IRS sent a letter <u>purporting</u> we owed back taxes._

en • crypt (en kript′) _vt._, encipher or encode. _The spy <u>encrypted</u> the message._

be noted, proved unable to enforce its rules restricting the types of code words that could be used in telegrams, and eventually abandoned them.)

On a simpler level, both the telegraph and the Internet have given rise to their own jargon and abbreviations. Rather than plugs, boomers, or bonus men, Internet users are variously known as surfers, netheads, or netizens. Personal signatures, used by both telegraphers and Internet users, are known in both cases as sigs.

Another parallel is the eternal <u>enmity</u> between new, inexperienced users and experienced old hands. Highly skilled telegraphers in city offices would lose their temper when forced to deal with hopelessly inept operators in remote villages; the same phenomenon was widespread on the Internet when the masses first surged on-line in the early 1990s, unaware of customs and traditions that had held sway on the Internet for years and capable of what, to experienced users, seemed unbelievable stupidity, <u>gullibility</u>, and impoliteness.

But while conflict and rivalry both seem to come with the on-line territory, so does romance. A general fascination with the romantic possibilities of the new technology has been a feature of both the nineteenth and twentieth centuries: On-line weddings have taken place over both the telegraph and the Internet. In 1996, Sue Helle and Lynn Bottoms were married on-line by a minister ten miles away in Seattle, echoing the story of Philip Reade and Clara Choate, who were married by telegraph 120 years earlier by a minister 650 miles away. Both technologies have also been directly blamed for causing romantic problems. In 1996, a New Jersey man filed for divorce when he discovered that his wife had been exchanging explicit e-mail with another man, a case that was widely reported as the first example of "Internet divorce."

After a period of initial skepticism, businesses became the most enthusiastic adopters of the telegraph in the

90

100

110

**words
for
everyday
use**

en • mi • ty (en′ mə tē) _n._, ill will, hostility, antagonism. _Until she stomped out he hadn't realized she felt such <u>enmity</u> toward him._

gul • li • bil • i • ty (gə lə bi′ lə tē) _n._, state of being easily deceived or cheated; naïveté. _Her <u>gullibility</u> made her believe him when he said the moon was bigger than the sun._

MARK THE TEXT

Underline or highlight the innovations that people thought would solve the world's problems.

nineteenth century and the Internet in the twentieth. Businesses have always been prepared to pay for premium
120 services like private leased lines and value-added information—provided those services can provide a competitive advantage in the marketplace. Internet sites routinely offer stock prices and news headlines, both of which were available over a hundred years ago via stock tickers[6] and news wires. And just as the telegraph led to a direct increase in the pace and stress of business life, today the complaint of information overload, blamed on the Internet, is commonplace.

The telegraph also made possible new business practices,
130 <u>facilitating</u> the rise of large companies centrally controlled from a head office. Today, the Internet once again promises to redefine the way people work, through emerging trends like teleworking (working from a distant location, with a network connection to one's office) and virtual corporations (where there is no central office, just a distributed group of employees who communicate over a network).

The similarities between the telegraph and the Internet— both in their technical underpinnings and their social impact—are striking. But the story of the telegraph
140 contains a deeper lesson. Because of its ability to link distant peoples, the telegraph was the first technology to be seized upon as a <u>panacea</u>. Given its potential to change the world, the telegraph was soon being hailed as a means of solving the world's problems. It failed to do so, of course— but we have been pinning the same hope on other new technologies ever since.

In the 1890s, advocates of electricity claimed it would eliminate the drudgery of manual work and create a world of abundance and peace. In the first decade of the twentieth
150 century, aircraft inspired similar flights of fancy: Rapid intercontinental travel would, it was claimed, eliminate international differences and misunderstandings. (One

---

6. **stock tickers.** Telegraphic receivers that print information, like stock prices, on paper

words for everyday use

fa • cil • i • tate (fə sil' ə tāt) vt., make easier. *Her research <u>facilitated</u> the discovery.*
pan • a • ce • a (pa nə sē' ə) n., universal remedy, cure-all. *Jokes are a <u>panacea</u> for sadness.*

commentator suggested that the age of aviation would be an "age of peace" because aircraft would make armies <u>obsolete</u>, since they would be vulnerable to attack from the air.) Similarly, television was expected to improve education, reduce social isolation, and enhance democracy. Nuclear power was supposed to usher in an age of plenty where electricity would be "too cheap to meter." The
160   <u>optimistic</u> claims now being made about the Internet are merely the most recent examples in a tradition of technological utopianism[7] that goes back to the first transatlantic telegraph cables, 150 years ago.

    That the telegraph was so widely seen as a panacea is perhaps understandable. The fact that we are still making the same mistake today is less so. The irony is that even though it failed to live up to the utopian claims made about it, the telegraph really did transform the world. It also redefined forever our attitudes toward new technologies.
170   In both respects, we are still living in the new world it <u>inaugurated</u>. ■

---

7. **utopianism.** Utopia is an imaginary place that has ideal laws and perfect social conditions. Utopianism refers to impossible schemes for social improvement.

words for everyday use	**ob • so • lete** (äb sə lēt´) *adj.*, no longer active or in use. *Cash is almost becoming <u>obsolete</u> because of credit and debit cards.*
	op • ti • mis • tic (äp tə mis´ tik) *adj.*, anticipating the best. *She was <u>optimistic</u> about graduating from college summa cum laude because she earned nearly all A's.*
	in • au • gu • rate (i nä´ gyə rāt) *vt.*, begin, introduce, or mark a start of. *She <u>inaugurated</u> her business by having an open house.*

Reflect ON YOUR READING

After Reading ➤ SYNTHESIZE MAIN IDEAS

When you finish reading, end your Note-Taking Chart with a statement that summarizes the main idea of the whole selection. Then, use that sentence as the thesis statement for a brief essay in which you summarize the main points of the selection. When you finish writing your essay, share it with a partner, and discuss similarities and differences in your interpretations of the selection's main ideas.

THINK-ALOUD
NOTES

_____

_____

_____

_____

_____

_____

_____

_____

_____

_____

_____

Reading Skills and Test Practice

COMPARE AND CONTRAST MODES OF COMMUNICATION
Discuss with a partner how to answer the following questions about comparing and contrasting.

1. Which of the following is *not* an example of how the telegraph and the Internet are similar?

   a. The public reacted with skepticism to both when they first appeared.
   b. People found ways to use both for illegal actions.
   c. Both became more popular among young people than among older generations.
   d. Both have been used enthusiastically by people in the business world.

What is the correct answer to the question above? How were you able to eliminate the other answers? How did your application of the reading strategy help you answer the question?

_____

_____

2. Which of the following statements is true and could be supported with details from the text?

   a. The Internet is simply a modern version of the telegraph.
   b. As did the telegraph, the Internet will fall into disuse someday.
   c. The telegraph was a more reliable means of communicating over long distances.
   d. While people in Victorian times were skeptical of the telegraph, people in modern times immediately embraced the Internet.

What is the correct answer to the question above? How were you able to eliminate the other answers? How did your application of the reading strategy help you answer the question?

_____

_____

Investigate, Inquire, and Imagine

RECALL: GATHER FACTS
1a. What were some of the negative effects of the Internet and the telegraph?

→ INTERPRET: FIND MEANING
1b. What ways to avoid these negative aspects were developed?

ANALYZE: TAKE THINGS APART
2a. What might be the point of comparing the design of a cutting edge technological development to one that is now almost obsolete?

→ SYNTHESIZE: BRING THINGS TOGETHER
2b. Identify the way the telegraph and the Internet are most fundamentally alike.

EVALUATE: MAKE JUDGMENTS
3a. What are some of the positive predictions about the Internet, and why does the article suggest that they are overly optimistic?

→ EXTEND: CONNECT IDEAS
3b. According to Sven Birkerts, who wrote "Into the Electronic Millennium," transitions brought about by technological innovation do not take place without "reweaving the entire social and cultural web." How does Birkerts's viewpoint compare with Standage's?

Literary Tools

COMPARISON-CONTRAST. **Comparison-contrast** presents similarities as it compares two things and presents differences as it contrasts them. Draw a Venn Diagram like the one below and complete it with examples from the text of the similarities between the telegraph and the Internet. Use your own ideas to identify differences between the telegraph and the Internet. Record these in the outer parts of the circles.

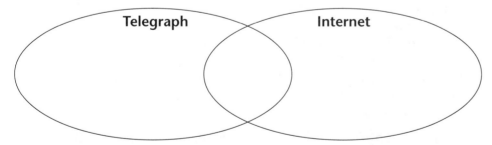

A comparison-contrast essay is usually organized in one of two ways: either presenting all the characteristics of one subject and then of the other, or by comparing and contrasting both subjects with regard to one characteristic and then another. Which of the two ways of organizing a comparison-contrast essay does Standage use.

_____

_____

WordWorkshop

PREFIXES AND SUFFIXES. Work with a partner to choose five words from the WordWatch box on page 429. Change each of the five words by adding or subtracting a prefix or suffix. Write the original word and then the new word. An example has been done for you.

EXAMPLE

encrypt   *encryption*

1._____   _____
2._____   _____
3._____   _____
4._____   _____
5._____   _____

Read-Write Connection

What will you remember from reading this selection? Explain.

_____

_____

_____

_____

Beyond the Reading

INTERNET RESEARCH LOG. Determine a topic of interest to you that you want to research on the Internet. Narrow your topic of research and write a statement about it, for example, "I want to find out what music has influenced singer John Mayer." Cite useful websites, following the format below. Evaluate each site in terms of accuracy and usefulness to your topic. After you have filled out your Internet Research Log and taken relevant notes, write a brief report on your topic and share it with a small group of your classmates.

DeMille, Justin. The Music Page. "Songwriter John Mayer Follows His Passion." 12 Oct. 2003, updated 4 Jan. 2004. http://www.musicpage.com/12469/.

GO ONLINE. Visit the EMC Internet Resource Center at **emcp.com** to find links and additional activities for this selection.

"The Roots of Genius?
The Odd History of a Famous Old Brain"

by Steven Levy

Active READING STRATEGY

VISUALIZE

Before Reading ➤ **PREVIEW THE SELECTION**

❑ Read the Reader's Resource.

❑ Study the diagram of Einstein's brain on page 441. Based on this diagram and the caption that accompanies it, predict what the article will say about Einstein's outstanding abilities.

❑ Preview the Time Line below. You will use this diagram to keep track of findings about Einstein's brain. As you read, you will mark events affecting Einstein's brain along this line. The first entry has been done for you.

Graphic Organizer

1955

removed from Einstein's body

CONNECT

Reader's resource

"The Roots of Genius? The Odd History of a Famous Old Brain" appeared in a 1999 issue of *Newsweek*. This article deals with the brain of famous scientist Albert Einstein. At the age of twenty-six, Einstein described his theory of relativity, which changed forever how scientists view matter, energy, and the measurement of time and distance. Einstein is considered one of the greatest geniuses of the twentieth century. As a result, neuroanatomists, or scientists who study the anatomy of the nervous system, are curious about whether or not his brain is different from the brains of most people. Could his genius be the result of a physical difference in his brain?

Reader's journal

What do you think determines a person's personality and ability level? Do you believe that your personality is a result of physical characteristics of your brain? of your genetic code? Or do you think that the personality is shaped more by life circumstances than by biology?

_____

_____

_____

VISUALIZE

❑ Read the selection on your own, referring to the diagram to help you understand what you read. Try to visualize the images of Einstein's brain segments, the glial cells, and the lobes.

❑ Keep track of the different scientists and their findings on your Time Line.

MARK THE TEXT

Underline what the *Lancet* article says about Einstein's brain.

NOTE THE FACTS

Where does Dr. Harvey keep the brain? What has he found in his study of it?

_____

_____

READ ALOUD

Read the highlighted paragraph aloud. What was found in the study prompted by Levy's article? What was found in the 1996 study? Record your answers on the Time Line.

The Roots of Genius?

THE ODD HISTORY OF A FAMOUS OLD BRAIN

Steven Levy

Albert Einstein's death, in 1955, hasn't stopped his brain from leading a lively existence. Its visit to McMaster University in Ontario, Canada, has led to an article in the June 19 *Lancet* (a British medical journal) affirming that maybe, just maybe, the secrets of relativity were due in part to unusual development of a lobe known for mathematical thought. And then again, maybe not.

It was just one more chapter in the twisted history of a brain that was born in 1879, hatched the secret of relativity in 1905 and was liberated from its body by a Princeton pathologist 50 years later. No further news came until the summer of 1978, when I came into the picture; my editor at a regional magazine asked me to find it. I deduced that it was still in the hands of the pathologist, Dr. Thomas Harvey. I tracked him to Wichita, Kans., where, after much cajoling, he sighed deeply and pulled from a cardboard box two glass jars with the sectioned pieces of Einstein's brain. Eureka! Harvey told me that so far in his ongoing study he'd found no variations from the norm.

My article encouraged Berkeley neuroanatomist Marian Diamond to get some samples from Harvey; she counted 73 percent more glial cells than the norm. (Glial cells help keep the network of neurons humming.) In 1996, another study indicated that the Nobel winner's cortex was "more densely populated with neurons." But there was no indication that the density led to $E=mc^2$.

The McMaster researchers, led by Sandra F. Witelson, began their work when Dr. Harvey sent them some samples in 1996, as well as photos of the brain before sectioning. Unlike brains in a control group of 35, Einstein's had a short sylvian fissure (a groove on the side), and a brain part known as the operculum was undeveloped. This may have allowed Einstein's parietal lobes, believed to affect math,

Mother Lobe

Einstein's brilliance may have been due to several distinctive brain features:

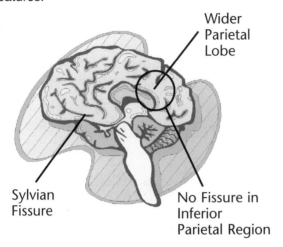

Wider Parietal Lobe

Sylvian Fissure

No Fissure in Inferior Parietal Region

FIX-UP IDEA

Tackle Difficult Vocabulary

If the scientific words in this article make it hard for you, read all the way through the article once to preview it. Then reread the article, using context clues and a dictionary to help you unlock word meanings. Finally, read the article one last time using the word meanings you discovered.

40 music and visual images, to grow 15 percent wider than average. "The thing that's compelling," says Witelson, "is that the differences occur in the region that supports psychological functions of which Einstein was a master."

The *Lancet* findings may well be a valuable jumping-off point for further research. But will taking the measure of parietal lobes really tell us why Einstein stands atop the scientific pantheon? His genius was unique, a control group of one. That's why his brain fascinates us, and has been the subject of "potboilers, poems, screenplays and paranoid cloning plots." And that's why, when I beheld Albert's brain matter bobbing in the formaldehyde like soggy tofu chunks, my own mind spun with amazement and wonder. When it comes to appreciating the most famous brain of our century, it ain't the meat—it's the emotion. ▪

THINK AND REFLECT

Why does the fact that Einstein is "a control group of one" cast doubt on the significance of the findings? **(Interpret)**

_____

_____

Reflect ON YOUR READING

Meet with a partner to compare your Time Lines. Fill in any missing information on yours. Then work with your partner to write a four-sentence summary of this article. Be sure to include what you think is the author's conclusion about Einstein's brain.

Reading Skills and Test Practice

DRAW CONCLUSIONS

Discuss with a partner how to answer the following questions that require you to draw conclusions.

1. The author appears qualified to write about this topic *mostly* because
   a. he is a scientist working on brain research.
   b. he wrote an influential article on the same topic twenty years earlier.
   c. he has consulted an overwhelming number of sources to validate his ideas.
   d. his profession is science writing.

What is the correct answer to the question above? How were you able to eliminate the other answers? How did your application of the reading strategy help you answer the question?

_____

_____

_____

_____

2. The author's final conclusion about Einstein's brain is that
   a. his genius is powerful beyond its physical features.
   b. Harvey is right that Einstein's brain is no different from the norm.
   c. the differences in Einstein's parietal lobes accounts for his genius.
   d. the findings of the scientists mentioned are invalid.

What is the correct answer to the question above? How were you able to eliminate the other answers? How did your application of the reading strategy help you answer the question?

_____

_____

_____

_____

THINK-ALOUD
NOTES

_____

_____

_____

_____

_____

_____

_____

_____

_____

_____

_____

_____

Investigate, Inquire, and Imagine

1a. What are scientists looking for when they study Einstein's brain?

1b. What assumption about where intelligence comes from are these scientists testing?

2a. List the differences various scientists have found between Einstein's brain and normal brains.

2b. What conclusions do these differences point toward?

3a. How reliable do you think the scientific findings are, based on the evidence in the article? How is the reliability affected by the fact that Einstein is "a control group of one"?

3b. Einstein once said that "the most beautiful and deepest experience a man can have is the sense of the mysterious." Given this opinion, what do you think Einstein would think about the studies on his brain?

Literary Tools

SCIENCE WRITING. **Science writing** is writing about scientific concepts and theories. Often, a science writer must make complex ideas understandable to an audience that knows little about the topic. How does the author create a friendly tone in this article?

_____

_____

_____

How does he make scientific terms understandable?

_____

_____

_____

How does his comparison of the brain segments to "soggy tofu chunks" help readers identify with the topic of the article?

_____

_____

_____

WordWorkshop

USING CONTEXT CLUES. When you come across unfamiliar words as you are reading, **context clues** can often help you estimate their meanings. Review the types of context clues on pages 20–21. Then, in the sentences below, use context clues to determine the meaning of the underlined word. Write the meaning and explain which clues helped you figure it out.

1. I tracked Dr. Thomas Harvey to Wichita, Kans., where, after much <u>cajoling</u>, he sighed deeply and pulled from a cardboard box two glass jars. . . .
   Meaning: _____
   Clue(s): _____

2. Marian Diamond counted 73 percent more <u>glial cells</u> than the norm. (Glial cells help keep the network of neurons humming.)
   Meaning: _____
   Clue(s): _____

3. Unlike brains in a <u>control group</u> of 35, Einstein's had a short sylvian fissure. . . .
   Meaning: _____
   Clue(s): _____

4. . . . . . Einstein's had a short sylvian <u>fissure</u> (a groove on the side), and a brain part known as the operculum was undeveloped.
   Meaning: _____
   Clue(s): _____

5. The thing that's <u>compelling</u> is that the differences occur in the region that supports psychological functions of which Einstein was a master.
   Meaning: _____
   Clue(s): _____

Read-Write Connection

Whose brain would you like to know more about? Why?

_____

_____

Beyond the Reading

READ ABOUT BRAINS. The brain is fascinating because there is so much we don't understand about it. In a newspaper or magazine, find an article about some aspect of brain research. Determine what the scientists have discovered. Then create a visual illustration of their findings. Use the diagram in this selection as a model or come up with your own creative way of illustrating the article's ideas.

GO ONLINE. Visit the EMC Internet Resource Center at **emcp.com** to find links and additional activities for this selection.

Unit 8 ⬤READING
Review

Choose and Use Reading Strategies

Before reading the excerpt below, review with a partner how to use each of these reading strategies.

1. Read with a Purpose
2. Connect to Prior Knowledge
3. Write Things Down
4. Make Predictions
5. Visualize
6. Use Text Organization
7. Tackle Difficult Vocabulary
8. Monitor Your Reading Progress

Now apply at least two of these reading strategies as you read the excerpt below from "The Rules of Chess." Use the margins and mark up the text to show how you are using the reading strategies to read actively.

When setting up the pieces, keep in mind two things. The light colored square goes on the player's right, and Queens go on their color next to the Kings on the center files.

You may not move a piece to a square already occupied by one of your own pieces. You may capture an opposing piece by replacing that piece with one of your own pieces, if the piece can legally move there.

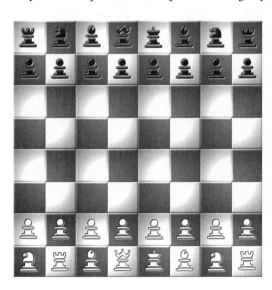

The King

The King is the most important piece. When it is trapped so it cannot move without being captured, then the game is lost. The trap is called checkmate. The King can move one square in any direction. A King can never move into check or onto a square where it can be captured by an opponent's piece.

WordWorkshop

UNIT 8 WORDS FOR EVERYDAY USE

analogous, 421	immune, 402	pigment, 402
anonymity, 409	imperative, 423	pliable, 420
burrow, 401	impinge, 424	plummet, 403
conglomerate, 421	inaugurate, 435	portend, 423
conjoining, 419	increment, 424	posit, 423
conspicuous, 419	inkling, 418	precursor, 404
corroboration, 418	innocuous, 402	prognosis, 403
derive, 404	intrinsically, 424	protocol, 430
detection, 402	juxtapose, 420	purport, 432
discourse, 423	laud, 431	quintessentially, 430
encrypt, 432	lesion, 402	ravage, 401
enmity, 433	malignant, 401	relevance, 425
eradicate, 420	morbid, 422	skepticism, 431
exalt, 424	obligatory, 410	stodgy, 419
explicitly, 432	obsolescence, 421	subsequently, 430
facilitate, 434	obsolete, 435	succumb, 425
generic, 430	omnipresence, 420	surmount, 423
gullibility, 433	optimistic, 435	vestigial, 418
hype, 431	panacea, 434	

ANTONYMS. **Antonyms** are words or phrases that are opposite in meaning. For each word below, select the appropriate antonym and write its letter in the blank.

_____ 1. subsequent
  a. conjoining   b. preceding   c. next

_____ 2 anonymity
  a. celebrity   b. evanescence   c. notoriety

_____ 3. skepticism
  a. corroboration   b. doubt   c. certainty

_____ 4. explicit
  a. vague   b. generic   c. clear

_____ 5. obsolete
     a. tangible   b. popular   c. archaic

_____ 6. pliable
     a. quiescent   b. bendable   c. rigid

_____ 7. discourse
     a. conversation   b. print   c. prognosis

_____ 8. imperative
     a. optional   b. mandatory   c. morbid

_____ 9. laud
     a. exalt   b. derive   c. criticize

_____ 10. tangible
     a. sweet   b. abstract   c. colorless

Literary Tools

Select the literary element from the column on the right that best completes each sentence on the left. Write the correct letter in the blank.

_____ 1. If you wrote a composition about the similarities and differences between your current job and your last one, you would be using _____.

_____ 2. _Time_ magazine has _____ about popular culture, politics, and entertainment.

_____ 3. You would probably expect a more academic and specialized _____ from a science professor than a middle-school student.

_____ 4. An article about a new discovery about black holes is an example of _____.

_____ 5. In her _____, the author of "Beware the Unruly Sun" presents facts about melanoma and its early detection.

a. exposition, 410

b. comparison-contrast, 430

c. science writing, 443

d. articles, 403

e. diction, 419

On Your Own

FLUENTLY SPEAKING. Find an informational or visual selection that focuses on a topic of interest to you. Read the article, and determine the tone of the author. **Tone** is the emotional attitude toward the reader or toward the subject implied by a literary work. For example, the tone might show wonder, optimism, familiarity with the reader, or seriousness, depending on the text you select. Practice reading aloud the last paragraph of the selection you have chosen. Use your voice to convey the tone of the selection. Finally, read your paragraph to the class.

PICTURE THIS. Find an informational or visual selection that focuses on a topic of interest to you. Read the article. Then draw a picture that captures some important bit of information, description, or exposition from the article.

PUT IT IN WRITING. Three of the selections in this unit—"How to Write a Letter," "Into the Electronic Millennium," and the excerpt from *The Victorian Internet*—are about communication. Find a fourth informational text about a form of communication—broadcasting, creating a website, writing a note, giving a presentation, or communicating in some other way. Then write a fictitious scene in which a character's life is impacted by this type of communication.

Unit NINE

Developing Vocabulary Skills

TACKLING DIFFICULT VOCABULARY AS YOU READ

To understand what you read, you need a set of tools for dealing with words you don't know. Glossaries and footnotes, context clues, prior knowledge of word parts and word families, and dictionaries are tools that can help you unlock the meaning of unfamiliar words.

Using Definitions, Footnotes, Endnotes, and Glossaries

Some textbooks, like this one, provide **definitions** of selected words on the page on which the word is used. **Footnotes**, like definitions, also appear on the same page as the words to which they refer. Specifically, footnotes appear at the foot, or bottom, of a page and are numbered to correspond to the words or phrases they explain. Sometimes footnotes cite a source of information. Other times they define uncommon words and phrases. If you see a superscripted number next to a word in the text you are reading (genii[3]), but can't find the footnote at the foot of the page, check the end of the article, chapter, or book. A footnote that comes at the end of a document is called an **endnote**. A **glossary** is an alphabetized list of important words and their definitions. Glossaries usually appear at the end of an article, a chapter, or a book.

To use definitions, footnotes, endnotes, and glossaries, follow these steps:

❶ Read the paragraph or short section containing the unfamiliar word to get a sense of the meaning.

❷ Check the definition, footnote, endnote, or glossary entry for the word.

❸ Reread the paragraph or section, this time keeping in mind the definition of the new word.

NOTE THE FACTS

What is the most effective way to use definitions given on the page or in a glossary?

_____

_____

_____

_____

Using Context Clues

You can often figure out the meaning of an unfamiliar word by using context clues. **Context clues**, or hints you gather from the words and sentences around the unfamiliar word, prevent you from having to look up every unknown word in the dictionary. The chart below defines the types of context clues and gives you an example of each. It also lists words that signal each type of clue.

THINK AND REFLECT

If someone says, "You have the *countenance* of my mother, who also had a rounded nose and a birthmark above her eye," what do you think *countenance* means? **(Apply)**

_____

_____

_____

Context Clues

comparison clue	shows a comparison, or how the unfamiliar word is like something that might be familiar to you
signal words	*and, like, as, just as, as if, as though*

EXAMPLE

The fan spoke *reverently* to the famous musician, as if she were meeting the Pope. (Someone would speak respectfully and humbly to the Pope, so *reverently* must mean "respectfully or with awe.")

contrast clue	shows that something contrasts, or differs in meaning, from something else
signal words	*but, nevertheless, on the other hand, however, although, though, in spite of*

EXAMPLE

In spite of my tendency to plan ahead, I agreed to the *spontaneous* trip to Central America. (The phrase "in spite of" signals a contrast between the speaker's usual behavior—planning ahead—and his or her spontaneous decision to travel to Central America. *Spontaneous* must mean "unplanned, impulsive, or sudden.")

restatement clue	uses different words to express the same idea
signal words	*that is, in other words, or*

EXAMPLE

Klista was *sequestered* after she got the chicken pox. She was secluded from her friends so that they wouldn't be exposed to the virus. (As the second sentence suggests, *sequestered* means "secluded or isolated.")

examples clue	gives examples of other items to illustrate the meaning of something
signal words	*including, such as, for example, for instance, especially, particularly*

EXAMPLE

Unfortunately, many *degenerative* diseases, such as Alzheimer's, multiple sclerosis, and cancer, transform once healthy individuals into invalids. (If you know enough about the diseases listed, you can guess that *degenerative* means "causing increasing deterioration of or reduction in health and vitality.")

CONTINUED

cause-and-effect clue	tells you that something happened as a result of something else
signal words	*if/then, when/then, thus, therefore, because, so, as a result of, consequently*

EXAMPLE

Because of the journalist's *exposé*, the public learned about hidden corruption in the city council. (If the exposé caused the public to know about something public officials didn't want known, *exposé* must mean "public exposure of a scandal.")

Using Your Prior Knowledge

You can often use your knowledge of word parts and other words to help you figure out the meaning of a new word.

BREAKING WORDS INTO BASE WORDS, WORD ROOTS, PREFIXES, AND SUFFIXES

Many words are formed by adding prefixes and suffixes to main word parts called **base words** (if they can stand alone) or **word roots** (if they can't). A **prefix** is a letter or group of letters added to the beginning of a word to change its meaning. A **suffix** is a letter or group of letters added to the end of a word to change its meaning.

Word Part	Definition	Example
base word	main word part that can stand alone	firm
word root	main word part that can't stand alone	liber
prefix	letter or group of letters added to the beginning of the word	hyper–
suffix	letter or group of letters added to the end of the word	–ish

When you encounter an unfamiliar word, check to see if you recognize the meaning of the prefix, suffix, base word, or word root. In combination with context clues, these meanings can help you unlock the meaning of the entire word. On the following pages are charts listing the meanings of the most common prefixes, suffixes, and word roots.

Reading STRATEGY REVIEW

READ WITH A PURPOSE. Rather than read the charts on the following pages all the way through from beginning to end, set a purpose for reading, and then let that purpose guide how you read the charts. For example, if you just want to become familiar with what prefixes, suffixes, and word roots are, read only a few lines from each chart, but read them carefully, studying how each word part contributes to the meaning of the words in the "Examples" column. Your teacher might set a purpose for you, too. If so, approach the charts as your teacher directs.

Common Prefixes

Prefix	Meaning	Examples
ambi–/amphi–	both	ambidextrous, amphibian
anti–/ant–	against; opposite	antibody, antacid
bi–	two	bicycle, biped
circum–	around; about	circumnavigate, circumstance
co–/col–/com–/con–/cor–	together	cooperate, collaborate, commingle, concentrate, correlate
counter–	contrary; complementary	counteract, counterpart
de–	opposite; remove; reduce	decipher, defrost, devalue
dia–	through; apart	dialogue, diaphanous
dis–	not; opposite of	dislike, disguise
dys–	abnormal; difficult; bad	dysfunctional, dystopia
em–/en–	into or onto; cover with; cause to be; provide with	embark, empower, enslave, enfeeble
ex–	out of; from	explode, export, extend
extra–/extro–	outward; outside; beyond	extraordinary, extrovert
hyper–	too much, too many, or extreme	hyperbole, hyperactive
hypo–	under	hypodermic
il–, im–, in–, ir–	not	illogical, impossible, inoperable, irrational
	in; within; toward; on	illuminate, imperil, infiltrate, irrigate
inter–	among or between	international, intersect
intra–/intro–	into; within; inward	introvert, intramural
meta–	after; changed	metamorphosis, metaphor
mis–	wrongly	mistake, misfire
non–	not	nonsense, nonsmoker
out–	in a manner that goes beyond	outrun, outmuscle
over–	excessive	overdone, overkill
per–	through, throughout	permeate, permanent
peri–	all around	perimeter, periscope
post–	after; later	postgame, postpone
pre–	before	prefix, premature

CONTINUED

Common Prefixes (continued)

Prefix	Meaning	Examples
pro–	before; forward	proceed, prologue
re–	again; back	redo, recall
retro–	back	retrospect, retroactive
semi–	half; partly	semicircle, semidry
sub–/sup–	under	substandard, subfloor, support
super–	above; over; exceeding	superstar, superfluous
sym–/syn–	with; together	sympathy, synonym, synergy
trans–	across; beyond	transatlantic, transfer, transcend
ultra–	too much, too many, extreme	ultraviolet, ultrasound
un–	not	unethical, unhappy
under–	below or short of a quantity or limit	underestimate, understaffed
uni–	one	unicorn, universe

Common Suffixes

Noun Suffixes	Meaning	Examples
–ance/–ancy/–ence/–ency	quality or state	defiance, independence, emergency
–age	action or process	marriage, voyage
–ant/–ent	one who	defendant, assistant, resident
–ar/–er/–or	one who	lawyer, survivor, liar
–dom	state or quality of	freedom, boredom
–es/–s	plural form of noun	siblings, trees
–ion/–tion	action or process	revolution, occasion
–ism	act; state; or system of belief	plagiarism, barbarism, Buddhism
–ist	one who does or believes something	ventriloquist, idealist
–itude, –tude	quality of, state of	multitude, magnitude
–ity/–ty	state of	longevity, infinity
–ment	action or process; state or quality; product or thing	development, government, amusement, amazement, ointment, fragment
–ness	state of	kindness, happiness

CONTINUED

Common Suffixes (continued)

Adjective Suffixes	Meaning	Examples
–able/–ible	capable of	attainable, possible
–al	having characteristics of	personal, governmental
–er	more	higher, calmer, shorter
–est	most	lowest, craziest, tallest
–ful	full of	helpful, gleeful, woeful
–ic	having characteristics of	scientific, chronic
–ish	like	childish, reddish
–ive	performs or tends toward	creative, pensive
–less	without	hapless, careless
–ous	possessing the qualities of	generous, joyous
–y	indicates description	happy, dirty, flowery
Adverb Suffixes	**Meaning**	**Examples**
–ly	in such a way	quickly, studiously, invisibly
–ward, –ways, –wise	in such a direction	toward, sideways, crosswise
Verb Suffixes	**Meaning**	**Examples**
–ate	make or cause to be	fixate, activate
–ed	past tense of verb	walked, acted, fixed
–ify/–fy	make or cause to be	vilify, magnify, glorify
–ing	indicates action in progress (present participle); can also be a noun (gerund)	running, thinking, being
–ize	bring about; cause to be	colonize, legalize

Common Word Roots

Word Root	Meaning	Examples
acr	highest point	acrobat
act	do	actor, reaction
ann/annu/enni	year	annual, bicentennial
aqu	water	aquarium, aquatic
aster, astr	star	asteroid, disastrous
aud	hear	audition, auditorium

CONTINUED

Common Word Roots (continued)		
Word Root	**Meaning**	**Examples**
bene	good	beneficial, benefactor
bibl, bibli	book	Bible
chron	time	chronic
cosm	universe; order	cosmic, cosmos
cred	believe; trust	credit, credible
cycl	circle	bicycle, cyclone
dem/demo	people	democracy
derm	skin	dermatologist
dic/dict	say	dictate, dictionary
duc/duct	lead; pull	conduct, reproduction
dyn	force, power	dynamic, dynamite
equ/equi/iqui	equal	equidistant, equitable, iniquity
fer	carry	transfer, refer
fin	end	finish, infinite
firm	firm, strong	confirm, reaffirm
flect/flex	bend	deflect, reflex, flexible
fort	strong	fortify, comfort
ge	earth	geode, geography
gress	go	progress, regress
hydr	water	hydrate
ign	fire	ignite, ignition, igneous
ject	throw	projector, eject
judic	judgment	prejudice, judicial
lect/leg	read; choose	lecture, election, collect
liber	free	liberate, liberal
loc	place	location, relocate
locut/loqu	speak	elocution, loquacious, colloquial
log/logue	word, speech, discourse	logic, dialogue
luc/lumin	shine; light	translucent, illuminate
mal	bad	malevolent
man/manu	hand	manufacture, manual

CONTINUED

Common Word Roots (continued)

Word Root	Meaning	Examples
metr	measure	metric
morph	form	morpheme, metamorphosis
mot	move	motor, emotion
mut	change	mutation, transmutable
nov	new	novelty, renovate
onym	name	synonym, antonym
path	feel; suffer; disease	sympathy, pathology
ped	foot, child	pedal, pediatrics
phon/phony	sound; voice; speech	symphony
phot	light	photography
physi	nature	physical, physics
pop	people	popular, populate
port	carry	transport, portable
psych	mind; soul	psychology, psychic
reg	rule	register, regulate
rupt	break	disrupt, interruption, rupture
scrib/script	write	describe, prescription
son	sound	sonic
spec/spect/spic	look	speculate, inspect, despicable
spir	breathe	spirit, inspiration
ter/terr	earth	inter, extraterrestrial, terrain
therm	heat	thermal
top	place	topography, topical
tract	draw; drag	retract, tractor, contract
typ	stamp; model	typical, type
ver	truth	veracity, verifiable
vert	turn	divert, introvert, extrovert
vid/vis	see	video, visual
viv	alive	vivacious, vivid
vol/volv	turn	evolution, revolve

The more meanings of prefixes, suffixes, and word roots you know, the better equipped you are to tackle difficult vocabulary words.

Even if you don't know the meaning of a word part, however, you can often figure out the meaning of a word using word parts. To do this, think of as many familiar words as you can that contain each part of the word.

For example, if you were tackling the word *ambivert*, you might first think of words beginning with the prefix *ambi–: ambidextrous*, *ambivalent*, and *ambiguous*. You know that ambidextrous means to be able to do things with both the right and left hand. You're pretty sure that the other two words also have something to do with taking up both positions or sides. (You could check out this hunch by looking in a dictionary.) Then you might think of words that contain *vert: divert*, *introvert*, and *extrovert*. Introvert and extrovert have to do with turning inward and turning outward, respectively. Divert also has something to do with turning. From this information, you might guess (correctly) that *vert* means turn. An ambivert is someone who turns both inward and outward, someone who has characteristics of both an introvert and extrovert!

This process is even easier when you work with a partner. Think aloud with your partner about how to break apart a word. Then discuss the meanings of each part and a possible meaning for the entire word.

RECOGNIZING COMBINING FORMS

Some word roots have become very common in English and are used all the time in combination with each other and with base words to create new scientific, medical, and technical terms. These combining forms can look like prefixes and suffixes, but contain more core meaning. The chart on the next page defines and gives examples of some common combining forms that will help you tackle new words.

NOTE THE FACTS

How can you use word parts to figure out the meaning of a new word?

_____

_____

_____

_____

_____

THINK AND REFLECT

Think aloud about how you would use word parts to figure out the meaning of the word *multitude*. Record notes from your think aloud here. (Apply)

_____

_____

_____

_____

_____

Combining Forms		
Word Part	**Meaning**	**Examples**
acro–	heights	acrophobia
anthropo–	human being	anthropologist
archaeo–/arche–	old	archeology
astr–/astro–	star	astronaut, astrology
audio–	hear	audiovisual
auto–	self	autobiography, automatic
bi–/bio–	life	biography, biosphere
bibli–/biblio–	book	bibliography
–centric	having such a center	egocentric
chron–/chrono–	time	chronology
–cracy	form of government; social or political class	aristocracy, democracy
ethno–	race; people; cultural group	ethnography
ge–/geo–	earth; soil	geography, geology
–graph/–graphy	something written, drawn, or represented by graphics	telegraph, photography
hydr–/hydro–	water	hydroelectric, hydrometer
–logy/–ology	study of	geology, biology
mal–	bad	malfunction, malnutrition
–mania	madness	kleptomania, megalomania
–metry	having to do with measure	geometry, symmetry
micro–	small; minute	microscope, microcosm
omni–	all	omnipresent, omnibus
–onym	name	synonym, antonym
–phile	one who loves	bibliophile
–phobe	one who has an irrational fear	arachnophobe, acrophobe
–phobia	exaggerated fear of	claustrophobia, photophobia
phon–/–phone/phono–	sound; voice; speech	telephone, phonograph
phot–/–photo–	light	photograph, telephoto
physi–/physio–	nature; physical	physiological
pseud–/pseudo–	false	pseudonym, pseudointellectual
psych–/psycho–	mind	psychiatrist, psychology
–scope/–scopy	view	telescope, microscopy
–ster	one who does or is	mobster, spinster
therm–/thermo–	heat	thermometer, thermodynamics
tel–/tele–	distant	telegram, telephone

EXPLORING WORD ORIGINS AND WORD FAMILIES

The English language expands constantly and gathers new words from many different sources. Understanding the source of a word can help you unlock its meaning.

One source of new words is the names of people and places associated with the thing being named. Words named for people and places are called **eponyms**.

EXAMPLES	
shrapnel	British Lieutenant General Henry Shrapnel invented a weapon consisting of a shell that released bullets or small shards of metal.
braille	Louis Braille, a French teacher of the visually impaired who was blind himself, developed a written language for the blind.

Another source for new words is **acronyms**. Acronyms are words formed from the first letter or letters of the major parts of terms.

EXAMPLES
scuba, from *self-contained underwater breathing apparatus*
HMO, from *health maintenance organization*

Some words in the English language are borrowed from other languages.

EXAMPLES
ramen (Japanese), **guerrilla** (Spanish), **tattoo** (Tahitian)

Many words are formed by shortening longer words.

EXAMPLES
movie, from *moving pictures*
pants, from *pantaloons*
zoo, from *zoological garden*

Brand names are often taken into the English language. People begin to use these words as common nouns, even though most of them are still brand names.

EXAMPLES
Q-tip   Coke   Band Aid

THINK AND REFLECT

How might understanding word origins help you unlock word meanings? **(Extend)**

_____

_____

_____

_____

_____

_____

Using a Dictionary

When you can't figure out a word using the strategies already described, or when the word is important to the meaning of the text and you want to make sure you have it right, use a dictionary.

There are many parts to a dictionary entry. Study the following sample. Then read the explanations of each part of an entry below.

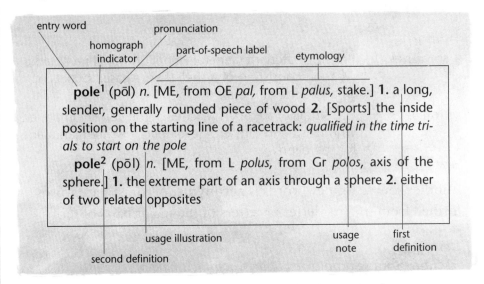

The **pronunciation** is given immediately after the entry word. The dictionary's table of contents will tell you where you can find a complete key to pronunciation symbols. In some dictionaries, a simplified pronunciation key is provided at the bottom of each page.

An abbreviation of the **part of speech** usually follows the pronunciation. This label tells how the word can be used. If a word can be used as more than one part of speech, a separate entry is provided for each part of speech.

An **etymology** is the history of the word. In the first entry, the word *pole* can be traced back through Middle English (ME) and Old English (OE) to the Latin (L) word *palus*, which means "stake." In the second entry, the word *pole* can be traced back through Middle English to the Latin word *polus*, which comes from the Greek (Gr) word *polos*, meaning "axis of the sphere."

Sometimes the entry will include a list of **synonyms**, or words that have the same or very similar meanings. The entry may also include a **usage illustration**, which is an example of how the word is used in context.

Understanding Multiple Meanings

Each definition in the entry gives a different meaning of the word. When a word has more than one meaning, the different definitions are numbered. The first definition in an entry is the most common meaning of the word, but you will have to choose the meaning that fits the context in which you have found the word. Try substituting each definition for the word until you find the one that makes the most sense.

If you come across a word that doesn't seem to make sense in context, consider whether that word might have another, lesser known meaning. Can the word be used as more than one part of speech, for example, as either a noun or a verb? Does it have a broader meaning than the one that comes to your mind? For example, in the legend *King Arthur and His Knights of the Round Table* (Unit 5, page 222), you will find this sentence: "In the forest not many leagues from here King Pellinore has set up his pavilion beside the high road . . ." The most common meaning of *leagues* is "groups of people with a common interest or goal," but that doesn't fit here. Consulting the footnote at the bottom of the page, you would discover that the word *league* can also mean "unit of measurement that is equal to about three miles."

Keep in mind that some words not only have multiple meanings but also different pronunciations. Words that are spelled the same but are pronounced differently are called **homographs**.

Understanding Denotation and Connotation

The **denotation** of a word is its dictionary definition. Sometimes, in order to understand a passage fully, it is helpful to know the connotations of the words as well. A **connotation** of a word is an emotional association the word has in addition to its literal meaning. For example, the words *persistent* and *stubborn* both denote "keeping at something in spite of difficulties," but *stubborn* has a negative connotation similar to *inflexible* or *difficult*, whereas *persistent* has a positive connotation involving being determined and loyal. The best way to learn the connotation of a word is to pay attention to the context in which the word appears or to ask someone more familiar with the word.

IMPROVING YOUR ACTIVE VOCABULARY

Keeping a Word Study Notebook

Keeping a **word study notebook** is a convenient way to log new words, their meanings, and their spellings, as well as prefixes, suffixes, word roots, and other concepts. In addition, you can use your word study

NOTE THE FACTS

What is the difference between a *denotation* and a *connotation*?

_____

_____

THINK AND REFLECT

How would it be different if one character called the other *stubborn* rather than *persistent*? What would that tell you about the relationship between the two characters? (**Apply**)

_____

_____

_____

_____

_____

In your word study notebook, record for each word:

- definition
- pronunciation
- etymology
- sample sentence or illustration

notebook to write down words that you have trouble remembering how to spell. You may even want to set aside a section of your notebook for word play. You can use this area to create jokes, silly rhymes, jingles, skits, acrostics, and games using the words you have logged.

When you record a new word in your notebook, include its definition, pronunciation, and origins, along with an example sentence or drawing to help you remember it.

Here is a sample page from a word study notebook.

Word: miasma (pl. miasmas or miasmata)

Pronunciation: \mī-az´-mə\

Origins: New Latin, from Greek word miainein, "to pollute"

Definition: Unhealthy, polluting vapor or fog

Sentence: The miasma created by tobacco smoke in that coffee shop makes me ill.

Review the words in your word study notebook and practice using the words in your speech and writing. Also, look for the words from your notebook as you read and listen. The more associations you develop and the more encounters you have with a word, the more likely you are to remember it.

Using Mnemonic Devices

A **mnemonic** (ni mä′ nik) **device** is a catchy phrase or striking image that helps you remember information. For example, you might have heard the phrase "the princiPAL is your PAL" as a trick for remembering the difference between *principal*, the person, and *principle*, the idea. The rhyme "*I* before *E* except after *C*" is a mnemonic for a spelling pattern.

Mnemonic devices are effective in learning new vocabulary words because you learn new information by linking it to words, images, and concepts that are already familiar to you. Vocabulary mnemonics can be sayings, drawings, jingles, or whatever works for you. To remember the definition of *neophyte*, you could say, "A neophyte fighter is new to fighting." To remember how to spell *museum*, you could associate the word with others like it: we are <u>amused</u> at the <u>museum</u>. A mental picture can also help you remember meaning and spelling.

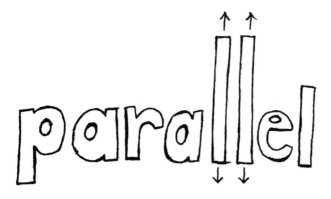

Categorizing and Classifying Words

Another technique for learning vocabulary words is categorizing and classifying the words. To categorize or classify a list of vocabulary words, sort them into groups that share a theme, topic, or characteristic. Then label each group. Like mnemonic devices, this technique works because it helps you create associations with and among new words.

For example, imagine that you need to learn the meanings of the following vocabulary words from the story "The Black Cat" (Unit 3, page 42).

allusion	cherish	deliberate
anomalous	conflagration	docility
apparition	conjointly	equivocal
atrocity	consign	expedient
aversion	constitute	expound
bravado	debauch	goaded

CONTINUED

NOTE THE FACTS

Why are mnemonic devices effective?

_____

_____

_____

THINK AND REFLECT

Why is the graphic to the left an effective mnemonic for remembering the meaning of *parallel*? (Interpret)

_____

_____

_____

imperceptible	lime	repose
inclination	odious	reverberation
incumbent	perverseness	solicit
inscrutability	premises	succinctly
intemperate	procure	succumb
jeopardize	remorse	uncongenial
latter	render	ungovernable

THINK AND REFLECT

In what other ways can these words be classified? **(Apply)**

_____

_____

_____

_____

_____

_____

_____

_____

_____

_____

_____

_____

_____

_____

_____

Here is how one student classified these words.

"The Black Cat" Vocabulary	
insult words	atrocity, aversion, bravado, debauch, intemperate, odious, perverseness, uncongenial, ungovernable
words about movement	consign, deliberate, expedient, expound, goaded, imperceptible, incumbent, procure, repose, reverberation, solicit, succumb
words about danger	anomalous, apparition, conflagration, jeopardize
words about going together or not	conjointly, constitute
words about caring or not	cherish, equivocal, remorse

Learning Synonyms, Antonyms, and Homonyms

A good way to expand your vocabulary is to learn synonyms, antonyms, and homonyms. As with using mnemonic devices and classifying or categorizing words, working with synonyms, antonyms, and homonyms will help you build associations for new words.

synonym	same (or nearly the same) meaning	harsh, scathing
antonym	opposite meaning	greedy, generous
homonym	same pronunciation but different meaning	sight, site, cite

One way of using synonyms and antonyms to make many connections to a new word is to create a **concept map**. In a concept map, you list synonyms, antonyms, examples, nonexamples, and a contextual sentence for the word you are studying. The best way to use a concept map is to fill it out with a small group or as a whole class. That way, you get to hear everyone else's associations with the word, too. Look at the concept map for *caustic* below.

THINK AND REFLECT

Add one more synonym, antonym, example, and nonexample to the boxes in the chart. (Apply)

_____

_____

_____

_____

Real-Life Contexts
Danger! <u>Caustic</u> chemicals may burn skin.
Mark Twain had a <u>caustic</u> wit.

Synonyms

burning
stinging
corrosive
biting
sharp
scathing
harsh
acrid

caustic

Antonyms

soothing
healing
bland
mild
pleasing
kind
gentle

Examples

insults
sarcasm
acid
critic

Nonexamples

compliment
lotion
pat on back
oatmeal
tea

Unit 9 VOCABULARY Review

Choose and Use Vocabulary Strategies

Before completing the vocabulary activities below, review with a partner how to use each of these vocabulary strategies.

TACKLING DIFFICULT VOCABULARY

- ❑ Use definitions, footnotes, endnotes, and glossaries
- ❑ Use context clues
- ❑ Use prior knowledge of word parts, word origins, and word families

- ❑ Use a dictionary
- ❑ Understand multiple meanings
- ❑ Understand connotation and denotation

IMPROVING YOUR ACTIVE VOCABULARY

- ❑ Keep a word study notebook
- ❑ Use mnemonic devices
- ❑ Categorize and classify words
- ❑ Learn synonyms, antonyms, and homonyms

Now read the passage below using the strategies from this unit to tackle difficult vocabulary in this excerpt from "Ice and Light" by Barry Lopez. After you finish the passage, answer the vocabulary questions that follow.

At first it seems that, except for a brief few weeks in autumn, the Arctic is without color. Its land of colors are the colors of deserts, the ochers and siennas of stratified soils, the gray-greens of sparse plant life on bare soil. On closer inspection, however, the monotonic rock of the polar desert is seen to harbor the myriad greens, reds, yellows, and oranges of lichens. The whites of tundra swans and of sunlit ice in black water are pure and elegant. Occasionally, there is brilliant coloring—as with wildflowers in the summer, or a hillside of willow and bearberry in the fall; or a slick of vegetable oils shining with the iridescent colors of petroleum on a tundra puddle, or the bright face of a king eider.[1] But the bright colors are more often only points in a season, not brushstrokes, and they are absorbed in the paler casts of the landscape.

Arresting color in the Arctic is found more often in the sky, with its vivid twilights and the aurora borealis. (The predominant colors of the aurora are a pale green and a soft rose. I turned over a weathered caribou antler once on the tundra and found these same two colors staining its white surface. Such correspondence, like that between a surfacing guillemot[2] and an Eskimo man rolling upright in his kayak, hold a landscape together.)

Arctic skies retain the colors of dawn and dusk for hours in winter. On days when the southern sky is barely lit for a while around noon, layers of deep violet, of bruised purples and dense blues, may stretch across 80° of the horizon, above a familiar lavender and the thinnest line of yellow gold.

---

1. **king eider.** Large sea duck of the north
2. **guillemot.** Any of several narrow-billed birds of northern seas

1. From this excerpt, the reader can guess that ochers and siennas are _____.
   a. geographical features
   b. animals
   c. plants
   d. colors

2. If *monolingual* means "knowing only one language," *monotonic* probably means _____.
   a. knowing many languages
   b. having only one color tone
   c. multicolored
   d. very dry

3. In this passage, *sparse* means _____.
   a. few and scattered
   b. rich and plentiful
   c. colorful and bright
   d. green and lush

4. The word *predominant* means _____.
   a. most common
   b. excessively eager
   c. urgent and loud
   d. quite rare

5. Imagine that your teacher has given you the following list of vocabulary words.

abalone	pervasive	tangible
evanescence	predominant	undulate
iridescent	quiescent	weathered
myriad	sienna	
ocher	sparse	

Use a dictionary and your knowledge of word parts to determine the meaning of each of these words. Then, on your own paper, do the following activities.

a. Create a word study notebook entry for one of the words.
b. Create a mnemonic device for one of the words.
c. Categorize the words.

On Your Own

FLUENTLY SPEAKING. Learn the pronunciations of each of the vocabulary words from the previous activity. Then practice reading the words aloud until you can read the entire list without stumbling. Use the Word Recognition Skills: Word Race form in Appendix A, page A-4. Record your personal best time.

PICTURE THIS. Choose a story, article, or poem that contains at least three words that are new to you. For each word, create a drawing that will help you remember its meaning. Then create a drawing that illustrates some aspect of the story, poem, or article and shows that you understand it.

PUT IT IN WRITING. Find and read a book, story, article, or poem that interests you. Create a list of vocabulary words from the text you have chosen. If the text doesn't have many difficult words in it, pick easy words and use a thesaurus to learn more difficult synonyms for those words. Then use these words to create a crossword puzzle, an acrostic, or some other word game. Look at the Word Workshop activities in the Unit Reading Reviews in this book for ideas. Write instructions for your puzzle or game. Then have a partner study the list of vocabulary words and complete your activity.

Unit TEN

TEST-TAKING Strategies

PREPARING FOR TESTS IN YOUR CLASSES

Tests are a common part of school life. You take tests in your classes to show what you have learned in each class. In addition, you might have to take one or more standardized tests each year. Standardized tests measure your skills against local, state, or national standards and may determine whether you graduate, what kind of job you can get, or which college you can attend. Learning test-taking strategies will help you succeed on the tests you are required to take.

These guidelines will help you to prepare for and take tests on the material you have covered in class.

Reading STRATEGY
REVIEW

CONNECT TO PRIOR KNOWLEDGE. Which of these test strategies do you already use? Which might help you on your next test?

_____
_____
_____
_____
_____
_____
_____
_____
_____
_____

Preparing for a Test

❏ **Know what will be covered on the test.** If you have questions about what will be covered, ask your teacher.

❏ **Make a study plan** to allow yourself time to go over the material. Avoid last-minute cramming.

❏ **Review the subject matter.** Use the graphic organizers and notes you made as you read as well as notes you took in class. Review any study questions given by your teacher.

❏ **Make lists** of important names, dates, definitions, or events. Ask a friend or family member to quiz you on them.

❏ **Try to predict questions** that may be on the test. Make sure you can answer them.

❏ **Get plenty of sleep** the night before the test. Eat a nutritious breakfast on the morning of the test.

Taking a Test

- ❑ **Survey the test** to see how long it is and what types of questions are included.
- ❑ **Read all directions and questions carefully.** Make sure you know exactly what to do.
- ❑ **Plan your time.** Answer easy questions first. Allow extra time for complicated questions. If a question seems too difficult, skip it and go back to it later. Work quickly, but do not rush.
- ❑ **Save time for review.** Once you have finished, look back over the test. Double-check your answers, but do not change answers too readily. Your first ideas are often correct.

Answering Objective Questions

An **objective question** has a single correct answer. This chart describes the kinds of questions you may see on objective tests. It also gives you strategies for tackling each kind of question.

MARK THE TEXT

Underline or highlight the guidelines in the chart that you want to try next time you take a test.

Questions Found on Objective Tests

Description	Guidelines
True/False. You are given a statement and asked to tell whether the statement is true or false.	■ If any part of a statement is false, then the statement is false. ■ Words like *all, always, never,* and *every* often appear in false statements. ■ Words like *some, usually, often,* and *most* often appear in true statements. ■ If you do not know the answer, guess. You have a 50/50 chance of being right.
Matching. You are asked to match items in one column with items in another column.	■ Check the directions. See if each item is used only once. Also check to see if some are not used at all. ■ Read all items before starting. ■ Match those items you know first. ■ Cross out items as you match them.
Multiple Choice. You are asked to choose the best answer from a group of answers given.	■ Read *all* choices first. ■ Rule out incorrect answers. ■ Choose the answer that is most complete or accurate. ■ Pay particular attention to choices such as *none of the above* or *all of the above*.

Short Answer. You are asked to answer the question with a word, phrase, or sentence.	■ Read the directions to find out if you are required to answer in complete sentences. ■ Use correct spelling, grammar, punctuation, and capitalization. ■ If you cannot think of the answer, move on. Something in another question might remind you of the answer.

Answering Essay Questions

An essay question asks you to write an answer that shows what you know about a particular subject. Read the following essay question on "The Necklace" (Unit 3, page 68).

> Compare and contrast the personalities of Mme. Loisel and her husband as they are revealed in the story.

A simplified writing process will help you tackle questions like this. Follow these steps:

1 ANALYZE THE QUESTION. Essay questions contain clues about what is expected of you. Sometimes you will find key words that will help you determine exactly what is being asked. See the list below for some typical key words and their meanings.

Key Words for Essay Questions	
analyze; identify	break into parts, and describe the parts and how they are related
compare	tell how two or more subjects are similar; in some cases, also mention how they are different
contrast	tell how two or more subjects are different from each other
describe	give enough facts about or qualities of a subject to make it clear to someone who is unfamiliar with it
discuss	provide an overview and analysis; use details for support
evaluate; argue	judge an idea or concept, telling whether you think it is good or bad, or whether you agree or disagree with it
explain	make a subject clearer, providing supporting details and examples
interpret	tell the meaning and importance of an event or concept
justify	explain or give reasons for decisions; be persuasive
prove	provide factual evidence or reasons for a statement
summarize	state only the main points of an event, concept, or debate

THINK AND REFLECT

Using the information in the chart, explain in your own words what the prompt above about "The Necklace" is asking you to do. **(Apply)**

_____

_____

_____

2 PLAN YOUR ANSWER. As soon as the essay prompt is clear to you, collect and organize your thoughts about it. First, gather ideas using whatever method is most comfortable for you. If you don't immediately have ideas, try freewriting for five minutes. When you **freewrite**, you write whatever comes into your head without letting your hand stop moving. You might also gather ideas in a **cluster chart**. (See Appendix B, page B-7, for an example of this kind of chart.) Then, organize the ideas you came up with. A simple outline or chart can help. For example, the following graphic organizer might help you organize the compare-and-contrast essay on "The Necklace" on the previous page.

	Mme. Loisel	M. Loisel
Similarity or Difference #1	strong personality; demands what she wants	weaker personality; never named in the story
Similarity or Difference #2		
Similarity or Difference #3		

Get to know other graphic organizers that might help you by reviewing those on the before-reading pages and in Appendix B of this book.

3 WRITE YOUR ANSWER. Start with a clear thesis statement in your opening paragraph. Your **thesis statement** is a single sentence that sums up your answer to the essay question. Then follow your organizational plan to provide support for your thesis. Devote one paragraph to each major point of support for your thesis. Use plenty of details as evidence for each point. Write quickly and keep moving. Don't spend too much time on any single paragraph, but try to make your answer as complete as possible. End your essay with a concluding sentence that sums up your major points.

4 REVISE YOUR ANSWER. Make sure you have answered all parts of the question and included everything you were asked to include. Check to see that you have supplied enough details to support your thesis. Check for errors in grammar, spelling, punctuation, and paragraph breaks. Make corrections to your answer.

NOTE THE FACTS

What is a thesis? Where should you put it?

_____

_____

_____

Reading TIP

Steps for answering essay questions:
1 Analyze the question
2 Plan your answer
3 Draft your answer
4 Revise your answer

TAKING STANDARDIZED TESTS

Standardized tests are given to large groups of students in a school district, a state, or a country. Statewide tests measure how well students are meeting the learning standards the state has set. Other tests, such as the Scholastic Aptitude Test, or SAT, are used to help determine admission to colleges and universities. Others must be taken to enter certain careers. These tests are designed to measure overall ability or skills acquired so far. Learning how to take standardized tests will help you to achieve your goals.

You can get better at answering standardized test questions by practicing the types of questions that will be on the test. Use the Reading Skills and Test Practice questions in this book and other sample questions your teacher gives you to practice. Think aloud with a partner or small group about how you would answer each question. Notice how other students tackle the questions and learn from what they do.

In addition, remember these points:

- ❑ **Rule out some choices** when you are not sure of the answer. Then guess from the remaining possibilities.
- ❑ **Skip questions that seem too difficult** and go back to them later. Be aware, however, that most tests allow you to go back only within a section.
- ❑ **Follow instructions exactly.** The test monitor will read instructions to you, and instructions may also be printed in your test booklet. Make sure you know what to do.

Answering Multiple-Choice Questions

On many standardized tests, questions are multiple choice and have a single correct answer. The guidelines below will help you answer these kinds of questions effectively.

- ❑ **Read each question carefully.** Pay special attention to any words that are bolded, italicized, written in all capital letters, or otherwise emphasized.
- ❑ **Read all choices** before selecting an answer.
- ❑ **Eliminate** any answers that do not make sense, that disagree with what you remember from reading a passage, or that seem too extreme. Also, if two answers have exactly the same meaning, you can eliminate both.

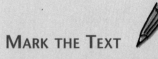

MARK THE TEXT

Underline or highlight the suggestions in this list that are new to you.

- ❏ **Beware of distractors.** These are incorrect answers that look attractive because they are partially correct. They might contain a common misunderstanding, or they might apply the right information in the wrong way. Distractors are based on common mistakes students make.
- ❏ **Fill in circles completely** on your answer sheet when you have selected your answer.

Answering Reading Comprehension Questions

Reading comprehension questions ask you to read a passage and answer questions about it. These questions measure how well you perform the essential reading skills covered in Unit 2 of this book.

The Reading Skills and Test Practice questions that follow each literature selection in this book are reading comprehension questions. Use them to help you learn how to answer these types of questions correctly. Work through each question with a partner using a **think aloud.** Say out loud how you are figuring out the answer. Talk about how you can eliminate incorrect answers and determine the correct choice. You may want to make notes as you eliminate answers. By practicing this thinking process with a partner, you will be more prepared to use it silently when you have to take a standardized test.

The following steps will help you answer the reading comprehension questions on standardized tests.

- ❏ **Preview the passage and questions** and predict what the text will be about.
- ❏ **Use the reading strategies** you have learned to read the passage. Mark the text and make notes in the margins.
- ❏ **Reread the first question carefully.** Make sure you know exactly what it is asking.
- ❏ **Read the answers.** If you are sure of the answer, select it and move on. If not, go on to the next step.
- ❏ **Scan the passage** to look for key words related to the question. When you find a key word, slow down and read carefully.
- ❏ **Answer the question** and go on to the next one. Answer each question in this way.

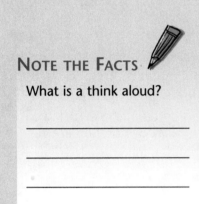

NOTE THE FACTS

What is a think aloud?

_____

_____

_____

Answering Analogy Questions

Analogy questions ask you to find the relationship between two words and then to recognize a similar relationship in another pair of words. Look at the example below.

CAMERA : PHOTOGRAPHY ::
a. paint : paintbrushes
b. easel : drawing
c. nail : hammer
d. writer : computer

In an analogy question, the symbols : and :: mean "is to" and "as." The example above would be read aloud as "*Camera* is to *photography* as. . . ." Follow these guidelines for answering analogy questions:

❑ Think of a sentence that relates the two words. For the example above, you might think "A camera is a tool used in photography."
❑ Try substituting the words from each answer pair in the sentence.
   "A paint is a tool used in paintbrushes."
   "An easel is a tool used in drawing."
   "A nail is a tool used in hammer."
   "A writer is a tool used in computer."
❑ Decide which sentence makes the most sense.
❑ If none of the options makes sense, try to think of a different sentence that relates the words, and work through the same process with the new sentence.

The following chart lists some common relationships used in analogy questions.

THINK AND REFLECT

Using the process described here, how would you answer the analogy question above? **(Apply)**

_____

_____

_____

Common Analogy Relationships

Relationship	Example
synonyms	amiable : friendly
antonyms	passionate : indifferent
cause and effect	drought : famine
effect and cause	cancer : smoking
general and specific	fruit : watermelon
less intense and more intense	healthy : robust
part to whole	vows : wedding
whole to part	wedding : vows
age	bud : blossom *CONTINUED*

gender	filly : colt
worker and tool	secretary : computer
worker and product created	writer : novel
tool and associated action	car : transport
scientist and object of study	oncologist : cancer
raw material and end product	coal : diamond
person and associated quality	seamstress : detailed
symbol and what it stands for	skull and cross bones : poison

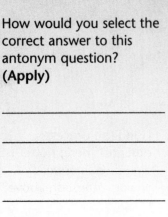

THINK AND REFLECT

How would you select the correct answer to this antonym question? **(Apply)**

_____

_____

_____

_____

_____

_____

_____

Answering Synonym and Antonym Questions

Synonym or antonym questions give you a word and ask you to select the word that has the same meaning (for a **synonym**) or the opposite meaning (for an **antonym**). You must select the best answer even if none is exactly correct. For this type of question, you should consider all the choices to see which is best. Always notice whether you are looking for a synonym or an antonym. You will usually find both among the answers. Think aloud with a partner about how to answer the following question:

Mark the letter of the word that is most nearly the OPPOSITE in meaning to the word in capital letters.

1. DESTITUTE
   a. degrading
   b. poor
   c. wealthy
   d. intelligent

THINK AND REFLECT

How would you select the correct answer to the sentence completion question? **(Apply)**

_____

_____

_____

_____

_____

_____

Answering Sentence Completion Questions

Sentence completion questions present you with a sentence that has two words missing. You must select the pair of words that best completes the sentence. The key to this kind of question is to make sure that both parts of the answer you have selected work well in the sentence. Think aloud with a partner about how to complete the following sentence.

2. The expansion of Cedar Hospital was largely _____ by the citizens of Minor county, even though it was a major _____ for the taxpayers.
   a. needed . . . contribution
   b. cheered . . . burden
   c. criticized . . . expense
   d. welcomed . . . dilemma

Answering Constructed-Response Questions

In addition to multiple-choice questions, many standardized tests include **constructed-response questions** that require you to write essay answers in the test booklet. Constructed-response questions might ask you to identify key ideas or examples from the text by writing a sentence about each. In other cases, you will be asked to write a paragraph in response to a question about the selection and to use specific details from the passage to support your answer. For example, the following prompt might occur after Coretta Scott King's "Montgomery Boycott," Unit 7, page 319.

> **Essay prompt:** What is the author's purpose for writing this selection?
>
> **Short response:** This article is an example of informative, or expository, writing. King's aim in writing this article is to inform the reader about the beginnings of the Civil Rights movement and all the various people who helped start the movement. She also depicts her husband as a great man, who, even though he was a great leader and was highly motivational, also had his own doubts and insecurities.

Other constructed-response questions ask you to apply information or ideas from a text in a new way. For example, imagine that you have just read "Something Could Happen to You" (Unit 7, page 377) on a standardized test. This excerpt from a memoir tells about the narrator's experience moving to New York from Puerto Rico. The question might ask you to imagine that you are the narrator and to write a letter about your experiences to a friend back home. Another question might ask you to use information from the text in a particular imaginary situation. For example, you might be asked to write the text for a brochure that will help children from other countries adjust to life in New York. As you answer these questions, remember that you are being evaluated based on your understanding of the text. Although these questions offer opportunities to be creative, you should still include ideas, details, and examples from the passage you have just read.

THINK AND REFLECT

How do constructed-response questions differ from multiple-choice questions? **(Infer)**

_____

_____

_____

_____

NOTE THE FACTS

How are constructed-response questions evaluated? What should you be sure to include?

_____

_____

_____

The following tips will help you answer constructed-response questions effectively.

Tips for Answering Constructed-Response Questions

- ❑ **Skim the questions first.** Predict what the passage will be about.
- ❑ **Use reading strategies** as you read. Underline information that relates to the questions and make notes. After you have finished reading, you can decide which of the details you have gathered to use in your answers.
- ❑ **List the most important points** to include in each answer. Use the margins of your test booklet or a piece of scrap paper.
- ❑ **Number the points** you have listed to show the order in which they should be included.
- ❑ **Draft your answer to fit** in the space provided. Include as much detail as possible in the space you have.
- ❑ **Revise and proofread** your answers as you have time.

Unit 10 / TEST-TAKING Review

Choose and Use Test-Taking Strategies

Before answering the sample test questions below, review with a partner how to use each of these test-taking strategies.

GENERAL STRATEGIES

- ❑ Know what will be on the test
- ❑ Make a study plan
- ❑ Review the subject matter
- ❑ Make lists
- ❑ Try to predict questions
- ❑ Preview the passage and questions
- ❑ Plan your time
- ❑ Use reading strategies to read the passage
- ❑ Come back later to questions that seem too difficult
- ❑ Save time for reviewing answers

STRATEGIES FOR OBJECTIVE TESTS

- ❑ Read each question carefully
- ❑ Read all answer choices before selecting one
- ❑ Scan the passage again if you are uncertain of the answer
- ❑ Rule out some choices
- ❑ Beware of distractors
- ❑ Understand how to answer analogy questions
- ❑ Understand how to answer synonym and antonym questions
- ❑ Understand how to answer sentence completion questions
- ❑ Fill in circles completely

STRATEGIES FOR ESSAY TESTS

- ❑ Understand how to answer constructed-response questions
- ❑ Analyze the question
- ❑ Plan your answer
- ❑ Write your answer
- ❑ Revise your answer

Now read the passage below and answer the questions that follow. Use the strategies from this unit to complete this practice test.

> The United Nations is an alliance that was established in 1945, right after World War II, by 51 countries who were committed to working together to preserve peace. They hoped that by joining together, they could develop friendly relations among nations, cooperate in solving international problems, and promote respect for human rights. Today, nearly every nation in the world belongs to the UN.

The United States is a powerful country, and it has an important role in the UN. In order to make sure the United States is doing all it can to help the UN, a special organization was formed called the United Nations Association of the United States of America (UNA-USA). The UNA-USA is a nonprofit organization that is not connected to any political party. Its sole purpose is to make the United Nations stronger because it believes no other group can more effectively bring about global problem-solving. The UNA-USA points out problems it sees in policies and offers alternative ways to resolve conflicts.

In helping the United Nations become a stronger force in achieving positive global change, UNA-USA tries to encourage people to participate in its cause. For example, UNA-USA offers programs that allow people to contribute to world peace and to help solve global crises. Adopt-a-Minefield is such a program. It allows Americans to contribute to the global effort of finding and eliminating hidden landmines in war-ridden countries such as Iran and Iraq. UNA-USA tries to make Americans aware of their role as individuals to influence our country's policy of peace and democracy toward other nations.

At the heart of these educational efforts is the annual National High School Essay Contest sponsored by UNA-USA and other partner organizations. Since 1986, high school students have been encouraged to think about America's role in world organization and global policies through this annual nationwide essay contest. It challenges students to think about their role as the future of our nation and our world. It also challenges students to analyze present outbreaks of violence, conflict, or chaos and propose ways to help <u>rectify</u> those situations by establishing peace. In doing so, the UNA-USA supports the UN's belief that establishing and maintaining peace must begin at the grassroots level—with individuals working in their communities. The organization believes that if it educates young people, it can prevent wars in the future. Essay topics such as "The United Nations and the Protection of Human Rights" (1998 essay topic) and "Who Needs Whom: Why the U.S. Needs the UN" (1999 essay topic) reflect these educational and awareness goals created by the UNA-USA.

1. With which statement would the author *most likely* agree?
   a. Teenagers should be involved in thinking about America's role in world organization and global policies.
   b. Teenagers should always be critical of how the government is handling its role in the United Nations.
   c. Teenagers should let adults handle political issues.
   d. Teenagers should not question global policies.

2. The UNA-USA encourages people to join their campaign by
   a. offering programs in which people contribute to world peace.
   b. using telemarketing tactics.
   c. giving lectures at high schools and middle schools.
   d. recruiting members.

3. In 2003, United States President George W. Bush launched a military attack on Iraq without the support of a United Nations resolution allowing that action. Based on this article, which viewpoint did the UNA-USA *probably* hold?
   a. It supported the United States completely.
   b. It criticized the United Nations for not agreeing with the United States.
   c. It supported Iraq completely.
   d. It criticized the United States for disregarding the United Nations.

4. Judging by the information in this article, what would be an appropriate essay topic for the United Nations Essay Contest? Identify a topic and explain why it is appropriate.

   _____

   _____

   _____

   _____

   _____

   _____

   _____

5. OLD : ANCIENT ::
   a. innocent : indict
   b. malleable : inflexible
   c. careful : superfluous
   d. destroy : annihilate

On Your Own

FLUENTLY SPEAKING. Review this unit and make a list of thirty key words about test taking. Use a word processor to key your words so that they are easy to read or use the Word Recognition Skills: Word Race form in Appendix A, page A-4. Then exchange lists with a partner. While your partner listens and times you with a stopwatch, read the list of words your partner gave you as quickly as you can without making errors. Then have your partner read the list of words you made while you time him or her. Practice reading the words until you can do it with no errors, and try to beat your partner's time.

PICTURE THIS. Find an informational article on a topic that interests you. After reading the article, come up with two essay questions. Practice planning answers for essay questions by constructing a graphic organizer that will help you organize your answer for each question. For more practice on planning responses to essay questions, exchange essay questions with a partner, and plan your answer for your partner's questions.

PUT IT IN WRITING. Find and read an informational article on any topic that interests you. After you have read the article, write three multiple-choice and two constructed-response questions that test reading comprehension. As models, use the sample questions in this unit as well as those in the Reading Skills and Test Practice section that follows every literature selection in this book. Finally, exchange your passage and questions with a partner, and take one another's tests.

Appendix A:
Building Reading Fluency

WORD RECOGNITION SKILLS: INCREASE YOUR AUTOMATICITY

WHAT ARE WORD RECOGNITION SKILLS? **Word recognition skills** are skills that help you recognize and decipher words. Learning how to read increasingly more words with faster recognition leads to **automaticity,** the ability to recognize words quickly and automatically. The activities below develop word recognition skills.

1 **CREATE A CROSSWORD PUZZLE.** Put together a crossword puzzle that includes clues for words you are studying and clues for facts everyone should know. Look at puzzles in the newspaper or a puzzle book to learn how to number your clues and add blank spaces. Here is how you might set up a puzzle.

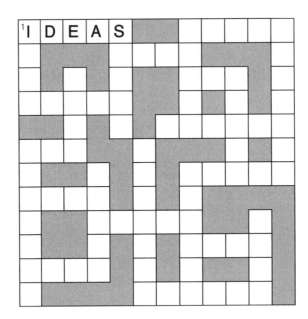

2 **CREATE A WORD RACE.** Make a list of 20 words you have studied. Practice reading the words aloud. Have a classmate keep track of how many seconds it takes you to read the entire list. Have another person keep track of the words you mispronounce. Have teams compete to see which team pronounces the same list of words the fastest with the fewest errors.

3 **CREATE A WORD MATRIX.** Choose vocabulary words that you find difficult to pronounce and place them in a chart. Add the same words to each row of your chart, but add the words to each row in a different order. Practice reading the words until you are comfortable pronouncing them. Have a partner time how many words in your chart you can read in 1 minute.

WORD RECOGNITION SKILLS: CROSSWORD PUZZLE

In a small group, list words to include in a crossword puzzle. Your list should contain 10 vocabulary words and 10 words that refer to facts that everyone knows. For instance, if the word *Washington* is on your "facts" list, add a CLUE ACROSS that says, *Our nation's first president.* Your first word down can come from one of the letters in *Washington*. For instance, the vocabulary word *wallow* can use the *w* in *Washington* with a CLUE DOWN that says, *Indulge oneself immoderately.* Use as many of the words on your list as you can (you may not be able to use all of them). Use your own paper for the CLUES ACROSS and CLUES DOWN. After you fill in your puzzle and finish your clues, make another blank, numbered puzzle. Exchange blank puzzles and clues with another group. See which group can solve their puzzle the fastest.

1.w	a	s	h	i	n	g	t	o	n										
a																			
l																			
l																			
o																			
w																			

WORD RECOGNITION SKILLS: WORD RACE

Create a list of 20 vocabulary words you have studied. Practice reading the list aloud. Have someone keep track of how many seconds it takes you to read the entire list. Have another person keep track of the words you mispronounce. After you have practiced the list, create teams. Have the team compete to see which team can pronounce the list the fastest with the fewest errors.

1.	11.
2.	12.
3.	13.
4.	14.
5.	15.
6.	16.
7.	17.
8.	18.
9.	19.
10.	20.

Keep track of the following data for each team member.

Number of seconds it took to read the list:

Number of words mispronounced:

WORD RECOGNITION SKILLS: WORD MATRIX

Choose 5 words that you find difficult to pronounce, and place them in the matrix below. Add the same words to each row, but use the words in a different order in each row. After a brief practice run-through, have a classmate use a clock or timer to see how many times you can make it through the chart in 1 minute. Have another classmate circle or check words you pronounce correctly. Use the second matrix below to run through your words a second time. Try to increase the number of words spoken correctly on your second reading.

Number of words correct in 1 minute: _____

Number of words correct in 1 minute: _____

SILENT READING SKILLS: INCREASE THE AMOUNT YOU READ

WHAT ARE SILENT READING SKILLS? **Silent reading skills** are skills you use as you read a text to yourself. Fluent silent readers can read a text quickly, easily, and smoothly. To build **silent reading fluency**, set aside time each day to read parts of a long selection or book. Most often, choose selections you consider easy and interesting. Vary the subject matter of selections you choose and, over time, include selections from several different genres—fiction, nonfiction, drama, short stories, poems, and informational and visual media. Use the charts below to keep track of your silent reading activity.

1 **FILL IN A FREE READING LOG.** Read silently for a sustained period several times a week. Write down what you read, the number of minutes you read, the number of pages you read, and your thoughts and reactions. Selections you read may be easy, moderate, or challenging.

2 **USE A PAGES-PER-MINUTE GRAPH.** Chart the number of pages you read in a 30-minute reading session. Try to increase the number of pages you read in each session. Be sure the selections you use for this activity are easy to read.

3 **USE A MINUTES-PER-SECTION GRAPH.** Each reading session, chart the time it takes you to read 5 pages of a selection. Try to decrease the number of minutes it takes to read 5 pages. Be sure the selections you use for this activity are easy to read.

SILENT READING SKILLS: HOW MUCH CAN YOU LEARN IN 10 MINUTES?

READING RATE. Pay attention to your silent reading rate. Do you vary your rate as you read? Do you slow down for difficult vocabulary and long sentences? Do you speed up when the ideas are easy to understand? Learn to use different reading rates with different tasks. Here are three methods to try.

Scan	Skim	Read closely
To locate particular information (to find a quotation, verify a statement, locate a word, or answer a question)	To get the overall picture (to preview or to review)	To absorb the meaning of a book you're reading for fun or a textbook on which you'll be tested (to read with understanding the first time)

Practice using different reading rates as you read silently for 10 minutes. How much can you learn in 10 minutes? Write what you learn below.

SILENT READING SKILLS: FREE READING LOG

Develop your silent reading fluency by reading silently for a sustained period several times a week. Keep track of what you read each day. List your reactions and thoughts about what you read.

Week of _____

Date/ Minutes Read	Title/Author	Pages Read From/To	Reactions/Thoughts

Total number of pages read this week:

Total number of minutes read this week:

Genres read this week: (circle)
Fiction   Nonfiction   Poetry   Drama   Informational or Visual Media   Other _____

Silent Reading Skills: Pages-per-Minute Graph

Choose an easy and interesting book. Read for 30 minutes, and count the number of pages you read. Record the number in the chart below. Try to read more pages in each practice session.

Over 10 pages										
9 pages										
8 pages										
7 pages										
6 pages										
5 pages										
4 pages										
3 pages										
2 pages										
1 page										
Practice Number	1	2	3	4	5	6	7	8	9	10
Number of Pages Read										

Silent Reading Skills: Minutes-per-Section Graph

Choose an easy and interesting book. Record in the chart below the time it takes you to read 5 pages of the book. Try to decrease the time it takes you to read 5 pages each time you read. You can time several 5-page sections in one reading by placing paper clips at 5-page intervals. Each time you reach a paper-clipped page, stop to record the time it took you to reach that page.

10 minutes										
9 minutes										
8 minutes										
7 minutes										
6 minutes										
5 minutes										
4 minutes										
3 minutes										
2 minutes										
1 minute										
Practice Number	1	2	3	4	5	6	7	8	9	10
Number of Minutes Read										

Oral Reading Skills: Perform Rereading Activities

WHAT ARE ORAL READING SKILLS? **Oral reading skills** are skills you use when you read aloud. Have you ever noticed how radio and television reporters read a news report? They do not read every word at the same speed and volume. They emphasize important points by putting more stress on some words. They use facial expressions and the tone of their voice to convey what words mean. They add pauses to give listeners time to think about what is being said. These news reporters exhibit **oral reading fluency**, the ability to read aloud smoothly and easily.

HOW CAN YOU BUILD ORAL READING SKILLS? To demonstrate that you are a fluent oral reader, you do not have to read fast without mistakes. Even the best news reporters mispronounce words or stumble over unfamiliar phrases. Good news reporters, however, use strategies that make the oral reading task easier. They read and reread material before they go on the air, and they vary their speed and vocal expression. The rereading activities below build oral reading skills.

1 PREPARE A REPEATED READING EXERCISE. Choose a 100–150-word passage that you consider difficult to read. With a partner, use the passage to prepare a repeated reading exercise. Read the passage aloud to your partner. Have your partner record the time it takes you to read the passage and the number of errors you make. Then have your partner read the passage to you while you record the time and number of errors. On your second reading see if you both can improve your initial time and error rate, and include more vocal expression. Reread the passage a third time, working to decrease your time and error rate and trying to increase your vocal expression.

2 PERFORM A CHORAL READING. Find a poem, song, or part of a story that would be fun for a group to read aloud. Practice reading the piece aloud. Everyone in the group should use the same phrasing and speed. Have group members add notes to the text that help them pronounce the words and pause at appropriate times. Poems such as "Dream Variations" on page 137, "Simple Song" on page 157, and "New Dog" on page 162 work well as choral readings.

3 THINK ALOUD. Read a selection aloud with a partner. As you read, discuss thoughts you have about what you are reading. Ask questions, make connections and predictions, and respond to the ideas in the selection. When you are finished with your oral reading, reread the selection again, either orally or silently.

4 PERFORM A PLAY. Read aloud a play you have previously read silently. Assign parts. In small groups, have each speaker rehearse his/her part several times. Present the play to an audience. Use props and costumes, if possible.

5 WRITE YOUR OWN PLAY. Rewrite a prose selection, or a part of a prose selection, as a play. Assign parts. In small groups, have each speaker rehearse his/her part several times. Present the play to an audience. Use props and costumes, if possible.

6 MAKE A RECORDING. Read a 100–150-word passage into a tape recorder or DVD player. Listen to your recording. Keep track of errors you make: mispronouncing a word, leaving a word out, or adding a word that is not there. Rerecord the passage. Try to decrease the number of errors you make, and increase the smoothness with which you read the passage. Rerecord the passage until you can read it smoothly without error.

7 **MEMORIZE A PASSAGE.** Memorize a 100–150-word passage from a selection you have read. Have a partner help you memorize the passage by chunking it. Memorize short sections at a time, and work up to repeating the entire passage from memory. Possible passages to memorize include lines from a speech or poem, such as Chief Seattle's "Yonder sky that has wept tears of compassion . . ." speech, or scenes from a short story or play such as Antony's monologue in act 3, scene 2 of *The Tragedy of Julius Cæsar*.

8 **MAKE A VIDEO.** Reread a selection with a partner. Prepare a video script that retells the selection. Record the retelling. Show the video retelling to an audience.

9 **EXPERIMENT WITH SPEED AND EXPRESSION.** Read a section of a selection silently. Reread the section aloud to a partner. Experiment with your speed and expression by rereading the section aloud in several different ways. Discuss which speed and means of expression work best.

10 **READ WITH A MASK.** Read silently, pretending that you are a character or the speaker in a selection. Reread aloud using a character or speaker mask that you hold in front of your face or wearing a costume that the character or speaker might wear.

11 **VIEW AND REENACT.** Watch a dramatic version of a selection on video. Read the print version, and reenact part of the selection.

ORAL READING SKILLS: REPEATED READING EXERCISE

❑ Choose a 100–150-word passage that you consider difficult to read. With a partner, use the passage to prepare a repeated reading exercise.

❑ Use a computer or a copier to make 6 copies of the passage: 3 for yourself and 3 for your partner.

❑ Read the passage aloud to your partner. Have your partner record the time you start reading, errors you make while reading, and the time you stop reading. Add this information to your Repeated Reading Record on page A-12.

❑ Have your partner read the passage to you. As your partner reads, record the time he/she starts reading, errors he/she makes, and the time he/she stops reading. See if your partner can improve your time and error rate. Record this information in your partner's Repeated Reading Record.

❑ Read the passage again. This time, work on varying your speed and vocal expression. Record the start/stop times and the number of errors you make, but this time your partner should listen for the meaning your words communicate. Have your partner comment on your speed and expression. For instance, your partner might note that "you read the first line too slow," "you had excellent pauses in the 2nd paragraph," or that you should "show more anger in the last line."

❑ Have your partner read the passage again. Record your partner's start/stop times and errors. Write down ways that your partner can vary his/her speed and vocal expression.

❑ You and your partner should reread the passage one more time. Continue to work on varying your speed and expression, and try to decrease your time and your number of errors. Record the information in your Repeated Reading Record.

ORAL READING SKILLS: REPEATED READING RECORD

Name:_____

Text Read: _____

Date	Evaluator	Errors	Time	Speed/Expression

ORAL READING SKILLS: REPEATED READING RECORD

Name:_____

Text Read: _____

Date	Evaluator	Errors	Time	Speed/Expression

ORAL READING SKILLS: PASSAGE FOR FLUENCY PRACTICE

from "The Open Window" by Saki, page 60

"You may wonder why we keep that window wide open on an October afternoon," said the niece, indicating a large French window that opened on to a lawn.

"It is quite warm for the time of the year," said Framton; "but has that window got anything to do with the tragedy?"

"Out through that window, three years ago to a day, her husband and her two young brothers went off for their day's shooting. They never came back. In crossing the moor to their favorite snipe-shooting ground they were all three engulfed in a treacherous piece of bog. It had been that dreadful wet summer, you know, and places that were safe in other years gave way suddenly without warning. Their bodies were never recovered. That was the dreadful part of it."

Here the child's voice lost its self-possessed note and became falteringly human. "Poor aunt always thinks that they will come back some day, they and the little brown spaniel that was lost with them, and walk in at that window just as they used to do . . .

Time started:_____   Number of errors:_____   Time stopped:_____
Comments about speed and expression:

"You may wonder why we keep that window wide open on an October afternoon," said the niece, indicating a large French window that opened on to a lawn.

"It is quite warm for the time of the year," said Framton; "but has that window got anything to do with the tragedy?"

"Out through that window, three years ago to a day, her husband and her two young brothers went off for their day's shooting. They never came back. In crossing the moor to their favorite snipe-shooting ground they were all three engulfed in a treacherous piece of bog. It had been that dreadful wet summer, you know, and places that were safe in other years gave way suddenly without warning. Their bodies were never recovered. That was the dreadful part of it."

Here the child's voice lost its self-possessed note and became falteringly human. "Poor aunt always thinks that they will come back some day, they and the little brown spaniel that was lost with them, and walk in at that window just as they used to do . . .

Time started:_____   Number of errors:_____   Time stopped:_____
Comments about speed and expression:

Oral Reading Skills: Passage for Fluency Practice

from *Almost a Woman* by Esmeralda Santiago, page 378

We came to Brooklyn in search of medical care for my youngest brother, Raymond, whose toes were nearly severed by a bicycle chain when he was four. In Puerto Rico, doctors wanted to amputate the often red and swollen foot, because it wouldn't heal. In New York, Mami hoped doctors could save it.

The day we arrived, a hot, humid afternoon had splintered into thunderstorms as the last rays of the sun dipped into the rest of the United States. I was thirteen and superstitious enough to believe thunder and lightning held significance beyond the meteorological. I stored the sights and sounds of that dreary night into memory as if their meaning would someday be revealed in a flash of insight to forever transform my life. When the insight came, nothing changed, for it wasn't the weather in Brooklyn that was important, but the fact that I was there to notice it.

One hand tightly grasped by Mami, the other by six-year-old Edna, we squeezed and pushed our way through the crowd of travellers. Five-year-old Raymond clung to Mami's other hand, his unbalanced gait drawing sympathetic smiles from people who moved aside to let us walk ahead of them.

Time started:_____   Number of errors:_____   Time stopped:_____
Comments about speed and expression:

We came to Brooklyn in search of medical care for my youngest brother, Raymond, whose toes were nearly severed by a bicycle chain when he was four. In Puerto Rico, doctors wanted to amputate the often red and swollen foot, because it wouldn't heal. In New York, Mami hoped doctors could save it.

The day we arrived, a hot, humid afternoon had splintered into thunderstorms as the last rays of the sun dipped into the rest of the United States. I was thirteen and superstitious enough to believe thunder and lightning held significance beyond the meteorological. I stored the sights and sounds of that dreary night into memory as if their meaning would someday be revealed in a flash of insight to forever transform my life. When the insight came, nothing changed, for it wasn't the weather in Brooklyn that was important, but the fact that I was there to notice it.

One hand tightly grasped by Mami, the other by six-year-old Edna, we squeezed and pushed our way through the crowd of travellers. Five-year-old Raymond clung to Mami's other hand, his unbalanced gait drawing sympathetic smiles from people who moved aside to let us walk ahead of them.

Time started:_____   Number of errors:_____   Time stopped:_____
Comments about speed and expression:

Appendix B:
Graphic Organizers for Reading Strategies

READING STRATEGIES CHECKLIST

Use at least one before-, during-, or after-reading strategy listed below.

Reading Strategy	Before Reading	During Reading	After Reading
READ WITH A PURPOSE	___ I write down my reason for reading. ___ I write down the author's purpose for writing.	___ I read with a purpose in mind.	___ I reflect upon my purpose for reading.
CONNECT TO PRIOR KNOWLEDGE	___ I write down what I know about a topic.	___ I use what I know. ___ I add to what I know.	___ I think about what I learned.
WRITE THINGS DOWN	___ I have the materials I need for writing things down.	___ I mark key points. ___ I use sticky notes. ___ I take notes. ___ I highlight. ___ I react to text.	___ I summarize.
MAKE PREDICTIONS	___ I preview. ___ I guess.	___ I gather more information. ___ I guess again.	___ I analyze my predictions.
VISUALIZE	___ I picture the topic.	___ I make a mind movie. ___ I continue my mind movie.	___ I sketch or summarize my mind movie.
USE TEXT ORGANIZATION	___ I skim the text.	___ I read sections or stanzas. ___ I pay attention to introductions and conclusions. ___ I use headings and signal words. ___ I read charts and graphic aids. ___ I study the pictures. ___ I follow familiar plot, themes, and hidden outlines.	___ I use the organization to review the text.
TACKLE DIFFICULT WORDS	___ I study words beforehand.	___ I use context clues. ___ I look at prefixes and suffixes. ___ I consult a dictionary. ___ I ask a teacher or friend for help.	___ I use the words and add them to my working vocabulary.
MONITOR YOUR READING PROCESS		**Fix-Up Ideas** ___ I reread. ___ I ask questions. ___ I read in shorter chunks. ___ I read aloud. ___ I take time to refocus. ___ I unlock difficult words. ___ I change my reading rate. ___ I create a mnemonic device.	

Read with a Purpose: Author's Purpose Chart

An author may write with the following purposes in mind:

- ❑ to inform (expository/informational writing)
- ❑ to entertain, enrich, enlighten, and/or use an artistic medium such as fiction or poetry to share a perspective (imaginative writing)
- ❑ to make a point by sharing a story about an event (narrative writing)
- ❑ to reflect (personal/expressive writing)
- ❑ to persuade readers or listeners to respond in some way, such as to agree with a position, change a view on an issue, reach an agreement, or perform an action (persuasive/argumentative writing)

The following types of writing reflect these purposes:

- ❑ Expository/informational: news article, research report
- ❑ Imaginative: poem, short story
- ❑ Narrative: biography, family history
- ❑ Personal/expressive: diary entry, personal letter
- ❑ Persuasive, argumentative: editorial, petition

Before Reading
Identify the author's purpose, the type of writing he or she uses, and the ideas he or she wants to communicate.

During Reading
Gather ideas that the author communicates to readers.

After Reading
Summarize the ideas the author communicates. Explain how these ideas help fulfill the author's purpose.

READ WITH A PURPOSE: READER'S PURPOSE CHART

Fill in the Reader's Purpose Chart at each stage of reading to set a purpose for reading and to help you attain it.

Before Reading
Set a purpose for reading. *(Example: I am going to determine the overall mood of this poem.)*

During Reading
Take notes on what you learn. *(Example: mournful owl—sounds sad)*

After Reading
Reflect on your purpose and what you learned. *(Example: I wanted to find the overall mood of this poem. From the notes that I took, I believe the mood is melancholy and sad.)*

CONNECT TO PRIOR KNOWLEDGE: K-W-L CHART

Connect to what you know and what you want to know by filling in the first two columns before you read. Fill in the last column after you read.

What I *Know*	What I *Want* to Learn	What I Have *Learned*

CONNECT TO PRIOR KNOWLEDGE: REACTIONS CHART

Since you cannot write in, mark up, or highlight text in a textbook or library book, use this chart to record your thoughts and reactions. As you read, ask yourself questions, make predictions, react to ideas, identify key points, and/or write down unfamiliar words.

Page #	Questions, Predictions, Reactions, Key Points, and Unfamiliar Words

WRITE THINGS DOWN: NOTE TAKING CHART

Take notes in the chart below as you read nonfiction or informational selections.

Section or Page	Main Ideas	My Reactions
Summary of My Notes		

WRITE THINGS DOWN: PRO AND CON CHART

As you read a persuasive or argumentative selection, take notes on both sides of each argument.

Arguments in Favor (PRO)	Arguments Against (CON)
Argument 1: Support:	Argument 1: Support:
Argument 2: Support:	Argument 2: Support:

WRITE THINGS DOWN: VENN DIAGRAM

Use a Venn diagram to compare and contrast ideas in one selection or to compare two selections.

Idea or Selection 1   Idea or Selection 2

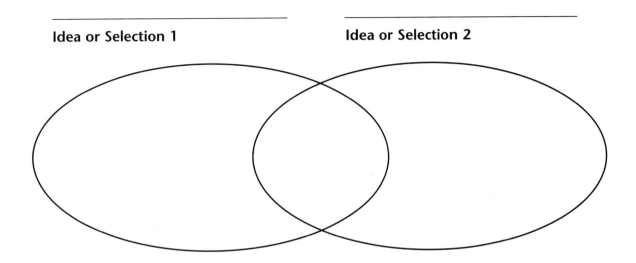

WRITE THINGS DOWN: CLUSTER CHART

Fill in the cluster chart below to keep track of character traits or main ideas. In the center circle, write the name of the character or topic. In the circles branching out from the center, write details about the character or topic.

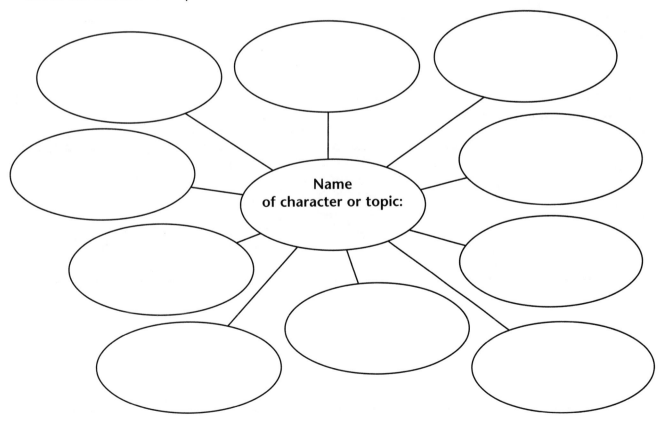

Name of character or topic:

WRITE THINGS DOWN: WRITING IDEAS LOG

Keep track of writing ideas inspired by what you read. Draw pictures or write brief notes that you can use later in a writing assignment.

Date	Idea	Inspired by

MAKE PREDICTIONS: PREDICTION CHART

Gather information before and during reading that helps you make predictions about a literature selection. Write your predictions in the "Guesses" column. Write reasons for your guesses in the "Reasons" column. As you read, gather evidence that either supports or disproves your predictions. Change your predictions and add new ones as you learn more about the selection.

Guesses	Reasons	Evidence

MAKE PREDICTIONS: CHARACTER CHART

A character is a person (or sometimes an animal) who figures in the action of a literary work. Choose one character from the selection and fill in the chart below based on what you learn about the character as you read.

Character's Name:	Physical Appearance	Habits/ Mannerisms/ Behaviors	Relationships with Other People	Other Characteristics
Your description of the character at the beginning of the story				
Your predictions for this character				
Your analysis of the character at the end of the story				

VISUALIZE: SENSORY DETAILS CHART

As you read, identify images or words and phrases that contain sensory details. Write each sensory detail beneath the sense to which it appeals.

Sight	Sound	Touch	Taste	Smell

VISUALIZE: FIGURATIVE LANGUAGE CHART

As you read, identify examples of figurative language. Write down examples of figurative language in the first column below. In the second column, write down the comparison being made by the figurative language, and in the third column, describe what the figurative language makes you envision.

Example of Figurative Language	What is Compared?	What You Envision
"The black canopy of nighttime sky was painted with dazzling jewels."	The night sky is described as a black canopy or painting. The stars are described as dazzling jewels.	A dark, cloudless night sky filled with bright, twinkling stars

USE TEXT ORGANIZATION: STORY STRIP

Story Strip. Draw pictures that represent key events in a selection. Then write a caption under each box that explains each event. Draw the events in the order in which they occurred.

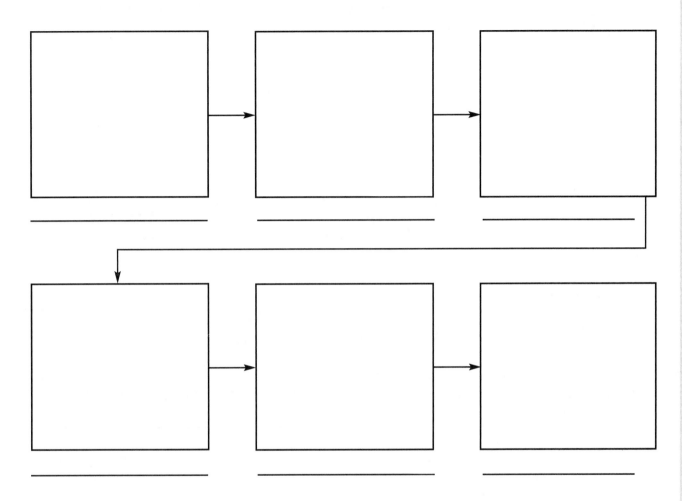

USE TEXT ORGANIZATION: TIME LINE

Use a time line to keep track of important events in a literature selection.

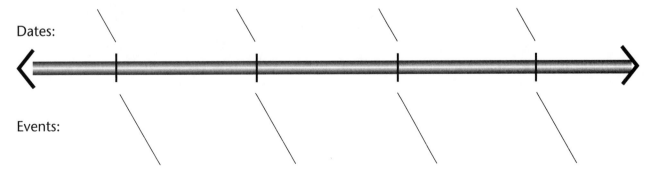

Dates:

Events:

Using Text Organization: Plot Diagram

Use the plot diagram below to chart the plot of a literature selection. In the spaces provided, describe the exposition, inciting incident, rising and falling action, climax, resolution, and dénouement. Be sure to include in the rising action the key events that build toward the climax of the selection.

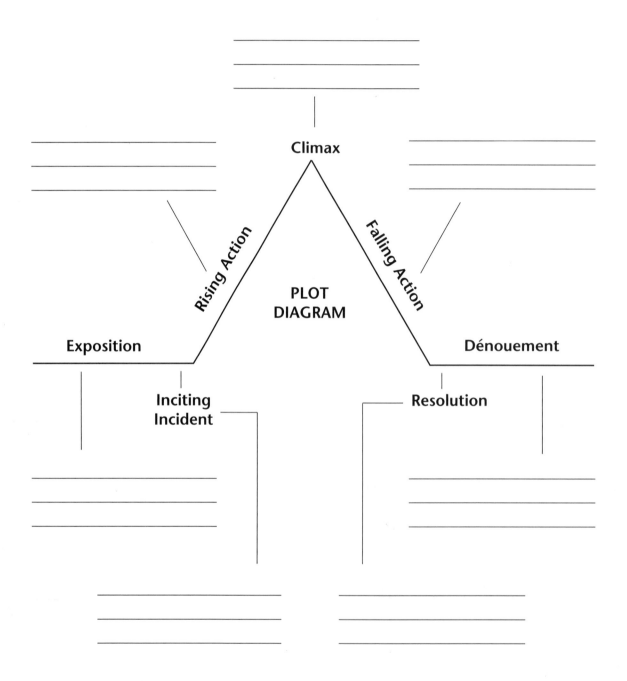

USE TEXT ORGANIZATION: CAUSE-AND-EFFECT CHART

Keep track of what happens in a story and why in the chart below. Use cause-and-effect signal words to help you identify causes and their effects. (Examples of cause-and-effect words: *as a result, because, if/then, since, therefore, this led to*.)

Cause →→→→→→→→→→→→ Effect

_____

_____

**Summary statement of what happened
in the selection and why:**

_____

_____

USE TEXT ORGANIZATION: SUMMARY CHART

Read and summarize short sections of a selection at a time. Then write a summary of the entire work.

Summary of Section 1:
Summary of Section 2:
Summary of Section 3:
Summary of the Selection:

USE TEXT ORGANIZATION: DRAWING CONCLUSIONS LOG

Draw conclusions about a selection by gathering supporting points for key ideas. Reread the supporting points and key ideas and draw a conclusion about the main or overall message of the selection.

Key Idea: Supporting Points:	Key Idea: Supporting Points:	Key Idea: Supporting Points:
Conclusion about Overall Message:		

MAIN IDEA MAP

To find the main or overall message of a whole selection or a part of the selection, gather important details into a Main Idea Map. Use the details to determine the main or overall message. Note: In fiction, the main idea is also known as the theme.

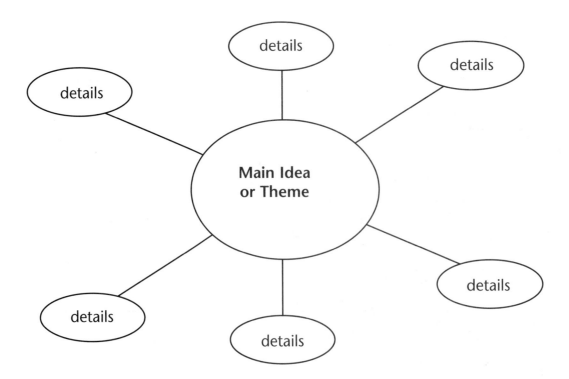

TACKLE DIFFICULT VOCABULARY: WORD SORT

Write one challenging word or phrase in each of the boxes below, along with its definition and part of speech. Cut the boxes apart. Then sort the words using one of the following methods.

- Same parts of speech
- Words with similar or opposite meanings
- Words with prefixes and suffixes
- Words that relate to each other or that can be used together
- My own sorting method: _____

Word: **Definition:** **Part of Speech:**	**Word:** **Definition:** **Part of Speech:**	**Word:** **Definition:** **Part of Speech:**
Word: **Definition:** **Part of Speech:**	**Word:** **Definition:** **Part of Speech:**	**Word:** **Definition:** **Part of Speech:**

TACKLE DIFFICULT VOCABULARY: WORD STUDY NOTEBOOK

Keeping a word study notebook is a convenient way to log new words, their meanings and their spelling, as well as prefixes, suffixes, word roots, and other concepts. When you record a new word, include its definition, pronunciation, and origins, along with an example sentence and a drawing to help you remember it.

Word: _____

Pronunciation: _____

Origins: _____

_____

Definition: _____

Sentence: _____

Drawing:

TACKLE DIFFICULT VOCABULARY: WORD STUDY LOG

Keep track of the words you gather in your Word Study Notebook in the log below.

100								
95								
90								
85								
80								
75								
70								
65								
60								
55								
50								
45								
40								
35								
30								
25								
20								
15								
10								
5								
Total Number of Words in My Word Study Notebook	Week of	Week of	Week of	Week of	Week of	Week of	Week of	Week of

TACKLE DIFFICULT VOCABULARY: WORD MAP

Write a challenging word or phrase in the first box below. Beneath the word or phrase, include its definition, word parts you recognize, and several synonyms. In the two boxes at the bottom, write a sentence that uses the word or phrase and create a drawing that helps you remember it.

A Challenging Word or Phrase

Definition

Word Parts I Recognize

Synonyms

A Sentence That Contains the Word or Phrase

A Picture That Ilustrates the Word or Phrase

MONITOR YOUR READING PROCESS: FIX-UP IDEAS LOG

Recognizing that you don't understand something is as important as knowing that you do understand it. Sometimes you may find yourself just reading the words but not actually comprehending or getting the meaning of what you are reading. If you are having trouble comprehending something you are reading, try using some of the fix-up ideas listed below to get back on track.

- Reread
- Ask a question
- Read in shorter chunks
- Read aloud
- Retell

- Work with a partner
- Unlock difficult words
- Change your reading rate
- Choose a new strategy
- Create a mnemonic device

Problems I Encountered While Reading	Fix-Up-Ideas I Used

MONITOR YOUR READING PROGRESS: YOUR OWN GRAPHIC ORGANIZER

Graphic organizers help you understand and remember information. Use your imagination to modify a graphic organizer in this appendix, or invent a new one. Use your graphic organizer to arrange ideas as you read and to guide your discussion and writing actions after you read. Graphic organizer possibilities are endless!

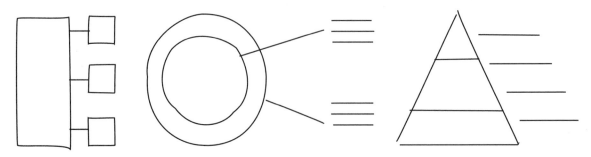

Monitor Your Reading Progress: Reading Strategies Evaluation Chart

My Evaluation of My Progress	My Teacher's Evaluation of My Progress
Things I Do Before Reading	My Actions Taken Before Reading
Things I Do During Reading	My Actions Taken During Reading
Things I Do After Reading	My Actions Taken After Reading

MONITOR YOUR READING PROGRESS: BOOKS I WANT TO READ

Keep track of books you want to read in the chart below. Whenever you read a book on your list, add a checkmark to the first column to indicate that you have read the book.

✔	Title	Author	Genre	Notes

LITERARY ACKNOWLEDGMENTS

Perseus Books, L. L.C. "Something Could Happen to You" from *Almost a Woman* by Esmeralda Santiago. Copyright © 1997 Canto-Media, Inc. Reprinted by permission of Perseus Book Publishers, a member of Perseus Books, L.L.C.

David Quammen. "The Last Bison" by David Quammen. This originally appeared in *Outside* magazine. Reprinted by permission of David Quammen. All rights reserved. Copyright © 1982 by David Quammen.

Random House, Inc. "Dead Men's Path" from *Girls at War and Other Stories* by Chinua Achebe, copyright © 1972, 1973 by Chinua Achebe. Used [in U.S.] by permission of Doubleday, a division of Random House, Inc. "Dream Variations" from *The Collected Poems of Langston Hughes* by Langston Hughes, copyright © 1994 by the Estate of Langston Hughes. Used by permission of Alfred A. Knopf, a division of Random House, Inc. "The Gazelle" copyright © 1982 by Stephen Mitchell, from *The Selected Poetry of Rainer Maria Rilke* by Rainer Maria Rilke, translated by Stephen Mitchell. Used by permission of Random House, Inc. "The Legend" from *The River of Heaven* by Garrett Hongo, copyright © 1988 by Garrett Hongo. Used by permission of Alfred A. Knopf, a division of Random House, Inc. "Short Assignments" from *Bird by Bird* by Anne Lamott, copyright © 1994 by Anne Lamott. Used by permission of Pantheon Books, a division of Random House, Inc. "Simple Song" from *Circles on the Water* by Marge Piercy, copyright © 1982 by Marge Piercy. Used by permission of Alfred A. Knopf, a division of Random House, Inc. "The Waking" from *The Collected Poems of Theodore Roethke* by Theodore Roethke, copyright 1953 by Theodore Roethke. Used by permission of Doubleday, a division of Random House, Inc.

Simon and Schuster. From *The Man Who Mistook His Wife for a Hat and Other Clinical Tales* by Oliver Sacks. Reprinted with the permission of Simon and Schuster Adult Publishing Group. Copyright © 1970, 1981, 1983, 1984, 1985 by Oliver Sacks.

Songtalk Publishing Company. "I Remember; I Believe" by Bernice Johnson Reagon. Copyright © Songtalk Publishing Co. (BMI). Reprinted with the permission of Bernice Johnson Reagon and Songtalk Publishing Co. (BMI).

University of Oklahoma Press. Excerpt from *Popol Vuh: The Sacred Book of the Ancient Quiche Maya*. English version by Delia Goetz and Sylvanus G. Morley from the translation of Adrian Recinos. Copyright © 1950 by the University of Oklahoma Press. "Yonder sky that has wept tears of compassion . . ." from *Indian Oratory: Famous Speeches by Noted Indian Chiefs*, by W. C. Vanderwerth, pp. 118-122. Copyright © 1971 by the University of Oklahoma Press. Reprinted by permission.

Walker Publishing Company, Inc. Excerpt from *The Victorian Internet* by Tom Standage, pp. 205-211. Copyright © 1998 by Tom Standage. Reprinted by permission of Walker Publishing Company, Inc.

We have made every effort to trace the ownership of all copyrighted material and to secure permission from copyright holders. In the event of any question arising as to the use of any material, we will be pleased to make the necessary corrections in future printings. We are grateful to the authors, publishers, and agents listed here for permission to use the materials indicated.

ART ACKNOWLEDGMENTS

Cover Illustration Works; **101** PhotoDisc; **142** © Kevin Schafer/CORBIS; **189** © Kevin Fleming/CORBIS; **211** © AFP/CORBIS; **242** © Nik Wheeler/CORBIS; **292** © Robert Holmes/CORBIS; **319** © Bettman/CORBIS; **351** © Yogi, Inc./CORBIS; **409** Julie Delton; **417** PhotoDisc; **430** PhotoDisc